HPB

The Extraordinary Life

and Influence of

Helena Blavatsky,

Founder of

the Modern Theosophical Movement

SYLVIA CRANSTON
& Carey Williams, Research Assistant

PATH PUBLISHING HOUSE
Santa Barbara, California

In cooperation with the

Institute of Noetic Sciences
Sausalito, California

Path Publishing House
3463 State Street
Suite 377
Santa Barbara, CA 93105-2603
email: cranwilliams@earthlink.net

Published in cooperation with the Institute of Noetic Sciences
475 Gate Five Road, Suite 300, Sausalito, CA 94965

Library of Congress Cataloging-in-Publication Data
(1st trade paperback edition)
Cranston, S. L.
    HPB : the extraordinary life and influence of Helena Blavatsky,
founder of the modern theosophical movement / Sylvia Cranston.
        p.   cm.
    Includes bibliographical references and index.
    ISBN 0-87477-769-0 (pbk: alk. paper)
    1. Blavatsky, H. P. (Helena Petrovna), 1831–1891.
    2. Theosophists—Biography. I. Title.
BP585.B6C73   1994   93-6229 CIP r92
299'.934'092—dc20
[B]

Text design by Tanya Maiboroda
Cover design by Johann Tafertshofer and Rochelle Voirol
Cover calligraphy by George Gilliland

Third and Revised Edition
ISBN 0-9662115-1-0

Printed in the United States of America
1   2   3   4   5   6   7   8   9   10

This book is printed on acid-free paper.
                    ∞

Grateful acknowledgment is hereby made to the following publishers, authors, and/or copyright holders for permission to quote from the following:

Bantam Doubleday Dell, New York, *Emergence, The Rebirth of the Sacred* by David Spangler, copyright 1984 by David Spangler, used by permission of Delacorte Press/Seymour Lawrence, a division of Bantam Doubleday Dell Publishing Group, Inc.

Blackwell Publishers, Oxford, England, *Philosophical Quarterly,* October 1953 issue, Russell Goldfarb cites Fussell's article *E. M. Forster's Mrs. Moore: Some Suggestions.*

David Bolt Associates, Surrey, England, *The Mysteries* by Colin Wilson, 1978.

Cassell, Ltd. London, *The Occult in Art* by Fred Gettings, copyright 1978 by Fred Gettings.

N. A. Fadeyev, Miscellaneous letters to H. P. Blavatsky, 1876–1878. Translated by Mary G. Langford.

HarperCollins, New York, *Unfinished Animal* by Theodore Roszak, copyright 1975 by Theodore Roszak. Reprinted by permission of HarperCollins Publishers.

Henry Holt & Co. Inc., New York, *The Forgotten Language* by Erich Fromm.

Levin, Garvett, & Dill, Southfield, MI, *Yeats: Man and Mask* by Richard Ellmann. Published by W. W. Norton, New York.

Little, Brown & Co., Boston, *Ireland's Literary Renaissance* by Ernest Boyd.

Geddes MacGregor, New York. Permission granted to quote from his writings.

Macmillan Publishers, New York, *The Star Rover* by Jack London; *Memoirs of Æ* by John Eglinton, 1975; *James Joyce* by Richard Ellmann.

P. C. Magazines, Ltd., London, *The New Scientist,* article discussing *Dr. David Bohm's Experiments,* November 11, 1982; article discussing *Experiments in Electrophysiology,* January 26, 1982.

Catherine S. Nekrasova, *Helena Andreyevna Hahn,* biographical sketch published in *Russkaya Starina,* August and September 1886. Translated by Mary G. Langford.

New York Times, January 12, 1990 issue, American Astronomical Society's report captioned *Found: A Continent of Galaxies That Draws Others Toward It.*

New York Times, Dr. Lewis Thomas' article dated July 15, 1989 on "The Moon Landing Walks and Varied Impressions it Evoked."

New York Times Magazine Group, extract in March 1970 issue of *McCall's* magazine, "The Mysterious Madame Blavatsky" by Kurt Vonnegut, Jr.

Pantheon Books, New York, *In My Own Way* by Alan Watts, copyright 1972 by Alan Watts, published by Pantheon Books, a division of Random House, Inc.

Penguin USA, New York, *Fantasia of the Unconscious* by D. H. Lawrence.

Kenneth Ring, *Heading Toward Omega,* New York, William Morrow, 1984; with special permission from Kenneth Ring.

Shambhala Publications, Inc., Boston, *An Art of Our Own: The Spiritual in Modern Art* by Roger Lipsey, copyright 1988 by Roger Lipsey. Reprinted by arrangement with Shambhala Publications, Inc., 300 Massachusetts Ave., Boston.

Jean-Louis Siemons: "A nineteenth-century explanatory scheme for the interpretation of near-death experience: the transpersonal model of death as presented in Madame Blavatsky's Theosophy." Copyright Jean-Louis Siemons, Paris, France.

Simon & Schuster, New York, *The Man Who Mistook His Wife for a Hat* by Dr. Oliver Sacks, copyright 1970, 1981, 1984, 1985 by Oliver Sacks. Reprinted by permission of Summit Books, a division of Simon & Schuster, Inc.

Society for Psychical Research, London, England. Dr. Harrison's Report, April 1986 (Vol. 53) issue of *SPR Journal.*

Theosophical Publishing House, Wheaton, IL, references quoted from *The Dawning of the Theosophical Movement* by Michael Gomes; *H. P. Blavatsky Collected Writings,* 15 volumes, edited by Boris de Zirkoff.

Time magazine, New York, selections from Dr. Freeman Dyson's book *Infinite in All Directions,* April 1988 issue.

Vera Zhelihovsky, *When I Was Small.* Translated by Catherine Young.

Vera Zhelihovsky, *My Adolescence.* Translated by Catherine Young.

Vera Zhelihovsky, booklet *H. P. Blavatsky and a Modern Priest of Truth.* Translated by Catherine Young.

Vera Zhelihovsky, *The Inexplicable or the Unexplained.* (series in *Rebus.*) Translated by Catherine Young.

Vera Zhelihovsky, *The Truth About H. P. Blavatsky* (series in *Rebus.*) Translated by Catherine Young.

Vera Zhelihovsky, from V. Solovioff's *A Modern Priestess of Isis,* Appendix A and B. Translated by Catherine Young.

Vera Zhelihovsky, *Enigmatical Tribes in the Light Blue Mountains, Durbar at Lahore,* by Radda-Bai (E. P. Blavatskaya) St. Petersburg, 1893. Translated by Mary G. Langford.

Vera Zhelihovsky, *Helena Petrovna Blavatskaya,* published in *Russkoe Obozrenie,* November and December 1891. Translated by Mary G. Langford.

To all friends, both near and far,
who helped in the preparation of this book.

Other books by Sylvia Cranston

REINCARNATION, AN EAST-WEST ANTHOLOGY
(with Joseph Head)

REINCARNATION IN WORLD THOUGHT
(with Joseph Head)

REINCARNATION: THE PHOENIX FIRE MYSTERY
(with Joseph Head)

REINCARNATION, A NEW HORIZON IN
SCIENCE, RELIGION AND SOCIETY
(with Carey Williams)

Contents

Part 3 MATURING YEARS

Part 4 AMERICA—LAND OF BEGINNINGS

Part 5 MISSION TO INDIA

Part 6 HORIZONS OPEN IN THE WEST

Part 7 THE CENTURY AFTER

Illustrations

Chronology

1831	Born August 12 at Dnepropetrovsk (Ekaterinoslav), Ukraine. Daughter of Col. Peter von Hahn and Helena Andreyevna, née de Fadeyev, renowned novelist who died young. Granddaughter on maternal side of Privy Councillor Andrey de Fadeyev and Princess Helena Pavlovna Dolgorukov, who supervised her education at Saratov and Tiflis, Caucasus. Endowed from childhood with remarkable psychic powers.
1849	Married Nikifor Blavatsky, a State Official, very much her senior.
1849–50	Left him and traveled in Turkey, Greece, Egypt, and France.
1851	Met her Master in London.
1852	Embarked for Canada later in the year; went to New Orleans, Mexico, South America, West Indies, thence via the Cape and Ceylon to India.
1853	Attempted but failed to enter Tibet. Returned to England via Java.
1854	Came to America again, crossing the Rockies with a caravan of immigrants. May have visited South America again.
1855	Left for India late in the year, via Japan and the Straits.
1856–57	Traveled throughout India, Kashmir, Ladakh, parts of Tibet, Burma.
1858	Returned to Europe via Java, staying in France and Germany. Then returned to Russia, reaching Pskov on Christmas Night.

Note: Chronology modified from Boris de Zirkoff's Chronology in the *H. P. Blavatsky Collected Writings*.

1860   Left for the Caucasus early in the year, where she traveled among the native tribes, remaining there until 1864–65. Experienced severe physical and psychic crisis acquiring complete control over her occult powers.

1866–67   Left Russia again and traveled extensively in Balkans, Egypt, Syria, Italy. Returned to Italy in 1867 and paid a short visit to southern Russia. Was present at the battle of Mentana, November 3, 1867, and was wounded.

1868   Went to India and Tibet with her Master.

1870   Returned to Greece.

1871   Embarked for Egypt and was shipwrecked near the island of Spetsai, July 4.

1871–72   Settled in Cairo. Traveled to Syria, Palestine, Lebanon in 1872, returning for a short time to Odessa.

1873   After brief travels in Eastern Europe, went to Paris in spring. On her Master's orders left for New York, landing July 7.

1874   Met Col. Henry Steel Olcott at the Eddy farmhouse, Chittenden, Vermont, October 14.

1875   September 8, founded the Theosophical Society, together with Col. Olcott, William Q. Judge, and others. Inaugural address of Col. Olcott delivered November 17.

1877   Published her first great work, *Isis Unveiled,* in the fall.

1878   Became an American citizen, July 8. Left for India with Col. Olcott, December 17, settling at Bombay.

1879   Launched her first magazine, *The Theosophist,* in October, which resulted in rapid growth of Theosophical work in India, 1879–83.

1882   Transferred headquarters to Adyar, Madras, India on December 19.

1884   Left for Europe, February 20, accompanied by Olcott and others. After visiting Nice, settled for a while in Paris to work on *The Secret Doctrine.* Briefly visited London. Moved to Elberfeld, Germany, in the fall. Went to London in October and soon after sailed to India, reaching Adyar December 21.

1885   Gravely ill, February. Sailed for Naples March 31, leaving India for good. After a brief stay at Torre del Greco, settled at Würzburg, Germany, where she wrote a large part of *The Secret Doctrine*.

1886   Moved to Ostende in July, visiting Elberfeld on her way.

1887   Transferred her residence to London in May, where the Blavatsky Lodge was established, and her second magazine, *Lucifer*, was launched in September.

1888   Published *The Secret Doctrine*, late fall. Founded the Esoteric School.

1889   Published *The Key to Theosophy* and *The Voice of the Silence*.

1890   Established European headquarters of the Theosophical Society, at 19 Avenue Road, London, where she died.

1891   Died May 8. Cremated at Woking Crematorium, Surrey, England.

Preface

A hundred years ago, a leading New York newspaper, the *Sun,* commenced a biographical account of the life of Helena Blavatsky with these words: "A woman who, for one reason or another, has kept the world—first her little child world and afterward two hemispheres—talking of her, disputing about her, defending or assailing her character and motives, joining her enterprise or opposing it might and main, and in her death being as much telegraphed about between two continents as an emperor, must have been a remarkable person."[1]

In a special issue on outstanding women in *Rikka* (Winter 1978), Dr. Paul Weinzweig, a director in the United Nations, spoke of Helena Blavatsky as

> a completely cultured woman in the renaissance ideal. . . . She was a scientist, poet, pianist, painter, philosopher, writer, educator, and above all, a tireless warrior for light. . . . In her quest for truth and universal brotherhood, H. P. Blavatsky earned much enmity, and many enemies. No one so ruffled the feathers of nineteenth century religious prejudice, spiritualistic charlatanism, and intellectual pomposity as she did. It was only natural, therefore, that her detractors should have accused her of the very qualities which she fought against almost single-handedly with such gargantuan strength, grace, and irreverent humor.

Charles Johnston, who taught Sanskrit at Columbia University, spoke of her in a different way:

> The first and earliest impression I received from Madame Blavatsky was the feeling of the power and largeness of her individuality; as though I were in the presence of one of the primal forces of Nature. . . . This sense of the power of individuality was not what one has felt in the presence of some great personality, who dominates and dwarfs surrounding persons into insignificance, and tyrannously overrides their independence. It was rather the sense of a profound deep-seated reality, an exhaustless power of resistance, a spirit built on the very depths of Nature, and reaching down to the primaeval eternities of Truth. Gradually apparent under this dominant impression of power, arose a subtle sense of great gentleness and kindliness, an unfailing readiness to forget herself entirely and to throw herself heartily into the life of others.[2]

Another tribute came from William Stewart Ross, a noted author and critic of HPB's day and editor of *The Agnostic Journal*. At the time of Blavatsky's death he wrote therein: "In spite of her tremendous attainments and unrivaled talent, she had not a vestige of pedantic assumption, and had the simple heart of a child. . . . Her followers are gnostic on grave issues of teleology, on which I am only agnostic. To me Mme. Blavatsky is dead, and another shadow has fallen athwart my life. . . . 'Impostor' indeed! She was almost the only mortal I have ever met who was *not* an impostor . . . and one of the very few who ever understood me."[3]

This last comment refers, no doubt, to the much-publicized Hodgson report published in December 1885 by the Society for Psychical Research in London, which concluded that Madame Blavatsky "has achieved a title to permanent remembrance as one of the most accomplished, ingenious, and interesting impostors in history." (Richard Hodgson, a man in his twenties, had gone to India to investigate her.)

This verdict has ever since been circulated in biographies and encyclopedias, and in the news media whenever her life and work are discussed. It is therefore especially noteworthy that in 1986, the centenary year of the Hodgson Report, the Society for Psychical Research itself issued a three-page press release to the newspapers and leading magazines in Great Britain, Canada, and the United States. It opened with these words.

MADAME BLAVATSKY, CO-FOUNDER OF THE THEOSOPHICAL SOCIETY
WAS UNJUSTLY CONDEMNED, NEW STUDY CONCLUDES
The "exposure" of the Russian-born occultist, Madame H. P. Blavatsky, by the SPR in 1885, is in serious doubt, with the publication in the SPR Journal (Vol. 53 April 1986) of a forceful critique of the 1885 report.

The case has been re-examined by Dr. Vernon Harrison, past president of The Royal Photographic Society and formerly Research Manager to Thomas De La Rue, who is an expert on forgery. The 1885 report was written mostly by Richard Hodgson, an Australian pioneer of both the British and American SPRs, who became widely known through the case.

The news release included one of the summarizing paragraphs of Dr. Harrison's twenty-five-page study: "As detailed examination of this report proceeds, one becomes more and more aware that whereas Hodgson . . . was prepared to use any evidence, however trivial or questionable, to implicate HPB, he ignored all evidence that could be used in her favour. His report is riddled with slanted statements, conjecture advanced as fact or probable fact, uncorroborated testimony of unnamed witnesses, selection of evidence and downright falsity."†

Harrison quotes from a statement issued by HPB shortly after Hodgson's report was published:

> That Mr. Hodgson's elaborate but misdirected inquiries, his affected precision, which spends infinite patience over trifles and is blind to facts of importance, his contradictory reasoning and his manifold incapacity to deal with such problems as those he endeavored to solve, will be exposed by other writers in due course—I make no doubt.[4]

Harrison adds: "I apologize to her that it has taken us one hundred years to demonstrate that she wrote truly."[5]

The press release mentioned that Blavatsky was co-founder of the Theosophical Society, founded in New York City in 1875. HPB had arrived in the United States in 1873 and five years later became a citizen. The other chief founders were Colonel Henry S. Olcott, who became president, and William Q. Judge. In early life Olcott achieved recognition as an agriculturist. After serving in the Civil War he was one of a three-man commission appointed by the government to investigate the assassination of Lincoln. He later became a lawyer. Judge, a young Irish-American lawyer, was later to play a leading role in the movement, particularly in America.

The gradually formulated threefold objects of the Society, although quite acceptable today, were viewed in Victorian times as radically innovative. The objects are:

1. To form the nucleus of a universal brotherhood of humanity, without distinction of race, creed, sex, caste, or color.
2. The study of ancient and modern religions, philosophies and sciences, and the demonstration of the importance of such study; and
3. The investigation of the unexplained laws of nature and the psychical powers latent in man.

Today, theosophical societies and associations holding to these Objects exist in over sixty countries.

In pursuance of the Third Object, HPB privately demonstrated occult phenomena to some of her students with a view to explaining the laws at work in their production. This was done at will, in full consciousness and under well-lighted conditions, while the opposite is the

---

† Reprinted in Vernon Harrison, *H. P. Blavatsky and the SPR: An Examination of the Hodgson Report of 1885*, Pasadena, California, Theosophical University Press, 1997.

case with mediums. Whenever phenomena are produced, however, suspicions as to their genuineness easily arise among those not present, as was the case with Hodgson, whose investigations were limited to interrogating witnesses or examining their reports.

H. G. Wells once wrote that he had always wondered at the phenomena produced by "Mahomet, the Yogis, and Madame Blavatsky. . . . Here we plumb some profounder law—deeper than the ordinary laws of nature."[6] The celebrated architectural critic and cultural historian Lewis Mumford spoke in his column in The New Yorker (May 23, 1964)[7] of HPB's uncanny foretelling of "the destruction of whole cities by nuclear blast."

HPB never assumed a leading role in administering the TS and for ten years held no higher position than corresponding secretary. A year before her death she was elected president of the European branches. Writing to her sister in Russia, she lamented: "But what is the use of all this to me? . . . Honors and titles are altogether out of my line."[8] Unlike many of the popular gurus today, she refused to accept money for her teachings, lived simply, and died without property.

HPB would object to the words "her teachings," as she never claimed them to be her own. She had learned them, she said, from teachers she met in her travels in the Orient. These gurus were referred to by her as adepts, masters of wisdom, or mahatmas (great souls). Whether they reside in the East or West, they are said to be global in work and vision. Blavatsky was the first in the West to speak openly of such advanced members of the human family as the natural product of evolution through reincarnation. Down through history, according to Theosophy, they have appeared as humanity's great teachers and saviors, such as Buddha, Krishna, Zoroaster, Moses, Abraham, and Jesus. As to the last, HPB wrote in her first book, Isis Unveiled (2:150), that he was "one of the grandest and most clearly-defined figures on the panorama of human history," one who "instead of growing paler will become with every century more pronounced and clearly defined."

Today, the idea of masters is so familiar that in Roget's International Thesaurus, under mahatma, the reader is directed to look up four synonyms: expert; good person; occultist; and wise man.[9] Theosophists hold that adeptship is attainable by women as well as men.[10]

How would the wisdom of a sage or master be classified? Is it religious, scientific, or philosophical? According to HPB's major work, The Secret Doctrine, subtitled "The Synthesis of Science, Religion and Philosophy," it is all three synthesized as one.

What has fascinated scientists who have studied The Secret Doctrine is that the author anticipated many later discoveries in their own fields.

When the physicists and chemists of her day were convinced that the atom was the ultimate building block of the universe, she affirmed its infinite divisibility. When anthropologists were grudgingly allowing man an antiquity of several hundred thousand years, she spoke, as present researchers do, in terms of millions. She considered as fact such later scientific discoveries as the convertibility of substance and energy; the transmutation of elements; the illusory nature of matter—that matter is not what we see; that space is not empty, there being no vacuity anywhere; that the moon was not torn from the earth as astronomers speculated, but was older than the earth. Scientists were astounded to discover that the moon rocks brought back by the astronauts were older than any found on the earth!

A niece of Einstein reported that a copy of *The Secret Doctrine* was always on his desk.[11] Another witness, Jack Brown, reports similarly in an article, "I Visited Professor Einstein."[12]

HPB had a number of friends among the scientific community, including Thomas Edison; Sir William Crookes, leading chemist and physicist of the nineteenth century; and Camille Flammarion, renowned French astronomer. All three were members of the Theosophical Society. Other members of note were the American philosopher William James and Major General Abner Doubleday, Civil War hero and reputed inventor of baseball. A learned scholar, Doubleday bequeathed his rare library to the TS, of which he had been vice-president. HPB knew him well when she lived in New York.

When she later lived in London, the poet William Butler Yeats, another TS member, was closely associated for several years with Blavatsky's work. In a letter to a friend he said that "she was the most living person alive."[13] An American reporter after interviewing her, wrote in the *Hartford Daily Times* (Dec. 2, 1878): "Madame laughed. When we write madame laughed, we feel as if we were saying, Laughter were present! For of all clear, mirthful rollicking laughter that we ever heard, hers is the very essence. She seems, indeed, the genius of the mood she displays at all times, so intense is her vitality." Unfortunately, her photographs usually disclose only the serious side of her nature.

To date there have been eighteen book-length biographies in English of H. P. Blavatsky. The present volume—commemorating the one hundredth anniversary of HPB's death—is the first large-scale biography to appear. Unlike most of its predecessors, it focuses on the teachings she transmitted as well as her life, for the latter cannot be understood apart from the former. Thus, in preparation for writing this biography all Blavatsky's books and articles, totaling almost ten thousand pages, have been examined.

Equally valuable are Blavatsky's letters. The writer was fortunate in receiving from Dara Eklund, executor of the estate of Boris de Zirkoff (editor of HPB's *Collected Writings*) photocopies of some six hundred letters collected by him over a period of fifty years. Also gratefully received was a large amount of other Blavatskyana he had been gathering as to facts in HPB's life not obtainable from usual sources.

Recently, much new material has been uncovered, including Blavatsky's long-lost correspondence with James Ralston Skinner, the learned author of the *Key to the Hebrew-Egyptian Mystery in the Source of Measures*. Although Skinner had mentioned their existence, no one knew what was in these letters. They were discovered in the archives of the Andover-Harvard Theological Library at Harvard University. The present writer played a small part in bringing them to light. Archivist Dr. Alan Seaburg wrote to her (January 30, 1984): "If you hear of other HPB letters needing a home, please think of Harvard. We would welcome them in our collection."

One invaluable source of information untapped by previous biographers is a large amount of material published in Russia but hitherto untranslated. Much of this has been rendered into English for the present work by a young Russian emigré, Cathy Young, honor graduate of Rutgers University and author of *Growing up in Moscow*.[14] The remainder has been translated by another native of Russia, Mary G. Langford, who, until her retirement, taught Russian at Occidental College in California.

The present volume, as the title indicates, concerns HPB's influence as well as her life. Author Paul Zweig was surprised to discover that "within only a few years, the Theosophical Society would revolutionize occult thinking in Europe and America. . . . Her Theosophical Society . . . would flourish in India and Ceylon, becoming a powerful factor in the Hindu and Buddhist revivals there. It would eventually have an important influence on the Indian independence movement."† (See "The Awakening of the East," in Part V of this book.)

As to HPB's influence in the West, social historian Theodore Roszak writes of one phase of it in his book *Unfinished Animal*. In an eight-page section, "Madame Blavatsky's Secret Doctrine," he refers to her as "one of the great liberated ladies of her day," adding:

She could not help but draw withering, critical fire by her every act and word, especially when she presumed to challenge the most entrenched intellectual orthodoxies of the age. Still today people

---

† "Talking to The Dead and Other Amusements," *New York Times Book Review*, October 5, 1980, 11.

who have never read a line she wrote remain adamantly convinced she was a fraud and a crank. . . . It is seldom remembered [that] in the years following publication of *The Origin of Species,* HPB was the first person to aggressively argue the case for a transphysical element in evolution against the rising Darwinian consensus.

In her two major works, he continues, are to be found "the first philosophy of psychic and spiritual evolution to appear in the modern West. Her effort, unlike that of the Christian fundamentalists, was not to reject Darwin's work, but to insist that it had, by its focus on the purely physical, wholly omitted the mental, creative, and visionary life of the human race; in short, it omitted *consciousness,* whose development followed a very different evolutionary path. Darwin simply did not go far enough; his was not a big enough theory to contain human nature in the round."

Viewing Blavatsky in perspective, Roszak observes that "with all criticisms weighed up against her, HPB stands forth as a seminal talent of our time. . . . Above all, she is among the modern world's trailblazing psychologists of the visionary mind."[15]

Other phases of HPB's influence are considered in Part VII, "The Century After," in the chapters on religion, psychology, literature, art, music, and the New Age, of which she has often been called the mother. The chapter "Science and *The Secret Doctrine*" includes not only her influence but indicates to what degree the teachings in that book anticipate subsequent scientific discoveries. It also predicts a great change that would take place in science between 1888 and 1897. The scientists of Blavatsky's day had been bemoaning the fact that all the great discoveries in physics, chemistry, and astronomy had already been made and there were no new worlds to conquer. Then, in 1895, '96, and '97, three discoveries were announced that opened up vast fields of research that continue to the present day, with no end in sight. This chapter furnishes a clue as to why Einstein and other scientists initially looked into *The Secret Doctrine.*

Today all of HPB's books are in print, many in several editions. Her writings have been translated into all the European languages, as well as Hebrew, Arabic, Tamil, Hindi, Chinese, Japanese, Vietnamese, and many others. This seems fitting, as in breadth of spirit she was more a citizen of the world than of any special country.

In Russia, Blavatsky's books were banned under Czarist rule during her life, as well as when the Soviets took over. This is no longer the case, as the following report reveals:

The motherland of Madame Blavatsky is now alive with interest in her life and work. . . . [In Moscow on June 18, 1990, and a year before the Soviet Union was dissolved,] an exhibition on HPB was opened in the imposing premises of the Writers Union. . . . Moscow press and television covered the event and several million viewers saw the opening on prime television time, when it was announced that 1991 would be celebrated as the International Year of Blavatsky, it being the 100th anniversary of her passing away.[16]

More will be said about this in the last chapter, "Not Without Honor." The year 1978 marked the one hundredth anniversary of HPB's becoming a citizen of the United States, a country, she said, she "loved for its glorious freedom."[17]

One exception to HPB's rejection by Russians at large appeared a year after her death in the distinguished *Critico-Biographical Encyclopedia of Russian Writers and Savants*. In a fourteen-page sketch of HPB's life, Zinaida Vengerova writes:

It is not possible to compile even an approximate list of everything that has been written on Blavatsky. Having created a great interest in her Theosophy in Western Europe, North America, and India, Blavatsky became the subject of a tremendous body of panegyrical and polemical literature: dozens of books, hundreds of magazine pieces, and thousands of newspaper articles. Her fame is so great that the esteemed London biographical dictionary, *Men of the Time,* which allots no more than a column to some of the best-known people of our day, devoted three to Blavatsky.[18]

HPB has been called "the Sphinx of the nineteenth century," and the familiar photograph in which her right arm rests under her chin, and her eyes look right through you, has also been called "the Sphinx." It may be of some significance that Time-Life Books selected that photograph in its campaign to promote the popular series *Mysteries of the Unknown.* Flashing on television screens, and reproduced in mailing circulars, millions of people have been seeing this unforgettable picture accompanied by the startling words COME FACE TO FACE WITH THE UNKNOWN—an unconscious confession, perhaps, that the world has yet to judge HPB aright.

In the present biography, witnesses to various events will be given opportunity to tell their tale in their own words wherever possible, lest in retelling the freshness and flavor of the original be lost. This policy, of course, holds good for our chief witness herself, Helena Petrovna Blavatsky.

The tidal wave of deeper souls,
Into our inmost being rolls,
And lifts us unawares,
Out of all meaner cares.

—Henry Wadsworth Longfellow

Part **1**

Life in
Russia

Chapter 1

Heritage

Reading through HPB's many letters, interviews, and voluminous writings, one finds only a few lines about her ancestors. Apparently she had no inclination to boast about her lineage, remarkable though it was. Researchers are obliged to go to other sources for information.

Her mother, Helena von Hahn, was a famous novelist whose books, as they appeared, "were regarded as extraordinary events in Russian literature. . . . She was recognized as the feminine equal of the great Lermontoff, and celebrated critics like Belinsky dedicated their articles to her."[1] She has been called the George Sand of Russian literature.[2] HPB's maternal grandmother, Princess Helena Pavlovna Fadeyev—with whom Blavatsky lived much of her childhood and youth—was a scientist and artist of note. The princess belonged to one of the ancient families of Russia, the Dolgorukovs, which goes back ten centuries to the Viking Prince Rurik, founder of what became the Russian empire. He is also known as the Prince of Rus, from which Russia derives its name.

In HPB's immediate hereditary background there is Russian, French Huguenot, and German stock. Going way back, there was Scandinavian as well, for surprisingly Rurik was not a Slav but a Viking. In the March 1985 *National Geographic,* under the caption "When the Rus Invaded Russia . . . Viking Trail East," one reads:

> Viking roots struck deep into Russian soil when Scandinavian warriors and traders, known as the Rus, created the land's first organized state and gave their name to a future empire. The legendary Rurik of the Rus became Prince of Novgorod in A.D. 862. A thousand years later his bronze figure adorns a huge monument in the Kremlin square of that city. By the 11th century a Rus state [and trade route] centered at Kiev stretched from the Baltic to the Black Sea.

The oldest chronicles indicate that Rurik and his two brothers did not *invade* Russia but were *invited* to come. Even an American guide-

book to the Soviet Union mentions this.[3] Blavatsky tells the legendary
story in her article on Turgenev's *Father and Sons*: "Implored by the
Slavs to come and reign over the country, Rurik is reported to have
been addressed by the delegates in these ominous words: 'Come with
us great prince . . . for vast is our motherland; but there is little order in
it.' " These words, HPB adds, "their descendants might well repeat
with as much, if not more, propriety."[4]

Among the descendants of Rurik in HPB's ancestral line was Prince
Yaroslav, the Wise and St. Michael of Chernigov, a canonized prince.
Later came Prince Yakov, the well-known favorite of Peter the Great.

The French element entered the family when HPB's great-grandfather, Prince Paul, married Countess Henriette de Plessis, daughter of
a persecuted French Huguenot nobleman, who emigrated to Russia
and served in the court of Catherine the Great. This French Huguenot
strain in Blavatsky's heraldry is usually passed over by writers without
comment, but the courage of the Huguenots in the midst of cruel
religious persecution surely must have had its effect.

It was the daughter of Prince Paul and Countess Henriette that
became HPB's maternal grandmother, Princess Helena Pavlovna. She
was a rarity in her time. Colleges and universities were not open then
to women in Russia and she was largely self-taught. Helena Pavlovna
was a superb artist and musician, speaking fluently five languages. She
studied classical as well as modern Greek, later teaching the basics of
both to HPB, who also was very proficient in foreign tongues.[5] The
grandmother's scientific work was in botany and archaeology. A famous British world traveler, Lady Hester Lucy Stanhope, wrote in a
book on Russia:

> In that barbarian land I met an outstanding woman-scientist, who
> would have been famous in Europe, but . . . there was none to
> recognize her scientific value.[6]

Helena Pavlovna's scientific work was recognized by several scientists of note, among them Alexander von Humboldt. She carried on an
extensive correspondence with geologist Sir Roderick Murchison, a
founder of the Royal Geographic Society in England.[7] The French
geologist Hommaire-de-Hell, who spent seven years in Russia, wrote
of her hospitality and achievements,[8] and named in her honor a newly
discovered fossil, *Venus Fadeef.* Even today Helena Pavlovna is appreciated in Russia, as one of our translators, Cathy Young, informs.

In 1813, at the age of twenty-three, the princess married Andrey
Fadeyev, who worked in the administrative field and eventually be-

came governor of a province.[9] His great-grandfather, a captain in the army of Peter the Great, was killed at the battle of Poltava, when Russia was invaded by the Swedish King Charles XII. Andrey's grandfather died of wounds from one of the Turkish wars, while his uncle was killed in the 1812 invasion by Napoleon. It must have been more than an academic history lesson for HPB when she read of these dreadful wars in which her own relatives perished.[10]

Despite a household of servants, Princess Helena reared her own children: first Helena Petrovna's mother, Helena Andreyevna; then Catherine, the future mother of Count Witte, who became the first premier of Russia; next Rostislav, renowned in his day as military general, historian, and social reformer;[11] and last Nadya or Nadyezhda, only three years older than Helena Petrovna and her beloved companion in their youth. Helena Andreyevna once said of her mother: "If I had to tell you that our mother was our nourisher, our caretaker, our teacher and our guardian angel, that still would not describe all her sacrificial, endless, selfless attachment by which she constantly gladdened our lives."[12] Later she was to do the same for her grandchild, the future Helena Blavatsky.†

Nor were her good deeds confined to her own family: A benefactor to the poor, Helena Pavlovna saved many families from starvation and set up a refuge for children.[13] As a Russian Orthodox Christian, the grandmother was deeply religious, and Helena Petrovna was similarly raised. The old lady would say: "God is all wise, the all good, who has created everything in the world in a beautiful and useful way."[14] One nineteenth-century writer recorded that the princess "lived to an extreme age [!] . . . dying at seventy-two."[15]

HPB's German heritage can be traced through her father, Peter von Hahn, back to the famous medieval crusader Count Rottenstern, whose life was once saved by the crowing of a cock when a Saracen entered his tent to kill him. In gratitude, the count added Hahn—the German word for cock—to his name.[16]

As counts and countesses, the Hahns were well known in Germany and later in Russia, where Peter's ancestors emigrated several generations before he was born. During the seventeenth and eighteenth centuries, it was not only the New World that attracted the persecuted and

---

† With three Helenas in HPB's family, it is fortunate for identification purposes that in Russia the second name is always the first name of the father, with an ending that means "son of" or "daughter of." Thus Helena Pavlovna was named after Paul; Helena Andreyevna after Andrey; and Helena Petrovna after her father, Peter. In Russia, Helena is usually spelled Yelena or Elena.

the adventurous, but Russia as well. HPB speaks of this occidental strain engrafted on Russian stock, the names of the emigrés "having been Russianized in some cases beyond recognition, for instance the English Hamiltons who became the 'HOMUTOFFS'!"[17]

Peter von Hahn made the military his career, becoming a colonel before he retired. His father, General Alexis von Hahn, received special recognition for winning a decisive battle in Switzerland, where he became commander of Zurich during the Russian occupation. He married Countess Elizabeth Maksimovna von Pröbsen, Helena Petrovna's German grandmother, from whom the granddaughter inherited her silvery, curly hair and vivacious, good-humored, carefree temperament.[18]

Helena Petrovna's father exhibited another kind of humor, the caustic wit of a confirmed skeptic. Cultured and well-read, he had little use for religion or things occult—"nursemaid's twaddle," he called them. His reactions to his daughter's burgeoning psychic powers will make interesting reading later.

On the father's side was Helena Petrovna's grandaunt,[19] Countess Ida Hahn-Hahn, a noted German author, whose works were published both on the continent and in Britain. By a strange coincidence, Helena Petrovna's mother and this grandaunt were engaged in a common cause. In the preface to the second edition of the mother's *Complete Works,* published in 1905, is the following:

> In the thirties of last century there appeared in France, Germany and Russia several novels, following each other in quick succession, in which were treated, for the first time in history, the questions concerning the social position of women, in all its aspects. To those novels one could actually trace the beginning of the so-called *feminist movement* and women's suffrage in the western world. Three women-writers were responsible for it: the famous George Sand in France, the Countess Ida H. Hahn-Hahn in Germany, and Helena Andreyevna Hahn in Russia [HPB's mother], writing under the nom-de-plume, Zenaida R-va. They tried to show in their writings the luckless destiny and miserable social position of women, who either were forced by circumstances to remain outside the circle of married happiness, or to survive the complete wreckage of their marriage.[20]

Helena Andreyevna considered in her writings other injustices besides those inflicted upon women, and she was among the first to do so in Russia. In her acclaimed novel *Theophania Abbiadzhio,* her heroine, passing one evening the houses of the rich, gazes through the windows and observes ladies overdressed in feathers and brilliants. Theophania involuntarily asks: "How did they merit these advantages? How do they justify them? For what are they given everything while others wander as outcasts from all diversions and joys . . . yet all the work, all the labor lies upon these outcasts?" Then passing through a poor street with small, miserable houses half buried in the ground, she sees "the awful faces of the coal stokers. . . . There live the movers of the entire city's activity, but they are invisible and forgotten by everybody." Not far away the wealthy are enjoying a display of fireworks, while "at a hundred paces distant, an entire family is dying of starvation on damp ground, and not one small spark turns into heavenly manna to fall on their heads in rescue. . . ."[21] In HPB's books we find the same deep concern for the sufferings of others. In *The Voice of the Silence,* which Tennyson is said to have had on his night table when he died,[22] are found these lines:

Let thy Soul lend its ear to every cry of pain like as the lotus bares its heart to drink the morning sun.

Let not the fierce Sun dry one tear of pain before thyself hast wiped it from the sufferer's eye.

But let each burning human tear drop on thy heart and there remain; nor ever brush it off, until the pain that caused it is removed.[23]

These tears, O thou of heart most merciful, these are the streams that irrigate the fields of charity immortal. 'Tis on such soil that grows the midnight blossom of Buddha,† more difficult to find, more rare to view, than is the flower of the Vogay tree. . . . Know that the stream of superhuman knowledge . . . thou hast won, must, from thyself . . . be poured forth into another bed. . . . Its pure fresh waters must be used to sweeter make the Ocean's bitter waves—that mighty sea of sorrow formed of the tears of men.[24]

Helena Andreyevna's career as a writer did not begin until her first child Helena Petrovna was five years old. We turn now to her birth, when the mother was only seventeen.

---

† Adeptship—"the blossom of Bodhisattva." [HPB.]

Chapter 2

Birth in Troubled Times

Helena Petrovna was born close to midnight in the early morning of August 12, 1831, in the Ukrainian town of Ekaterinoslav (Glory of Catherine), which was built for Catherine the Great. The Russians renamed it Dnepropetrovsk in honor of Peter the Great and the river that flows through it, the Dneiper.

The Dneiper has special significance in Russian history. It was along this river, the second largest in Russia, that the Rurik dynasty grew. By the eleventh century the Rus state centered at Kiev stretched from the Baltic to the Black Sea. The river became a major trade route to Constantinople (now Istanbul).

The river has important religious associations as well. It was at Kiev that a descendant of Rurik, the reigning Prince Vladimir, newly converted to Christianity, ordered his people to be herded into the Dneiper while priests administered mass baptism. Vladimir was canonized for converting pagan Russia to the Christian faith.[25] It seems ironic that eight centuries later another descendant of Rurik, born in a town on the same river, should publicly question—as HPB did in her writings—the efficacy of church sacraments, such as baptism, in conferring salvation upon the participants, nonparticipants being forever damned. HPB, however, was not anti-Christian in the least. In her first major work, *Isis Unveiled,* she discloses that the book "contains not one word against the pure teachings of Jesus, but unsparingly denounces their debasement into pernicious ecclesiastical systems. . . ."

The circumstances surrounding Helena Petrovna's own baptism are worthy of note. When she was born in 1831 there was great suffering in Russia. Asiatic cholera, the most cruel and fatal of all plagues, had first appeared in Western lands a year earlier, and soon its ravages spread throughout the Russian empire, then through much of Europe. Whole populations were wiped out in its deadly path. The brother of Czar Nicholas, the Grand Duke Constantine, was a victim. In the southern Russian household of Helena Petrovna's grandparents, where she was born, there had been several fatalities. Coffins were piled high everywhere, awaiting burial. It was a bad omen to be born at such a time, the peasants thought.

In all the excitement, Helena was born prematurely and in such delicate health that the family decided on immediate baptism lest she die "with the burden of original sin on her soul." A dramatic portrayal of what occurred is told by the relatives:

> The ceremony of baptism [in] "orthodox" Russia is attended with all of the paraphernalia of lighted tapers and "pairs" of god-mothers and god-fathers, every one of the spectators and actors being furnished with consecrated wax candles during the whole proceedings. Moreover, everyone has to stand during the baptismal rite, no one being allowed to sit in the Greek religion as they do in Roman Catholic and Protestant Churches, during the church and religious service. The room selected for the ceremony in the family mansion was large, but the crowd of devotees eager to witness it was still larger.
>
> [Aunt Nadya, the child-aunt of the baby], only a few years older than her niece aged twenty-four hours—placed as "proxy" for an absent relative, was in the first row immediately behind the venerable *protopope*. Feeling nervous and tired of standing still for nearly an hour, the child settled on the floor unperceived by the elders, and became probably drowsy in the overcrowded room on that hot August day. The ceremony was nearing its close. The sponsors were just in the act of renouncing the Evil One and his deeds, a renunciation emphasized in the Greek Church by thrice spitting upon the invisible enemy, when the little lady, toying with her lighted taper at the feet of the crowd, inadvertently set fire to the long flowing robes of the priest, no one [noting] the accident till it was too late. [Several persons, including the old priest, suffered burns.]
>
> That was another bad omen, according to the superstitious beliefs of orthodox Russia; and the innocent cause of it—the future Mme. Blavatsky—was doomed from that day in the eyes of all the town to an eventful life, full of vicissitude and trouble.[26]

But there was a good omen also. According to the old Julian calendar then current in Russia, the child was born around midnight of July 30/31. In the annals of Russian folklore, such a person was endowed with power over evil forces, including demons and witches.[27]

Some may question whether it really is a bad sign to be born amidst great suffering, whether from illness or any other cause. One recalls a celebrated passage in the *Bhagavad-Gita,* wherein the sage Krishna addresses his disciple thus:

> Both I and thou have passed through many births. . . . Mine are known unto me, but thou knowest not of thine. . . . I produce myself among creatures . . . whenever there is a decline of virtue and an insurrection of vice and injustice in the world; and thus I incarnate from age to age for the preservation of the just, the destruction of [wickedness], and the establishment of righteousness.[28]

The Fadeyev grandparents moved into their mansion in Ekaterinoslav sixteen years before Helena Petrovna's birth, when her grandfather Andrey became president of the Office of Foreign Settlers and her mother was one year old. Helena Petrovna, herself, was born in this home.[29] It still exists and, in 1991, the hundredth anniversary of her death, the visitor will find a plaque designating the mansion a historic site.

Peter von Hahn was in Poland to quell the uprising against that country's Russian conquerors at the time of his daughter's birth. He returned when Helena was six months old. One year later, the von Hahns moved to Romankov, an army town not far from the grandparents in Ekaterinoslav, and lived in a house of their own.

Chapter 3

Army Camp Life

The von Hahns did not remain in Romankov long; they soon moved to other parts of the Ukraine. As captain of a horse artillery battery, Peter frequently moved from place to place. Grandfather Andrey, in his administrative work, would likewise be moving to various parts of Russia. And as Helena Andreyevna and her children sometimes lived with Peter and other times with the grandparents, Helena Petrovna from an early age began a life of travel and wide experience of varying cultures and peoples, perhaps preparatory for her future world travels.

When Helena was two years old,[30] the first great sorrow overtook the family, which had moved to another army-occupied town far from the grandparents. Her baby brother, Sasha, became seriously ill, and no medical aid was available. The spring rains had so muddied the roads that travel by foot or horse was impossible. Thus the poor mother witnessed the slow death of her child, with no doctor to cure him or relieve his sufferings.[31]

While pregnant with her next child, Helena Andreyevna moved temporarily to Odessa, a renowned cultural center and resort on the Black Sea. Andrey was now there, serving on the board of trustees for the colonizers, adventurous families coming from as far away as Germany to settle in newly acquired Russian territory. When Helena was three-and-a-half, her sister, Vera, was born.

It was not long before Helena Andreyevna rejoined her husband and again the family was on the move from hamlet to hamlet in the Ukraine. This constant uprooting of family life would be an exhausting trial for any mother, but was especially so for one in fragile health. Furthermore, the wandering life with Peter "was ever like a dark cloud over her head," relates de Zirkoff. "As soon as she became settled and attached to her home, as soon as sweet friendships had taken root and things became dear to her heart, the nightmare of the frightening word 'transferred' would descend upon her and would force her once more to leave all this behind, moving on and on to strange and lonely places. Small, dirty provincial towns, boring dinners and tea-parties with their heavy smoke of cigarettes, the eternal conversations about horses, dogs, guns, and the like."[32]

Chapter 4

A Joyous Respite

In the spring of 1836 came splendid news that Peter and his company had been transferred to St. Petersburg. Russia as yet had no railroads. The nine-hundred-mile journey in horse-drawn vehicles was probably a great adventure for Helena Petrovna, but for the mother with a baby and a five-year-old to care for, it was another matter. She was thrilled, however, by the prospect of sharing in the cultural life of the nation's capital—the most European city in Russia, almost on par with London and Paris.

St. Petersburg was no novelty to Peter, who had grown up there and whose family still lived there. In his absence at work, his brothers obligingly escorted their sister-in-law to museums, the theater, and opera. "Here in Petersburg," remarks writer Nekrasova, "it was possible to find oneself suddenly face to face with people about whom one knew only through books; it was possible to see 'great poets' in person."[33] At a private gallery Helena Andreyevna had a great surprise and wrote Catherine:

> I stumbled upon a figure which seemed familiar to me. . . . Upon second glance, I recognized Pushkin. I had imagined him a dark brunette, but his hair is not darker than mine—it is long and tousled. He is short in stature, with a bewhiskered face, not handsome, but his eyes sparkled like coals and incessantly. . . . He glanced at me several times and smiled—obviously there was an expression of adoration on my face.[34]

With all these exciting possibilities available, however, Nekrasova writes that the mother did not neglect her children: "As before, she played piano duets with Lolo [Helena], sang songs with her, taught her to read and write, and delighted in the extraordinary aptitudes and mind of her five-year-old girl."[35] (Helena Petrovna's pet names—Lolo, Lyolya, and Lyolinka—are all diminutives of Helena.[36])

From birth, Helena "became the object of her Mother's affectionate solicitude," and "in spite of Helena Andreyevna's seventeen years, she fed and tended the child herself," writes Catherine Nekrasova in her biographical sketch of the mother, published in the 1880s in *Russkaya Starina,* a historical journal. This has never been translated for use in any biography of HPB and is of special value, as it is largely based on Helena Andreyevna's letters to her older sister Catherine, the only letters of HPB's mother that have apparently survived. Up to now any biographer of HPB could speculate as they pleased upon the relationship of HPB and her mother. Thus Marion Meade in her 1980 biography *Madame Blavatsky: The Woman Behind the Myth* could state with impunity that the mother, involved in her career as a novelist, was "always remote" to Helena Petrovna, abandoning her to the care and discipline of governesses. Meade then makes the extraordinary claim that the child always viewed her mother with "deep hostility" and was determined "to kill her prematurely."[37]

While in St. Petersburg, the mother continued her own studies. She read books in German, Italian, and English, in all of which languages she was self-taught. English she especially loved. After reading Bulwer-Lytton's recent novel, *Godolphin,* Helena Andreyevna decided to translate excerpts into Russian and timidly submitted her work for publication in a popular magazine, *Library for Reading.* She was overjoyed by its acceptance, and the editor encouraged her to write something of her own. Thus began her career as an author.

Several of Helena Andreyevna's novels concern the plight of unhappily married women. They were partly autobiographical, for her life with Peter, who was twice her age, had proved a great disappointment.[38] In *The World's Judgment,* she wrote:

> The fine, sharp and fast mind of my husband, as a rule accompanied by a cutting irony, smashed every day one of my brightest, most innocent and pure aspirations and feelings. All that I admired, all that I aspired to from my childhood, all that was sacred to my heart was either laughed at, or was shown me in the pitiless and cynical light of his cold and cruel reasoning.[39]

The time approached for Peter to be transferred from St. Petersburg to the Ukraine, and his wife was terrified at the thought. In her last letter to her sister Catherine from St. Petersburg she wrote: "I admit that it is awful to remember it will be necessary to return to some Romankov or Oskol! Oh, God, give me endurance." She soon concluded it was *not* necessary; the time had come to separate from her husband, at least temporarily, and she went to live with her parents.

Her decision coincided with a major change in the Fadeyev family's life. Andrey had just been appointed trustee of the Kalmuck Buddhist tribes in Astrakhan, as well as for the German colonizers there. This semi-Oriental city is strategically located at the mouth of the Volga, where the river flows into the Caspian Sea. Centuries before, HPB's Viking ancestors passed this way en route to trade markets in Iran and the Far East.

Andrey had been ordered by his superiors to proceed to St. Petersburg for instructions on his new position, and he happened to arrive at the very time the von Hahns were there. When he departed for Astrakhan, Helena Andreyevna and her children went with him. HPB's mother related, "She started off, under the protection and patronage of her father, for the other end of Russia. Neither the distance of a thousand miles, nor the difficult, murderous roads frightened her."[40] Andrey Fadeyev's trusteeship over a hundred thousand Buddhists brought Helena Petrovna for the first time in contact with an Oriental religion.

The Kalmucks had come originally from China in the 1600s. When the Fadeyevs and von Hahns lived in Astrakhan they visited the Kalmuck leader, Prince Tumen, who lived in a European-style house on one of the islands in the delta. His days were spent in prayer in a Buddhist temple, which he had built. In his younger days, after the defeat of Napoleon by the Russians, he had organized a regiment of his people and joined the Russian army in its triumphant march into Paris, for which the prince received many decorations from the Czar.[41]

Helena Andreyevna lived in Astrakhan for a year and wrote two novels there, one on Kalmuck life—later translated into French—and the other set in the Caucasus, where the family had lately gone for mineral baths in the hot springs, for which that region is famous.

Chapter 5

On the Road Again

Chastened by his wife's departure and lonesome for his precious children, Peter von Hahn pleaded with her to return. Soon they resumed their life together wandering from one military garrison to another.

The first place the family settled in was Poltava, where they remained longer than usual. Here the mother's burdens were immeasurably lightened when a governess, Antonia Kühlwein, offered to take charge of the children. She remained with the family for many years as a teacher and beloved companion. Helena Andreyevna continued with her elder daughter's piano lessons, professional teachers being engaged later, for the pupil excelled in music. Helena Andreyevna had a beautiful voice and in the evenings would play the piano and sing Russia's favorite folk songs, while Antonia taught the children to dance. It was a jolly time, to provide the children with golden memories of their childhood days.[42]

Fortunately, much of what occurred during the children's growing years was recorded by Helena Petrovna's younger sister, Vera. At the age of ten she started a diary, reconstructing the previous years while her memory was fresh.[43] Her diaries became the basis for two autobiographies, *When I Was Small* and *My Adolescence*. Both have been translated into English for use in the present biography, as they contain useful information about Helena Petrovna's activities and the fortunes of the family as a whole. Later, when the sisters were mature women, Vera continued to write about Helena "as a woman with her good and bad sides." Though she "loved her ardently, she was not inclined to exaggerate her worth." She "was not hostile to her teachings but also not carried away to the point of forgetting the ideals and higher truths of Christianity in the light of which," she believed, "all the lofty and moral teachings of antiquity had been submerged."[44]

Vera became a noted author in her own right. Her stories for young people, like those of Louisa May Alcott for American youth, inspired several generations of Russian children. As reported in London's *Review of Reviews,* Vera also wrote for an adult audience; her works include twelve novels, sixty stories, two plays—a drama and a comedy, both of which won first prize at the New Russian University, and "books for the people" read in all the town halls of the land.[45] She wrote under the name of Vera Zhelihovsky, the latter being her second husband's name.

During the Poltava days, Vera was only two. She recalled the time in *When I Was Small,* where she wrote:

> I remember that mama was often ailing, and when in good health she would sit for hours behind her green calico screen and write. The space behind the screen was called "Mama's study," and neither myself nor my older sister Lyolya ever *dared touch anything in this corner,* separated from the nursery by nothing but a curtain. We did not know what it was that mama spent her days doing there. All we knew was that she was writing something.

When Vera was six, she was amazed to learn from Antonia that her mother was writing books, and that they first appeared in serialized form in a magazine together with the writings of other authors who were paid for their contributions.

"Does mama get paid, too?" Vera asked.

"Yes, a lot of money. She uses the money to pay the governesses and the teachers their salaries and to buy books needed for herself or for us."

"Does she pay you, too?"

"No," Antonia answered, "she doesn't pay me anything. I get money from the czar, and am living with your family just because I love your mother more than anyone else in the world."

The story of how Antonia became recipient of funds from the czar is a Cinderella tale more pitiful than the classic story of that name. Fortune finally smiled when she was accepted in the Catherine Institute in St. Petersburg, founded by Catherine the Great for daughters of good families. Antonia graduated with honors and at the commencement Czar Nicholas I presented her with a gold medal. Inquiring about her family, and learning she had none, he offered her a choice. She could become a ward of the school or receive a pension from him for life. She chose the latter, as she longed to see the world.[46]

Peter's battery moved from Poltava to other parts of the Ukraine. In the spring of 1839, his ailing wife went with the children to Odessa for mineral water treatments. While there, Helena Andreyevna consum-

mated a long-held plan to find a governess to teach her children English—a language she deemed essential to a good education. But who
would accompany the family on their travels to lonely and desolate
places? A young Yorkshire woman, Augusta Jeffers, agreed to "bear all
the misfortunes of travel" and to remain with the family "for always."
When Miss Jeffers left after several years, a Russianized English girl was
engaged so the children would not forget English.[47]

Chapter 6

Year with Grandparents

A fter the family's stay in Odessa, a dreary summer was spent in Poland, where Peter von Hahn was transferred. Helena Andreyevna's health did not improve. Furthermore, she was expecting another child. Vassily Benzenger, a young doctor provided by her parents, was henceforth in constant attendance and lived with the family.[48] When Helena Andreyevna's parents moved from Astrakhan to Saratov, a large town on the Volga, where her father became governor of the province, she and the children left Peter in Poland and went to live with them, where they spent a happy year in ideal surroundings. Her health improved remarkably and there was ample opportunity to write. A baby boy, Leonid, was born in June 1840.[49]

It is only at this point, when Helena Petrovna is nine, that we begin to learn about her personal characteristics. Vera thus far has been of no help, being four years her junior, but Aunt Nadya, two years Helena's senior, appears to have remembered a good deal. She informed A. P. Sinnett, Helena's first biographer:

> [In Helena's] childhood all her sympathies and attractions went out towards people of the lower class. She had always preferred to play with her servants' children rather than with her equals and . . . had to be constantly watched for fear she should escape from the house to make friends with ragged street boys. So, later on in life, she continued to be drawn in sympathy towards those who were in a humbler station of life than herself, and [she] showed a pronounced indifference to the "nobility" to which by birth she belonged.[50]

> She was the strangest girl, one with a distinct dual nature. One mischievous, the other mystical, and metaphysically inclined. . . . No schoolboy was ever more uncontrollable or full of the most unimaginable pranks. . . . At the same time, when the paroxysm of mischief-making had run its course, no old scholar could be more assiduous in his study; and she could not be prevailed upon to give up her books, which she would devour night and day as long as the impulse lasted. The enormous library of her grandparents seemed then hardly large enough to satisfy her cravings. . . .[51]

One thing particularly caused trouble: Helena had the uncomfortable habit of telling people to their faces what she thought of them—something not done in polite society. This "embarrassed many and placed her own relatives in a very awkward situation." Yet "she was so kind and so daring, that she was ready to give everything away to the needy, to do everything for a friend, and to decide upon any action in defense of the injured," while "she never remembered evil or injury to herself."[52]†

† Years later one of her students recalled: "One thing was remarkable about HPB. She *never, never* bore malice, resented criticism in private, or made one feel that there remained even a trace of annoyance or disapproval in her mind, or even a shadow of feeling about anything past. . . . Everything was just wiped clean out and wholly forgotten once it was past." (Bertram Keightley, *Reminiscenses of H. P. Blavatsky,* 25.)

Chapter 7

Christmas in the Ukraine

The following spring the von Hahn family was re-united in Malarossa, in the Ukraine, where the climate was pleasant and warm. Helena Andreyevna had spacious quarters in which to write. Vera relates that her mother's "sole recreation was her writing; her only solace and joy were the growing children on whom all her hopes and care were directed."[53]

Helena Petrovna decided to study German and Antonia gave her lessons three times a week. Such excellent progress was made that her father exclaimed: "A worthy descendant of her glorious ancestors, the German knights of Hahn-Hahn von der Roeter Hahn, who never knew any language but German."[54]†

In the fall, Helena Andreyevna became seriously ill. Dr. Benzenger advised that she should go immediately to Kharkov for medical treatments, but she chose to wait until spring and go to Odessa, where she had many friends.

Vera's autobiography, *When I Was Small*,‡ provides this intimate picture of the children's last Christmas with their mother.[55]

> Winter came. All the fields and all the roads were now snow-bound. . . . Doors and windows were locked up and sealed, firewood crackled in stoves, burning bright; evenings were long, and days were grey and so short that our lessons had to be finished by candlelight. Right up to the Christmas holiday season, there wasn't a single memorable occasion to break the monotony of our life. Before Christmas, Papa made a trip to Kharkov and came back with many gifts for us. He also brought plenty of something that was taken to Mama's room as "kitchen supplies." Busy examining our illustrated books, we paid no attention to that altogether.

---

† Meade's biography not only portrays HPB's mother as indifferent to her daughter but her father as cold to her. To compensate for his rejection, Meade claims that Helena fantasied he took her on a three-month trip with him to London and Paris.

‡ Vera's stories were first written for her children. A few years later, Russian children everywhere were reading the adventures of Vera and Helena (Lyolya or Lolo).

That evening we were summoned to the sitting-room; we saw everyone assembled there by the light of one candle, and Papa snuffed even that one out as soon as we came in.

"What's that? Why are there no lights on?" we asked.

"Wait and you'll see why," Mama replied.

"Don't move!" Antonia said, turning me by the shoulders. "Stand still and look straight before you." We stood stock-still, in a total silence. I stared, my eyes wide open but I couldn't see anything.

All of a sudden, there was a rustling, and a blue fiery pattern ran across the wall like a lightning.

"What is that?" we exclaimed.

"Look! Look what a fiery pencil Mama has! Look what she's drawing!" came Papa's joyful voice.

A face with an aquiline nose and asinine ears flashed on the wall, then another shape, a third one. . . . As Mama's hand moved swiftly, patterns and pictures appeared and gleamed. . . . "Read!" she said.

And we read the fiery, instantly disappearing words, "Lolo [H.P.B.] and Vera are little fools!"

"Well, that's something!" Lyolya [H.P.B.] shouted and burst out laughing. She dashed towards Mother. "Show me that, Mommie! What's that? What are you writing with?"

"Here it is!" Mama said and, with a stronger stroke on the wall, lit *the first phosphoric match we had ever seen.* Sulphur matches came into use in Russia in the early forties. Before that, fire was lit with flintstone. . . .

Then came the eve of January 1842 [the Russian Christmas]. A dull, grey, sad day it was! . . . We were alone almost throughout the day; we were told Mama was ailing, and as we knew she often stayed in her bedroom when sick, we were not surprised either at Antonia's staying with her all day long, or even Papa's almost constant absence. He only came when we were having dinner with Miss Jeffers, ate his borscht hastily, beamed at us through his spectacles, pinched my cheek, teased Lyolya and then said he was very busy and left us again. After dinner Miss Jeffers, too, was nowhere to be seen.

Lyolya and I settled quietly in the semi-dark room, sighing secretly for our festivities of yesteryear, recalling Grandmother's gifts, Gorov's marvelous Christmas party, and wondering if they would make a Christmas party in Saratov without us or, on the contrary, deem Nadya too grown-up for childish entertainment like a Christmas tree. . . .

Outside, in the yellow dusk, snowflakes were flying and the wind was already howling in the chimney, wailing out its dreary nightly song.

Even Lyolya, always so carefree and cheerful, looked somewhat depressed. . . .

Suddenly the door opened, and Annushka came in with Leonid in her arms, flanked by her fat sister Marya . . . our seamstress and housekeeper. Both of them sat down by the wall, smiling and glancing now at us, now at the door, as if waiting for something. . . . When the door opened once more Mama's maid Masha came in. . . .

"Come on, young ladies!" she said. "Mama wants to see you!"

"Oh!" Lyolya cried out and slapped herself on the forehead. "I know what it's all about!" She darted towards the door and ran to Mama's room. Naturally, I ran after her; but only when I reached the bedroom did I realize what was going on. A beautifully decorated unexpected Christmas tree was glistening with lights right in the middle of the room. There were toys under the tree, and Mama, Antonia, Papa, Miss Jeffers and all the rest were standing around it and smiling at the thought of having spent the whole day fussing with the Christmas tree and yet tricked us so successfully![56]

Chapter 8

A Sad Departure

S pring came and as Helena Andreyevna's health had not improved, everyone accompanied her to Odessa, save her husband, who could not leave his job.

When writing the story of HPB's mother, Catherine Nekrasova interviewed both Dr. Benzenger and Vera and reported:

> In spite of all the care and efforts of the then renowned Dr. Geno in Odessa, she became worse with every day, particularly from the bloodlettings in which medicine of that day believed so strongly. . . . Weak without these, she became yet weaker and closer to the grave. She was afraid she would not last until the arrival of her parents, and began writing her farewell letter. . . . She thanked her parents warmly for everything and implored her mother not to forsake the children.[57]

The arrival of her parents and sisters inspired her with new life, and for a glorious month she was almost her old self again. As recovery seemed imminent, plans were made for everyone to return to Saratov and live there permanently.[58] Helena Andreyevna's mother and sisters, Cathy and Nadya, all strong swimmers, took time out to bathe in the beautiful Black Sea, and Helena Petrovna became an expert swimmer too.

Soon thereafter, however, Helena Andreyevna's health declined quickly, and she died in her own mother's arms on June twenty-fourth, in the twenty-ninth year of her life. The family was shattered with grief and the children were inconsolable.[59] Among the reading public in Russia, Helena Andreyevna's death was universally mourned. Belinsky penned this epitaph:

> Peace be unto your ashes, extraordinary woman, victim of the rich talents of your own lofty nature! . . . We thank you for your short life. Not in vain did it bloom like a luxurious, fragrant flower of profound feelings and lofty thoughts. Your soul is in this flower and there will be no death for it![60]

In the months before her death, Helena Andreyevna was plagued by

23

thoughts of her children. Nekrasova relates that in a letter to Catherine (November 18, 1841) she expressed worries about their future, "for it seemed to her that she would soon die," adding: "The question of their upbringing gave her no peace; she so wanted to give them a good 'fundamental' education, but 'there were no means whatsoever but her pen.'" Nekrasova notes that she worried especially about Helena Petrovna:

> Governesses for her eldest daughter were useless as she quickly outgrew them. Helena Andreyevna began thinking of sending her to Odesskii Institute, even though the education of the Institute was contrary to her fundamental convictions; but of the two evils this would be the lesser. The thought of her own illness tormented her, particularly because of this.[61]

Vera reports that over the years, her mother worried most about Helena, "the one gifted from childhood with an exceptional nature,"[62] and that when she lay dying uttered these prophetic words: "Ah well! perhaps it is best that I am dying, so at least I shall be spared seeing what befalls Helena! Of one thing I am certain, her life will not be as that of other women, and that she will have much to suffer."[63]

What did she fear her daughter would suffer? Perhaps these words from her novels *The Ideal* and *The Vain Gift* provide an answer:

> Every outstanding woman, especially a writer, will be persecuted by the world. . . . The man with a higher intellect is intolerable enough to this world, but the position of a woman, who has been placed by Nature itself above the crowd is verily desperate.
>
> The Hundred-headed monster of public opinion will declare her immoral, will throw dirt on her noblest feelings, . . . Her gifts of intellect, her talents all are in vain before the crowd; she will be like a criminal rejected by Society.[64]

Helena Andreyevna herself had experienced this kind of malevolence from provincial minds.[65]

In another of her novels, *The Judgment of the World,* the heroine, in a death testament, declares that the "members of this awful tribunal are all cowardly people. From the shameful block on which it has laid my head . . . I still implore you with the final words of my lips: 'Do not fear it! It is the slave of the strong and ruins only the weak.'"[66] These are words Helena Petrovna must have read and cried over, as well as all of her mother's other stories, which appeared in a handsome four-volume edition a year after Helena Andreyevna's death—a living legacy for her children.

Chapter 9

Saratov Days

S oon after Helena Andreyevna died, her children moved permanently to Saratov. The awesome journey over the vast steppes of Russia helped assuage their grief. Deserts, too, were traversed, and the horses of the Fadeyevs' two massive coaches were exchanged for camels, to the delight of the children.

A day and a night were spent at the summer quarters of the Kalmuck Buddhists from Astrakhan. Prince Tumen extended a royal welcome to his old friends and provided a fascinating glimpse of nomadic life in the desert. Princess Helena, well versed in Kalmuck Buddhist customs, explained them to her grandchildren. She said of the prayer wheel: "If the Buddhists are too tired or too busy to pray, they just turn the handle as fast as they can, unrolling the prayers and then rolling them back again."

"The fools!" Vera declared. Helena retorted: "Well, there are fools among our own people too. Isn't it the same thing to turn a handle as to mumble your prayers without any thought . . .?" When she reminded them of how the Fadeyev housekeeper, while praying before icons, would shout at the maids or box their ears, everyone laughed.

In the new phase of their life at Saratov the children had three new teachers, in addition to Antonia. One was a French governess, Henriette Peigneur, a distinguished beauty in the days of the French revolution. Writes Sinnett:

> Her favourite narrative to the children consisted in the description of those days of glory and excitement when, [she was] chosen by the "Phrygian redcaps," the *citoyens rouges* of Paris to represent in the public festivals the goddess of Liberty, she had been driven in triumph, day after day, along the streets of the *grande ville* in glorious processions. The narrator herself was now a weird old woman, bent down by age, and looked more like the traditional *Fée Carabosse* than anything else. But her eloquence was moving, and the young girls that formed her willing audience were greatly excited by the glowing descriptions . . . [Helena Petrovna] declared then and there that she meant to be a "Goddess of Liberty" all her life.[67]

The following summer, Helena discovered her own "Hall of Liberty." The family had rented a great country mansion full of subterranean galleries, long abandoned passages, turrets, and weird nooks and corners. Vera writes:

> We had been permitted to explore [them] under the protection of half-a-dozen male servants [with] torches and lanterns. . . . Helena would not remain satisfied with one solitary visit, nor with a second. She had selected the uncanny region as a Liberty Hall, and a safe refuge where she could avoid her lessons. A long time passed before her secret was found out. . . . She had erected for herself a tower out of old broken chairs and tables in a corner under an iron-barred window, high up in the ceiling of the vault, and there she would hide for hours, reading a book known as "Solomon's Wisdom," in which every kind of popular legend was taught. . . .
>
> [As to fairy tales,] there was, among the numerous servants of the Fadeyev family an old woman, an under-nurse, who was famous for telling them. . . . Only, while all we children forgot those tales as easily as we had learned them, Helena never either forgot the stories or consented to recognize them as fictions. She thoroughly took to heart all the troubles of the heroes, and maintained that all their most wonderful adventures were quite natural.[68]

Helena, however, not only immersed herself in the stories she heard or read, she told her own. Vera relates:

> At about ten versts [roughly seven miles] from the governor's villa there was a field, an extensive sandy tract of land, evidently once upon a time the bottom of a sea or a great lake, as its soil yielded petrified relics of fishes, shells, and teeth of some (to us) unknown monsters. Most of these relics were broken and mangled by time, but one could often find whole stones of various sizes on which were imprinted figures of fishes and plants and animals of kinds now wholly extinct, but which proved their undeniable antediluvian origin. The marvellous and sensational stories that we, children and schoolgirls, heard from Helena during that epoch were countless. I well remember when stretched at full length on the ground, her chin reclining on her two palms, and, her two elbows buried deep in the soft sand, she used to dream aloud, and tell us of her visions, evidently clear, vivid, and as palpable as life to her! . . . How lovely the description she gave us of the submarine life of all those beings, the mangled remains of which were now crumbling to dust around us. How vividly she described their past fights and

battles on the spot where she lay, assuring us she saw it all; and how minutely she drew on the sand with her finger the fantastic forms of the long dead sea monsters, and made us almost see the very colors of the fauna and flora of those dead regions. . . .[69]

Helena spoke of reincarnation even in those early days:

It was her delight to gather around herself a party of us younger children at twilight, and, after taking us into the large dark museum [of her grandmother's house] to hold us there spellbound with her weird stories. . . . Each of the stuffed animals in the museum had taken her in turn into its confidence, had divulged to her the history of its life in previous incarnations or existences. Where had she heard of reincarnation, or who could have taught her anything of the superstitious mysteries of metempsychosis in a Christian family? Yet, she would stretch herself on her favorite animal, a gigantic stuffed seal, and caressing its silvery, soft white skin, she would repeat to us his adventures as told to her by *himself,* in such glowing colors and eloquent style, that even grown up persons found themselves interested involuntarily in her narratives.[70]

Among Helena's audience were some of the children of serfs. Serfdom existed in Russia until 1861, one and a half years before Lincoln freed the slaves.[†] The serfs in the Fadeyev household, however, were more like members of the family than servile underlings, and Princess Helena would not tolerate their being abused in any way, as Helena Petrovna bitterly discovered one day. Years later, HPB told the story to Colonel Henry Steel Olcott, President of the Theosophical Society, who recorded it in his *Old Diary Leaves:*

. . . on one occasion, in a fit of temper at her nurse, a faithful old serf who had been brought up in the family, she struck her a blow on the face. This coming to her grandmother's knowledge, the child was summoned, questioned, and confessed her fault. The grandmother at once had the castle bell rung to call all the servants of the household, of whom there were scores, and when they were assembled in the great hall, she told her granddaughter that she had acted as no lady should, in unjustly striking a helpless serf who would not dare defend herself; and she ordered her to beg her pardon and kiss her hand in token of sincerity.

The child at first, crimson with shame, was disposed to rebel; but the old lady told her that if she did not instantly obey, she would

† The United States Emancipation Proclamation occurred on September 22, 1862.

send her from her house in disgrace. She added that no real noble lady would refuse to make amends for a wrong to a servant, especially one who by a lifetime of faithful service had earned the confidence and love of her superiors.

Naturally generous and kind-hearted towards the people of the lower classes, the impetuous child burst into tears, kneeled before the old nurse, kissed her hand, and asked to be forgiven. Needless to say that she was thenceforth fairly worshipped by the retainers of the family. She told me that lesson was worth everything to her, and had taught her the principle of doing justice to those whose social rank made them incapable of compelling aggressors to do rightly towards them.[71]

As to Helena's volatile temperament, this would flare up at times even when she was an adult. Olcott once appealed to her mahatmic teachers about this: "I asked why a permanent control was not put upon her fiery temper, and why she should not always be modified into the quiet Self-centered sage" she was on certain occasions. The answer was that "such a course would inevitably lead to her death by apoplexy; the body was vitalized by a fiery impetuous spirit, one which from childhood brooked no restraint; and if vent were not allowed for the excessive corporeal energy, the result must be fatal." Olcott continues:

I was told to look into the history of her kinsfolk, the Russian Dolgorukovs, and I would understand what was meant. I did so and found that this princely and warlike family, tracing back to Rurik had always been distinguished by extreme courage, a daring equal to every emergency, a passionate love of personal independence, and a fearlessness of consequences in the carrying out of its wishes.

Strange Happenings

" or Helena, all nature seemed animated with a mysterious life of its own," Vera relates. "*She heard the voice of every object and form, whether organic or inorganic;* and claimed consciousness and being, not only for some mysterious powers visible and audible to herself alone in *what was to everyone else empty space,* but even for visible but *inanimate things such as pebbles, moulds, and pieces of decaying phosphorescent timber.*"[72]

It may be owing to such experiences that Helena was drawn to a centenarian by name of Baraniy Bouyerak, who dwelt close to Saratov. He was revered by the people in that area as a holy person, a healer, and a magician. His house was in a wild ravine of a neighboring forest. "He was greatly versed in the knowledge of the occult properties of plants and flowers," reports Vera, "and could read the future, it is said." Bouyerak had "an irresistible attraction" for Helena, Vera continues:

[She] visited the strange old man whenever she could. . . . Once there, she would put questions and listen with a passionate earnestness to the old man's replies and explanations as to how to understand the language of bees, birds and animals. . . . He used to say of her constantly to us: "This little lady is quite different from all of you. There are great events lying in wait for her in the future. I feel sorry in thinking that I will not live to see my predictions of her verified; but *they will all come to pass!*"[73]

A wise personage of another order than Bouyerak, it seems, was interested in Helena's welfare. "From her earliest recollections," Sinnett remarks, "she would sometimes have visions of a mature protector, whose imposing appearance dominated her imagination from a very early period. This protector was always the same, his features never changed; in [later] life she met him as a living man, and knew him as though she had been brought up in his presence."[74]

There is no indication that Helena spoke to her family about this personage, but Vera says that as a girl Helena would say: "Wise men had existed in all ages and existed even in our days, making themselves known only to those who were worthy of knowing and seeing them, and who believed in, instead of laughing at them."[75]

It may be that to her so-called protector she owed her invulnerability to harm, if such examples that follow, retold by Sinnett, are to be credited. The first occurred in the family gallery that housed the portraits of the Dolgorukov ancestors. One picture excited Helena's curiosity. It was covered by a curtain and placed high on the wall out of reach. Her relatives refused to say who it was, so Helena stole into the room one day when no one was around. In Sinnett's words:

> She dragged a table to the wall, and contrived to set another small table on that, and a chair on the top of all, and then gradually succeeded in mounting up on this unstable edifice. She could just manage to reach the picture . . . and leaning with one hand against the dusty wall, contrived with the other to draw back the curtain. The effect wrought upon her by the sight of the picture was startling, and the momentary movement back upset her frail platform. But exactly what occurred she does not know. She lost consciousness from the moment she staggered and began to fall, and when she recovered her senses she was lying quite unhurt on the floor, the tables and chair were back again in their usual places, the curtain had been run back upon its rings, and she would have imagined the whole incident some unusual kind of dream but for the fact that the mark of her small hand remained imprinted on the dusty wall high up beside the picture.[76]

On another occasion, reports Sinnett, Helena's life was saved under equally strange circumstances: "A horse bolted with her—she fell, with her foot entangled in the stirrup, and before the horse was stopped she ought, she thinks, to have been killed outright but for a strange sustaining power she distinctly felt around her, which seemed to hold her up in defiance of gravitation."

Sinnett comments in his *Incidents in the Life of Madame Blavatsky:* "If anecdotes of this surprising kind were few and far between in Mme. Blavatsky's life, I should suppress them in attempting to edit her memoirs, but as will be seen later, they form the staple of the narratives which each person in turn, who has anything to say about her, comes forward to tell."

As to the strange happenings recounted in this chapter, HPB apparently was not satisfied to be merely the visible focus for such manifestations, she wished to *understand* them, as well as her own developing psychic powers. Were there books available that she could study on such subjects? In a letter to a friend of her youth, Prince Alexander Dondoukov-Korsakov, HPB speaks of a library that her grandmother had inherited from her father, Prince Paul. It contained hundreds of books on alchemy, magic, and other occult sciences. "I had read them with keenest interest before the age of fifteen, . . ." she writes. "Soon neither Paracelsus, Kunrath, nor C. Agrippa would have anything to teach me."[77] It is only later, however, when she traveled in the East that she found more light on these subjects.

In this chapter, the words *magician, magic,* and *occult* appear. HPB's use of them in her writings requires explanation. In her *Theosophical Glossary,* under *magician* she quotes from her book *Isis Unveiled:*

> This term, once a title of renown and distinction, has come to be wholly perverted from its true meaning. Once the synonym of all that was honourable and reverent, of a possessor of learning and wisdom, it has become degraded into an epithet to designate one who is a pretender and a juggler; a charlatan, in short, or one who has "sold his soul to the Evil One," who misuses his knowledge, and employs it for low and dangerous uses, according to the teachings of the clergy. . . . The word is derived from *Magh, Mah,* in Sanskrit *Maha*—great; a man well versed in esoteric knowledge.

HPB adds that in Latin the word used is *Magi,* which we all recognize from the story of the birth of Christ and the three Wise Men, or Magi, who saw his star, the star of Bethlehem.[78]

HPB defines *White Magic,* or *Beneficent Magic,* as "*divine* magic, devoid of selfishness, love of power, of ambition, or lucre, and bent only on doing good to the world in general, and one's neighbour in particular. The smallest attempt to use one's abnormal powers for the gratification of self, makes these powers sorcery or black magic."

White and black magic, of course, have nothing to do with the color of one's skin. In HPB's article "Practical Occultism" (*Lucifer,* August 1888) she writes that "it is the motive and *the motive alone,* which makes an exercise of power become black, malignant, or white, beneficent magic."

The dictionary reveals that the word *occult* is derived from the Latin word *occultus,* meaning "hidden." HPB indicates that true occultism is not the same as the occult arts, such as alchemy, mesmerism, and the cultivation of various psychic powers. True occultism, called *Atma Vidya* in India, is defined by the Orientalist simply as "knowledge of the Soul" or "true wisdom," but it means far more. One who follows this path becomes "a beneficent force in Nature . . . 'not for himself, but for the world he lives.' " It is when the personal selfish self is reduced "to a cypher, that the union with the 'Higher Self' can take place. . . . Then the brilliant *Augoeides,* the divine SELF, can vibrate in conscious harmony with both the poles of the human Entity—the man of matter purified, and the ever pure Spiritual Soul" and becomes "blended, merged into, and one with It forever."[79]

Chapter **11**

Expanding Horizons

The years 1845 and 1846, when Helena was fourteen
and fifteen, were a time of worry and unrest for the
Fadeyevs. Grandfather Andrey was being replaced as governor of
Saratov. His future uncertain, he spent months in St. Petersburg seeking reassignment. An old friend, Prince Vorontzov, viceroy of the
Caucasus, came to his rescue and appointed him state treasurer of the
newly conquered land formerly owned by the Turks, and before them
by the Iranians. Later he held other positions.

For the family to leave their beloved Russia to go to that "heathen
Asia," as some called it, was an ordeal. Traveling there was dangerous
and required an armed escort part of the way. A hundred thousand
Russian soldiers were quartered in the Caucasus to protect the borders
and to fight off the Circassian mountaineers who ravaged the population.[80] A decade or two later, Helena's uncle Rostislav wrote *Sixty
Years of Caucasian Wars,* a classic source of information about the wars
and the many ethnic and religious groups that lived in this exotic semi-
tropical land with its gorgeous vegetation and magnificent snow-
capped peaks. In time, these wonders, and fascinating relics of ancient
Iranian and Islamic culture, attracted such notables as Pushkin, Tolstoy,
Chekov, and Tchaikovsky.[81]

The grandparents and young Nadya left Saratov first to make preparations for the others to follow. Crowds of German immigrants who
remembered Andrey for his integrity and fair dealings ten years earlier
gathered to greet him each time the boat docked for firewood and
supplies as it neared Astrakhan, at the mouth of the Volga.

After weeks of travel by sea and land, the party reached its destination, the capital of Georgia, Tiflis, now called Tbilisi. For those back
home there was much anxiety waiting to hear of their safe arrival, as it
took months to receive a letter.

Almost a year passed before the von Hahn children, their aunt
Catherine, Yuli de Witte, her husband, and their two boys would be
reunited with the others. Meanwhile they had some novel experiences
of their own.

33

The summer and fall were spent on the other side of the Volga, where the children's uncle Yuli managed a large state farm. Vera wrote:

> Those vast, trans-Volgian steppes looked so green, boundless, quiet, peaceful and blissful to us children unaccustomed to real country. . . . There were no guests or noisy gatherings of friends, no fireworks, acrobats, or music with which we had been entertained in the last years at Saratov. Simple country life with its work on the farm and in the fields, of which we had never had any idea, came very close to us. . . . Helena, carried away by her fantasies, gave me the idea that we were "just common girls now," our uncle was "a common farmer" just like "Farmer Gray" in the English story by that title.

The children were overwhelmed by "the simple, healthy vigor" of their new life.[82]

When winter came the families moved back to Saratov, not to the spacious governor's mansion but to a tiny house with rooms like closets. Helena complained, "This is real poverty!" With sadness the young people passed their old home, now occupied by the new governor.[83]

In May 1847, the time at last arrived to go to Tiflis. In her memoirs, Vera provides a fascinating account of their eventful journey and of the first years spent in the Caucasus.[84]

The first house the families lived in was a newly built, magnificent palace, on the outskirts of the city, owned by an Armenian merchant. After a year, they moved to a mansion formerly owned by Prince Chavachavadze. Here the Fadeyevs and the de Wittes lived for twenty years, returning to Odessa after the grandparents and Uncle Yuli died.

Tiflis was an inferno in the summer, and those that could fled to the mountains. Thus during the next few years the von Hahn children, with their elders, visited the many mountain retreats and mineral spas for which the Caucasus is noted.[85] Vera tells how on one trip, Helena, Nadya, Catherine, and her husband narrowly escaped death: "Early in summer, the masses of snow on the peaks of the giant mountains of Caucasus begin to melt, and sometimes they collapse, obstructing roadways and burying ill-starred travellers. In those years, hundreds of people died in accidents in the mountains." On this occasion the family saw an avalanche slide down the Mayorsha peak from which they were saved by luck: "Fortunately, Uncle Yuli having felt sorry for the exhausted horses who had been dragging the coach up the Kaischaur slope, gave them a short rest." And so the party just missed being buried in a mountain precipice.[86]

Chapter 12

Parting of the Ways

Helena Petrovna's sixteenth year appears to have been a period of transition in her life. Since that time, she claimed, "I have always lived a *double* existence, mysterious, incomprehensible even to myself, until I met for the second time my still more mysterious Indian."[87] She had hitherto lived an active social life, loving to dance and attend parties.[88] Madame Yermolov, the wife of the governor of Tiflis, told a friend, H. F. Pissareff, that Helena "was a brilliant very wilful young lady." Pissareff adds: "Those who knew her in her earlier days remember her with delight—unswerving, impetuous, merry, sparkling with acute humor and witty conversation. She loved to joke, tease, to create a commotion."[89] But now Helena was more deeply occupied than ever with the mystical books in the library of her great-grandfather. Around this time she met someone with whom she could discuss such subjects: Prince Alexander Golitsyn, elder son of an old family friend of the Fadeyevs, Prince Vladimir S. Golitsyn, cousin of the wife of the viceroy. Vera says Alexander was a frequent visitor at her grandparents' home. A recent article, "Russian Ways to Theosophy" by Dr. Dmitri L. Spivak, of the Academy of Sciences of the USSR, refers to Prince Alexander as a "famous freemason and mystic." After several months or so the prince left Tiflis, and it is not known whether HPB ever met him again.[90]

Alexander evidently was a man of wide experience in areas Helena ardently wished to investigate, such as sacred places in Greece, Egypt, Iran, and even India. A person of her leanings could not help being smothered by the narrow life and conventional obligations allotted in those days to women. Then, suddenly, something happened that at first seemed to bind her more than ever to a constricted existence.

During the winter of 1848–49, Helena, now seventeen, astounded her family by announcing that she was engaged to be married. Even more startling was her choice of a husband. Nadya explained how the engagement came about: Helena had been "defied one day by her governess to find any man who would be her husband, in view of her temper and disposition. The governess, to emphasize the taunt, said that even the old man she had found so ugly, and had laughed at so much, calling him 'a plumeless raven'—that even he would decline her for a wife! That was enough: three days after she made him propose."[91]

Soon thereafter, frightened at what she had done, Helena tried to induce her relatives to stop the marriage. They refused, and her grandmother was too ill to intervene.[92] Next she asked her fiancé to release her: "You make a great mistake in marrying me. You know perfectly well that you are old enough to be my grandfather." Her plea did not work. In desperation, Helena ran away from home, but she returned after a few days. Where she went nobody knows, but her absence excited gossiping minds, and her relatives were more anxious than ever to get her married and settled. Surprisingly, she no longer resisted. It dawned upon her, as she told intimate friends, that as a married woman she would be free from the constant supervision to which single girls and women in aristocratic families were then subject.[93]

Helena married Nikifor Blavatsky in a small town near Erivan on July 7, 1849, shortly before her eighteenth birthday.[94] It was a gala affair and many wedding guests came from Tiflis. Also present were twenty dashing Kurd horsemen, who had accompanied Nikifor to meet his future wife when they learned that their former superintendent was getting married.[95]

That morning, relates Nadya:

> There had been a distinct attempt to impress her with the solemnity of marriage, with her future obligations and her duties to her *husband,* and married life. A few hours later, at the altar, she heard the priest saying to her: "Thou shalt honor and obey thy husband," and at this hated word "shalt," her face was seen to flush angrily, then to become deadly pale. She was overheard to mutter in response, through her set teeth—"Surely, I *shall not.*"[96]

Vera completes the story:

> On the same day, after the reception, the newlyweds left for Daichichag, the mountain residence of all Erivan officials for the summer. They rode up the Bezobdal slope, along a steep zigzagging path, on horseback. Besides their exotic cortege [of Kurds] they were accompanied by many of the wedding guests. . . . When they reached the lowest ledge, everyone stopped; Helena waved her handkerchief to us, the Kurds raised their feathered spears, bidding us goodbye, some shot into the air—and the train was gone.
>
> I burst into tears. My sister and I had never been very good friends, because of the differences of our age and personalities; but

we had always great affection for each other. This was our first parting, and a sad one . . . the end of my childhood and of my adolescence, of everything I had loved and held dear and thought to be inseparable from myself.[97]

For Helena, it seemed, the parting from her beloved family might be forever. She planned that very day to escape from Nikifor and leave Russia via the Iranian border. A Kurd warrior was ostensibly induced to fall in with her plans, but instead he told the husband. After that she was carefully guarded.[98]

For the three months the couple lived together there was a battle of wills most of the time, with Nikifor demanding his conjugal rights and Helena refusing them. The first two months were spent in Daichichag ("the land of flowers"). The couple was visited by the grandparents, Nadya, and Catherine at the end of August, after which everyone went to Erivan.[99] It was here that Helena spent the last month with her husband, now acting governor of the province, and as such they lived in the fabulous Palace of Sardar, where the former Turkish rulers dwelt.

Dominating the landscape at Erivan was the distant Mount Ararat of biblical fame. Accompanied by her guard, the Kurd tribal chief Sahar Ali Bek—who HPB says once saved her life—Helena crossed the Turkish border several times and encircled the mountain on horseback.[100]

Relations with Nikifor worsened as the weeks dragged on, and one day in September, giving her guard the slip, Helena rode back to Tiflis—a hazardous journey for a lone woman on horseback in those troubled times. "I went into hiding with my grandmother," she wrote. "I swore that I would kill myself if I was forced to return" to Blavatsky.[101]

Sinnett learned from HPB that "family councils followed and it was settled that the unmanageable bride should be sent to join her father." He arranged to meet her at Odessa, and she was dispatched in the care of an old manservant and a maid to board at Poti, a port on the Black Sea, a steamer that would take her to her destination. But, according to Sinnett:

Her desperate passion for adventure, coupled with apprehensions that her father might endeavor to refasten the broken links of her nuptial bond, led her to design in her own mind an amendment to this program. She so contrived matters on the journey through Georgia . . . that she and her escort missed the steamer at Poti. But a small English sailing vessel was lying in the harbor. Mme. Blavatsky went on board this vessel—the *Commodore* she believed was the name—and, by a liberal outlay of roubles, persuaded the skipper to fall in with her plans.

The *Commodore* was bound first to Kerch [in the Crimea], then to Taganrog in the Sea of Azof, and ultimately to Constantinople. Mme. Blavatsky took passage for herself and servants, ostensibly to Kerch. On arriving there, she sent the servants ashore to procure apartments and prepare for her landing the following morning. But in the night, having now shaken herself free of the last restraints that connected her with her past life, she sailed away in the *Commodore*. . . .

The little voyage itself seems to have been full of adventures. . . . The harbor police of Taganrog visiting the *Commodore* on her arrival, had to be so managed as not to suspect that an extra person was on board. The only available hiding place, amongst the coals, was found unattractive by the passenger, and was assigned to the cabin boy, whose personality she borrowed for the occasion, being stowed away in a bunk on pretense of illness. Later on when the vessel arrived at Constantinople further embarrassments had developed, and she had to fly ashore precipitately in a caique† with the connivance of the steward to escape the persecutions of the skipper. [The nature of the persecutions is not mentioned.]

At Constantinople, however, she had the good fortune to fall in with a Russian lady of her acquaintance, the Countess K[isselev], with whom she formed a safe intimacy, and traveled for a time in Egypt, Greece, and other parts of Eastern Europe.[102]

---

† A light skiff used on the Bosporus.

Part **2**

World
Search

First Wanderings

W as it only a passion for adventure, and the desire to escape her husband, that led Helena Petrovna Blavatsky to abandon a life of ease and luxury to face the nameless hardships a woman might encounter in a friendless world?

Her letters to Prince Dondoukov-Korsakov, whom she first knew in Tiflis, may provide an answer. Then aide-de-camp to the viceroy, subsequently he would become governor general of Kiev and other provinces. When HPB wrote to him from India in the 1880s he was back in Tiflis as governor general of the Caucasus.[1]

It would be seventy years before these letters became public. After the prince died, they ultimately came into the possession of Leo Séméré, a Hungarian of unknown ancestry. With a view to selling the letters, he contacted several Theosophical societies but then would disappear and cease negotiations. He had come to believe the letters to be a talisman and that so long as he kept them, he would not die. Séméré was fleeing the Nazis as a Hungarian political activist, and so moved from place to place. Only when he had become mortally ill did he release the correspondence.[2]

In one letter to the prince, HPB answers his query as to the circumstances that led to her eventually meeting in the flesh her "mysterious Indian teacher," whom hitherto she had seen only in dreams and visions. "I was in search of the *unknown*," she said. "If I began to speak to you of alchemy, of union or 'marriage of the red *Virgin*' with the 'Astral Mineral,' of the philosopher's stone (union of the Soul and the Spirit), would you send me to the devil? Yet, when I expound a subject, surely I must use the appropriate terms befitting that subject?"

It was in this letter that she revealed her studies of the books in her great-grandfather's library on "alchemy, magic, and other occult sciences." "Paracelsus, Kunrath, and Agrippa," she wrote, "all spoke of the 'marriage of the red Virgin with the Hierophant,' and of that of the 'astral mineral with the sibyl,' of the combination of the feminine and masculine principles,"[3] or what the East calls the harmonizing of the yin and the yang.

41

In HPB's day the alchemists' obscure jargon was laughed at by intelligent people, but not so today. Carl Jung's major preoccupation during the last thirty years of his life was with "alchemy in its psychological and religious implications."[4] "I must confess," Jung wrote, "that it cost me quite a struggle to overcome the prejudice, which I shared with many others, against the seeming absurdity of alchemy. . . . But my patience has been richly rewarded. . . . True alchemy was never a business or a career, but a real *opus* that a man carried on in silent self-sacrificing labor."[5] In Jung's *Alchemical Studies,* it is evident that the truest practitioners of alchemy were "seeking not the vulgar gold, but the golden understanding; not the transmutation of base metals, but the psychic transformation of their own personalities; not the elixir of immortality, but the philosopher's stone, the mysterious *lapis* that symbolized the total man."[6] Blavatsky wrote that mystically "the philosopher's stone symbolizes the transmutation of the lower animal nature of man into the highest and divine." The latter she calls "the universal solvent of everything."[7]

The *red* Virgin requires explanation, because we usually associate that color with passion. Jung asserts that "red and white are alchemical colors; red signifies the sun and white the moon."[8] Similarly, HPB mentions "the transcendent red or golden orange of the sun" and that "this must not be confused with the scarlet kama-rupan redness."[9] (*Kāma-rūpa* is a Sanskrit compound word for a man's passionate nature.) Jung intriguingly writes that the trinity of body, soul, and spirit "must change into a circle, that is, into *unchangeable redness* or '*an everlasting fire*'." (Italics added.)[10]

After her departure from Russia, HPB's life is not easy to document. She kept no diary, and her relatives were not standing by to report her doings. Nadya writes: "For the first eight years she gave her mother's family no sign of life for fear of being traced by her legitimate 'lord and master.'" As to her father, he "alone knew of her whereabouts. Knowing, however, that he would never prevail upon her to return to [Nikifor], he acquiesced in her absence, and supplied her with money whenever she came to places where it could safely reach her."[11]

HPB's critics find it difficult to believe that a woman in those days could safely travel to the places she claimed to have visited. Privately, she wrote the following to Sinnett when he was preparing her memoirs:

Suppose I was to tell you that [in India] I was in man's clothes (for I was very thin then) which is the solemn truth, what would people say? So I was in

Egypt with the old Countess [Kisselev] who liked to see me dressed as a man student, *"gentleman student" she said. Now you understand my diffi- culties? That which would pass* [elsewhere, save in the prudish West] *as an eccentricity, oddity, would serve now only to* incriminate *me.* . . .[12]

In Cairo, HPB met Dr. Albert Leighton Rawson, then a young art student from the United States. As he also saw her two or three years later in New York, and again in that city in the 1870s, he is an important witness as to some of her journeyings. Rawson has an interesting history, as disclosed in *Who Was Who in America* (1607–1896) and in the *Twentieth Century Biographical Dictionary of Notable Americans*. He stud- ied law and also engaged in archaeological explorations. He received his doctorate of divinity and LL. D at Oxford and a medical degree at the Sorbonne in Paris. Author of many books on religion, philology, and archaeology, he traveled four times to the Orient.

Rawson described his meeting with HPB in Cairo in an article written after her death. She revealed to him that she was engaged in a work that would someday free mankind from mental bondage. He commented that "her disinterestedness in her mission was sublime, for she frequently said 'This work is not mine, but his that sent me.' [Book of John vii:16]"[13]

HPB's travels in the Middle East proved disappointing. She wrote Prince Dondoukov:

At Athens, in Egypt, on the Euphrates, everywhere I went I sought my [philosopher's stone], . . . I have lived with the whirling Dervishes, with the Druses of Mt. Lebanon, with the Bedouin Arabs and the Marabouts of Damascus. I found it nowhere! I learned necromancy and astrology, crystal- gazing and spiritualism—of "red Virgin" no trace whatsoever![14]

After this, as HPB mentioned later to a French correspondent, she traveled with her father in Europe.[15] This may be the time she went with him to London. Elsewhere, she speaks of the trip as occurring in 1844 or 1845, but she was poor at remembering dates.[16] From Vera's catalog of events, neither Helena, then in Saratov, nor her father, still in military service, could have spent several months abroad during that period,[17] although in 1850 the stay in London was possible.

The purpose of the visit may have been to obtain advanced musical instruction. HPB spoke of receiving a few lessons from "old Mos- cheles," the noted pianist-composer who was then teaching in the Leipzig Conservatory. All this suggests she contemplated earning a living as a professional pianist. Several years later, it is said, she did give some concerts in England and on the continent.[18]

HPB appears not to have stayed long with her father. She went to Paris, where Sinnett says she knew "many literary celebrities of the time, and where a famous mesmerist, still living as I write, though an old man now, discovered her wonderful psychic gifts, and was very eager to retain her under his control as a sensitive. But the chains had not yet been forged that could make her prisoner, and she quitted Paris precipitately to escape this influence."[19]

In early 1851, HPB was in London, employed as companion to a family friend, Countess Bagration. They were staying in Mivart's Hotel, now called The Claridge. Two years had elapsed since leaving Russia, and HPB was in a deep depression. What Voltaire once said of himself seemed to echo her own thoughts: "I have consumed forty years of my pilgrimage . . . seeking the philosopher's stone of truth . . . and still remain in ignorance."[20]

To Dondoukov-Korsakov, she recalled the period thirty years later:

> *When sick of everything, tired of poor old Countess Bagration who held me confined in "Mivart's Hotel," making me read the* Chitaminyi *and the Bible, I escaped on to Waterloo Bridge, for I was seized with a strong desire to die. I had long felt the temptation approaching. This time I did not seek to resist it and the muddy water of the Thames seemed to me a delicious bed. I was seeking eternal repose not being able to find the "stone" and having lost the "Virgin."*[21]

Then, looming up before her appeared the figure of her teacher and protector. He "woke me up and *saved* me and, to console me with life, promised me 'the Stone and the Virgin.'"[22]

Chapter 2

A Memorable Night

E ighteen fifty-one was the year of the Great Exhibition in Hyde Park, London, and its fabulous Crystal Palace housing "the Works of All Nations," including the latest inventions of science and technology. Queen Victoria opened the exhibit in May, and when it closed in October there had been over six million visitors from all parts of the world. Whether HPB was impressed by this event of the century is not known, but it provided the backdrop for the most extraordinary experience of her life. Accompanying one of the Indian delegations came the teacher of her dreams! "Saw him twice," she wrote Sinnett. "Once he came out of the crowd, then He ordered me to meet Him in Hyde Park. I *cannot, I must not* speak of this. I would not publish it for the world."[23]

Two years after HPB died, the meeting became public knowledge when the book *Reminiscences of H. P. Blavatsky and The Secret Doctrine* appeared. The author, Countess Constance Wachtmeister, widow of a former Swedish ambassador to London, had lived with HPB in Germany and Belgium during the writing of *The Secret Doctrine*. The countess wrote:

> In Würzburg a curious incident occurred. Madame Fadeyev—HPB's aunt—wrote to her that she was sending a box to the Ludwigstrasse containing what seemed to her a lot of rubbish [which HPB had left behind when leaving Russia in the 1860s]. The box arrived and to me was deputed the task of unpacking it. As I took out one thing after another and passed them to Madame Blavatsky, I heard her give an exclamation of delight, and she said, "Come and look at this which I wrote in the year 1851, the day I saw my blessed Master"; and there in a scrapbook [sketchbook] in faded writing, I saw a few lines in which HPB described the meeting.[24]

The sketchbook still exists, and here is a reproduction of the page.†

† *Original in French:* Nuit mémorable! Certaine nuit, par au clair—de lune qui se couchait a Ramsgate 12 Aout: 1851* lorsque je rencontrais M ∴ le Maître—de mes rêves!!
Le 12 Aout c'est Juillet 31 style russe jour de ma naissance—*Vingt ans!*

English translation: Memorable night! On a certain night by the light of the moon that was setting at Ramsgate on August 12, 1851,* when I met M ∴ the Master of my dreams!!
August 12 is July 31 in the Russian calendar, the day of my birth—*Twenty years!*

2. *1851 boat scene; the day Blavatsky first met her Master.*
(The Theosophist, *August 1931, 558, Theosophical Society, Adyar Archives*)

The countess asked HPB why Ramsgate (a resort on the North Sea) was mentioned, instead of London, where she previously had told her she met her teacher. She writes: "HPB told me that it was a blind, so that anyone casually taking up her book would not know where she had met her Master."

On this previous occasion, HPB provided the countess with the following description of the meeting:

She was one day out walking when, to her astonishment, she saw a tall Hindu in the street with some Indian princes. She immediately recognized him. . . . Her first impulse was to rush forward to speak to him, but he made her a sign not to move. She there stood as if spellbound while he passed on. The next day she went to Hyde Park for a stroll to be alone and free to think over her extraordinary adventure. Looking up, she saw the same form approaching her, and then her Master told her that he had come to London with the Indian princes on an important mission, and he was desirous of meeting her personally, as he required her cooperation in a work

which he was about to undertake [the nature of which he outlined].
To prepare for the important task . . . [she would] have to spend
three years in Tibet.[25]

The countess herself was "in England at the time of the visit of the
Indians and remembered hearing that they and their suite were a fine
set of men and one of them immensely tall."[26] HPB's teacher was said
to be six-foot-eight.[27]

Before leaving for India, HPB consulted her father. Wachtmeister
was of the impression that he was in London then, but HPB explicitly
told Sinnett this was not the case.[28] Thus, whatever approval she received must have been by mail. Once received, she immediately left
for India, reports the countess.[29] More correctly, it would appear, she
left for India via the Americas, as she yearned to see the New World
first.

Chapter 3

The New World
and Mother India

The reason HPB was desirous of visiting the New World was to learn the wisdom of the Native Americans.[30] Years later, in retrospect, she may have viewed her choice in a larger context. *The Secret Doctrine* teaches:

> Even now, under our very eyes, the new Race and Races are preparing to be formed, and . . . it is in America that the transformation will take place, and has already silently commenced. Pure Anglo-Saxons hardly three hundred years ago, the Americans of the United States have already become a nation apart, and owing to a strong admixture of various nationalities and intermarriage, almost a race *sui generis,* not only mentally, but also physically. . . .
>
> Thus it is the mankind of the New World . . . whose mission and karma it is, to sow the seeds for a forthcoming, grander, and far more glorious Race than any of those we know of at present. Cycles of matter will be succeeded by cycles of spirituality and a fully developed mind.[31]

What drew HPB to the New World in 1851 were the Native Americans she had read about in James Fenimore Cooper's novels. Taking passage to Canada, she went to Quebec and was introduced to a party of Native Americans from whom she hoped to learn the secrets of the medicine men. One day they disappeared with some of her possessions, including a prized pair of boots.[32] In *Isis Unveiled* she speaks of "the sad examples of the rapid demoralization" of Native Americans "as soon as they are made to live in close proximity with *Christian* officials and missionaries."[33]

A new program of travel was devised. Sinnett writes:

> In the first instance, [HPB] thought she would try to come to close quarters with the Mormons, then beginning to excite public attention; but their original city Nauvoo, in Missouri, had just been

destroyed by the unruly mob of their less industrious and less prosperous neighbors, and the survivors of the massacre in which so
many of their people fell were then streaming across the desert in
search of a new home. Mme. Blavatsky thought that under these circumstances Mexico looked an inviting region in which to risk her life
next, and she made her way, in the meanwhile, to New Orleans.[34]

Here she investigated the Voodoos but was warned in a vision that
the sect was engaged in dangerous practices, and she left immediately.
Sinnett continues:

> She went through Texas to Mexico, and contrived to see a good deal
> of that insecure country, protected in these hazardous travels by her
> own reckless daring, and by various people who from time to time
> interested themselves in her welfare. She speaks with special grati-
> tude of an old Canadian, a man known as Pere Jacques, whom she
> met in Texas, at the time she was quite without any companionship.
> He saw her safely through some perils to which she was then ex-
> posed.[34]

Her travels during 1852 brought her to Central and South America
where she visited ancient ruins. Some of these explorations are described in *Isis*.[35]

Having decided it was now time to go to India, Sinnett writes, "she
wrote to a certain Englishman, whom she had met in Germany two
years before, and whom she knew to be on the same quest as herself, to
join her in the West Indies, in order that they might go to the East
together." Another fellow traveler was added to the party, a Hindu
whom Blavatsky met in Honduras. He proved to be a *chela,* or pupil of
the Masters. "The three pilgrims of mysticism went out via the Cape
[of Good Hope] to Ceylon, and thence in a sailing ship to Bombay,"
arriving at the end of 1852. The party then dispersed, "each being bent
on somewhat different ends."[36]

More information about HPB's first stay in India was disclosed in a
letter to Prince Dondoukov, in which she speaks of her teacher:

> *In England I saw him only twice and at our last interview he said to me:
> "Your destiny lies in India, but later, in twenty-eight or thirty years. Go
> there [now] and see the country." I came there—why, I do not know! I was
> as in a dream. I stayed nearly two years, traveling about and receiving money
> each month—from whom I have no idea, and following faithfully the
> itinerary given to me. I received letters from this Hindu, but I did not see
> him a single time during those two years.*[37]

Before leaving India, an attempt was made to enter Tibet through Nepal, but it was unsuccessful owing to the opposition of the British Resident.[38] This and other information about her travels was given to Sinnett by HPB thirty years after their occurrence, when verification was difficult, thus providing skeptics an excuse for doubting her veracity. One major contention is that her first visit to India was not made until much later in her career. However, support for the British Resident story surprisingly surfaced two years after she died.

In 1893, Olcott and a friend were traveling by train in India and met a retired army officer, Major General Charles Murray. During the course of conversation Olcott's association with the Theosophical Society was mentioned, and Murray remarked that years ago he had prevented HPB from entering Tibet. Olcott wrote down the following details of the detention on the back of his diary for 1893, and Murray attested the statement with his signature:

> On the 3rd of March, 1893, S. V. Edge and I met in the train between Nalhati and Calcutta, Major General C. Murray (retired), late of the 70th Bengal Infantry, now Chairman of the Monghyr Municipality, who met HPB in 1854 or '55, at Punkabaree, at the feet of the Darjeeling Hills. He was then a Captain commanding the Sebundy Sappers and Miners. She was trying to get into Tibet via Nepal "to write a book," and to do it, she wished to cross the Rungit river. Captain Murray had it reported to him by the guard that a European lady had passed that way, so he went after and brought her back. She was very angry, but in vain. She stopped with Captain and Mrs. Murray for about a month when, finding her plan defeated, she left, and Captain Murray heard of her as far as Dinajpore. She was then apparently about thirty years of age.
>
> The above memo is correct
> C. Murray, Major General

As the foregoing was immediately inserted in the April 1893 issue of *The Theosophist,* published in India,[39] Murray had ample opportunity to see his attestation in print and could have contested it if it were not correct. Apparently no one bothered to check Olcott's story against the major general's military record until in 1952, a Mrs. Stanley in London wrote for details.[40] For the years 1854 and 1855, the records state that Murray was "commandant of the Sebundy Sappers and Miners." Marion Meade reports that Murray "told Olcott in 1854 or '55 a European woman had tried to cross the border but had been brought back by guards."[41] That Murray specifically named Blavatsky is withheld for a reason that is apparent. Meade claims, as do many of HPB's biographers, that during the ten years she was away from Russia she never set foot in India but was leading an immoral life in the capitals of Europe, and hence that her stories of her travels were clever cover-ups and her teachers nonexistent.

Dr. Rawson provides evidence of both HPB's stays in the United States and in India during the period in question. As to India, he wrote the following letter, published in 1878, to refute a critic's charges that she had hitherto never been in the Orient:

> [Some] of my acquaintances have met Madame Blavatsky in the far east; others have heard of her residence there; for instance, the eminent physician and surgeon, David E. Dudley, M.D. of Manila; [and] Mr. Frank A. Hill of Boston, Mass., who was in India some years since. . . . The editor of the Builder of this city [New York], Mr. William O'Grady, a native of Madras, India, visits Madame Blavatsky frequently [in New York], having known her in India.
>
> Why repeat these evidences? One accepted testimony is sufficient—a thousand insufficient to the unwilling soul.[42]

In 1854, after HPB's plan to enter Tibet was thwarted by Murray, she left India. To Prince Dondoukov she explained that when her teacher wrote "Return to Europe and do what you like but be always ready to return," she took "passage on the *Gwalior* which was wrecked near the Cape but I was saved with some twenty others."[43] No details of what occurred are available.

Chapter 4

Second Time Around

W hen HPB returned to England, the Crimean War between Turkey and Russia was underway. In January 1854 British and French fleets entered the Black Sea and, in February, Czar Nicholas I withdrew his ambassadors from London and Paris. It was an embarrassing time for a Russian to be in England, but Vera says HPB was detained there by a contract (presumably to give concerts): "Having distinguished herself by her musical talents, she became a member of the Philharmonic Society."[44]

In June of 1854, HPB appears to have again met her teacher in England. She writes: "I met him in the house of a stranger in England, where he had come in the company of a dethroned native prince, and our acquaintance was limited to two conversations which, although producing on me a strong impression by their unexpectedness, their strange character, and even their severity, have, nevertheless, like so many other things, sunk beneath the waters of Lethe."[45] By "a dethroned native prince" she probably meant Dalip Singh, the deposed maharajah of Lahore. He arrived in Southampton on June eighteenth and was presented to Queen Victoria on July first.[46] Thereafter HPB left England for New York.[47]

In New York she renewed her acquaintance with Dr. Rawson. He gives the year as 1853, but 1854 seems more likely. When, as a young artist, he met her in Cairo she was nineteen. Now, "at twenty-two or twenty-three," Rawson said:

> Her face was full, moon-shaped—the outline so prized in the Orient; she had bright, clear eyes, mild as a gazelle's in repose, but flashing like a serpent's in anger or excitement. Her youthful figure, until she was thirty, was supple, muscular and well rounded, fit to delight an artist. Her hands and feet were so small and delicately molded as to suggest the fullness and softness of youth, and they never lost entirely those qualities.
>
> [She] was almost irresistible in society, for she could win at a single interview the admiration of any man who had ever lived

outside of himself long enough to discover that he was not three-quarters of the universe.

She cared very little for the admiration of men for herself merely as a woman, he said. "As a student," Rawson found her "ever at work and tireless, never satisfied. More light, more facts, advanced theories, different hypotheses, further suggestions, always pushing toward an ideal." [*Frank Leslie's Popular Monthly*, February, 1892]

From New York, Sinnett reports, HPB "went first to Chicago, then an infant city . . . and afterwards to the Far West," proceeding "across the Rocky Mountains with emigrants' caravans, till ultimately she [reached] San Francisco," where she embarked for the Orient.[48]

According to John Unruh's classic work *The Plains Across*, "the experiences of the overlanders during the 1850s," when HPB traveled West, were "extremely challenging." Ferrying across raging rivers and passing through vast stretches of torrid, waterless deserts were some of the difficulties. When a wagon wheel broke, or the oxen succumbed to exhaustion, the travelers were in dire trouble. The Rockies were crossed at South Pass, Wyoming, at an elevation of seven thousand feet.

After crossing the Rockies, many of the travelers, of whom it is said HPB was one, rested and replenished supplies at Salt Lake City. She is reported to have stayed overnight at the house of a Mormon woman, Mrs. Emmeline B. Wells (1828–1921), publisher and editor of *The Woman's Exponent*. Mrs. Wells informed her granddaughter, Mrs. Daisy Woods, that HPB was wearing men's shoes as she intended to travel over rugged country. The impression conveyed was she was en route to Mexico.[49] Unruh mentions that "hotels and eating houses notwithstanding, a great many overland emigrants boarded with Mormon families during their stay in Salt Lake City."[50] If HPB did go to Mexico, and perhaps other countries in Central and South America, she could have boarded one of the numerous coastal boats destined for San Francisco, and there obtain passage to the Orient.[51]

The first glimpse of the Pacific Ocean is often an awesome experience to travelers. Walt Whitman memorialized his own view with a reincarnation poem, "Facing West from California's Shores," telling how ages ago he began his pilgrimage westward from ancient India; and now:

Facing west from California's shores,
Inquiring, tireless, seeking what is yet unfound.
I, a child, very old . . .
towards the house of maternity . . . look afar,
Look off the shores of my Western sea,
the circle almost encircled;
For starting westward from Hindustan,
from the vales of Kashmere . . .
Long having wander'd since,
round the earth having wander'd,
Now I face home again, very pleas'd and joyous,
(But where is what I started for so long ago?
And why is it yet unfound?)[52]

As HPB crossed the Pacific, reaching Calcutta sometime in 1855 or 1856,[53] perhaps she asked the same question regarding her present life's quest: Why is it yet unfound?

Chapter 5

Sages of the Orient

I t will be recalled that on HPB's first trip to India, although she went there under direction of her teacher,
she never saw him. On this trip it was to be different. In the selections
that follow from *Isis Unveiled,* HPB appears to merge both visits into
one:

> When, years ago, we[†] first traveled over the East, exploring the
> penetralia of its deserted sanctuaries, two saddening and ever-recur-
> ring questions oppressed our thoughts: *Where, Who, What is God?*
> *Whoever saw the Immortal Spirit of man, so as to be able to assure himself of*
> *man's immortality?*
>
> It was while most anxious to solve these perplexing problems
> that we came into contact with certain men, endowed with such
> mysterious powers and such profound knowledge that we may truly
> designate them as the sages of the Orient. . . . They showed us that
> by *combining science with religion* [italics added], the existence of God
> and immortality of man's spirit may be demonstrated like a problem
> of Euclid.
>
> For the first time we received the assurance that the Oriental
> philosophy has room for no other faith than an absolute and im-
> movable faith in the omnipotence of man's own immortal self. We
> were taught that this omnipotence comes from the kinship of man's
> spirit with the Universal Soul—God! The latter, they said, can never
> be demonstrated but by the former. Man-spirit proves God-spirit, as
> the one drop of water proves a source from which it must have
> come. (p. vi)

Thus, she adds, when one sees human beings, such as these sages of
the Orient "displaying tremendous capabilities, controlling the forces
of nature and opening up to view the world of spirit, the reflective
mind is overwhelmed with the conviction that if one man's spiritual

---

† Throughout *Isis Unveiled,* HPB uses the editorial "we."

Ego can do this much, the capabilities of the FATHER SPIRIT† must be relatively as much vaster as the whole ocean surpasses the single drop in volume and potency. *Ex nihilo nihil fit;* prove the soul of man by its wondrous powers—you have proved God! . . . Such knowledge is priceless; and it has been hidden only from those who overlooked it, derided it, or denied its existence."[54]

As to HPB's stay in India in 1856, she wrote Sinnett: "Traveled from place to place, never said I was Russian, people taking me for what I liked. . . . Were I to describe my visit to India only in that year, that would make a whole book."[55]

Some of it did become a book, *Caves and Jungles of Hindostan.* Originally this was a series of articles, which she wrote from 1878 to 1886 under the pen name Radda Bai and which first appeared in the *Moscow Chronicle,* edited by the famous Russian journalist M. N. Katkov. They created so much interest that in 1883 the series thus far published was reprinted in the Supplement to Katkov's *Russky Vyestnik (Russian Messenger),* and then continued. Tolstoy, Turgenev, and other noted authors were frequent contributors to this periodical.

The stories, in fictionalized form, record in part HPB's travels with her teacher, who in *Caves and Jungles*[56] appears under the pseudonym of Gulab Singh.[57] I "give there true *facts* and true personages," she wrote Sinnett, "only bringing in together within three or four months' time facts and events scattered all throughout years as some of Master's phenomena."[58] Many of them, she said, occurred during her second visit to India. A review of the series was written by Zinaida Vengerova in her article on HPB's life in the *Critico-Biographical Encyclopedia of Russian Writers and Savants* (1892).

Critical of some phases of HPB's career, Vengerova has only praise to lavish on the book under review:

> *Caves and Jungles of Hindostan* cannot be included among ordinary, picturesque descriptions of foreign lands. The author is not just a curious tourist describing the wonders she has seen but rather a member of a scientific expedition, with the purpose of studying the basics of human history through India's fixed civilization. This specific purpose is always there in Radda-Bai's narrative, which gives it a peculiar charm. The author emphasizes everything that points to the great past of that now-enslaved nation. She gives

---

† In later writings HPB speaks of God as sexless. In *The Secret Doctrine* (1:295 fn) she remarks that the expression "God 'the Father'" is "anthropomorphic fiction."

simple but most artistic descriptions of the magnificent buildings scattered through India since time immemorial and untarnished by the millennia that have gone by. . . . But more than all the works of art that show the heights of Hindu civilization, or the luxurious landscapes portrayed by Blavatsky, where reality dwarfs one's wildest imagination, it is the native's life style that captures her attention . . . for wherever she went she lived not in the European sections of cities but in Hindu homes (bungalows), among natives. . . .

When reading her book, one should not forget for a moment that Radda-Bai is first and foremost a theosophist, that she went to India in search of the secret knowledge of the East, and her attention is riveted, above all, upon the teachings of Hindu sages. . . . She is especially interested in the mysterious school of the Raja-Yogis, holy wise men, who, by a special training of their spiritual powers, achieve the ability to work unquestionable miracles, thus Raja-Yogi Gulab Singh, whom Blavatsky knew personally . . . answered her unspoken questions; disappeared and reappeared when no one expected it; opened before the travelers secret entrances into mountains leading to wonderful underground temples, and so on. And all of this he did quite easily, always providing a natural explanation for his actions. Many of Gulab Singh's phenomena as described by Blavatsky are not unlike what she later performed herself. Could it be from the mysterious Gulab Singh that she borrowed the ability to "create" and disintegrate objects?[59]

The first English translation of *Caves and Jungles* appeared in 1892 but was not complete. It was done by Vera Johnston, HPB's niece. A new translation, numbering over seven hundred pages, is now available in Blavatsky's *Collected Writings* series. A second volume of Russian writings, which will complete the series, is still to be published.

Having been unsuccessful in entering Tibet through Nepal on her first visit to India, this time HPB tried through Kashmir. In Colonel Olcott's report of his meeting with Major General Murray, who sabotaged the first attempt, the colonel added:

I got trace of another of her Tibetan attempts from a Hindu gentleman living at Bareilly, while on one of my North Indian official tours. The first time HPB came to that station after our arrival in India (in 1879) this gentleman recognized her as the European lady who had been his guest many years before, when she was going northward to try and enter Tibet via Kashmir. They had a pleasant chat about old times.[60]

Kashmir is in the northwestern part of India, and parts of it were once called Little Tibet. Further north lies western Tibet, which HPB claimed to penetrate on this trip. However, she failed to realize her main objective: to reach the occult center in eastern Tibet where her teacher and his fellow adepts often lived. Eastern Tibet includes Lhasa, the country's capital and the seat of the Dalai Lama.

Sinnett reports that prior to entering western Tibet, HPB was overtaken in Lahore by a German friend of her father, an ex-Lutheran minister by the name of Külwein [Kühlwein]. As he had planned a trip to the East with two friends, Colonel Hahn, anxious about his daughter's welfare, asked him to locate her.[61]

The four traveled together through Kashmir in the company of the Tartar shaman, who was en route to his home in Siberia after twenty years' absence. The shaman attached himself to HPB, believing she could be influential with the Russian authorities in permitting his return.

Using various disguises, the party sought to enter Tibet. Külwein became ill and remained behind. His two friends were turned back by the guards, but the shaman and HPB were allowed to proceed. Her Mongolian features were perhaps her best disguise. The story of some of their adventures is told in *Isis*. One incident concerns a talisman the shaman wore under his left arm:

> "Of what use is [the talisman], and what are its virtues?" was the question we often offered to our guide. To this he never answered directly, but evaded all explanation, promising that as soon as an opportunity was offered, and we were alone, he would ask the stone *to answer for himself.* With this very indefinite hope, we were left to the resources of our own imagination. But the day on which the stone "spoke" came very soon. It was during the most critical hours of our life; at a time when the vagabond nature of a traveler had carried the writer to far-off lands, where neither civilization is known, nor security can be guaranteed for one hour.

The villagers with whom they lived had left one day en masse to witness a Buddhist ceremony, and it was opportune for the shaman to demonstrate the powers of the stone:

> . . . placing his hand in his bosom he drew out the little stone, about the size of a walnut, and, carefully unwrapping it, proceeded,

as it appeared, to swallow it. In a few moments his limbs stiffened, his body became rigid, and he fell, cold and motionless as a corpse. But for a slight twitching of his lips at every question asked, the scene would have been embarrassing, nay dreadful. . . . For over two hours the most substantial, unequivocal proofs that the shaman's astral soul was traveling at the bidding of our unspoken wish were given us.

One request of HPB was to visit a friend, a Rumanian lady of Walachia, and to bring back that person's present thought. The voice announced that the old woman was sitting in her garden reading a letter. HPB hastily secured paper and pencil to write down the words slowly given phonetically in the Walachian language, of which she knew nothing save to recognize it. The letter was later mailed to the woman with an inquiry as to what she was doing during the day in question. This woman, "a mystic by disposition, but a thorough disbeliever in this kind of occult phenomena," replied that "she was sitting in the garden on that morning prosaically occupied in boiling some conserves; the letter HPB sent to her was word for word the copy of the one received by her from her brother; all at once—in consequence of the heat, she thought—she fainted, and remembered distinctly *dreaming* she saw the writer in a desert place which she accurately described, and sitting under a 'gypsy's tent,' as she expressed it. 'Henceforth,' she added, 'I can doubt no longer!' . . . The hour in Bucharest corresponded perfectly with that of the country in which the scene had taken place."

HPB continues:

But our experiment was proved still better. We had directed the shaman's inner *ego* to the same friend heretofore mentioned in this chapter, the Kutchi of Lhasa, who travels constantly to British India and back. *We know* that he was apprised of our critical situation in the desert; for a few hours later came help, and we were rescued by a party of twenty-five horsemen who had been directed by their chief to find us at the place where we were, which no living man endowed with common powers could have known. The chief of this escort was a Shaberon, an "adept" whom we had never seen before, nor did we after that, for he never left his *soumay* (lamasery), and we could have no access to it. But *he was a personal friend of the Kutchi.*[62]

"This incident," says Sinnett, "put an end to Madame Blavatsky's wanderings in Tibet," and "she was conducted back to the frontier by roads and passes of which she had no previous knowledge. . . ." He adds that she "was directed by her occult guardian to leave the country shortly before the troubles which began in India in 1857." This refers to the Sepoy Mutiny, which erupted in May and became so widespread that British rule was seriously threatened. HPB left from Madras in a Dutch vessel and went to Java, on orders from her teacher "for a certain business."[63] She then returned to Europe.

Part 3

Maturing Years

Chapter 1

Back in Russia

It was Christmas night and the year 1858 was coming to a close. HPB's sister, Vera, and their father, Colonel Hahn, were at a wedding party in the town of Pskov, not far from St. Petersburg. The sister, now a young widow with two small boys, was spending the winter on the estate of her in-laws, the Yakhontovs, and it was there that the wedding reception was taking place.

"They were all sitting at supper," Vera recalls, "carriages loaded with guests were arriving one after the other, and the hall bell kept ringing without interruption. At the moment when the bridegroom's best men arose, with glasses of champagne in their hands, to proclaim their good wishes for the happy couple—a solemn moment in Russia—the bell was again rung impatiently." Vera, "moved by an irrepressible impulse, and notwithstanding that the hall was full of servants, jumped up and, to the amazement of all, rushed herself to open the door. She felt convinced . . . it was her long lost sister!" And there, standing at the door, was Madame Blavatsky![1]

On returning from India, HPB had spent several months in France and Germany, and then some time in St. Petersburg contacting her relatives. The first relative she reached was Nadya, who was asked not to tell the others. HPB was apprehensive that her husband might now claim his marriage rights, so she asked Nadya, in Tiflis, to contact Nikifor. He replied:

> You may assure H. P. on my word of honor I will never pursue her. . . . Since the time of my misfortune, and in consequence of it, I have been working on my character in order that I may become unaffected by anything. Very often I even laugh at the stupidities which I committed. . . . One can become accustomed to anything. So I have got used to a joyless life in Erivan [without Helena].[2]

After her sister's arrival at Pskov, Vera naturally expected a full account of her travels but learned only that Helena "traveled all over Europe, America and Asia."[3] Later, explaining her reticence to Sinnett,

HPB wrote: "From 17 to 40 I took care during my travels to sweep away all traces of myself wherever I went. . . . I never allowed people to know *where* I was and *what* I was doing. Had I been a common p—— [my relatives] would have preferred it to my studying occultism." Such studies would mean to them she was "*sold to Satan.*"[4]

After the Theosophical Society was founded, she responded to her detractors' prying questions about her past:

> To even my best friends I have never given but fragmentary and superficial accounts of [my] travels, nor do I propose to gratify anyone's curiosity, least of all that of my enemies. The latter are quite welcome to believe in and spread as many cock-and-bull stories about me as they choose, and to invent new ones as time rolls on and the old stories wear out. Why, again, should they not, since they disbelieve in the theosophical adepts [or masters of wisdom]?[5]

To friendly correspondents, HPB wrote in a different vein: "There are several 'pages of the history of my life' which I will never mention, and die first, not because I am ashamed of them, but because they are too sacred."[6]

Chapter 2

Occult Wonders

W rites Vera Zhelihovsky, in a series of articles about
her sister published in the Russian magazine *Rebus*:

People who read newspapers and magazines have more than once
come across the name of Helena Petrovna Blavatsky. It would be
impossible to recount all the calumnies and absurdities that her own
compatriots have flung at her—from fraud and quackery to serious
crimes. We are well acquainted with H. P., having known her
intimately since her early childhood and into her mature years. We
have long sought an opportunity to present a few cursory essays
about her to those interested in this outstanding personality.
Whether or not our true story will be believed, we do not care, and
are content to know that we are telling the truth—the only truth, it
seems, to have been told about her in Russia.

Both series were so popular that they soon appeared in two booklets.

When HPB returned to Russia in 1860, Vera relates that "she was
surrounded by a mysterious atmosphere of visible and audible manifestations, perceptible but totally abnormal and incomprehensible to
all those around her."[7] HPB later told W. Q. Judge, a co-founder of
the Theosophical Society, that "this was a period when she was letting
her psychic forces play, and learning fully to understand and control
them."[8]

Vera writes:

All those who were living in the house remarked that strange things
were taking place in it. Raps and whisperings, sounds, mysterious
and unexplained, were now being constantly heard wherever the
newly arrived inmate went. That such raps could be increased or
diminished, and at times even made to cease altogether by the mere
force of her will, she acknowledged, proving her assertion generally
on the spot. . . .

The sounds were not simple raps . . . as they showed extraordinary intelligence, disclosing the past as well as the future to those

who held converse through them. . . . More than that, for they showed the gift of disclosing unexpressed thoughts, *i.e.,* penetrating freely into the most secret recesses of the human mind, and divulging past deeds and present intentions.

The relatives of Madame Blavatsky's sister were leading a very fashionable life, and received a good deal of company in those days. Her presence attracted a number of visitors, no one of whom ever left her unsatisfied, for [at times] the raps she evoked gave answers, composed of long discourses in several languages, some of which were unknown [to HPB].

It was her usual habit to sit very quietly and quite unconcerned on the sofa, or in an arm chair, engaged in some embroidery, and apparently without taking the slightest interest or active part in the hubbub which she produced around herself. And the hubbub was great indeed. One of the guests would be reciting the alphabet, another putting down the answers received, while the mission of the rest was to offer mental questions.[9]

The rap phenomena was a slow process. [My] sister could have used direct writing, which was much faster, but she was "afraid to employ it, fearing, as she explained, uncalled for suspicion from foolish people, who did not understand the process."[10]

As to using raps, HPB provided this explanation of the process:

Whenever the thought of a person had to be communicated through raps . . . she had to read first of all . . . the thought of the querist, and having done so, to remember it well after it had often disappeared; watch the letters of the alphabet as they were read or pointed out, prepare the will-current that had to produce the rap at the right letter, and then have it strike at the right moment, the table or any other object chosen to be the vehicle of sounds or raps. A most difficult process, and far less easy than *direct writing.*[11]

Says Vera:

The most absurd hypotheses were offered by the skeptics. For instance, it was suggested that she might produce her loud raps by the means of a machine in her pocket, or that she rapped with her nails; the most ingenious theory being that "when her hands were visibly occupied with some work, she did it with her toes."

To put an end to all this, she allowed herself to be subjected to the most stupid demands; she was searched, her hands and feet were tied with string, she permitted herself to be placed on a sofa, to have her shoes taken off and her hands and feet held fast against a soft pillow, so that they should be seen by all, and then she was asked that the knocks and rappings should be produced at the further end of the room. Declaring that she would try but would promise nothing, her orders were, nevertheless, immediately accomplished, especially when the people were seriously interested. These raps were produced at her command on the ceiling, on the window sills, on every bit of furniture in the adjoining room, and in places quite distant from her.

At times she would wickedly revenge herself by practical jokes on those who so doubted her. Thus, for example, the raps which came one day inside the glasses of the young professor, M_____, while she was sitting at the other side of the room, were so strong that they fairly knocked the spectacles off his nose, and made him become pale with fright. At another time, a lady, an *esprit fort,* very vain and coquettish, to her ironical question of what was the best conductor for the production of such raps, and whether they could be done everywhere, received a strange and very puzzling answer. The word, "Gold," was rapped out, and then came the words, "We will prove it to you immediately."

The lady kept smiling with her mouth slightly opened. Hardly had the answer come, then she became very pale, jumped from her chair, and covered her mouth with her hand. Her face was convulsed with fear and astonishment. . . . the lady had felt a violent commotion and raps *in the gold* of her artificial teeth! The woman fled from the room, her secret revealed.[12]

At the time, Vera and most others ascribed these phenomena to her sister's mediumistic powers, but HPB always denied it:

> My sister spent most of her ten-year sojourn abroad in India, where, as most people know, spiritualist theories of claiming to contact the dead are held in great contempt. The phenomena we call mediumistic are explained there by completely different causes—a source my sister considers beneath her dignity to draw from. . . . She still insists that she was possessed then, as now, of a different power—the kind used by the Hindu sages, the Raja-Yogis. She even claims that the shadows she has been seeing throughout her life were not ghosts or spirits of the dead but appearances of those all-powerful friends of hers in their astral bodies.
>
> Anyway, whatever force it was that produced the phenomena, these phenomena occurred constantly during the whole time that my sister Helena and I stayed at the Yakhontovs, before the eyes of believers and non-believers alike, bewildering everyone.[13]

The two exceptions were Peter von Hahn, their father, and Leonid, their brother. The latter's doubts were shattered one evening when the Yakhontov's drawing room was filled with visitors. Vera's story is condensed, but only her own words are used:

The brother was a strong, muscular youth, saturated with the Latin and German wisdom of the University, and believed, so far, in no one and nothing. He stopped behind the back of his sister's chair, and was listening to her narratives of how some persons, who called themselves mediums, made light objects become so heavy that it was impossible to lift them; and others which were naturally heavy became again remarkably light.

"And you mean to say that you can do it?" ironically asked the young man.

"Mediums can, and I have done it occasionally; though I cannot always answer for its success," coolly replied Mme. Blavatsky.

"But would you try?" asked somebody in the room; and immediately all joined in requesting her to do so.

"I will try," she said, "but I beg of you to remember that I promise nothing. I will simply fix this chess table. He who wants to make the experiment, let him lift it now, and then try *again after I shall have fixed it.*"

"Do you mean to say that you will not touch the table at all?"

"Why should I touch it?" answered Mme. Blavatsky with a quiet smile.

Upon hearing the extraordinary assertion, one of the young men went determinedly to the small chess table and lifted it up as though it were a feather.

"All right," she said. "Now kindly leave it alone, and stand back!"

The order was at once obeyed, and a great silence fell upon the company. All, holding their breath, anxiously watched for what Mme. Blavatsky would do next. She apparently, however, did nothing at all. She merely fixed her large blue eyes upon the chess table, and kept looking at it with an intense gaze. Then without removing her gaze, she silently, with a motion of her hand, invited the same young man to remove it. He approached, and grasped the table by its leg with great assurance. The table *could not be moved!* He then seized it with both his hands. The table stood as though screwed to the floor. He grew red with the effort, but all in vain!

There was a loud burst of applause. The young man, looking very much confused, slowly said, "Well, this is a good joke!"

"Indeed, it is a good one!" echoed Leonid. A suspicion had crossed his mind that the young visitor was acting in secret confederacy with his sister. "May I also try?" he suddenly asked her.

"Please do, my dear," was the laughing response.

Her brother upon this, approached, smiling, and seized the table by its leg. But the smile instantly vanished, to give place to an expression of mute amazement. He gave it a tremendous kick, but the little table did not even budge. Applying to its surface his powerful chest he enclosed it. "How strange!" he said, with a wild expression of astonishment.

Addressing him with her usual careless laugh, HPB said, "Try and lift it now." Pulling it upward by a leg, Leonid nearly dislocated his arm. It lifted like a feather![14]

Sinnett reports:

Madame Blavatsky has stated that this phenomenon could be produced in two different ways: 1st. Through the exercise of her own will directing the magnetic currents so that the pressure on the table became such that no physical force could move it; and 2nd, through the action of those beings with whom she was in constant communication, and who, although unseen, were able to hold the table against all opposition.[15]

Chapter 3

St. Petersburg and Rugodevo

I n the spring of 1859 HPB, her father, and Vera were in St. Petersburg on a business trip. They stayed at the Hotel de Paris. Their forenoons were occupied with business and their afternoons and evenings with making and receiving visits, and there was no time for, or even mention of, phenomena.

One night they received a visit from two old friends of Peter von Hahn. Both were much interested in spiritualism and were, of course, anxious to see some phenomena. According to Vera:

After a few successful phenomena, the visitors declared themselves positively delighted, amazed, and quite at a loss what to make of Madame Blavatsky's powers, but they could not understand her father's indifference. There he was, coolly laying out his *"grande patience"* with cards, while phenomena of such a wonderful nature were occurring around him. Taken to task, he answered that it was all bosh. The rebuke left the two old gentlemen unconcerned, and they insisted that Colonel Hahn go to another room, write a question on a piece of paper, and put it in his pocket without letting anyone see it.[16] Finally consenting, he returned to his solitaire, assuring his friends that before he would believe in such nonsense, "I shall be ready to believe in the existence of the devil, undines, sorcerers, and witches; and you may prepare to offer me as an inmate of a lunatic asylum."

By the means of raps and alphabet we got *one word,* but it proved such a strange one, so grotesquely absurd as having no evident relation to anything that might be supposed to have been written by her father, that all of us who had been in the expectation of some complicated sentence looked at each other, dubious whether we ought to read it aloud. To our question, whether that was all, the raps became more energetic: Yes! . . . yes, yes, yes!!!

[Noting] our agitation and whispering, Madame B.'s father looked at us over his spectacles, and asked: "Well! have you any answer? It must be something very elaborate and profound indeed!"

"We only got *one* word, *Zaitchik.*"

It was a sight indeed to witness the extraordinary change that came over the old man's face at this *one* word! He became deadly pale. Taking out of his pocket the paper he had written upon in the adjoining room, he handed it in silence to his daughter and guests. They read: "What was the name of my favorite war horse which I rode during my first Turkish campaign?" and lower down, in parenthesis, ("Zaitchik").

This solitary word had an enormous effect upon the old gentleman. As it often happens with inveterate skeptics, once that he had found out that there was indeed *something* in his eldest daughter's claims, and that it had nothing to do whatever with deceit or juggling, he rushed into the region of phenomena with all the zeal of an ardent investigator.[17]

After the visitors left, they spread the word of what they had witnessed. Soon crowds of people were visiting to see for themselves. The most successful phenomena took place during those hours when we were alone, when no one cared to make experiments or sought useless tests, and when there was no one to convince or enlighten. . . . I well remember how, during a grand evening party, when several families of friends had come from afar off to witness phenomena, HPB produced nothing,[†] but hardly had they left, everything in the room seemed to become endowed with life. The furniture acted as though every piece of it was animated and gifted with voice and speech, and we passed the rest of the evening and the greater part of the night as though we were between the enchanted walls of the magic palace of some Scheherazade.

It is far easier to enumerate the phenomena that *did not* take place during those forever memorable hours than to describe those that did. At one moment as we sat at supper in the dining room, there were loud chords played on the piano which stood in the adjoining apartment, and which was closed and locked, and so placed that we could all of us see it from where we were through the large open doors.

Then at the first command and look of Madame Blavatsky there came rushing to her through the air her tobacco pouch, her box of matches, her pocket handkerchief, or anything she asked, or was made to ask for.

† When the above was translated into English for Sinnett, HPB added: "Simply because she was tired and disgusted with the ever growing thirst for phenomena. As in 1880—so in 1850 and 1860. People are never satisfied with what they get but ever crave more." (Blavatsky, *Collected Writings* 14:479.)

Then, as we were taking our seats all the lights in the room were suddenly extinguished, both lamp and wax candles, as though a mighty rush of wind had swept through the whole apartment; and when a match was instantly struck, there was all the heavy furniture, sofas, arm chairs, tables standing upside down, as though turned over noiselessly by some invisible hands. . . .[18]

As HPB was later to explain, the expression "invisible hands" is correct. It was her own astral hands and arms at work.[19] The astral body, it is claimed, can be extended a number of feet from its physical counterpart.

The business that brought the family to St. Petersburg being accomplished, they moved to the village of Rugodevo, which had recently been bought by Vera's late husband. Here HPB remained for about a year.

Vera writes:

Once we settled down in my village, we seemed to have entered a magical world and grew so used to the inexplicable movements of furniture, to things being transported from one place to another, and to the interference into our everyday life of an unknown but *rational* force, that we soon began to regard that force as something rather ordinary, often paying little attention to things that struck other people as miraculous. Habit, indeed, becomes second nature! . . .

One morning father came down for his morning tea, with a strange look on his face. I was frightened to see him so worried and pale, as though he was ill, but he reassured me. "I'm not ill but I am very upset. I haven't slept all night. Right after I went to bed *your mother came to my room*. I saw her all of a sudden, staring at me, calmly and affectionately. I sat up and was about to jump towards her but she held out her hand and asked me not to touch her. . . . The voice, the face, the way she behaved, everything was hers. Even that habit of frowning a little when talking!"

He said he remembered every word of the conversation, but refused to reveal what she said. Several times later, he expressed the wish to see her again, but it never happened.[20]

The quiet life of the sisters at Rugodevo was brought to an end by a terrible illness which befell Madame Blavatsky. Years before, perhaps during her solitary travels in the steppes of Asia, she had received a remarkable wound. We could never learn how she had met with it. Suffice to say that the profound wound reopened occasionally, and during that time she suffered intense agony, often bringing on convulsions and a death-like trance. The sickness used to last from three to four days, and then the wound would heal as suddenly as it had reopened, as though an invisible hand had closed it, and there would remain no trace of her illness. But the affrighted family was ignorant at first of this strange peculiarity, and their despair and fear were great indeed. A physician was sent for to the neighboring town; but he proved of little use, not so much indeed through his ignorance of surgery, as owing to a remarkable phenomenon, which left him almost powerless to act through sheer terror at what he had witnessed. He had hardly examined the wound of the patient prostrated before him in complete unconsciousness, when suddenly he saw a large, dark hand between his own and the wound he was going to anoint. The gaping wound was near the heart, and the hand kept slowly moving at several intervals from the neck down to the waist. To make his terror worse, there began suddenly in the room such a terrific noise, such a chaos of noise and sounds from the ceiling, the floor, window panes, and every bit of furniture in the apartment, that he begged he might not be left alone in the room with the insensible patient.[21]

After HPB recovered, the doctor attributed the appearance of the dark hand to uncertain light in the room and the flickering flame of candles, an explanation which became a subject for laughter throughout the countryside for months to come.

Vera continues: "In the spring of 1860 both sisters left Rugodevo for the Caucasus, on a visit to their grandparents. . . . During the three weeks' journey from Moscow to Tiflis . . . there occurred many a strange manifestation," but, she notes the most outstanding took place "at Zadonsk . . . a place of pilgrimage where the holy relics of St. Tilhon are preserved." What happened, however, was suppressed by the Russian censor who prevented its publication in "The Truth about H. P. Blavatsky." Fortunately it was rescued from Vera's original manuscript when Sinnett's *Incidents* was being prepared. Here is what the censor omitted:

[At Zadonsk] we halted for rest, and I prevailed upon my lazy sister to accompany me to the church to hear the mass. We learned that on that day church service would be conducted near the said relics by [one of the three "Popes" of Russia] the Metropolitan of Kiev, the famous and learned Isidore, whom both of us had well known in

our childhood and youth at Tiflis, where he was . . . the spiritual
chief of all the archbishops and the head of the church in Georgia. . . . During service the venerable old man recognized us, and
immediately dispatched a monk after us, with an invitation to visit
him at the Lord Archbishop's house. He received us with great
kindness. But hardly had we taken our seats in the drawing room of
the Holy Metropolitan than a terrible hubbub, noises, and loud raps
in every conceivable direction burst suddenly upon us with a force
to which even we were hardly accustomed: every bit of furniture in
the big audience room cracked and thumped—from the huge chandelier under the ceiling, every one of whose crystal drops seemed to
become endowed with self-motion, down to the table, and under
the very elbows of his holiness, who was leaning on it.

Useless to say how confused and embarrassed we looked—
though, truth compels me to say that my irreverent sister's embarrassment was tempered with a greater expression of fun than I would
have wished for. The Metropolitan Isidore saw at a glance our
confusion, and understood, with his habitual sagacity, the true cause
of it. He had read a good deal about the so-called "spiritual"
manifestations, and on seeing a huge arm chair gliding toward him,
laughed, and felt a good deal interested in the phenomenon.

Upon ascertaining which of the sisters "had such a strange power,"
the metropolitan received HPB's permission to ask a serious question
from her "invisibles." The answer was so pertinent that he continued
the conversation for several hours, in Vera's words, "expressing all the
while his profound astonishment at their "all-knowledge."[22]

Years later, Vera repeated the story in a Russian sketch of HPB's life,
and this time it escaped the wary eye of the censor. It ends thus:

Isidore blessed and counseled my sister about the exceptional gift
she was given and added precious and memorable words which
remained with her forever as the opinion of an enlightened priest of
the orthodox church. He said: "There is no power that is not from
God! You need not be troubled unless you misuse the special power
given you. Are there not many unexplained powers in nature? Man
is not forbidden to learn them. In time they all will be mastered and
used for the benefit of all mankind. May God bless you for all things
good and kind."[23]

Chapter 4

Return to the Caucasus

A rriving in Tiflis in the spring, HPB lived with the Fadeyevs for a year, but the reunion with her beloved grandmother did not last beyond August, when the grand old lady passed away.

A fascinating glimpse of life in their household is provided by a frequent visitor, General P. S. Nikolayeff:

> They were living in the ancient mansion of the Prince Chavcha-vadze, the very building itself carrying the imprint of something peculiar, something that evoked the epoch of Catherine the Great. A long and gloomy hall, with the family portraits of the Fadeyevs and the Princes Dolgorukov; then the drawing room, its wall covered with Gobelins [tapestry], a present from the Empress Catherine to Prince Chavchavadze; this was adjoined by the apartment of Miss N. [Nadya] A. Fadeyev, in itself one of the most remarkable museums, [and] a very rare and precious library.
>
> The emancipation of the serfs altered in no way the life of the Fadeyevs, their enormous retinue of domestics remaining with them as hired people and everything went on as of yore, comfortably and in plenty. I loved to spend my evenings with them. At a quarter of eleven, the [grandfather] would retire . . . supper would be brought into the drawing room, the doors would be tightly shut, and an animated conversation would ensue. At times it was contemporaneous literature or current problems of Russian life that were being analyzed; at other times one listened to the narrative of some traveler, or the account of some sunburnt officer just back from the battlefield . . . or again it was Radda-Bai (Helena Petrovna Blavatsky, granddaughter of A. M. de Fadeyev) who called forth from her past, stormy episodes of her life in America.

At times the conversation would take a mystical turn; Radda-Bai would seem to call forth invisible presences: "The candles would glimmer low, the figures on the . . . [tapestry] would appear to come to life, unwittingly one felt a creepy sensation, while the Eastern sky was already lighting up against the dark background of the southern night."[24]

HPB went for a while to Zugdidi and Kutais, after which she then returned to live another year with her grandfather.[25] She supported herself by engaging in various commercial enterprises. Vera tells us that her sister "was a master of needlework and skilled in making beautiful artificial flowers," adding:

> To sell these she at one time opened a prosperous workshop. Later she undertook a broader field of commerce in rafting walnut logs abroad, for which she moved to Mingrelia on the shore of the Black Sea[†]. . . . While in Mingrelia, she bought a home.
>
> Her occult powers, all this while, instead of weakening, became every day stronger, and she seemed finally to subject to her direct will every kind of manifestation. The whole country was talking of her. The superstitious Gooriel and Mingrelian nobility began very soon to regard her as a magician, and people came from afar off to consult her about their private affairs [and also to be healed]. She had long since given up communication through raps, and preferred— what was a far more rapid and satisfactory method—to answer people either verbally or by means of direct writing.[26]

When translating the foregoing for Sinnett, HPB appended an intriguing explanation of how she read people's thoughts. Writing in the third person, she said:

> This was done always in full consciousness and simply by watching people's mental thoughts as they evolved out of their heads in *spiral* luminous smoke, sometimes in jets of what might be taken for some radiant material . . . [which] settled in distinct pictures and images around them. Often such thoughts and answers to them would find themselves impressed in her own brain, couched in words and sentences, in the same way as original thoughts [do]. But, so far as we are able to understand—the former visions are always more trust-worthy, as they were independent and distinct from her own im-pressions, belonging to pure clairvoyance not "thought transference" which is a process always liable to get mixed up with one's own more vivid mental impressions.[27]

While in Mingrelia HPB contracted a mysterious illness and gradu-ally wasted away to a living skeleton. The local physician ordered her

---

† Vera adds that "still later [probably in Odessa] she became involved in a cheap process of ex-tracting ink, which venture succeeded, though she finally sold it."

return to Tiflis. Traveling in a native boat down the river Rion to Kutais, she arrived at Tiflis close to death. Vera reports:

> She never talked upon that subject [her illness] with anyone. But as soon as she was restored to life and health, she left the Caucasus. Yet it was before her departure from the country in 1863 [1864] that the nature of her powers seems to have entirely changed.[28]
>
> . . . for nearly five years we had a personal opportunity of following the various and gradual phases in the transformations of Helena's psychic force. At Pskoff and Rugodevo, it happened very often that she could not control, nor even stop its manifestations. After that she appeared to master it more fully every day, until after her extraordinary and protracted illness at Tiflis she seemed to . . . subject it entirely to her will.[29]

The five years in Russia were years of intensive training for Blavatsky. However, from perusal of her ink sketch that follows it appears that there were lighter moments too. In April of 1862, HPB attended the Tiflis Opera House to see Gounod's *Faust,* which only four years earlier had had its world premiere in Paris. Two of the leading singers at this Tiflis production, Agardi and Teresina Mitrovich or Metrovich, were very good friends of HPB. Teresina played the part of Marguerite, and her husband—a famous basso at the time—played the part of Mephistopheles.

3. *The Metrovitches in "Faust," 1862. (Theosophical Society, Adyar Archives)*

Chapter 5

Travels Resumed

A s when she left Tiflis more than a decade previously, HPB says she again fled "because I was sick at heart and my soul needed space." It was the boredom of conventional life in Russia and the absence of real freedom that drove her away.[30] She went to Odessa for a while. Thereafter one cannot speak with certainty as to the sequence of her travels, but besides Iran, Syria, Lebanon, and Jerusalem, HPB appears to have been more than once in Egypt, Greece, and Italy. It may be during this time that she studied the Kabbalah under a learned rabbi. She corresponded with him until he died, and his portrait was always a treasured relic.

In 1867, HPB spent several months traveling through Hungary and the Balkans. The towns visited were recorded in a travel diary that still exists.[31] Her last stops were in Venice, Florence, and Mentana.[32] A small town northeast of Rome, Mentana has special historic significance: In Italy's long struggle for freedom, on November 3, 1867 it was the site of an important battle waged between the forces of the Italian liberator, Garibaldi, and those of the papists and the French.

When eight years later HPB was in New York, a reporter heard about her participation in this battle. He wrote under the caption "Heroic Women":

Her life has been one of many vicissitudes, and the area of her experiences is bounded only by the world. . . . in the struggle for liberty [she] fought under the victorious standard of Garibaldi. She won renown for unflinching bravery in many hard-fought battles, and was elevated to a high position on the staff of the great general. She still bears the scars of many wounds she received in the conflict. Twice her horse was shot under her, and she escaped hasty death only by her coolness and matchless skill.

Altogether Madame Blavatsky is

AN ASTONISHING WOMAN

78

When HPB included the clipping in her scrapbook she inked in these words: "Every word is a *lie*. Never was on 'Garibaldi's staff'. . . ."

To Sinnett, she wrote: "The Garibaldis (the sons) are alone to know the whole truth; and [a] few more Garibaldians with them. What I did, you know partially; you do not know all."[33] On another occasion she remarked, "[W]hether I was *sent* there, or found myself there by accident, are questions that pertain to my private life."[34] One of Blavatsky's inveterate critics, René Guenon, admits that a high-ranking Mason, John Yarker (whose writings HPB commends in *Isis*), was "a friend of Mazzini and Garibaldi" and "had once seen Madame Blavatsky in their entourage."[35]

HPB told Olcott she was at Mentana as a volunteer with a number of other European ladies. He recalls "In proof of her story she showed me where her left arm had been broken in two places by a sabre stroke, and made me feel in her right shoulder a musket bullet, still embedded in the muscle, and another in her leg." In all, five wounds were received and she was picked up out of a ditch for dead. Olcott is of the opinion that this near-death was a critical stage in her development, wherein she was able to use her personal self more effectively as a vehicle for the higher self within.

In the early part of 1868, apparently recovered from her wounds, HPB was in Florence. Then via northern Italy she crossed over to the Balkans, according to her account spending some time there awaiting orders from her teacher. Finally word came to proceed to Constantinople and then on to India,[36] after which she journeyed to eastern Tibet. This trip is said to mark her first prolonged stay in that mysterious realm.

Chapter 6

Tibetan Sojourn
Part 1

When HPB first met her teacher in London, in 1851, she was told that as preparation for a work he was about to undertake—one in which he needed her cooperation—she would have to spend three years in Tibet. In a letter to an inquirer who asked why she was sent there, HPB answered:

True, there is absolutely no need of going to Tibet or India to find some knowledge and power "which are latent in every human soul"; but the acquisition of the highest knowledge and power require not only many years of the severest study enlightened by a superior intelligence, and an audacity bent by no peril, but also as many years of retreat in comparative solitude, and association with but students pursuing the same object, in a locality where nature itself preserves like the neophyte an absolute and unbroken stillness if not silence! Where the air is free for hundreds of miles round of all mephytic influence; the atmosphere and human magnetism absolutely pure, and—no animal blood is spilt.[37]

Even in remote parts of China such places exist, if the letter that follows is to be credited. It was received at the Adyar TS nine years after HPB's death and was published in *The Theosophist* in August 1900, with this introduction: "Through the kindness of an Indian Prince, we have received a letter written by a gentleman from Simla who was travelling in China, to an Indian friend. The reference to HPB makes it specially interesting. We omit the names from the original letter, which is in our possession."

> *Rung Jung*
> *Mahan, China*
> *1st January 1900*

My Dear—

Your letter addressed through His Highness Raja Sanhib Hira Singh, reached me while traversing the Spiti mountains. Now I have crossed these

80

*mountains and am in the territory of Mahan, China. This place is known by
the name of Rung Jung and lies within the territory of the Chinese empire.
The place has a great cave and is surrounded by high mountains. It is the chief
haunt of Lamas and the favourite resort of the Mahatmas. Great Rishis have
chosen it on account of its antiquity and beautiful and charming scenery. The
place is suited for divine contemplation. A man can nowhere find a place
better suited for focusing one's mind.*

*The great Lama [here is] Kut Tĕ Hum . . . the guru of all Lamas. . . .
His chelas (disciples) also are ever meditating and trying to absorb themselves in the Great Divine. From conversation with them I came to know that
Madame Blavatsky had visited this place and meditated here for some time.
Formerly I had doubts as to her arrival here, but all my misgivings
have now been removed and I feel confident of her divine contemplation at
this holy and sacred place. The lesson and Updesha I received from these
Lamas show that the views of the* Theosophical Society *are not merely
visionary and theoretical but are practical schemes. . . .*

Before they descended into what is now called India, the Brahmans
lived far to the north and, according to HPB, claimed their scriptures,
the Vedas, were compiled on the shores of Lake Manasarovara in
Tibet.[†] Buddha himself was born in Kapilavastu, now in modern-day
Nepal, a kingdom bordering "the roof of the world," as Tibet has been
called.

During the twenty-five hundred years since the Buddha died, his
followers have spread his philosophy throughout Asia and elsewhere,
forming a great number of schools whose practices and interpretations vary widely.[38] Among the most subtle and perplexing of Buddha's teachings has been his doctrine of "no-self" (anātman), that is, of
no permanent, unchanging soul in man separate from the vast totality
of life. Many people, especially in the West, have taken this to mean
that Buddha did not believe in an immortal inner self that reincarnates
from life to life. The fourteenth Dalai Lama, the titular head of Tibetan
Buddhists, commented upon this notion on his first visit to the United
States, when he lectured at Harvard University's Center for the Study of
World Religions on October 17, 1979. He affirmed that "by our
own experience it is established that the self exists. . . . If we did assert total selflessness, then there would be no one who could culti-

---

[†] For additional information see *H. P. Blavatsky Collected Writings,* compiled by Boris de
Zirkoff (Wheaton, Illinois, The Theosophical Publishing House, 1950–91), 3:419; and
"Vedas," in H. P. Blavatsky, *The Theosophical Glossary* (Los Angeles, California, The Theoso-
phy Company, 1973), 361–63.

vate compassion." Even in nirvana, he added, "the continuum of consciousness goes on . . ."[39] HPB taught similarly.[40]

≈

The usual argument against HPB's having lived in Tibet is that the country had been closed to foreign intrusion for several centuries. Furthermore, considering the hazardous travel conditions and the high mountain passes to be traversed, how could a lone woman survive?

Some little-known facts are important to counter the first objection. In *Tibet, the Sacred Realm,* to which the Dalai Lama wrote the introduction, the author, Lobsang Lhalungpa, writes:

> Although Tibet was relatively isolated—its history made it wary of foreigners and Lhasa was known in the West for centuries as "The Forbidden City"—it was always open to neighboring peoples, and saw a continuous stream of visitors, pilgrims, and traders from as far away as Mongolia, China, Bhutan, India, and Ladakh. During the major Buddhist festivals the city swelled to more than twice its size, as tens of thousands of monks and pilgrims crowded into the ancient citadel.[41]

HPB, with her Mongolian face and olive-yellow skin, might have had little difficulty living in Lhasa or elsewhere in Tibet.

As to the second objection, HPB never claimed she journeyed alone or on foot, as her critics presume. It is likely she was accompanied by her teachers, who traveled by horse. Heinrich Harrer, in *Seven Years in Tibet,* reports that women on horseback were a common sight in Tibet.[42] HPB herself was a superb horsewoman. One of her teachers wrote to A. P. Sinnett: "Those whom we desire to know us will find us at the very frontier." Others, he noted, "would not find us were they to go [to] Lhasa with an army."[43] It is also possible to enter Tibet on a less strenuous route than the overland one, which requires massive supplies and sufficient native bearers to carry them. Harrer traveled via the Indus River. Furthermore, the availability of food markets would make carrying huge food supplies unnecessary.

It should be explained that HPB's teachers were not Tibetans, but Indians. Her special guru, Mahatma Morya (usually called Master M) was born in the Punjab; his colleague, Mahatma Koot Hoomi (Master KH), was born in Kashmir. HPB wrote:

There is beyond the Himalayas† a nucleus of Adepts, of various nation-
alities, and the Teshu [Panchen] Lama knows them, and they act together,
and some of them are with him and yet remain unknown in their true
character even to the average lamas—who are ignorant fools mostly.[44] *My*
Master and KH and several others I know personally are there, coming and
going, and they are all in communication with Adepts in Egypt and Syria,
and even Europe.[45]

The Teshu, or Panchen Lama lived in the monastery town of
Tashilunpo near Shigatse, and it apparently was here that HPB went at
the outset of her present stay in Tibet. Lhasa was much farther from the
Indian border. However, whether one's destination was Lhasa or
Shigatse, some of the passes to be traversed were fourteen thousand
feet above sea level and the journey would seem to be wearisome in the
extreme. However, Sven Hedin, Swedish explorer of Tibet and Central
Asia, writes of his travels through the "glorious mountain giants with
snow-capped peaks and labyrinths of winding valleys,"—which he
deems the most magnificent scenery of the world:

> We penetrated deeper and deeper into the unknown, putting one
> mountain chain after the other behind us. And from every pass a
> new landscape unfolded its wild, desolate vistas, towards a new and
> mysterious horizon, a new outline of rounded or pyramidal
> snow-capped peaks. Those who imagine that such a journey in vast
> solitude and desolation is tedious and trying are mistaken. No
> spectacle can be more sublime. Every day's march, every league
> brings discoveries of unimagined beauty.[46]

It is unsurprising that HPB once exclaimed that she would rather live
in a cave in Tibet than in any so-called civilized country in the world!
    In considering what evidence exists, if any, to support Blavatsky's
claims to having lived in Tibet, one must be aware that her knowledge
of Tibetan Buddhism was greater than was then available to the public
or even to Western scholars. Dr. G. P. Malasekera, founding president
of the World Fellowship of Buddhists, states under "Blavatsky" in his
monumental *Encyclopedia of Buddhism:* "Her familiarity with Tibetan
Buddhism as well as with esoteric Buddhist practices seems to be

---

† "Beyond the Himalayas" does not necessarily refer to Tibet. HPB never claimed that Tibet
was the *chief* headquarters of the "fraternity of perfected adepts." In *The Secret Doctrine* she
indicates that Tibet is only one of several esoteric schools, "the seat of which is beyond the
Himalayas, and whose ramifications may be found in China, Japan, India, Tibet, and even in
Syria, besides South America. . . ." (1:xxiii.)

beyond doubt."[47] The Japanese philosopher and teacher, D. T. Suzuki, who brought Zen Buddhism to the West, believed that "undoubtedly Madame Blavatsky had in some way been initiated into the deeper side of Mahayana teaching. . . ."[48] As to Suzuki's credentials for making such an evaluation, in 1966, when he died at the age of ninety-five, the *London Times* wrote:

> Dr. Suzuki was a remarkable figure in the field of Oriental philosophy, for he was at the same time a scholar of international rank, a spiritual teacher who had himself attained the enlightenment he strove to hand on, and a writer who in some twenty volumes taught the West the nature and purpose of Zen Buddhism. As a scholar he was a master of Sanskrit and Chinese Buddhist texts, with an up-to-date knowledge of European thought in several languages.

Suzuki not only influenced the Zen generation, but many professional people as well. When he conducted seminars at Columbia University in the late 1950s, his students included psychoanalysts and therapists such as Erich Fromm and Karen Horney, as well as artists, composers, and writers.[49] Some fifty American psychiatrists and psychologists spent a week with him in the summer of 1957. An outgrowth of the conference was the volume *Psychoanalysis and Zen Buddhism,* by Fromm, Suzuki, and DeMartino, published by Harper and Row.

In reviewing Suzuki's contact with HPB's writings, it should be mentioned that up until 1927, when his essays first appeared, practically all of the Buddhist scriptures the West knew and studied were translated ones of the Theravada school of Southern Buddhism. Consequently, when in 1910 Dr. Suzuki came across HPB's translation of *The Voice of the Silence,* published in 1889, he was amazed. "I saw *The Voice of the Silence* for the first time when at Oxford," he later told a friend. "I got a copy and sent it to Mrs. Suzuki (then Miss Beatrice Lane) at Columbia University, writing to her: 'Here is the real Mahayana Buddhism.'"[50] Many Western scholars, incidentally, do not accept *The Voice of the Silence* as genuine, because they have never seen the original work from which it was taken.

Another evidence of Dr. Suzuki's high regard for HPB came when he visited the United States in 1935. Boris de Zirkoff had been in contact with Suzuki about some Buddhist writings and upon learning of his impending visit to the country, made arrangements through Nyogen Senzaki, a Buddhist monk and teacher in Los Angeles, for Suzuki to visit de Zirkoff at his office in the TS International Headquarters at Point Loma, California. When the Japanese philosopher walked in he was immediately attracted by a picture of HPB on the wall, and after standing before it in silent meditation, turned to his host and said: "She was one who attained."[51]

In 1989, the hundredth anniversary of *The Voice of the Silence* was celebrated and a special edition of the work was printed, to which the present Dalai Lama wrote the foreword.[52] This was the year that he received the Nobel Prize for Peace and the Raoul Wallenberg Human Rights Award. The foreword reads:

FOREWORD

THE BODHISATTVA PATH

I first met the members of the Theosophical Society more than thirty years ago, when I visited India to attend the celebrations of the 2500th anniversary of the Buddha. Ever since, I have had the pleasure of sharing my thoughts with Theosophists from various parts of the world on many occasions. I have much admiration for their spiritual pursuits.

I believe that individuals can be good human beings without necessarily being spiritual. I also accept their right in not wanting to be spiritual or to believe in a particular religion. At the same time, I have always believed that inner or spiritual development is necessary for greater human happiness and to increase our capacity to benefit others. I am therefore happy to have this long association with the Theosophists and to learn about the Centenary Edition: THE VOICE OF THE SILENCE which is being brought out this year. I believe that this book has strongly influenced many sincere seekers and aspirants to the wisdom and compassion of the Bodhisattva Path. I very much welcome this Centenary Edition and hope that it will benefit many more.

THE XIVth DALAI LAMA

April 26, 1989

4. The seal and signature of the XIVth Dalai Lama, included in the foreword of The Voice of the Silence. *(Concord Grove Press, Santa Barbara, California)*

Following this foreword in the centenary edition is a message from the Ninth Panchen Lama (1883–1933), which he wrote for *The Voice of the Silence,* published in English, in 1927, by the Chinese Buddhist Research Society in Beijing.[53] The message, or sutra, as it is called in Buddhism, was penned by the Panchen Lama in Tibetan calligraphy:

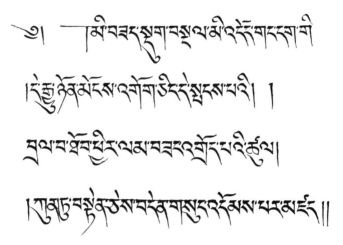

5. *Tibetan calligraphy of the Panchen Lama; sutra for 1927 Chinese edition of HPB's* The Voice of the Silence. *(The Chinese Buddhist Research Society, Peking, China, 1927)*

The above sutra was composed and penned in Tibetan characters by the Ninth Panchen Lama and was included at his request in the 1927 Peking, China, edition of H. P. Blavatsky's *The Voice of the Silence.* Translation:

> All beings desire liberation from misery.
> Seek, therefore, for the causes of misery
> and expunge them.
> By entering on the path, liberation
> from misery is attained.
> Exhort, then, all beings to enter the path.

The Editorial Foreword to the 1927 edition states that the edition was printed at the Panchen Lama's request and that his staff, together with several Chinese scholars, verified Madame Blavatsky's translation of Tibetan words. The foreword also mentions that she studied for several years at Tashilunpo and knew the previous Panchen Lama very well.

It was during HPB's present stay in Tibet that she may have first studied *The Voice of the Silence.* In the preface she writes:

> The following pages are derived from "The Book of the Golden Precepts," one of the works put into the hands of mystic students in the East. The knowledge of them is obligatory in that school, the teachings of which are accepted by many theosophists. Therefore,

as I know many of these Precepts by heart, the work of translating has been relatively an easy task for me. . . .

The work from which I here translate forms part of the same series as that from which the "Stanzas" of the *Book of Dzyan* were taken, on which *The Secret Doctrine* is based. . . . The original *Precepts* are engraved on thin oblong squares; copies very often on discs. These discs, or plates, are generally preserved on the altars of the temples attached to centres where the so-called "contemplative" or Mahayana (Yogacharya) schools are established. They are written variously, sometimes in Tibetan but mostly in ideographs.

"The Book of the Golden Precepts"—some of which are pre-Buddhistic while others belong to a later date—contains about ninety distinct little treatises. Of these I learnt thirty-nine by heart, years ago. To translate the rest, I should have to resort to notes scattered among a too large number of papers and memoranda collected for the last twenty years and never put in order, to make of it by any means an easy task. Nor could they be all translated and given to a world too selfish and too much attached to objects of sense to be in any way prepared to receive such exalted ethics in the right spirit. For, unless a man perseveres seriously in the pursuit of self-knowledge, he will never lend a willing ear to advice of this nature. Therefore . . . it has been thought better to make a judicious selection only from those treatises which will best suit the few real mystics in the Theosophical Society, and which are sure to answer their needs.[54]

HPB did more than translate *The Voice of the Silence* into English. She appended notes and commentaries to assist readers in understanding and using the precepts.

Some ten years ago, friends of the writer, Jerome and Roseva Muratore, invited the Tibetan Lama, Geshe,[†] Lozang Jampsal, to their home in New Jersey. He had lived and studied at Tashilunpo before escaping from Tibet. The Lama was Roseva's Sanskrit teacher at Columbia University. During the course of the visit the Muratores showed him *The Voice of the Silence,* directing his attention especially to the notes. The effect was electrifying. He confessed amazement that such information was available in the West. As to HPB, he said, "She must be a *bodhisattva*" (a person close to Buddhahood).

---

† "Geshe" is a title accorded Tibetan lamas who have progressed to an advanced degree in their Buddhist studies.

Chapter 7

Tibetan Sojourn
Part 2

From testimonials pertaining to HPB's knowledge of Tibetan Buddhism, we turn to other possible evidence of her reputed stay in Tibet. The first was reported by Margaret Cousins, who achieved recognition in the late 1920s for visiting the sacred cave of Amarnath in the Himalayas, fourteen thousand feet above sea level. Her article "A Pilgrimage in the Himalayas" describes with such depth of feeling the magnificent sights witnessed, one regrets it is buried in the pages of an old magazine.[55] In a subsequent issue the following was published:

> When Mrs. Cousins returned safely to Srinagar, the capital of Kashmir State, she was invited by a prominent *sadhu* (spiritual teacher) then visiting Srinagar to call on him, as he was much impressed with the courage of a lady who could make the long and perilous journey almost alone and outside the usual season for the pilgrimage. In the course of their conversation, which ranged over religion, philosophy and art, Mrs. Cousins asked the *sadhu* if he had known of any Europeans penetrating into the inner recesses of the Himalayas and getting contact with the great Rishis and their wisdom. He replied that "he had known of very few such, as those who came to the hills did not come on the highest quest, and were not physically or spiritually prepared."

He then recalled that "in the early days of his lifetime of discipline in the Himalayas, a lady had found the high teachers and received the Ancient Wisdom. Going back through his memory, he ultimately recalled that she was not British, but Russian, and he finally remembered her name—Blavatsky. He had not himself met her, but had heard her achievement spoken of by fellow ascetics."[56]

A very different sort of evidence concerning HPB's presence in Tibet involves an experiment conducted in Austria in 1886 by a prominent theosophist, Franz Hartmann, MD. The experiment was carried on through a clairvoyant, a German woman, who was at one time a servant in the house of Hartmann's parents when he was a child. He had accidentally met this woman on his return to Austria, after living at the headquarters of the Theosophical Society in Adyar for a year. She invited him to her house, where she was engaged in the practice of medicine among poor people. Himself a physician of wide experience, Hartmann discovered that the woman had an astonishing ability to correctly diagnose illnesses clairvoyantly by the examination of a patient's urine. To her, the diseased organs became clearly visible. By placing her hands on Hartmann's spine, she enabled the doctor to share her vision. He wrote a paper about her work, "Clairvoyant Medical Diagnosis" (*The Theosophist,* February 1887, 291–92). What concerns us especially, however, is his follow-up article, "Psycho-metrical Experiments" (*The Theosophist,* March 1887, 354–58), from which the following is taken:

My last paper contained an account regarding the clairvoyant powers of a German peasant woman, residing in the suburbs of this town, Kempten. After mailing it, it occurred to me to test her psy-chometrical powers with letters, and I therefore went to her house, armed with the following documents:

1. A letter from Mrs. Rhoda Batchelor of Ootacamund [India].

2. A letter from Col. H. S. Olcott [of Adyar, Madras].

3. A letter from the Countess Wachtmeister of Ostende [Belgium].

4. An "occult letter," purporting to come from an Adept, and bearing neither postmark, nor any other indication regarding the place where it had been written.

I gave to the woman letter No. 1, and requested her to hold it to her forehead, and to remain entirely quiet and passive; not to think of anything, and then to tell me after awhile what she saw. She said that she did not think she would see anything, and that she never had heard of such an experiment before; but that she was willing to try.

After a little while she began to describe a cottage with a veran-dah, standing at the side of a hill, and having a high room with a bay window in one corner. She described the furniture of that room and some trees which could be seen from the verandah; such as do not grow in this country, but look somewhat like poplars. In short, I easily recognized in her description the residence of Mrs. Batchelor, called *The Laurels* (at Ooty) and the *Eucalyptus* trees in its vicinity.

She also described a lady in a grey dress, but the latter is unknown to me.

I then handed her letter No. 2, written by Col. Olcott. I supposed that this letter had been written in the Colonel's private room, and if thought-transfer had been the cause of these psychometric imaginings, I should probably have received a description of that room. But instead of that she gave me a description of a large, high hall with pillars and benches, corresponding to the appearance of the entrance hall of the [Theosophical] Headquarters at Adyar. She also described the gravel-walks, the trees, and the river, with astonishing correctness, and spoke of an adjoining room where "a man with a beard" was writing, and near that place, towards the river, a sort of a "cage," the use of which neither she nor I could make out.

At this point, Olcott, as editor of *The Theosophist,* added this footnote to Hartmann's article: "Probably since the cage was described as 'towards the river,' the description refers to a heap of the peculiar wide native ladders, some of which, having been used in the building of a new Sanskrit Library, were so stacked for a time on the river bank as to present exactly the appearance of a cage; but of this accidental arrangement of course Dr. Hartmann knew nothing."

Hartmann continues:

Next came the letter of the Countess Wachtmeister, and I received a very good description of the "fair and blue-eyed" countess, and of a "stately and extremely pleasant-looking old lady," in whom I easily recognized Madame Blavatsky. The woman furthermore gave a description of the house where these ladies resided; of a great many manuscripts "in some foreign language"; and of the furniture of the rooms. [HPB was writing *The Secret Doctrine* at this time.] The most remarkable feature was that she saw a number of statues and busts about the house; a circumstance which I cannot verify at present as I never was at Ostende and the said house is unknown to me.

Here the doctor inserted a note: "Since writing the above I received a letter from the Countess in answer to my inquiry. She says: 'The woman was quite right about the statuary here. There are many busts in the house.'"

The crucial experiment for Hartmann and one that greatly worried him was No. 4, the occult letter from an adept. Was it genuine? Do the Masters of Wisdom really exist? Hartmann continues:

This letter was one which I took at random out of my box containing letters of a similar kind. After the experiment was over I examined it and saw that it was one which I had found one day upon my table in my room at Adyar, where a moment before no such letter had been. . . .

Now with a heart full of sad misgivings and forebodings of evil tidings, I handed her the *"occult letter."* Her first exclamation was one of surprise, wonder and joy. "Ah!"—she exclaimed—"What is this? I never saw anything so beautiful in my life!"

Here follows Hartmann's translation of the woman's remarks, leaving out merely unimportant details:

"I see before me a high but artificially made elevation or hill, and upon that hill a building which looks like a *temple,* with a high *Chinese* roof. The temple is of a splendid white, as if it were made of pure white marble, and the roof is resting upon three pillars. On the top of a roof there is a shining sun;—but no!—it only looks like a sun; it seems to be some kind of an animal. I do not know how to describe it; I never saw such a thing before; but it shines like a sun.

"There is a beautiful walk of smooth stones and some steps leading up to that temple, and I am going up to it. Now I am there, and lo! the floor is a lake, in which the light of that sun on the top of the roof is reflected! But no—I am mistaken; it is no water at all; it is a kind of yellowish marble, which shines like a mirror. Now I see it plainly! It is a square marble floor, and in the centre there is a dark round spot. This is all so very beautiful. It looks to a certain extent like the *Walhalla* near Regensburg.

"Now I am in that temple, and I see two gentlemen looking at something on the wall. One is a very fine-looking gentleman, but he is dressed quite differently from the people in this country. He is dressed in a loose flowing robe of pure white, and the forepart of his shoes is pointed upwards. [As previously indicated, HPB's teachers were said to be Indians, not Tibetans.] The other one is smaller and bald-headed; he wears a black coat and silver buckles (ornaments?) on his shoes.

"They are looking at a picture on the wall. The picture represents a vase with some tropical plants; something like prickly-pear leaves; but very different from all the prickly-pears I ever saw. The vase is not a painting, but a real vase. I first thought it was painted. It stands in a corner, and there are ornamental paintings on it.

"There are some paintings and drawings on the wall. Below the ceiling, where the roof begins, there is a field, or panel, on which there are some curious figures. Some look like a 1 5 and one like a V, and others like squares and ciphers; with all sorts of garnishes between them. They look as if they were numbers; but I do not think they are. They may be some strange letters or characters. Above that field or panel there is another one, on which there are some square pictures or plates, with some very queer things painted upon them. They are movable; at least I think that they are; but I am not quite certain. . . ."

I afterwards asked the woman to draw the figures she had seen on a paper. Being no artist, she could do so only in a very imperfect manner, but she said she did it as well as she could. The accompanying illustration is a copy of what she drew. The woman informs me, that if she merely *imagines* a thing, the memory of it soon leaves her; but if she once sees a thing clairvoyantly, it remains in her mind, and she can recall it with all its details whenever she pleases.

The complete drawing was reproduced as the frontispiece of *The Theosophist* issue (March 1887) containing Dr. Hartmann's paper. Below are the pertinent parts:

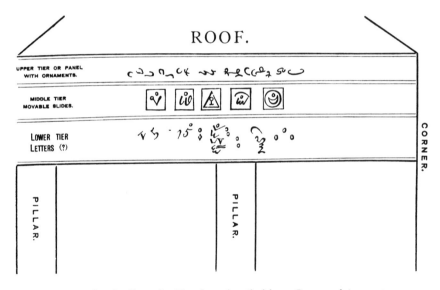

6. *Roof and pillars of a Temple as described by a German clairvoyant.*
(The Theosophist, *March 1887, Frontispiece*)

The woman continues: "Now these two gentlemen are going out, and I am following them. There are a great many trees looking like pine trees. I think they are pines. There are others with big fleshy leaves and spikes something like prickly-pears. There are mountains and hills and a lake. They are taking me away from that temple. I am afraid I cannot find my way back to it. There is a big ravine, and there are some trees which I take to be olive trees; but I am not sure of it, for I never saw any olive-trees. Now I have arrived at a place, where I can see over a wide expanse of country. The two gentlemen have gone away. Here there is some antiquity looking like an old ruined wall, and something like what I saw on that paper you showed me. I believe you call it a *Sphinx*. [Hartmann had previously shown her the cover of a German magazine, *The Sphinx*.] There is sort of a pillar, and on the top of it is a statue, whose upper part looks like a woman, while the lower part of her body seems to be a fish. She seems to be holding some moss in her hands, or resting them upon it."

Here [the clairvoyant] began to laugh, and when I asked her what was the matter, she answered: "What a funny sight! There are lots of queer people! They are little women and children. They wear such funny dresses, and have fur caps on their heads. They have *soles* tied to their feet! [The clairvoyant had never seen sandals before.] They are collecting something from the shore and putting it into baskets. Now the whole scene dissolves into a cloud."

Thus ended this important experiment. . . .[57]

Before Hartmann forwarded his paper to *The Theosophist* for publication, he sent it to Ostende for analysis by HPB. *However, he did not send the woman's drawing.* Here is HPB's reply, dated December 5, 1886:

My Dear Doctor: You must really forgive me for my seeming neglect of you, my old friend. I give you my word of honor, I am worried to death with work. Whenever I sit to write a letter all my ideas are scattered and I cannot go on with the Secret Doctrine *that day. But your letter (the last) is so interesting that I must answer it as asked. You will do an excellent thing to send to the* Theosophist *this experiment of yours. It has an enormous importance in view of Hodgson's lies and charges, and I am happy you got such an independent corroboration; [the] astral light, at any rate, cannot lie for my benefit.[†]*

I will only speak of number 4, as the correctness about the other three letters you know yourself. This looks like the private temple[58] of the Teshu

---

† In *Isis Unveiled* (1:184), HPB explains: "When the psychometer examines his specimen, he is brought in contact with the current of the astral light, connected with that specimen, and which retains pictures of the events associated with its history. These pass before his vision with the swiftness of light."

[Panchen] Lama, near Tchigadze—made of the "Madras cement"—like material; it does shine like marble and is called the snowy "Shakang" [temple]†—as far as I remember. It has no "sun or cross" on the top, but a kind of algiorna dagoba, triangular, on three pillars, with a dragon of gold and a globe. But the dragon has a swastica‡ on it and this may have appeared a "cross," I don't remember any "gravel walk"—nor is there one, but it [the temple] stands on an elevation (artificial) and a stone path leading to it, and it has steps—how many I do not remember (I was never allowed inside); saw from the outside, and the interior was described to me. The floors of nearly all of Buddha's (songyas) temples are made of yellow polished stone, found in those mountains of Oural and in northern Tibet toward Russian territory. I do not know the name, but it looks like yellow marble.

The "gentleman" in white may be Master, and the "bald-headed" gentleman I take to be some old "shaven-headed" priest. The cloak is black or very dark generally—(I brought one to Olcott from Darjeeling), but where the silver buckles and knee-breeches come from I am at a loss. They wear, as you know, long boots—up high on the calves, made of felt and embroidered often with silver. . . . Perhaps it is a freak of astral vision mixed with a flash of memory (by association of ideas) about some picture she saw previously.

In those temples there are always movable "pictures," on which various geometrical and mathematical problems are placed for the disciples who study astrology and symbolism. The "vase" must be one of many Chinese queer vases about in temples, for various objects. In the corners of the temples there are numerous statues of various deities (Dhyanis). The roofs are always (almost always) supported by rows of wooden pillars dividing the roof into three parallelograms, and the mirror "Melong" of burnished steel (round like the sun) is often placed on the top of the Kiosque on the roof. I myself took it once for the sun. Also on the cupolas of the [dagoba] there is sometimes a graduated pinnacle, and over it a disk of gold placed vertically and a pear-shaped point and often a crescent supporting a globe and the swastica upon it.

Ask her whether it is this she saw, Om tram ah hri hum, which figures are roughly drawn sometimes on the Melong "mirror"—(a disk of brass) against evil spirits—for the mob. [Remember, HPB had not seen the woman's drawing, reproduced on page 92, yet the resemblance is almost exact.] Or perhaps what she saw was a row of slips of wood (little cubes), on which such things are seen:

---

† The correct spelling of a Tibetan temple is *lhakang.* HPB's handwritten "*l*" may have been mistaken for an "s." Sven Hedin translates *lha kang* as "God's house." (Hedin, *Trans-Himalaya* 1:405. See also plates 124, 129.)

‡ Swastikas are widely used in Tibet. (Hedin 404; Lhalungpa 65, 77).

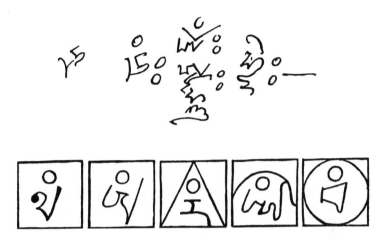

7. *Tibetan characters drawn by HPB, confirms clairvoyant's vision.* (The Path, *January 1896, 298*)

If so, then I will know what she saw. "Pine woods" all round such temples, the latter built expressly where there are such woods, and wild prickly pear, and trees with Chinese fruit that the priests use for making inks. A lake is there, surely, and mountains plenty—if where Master is; if near Tchigadze—only little hillocks. The statues of Meilha Gualpo, the androgyne Lord of the Salamanders or the Genii of Air, looks like this "sphinx"; but her lower body is lost in clouds, not fish, and she is not beautiful, only symbolical. Fisherwomen do use soles alone, like the sandals, and they all wear fur caps. That's all; will this do? But do write it out.[59]

One special problem in the foregoing was to decipher, or rather identify, the strange characters appearing in both the German woman's drawing and in HPB's letter, for they had no resemblance to Tibetan printed characters. To solve this conundrum I had recourse to the kind assistance of Wesley Needham in charge of Yale University's comprehensive Tibetan collection and an expert in that language. Both Hartmann's paper and HPB's letter accompanied the query. On December 8, 1986, Needham replied.

I have read with much interest the psychometrical experiments and can report that on page 299 of "Letters of HPB to Hartmann," the Tibetan letters are Om tram ah hri hum in the top group arranged like this:

OM
tram ah hri   *All Sanskrit mantras*
hum   *in Tibetan characters*

The lower group in squares appear to be the mantras related to the five
Dhyani Buddhas:

[Tibetan]	[Sanskrit]
Lam	*Ratnasambhava*
Yam	*Amoghsiddhi*
Ram	*Amitabha*
Kham	*Vairocana*
Vam	*Aksobhya (Vajrasattva)*

On the page marked ROOF, the characters in squares are different from
those on page 299, and are beyond me. [The latter are the movable slides,
some examples of which were given by HPB, who had not seen the clair-
voyant's drawing.]

Below these squares are Om tram ah hri hum, again the same Sanskrit
mantras in Tibetan characters, same arrangement. They are called seed-
syllables, *not intended to be translated [in usual Tibetan printed type].*
They are also related to the five Dhyani Buddhas.

Thus it is confirmed that an unlearned German woman could reproduce in Tibetan seed-syllables a sacred Buddhist mantra of which
she had no likely previous knowledge. The catalyst for this remarkable
feat and her accompanying visions was, as we have seen, an occult
letter reputed to be from one of HPB's teachers in Tibet.

One more step needs to be taken to complete Hartmann's experiment, and that is to ascertain whether HPB's statements of what the
woman saw, some of which already have been verified in the previous
pages, are correct. Again Wesley Needham of Yale was approached for
help. A list of a number of items requiring identification was sent him.
Although he had available to him the large Tibetan collection at Yale,
he could verify only two of the items: first, that "in Tibetan temples
are numerous images of Dhyani Bodhisattvas and Buddhas, also
wrathful protective divinities." Second, "the graduated pinnacle and
disk is obviously the common Chorten. See Ippolito Desidere, *An
Account of Tibet,* Plate IV, opp. page 132." Needham suggested that for
the remaining items I should check with the Dalai Lama's brother,
Professor Thubten J. Norbu of Indiana University at Bloomington.
Norbu was unable to help.

Sometime later I learned that two friends, Angiola Sartorio and Terry
Dickinson, and a third companion, a researcher in Buddhism, were

going to India, and among various places were visiting Dharamsala to see the Dalai Lama. They volunteered to continue the search there for the needed information, but it was not available, and the Dalai Lama's secretary suggested they visit several lamas originally from Tashi-lunpo monastery in Tibet, which had been destroyed by the Chinese Communists. The secretary phoned for an appointment and my friends were granted an audience with seven lamas in residence, headed by the Venerable Kachan Lhadkor. The questions asked were given careful attention, for one by one, some required recovering memories of scenes from many years earlier.

Two negative replies were received: the floors of Buddhist temples were not of yellow marble, and the lamas did not recognize "Snowy Lhakang" as a name of the private temple of the Panchen Lama. As to all the rest, affirmative replies were given: there were pine woods and wild prickly pear plants around the Buddhist temples in that area and trees from which the monks made ink. There were statues of Meilha Gualpo on pillars, and on the roofs could be found dragons of gold, holding a globe, as well as huge mirrors (melongs) of burnished steel, round like the sun, often with the invocation engraved thereon of "Om tram ah hri hum." The lamas added that the melongs were made of "multiple metals."

The lamas may have failed to identify the sacred retreat of the Panchen Lama mentioned by HPB either because they were unaware of its existence or are not initiated lamas, or because they are initiated and hence were unable to speak of its existence. What gives rise to this speculation is the description given by HPB of the private retreat of the Panchen Lama, a secret school near Shigatse founded by Tsong-ka-pa, who was in charge of it. There are preserved valuable occult works used in the preparation of *The Secret Doctrine*.[60]

One place HPB never publicly claimed to have visited in Tibet was the forbidden city of Lhasa. Since the time of Abbe Huc's brief stay in 1847 and until 1904, when the British invaded Tibet for a short period, no person from the West is known to have been there. The first woman was the French explorer Alexandra David-Neel, who, in her fifth journey to Tibet (1923–24), achieved what until then had been believed the impossible. However, according to HPB's sister, Vera, "it is authentic that Helena was in Lhasa, the capital of Tibet, and its main religious center, Shigatse . . . and in the Karakoram Mountains in the Kunluns. Her vivid stories about these places proved this to me many times."[61]

If HPB was in Tibet for almost three years during this period, it would be incredible if she *did not* go to Lhasa, the great mecca of the Buddhist world. Her teachers could easily have taken her disguised as a pilgrim, as her Asiatic features would excite no attention. But to claim publicly later that she was there might cause embarrassment to her guardians. The Panchen Lama and the Dalai Lama in those days were not in agreement on the policy of isolating Tibet from the rest of the world. The explorer Sven Hedin attests to that: though he visited the Panchen Lama and was warmly received, he could never enter Lhasa and meet the Dalai Lama.[62]

If HPB in fact was the first Westerner since Huc to visit Lhasa, that should not detract from the magnificent achievement of Madame David-Neel,[†] whose book *My Journey to Lhasa* the London *Times Literary Supplement* calls "one of the epic journeys of our time."

An undated entry in David-Neel's diary refers to a British friend, Elisabeth Morgan: "One day while writing [to me], Elisabeth let drop the word Theosophy with the name Blavatsky." This, David-Neel added, opened "a new phase of my life."[63] From another source it is learned that she thereafter attended lectures on oriental religions, "especially Buddhism at the Paris Theosophical Society," and developed a burning ambition to explore the East.[64]

---

† Mlle. Alexandra David received her TS diploma in London, on June 7, 1892. According to a letter from Annie Besant dated March 17, 1893, she also applied to enter the ES. (Daniel Caracostea, "Alexandra David-Neel's Early Acquaintances With Theosophy, Paris 1892," tr. by Diana Dunningham-Chapotin, *Theosophical History,* July–October 1991, 209–13.)

Tibetan Sojourn
Part 3

During the final period of HPB's stay in Tibet, it seems that she was in the Karakoram Mountains, north of Kashmir and part of the great Himalayan range, far west of Shigatse and Lhasa. According to her sister, Vera, she stayed there with the Mahatma KH, who lived with his sister and nephew. "Mahatma Morya," Vera wrote, "her own guru, did not have a permanent residence . . . and traveled constantly living where at the moment he was most needed."[65] KH also was frequently away on missions and often at Tashilunpo.[66] HPB said she met him first in 1868.[67]

In a letter to Mrs. Hollis Billings (October 2, 1881), HPB wrote that KH's home "is in Little Tibet and belongs now to Kashmir. It is a large wooden building in the Chinese fashion, pagoda-like, between a lake and a beautiful mountain." She added that Master M often dwelt there. Both of these teachers, she said, rarely came out openly in the world, "but they can project their astral forms anywhere."[68]

KH's home, or ashram, as Olcott called it, had more than one purpose, as intimated in letters to William Q. Judge from the Hindu Theosophist Damodar, who, in an out-of-body experience, was taken there. Damodar writes:

I was in a peculiar place. It was the upper end of Kashmir at the foot of the Himalayas. . . . there were only two houses just opposite to each other and no other sign of habitation. From one of these came out . . . Koot Hoomi. It was his house. Opposite him stood [Master M]. Brother K ordered me to follow him. After going a short distance of about a half a mile we came to a natural subterranean passage which is under the Himalayas. [This] is a natural causeway on the River Indus which flows underneath in all its fury. Only one person can walk on it at a time and one false step seals the fate of the traveler. . . .

After walking a considerable distance through this subterranean passage we came into an open plane in L⸺k. There is a large massive building. . . . This is the Chief Central Place where all those of our Section who are found deserving of Initiation into Mysteries have to go for their final ceremony and stay there for the requisite period. I went up with my Guru to the Great Hall. The grandeur and serenity of the place is enough to strike anyone with awe. . . . The splendor of the Chief's Throne is incomparable [and] has around it an indescribable glory, consisting of an effulgence which seemed to radiate from the one who occupied it.[69]

As Damodar was under HPB's tutelage when he underwent this experience—and also a few years later, when he appears to have also undergone it in his waking body[70]—one might suspect that some of her own initiations took place there, not only in her present stay in the East but in the previous one, too, when, it will be recalled, HPB claimed to have entered Tibet through Kashmir.

As to her present stay in Tibet, HPB once afforded, in a letter to Sinnett, a glimpse of her training when she lived in KH's home. It was written after a vivid flashback dream that returned to consciousness all of the details of her daily life there.

Much of Blavatsky's time had been engaged in learning two languages. One was Senzar, which she defines as "the mystic name for the secret sacerdotal language, or the 'mystery speech' of the initiated adepts, all over the world."[71] It was in this language that the stanzas forming the basis of *The Secret Doctrine* and *The Voice of the Silence* were claimed to be originally written.[72]

The second language was English. It seems incongruous that HPB should have gone all the way to Tibet to learn English! Did she not study it as a child, and later speak it in England and America? Conversational English, yes, but not much above the level of the Farmer Brown stories her Yorkshire governess taught her, and even this she avoided speaking, because her acquired Yorkshire accent made people laugh!

"I remember," Blavatsky tells Sinnett, "how difficult it was for me to understand a well-written book in English so far back only as 1867 in Venice." In presenting theosophical ideas to the world, she had the enormously difficult task of rendering the subtleties of esoteric philosophy and metaphysics into a Western tongue not equipped to express such ideas. One of her daily tasks was to translate sentences from Senzar into English. Master KH, who knew both languages, corrected her. Also, during that time HPB conversed only in English, even with her own teacher, but whether her speech "was good or bad," she says, "was the same for him as he does not speak it but understands every word I say out of my head. . . ."

In Blavatsky's dream "the scene changes and I am going away with Master who is sending me off, back to Europe."[73] One source indicates the parting took place from the Manasarovara Hills in Tibet.[74] Maps record this famous area as south of the Karakoram Mountains.

Chapter 9

A Strange Visitation

W hile HPB was still in Tibet, her aunt Nadya had a strange experience in Odessa. Years later, when in Paris, Nadya wrote of it to Olcott, who was then in London. Her letter, dated June 26, 1884, translated from the French, reads in part:

> *. . . when my niece was at the other side of the world . . . not a soul knew where she was—which grieved us greatly. All our researches had ended in nothing. We were ready to believe her dead, when—I think it was about the year 1870, or possibly later—I received a letter from him, whom I believe you call "KH," which was brought to me in the most incomprehensible and mysterious manner, by a messenger of Asiatic appearance,* who then disappeared before my very eyes. *This letter, which begged me not to fear anything, and which announced that she was in safety—I have still at Odessa. Immediately upon my return I shall send it you, and I shall be very pleased if it can be of any use to you.*
>
> *Pray excuse me, but it is difficult, not to say impossible for me, to comprehend how there can exist people so stupid as to believe that either my niece or yourself have invented the men whom you call the Mahatmas! I am not aware if you have personally known them very long, but my niece spoke of them to me, and at great length, years ago. She wrote me that she had again met and renewed her relations with several of them, even before she wrote her* Isis. *Why should she have invented these personages? For what end and what good could they have done her if they had no existence? . . .*
>
> *If I, who have ever been, and hope ever to continue to be a fervent Christian, believe in the existence of these men—although I may refuse to credit all the miracles they attribute to them—why should not others believe in them? For the existence of at least one of them, I can verify. Who, then, could have written me this letter to reassure me at the moment when I had the greatest need for such comfort, unless it had been one of those adepts mentioned? It is true that the handwriting is not known to me; but the manner in which it was delivered to me was so phenomenal, that none other than an adept in occult science could have so effected it. It promised me the return of*

*my niece—and the promise was duly fulfilled. However, I shall send it to
you, and in a fortnight's time you shall receive it at London.*[75]

Ten days later, the letter and its accompanying addressed envelope
were sent to Olcott. Both were written in French on handmade rice
paper used in Kashmir and Punjab. They read:

*To the Honorable
    Most Honorable Lady—
    Nadyejda Andreewna
        Fadeew
        Odessa*

*The noble relatives of Mad. H. Blavatsky have no cause whatsoever for grief.
Their daughter and niece has not left this world at all. She is living and
desires to make known to those whom she loves that she is well and feels very
happy in the distant and unknown retreat she has selected for herself. She has
been very ill, but is so no longer; for owing to the protection of the Lord
Sangyas*[†] *she has found devoted friends who take care of her physically and
spiritually. Let the ladies of her house, therefore, remain calm. Before 18 new
moons shall have risen—she will have returned to her family.*[76]

On the envelope, in Nadya's handwriting in Russian, are the words
in pencil "Received at Odessa, November 7 [Russian calendar], about
Lyolinka, probably from Tibet, November 11, 1870, Nadejda F."[77]
    The communication was published in an 1885 report of the General
Council of the Theosophical Society and included this comment:

Both the note and envelope are written in the now familiar handwriting of the Mahatma KH, so that those who pretend that
Madame Blavatsky later invented both Mahatma and writing, have
to disprove the fact that both were known to the family of Madame
Blavatsky . . . five years before the Theosophical Society was
founded in America.
    Many persons, both in Europe and India, have carefully com-
pared this note with others received through the Adyar shrine and in
various other places phenomenally, as well as with the voluminous
[KH] letters in Mr. Sinnet's possession, and find the handwriting
absolutely identical.[78]

Even Frederic Myers of the Psychical Research Society concurred,

† "Lord Sangyas" is the Tibetan title for Buddha.

reporting on the letter to HPB's aunt. "I have seen this letter," he states, "which certainly appears to be in the KH handwriting."[79]

In a letter dated October 29, 1877, to her relatives (once in the possession of the Earl of Crawford and now at Adyar), HPB wrote that her Master had a deep respect for the spirit of Christ's teachings and further, that she had once spent seven weeks in a forest not far from the Karakoram Mountains, where she had been isolated from the world and where her teacher had visited her daily, though whether astrally or otherwise she did not state. Judge states that while there she had been shown in a cave-temple a series of statues representing the great teachers of the world.[80†] "A colossal bronze statue of Jesus, forgiving Mary Magdalen, stands in one of the underground Temples. Near it a statue of Gautama giving water to a beggar from his cup, and of Ananda his pupil and brother. And of Buddha who drinks at a well out of a vessel extended to him by a pariah and a prostitute. *This I know*" (*H.P.B. Speaks* 1:223–24).

† *The Path* situates the forest near the Karakorams, though they are not mentioned in the letter. This information may be based on HPB's comments to Judge. See also *H.P.B. Speaks*, 1:193.

Chapter 10

A Time of Waiting

It would be over a year after leaving Tibet before HPB was reunited with her relatives in Odessa. Meanwhile, she traveled in the Near and Middle East. She speaks of going to Cyprus and to Greece, where she met for the first time the Master Hilarion.[81] According to Madame Blavatsky, she studied under several masters in Syria and Egypt, and came in contact with many of the Brotherhood.[82]

"There is no doubt in my mind," writes Dr. Rawson, "that Madame Blavatsky was made acquainted with many, if not quite all, of the rites, ceremonies, and instructions practiced among the Druzes of Mount Lebanon in Syria, for she speaks to me of things that are only known by the favored few who have been initiated."[83] Rawson, himself, had been initiated therein according to *Who Was Who in America* (the edition that covers three centuries, 1607–1896).

In Greece, at the Port of Piraeus, HPB boarded the SS *Eunomia,* bound for one of the Ionian islands. Her ultimate destination was Cairo. However, the ship, carrying gunpowder and fireworks, blew up in midvoyage. At the time, Lloyds of London gave the date as July 6, 1871. Of the four hundred passengers only sixteen escaped.[84] HPB's money and possessions were lost. The Greek government provided the survivors with passage to their destinations.[85]

Based on letters shown him by her relatives, Sinnett tells the story of what occurred during this period:

In 1871 Mme. Blavatsky wrote from Cairo to tell her friends that she had just returned from India and had been wrecked somewhere *en passant* (near Spezzia). She had to wait in Egypt for some time before she returned home, meanwhile she determined to establish a *Société Spirite* for the investigation of mediums and phenomena according to Allan Kardec's theories and philosophy, since there was no other way to give people a chance to see for themselves how mistaken they were. She would first give free play to an already established and accepted teaching and then, when the public would see that nothing was coming out of it, she would offer her own explanations. To accomplish this object, she said, she was ready to go to any amount of trouble—even to allowing herself to be regarded for a time as a helpless medium. "They know no better, and it does me no harm— for I will very soon show them the difference between a passive medium and an active doer," she explains.

A few weeks later, says Sinnett, a second letter was sent to her friends:

> In this one she showed herself full of disgust for the enterprise, which had proved a perfect failure. She had written, it seems, to England and France for a medium, but without success. *En désespoir de cause,* she had surrounded herself with amateur mediums— French female spiritists, mostly beggarly tramps, when not adventuresses in the rear of M. de Lesseps' army of engineers and workmen on the canal of Suez.
>
>   "They steal the society's money," she wrote, "they drink like sponges, and I now caught them cheating most shamefully our members, who came to investigate the phenomena, by bogus manifestations. I had very disagreeable scenes with several persons who held me alone responsible for all this. So I ordered them out. . . . The *Société Spirite* has not lasted a fortnight—it is a heap of ruins— majestic, but as suggestive as those of the Pharaoh's tombs. . . . To wind up the comedy with a drama, I got nearly shot by a madman— a Greek, who had been present at the only two public seances we held, and got possessed, I suppose, by some vile spook."[86]

The original of the last letter is in the archives of the Theosophical Society in Adyar and concludes with these words: "I swear to put an end forever to such seances—they are too dangerous and I am not practised and strong enough to control the wicked spooks that may approach my friends during such sittings."[87]

After leaving Cairo, Blavatsky traveled in Syria,[88] Palestine, and Constantinople, finally reaching her family in Odessa in July 1872, where she remained for nine months, until April 1873.[89] About all that is known of this period is one incident, which HPB later recalled in a letter to Nadya:

> *I shall never forget one characteristic day, or rather night, in Odessa, in your house at a dinner. Aunt [Catherine de Witte] was quarreling with me about religion, and was firmly stating that no Jew or idol-worshipper can ever enter the Kingdom of Heaven and will never be found there. From this very moment I began to brood over these words. "If even Aunt," I thought, "such a good, noble and just woman, is so blinded by Christian faith that she can*

believe in such a terrible, horrifying injustice of God, then what must be [the beliefs of] other Christians, many of whom are not worthy of her little finger?"

. . . The differences in religious dogmas, were created not by saints but by all-sinful mortals . . . [and] divide humanity into inimical nations and races.

If there were no dogmas, there would also be no Protestants, Catholics, Buddhists, Brahmanists, etc.; all would believe in One God . . . all would regard themselves as brothers, . . . they would be ashamed before the rest of their brothers to kill and slaughter each other in wars, to torture each other like wild beasts, and to create a hell *for another.*[90]

From Odessa, HPB went to Bucharest to visit a friend, and then to Paris where she lived with her cousin Nikolay von Hahn. Among her friends was a physician, Dr. Lydia Marquette, who two years later, in New York, described Blavatsky's activities while in the French capital. This was done at the request of Colonel Olcott, who had been disturbed by innuendoes that HPB "led a wild life" in Paris. The doctor wrote:

New York, December 26, 1875

Dear Sir:

In reply to your inquiries, I have to say that I made Madame Blavatsky's acquaintance in Paris in the year 1873. She was living in the Rue Du Palais in an apartment with her brother [cousin] M. Hahn, and his intimate friend M. Lequeux. I was with her almost daily, and, in fact, spent a good part of my time with her when I was not in the hospitals or attending the lectures. I am, therefore, able to state from positive knowledge, what her behavior was. It gives me great pleasure to say that that behavior was unexceptionable, *and such as to entitle her to every respect. She passed her time in painting and writing, seldom going out of her room. She had few acquaintances, but among the number were M. and Mme. Leymarie. Mme. Blavatsky I esteem as one of the most estimable and interesting ladies I ever met, and since my return from France, our acquaintance and friendship have been renewed.*

Yours respectfully,
(Sd.) L. M. Marquette, M.D.[91]

Olcott relates how it came about that Blavatsky left Paris for New York: "HPB told me that she had come to Paris intending to settle down for some time under the protection of a relative of hers, but one day received from [her Teachers] a peremptory order to go to New York to await further orders. The next day she had sailed with little more than money enough to pay her passage."[92]

Vera wrote similarly: "In June [1873] she [HPB] was in Paris, where she had intended to reside for some time, when suddenly she received a letter—'an advice I have neither the desire nor possibility of resisting' as she explained to us in her correspondence—from one of her teachers in the Far East to go to America."

Toward the end of June, HPB sailed for New York. An incident that occurred when she was boarding ship was reported years later in the *New York Times* (January 6, 1889). W. Q. Judge, having just returned from a visit to her in London, was interviewed by a reporter. In describing her appearance, he said:

The characteristics that are most apparent in her countenance are, in equal blending, energy and great kindness. Looking at her one can realize that she is just the sort of woman who would do what she did a dozen years ago when she was coming over here from France. She reached Havre with a first class ticket to New York, and only two or three dollars over, for she never carried much money. Just as she was going aboard the steamer she saw a poor woman, accompanied by two little children, who was sitting on the pier weeping bitterly.

"Why are you crying?" she asked.

The woman replied that her husband had sent to her from America money to enable her and the children to join him. She had expended it all in the purchase of steerage tickets for herself that turned out to be utterly valueless counterfeits. Where to find the swindler who had so heartlessly defrauded her she did not know, and she was quite penniless in a strange city. "Come with me," said Madame Blavatsky, who straightaway went to the agent of the steamship company and induced him to exchange her first-class ticket for steerage tickets for herself, the poor woman, and the children.

Anybody who has ever crossed the ocean in the steerage among a crowd of emigrants will appreciate the magnitude of such a sacrifice to a woman of fine sensibilities . . .[93]

Marion Meade learned that during the crossing the boat "experienced extremely heavy westerly gales and head seas," causing engine damage and a four-day delay at sea. "On emigrant ships," she adds, "steerage could only be reached by climbing down a ladder through a hole in a hatchway deck. These hatches provided almost no ventilation and, in rough weather when air was most needed, they were kept shut. Two weeks of airlessness, overcrowding, lack of sanitary facilities, contamination of food and water, as well as the ever-present possibility of shipwreck, added up to downright misery. Remembering HPB's traumatic experience aboard the SS *Eumonia,* one can only assume that the Atlantic crossing was a nightmare."[94]

For one woman and her children, however, it was far better to be aboard than stranded penniless in a foreign city.

Part **4**

America —
Land of
Beginnings

Chapter 1

Early Days in New York

Whenin the summer of 1873 HPB came to New York,
it was not with the wonderment and trepidation of
an immigrant, for she had been there before. Would it be another
traveling adventure, or did she come to stay? Did she herself know? The
only information we have is that the same year, on September twenty-
second, she took out her first naturalization papers to become a citizen
of the United States.[1]

In view of her history of constant travel, Blavatsky's relatives were
astonished. Reminiscing later, Vera observed: "Once she found a
purpose worthy of all her efforts, she instantly stopped, like a roving
ship that pulls into the right harbor, confidently drops its anchor, to
roam no more. . . . To this work she remained faithful all her life. She
gave it her health, time, and soul, having recognized in it the task for
which she was destined. . . . 'Ideals and faith have been lost almost
everywhere,' she used to say. 'Pseudo-science has destroyed them.
People in our century demand a *scientific* bulwark, scientific proofs of
the spirit's immortality. Ancient esoteric science will give it to them.'"[2]

HPB's story of having left France on a day's notice was not, as some
believe, an invented afterthought, but the simple truth, and it received
corroboration after her death. Olcott writes: "We have had staying at
Adyar an American lady, Miss Anna Ballard, a veteran journalist, a life
member of the New York Press Club, who, in the course of professional duty, met HPB in the first week after her arrival at New York. In
the course of conversation, amid a variety of less important facts, Miss
Ballard casually mentioned to me too that I at once begged her to put in
writing. . . ." Here is what she wrote:

Adyar, 17th January, 1892

Dear Col. Olcott:

*My acquaintanceship with Mme. Blavatsky dates even further back than
you suppose. I met her in July, 1873, at New York, not more than a week
after she landed. I was then a reporter on the staff of the* New York Sun,

and had been detailed to write an article upon a Russian subject. In the course of my search after facts the arrival of this Russian lady was reported to me by a friend, and I called upon her; thus beginning an acquaintance that lasted several years.

At our first interview she told me she had had no idea of leaving Paris for America until the very evening before she sailed, but why she came or who hurried her off she did not say. I remember perfectly well her saying with an air of exultation, 'I have been in Tibet.' Why she should think that a great matter, more remarkable than any other of the travels in Egypt, India, and other countries she told me about, I could not make out, but she said it with special emphasis and animation. I now know, of course, what it means.

Anna Ballard.[3]

Paging through the newspapers of that period, Fritz Kunz, editor of *Main Currents,* discovered an item on HPB in the New York *Tribune* (September 26, 1873) and writes: "The woman was striking long before any occult glamour arose about her. The *Tribune* staff writer turns in a story of a Russian noblewoman arriving by steerage because she had shared her [first] class passage with a poor stranded immigrant."[4]

As to the circumstances of Blavatsky's life and the people with whom she lived during this period, little was known until Elizabeth Holt's "A Reminiscence of H. P. Blavatsky in 1873" appeared in the December 1931 *Theosophist.* From Miss Holt's description of New York in the 1870s, that city would appear a poor choice for the birthplace of a world movement, when London and Paris were the acknowledged centers of Western culture:

New York in 1873, as compared to the present city, was small. You reached the north end of Manhattan Island by horse-drawn vehicles, the public horse cars taking hours for the trip; there were no bridges over the rivers, East or Hudson; if necessary to cross, you used a ferry boat. There were, of course, no skyscrapers—the down-town city was dominated by the Trinity Church steeple, the most conspicuous landmark for miles around. The north end of the Island was mostly granite cliffs, not yet excavated into streets, even as far down as East Fortieth Street. There was a solid boulder from Third to Second Avenues, on which squatters had built for themselves nondescript shanties, and over which goats and squatter children played. Second and Third Avenues were not built up, in some sections not yet reclaimed from the East River waters. [Fifth Avenue and Broadway were well traveled and when Central Park was opened, the year of HPB's arrival, there were ten million visitors.]

The habits and thoughts of the people resembled today's as little
as that city of small homes resembles the present skyscraper city.
Darwin and the evolutionary theory were live subjects of angry
dispute. I remember the sermon preached by our clergyman—a
most kindly old gentleman—upon a horror which had shocked the
city. A theatre in Brooklyn had been burned down the previous
week and some three hundred people, mostly women and children,
had been burned to death. The clergyman told us that God, in His
just anger, had sent the fire to punish the frivolous who were
spending their time in so evil a place.

Even in social affairs we were very respectable Victorians. There
were, of course, no women in business; a few, a very few, were
beginning to be heard, clamoring for their "rights"; but the women
who had to go out into the world to earn a living were teachers,
telegraphers, sewers of various kinds and workers at small trades
which paid very badly. A lady traveling alone was not received in the
better hotels, being looked upon as under suspicion when unac-
companied by a male relative.

It was probably this difficulty of finding proper accommodation
that led HPB to the house in which I met her. I have always wondered how she, a stranger coming into New York, had discovered it.
The house itself was unique and a product of that particular era. In
those days it was hard for respectable women workers of small
means to find a fitting place in which to live; so it happened that
some forty of them launched a small experiment in cooperative
living. They rented a new tenement house, 222 Madison Street [on
the Lower East Side], one of the first built in New York, I think.
The cooperative experiment, having neither capital nor business
efficiency behind it, failed, lasting in all only some months.

My mother and I had spent the summer of 1873 in Saratoga. In
order to be ready for school when it opened, I was sent home in August to the Madison Street house, where we had a friend who would
take me somewhat under her friendly protection, and there I found
Madame Blavatsky. So far as I know, this was her first stopping place
in New York. She had a room on the second floor and my friend had
a duplicate room next to hers, so that they became very friendly
neighbors. Being a cooperative family, we all knew one another
familiarly, and kept a room next to the street door as a common
sitting room or office. My small apartment was directly opposite, so
that I saw a good deal of Madame Blavatsky, who sat in the office a
large part of her time, but she seldom sat alone; she was like a
magnet, powerful enough to draw round her everyone who could

possibly come. I saw her, day by day, sitting there, rolling her cigarettes and smoking incessantly. She was certainly an unusual figure. I think she must have been taller than she looked, she was so broad.[†] Her whole appearance conveyed the idea of power. There was a sort of suppressed excitement in the house because of her presence, an excitement wholly pleasant and yet somewhat tinged a little with awe.

I never looked upon Madame as an ethical teacher. For one thing she was too excitable; when things seemed wrong to her, she could express her opinion about them with a vigor which was very disturbing. I never saw her angry with any person or thing at close range. Her objections had an impersonality about them. In mental or physical dilemma, you would instinctively appeal to her, for you felt her fearlessness, her unconventionality, her great wisdom and wide experience and hearty goodwill—her sympathy with the underdog.

My friend, Miss Parker, a logical, level-headed Scotch-Irish lady, in her early thirties, was greatly startled when Madame told her incidents in her life which, my friend said, were known only to herself and to the dead. Miss Parker had lost her mother many years before, and when she asked Madame to put her into communication with her mother, Madame said it was impossible for her to do so as her mother was absorbed in higher things and had progressed beyond reach.

Madame continually described herself as being under the authority of unseen powers; there was quite a vogue of Spiritualism at that time and the people around her thought that these unseen powers were her "Spirit Guides." This was the most natural conclusion for people to reach who had never heard of unseen directing powers outside of the church or among the Spiritualists.

At this time Madame was greatly troubled about money; the income she had received regularly from her father in Russia had stopped, and she was almost penniless. Some of the more conservative people in our house suggested that she was, after all, an adventuress, and the want of money was only what might be expected; but my friend Miss Parker, whom she took with her to the Russian Consul, assured me that she was really a Russian Countess;[‡] that the Consul knew of her family, and had promised to do all he could to

---

† Dr. Alexander Wilder speaks of her being tall (*The Word,* July 1908, 80). So does her sister, Vera (*Russkoye Obozreniye,* Dec. 1891, 578).

‡ When traveling in Europe, both HPB and her aunt Nadya signed the hotel registers as countesses. HPB's cousin was Count Witte.

get into touch with them and find out what was the difficulty. I may say here that the holding up of her income was caused by the death of her father and the consequent time required to settle up his affairs, and that this delay continued until Madame had left 222 Madison Street.

The owner of our house was a Mr. Rinaldo, who personally collected his rents, and so became acquainted with our people. Like everyone else he became interested in HPB and introduced two young friends of his to her. They came very often to see her and were of practical aid to her in suggesting and giving her work. They got her to design picture advertising cards for themselves and for others; I think these gentlemen had a collar and shirt factory, for the card I remember best was of little figures dressed in the collars and shirts of their manufacture. I think these were the first picture advertising cards used in New York. Madame also tried ornamental work in leather, and produced some very fine and intricate examples, but they did not sell and she abandoned the leather work.

Olcott relates that when HPB was living on Madison Street she also "supported herself by making cravats or artificial flowers—I forget which now—for a kindhearted Hebrew shopkeeper. She always spoke to me with gratitude about this little man."[5]

Miss Holt recalls that sometime later "I heard that HPB went to Ithaca to give to Professor Corson of Cornell University a ring entrusted to her by one of her mysterious directors, which would identify her as an authentic messenger from them." Hiram Corson was a leading spiritualist. His son, Eugene, a medical doctor, published a volume of HPB's correspondence with his father. In her second letter, postmarked February 16, 1875, Blavatsky wrote:

I am here, in this country, sent by my Lodge, on behalf of Truth in modern spiritualism, and it is my most sacred duty to unveil what is and expose what is not. Perhaps did I arrive here 100 years too soon . . . for people seem to care every day less for truth and every hour more for gold, [and so] my feeble protest and endeavors will be of no avail.

She assured the professor that her interest in spiritualism arose "not through the agency of the ever lying, cheating mediums, miserable instruments of the undeveloped spirits of the lower sphere, the ancient *Hades*. My belief is based on something older than the Rochester knockings, and springs out from the same source of information that was used by Raymond Lully, Pico della Mirandola, Cornelius

Agrippa, Robert Fludd, Henry More, etc., etc., all of whom have ever been searching for a system that should disclose to them the 'deepest depths' of divine nature and show them the *real tie which binds all things together.* I found at last—and many years ago—the cravings of my mind satisfied by this theosophy† taught by the angels and communicated by them . . . for the aid of human destiny [this is a typical Judeo-Christian and Kabbalistic phrase]."[6]

---

† Nine months later, on November 17, the Theosophical Society was founded. Subsequently several persons have taken credit for introducing the term *theosophy* at that time. In the above we find HPB using it to identify the teachings she received from her instructors—not angels in the Christian sense, but living men who normally function in higher states of consciousness while living in bodies of flesh and blood.

Chapter 2

The Heyday of Spiritualism

S piritualism is repugnant to many people because of its association with weird practices, but the word itself is blameless. It is merely the opposite of materialism, as HPB makes plain in her *Theosophical Glossary:*

SPIRITUALISM. In philosophy, the state or condition of mind opposed to materialism or a material conception of things. Theosophy, a doctrine which teaches that all which exists is animated or informed by the universal soul or spirit, and that not an atom in our universe can be outside of this omnipresent Principle—is pure spiritualism. As to the belief that goes under that name; namely, belief in the constant communication of the living with the dead, whether through the mediumistic powers of oneself or a so-called medium—it is no better than the materialization of spirit, and the degradation of the human and divine souls. Believers in such communications are simply dishonoring the dead and performing constant sacrilege. It was well called "necromancy" in days of old. But our modern spiritualists take offence at being told this simple truth.

Modern spiritualism began in 1848 with what is known as "the Rochester knockings," or psychic manifestations surrounding the Fox sisters who lived in Hydeville, New York, not far from Rochester.

In his two-volume *History of Spiritualism,* Sir Arthur Conan Doyle observes that "either this power was contagious or else it was descending . . . like some psychic cloud on high showing itself on those persons who were susceptible. . . . In an incredibly short space of time the movement, with many eccentricities and phases of fanaticism" swept around the country.[7] Orthodox religions had hitherto offered only platitudes about immortality and life after death; the spiritualists believed they had proof.

Professor R. Laurence Moore observes that "it was not just the half-baked, the uneducated, and the credulous who appeared at séances or spirit circles. The number of prominent people who attended spiritualist meetings" was impressive.[8] Even distinguished scientists, as will be seen, became convinced of the genuineness of the phenomena after conducting controlled experiments.

Spiritualism flourished not only in the United States but in England, France, Germany, and Russia. The famous medium Daniel Home was largely responsible for its success in Europe. Conan Doyle writes that "the Emperor Napoleon III, the Empress Eugenie, the Czar Alexander, the Emperor William the First of Germany, and the Kings of Bavaria and Wurttemberg were all equally convinced by his extraordinary powers."[9]

Spiritualism was the rage in Russia in the 1850s, and Vera and Nadya engaged in spirit-writing and table-turning (levitation). Even sedate and very proper Aunt Catherine joined the circles.[10] HPB was then far from home.

In the 1860s, séances were held in the White House. One such is reported in Carl Sandburg's biography of Abraham Lincoln, at which the president permitted a journalist to be present, along with Secretary of War Stanton and Secretary of Navy Wells. Sandburg quotes the lengthy news item reprinted in scores of newspapers and headed "Spiritualism in the White House."[11]

Mrs. Lincoln was an ardent spiritualist, and the president had access through her to a remarkable medium, Nettie Colburn, whom, it appears, he consulted when serious crises arose in the struggle to preserve the union and free the slaves.[12] He was asked once what he thought of the source of a message received. According to a witness, he replied: "I am not prepared to describe the intelligence that controls this young girl's organism. She certainly could have no [waking] knowledge of the facts communicated to me, nor of what was transpiring in my Cabinet meeting prior to my joining this circle, nor of affairs at the front, nor regarding transpiring events which are known to me only and which I have not imparted to anyone, and which have not been made public."[13]

"We remember," one witness of this period remarked, "what a general uproar in public opinion, and what unrest among scientists, Spiritism called out at the time. . . . It represented that battering ram which made the first breach in materialism filling people's minds, and made them think. . . . Belief in the existence of the physical world alone was shaken."[14]

HPB applauded the scientific investigation of spiritualism and, in her article "The Evidence of Science" in the July 1881 *Theosophist,* assembles an impressive list of distinguished scientists in this field. One was Alfred Russel Wallace, who, independently of Darwin, developed the theory of evolution. In his preface to *Miracles and Modern Spiritualism,* he writes:

> Up to the time when I first became acquainted with the facts of spiritualism, I was a confirmed philosophical sceptic. . . . I was so thorough and confirmed a materialist that I could not at that time find a place in my mind for the conception of spiritual existence. . . . Facts, however, are stubborn things. . . . The facts beat me. They compelled me to accept them as facts . . . [and] led me to accept spiritualism.

Also on HPB's list was the celebrated chemist and physicist Sir William Crookes, who, as the *Encyclopaedia Britannica* informs, "maintained his belief in the reality of occult phenomena from the 1870s until his death."[15] In 1897 he became president of the Society for Psychical Research, and he was knighted the same year. On the fiftieth anniversary of his passing, *The Scientific American* (April 1969) wrote: "In Sir William Crookes we have a man who was a direct descendant of the giants of old, men who could turn their attention with equal ease to several of the great divisions of science and achieve work of lasting importance in each. Sir William's striking combination of diverse gifts, keen observation, patient and inexhaustible experimental skill, together with the glowing mind and imagination of a poet, have assured him for all time a settled place in the great list of English men of science."

In his book *Researches in Spiritualism,* Crookes describes thirteen classes of phenomena he witnessed, and comments: "With very few exceptions, the many hundreds of facts I am prepared to attest—facts which to imitate by known mechanical or physical means would baffle the skill of [the magicians] Houdin, a Boscoe, or an Anderson, backed with all the resources of elaborate machinery and the practice of years—have all taken place in my own house, at times appointed by myself, and under circumstances which absolutely precluded the employment of the very simplest instrumental aids."[16]

Blavatsky, Olcott, and Sinnett were good friends of Crookes. Crookes and his wife joined the Theosophical Society on November 20, 1883, and the next year he became a Councilor of the TS lodge in London.[17]

HPB concludes her "Evidence of Science" article by citing from professor Zöllner's book on spiritualism, *Transcendental Physics,* the published confessions of two noted magicians of the day: "Messrs. Maskelyne of London, and Samuel Bellachini, court conjurer at Berlin—who repeat that which the celebrated Robert Houdin, the French conjurer, had already stated before; namely, that 'levitations without contact as produced in the presence of mediums were feats utterly beyond the power of the *professional* juggler'; that it was the work of *no human agency,* whatever else that agency might be."†

Maskelyne emphasizes that he "never denied that such manifestations are genuine, but I contend that in them there is not one iota of evidence which proves that departed spirits have no better occupation than lifting furniture about."

The phenomenon of levitation is not difficult to explain, says HPB. Change the polarity of either an object or the human body and it will rise, for its attraction to the earth's magnetic center—which causes the illusion of weight—has been broken.[18] This can be done in various ways, one of which has been indicated earlier by HPB in a letter of April 3, 1886, to Hartmann. It bears repetition here, this time in full context, as we now approach the period when HPB met Olcott for the first time. This was at the famed Eddy farmhouse in Vermont:

> *I was sent to America on purpose and sent to the Eddys. There I found Olcott in love with spirits, . . . I was ordered to let him know that spiritual phenomena without the philosophy of Occultism were dangerous and misleading. I proved to him that all the mediums could do through [so-called] spirits others could do at will without any spirits at all; that bells and thought reading, raps and physical phenomena, could be achieved by anyone who had a faculty of acting in his physical body through the organs of his astral body; and I had that faculty ever since I was four years old, as all my family know. I could make furniture move and objects fly apparently, and my astral arms that supported them remained invisible; all this ever before I knew even of Masters. Well, I told [Olcott] the whole truth. I said to him that I had known Adepts, the "Brothers," not only in India and beyond Ladakh, but in Egypt and Syria,—for there are "Brothers" there to this day.[19]*

_____

† This appears to dispose of—or at least call into serious question—the frequent boast of a famed magician of our day, James Randi, that he can duplicate on the stage any mediumistic phenomenon, thus proving it a hoax.

Chapter 3

An Auspicious Meeting

W hen at the age of forty-two Henry Steel Olcott first met HPB, he was a man of wide experience. Born in Orange, New Jersey, of Puritan stock, Olcott attended college in New York for a year and then worked for two years on a farm in Ohio, after which he returned to New York to study scientific agriculture. In his early twenties he received international recognition for his work on the Model Farm of Scientific Agriculture, in Newark, New Jersey. The Greek government offered him the chair of agriculture at the University of Athens, and the United States government a directorship of agriculture, but he preferred to work independently. Olcott became associate editor of agriculture on the New York *Tribune.*

When the Civil War broke out, Olcott enlisted and first served in several campaigns under General Burnside, and then was appointed Special Investigator to root out corruption and graft in the War Department.[†] This earned him a colonelship. On completion of one case, Secretary of War Stanton telegraphed him:

I heartily congratulate you upon the result of today's trial. It is as important to the government as the winning of a battle.

Olcott did similar work for the Navy. Then, when Lincoln was shot, he was one of a three-member panel to investigate the assassination.

After the war, Olcott studied law for three years and was admitted to the Bar in New York in 1868. He codified confusing insurance law practices and became a specialist in customs, revenue, and insurance cases, thereby aquiring a large and prosperous clientele.[20]

Olcott's interest in spiritualism stemmed from his farming days in

† Olcott was especially clever at detecting fraud. Thus later when investigating spiritualism, he was adequately equipped to detect charlatanism, as will be seen later.

Sir Arthur Conan Doyle, the creator of the phenomenally acute *Sherlock Holmes,* admired Olcott's work in his investigation of spiritualism. Good examples will be found in his *People from the Other World,* 106–119, 174–176. The Psychical Research Society, however, pictured Olcott as a gullible witness to HPB's phenomena. (This is not true, although his memory is sometimes faulty when recording events that occurred years prior.)

Ohio, when he visited three uncles who were ardent spiritualists.[21] Henry had been reared as a strict Presbyterian.

As to the circumstances that led to his meeting with HPB, Olcott wrote in *Old Diary Leaves:*

> One day, in the month of July, 1874, I was sitting in my law office thinking over a heavy case in which I had been retained by the Corporation of the City of New York, when it occurred to me that for years I had paid no attention to the spiritualist movement. I do not know what association of ideas made my mind pass from the mechanical construction of water metres to modern spiritualism, but at all events, I went around the corner to a dealer's and bought a copy of the *Banner of Light.* In it I read an account of a certain incredible phenomena, viz., the solidification of phantom forms, which were said to be occurring at a farm house in the township of Chittenden, in the state of Vermont, several hundred miles distant from New York. I saw at once, that, if it were true that visitors could see, even touch and converse with deceased relatives who had found means to reconstruct their bodies and clothing so as to be temporarily solid, visible, and tangible, this was the most important fact in modern physical science. I determined to go and see for myself. I did so, found the story true, stopped three or four days, and then returned to New York.
>
> I wrote an account of my observations to the New York *Sun,* which was copied pretty much throughout the whole world, so grave and interesting were the facts. A proposal was then made to me by the editor of the New York *Daily Graphic* to return to Chittenden in its interest, accompanied by an artist to sketch under my orders, and to make a thorough investigation of the affair. The matter so deeply interested me that I made the necessary disposition of office engagements, and on September 17th was back at the "Eddy Homestead," as it was called from the name of the family who owned and occupied it. I stopped in that house of mystery, surrounded by phantoms and having daily experiences of a most extraordinary character, for about twelve weeks—if my memory serves me. Meanwhile, twice a week there appeared in the *Daily Graphic* my letters about the "Eddy ghosts," each one illustrated with sketches of spectres actually seen by the artist, Mr. Kappes, and myself, as well as by everyone of the persons—sometimes as many as forty—present in the séance room.[22]

The Eddy brothers, William and Horatio, were uneducated farmers. A long history of mediumship existed in the family. A grandmother four times removed was condemned as a witch during the Salem, Massachusetts trials of 1692. William's séances took the form of supposed materializations of the dead, while Horatio's were of a different character. No fee was charged for their demonstrations, only for inexpensively boarding and feeding their many guests.

The *Globe,* a newspaper in nearby Rutland, wrote:

> Colonel Henry S. Olcott, the commissioner of the *Daily Graphic,* to investigate and report upon the Eddy "manifestation" has stirred up a breeze throughout the country. Before his first letter from Rutland appeared, the subject of spiritualism had not been even mentioned in the secular papers since the appearance of Mr. Crookes' articles and Mr. Alfred Wallace's pamphlet in England set Europe agog. Now the New York dailies discuss the subject editorially—nearly all have sent reporters to Chittenden and their example has been imitated by the journals of Chicago, Hartford, Rochester, Albany, and many other cities. Whatever may be the truth about the Eddy affair, there can be no question that the public mind is very much excited upon the question whether the spirits of the dead return to us or not.[23]

Back in New York, Olcott's articles were in such demand the *Graphic* was selling at a dollar a copy, which was what HPB paid for hers. She traveled with a French woman to the Eddys, arriving October fourteenth, and remained two weeks. Olcott recalls:

> I remember our first day's acquaintance as if it were yesterday; besides which I have recorded the main facts in my book (*People from the Other World,* 293 *et seq.*).[†] It was a sunny day and even the gloomy old farm house looked cheerful. It stands amidst a lovely landscape, in a valley bounded by grassy slopes that rise into mountains covered to their very crests with leafy groves.

> The dinner hour at Eddys was noon, and it was from the entrance door of the bare and comfortless dining room that Kappes and I first saw HPB. She had arrived shortly before noon with a French Canadian lady, and they were at the table as we entered. My eye was first attracted by a scarlet Garibaldian shirt the former wore, as in vivid contrast with the dull colors around. Her hair was then a thick blond mop, worn shorter than the shoulders, and it stood out from her head, silken-soft and crinkled to the roots, like the fleece of a

---

† "In *People from the Other World,*" Olcott says, "I have described all the phenomena and the tests against fraud I invented and employed." "It is difficult to suggest any precaution he has omitted," commented Conan Doyle. (*History of Spiritualism,* 1:255.)

Cotswold ewe. This and the red shirt were what struck my attention before I took in the picture of her features. It was a massive Calmuck face, contrasting in its suggestion of power, culture, and imperiousness, as strangely with the commonplace visages about the room as her red garment did. . . . Pausing on the door-sill, I whispered to Kappes, "Good gracious! look at that specimen, will you." I went straight across and took a seat opposite her to indulge my favorite habit of character study. The two ladies conversed in French. . . .

Dinner over, the two went outside the house and Madame Blavatsky rolled herself a cigarette. . . . I said "Permettez moi, Madame," and gave her a light for her cigarette; our acquaintance began in smoke, but it stirred up a great and permanent fire. . . . My remark having been made in French, we fell at once into talk in that language. . . . Strolling along with my new acquaintance, we talked together about the Eddy phenomena and those of other lands. I found she had been a great traveler and seen many occult things and adepts in occult science, but at first she did not give me any hint as to the existence of the Himalayan Sages or of her own powers. She spoke of the materialistic tendency of American spiritualism, which was a sort of debauch of phenomena accompanied by comparative indifference to philosophy. . . .[24]

In *People from the Other World,* written soon thereafter, Olcott adds:

I gradually discovered that this lady, whose brilliant accomplishments and eminent virtues of character, no less than her exalted social position, entitle her to the highest respect, is one of the most remarkable mediums in the world. At the same time, her mediumship is totally different from that of any other person I ever met; for, instead of being controlled by spirits to do their will, it is she who seems to control them to do her bidding. Whatever may be the secret by which this power has been attained, I cannot say, but that she possesses it I have had too many proofs to permit me to doubt the fact.[25]

This power, he learned later, was conscious mediatorship rather than passive mediumship, the first hint of which was that Will Eddy's manifestations changed radically when she was present. Quoting again from *Old Diary Leaves:*

Up to the time of HPB's appearance on the scene, the figures which had shown themselves were either Red Indians, or Americans, or

Europeans . . . . But on the first evening of her stay, spooks of other nationalities came before us. There was a Georgian servant boy from the Caucasus; a Musselman merchant from Tiflis; a Russian peasant girl and others. Another evening there appeared a Kourdish cavalier armed with scimitar, pistols, and lance . . . and a European gentleman wearing the cross and collar of St. Anne, who was recognized by Madame Blavatsky as her uncle.[26]

The advent of such figures in the séance room of those poor, almost illiterate Vermont farmers, who had neither the money to buy theatrical properties, the experience to employ such if they had them, nor the room where they could have availed of them, was to every eyewitness a convincing proof that the apparitions were genuine. . . .[†]

It was long afterwards that I was informed that she had evoked them by her own developed and masterful power. She even affirms the fact in a written note in our *T. S. Scrapbook,* Vol. 1, appended to a cutting from the [London] *Spiritualist* of January, 1875.[27]

The cutting was an article, "Materialized Spirit Forms," by Benjamin Coleman, in which the following concerned HPB: "The countess' presence at several of the Eddy séances led to most surprising manifestations, including the appearance of several spirits of persons known to her in foreign countries." HPB added in ink: "Yes; for I have called them out MYSELF."[28]

Olcott reports that while at the Eddys "HPB tried her best to make me suspect the value of William Eddy's phenomena as proofs of the intelligent control of a medium by spirits; telling me that, if genuine, they must be the double of the medium escaping from his body and clothing itself with other appearances [projected unconsciously by the sitters desiring to see their loved ones]; but I did not believe her. I contended that the forms were of too great diversities of height, bulk, and appearance to be masquerades of William Eddy; they must be what they seemed, *viz.,* the spirits of the dead. Our disputes were quite warm on occasions, for at that time I had not gone deep enough into the question of the plastic nature of the human Double to see the force of her hints, while of the eastern theory of Maya I did not know the least iota."[29]

---

† The apparitions were minutely sketched by the artist Kappes for the *Graphic* and are featured in *People from the Other World.* The book is currently available in a handsome edition by a Rutland, Vermont publisher, Charles E. Tuttle Co. (1972).

HPB remarks that "even the materialized form of my uncle at the Eddys was [a] picture; it was I who sent it out from my own mind, as I had come out to make experiments without telling it to anyone. It was like an empty outer envelope of my uncle that I seemed to throw on the medium's [projected] astral body. I saw and followed the process, I knew Will Eddy was a genuine medium, and the phenomena as real as it could be, and, therefore, when days of trouble came for him I defended him in the papers."[30]

One of her experiments succeeded too well: "I actually evoked among them the form of one *whom I believed dead* at the time, but who, it now appears, was up to last year, alive and well: viz., 'Michalko,' my Georgian servant! He is now with a distant relative at Kutasis [Kutais], as my sister informed me two months ago, in Paris. He had been reported, and I thought him, dead, but had got well at the hospital. So much for 'spirit identification.'"[31]

Unfortunately, the explanation given for the materialization of the dead apparently does not apply to some cases. It is here the gruesome aspect of spiritualism enters. This is where the thoughts of the sitters attract to the medium the disintegrating astral remains of the deceased, cast off by the soul as it rises to higher states of consciousness between lives. HPB writes of this to her sister:

The more I see of mediums—for the United States is a true nursery, the most prolific hot bed for mediums and sensitives of all kinds, genuine and artificial—the more I see the danger humanity is surrounded with. . . . You remember, Vera, how I made experiments for you at Rugodevo, how often I saw the ghosts of those who had been living in the house, and described them to you, for you could never see them. . . . Well, it was the same daily and nightly in Vermont. I saw and watched these soulless creatures, the shadows of their terrestrial bodies, from which, in most cases, soul and spirit had fled long ago, but which throve and preserved their semimaterial shadows, [by feeding on the vital energies of] the hundreds of visitors that came and went, as well as of the mediums. . . .

It was ghastly to watch the process! It made me often sick and giddy, but I had to look at it, and the most I could do was to hold the disgusting creatures at arm's length. But it was a sight to see the welcome given to these umbrae by the spiritualists! They wept and rejoiced around the medium, clothed in these empty materialized shadows. . . . [It] made my heart bleed for them. "If they could but see what I see," I often wished. If they only knew that these simulacra of men and women are made up wholly of the terrestrial passions, vices, and worldly thoughts of the residuum of the personality that was; for these are only such dregs that could not follow the liberated soul and spirit, and are left for a second death in the terrestrial atmosphere† that can be seen by the average medium and the public.[32]

This is why, says HPB elsewhere, the Hindus and Buddhists from ancient times warned of the dread influences arising from communicating with the dead.[33]

In contrast to these "lower order of manifestations . . . and the platitudes and common talk of mediums," HPB remarks that there are "truly wonderful phenomena of a higher order, in which undeniable intelligence and knowledge are exhibited." These, she says, are due to the activity of the inner or higher self of the sensitive.[34] In other cases, an advanced soul may use a pure channel to accomplish some beneficent purpose. An example, perhaps, is Abraham Lincoln's experience with the medium recounted earlier.

One basic reason that theosophists discourage the notion that the dead communicate with the living is that such constant involvement of the dead in our world, with all its miseries and cruelties, would make afterlife a hell, not a heaven. The soul requires peace and spiritual refreshment between lives.[35] This, however, does not mean we are cut off from our loved ones who have died. In *The Key to Theosophy*, Blavatsky writes:

> We are with those whom we have lost in material form, and far, far nearer to them now, than when they were alive. . . . For pure divine love is not merely the blossom of a human heart, but has its roots in eternity. . . . Love beyond the grave, illusion though you may call it, has a magic and divine potency which reacts on the living. . . . It will manifest in their dreams, and often in various events—in providential protections and escapes, for love is a strong shield and is not limited by space and time. [Furthermore] karma brings sooner or later all those who loved each other with such a spiritual affection to incarnate once more in the same family group.[36]

† Professor Huston Smith remarks that reports from mediums "should be approached with great suspicion, for the 'controls' in question are not integrated souls or even integrated minds; they consist mostly of 'psychic residues' that minds leave in their wake as they traverse the psychic plane. . . ." (*Forgotten Truth,* New York, Harper Row 1976, 72–73.)

Chapter 4

First Public Work

In the interim year before the founding of the Theo-sophical Society, we find HPB working with the spiritualists as a champion of their cause. In view of her real feelings—as to the dangers of their practices—it is puzzling why she did this. But as a friendly voice in their midst, perhaps she saw a possibility of weaning them away from these practices and awakening the more enlightened to a rational philosophy that not only explained the phenomena, but also the manifold mysteries around us.[37]

Her public defense of the spiritualists began, as Olcott recalls, immediately upon her return to New York from Vermont:

A well-known physician of New York, a Dr. Beard, attracted to Chittenden by my *Graphic* letters, had come out with a bombastic and foolish explanation of the Eddy ghosts as mere trickery, and she had flayed him alive in a reply, dated October 27th and published in the *Graphic* of October 30th. Her letter was so brave and sparkling a defence of the Eddy mediums, and her testimony as to the seven "spirit-forms" she herself had recognized so convincing, that she at once came into the blaze of a publicity which never afterwards left her. . . .[38]

She carried a tone of breeziness, defiant brusqueness, and *camaraderie* throughout all her talk and writing in those days, fascinating everybody by her bright wit, her contempt for social hypocrisies, and all "caddishness," and astounding them with her psychical powers. The erudition of *Isis Unveiled* had not yet overshadowed her, but she constantly drew upon a memory stored with a wealth of recollections of personal perils and adventures, and of knowledge of occult science, not merely unparalleled but not even approached by any other person who had ever appeared in America, so far as I have heard. She was a totally different personage then from what she was later on, when people saw her settled down to the serious life work for which her whole past had been a preparatory school.[39]

HPB's letter to Beard opens Volume One of her scrapbooks. Theosophical historian, Michael Gomes remarks:

Mme. Blavatsky remains the greatest chronicler of the Theosophical Society. The Archives at Adyar contain twenty large scrapbooks of press clippings covering the years 1874 to 1884, which were undoubtedly put together by HPB. The first seven volumes, with over 1,000 articles and references to the Theosophists in New York, are the most heavily annotated by her, and are divided into thematic volumes, often bearing titles like the "Ante and Post Natal History of the Theosophical Society."[40]

After the tilt with Beard, HPB turned her attention to minimizing the effects of the greatest scandal to overtake the spiritualist movement. A leading spiritualist, Robert Dale Owen, former U.S. Congressman and foreign ambassador, had publicly admitted being duped by séances conducted by the mediums Jennie Holmes and her husband Nelson, wherein the famed spirit Katie King had supposedly been appearing. The spirit had previously manifested in séances held by Sir William Crookes, in England, and when she appeared in the United States the whole country was agog with excitement. The bubble burst when a woman, Eliza White, confessed to having masqueraded as Katie.[41] Robert Owen had lent his powerful support to the genuineness of the manifestations.

To save the situation, the Holmeses, through Owen, appealed to Olcott to test their powers.[†] He agreed and was accompanied by HPB already in Philadelphia, where the mediums lived. The first séance was held on January 11, 1875; the last, on the twenty-fifth. On the whole, they were successful; but only on the final night did a full materialization of Katie appear, thus apparently establishing credibility for Jennie Holmes's mediumship.[42] Years later, to his surprise, Olcott learned that credit belonged elsewhere. Paging through Volume One of HPB's scrapbook, he came across the following handwritten note, which, because of its contents, he concluded was "meant to be published after her death":

IMPORTANT NOTE

Yes. I am sorry to say that I *had* to identify myself during that shameful exposure of the *mediums* Holmes with the Spiritualists. I had to save the situation, for I was sent from Paris on purpose to America to *prove* the phenomena and their reality and—show the

† In a letter to General Lippitt, received March 9, 1875, HPB remarks that the Holmeses were genuine mediums only when in deep trance, which apparently was not very often. At other times they cheated. (*HPB Speaks,* 1:55–56.) Among professional mediums this frequently happened when their powers were at low ebb, and an angry audience demanded their money's worth.

fallacy of the Spiritualistic theories of "Spirits." But how could I do it best? I did not want people at large to know that I could *produce the same thing at will.* I had received ORDERS to the contrary, and yet, I had to keep alive the reality, the genuineness and *possibility* of such phenomena in the hearts of those who from *Materialists* had turned *Spiritualists* and now, owing to the exposure of several mediums fell back again, [and] returned to their skepticism.

This is why, selecting a few of the faithful, I went to the Holmeses and helped by M ∴ and *his power,* brought out the face of John King and Katie King [from] the astral light, produced the phenomena of materialization and—allowed the Spiritualists at large to believe it was done thro' the mediumship of Mrs. Holmes. She was terribly frightened herself, for she knew that *this once* the apparition was real.

Did I do wrong? The world is not prepared yet to understand the philosophy of Occult Science—let them assure themselves first of all that there are beings in an invisible world, whether "Spirits" of the dead or *Elementals;* and that there are hidden powers in man, which are capable of making a *God* of him on earth.

When I am dead and gone people will, perhaps, appreciate my disinterested motives. I have pledged my word to help people on to *Truth* while living and—will keep my word. Let them abuse and revile me. Let some call me a MEDIUM and a Spiritualist, and others an *imposter.* The day will come when posterity will learn to know me better.

O poor, foolish, credulous, wicked *world!*

M ∴ brings orders to form a Society—a secret society like the Rosicrucian Lodge. He promises to help.

H. P. B.[43]

From the last sentence, the note must have been written shortly before September 1875, when the formation of the TS was first announced. There was a relatively brief period when its teachings were secret, because of distortion and ridicule that ensued when the newspapers and detractors of the movement heard of them.[44]

Who is the John King just mentioned? As HPB was ordered not to reveal at first that the phenomena occurring in her presence were performed by herself, she had to attribute them to someone, and John King, a familiar name in spiritualistic circles, was chosen. This satisfied Olcott, who was still a staunch spiritualist. He comments: "Must not babes be fed with milk? . . . Was not I at first made to believe that I was dealing with disincarnate spirits; and was not a stalking-horse put forward to rap and write, and materialize forms for me under the pseudonym of John King?" The name was also used by HPB at this time as a blind for her teachers and their agents. "Little by little," Olcott adds, "HPB let me know of the existence of Eastern adepts and their powers, and gave me by a multitude of phenomena the proofs of her own control over the forces of nature [hitherto] ascribed to John King."[45]

Simultaneously she began to teach him esoteric philosophy and metaphysics. To him she wrote: "I have been entrusted with an arduous and dangerous task, Henry, to 'try' and teach you, having to rely solely on my poor, lame English. They *must* have tremendous hopes in your *intuitional* gifts, for 'pon my word I put very little hope myself in my powers of elocution and *clear,* definite explanations. Do *you* understand, friend? Well, I proceed as I can. . . ."[46]

Olcott was not the only recipient of these private teachings. In *The Secret Doctrine* (1:xviii–xix), Blavatsky relates that "a considerable part of the philosophy" later expounded when she went to India was "taught in America, even before *Isis Unveiled* was published, to two Europeans and to my colleague, Colonel H. S. Olcott. . . ." One of these individuals was William Q. Judge; the other may have been a barrister, C. C. Massey, who had come over from London for a while.

After the Holmeses' séances in Philadelphia, HPB remained there for many months. During this period she married Michael Betanelly, a Georgian from the Caucasus; her first husband, from all reports, was dead.[†] Olcott tells the story:

One of my Chittenden letters in the *Daily Graphic* aroused the interest of this Mr. B.—a Russian subject—and led him to write me from Philadelphia[47] expressing his strong desire to meet my colleague and talk over spiritualism. No objections being made by her, he came over to New York toward the end of 1875 [actually 1874] and they met. It turned out that he fell at once into a state of profound admiration, which he expressed verbally, and later, by letter, to her and to me. She persistently rebuffed him when she saw that he was matrimonially inclined, and grew very angry at his persistence. The only effect was to deepen his devotion, and he finally threatened to take his life unless she would accept his hand. . . . He

† Twelve years later it was discovered that Blavatsky had retired to his brother's estate and was very much alive!

declared he would ask nothing but the privilege of watching over her, that his feeling was one of unselfish adoration for her intellectual grandeur, and that he would make no claims to any of the privileges of wedded life. He so besieged her that—in what seemed to me a freak of madness—she finally consented to take him at his word and be nominally his wife; but with the stipulation that she would retain her own name, and be as free and independent of all disciplinary restraints as she then was. . . . The inevitable result was that this ill-starred couple dwelt together but a few months. The husband forgot his vows of unselfishness . . . she left him and would not go back.

Betanelly sued for divorce on the grounds of desertion and this was granted. Several years later, his business having failed, he returned to Georgia.[48]

"Her time during the period" of her marriage, says Olcott, "was fully engrossed with writing for the public press, upon western spiritualism at first, and later upon [the occultism] of the East."[49] Much of this activity was carried on when HPB was seriously ill from a leg injury received early in the year when she fell on the pavement. Deeply concerned, Betanelly wrote to General Lippitt: "Dr. Pancoast, who was attending and curing her, gave her up, saying that he hardly could do anything, as paralysis is approaching or even worse, amputation of the leg might be found necessary. I do not know what to do. And imagine at this very time when she is so ill she keeps on writing, working and corresponding all the time, when by Dr.'s advice she must keep quiet and not worry her brain. I believe her illness partially is caused by her own carelessness for herself and overworking. Although she helps others, she cannot or will not help herself, even to cure her leg."[50]

It was a time of deep depression and inner trial for HPB, when, as one of her teachers indicated, her future seemed to hang in the balance.[51]

Chapter 5

New Developments

I n July of 1875, an article by HPB was published that she labeled in her scrapbook "My First *Occult* Shot."[52] It was published under the title "A Few Questions to Hiraf" and would never have been written had she not acquired farm property on Long Island the previous summer. The co-owner of the property, Clementine Gerebko, breached the contract and Blavatsky sued to recover her losses. The firm of Bergen, Jacobs and Ivins handled the case. William Ivins was HPB's attorney at the trial, which took place before a jury on April 26, 1875. As a young lawyer at the time, he later became prominent in his professional and civic affairs. During this period he recorded some of the circumstances of the trial:

> Long Island in those days was a long way from New York City, for traveling facilities were limited. The calendar of this particular term was very slow, and all the parties were kept there waiting their turn to be heard. As many of the documents and witnesses were French, and there was no interpreter to the court, William S. Fales, a student in the law firm of General Benjamin Tracy, was made special interpreter, and he reported HPB's testimony which was given in French. For two weeks the Judge, the lawyers, clerks, clients and interpreter were guests in a dull country hotel. . . .[53]

Ivins reports that while waiting for her case to be tried, HPB was translating into Russian H. T. Buckles's *History of Civilization in England* and Darwin's *Origin of Species*.[54] Other things happened too, adds de Zirkoff, in her *Collected Writings:* "Ivins, in addition to being a brilliant lawyer, was a bookworm with a phenomenal memory. More as a joke than in earnest, he deluged his client with [questions on] occultism, gnosticism, Kabbalism, and white and black magic. Fales, taking his key from Ivins, gave long dissertations on mystical arithmetic, astrology, alchemy, medieval symbolism, neo-platonism, rosicrucianism, and quaternions."[55]

As to the trial, some details are given by Charles R. Flint, a longtime friend of Ivins and Fales, in his book *Memories of an Active Life:*

. . . Madame, who was her own principal witness, testified quite contrary to the way in which her attorneys assumed she would testify. . . . As cautious lawyers, they had gone over the testimony with Madame before the trial, and had advised her as to what points she should emphasize; but to their great discomfiture, on the witness stand she took the bit in her teeth and galloped along lines of evidence quite opposed to their instructions, giving as a reason, when they complained of her testimony that her "familiar," whom she called Tom [John] King, stood at her side (invisible to everyone but her), and prompted her in her testimony. After the court had taken the matter under advisement, Madame left the city, but wrote several letters to Ivins asking him as to the progress of the suit, and finally astonished him by a letter giving an outline of an opinion which she said the court would render in the course of a few days, in connection with a decision in her favor. In accordance with her prediction, the court handed down a decision sustaining her claim upon grounds similar to those which she had outlined in her letter.[56]

Now Ivins and Fales belonged to a prestigious debating society in Brooklyn and one evening met with three other members, Frederick Hinrichs, James Robinson, and Charles Adams. Years later, Hinrichs, by then a noted political reformer, wrote the following concerning this meeting:

[They] jocularly suggested to one another the writing of a mystic article on Theosophy, esoteric science and what not. I had been reading *Zanoni,* a book on Rosicrucianism; and the life of Paracelsus—so that I wrote, especially, along those lines. The Madame [HPB] claimed to be a Rosicrucian, [so Fales] dubbed the article, which he compounded out of our three or four separate unrelated contributions—"Rosicrucianism." Fales also created the acrostic "Hiraf" out of our initials, [and gave that name as the author]. We all laughed heartily over the compounded article and sent it to the Madame in Boston. She published it in two numbers of her periodical, as I recall it, and wrote two very flattering editorials on "Hiraf." I have been told by Theosophists here that we young men had written better than we knew, and that we were probably inspired by higher powers. Of this, I know nothing, *although this may be so.* Certain it is that "Hiraf" has been quite extensively quoted as authority in various printed publications. . . .[57]

The periodical to which Hinrichs refers is *The Spiritual Scientist,* published in Boston by its editor, E. Gerry Brown. Attracted by his courageous criticism of evils in spiritualism, Blavatsky and Olcott contributed articles and financial support.[58]

The "Hiraf" essay was published in the July 1 and 8 issues of *The Spiritual Scientist,* and HPB's reply followed in the next two issues. It was her first public disclosure of the existence of brotherhoods of adepts. "I am telling," she says, "a little of the little I picked up in my long travels throughout the length and breadth of the East—that cradle of occultism." A few extracts follow:

> Among the numerous sciences pursued by the well-disciplined army of earnest students of the present century, none has had . . . more scoffing than the oldest of them—the science of sciences, the venerable mother-parent of all our modern pygmies [occultism]. As a rule, occultism is a dangerous, double-edged weapon for one to handle who is unprepared to devote his whole life to it. The theory of it, unaided by serious practice, will ever remain in the eyes of those prejudiced against such an unpopular cause, an idle, crazy speculation, fit only to charm the ears of ignorant old women. When we cast a look behind us and see how for the last thirty years, modern spiritualism has been dealt with . . . how can we hope that Occultism . . . which stands in relation to Spiritualism as the infinite to the finite . . . will easily gain ground where Spiritualism is scoffed at? . . .
>
> Hiraf doubts whether there are in existence, in England or elsewhere, what we term regular colleges for the neophytes of this Secret Science. I will say from personal knowledge that such places there are in the East—in India, Asia Minor, and other countries. . . .
>
> The real, the complete [Oriental] Kabbalah of the first ages of humanity is in possession . . . of but a few Oriental philosophers; where they are, who they are, is more than is given me to reveal. . . . The only thing I can say is that such a body exists, and that the location of their Brotherhoods will never be revealed to other countries until the day when humanity shall awake in a mass from its spiritual lethargy and open its blind eyes to the dazzling light of Truth.[59]

Olcott commented that at a time when the Western world was enamored by the phenomenal rise of modern science, it astounded people to hear that ancient science existed and that there were human beings living in the world who knew its secrets.

Other HPB articles on Eastern occultism followed. One writer observes:

The Spiritualists of 1875 knew nothing of these matters; one need only turn the pages of the journals devoted to spiritualistic phenomena and religion to discover the striking contrast between the philosophic vigor of the writings of Madame Blavatsky and the psychic fancies of conventional spiritualism. . . . twenty-seven years of séances had brought no genuine progress, but only a vast accumulation of trivial psychic messages, of no particular importance save for the miraculous manner of their communication.[60]

Of the five Hiraf men, three—Ivins, Hinrichs, and Robinson (until his early death)—continued contact with Blavatsky. In 1912, conversing with a mutual friend, Ivins spoke of her as a "wonderful woman [who] had, all in all, the most brilliant attainments of any woman he had ever met. He deplored her decision to devote her life to building up a society, and thought that had she given her time exclusively to pen work, she would have won renown and lived a much more tranquil life. He conceded that she possessed psychic gifts of great power, but thought she should have used her talents in the service of general literature and not gone off to India to teach religion. . . . He had seen her perform too many phenomena to question her supreme gift in that line. His only criticism was of her good judgment in undertaking the thankless task of convincing people of other planes of existence."[61]

Had HPB followed his advice she certainly would have lived a more tranquil life and earned fewer enemies, especially among the spiritualists; for when she began writing openly of the dangers of mediumship, the spiritualist papers conducted an appallingly vindictive smear campaign regarding her personal character for years thereafter. When she died in 1891, the *Religio-Philosophical Journal* wrote that "as a moral monstrosity she stands without peer among the sex in this country. The spurious fakes which she originated to gratify her love of deception and ambition, and to cover up her real sins, has ended with her death."[62]

In the spring of 1875, Blavatsky penned in her scrapbook:

Ordered to begin telling the public the *truth* about the phenomena & their mediums. And *now* my martyrdom will begin! I will have all the Spiritualists against me in addition to the Christians & the Skeptics! Thy Will, oh M ∴ be done!

HPB wrote to Professor Corson's wife, Caroline, in March 1876, about the slanders emanating from "my worst enemies, the spiritualists and the mediums . . . [who] will not stop at any baseness, any infamy. . . . Indeed happy am I, if, in losing my reputation, I save millions who are lost now in the illusion that all the spirits who communicate with them are angels of purity, *disembodied spirits.* . . . Truth comes slowly into the light, very slowly; but it is impossible to hide the light under a bushel."[63]

Chapter 6

Another Colleague Arrives

Not long after Henry Steel Olcott and HPB had re- turned to New York in the summer of 1875 (July or August), another future co-founder of the Theosophical Society ar- rived on the scene. He was twenty-four-year-old Irish-born William Q. Judge. Judge had been reading Olcott's *People from the Other World* (a series of articles about the Eddy's, published in the *Daily Graphic*) and, after writing to its author, was invited to call upon HPB at her home at 46 Irving Place.† He was later chiefly responsible for the widespread growth of the Theosophical Society in America.

Judge was in intimate contact with the Dublin theosophists and was regarded as their special hero. Actively associated with the Dublin TS were William Butler Yeats and George Russell (Æ), the principal leaders of the influential Irish Literary Revival.[64] In *Ulysses,* James Joyce speaks of the group's regard for "Judge, the noblest Roman of them all."[65] Long after his death, Russell wrote: "Judge was the most impressive man I ever met, not by any air of dignity but simply from what he was."[66]

As to Judge's youth, not very much is known. He was born in Dublin, on April 13, 1851. His mother, Alice Mary Quan, died in early life

---

† Conflicting dates of the year in which W. Q. Judge first met HPB have been published, as she resided on Irving Place very briefly in November 1874 as well as summer through fall of 1875. The 1875 date, however, is clearly implied by Judge's and others' statements. See *The Path,* June 1891, 66; *Lucifer,* June 15, 1891, 290; A. P. Sinnett, *Incidents in the Life of Madame Blavatsky,* 186–87; *The Theosophist,* November 1892, 72; *The Irish Theosophist,* March 15, 1896, 112–13; *Theosophy,* June 1896, 76; Michael Gomes, *The Dawning of the Theosophical Movement,* 84, Eek and de Zirkoff, *William Quan Judge: Theosophical Pioneer,* 6.

From a handwritten letter of William Q. Judge to Mrs. Cape [we think it was written in October 1893]: "In 1874, thought of looking up spiritualism and finding Col. Olcott's book 'People from the Other World', I wrote him asking for the address of a medium. He replied that he did not then know, but had a friend Mme. Blavatsky who asked him to ask me to call. I called at 46 Irving Place New York and made her acquaintance. Very soon after at a gathering of people there H. P. Blavatsky asked me to ask Col. Olcott then at the other side of the room to found a Society. I asked him and then I called the gathering to order assumed the chairmanship and nominated Olcott as permanent chairman, as [sic] which he was elected. He then took the chair and nominated me as Secretary and was elected. This was the beginning of the Theosophical Society."—William Q. Judge at the birth of her seventh child. His father, Frederick Judge, was a Mason and was interested in mysticism. William became mortally ill when he was seven. It is reported in a sketch of Judge's life that "the physician declared the small sufferer to be dying, then dead; but, in the outburst of grief which followed the announcement, it was discovered that the child had revived. . . ."[67]

> During convalescence, the boy showed aptitudes and knowledge never before displayed, exciting wonderment and questioning among his elders as to when and how he had learned all these new things. He seemed the same, and yet not the same; he had to be studied anew by his family, and while no one knew that he had ever learned to read, from his recovery in his eighth year, we find him devouring the contents of all the books he could obtain, relating to Mesmerism, Phrenology, Character Reading, Religion, Magic, Rosicrucianism, and deeply absorbed in the Book of Revelation [in the Bible] trying to discover its real meaning. . . .
>
> Without being sickly, he was frail, but indomitable and persevering beyond his years. An anecdote of his boyhood illustrates these traits. He was with other boys upon the bank of a stream. His companions swam to an island a little way off from the bank, from which vantage-ground they jeered and mocked their younger comrade, who could not swim. . . . He plunged into the water, resolved to get to that island or perish. When out of his depth he let himself sink, touched bottom, ran a few steps on the river's bed, rose, of course, kicked, sank, took a step and another, repeated the process, and thus struggling, rising, sinking, scrambling, and, above all, holding his breath, he actually reached the margin of the island to be drawn out, half unconscious, by his astonished playfellows.[68]

This expression of fearless, indomitable persistence, manifested later, when Judge underwent great trials and difficulties to carry out the work in the United States with no one else to help.

When William was thirteen, the Judge family emigrated to the United States and settled in Brooklyn, New York. William managed to finish his schooling before going to work. He eventually became a clerk in the law office of George P. Andrews, who later became Judge of the Supreme Court of New York. In April 1872, he became naturalized, and he was admitted to the State Bar of New York one month later.

At the time HPB died, Judge wrote of his first meeting with her:

It was her eye that attracted me, the eye of one whom I must have known in lives long passed away. She looked at me in recognition at that first hour, and never since has that look changed. Not as a questioner of philosophies did I come before her, not as one groping in the dark for lights that schools and fanciful theories had obscured, but as one who wandering many periods through the corridors of life, was seeking the friends who could show where the designs for the work had been hidden. And true to the call she responded, revealing the plans once again, and speaking no words to explain, simply pointed them out and went on with the task. It was as if but the evening before we had parted, leaving yet to be done some detail of a task taken up with one common end; it was teacher and pupil, elder brother and younger, both bent on one single end,† but she with the power and the knowledge that belong but to lions and sages. So, friends from the first I felt safe. Others I know have looked with suspicion on an appearance they could not fathom, and though it is true they adduce many proofs which, hugged to the breast, would damn sages and gods, yet it is only through blindness they failed to see the lion's glance, the diamond heart of HPB.[69]

According to a close friend, Judge often said "he never had a really conscious existence until 'Isis' was unveiled to him."[70] HPB was known by that name among her intimate acquaintances in New York.

---

† HPB once said of Judge that he was "part of herself for several aeons." *Letters That Have Helped Me,* 277. Letter from HPB in London to Judge on October 23, 1889; reprinted in *The Theosophical Forum,* June 1932, 192–93, original in the TS Archives, Pasadena, California.

Chapter 7

Birth of a Movement

In paging through HPB's scrapbook, the following entry is found in her handwriting under date of July 1875:

> Orders received from India direct to establish a philosophico-religious Society & choose a name for it—also to choose Olcott.[71]

On September 7, 1875, sixteen or seventeen persons joined HPB in her rooms at 46 Irving Place to hear a lecture by George H. Felt, an engineer and architect, on "The Lost Canon of Proportion of the Egyptians, Greeks and Romans."[72] The talk was enthusiastically received, and Olcott wrote on a slip of paper: "Would it not be a good thing to form a society for this kind of study?" He handed it to William Q. Judge to pass to HPB, who nodded assent. Judge moved that Olcott be elected chairman, and he, in turn, moved that Judge be appointed secretary. The meeting was then adjourned until the following evening.

A report of the first meeting appeared in a New York newspaper and was reprinted in Emma Hardinge Britten's *Nineteenth Century Miracles,* from which this is taken:

> One movement of great importance has just been inaugurated in New York, under the lead of Colonel Henry S. Olcott, in the organization of a society, to be known as the Theosophical Society.†
> The suggestion was entirely unpremeditated, and was made on the evening of the 7th inst. in the parlors of Madame Blavatsky, where a company of seventeen ladies and gentlemen had assembled to meet Mr. George Henry Felt, whose discovery of the Geometrical figures of the Egyptian Kabbalah may be regarded as among the most surprising feats of the human intellect. The company included several persons of great learning and some of wide personal influence. The Managing Editors of two religious papers; the co-editors of two literary magazines; an Oxford LL.D.; a venerable Jewish scholar and

† The name was not decided upon until the following meeting of September thirteenth.

traveler of repute; an editorial writer of one of the New York morn-
ing dailies; the president of the New York Society of Spiritualists;
Mr. C. C. Massey, an English visitor [barrister-at-law]; Mrs. Emma
Hardinge Britten and Dr. Britten; two New York lawyers besides
Colonel Olcott; a partner in a Philadelphia publishing house; a well-
known physician [Dr. Seth Pancoast] and, most notable of all,
Madame Blavatsky herself, comprised Mr. Felt's audience. . . .[73]

8. Original minute book of the Theosophical Society's
first meeting in New York City, September 8, 1875.
(Archives of the Theosophical Society, Pasadena, California)

Among those present, but not named in the foregoing report, were
William Livingston Alden, an editorial writer for the *New York Times;*
John Storer Cobb, editor of the *New Era,* organ of reformed Jews; and
Charles Sotheran, scholarly editor of the *American Bibliopolist* and a
high-ranking mason.

At subsequent meetings bylaws were decided upon and officers elected. Olcott was chosen president, and Dr. Pancoast and George Felt vice presidents. HPB agreed to serve as corresponding secretary, Sotheran as librarian, and Judge as counsel. The selection of a name for the society was difficult. Turning the pages of a dictionary, Sotheran came across *Theosophy,* which was unanimously adopted.

The word has a venerable history going back to the Neoplatonists and was later used by Christian mystics.[74] Derived from the Greek words *theos,* "god," and *sophia,* "wisdom," it means godlike wisdom, or, according to HPB, "Divine *Wisdom* such as that possessed by the gods."[75]

To attempt to define the term more specifically is an unrewarding task, as Professor Ralph Hannon admits in an article on the subject:

> To ask the question "What is Theosophy?" has been part of the history of the Theosophical Society since the beginning. In the very first issue of *The Theosophist,* Madame Blavatsky wrote a long article responding to this question. Numerous attempts have followed. On many occasions I have been asked this same question by members as well as nonmembers. I'm afraid my various answers have always left a degree of self-doubt. Only recently have I come to realize that I had been trying too hard. The answer, as with all things, is really a hierarchy; a multilevel system that is limited only by our ability to comprehend. In other words, "What is Theosophy?" is a koan. We are told in Zen that "a koan is a formulation . . . pointing to ultimate truth. Koans cannot be solved by recourse to logical reasoning but only by awakening a deeper level of the mind beyond the discursive intellect."[76]

Professor Hannon heads his article with a selection from Mr. Judge's writings:

> The strength of theosophy lies in the fact that it is not to be defined. This means that evolution, slowly progressing, will bring out new truths and new aspects of old truths, thus absolutely preventing any dogmas or "unequivocal definitions."[77]

As a practical, ethical philosophy, however, Theosophy *can* be defined, as Blavatsky indicates in a letter to the 1888 yearly Convention of American Theosophists:

> *Many who have never heard of the Society are Theosophists without knowing it themselves; for the essence of Theosophy is the perfect harmoniz-*

ing of the divine with the human in man, the adjustment of his god-like qualities and aspirations, and their sway over the terrestrial or animal passions in him. Kindness, absence of every ill feeling or selfishness, charity, goodwill to all beings, and perfect justice to others as to oneself, are its chief features. He who teaches Theosophy preaches the gospel of goodwill, and the converse of this is true also—he who preaches the gospel of goodwill teaches Theosophy.[78]

Elsewhere she observes that "there is one notable difference between the Christian Churches and our Society, and it is this: Whereas every baptized child or adult is called a *Christian,* we have always drawn a clear and broad line between a *Theosophist* and a simple member of the TS. A Theosophist, with us, is *one who makes Theosophy a living power in his life.*"[79] On another occasion, quoting the saying "handsome is who handsome does," she paraphrased it to read: "Theosophist is who Theosophy does."[80]

One may wonder what good works of a practical nature the Theosophical Society itself performed in carrying out the objects. In the same 1888 letter HPB answers:

Theosophists are of necessity the friends of all movements in the world, whether intellectual or simply practical, for the amelioration of the condition of mankind. We are the friends of all those who fight against drunkenness, against cruelty to animals, against injustice to women, against corruption in society or in government, although we do not meddle in politics. We are the friends of those who exercise practical charity, who seek to lift a little of the tremendous weight of misery that is crushing down the poor. But, in our quality of Theosophists, we cannot engage in any one of these great works in particular. As individuals we may do so, but as Theosophists we have a larger, more important, and much more difficult work to do. . . .

*   The function of Theosophists is to open men's hearts and understandings to charity, justice, and generosity, attributes which belong specifically to the human kingdom and are natural to man when he has developed the qualities of a human being. Theosophy teaches the animal-man to be a human-man; and when people have learned to think and feel as truly human beings should feel and think, they will act humanely, and works of charity, justice, and generosity will be done spontaneously by all.*[81]

The Theosophical Movement has three objects as already stated in our Preface. They are as follows:

1. To form the nucleus of a universal brotherhood of humanity, without distinction of race, creed, sex, caste, or color.

2. The study of ancient and modern religions, philosophies and sciences, and the demonstration of the importance of such study; and

3. The investigation of the unexplained laws of nature and the psychical powers latent in man.

Sympathy with the first object was all that was required to join the TS. One need not believe in karma, reincarnation, or the existence of Masters or any other teaching. That the Society had no creed was affirmed in the 1880s by an American court of law, when a decree of incorporation was granted the St. Louis Theosophical Society. Judge August W. Alexander ruled: "The petitioner is not a religious body . . . merely teaching religions is not a religious work in the statutory sense. It will be noted that in Art. 2 of this Society's constitution the word religion is used in the plural. To teach religions is educational, not religious. 'To promote the study of religions' is in part to promote the study of the history of man. I add the subordinate finding that the Society has no religious creed and practices no worship."[82]

The official birth date of the TS is generally regarded as November 17, 1875, when its president delivered his inaugural address, seventy days after the Society was first proposed. The opening words proved prophetic: "In future times, when the impartial historian shall write an account of the progress of religious ideas in the present century, the formation of this Theosophical Society, whose first meeting under its formal principles we are now attending, will not pass unnoticed."

When HPB included in her scrapbook the newly issued *Preamble and By-Laws of The Theosophical Society,* she exultingly wrote:

The Child is Born! Hozannah![83]

Fifteen years later, when HPB was living in London, she was invited by the publisher of a leading U.S. publication, *The North American Review,* to contribute a paper on "recent progress of theosophy." Under that title her article appeared in the August 1890 issue and described the phenomenal achievements thus far effected in various fields of human thought. Here we are concerned only with the contributing causes for such success. She remarked:

The theosophical movement was a necessity of the age and it has spread under its own inherent impulsion, and owes nothing to adventitious methods. From the first it has had neither money, endowment, nor social or governmental patronage to count upon. It appealed to certain human instincts and aspirations, and held a certain lofty ideal of perfectability, with which the vested extraneous interests of society conflicted, and against which these were fore-doomed to battle. . . .

Accepting thankfully the results of scientific study and exposure of theological error, and adopting the methods and maxims of science, its advocates try to save from the wreck of cults the precious admixture of truth to be found in each. Discarding the theory of miracle and supernaturalism, they endeavor to trace out the kinship of the whole family of world-faiths to each other, and their common reconciliation with science. . . .

For many a long year the "great orphan," Humanity, has been crying aloud in the darkness for guidance and for light. Amid the increasing splendors of a progress purely material, of a science that nourished the intellect, but left the spirit to starve, Humanity, dimly feeling its origin and presaging its destiny, has stretched out towards the East empty hands that only a *spiritual* philosophy can fill. Aching from the divisions, the jealousies, the hatreds, that rend its very life, it has cried for some sure foundation on which to build the solidarity it senses, some metaphysical basis from which its loftiest social ideals may rise secure. . . . Such is the goal which theosophy has set itself to attain.

Chapter 8

A Psychophysiological Change

L ate in the spring of 1875 and before the Theosophical
Society was founded, HPB underwent what Olcott
called "a wonderful psycho-physiological change . . . that I am not at
liberty to speak about."[84] Unknown to him, however, she spoke of it
on several occasions to her relatives when in 1876, after a near three-
year lapse, her correspondence with them was resumed. She had failed
to inform them of her many changes in address and their inquiries
proved of no avail.[85]

Bringing Vera up to date, HPB informed her of the serious leg
injury she suffered in early 1875, which her Hindu teacher completely
cured on the eve of amputation, continuing:

*And just about this time I [began] to feel a very strange duality. Several times
a day I feel that beside me there is someone else, quite separable from me,
present in my body. I never lose the consciousness of my personality; what I
feel is as if I were keeping silent and the other one—the lodger who is in me—
were speaking with my tongue.*

*For instance, I know that I have never been in the places which are
described by my 'other me,' but this other one—the second me—does not lie
when he tells about places and things unknown to me, because he has actually
seen them and known them well. I have given it up; let my fate conduct me at
its own sweet will; and besides, what am I to do? It would be perfectly
ridiculous if I were to deny the possession of knowledge avowed by my No. 2,
giving occasion to the people around me to imagine that I kept them in the
dark for modesty's sake.*

*In the night, when I am alone in my bed, the whole life of my No. 2 passes
before my eyes, and I do not see myself at all, but quite a different person—
different in race and different in feelings. But what's the use of talking about
it? It is enough to drive one mad. I try to throw myself into the part, and to
forget the strangeness of my situation. This is no mediumship, and by no
means an impure power; for that, it has too strong an ascendancy over us all,
leading us into better ways.*[86]

Later she informed her family concerning No. 2, or her teacher:

I see this Hindu every day, just as I might see any other living person, with the only difference that he looks to me more ethereal and more transparent. Formerly I kept silent about these appearances, thinking that they were hallucinations. But now they have become visible to other people as well. He (the Hindu) appears and advises us as to our conduct and our writing. He evidently knows everything that is going on, even to the thoughts of other people, and makes me express his knowledge. Sometimes it seems to me that he overshadows the whole of me, simply entering me like a kind of volatile essence penetrating my pores and dissolving in me.† Then we two are able to speak to other people, and then I begin to understand and remember sciences and languages—everything he instructs me in, even when he is not with me any more.[87]

Apparently, the source of inspiration is not solely to be attributed to her teachers, for HPB told Vera that at times "it is not I who talk and write; it is something within me, my higher and luminous Self, that thinks and writes for me."[88]

The degree to which HPB's family were at first alarmed by these and other letters from her was revealed by Vera after her sister's death in an article in a periodical, *The Russian Herald*, "H. P. Blavatsky—A Biographical Sketch":

She surprised us with tales of "The Society of Universal Brotherhood," planned by her, of her studies of ancient philosophy of the peoples of the East—about which she had begun to write a large treatise (*Isis Unveiled*). I remember, as if it happened now, to what degree this news flabbergasted us. I positively did not know what to think, how to explain such fantasies. . . . Her relatives at first did not believe in them at all and for a long time afterwards regarded her writings skeptically, seeking explanation for them—to speak honestly—in forgery and fraud! . . . I always knew my sister to be an intelligent, capable woman, but to suddenly write about this science, unknown till then, I feared she had lost her mind . . . I was relieved a bit only by the fact that Helena Petrovna occasionally sent me her articles in the American papers together with reviews of them, which assured me that there was no need for her immediate removal to a lunatic asylum.

† This ensouling, at times, of a human body by a sage is known in India as *Āveśa*, and in Tibet as *Tulku*. (Olcott, *Old Diary Leaves* 1:269–70; Barborka, *H. P. Blavatsky, Tibet and Tulku*; Blavatsky, *Isis Unveiled*, ed. de Zirkoff, Introductory [11–12].)

As to HPB's teacher Vera wrote:

She who had never submitted to anyone, who from early childhood favored only her own will in everything—she, suddenly, found a man, a lord and sovereign to whose will she yielded silently! And, at that, what sort of a man! Some kind of sorcerer, a half-mystical Hindu from the shores of the Ganges! I understood nothing! . . . I must admit that my lack of understanding continues even to the present day. In spite of my visits with her, almost every year during the past five years—visits which lasted for months under her roof—I have understood very little from all her zealous explanations. And today, as fifteen years ago, I marvel far more at the inexplicable phenomena of her profound learning which had descended upon her as if from heaven, than at all the wonders ascribed to her by the theosophists.[89]

Olcott, too, was puzzled by HPB's newly acquired learning when writing *Isis* and, without informing her, he wrote a long letter in French to Nadya inquiring about her niece's educational background.[90] Here is her reply, dated May 8, 1877:

[HPB] received the education of a girl of good family. She was well brought up, but was not at all learned, and as for scholarship, of that there was no question. But the unusual richness of her intellectual nature, the delicacy and swiftness of her thought, her marvelous facility in understanding, grasping and assimilating the most difficult subjects, such as would require from anybody else years of laborious study; an eminently developed intelligence, united with a character loyal, straightforward, frank, energetic—these gave her such an unusual superiority, raised her so high above the ordinary level of the insipid majority of human societies, that she could never avoid attracting general attention, and the consequent envy and animosity of all those who, in their trivial inferiority, felt wounded by the splendor of the faculties and talents of this really marvelous woman.

You ask what languages she has studied. From childhood, in addition to Russian, her native tongue, she knew only French and English. Long afterwards, during her travels in Europe, she picked up a little Italian. The last time that I saw her, four years [ago], that was all she knew in the way of languages; of that I am positively certain, I can assure you. As to the unfathomable depths of her erudition four years after, as I say, there was no shadow of it, not even the least promise thereof.[91]

If, in fact, HPB studied all these subjects on her own, does it not seem astounding she accords credit for all her learning to mythical mahatmas, taking none of the laurels to herself? Two years before her death she expressed regret for being the first to introduce to the West the existence of such advanced souls on the earth. In *The Key to Theosophy* she wrote:

> Every bogus swindling society, for commercial purposes, now claims to be guided and directed by "Masters." . . . Thousands of men have been held back from the path of truth and light through the discredit and evil report which such shams, swindles, and frauds have brought upon the whole subject. [The author] would rather people should seriously think that the only Mahatmaland is the grey matter of her brain, and that, in short, she has evolved them out of the depths of her own inner consciousness, than that their names and grand ideal should be so infamously desecrated as they are at present. . . . It is only her unwillingness to pose in her own sight as a crow parading in peacock's feathers that compels her to this day to insist upon the truth [as to the source of her knowledge].[92]

Chapter 9

Writing of Isis Unveiled

"**N**othing could have been more commonplace and [less] ostentatious than the beginning of *Isis*," recalls Colonel Olcott. "One day in the summer of 1875, HPB showed me some sheets of manuscript she had written and said: 'I wrote this last night "by order," but what the deuce it is to be I don't know. Perhaps it is for a newspaper article, perhaps for a book, perhaps for nothing; anyhow, I did as I was ordered.' And she put it away in a drawer, and nothing more was said about it for some time."[93]

That she had in mind doing some serious writing seems evident from a letter written earlier in 1875 to Professor Corson: "The indications are, that we are about at the threshold of an epoch when, a thousand mysteries shall be revealed, and it depends, at least in some degree, upon such very feeble mortal agencies as your pen and mine and those of other zealous workers, how soon the world shall be enlightened."[94]

In September of that year Blavatsky spent several weeks at Corson's home in Ithaca, and there the work on *Isis* continued. New information concerning this visit has recently been discovered by Michael Gomes in the Corson papers preserved at Cornell.[95] Hitherto, the main source of information was the volume published and annotated by Corson's son, Eugene, of HPB's letters to his father. Regarding the professor's status at Cornell, Dr. Andrew White, its president, wrote that he was "in many respects the most important professor Cornell University has ever had, enjoying a great reputation for his lectures and writings in English literature."[96]

Corson had been led to spiritualism by the sudden death of his sixteen-year-old daughter, and one reason for inviting HPB to his home was to contact this girl. He wrote his son at the time: "I had expected we should get some 'sittings' together, but she is not only not disposed but is decidedly opposed to anything of the kind." His first impression was that "she is a smart woman, but ignorant of all the graces and amenities of life. She is a Russian bear."[97]

Eugene reports that HPB "spent her time at her desk, writing, writing, writing most of the day and way into the night, carrying on a huge correspondence by long letters. Here she started *Isis Unveiled,* writing about twenty-five closely written foolscap pages a day. She had no books to consult, my father's extensive library was almost wholly on English literature . . . and she rarely consulted him about anything."[98] In an interview with writer Charles Lazenby, Professor Corson confirms this:

> She continually filled me with amazement and curiosity as to what was coming next. She had a profound knowledge of everything, and her method of work was most unusual. She would write in bed, from nine o'clock in the morning, smoking innumerable cigarettes, quoting long verbatim paragraphs from dozens of books of which I am perfectly certain there were no copies at that time in America, translating easily from several languages, and occasionally calling out to me, in my study, to know how to turn some old-world idiom into literary English, for at that time she had not attained the literary fluency of diction which distinguished *The Secret Doctrine.*[99]

The professor's granddaughter, Mrs. Pauline Corson Coad, recalled being told that her grandfather could not understand how HPB obtained her statistics, but very soon they found out that a slim brown Indian hand would reach up from underneath the table cover and jot down the notes that she needed, which, when checked, were always found to be correct.[100]

As to HPB's quotations in *Isis,* Professor Corson remarks:

> She herself told me that she wrote them down as they appeared in her eyes on another plane of objective existence, that she clearly saw the page of the book, and the quotation she needed, and simply translated what she saw into English. . . . The hundreds of books she quoted were certainly not in my library, many of them not in America, some of them very rare and difficult to get in Europe, and if her quotations were from memory, then it was an even more startling feat than writing them from the ether. The facts are marvelous, and the explanation must necessarily bewilder those whose consciousness is of a more ordinary type.[101]

Olcott reports that when continuing the work on *Isis* in New York, Blavatsky did use books wherever available, some being from his own library. As to the rest, he says she drew from the Astral Light, or from her adept teachers, or by using her soul senses. He comments: "How do I know it? By working two years with her on *Isis* and many more years on other literary work."[102]

Marion Meade contends that the Corson visit ended in a rift and HPB lost the professor's friendship. Meade's proof is adduced from Blavatsky's letter to Corson: "This is the third letter I write you and not a word in response. Are you angry?"[103] But now we have Corson's reply. In it he assured her his reply must have gone astray: "What on earth have I to be angry about? Didn't we part the best of friends? Didn't we grow better friends together? And I've felt lonely ever since you have gone and have wished you back." When years later he was asked about the most outstanding of the remarkable people he met, he named Madame Blavatsky.[104]

Once back in New York, the work on *Isis* continued at an accelerated pace, and HPB did not go out for six months at a time. She wrote Nadya that she worked seventeen hours a day and lived on oatmeal. "Better than oatmeal," the aunt replied, "eat roast beef and ham, but do not ruin yourself. . . ."[105]

Despite the enormous labors involved in producing *Isis*—it ran to over twelve hundred pages in small print—HPB apparently had no ambition to become a popular or successful author, for here is what she says in the preface:

> To show that we do not all conceal from ourselves the gravity of our undertaking, we may say in advance that it would not be strange if the following classes should array themselves against us:
>
> The Christians, who will see that we question the evidences of the genuineness of their faith.†
>
> The Scientists, who will find their pretensions placed in the same bundle with those of the Roman Catholic Church for infallibility, and, in certain particulars, the sages and philosophers of the ancient world classed higher than they.
>
> Pseudo-Scientists will, of course, denounce us furiously.
>
> Broad Churchmen and Freethinkers will find that we do not accept what they do, but demand the recognition of the whole truth.
>
> Men of letters and various *authorities,* who hide their real belief in deference to popular prejudices.

† In the preface to Volume Two, *Theology,* HPB wrote: "It contains not one word against the pure teachings of Jesus, but unsparingly denounces their debasement into pernicious ecclesiastical systems that are ruinous to man's faith in his immortality and his God, and subversive of all moral restraint." (2:iv.)

The mercenaries and parasites of the Press, who prostitute its more than royal power, and dishonor a noble profession, will find it easy to mock at things too wonderful for them to understand; for to them the price of a paragraph is more than the value of sincerity.

From many will come honest criticism; from many—cant. But we look to the future . . . we are laboring for the brighter morrow.[106]

That brighter morrow, she indicates elsewhere, was not just around the corner, nor even in the twentieth century. The twenty-first had possibilities, she thought, if certain conditions were fulfilled.[107]

Chapter 10

"A Book with a Revolution in It"

O ne afternoon in the autumn of 1876, Professor Alexander Wilder,[108] an eminent Platonic philosopher,
archaeologist, author, educator, and practicing physician, was at his
home in Newark, New Jersey, when the doorbell rang and in came an
uninvited visitor, Colonel Olcott. In Wilder's article "How Isis Was
Written," published in 1908, he relates that Olcott "had been referred
to me by Mr. J. W. Bouton," a publisher for whom Wilder had edited
some books. Olcott explained to him that "Madame Blavatsky had
compiled a work upon occult and philosophic subjects, and Mr. Bouton had been asked in relation to undertaking its publication. Why it
had been referred to me I could never understand," for no one suspected "I took any interest whatever in unusual subjects" and had "an
ardent passion for mystic speculation, and the transcendental philosophy. I think that Colonel Olcott had himself been taken somewhat by
surprise."

Wilder continues:

> Mr. Bouton had taken passage for England a few days before, and I
> had visited him several times, even going over from Newark to bid
> him farewell the morning that he left. Yet he had not said a word to
> me about the manuscript. Did he really expect me to read it, or was
> he merely endeavoring to shirk having anything to do with it with-
> out actually refusing outright? I am now inclined to the opinion that
> he referred Colonel Olcott to me to evade saying "No." At the time,
> however, I supposed that although the mode of proceeding was not
> that of a man of business, Mr. Bouton really meant that I should
> examine the work, and I agreed to undertake the task.
>
> It was truly a ponderous document and displayed research in a
> very extended field, requiring diligence [and] familiarity with the
> various topics. . . . Regarding myself as morally obligated to act for
> the advantage of Mr. Bouton, I showed no favor beyond what I

believed justice to demand. I regarded it a duty to be severe. In my report to him, I stated that the manuscript was the product of great research, and that so far as related to current thinking, there was a revolution in it, but I added that I deemed it too long for remunerative publishing. Mr. Bouton, however, presently agreed to publish the work.

As the manuscript was too long, Wilder's job was to abridge the work, but he removed "only such terms and matters as might be regarded as superfluous . . . it proved to be only a 'labor of love.'"
He continues:

Colonel Olcott was very desirous that I should become acquainted with Madame Blavatsky [and after much hesitation] I accompanied him to their establishment in Forty-seventh Street. . . . She did not resemble in manner or figure what I had been led to expect. She was tall, but not strapping; her countenance bore the marks and exhibited the characteristics of one who had seen much, thought much, traveled much, and experienced much. . . . She was a superior conversationalist and at home on every matter about which we discoursed. She spoke the English language with the fluency of one perfectly familiar with it, and who thought in it. It was the same to me as though talking with any man of my acquaintance. She was ready to take the idea as it was expressed, and uttered her own thoughts clearly, concisely and often forcibly. . . . Anything which she did not approve or hold in respect she promptly disposed of as "flapdoodle." I have never heard or encountered the term elsewhere.
   After the work had been printed and placed on sale, there was discussion in regard to actual authorship. Many were unwilling to acknowledge that Madame Blavatsky could be sufficiently well informed or intellectually capable of such a production. . . . A clergyman in New York, a member of the Russian Greek Church, I have been told, affirmed that I was the actual author . . . nobody familiar with my style of writing would ever impute to me the authorship of *Isis Unveiled.*[109]

Wilder also discountenanced the rumor circulated by the spiritualists, and perpetuated as fact in modern HPB biographies, that *Isis* was taken from the manuscripts of Baron Joseph Henry Louis de Palm left in his trunk when he died.[110] The ailing baron had been befriended by the Theosophists, and Olcott had even sheltered him in his home. The contents of the trunk were worthless stocks and deeds to underwater property, left by will to the TS, as well as some shirts the baron had stolen from Olcott, with the latter's name effaced. Upon investigation Olcott discovered he was a wanted man in several European cities.

One thing de Palm left behind proved of inestimable value to future generations of Americans: he willed to Olcott, as president of the TS, his corpse, the first body to be cremated in the United States. This created a sensation on two occasions—first, his funeral at the Masonic Temple in New York City, on May 29, 1876, and second, six months later, when his body was incinerated in the newly built crematorium of Dr. Francis Le Moyne, planned for his personal use when he died. The cremation on December sixth in the town of Washington in western Pennsylvania was featured in seven thousand journals in the United States and abroad.[111] The TS was widely condemned for introducing a sacrilegious heathen custom.

Olcott attended, and some researchers report HPB's presence, too. But on the very day of the event she wrote to Wilder: "Olcott will be home by Friday night, I think, I could *not* go, though they expect me there today. To tell you the truth, I do not see the fun of spending $40 or $50 for the pleasure of seeing a man burnt. I have seen burnings of dead and living bodies in India sufficiently."[112]

It was around this time a title was selected for *Isis*. Its significance lay in the well-known ancient inscription on a statue of Isis: "I am all that has been, all that is, all that ever shall be, and no mortal has ever lifted my veil." The title chosen was not *Isis Unveiled,* but a more modest one. "My title was *The Veil of Isis,*" wrote HPB, "and that heading runs through the entire first volume"—and still does to this day.[113] But before the second volume was stereoplated she received from Bouton the following letter, dated May 8, 1877:

> *Our mutual friend Sotheran called upon me yesterday and during our conversation suggested something, which, considering its source, is really worth considering. It appears that there has been another, and a very good book published in England under the title of the "Veil of Isis.". . . Strange as it may appear, the idea struck Sotheran and myself simultaneously that it will be better to change our title a little, and we both hit upon exactly the same one, viz.—*Isis Unveiled, *which it seems to me in many respects much better than the other title, for in itself it has a distinct meaning which the other has not.*[114]

The extravagantly worded subtitle was probably also of Bouton's invention: "A Master-Key to the Mysteries of Ancient and Modern Science and Theology." HPB disapproved of both title and subtitle:

"[W]ho ever claimed that the book was that, or anything like that? Not the author, certainly."[115] (The copyright was in Bouton's name, and Blavatsky never gained control over the plates.)

In presenting a copy to the scientist Alfred Russel Wallace, HPB wrote:

> My title is really a misnomer for I *do not* reveal the arcane *secrets* of the dread goddess—Isis. Needless to tell you who have lived in the East that the *final* mysteries and secrets are never given to the general public. . . . If I do not uncover altogether the Saitic goddess, I hope to have at least sufficiently indicated where the Veil of her shrine can be raised [for] there alone can be discovered the secret of secrets: what is man, his origin, his powers and his destiny.[116]

Wallace replied:

> > . . . *Surrey*
> > *January 1st, 1878.*
>
> *Dear Madam,*
>
> *I return you many thanks for the handsome present of your two very handsome volumes. I have as yet only had time to read a chapter here and there. I am amazed at the vast amount of erudition displayed in them and the great interest of the topics on which they treat. Moreover, your command of all the refinements of our language is such that you need not fear criticism on that score. Your book will open up to many spiritualists a whole world of new ideas, and cannot fail to be of the greatest value in the enquiry which is now being so earnestly carried on. . . .*
>
> > (signed) *Alfred R. Wallace.*[117]

Isis was published in September 1877, and the two volumes were dedicated to "The Theosophical Society, which was founded at New York, A.D. 1875, to study the subjects on which they treat." It was an instant success, about which no one was more surprised than Helena Blavatsky. The *American Bookseller* wrote: "The sale . . . is unprecedented for a work of its kind, the entire edition" of a thousand copies "having been exhausted within ten days of the date of publication. . . . The demand for it is quite remarkable, and far beyond the expectations of its publishers."[118] Several more printings followed. (*Isis* has never been out of print and currently is published by three different houses.) Here are some of the American reviews:

It must be acknowledged that she is a remarkable woman, who has read more, seen more, and thought more than most wise men. Her work abounds in quotations from a dozen different languages, not for the purpose of a vain display of erudition, but to substantiate her peculiar views. . . . Her pages are garnished with foot-notes establishing, as her authorities, some of the profoundest writers of the past. . . . [The work] demands the earnest attention of thinkers, and merits an analytic reading.   —*Boston Evening Transcript.*

An extremely readable and exhaustive essay upon the paramount importance of reestablishing the Hermetic Philosophy in a world which blindly believes that it has outgrown it. —*N. Y. World.*

A marvelous book both in matter and manner of treatment. Some idea may be formed of the rarity and extent of its contents when the index alone comprises 50 pages, and we venture nothing in saying that such an index of subjects was never before compiled by any human being. . . . [It] will certainly prove attractive to all who are interested in the history, theology, and the mysteries of the ancient world.   —*Daily Graphic.*

One who reads the book carefully through, ought to know everything of the marvelous and mystical, except perhaps, the passwords. . . . It is easy to forecast the reception of this book. With its striking peculiarities, its audacity, its versatility, and the prodigious variety of its subjects which it notices and handles, it is one of the remarkable productions of the century.   —*New York Herald.*

The editor of the *New York Times* wrote Bouton they were sorry they could not review *Isis* as they "have a holy horror of Mme. Blavatsky and her letters."[119] Yet in London, *Public Opinion,* whose severe criticisms were feared everywhere by writers and artists, called it "one of the most extraordinary works of the nineteenth century."[120] The renowned British publisher and bookseller Bernard Quaritch wrote to Bouton (December 27, 1877) that "the book will evidently make its way in England and become a classic. I am very glad to be the English agent."[121] One would hardly suspect that Britain's celebrated philosopher Herbert Spencer would read *Isis.* Here is HPB's entry in Olcott's diary, penned by her in his absence:

October 19, [1878]. A Miss Potter, tall, young, intellectual daughter of a millionaire came with a card of introduction from E. K. [Emily Kislingbury], London. Insisted on seeing me. Lived half her life in

Herbert Spencer's family. Knows Huxley and Tyndall. Interested in Theosophy; doubts Spiritualism. She and her *eight* sisters all materialists. Herbert Spencer read *Isis* and found some beautiful and *new original ideas.*[122]

Dr. John A. Weisse, the learned author of *Origin, Progress, and Destiny of the English Language and Literature,* states therein that *Isis* is "a thesaurus of new phrases and facts, so sprightfully related that even the uninitiated may read them with interest." In his analytical table, he compared the language used by a number of distinguished authors and found HPB's English, as Olcott comments, "practically identical with that of Dr. Samuel Johnson, which one might say is as nearly classically perfect as one could ask."[123]

"Many honors were showered upon HPB as a result of the publication of *Isis Unveiled,*" reports W. Q. Judge. One was the gift of a very ancient copy of the *Bhagavad-Gita,* in a mother-of-pearl and gold binding, from an Indian prince.[124]

Another recognition created a sensation among American Masons when they learned that the famous Madame Blavatsky had received a diploma from brother Masons in England conferring membership in a Masonic order. Some doubted the award had been given. HPB answered the skeptics in a Masonic journal, taking the occasion to contrast eastern Masonry with its Western counterpart. Recent researches have uncovered additional facts concerning the award. Gomes writes:

> Sotheran had written enthusiastically of her to his fellow Masons in England, including John Yarker, Grand Master of the Ancient and Primitive Rite of Freemasons. In recognition of the erudition displayed in *Isis,* Yarker sent Blavatsky the certificate of the highest rank of Adoptive Masonry, that of a Crowned Princess. . . . Sotheran solemnly informed the readers of the *Banner of Light* [February 2, 1878], "No higher mark of Masonic honor could be conferred upon a woman, and its bestowal should be remembered by the craft as a historical event of importance." When her fitness to receive these degrees was questioned, Yarker himself stated, "I gave to Madame Blavatsky *no degrees beyond what she was entitled to receive* by all international rules and regulations of what is called *high-grade* Masonry. At the same time I am quite well aware that from older sources she was in possession of much that was not given by myself."[125]

Isis Unveiled is in two volumes, the first being titled *Science* and the second, *Theology.* The preface to Volume One opens with these words:

The work now submitted to public judgment is the fruit of a some-what intimate acquaintance with Eastern adepts and study of their science. It is offered to such as are willing to accept truth wherever it may be found, and to defend it, even looking popular prejudice straight in the face. It is an attempt to aid the student to detect the vital principles which underlie the philosophical systems of old. . . . It is meant to do even justice, and to speak the truth alike without malice or prejudice. But it shows neither mercy for enthroned error, nor reverence for usurped authority. It demands for a spoliated past, that credit for its achievements which has been too long withheld. It calls for a restitution of borrowed robes, and the vindication of calumniated but glorious reputations. Toward no form of worship, no religious faith, no scientific hypothesis has its criticism been directed in any other spirit. Men and parties, sects and schools are but the mere ephemera of the world's day. Truth, high-seated upon its rock of adamant, is alone eternal and supreme.

In the preface to Volume Two, HPB writes:

Were it possible, we would keep this work out of the hands of many Christians whom its perusal would not benefit, and for whom it was not written. We allude to those whose faith in their respective churches is pure and sincere, and those whose sinless lives reflect the glorious example of that Prophet of Nazareth, by whose mouth the spirit of truth spoke loudly to humanity. . . . These have ennobled Christianity, but would have shed the same lustre upon any other faith they might have professed. . . . They are to be found at this day, in pulpit and pew, in palace and cottage; but the increasing materialism, worldliness and hypocrisy are fast diminishing their proportionate number. Their charity, and simple, child-like faith in the infallibility of their Bible, their dogmas, and their clergy, bring into full activity all the virtues that are implanted in our common nature. . . . We have always avoided debate with them, lest we might be guilty of the cruelty of hurting their feelings; nor would we rob a single layman of his blind confidence, if it alone made possible for him holy living and serene dying.

In the last chapter of *Isis* is to be found HPB's famous "Ten Points of Isis," which she introduces thus:

To comprehend the principles of natural law involved . . . the reader must keep in mind the fundamental propositions of the Oriental philosophy which we have successively elucidated. Let us recapitulate very briefly:

1st. There is no miracle. Everything that happens is the result of law—eternal, immutable, ever active.

2nd. Nature is triune: there is a visible, objective nature; an invisible, indwelling, energizing nature, the exact model of the other, and its vital principle; and, above these two, *spirit,* source of all forces, alone eternal and indestructible.

3rd. Man is also triune: he has his objective, physical body; his vitalizing astral body (or soul), the real man;† and these two are brooded over and illuminated by the third—the sovereign, the immortal spirit. When the real man succeeds in merging himself with the latter, he becomes [a conscious] immortal entity.

4th. Magic, as a science, is the knowledge of these principles, and of the way by which the omniscience and omnipotence of the spirit and its control over nature's forces may be acquired by the individual while still in the body. Magic, as an art, is the application of this knowledge in practice.

5th. Arcane knowledge misapplied is sorcery; beneficently used, true magic or Wisdom.

6th. Mediumship is the opposite of adeptship; the medium is the passive instrument of foreign influences, the adept actively controls himself and all inferior potencies.

7th. All things that ever were, that are, or that will be, having their record upon the astral light, or tablet of the unseen universe, the initiated adept, by using the vision of his own spirit, can know all that has been known or can be known [in our solar universe].

8th. Races of men differ in spiritual gifts as in color, stature, or any other external quality; among some peoples seership naturally prevails, among others mediumship. . . .

9th. One phase of magical skill is the voluntary and conscious withdrawal of the inner man (astral form) from the outer man (physical body). In the cases of some mediums withdrawal occurs, but it is unconscious and involuntary. . . . To the movements of the wandering astral form neither time nor space offer obstacles. The thaumaturgist, thoroughly skilled in occult science, can cause himself (that is, his physical body) to *seem* to disappear, or to apparently take on any shape that he may choose. He may make his astral form visible, or he may give it protean appearances. . . .

10th. The cornerstone of Magic is an intimate practical knowl-

---

† Later, a sevenfold division is given in Theosophical philosophy, which will clarify the statements made in number 3 above. See page 240.

edge of magnetism and electricity, their qualities, correlations, and potencies.

To sum up all in a few words, Magic is spiritual Wisdom; nature, the material ally, pupil and servant of the magician. One common vital principle pervades all things, and this is controllable by the perfected human will. . . . The adept can control the sensations and alter the conditions of the physical and astral bodies of other persons not adepts; he can also govern and employ, as he chooses, the spirits of the elements. He cannot control the immortal spirit of any human being, living or dead, for all such spirits are alike sparks of the Divine Essence, and not subject to any foreign domination.[126]

While reincarnation is clearly taught in *Isis,* the author does not feature it as she does in subsequent works but contents herself with merely paving the way in an antireincarnationist society for a more sympathetic appreciation of this ancient tenet. Where it does appear, HPB refers to it under the word *metempsychosis.* This word had been used for centuries in the West for the teaching that human beings live many lives before reaching perfection. Another word used in the Occident for rebirth is *transmigration.* But this word has drawbacks, for it often is used to indicate that a human being can regress to the lower kingdoms. In the Orient this idea is prevalent, because it is used as a threat by priests that people will return as an animal if they do not obey strict caste practices. Theosophy holds that "once a human being, always a human being." Once self-conscious awareness has awakened in an individual and he has become a responsible entity he cannot revert to the animal stage; he has reached a point of no return.

At the time *Isis* was written, HPB avoided using the word *reincarnation,* because it was used by the French spiritist Allan Kardec, who believed in immediate rebirth with no period of rest between.[127] When, therefore, HPB uses the word *reincarnation* in *Isis* on several occasions, she denies the veracity of such teaching. Consequently, some of her critics say Blavatsky did not believe in reincarnation until she left the United States in 1878 and lived in India. The following words from *Isis* reveal otherwise:

The doctrine of *Metempsychosis* has been abundantly ridiculed by men of science and rejected by theologians, yet if it had been properly understood in its application to the indestructibility of matter and the immortality of spirit, it would have been perceived that it is a sublime conception. . . . There was not a philosopher of any notoriety who did not hold to this doctrine of metempsychosis, as taught by the Brahmans, Buddhists, and later by the Pythagoreans. . . .

[The church fathers] Origen and Clemens Alexandrinus, Synesius and Chalcidius, all believed in it; and the Gnostics, who are unhesitatingly proclaimed by history as a body of the most refined, learned, and enlightened men, were all believers in metempsychosis. . . . If the Pythagorean metempsychosis should be thoroughly explained and compared with the modern theory of evolution it would be found to supply every "missing link" in the chain of the latter. But who of our scientists would consent to lose his precious time over the vagaries of the ancients.[128]

The purpose of human evolution through reincarnation is indicated in another *Isis* reference:

This philosophy teaches that nature never leaves her work unfinished; if baffled at the first attempt, she tries again. When she evolves a human embryo, the intention is that a man shall be perfected—physically, intellectually, and spiritually. His body is to grow mature, wear out, and die; his mind unfold, ripen, and be harmoniously balanced; his divine spirit illuminate and blend easily with the *inner* man. No human being completes its grand cycle, or the "circle of necessity," until all these are accomplished. . . . As the laggards in a race struggle and plod in their first quarter while the victor darts past the goal, so, in the race [toward conscious] immortality, some souls outspeed all the rest and reach the end, while their myriad competitors are toiling under the load of matter, close to the starting point. Some unfortunates fall out entirely, and lose all chance of the prize; some retrace their steps and begin again. . . . Thus, like the revolutions of a wheel, there is a regular succession of death and birth. . . .[129]

The publisher of *Isis* was so "surprised and pleased" with its sale, writes Olcott, "that on Sunday, Feb. 10, 1878, in my presence, he offered [HPB] $5,000 as copyright on an edition of a book in one volume, if she would write it [and] a little more unveil *Isis*. He intended to print only 100 copies and make the price $100 per copy." "Though she needed money badly enough," said Olcott, "she refused the offer on the ground that she was not permitted at that time to divulge any more arcane secrets than she had done in *Isis*."[130] However, there appears to be more in the two volumes of *Isis* than meets the eye, for "in *Isis*," she once remarked, "the explanations of a hundred mysteries lie but half buried. . . . only waiting for the application of intelligence guided by a little Occult knowledge to come into the light of day."[131]

At another time she wrote that "regardless of its minor shortcomings" she maintained that *Isis Unveiled* "contains a mass of original and never hitherto divulged information on occult subjects. . . . I defend the ideas and teachings in it, with no fear of being charged with conceit, since *neither ideas nor teachings are mine,* as I have always declared; and I maintain that both are of the greatest value to mystics and students of Theosophy."[132]

Chapter 11

The Lamasery

" **F**rom the close of 1876 to that of 1878, the Theosophical Society as a body was comparatively inactive," reports Olcott, continuing:

> Its By-laws became a dead letter, its meetings almost ceased. . . .
> The signs of its *growing influence* are found in the increase of the
> founders' home and foreign correspondence, their controversial
> articles in the press, the establishment of Branch societies at London
> and Corfu, and the opening up of the relations with sympathisers in
> India and Ceylon. The influential spiritualists who joined us at first
> had all withdrawn; our meetings in a hired room—the Mott Memorial Hall, on Madison Avenue, New York—were discontinued;
> the fees formerly exacted upon entrance of members were abolished . . . yet the idea was never more vigorous, nor the movement
> more full of vitality, than when it was divested of its external
> corporateness, and its spirit was compressed into our brains, hearts,
> and souls.

The real headquarters was HPB's home on Eighth Avenue and
Forty-Seventh Street, which became "the most attractive *salon* in the
metropolis." HPB had moved there in June of 1876, or perhaps a
month or two later.[133] A New York reporter dubbed it "the Lamasery
in New York."[134] Olcott observes:

> I am not exaggerating when I say that a more unworldly tone would
> not be found in any other home in New York. The social distinctions of our visitors were left outside our threshold; and rich or poor,
> Christian, Jew, or Infidel, learned or unlearned, our visitors received
> the same hearty welcome and patient attention to their questions
> upon religious and other subjects. HPB was born so great an aristocrat as to be at ease in the highest society, and so thorough a
> democratic altruist as to give cordial hospitality to the humblest
> caller.[135]

David Curtis, one of New York's cleverest reporters, recalled that one might meet "Roman Catholic priests, actresses, army doctors, merchants, foreign countesses, artists, physicians and occasional Asiatics" at HPB's rooms, adding:

> Nearly all were unspeakably heathen. Nearly all were intellectually brilliant. Nearly all were rebels against conventionality in some direction, whether outspoken or secret Bohemians. And all acknowledged Mme. Blavatsky as an undoubted leader in intellectual rebellion. . . . Every imaginable subject on earth, in the heavens above the earth, and in the profoundest depths below was discussed there with a curious mixture of wit and philosophy that is by no means to be found in the huge volumes of *Isis Unveiled*.[136]

Rabbis came too, remarks Olcott: "I have known a Jewish Rabbi pass hours and whole evenings in her company, discussing the Kabbalah and have heard him say to her that although he had studied the secret science of his religion for thirty years, she had taught him things he had not even dreamed of, and thrown a clear light upon passages which not even his best teachers had understood."[137]

Among the rebellious spirits that visited the Lamasery, HPB drew the line where violence was advocated. She included in her scrapbook a clipping headed "In Open Revolt," from the *New York Herald* (September 6, 1878) in which Charles Sotheran was quoted as exhorting a group of strikers to use extreme measures. She commented: "A Theosophist becoming a rioter, encouraging revolution and *murder*, a friend of communards—is no fit member of our Society. *He has to go*."[138] Scattered through her writings are found similar strong words against the activities of anarchists and nihilists, particularly in Russia, where they gave rise to communism.

An intriguing portrait of HPB from the pen of a Connecticut reporter who visited the Lamasery appeared in the *Hartford Daily Times* (December 2, 1878):

> A rare, strange countenance is hers. A combination of moods seems to constantly play over her features. She never seems quite absorbed by one subject. There is a keen, alert, subtle undercurrent of feeling and perception perceivable in the expression of her eyes. It impressed us then, and has invariably, with the idea of a double personality; as if she were here and not here; talking, and yet thinking, or acting far away. . . . Her whole personality is expressive of self-possession, command and a certain *sang froid* which borders on

masculine indifference, without for a moment overstepping the bounds of a womanly delicacy. . . .

Glancing at a pile of letters which the servant had just brought, [I] exclaimed: "What an immense correspondence must be yours, madame! And in so many different languages! Tell us; what language do you *think* in?"

"In a language of my own, which is neither Russian, French, nor any you know."

Olcott interjected: "It may be in the Pythagorean numbers, who can tell; or in some dead language employed by races who had attained to a civilization of which the present phonograph may have been but the merest commonplace to them. Who knows but madame may sometime find a sheet of tinfoil† in some future museum of 'recent excavation,' which [will] talk to her in the very language of her thoughts?"

It was the following evening . . . that madame displayed to us her much treasured album containing portraits of foreign members of the Theosophical Society. It was, indeed, one of the finest collections of intellectual, cultured, refined faces that it had ever been our pleasure to examine. Men and women of every nation were there represented. Every type of countenance, from the veteran English general to the Indian philosopher, with his delicate features, clean-cut, expressive countenance and wonderfully perfect form. . . .

The sketch on the facing page was drawn by J. A. Knapp of the building where the Lamasery existed. The building still stands.[139] Its narrow front is on Eighth Avenue, and on the first floor over the shop was HPB's suite of rooms—one of the two flats on that floor. The two front windows on the right, and the one around the corner, open on the large room where callers gathered and where HPB did her writing. A reproduction of Knapp's drawing appeared in a series in Judge's *Path* magazine, "Habitations of HPB," where he remarked:

It was in this flat, in the larger front room that *Isis Unveiled* was written and finished. There so many extraordinary phenomena had taken place that volumes would be required to describe them. Here the "astral music and bells" were so often heard, which self-styled wise critics have assumed were produced by a maid walking up and down the hall with an instrument: an absurdity for those who, like myself, were there and heard all such things. Here, in the corner of the room over Eighth Avenue, the stuffed owl stood and sometimes

† Tinfoil was used in recordings in those days.

blinked. . . . It is a modest place in a modest, busy part of a great city; yet how much was done there and what mighty forces played within those four walls while the immense personality known as Helena P. Blavatsky dwelt therein![140]

9. Drawing of "The Lamasery" building in New York City by J. A. Knapp. (The Path, *November 1893, 238*)

Olcott also lived at the Lamasery. His sister, Belle Mitchell, lived with her husband and children on the floor above. They had also lived in the apartment house on West Thirty-fourth Street where Blavatsky and Olcott had lived. Belle was very attached to HPB, and when a Mrs. Frederica Showers in England wrote an abusive letter to the London *Spiritualist* (March 8, 1878) attacking HPB's veracity and character, Belle penned an indignant reply. Olcott may have thought it too long for publication and never forwarded it to *The Spiritualist*, but he later published it in *The Theosophist*. Quoting therefrom:

10. Dining room at "The Lamasery."

I am neither Buddhist, Brahminist, Theosophist nor Spiritualist, but simply a communicant in the Presbyterian Church, in which body I was brought up and expect to die. I am the sister of Col. H. S. Olcott, a wife, and mother of a family; and I may add, that I am neither a dupe of, nor "psychologized" by, Madame Blavatsky. But I am a woman calling for justice to a woman. . . . I have enjoyed the friendship of Madame Blavatsky for some three years past, during a portion of the time (as at present) occupying an apartment with my family under the same roof with her. Could you believe that a mother would have her children housed with such a monster as Mrs. Showers depicts her to be? With me she is at all times friendly, unrestrained and familiar; and I can affirm that I, and I only, have free entrance to her rooms by day or by night . . . and when in her busiest moments everyone else is excluded, she permits me the freest access to her.

I find Madame Blavatsky a true, honest woman, entirely devoted, body and soul, to what she deems a sacred cause; counting no sacrifice too great to further it, and influencing all about her to a pure, charitable and good life. . . . Of the curious and wonderful phenomena that I have seen produced by Madame Blavatsky without premeditation or preparation, it is not necessary for me to speak.[141]

She later described some of the phenomena she witnessed in an article, "Madame Blavatsky."[142]

Demonstrations of psychic laws and forces by HPB were always done in private. The early members of the TS dropped off, says Olcott, because she "refused to do the slightest phenomena at our meetings."[143] In a letter to Alexander Aksakov in St. Petersburg, Russia, written in April 1875, six months before the TS was founded, Blavatsky wrote: "I have learned that there is no convincing people with suspicious facts only, and that even every genuine fact always presents some weak side or other on which it is easy for opponents to fasten. This is why I have laid down the rule never in any case to permit outsiders to utilize my psychic powers. Except Olcott and two or three very intimate friends, no one has seen what happens around me."[144]

The number of witnesses increased later after *Isis* was written. Olcott wrote C. C. Massey and W. Stainton Moses in London that at times six or eight people were present and that the variety and number of phenomena exceeded all he had seen before.[145]

In Olcott's memorial tribute to HPB, he speculated on the reason she performed phenomena for him:

[The production of *Isis*] with its numberless quotations and its strange eruditions, was quite miracle enough to satisfy me, once and for all, that she possessed psychical gifts of the highest order. But there was far more proof than even that. Often and often, when we two were working alone at our desks far into the night, she would illustrate her descriptions of occult powers in man and nature by impromptu experimental phenomena. Now that I look back to it, I can see that these phenomena were seemingly chosen with the specific design of educating me in psychical science, as the laboratory experiments of Tyndall, Faraday, or Crookes are planned so as to lead the pupil *seriatim* through the curriculum of physics or chemistry. . . . She merely wanted my literary help on her book; and, to make me comprehend the occult laws involved in the moment's discussion, she experimentally proved the scientific ground she stood upon.[146]

In Olcott's letter to HPB's aunt Nadya, he described some of the phenomena her niece was performing during this period. Nadya responded on May 8, 1877:

They are very curious and wonderful, veritable marvels; but they are not exceptional or unique. Many times have I been told of, and I have often read in works dealing with spiritualism, sacred and profane, astonishing accounts of phenomena resembling those which you mentioned in your letter, but they have generally been isolated occurrences, or coming from different sources. But so much force concentrated in a single individual—a whole group of the most extraordinary manifestations emanating from a single source, as in the case of Madame Blavatsky—that is certainly exceedingly rare and perhaps unparalleled. I have long known her to be possessed of [such] power, the greatest with which I have met, but when she was here this power was in a condition far inferior to that which it has now reached.[147]

Many of the phenomena during this period are described in Volume 1 of *Old Diary Leaves*. The famed founder of the Gotham Book Mart in New York, Frances Steloff, once sent a copy of the volume to the Russian mathematician P. D. Ouspensky, author of *Tertium Organum* and leading disciple of Gurdjieff. He replied:

Dear Miss Steloff,

I thank you very much for your book and for your desire to help me, but I already got a copy of this book. So I return your book with great thanks. I have this book in England and I read it first the year Olcott died, 1907. I always consider it the strangest book in the universe, because in spite of all that people can say I always feel that Olcott did not lie, and this is the most remarkable.

> *Yours very sincerely,*
> *P. D. Ouspensky*[148]

Olcott provides a sevenfold classification of the phenomena HPB produced in those days:

1. Those whose production requires a knowledge of the ultimate properties of matter, of the cohesive force which agglomerates the atoms; especially a knowledge of Akasha, its composition, contents, and potentialities.

2. Those which relate to the powers of the elementals [invisible forces of nature] when made subservient to human will.

3. Those where hypnotic suggestion through the medium of thought-transference creates illusive sensations of sight, sound, and touch. [In *Isis* II, 588, this is called "mesmeric hallucination."]

4. Those which involve the art of making objective images, pictorial, or scriptory . . . for instance, the precipitation of a picture or writing upon paper or other material surface, or of a letter, image, or other mark upon the human skin.

5. Those pertaining to thought-reading and retrospective and prospective clairvoyance.

6. Those of the intercourse at will between her mind and the minds of other living persons equally or more perfectly gifted, psychically, than herself. . . .

7. Those, of the highest class, were by spiritual insight, or intuition, or inspiration . . . she reached the amassed stores of human knowledge laid up in the [higher] registry of the Astral Light, called the akashic record.[149]

Judge also witnessed many of the phenomena performed in New York. In a March 1, 1884 letter to Damodar, one of the active Theosophical workers in India, he wrote:

I have seen her cause objects in the room to move without aid from anyone. Once a silver spoon came from the furthest room through two walls and three rooms into her hands before our eyes, at her simple silent will. Another time, she-or-he produced out of the wall a dozen bottles of paint that I desired to use in making a picture in her room. At another time a letter was taken by her unopened, sealed, and in a moment the letter lay in her hand, while the envelope was unbroken; again the same letter was taken in the fingers and instantly its duplicate was lifted off it, thus leaving in her hands two letters, facsimiles of each other. Still further, her three-stoned sapphire ring was taken off, given to a lady who wanted it to wear for a while, taken away by her, and yet on her departure the real ring remained on HPB's finger, only an illusion was taken by the lady. And so on for hundreds of instances.

But all that paled and grew dim before the glorious hours spent in listening to the words of those illuminated Ones who came often late at night when all was still, and talked to H. S. O. and myself by the hour. . . . It was after twelve midnight until 4 a.m. that I heard and saw most while with her in New York.[150]

Most of the phenomena just mentioned falls under the first item in Olcott's sevenfold classification. Rationale for these phenomena was strikingly explained by a *chela* of one of the adepts in a letter to the Honorable John Smith, professor of chemistry at the University of Sydney and president of the Royal Society in New South Wales. It was published in *The Theosophist* in October 1883 (p. 22). In August 1959, sixty years later, it was excerpted in *Proceedings of the Royal Australian Chemical Institute* in a paper entitled "Professor John Smith and Theosophy," by J. L. Davidge. Quoting from the chela's letter:

> The phenomenon of "osmosing" (extracting, *Ed.*) your note from the sealed envelope in which it was sewn with thread, and substituting for it [the Master's] own reply, without breaking either seal or thread, is to be considered first. It is one of those complete proofs of the superior familiarity with and control over atomic relations among our Eastern Adepts as compared with modern Western men of science, . . . It was the same power as that employed in the formation of the letter in the air of your room at [Bombay, February 1, 1882]; in the case of many other airborne letters; of showers of roses; of the gold ring which leaped from the heart of a moss-rose . . .; of a sapphire ring doubled for a lady of high position here, a short time ago, and of other examples. The solution is found in the fact that the "attraction of cohesion" . . . can be interrupted and again set up as regards any given group of atoms. . . . Matter may be defined as condensed Akasa (Ether); and in atomizing, differentiates, as the watery particles differentiate from superheated steam when condensed. Restore the differentiated matter to the state *ante* of undifferentiated matter, and there is no difficulty in seeing how it can pass through the interstices† of a substance in the differentiated state, as we easily conceive of the travel of electricity and other forces through their conductors. The profound art is to be able to interrupt at will and again restore the atomic relations in a given substance: to pull the atoms so far apart as to make them invisible, and yet hold them in polaric suspense, or within the attractive radius, so as to make them rush back into their former cohesive affinities, and re-compose the substance.[151]

Once disintegrated and made invisible, adds Judge, an object can then be sent "along a current formed in the ether to any distance on earth. At the desired point the dispersing force is withdrawn, when immediately cohesion reasserts itself and the object appears intact."[152]
There are two ways of accomplishing the phenomena of passing matter through matter, such as a stone through a solid wall, explains Judge: first, "when a small object is disintegrated by occult means, and is passed through other objects," or second, "if it is to be transported

† Modern science teaches that the interstices between atoms in a solid object are as great, relatively speaking, as the space between the planets! Consequently *solid* matter is an illusion.

without disintegration, then any dense intervening obstacle is disintegrated for a sufficient space to allow it to pass." To cite an example, he notes that HPB "has taken in my sight a small object such as a ring, and laying it on the table caused it to appear without her touching it inside of a closed drawer nearby. Now in that instance either she disintegrated it and caused it to pass into the drawer, or disintegrated the drawer for a sufficient space" so the ring could pass through.[153]

It was not always ponderous philosophy or phenomena that engaged HPB's attention when living at the Lamasery, as this story told by Olcott reveals:

The astral bell once rang with pathetic effect, when her pet canary died, and she broke down and wept. "It was just an ordinary little hen canary," Olcott recalls, "not much to look at for beauty, but an amazingly industrious housewife. . . ." He bought her a mate, a splendid singer, and says of the pair:

We used to let them fly about the room at their pleasure, and the male bird would reward us by perching on a picture frame near our work table and singing most melodiously. The hen would light upon our table in the most fearless way, walk, chirping, right under our noses, and pick up and carry away for nest-building near the ceiling, up in the bronze ornament on the chandelier pipe, any ends of twine or other likely materials. She seemed especially to value the long thin snippings of paper cut off by HPB when pasting and readjusting her foolscap MSS. sheets. Little "Jenny" would sometimes wait until her mistress had cut off a piece of paper and dropped it on the table or floor, and then hop to it and carry it off, to the approving song of her handsome husband, "Pip."

The nest-building was finished at last, and then Jenny began sitting up aloft over our table, her little head showing beyond the edge of the bronze cup, or ornament, on the gas pipe. Pip sang his sweetest, and we waited for the hatching out of the eggs with pleasurable interest. The weeks passed on and Jenny still sat and we waited, but no young birds twittered, and we wondered what could be up. At last one day when the bird was away after seed and water, I placed a chair on our writing table, HPB held it, and I mounted for a peep. The nest was absolutely empty. . . . HPB gave the only possible explanation: "Jenny had been sitting on her illusions" . . . she had persuaded herself that she had laid eggs, and it was her duty to hatch them out.[154]

Pip's singing was not the only music heard at the Lamasery. Occasionally HPB would play the piano. Olcott writes:

> She was a splendid pianist, playing with a touch and expression that were simply superb. Her hands were models—ideal and actual—for a sculptor, and never seen to such advantage as when flying over the keyboard to find its magical melodies. She was a pupil of Moscheles. . . . She would sit in the dusk sometimes, with nobody else in the room beside myself, and strike from the sweet-toned instrument improvisations that might well make one fancy he was listening to the Gandharvas, or heavenly choristers.[155]

Dr. Eugene Corson relates that his mother told him "how HPB would sit down and improvise at the piano with great skill, showing remarkable efficiency for one who played but at odd times, as the spirit might move her."[156] This was at Ithaca, New York, in 1875.

Chapter 12

A Major Decision

In Volume One of *Old Diary Leaves,* Olcott recounts an experience that "was the most momentous in its consequences upon the course of my life":

Our evening's work on *Isis* was finished, I had bade good-night to HPB, retired to my own room, closed the door as usual, sat me down to read and smoke, and was soon absorbed in my book; which, if I remember aright, was Stephens' *Travels in Yucatan.* . . . My chair and table were to the left in front of the door, my camp-cot to the right, the window facing the door, and over the table a wall gasjet.

I was quietly reading, with all my attention centered on my book. . . . All at once, as I read with my shoulder a little turned from the door, there came a gleam of something white in the right-hand corner of my right eye; I turned my head, dropped my book in astonishment, and saw towering above me in his great stature an Oriental clad in white garments, and wearing a head-cloth or turban of amber-striped fabric, hand-embroidered in yellow floss-silk. Long raven hair hung from under his turban to the shoulders; his black beard, parted vertically on the chin in the Rajput fashion, was twisted up at the ends and carried over the ears; his eyes were alive with soul-fire; eyes which were at once benignant and piercing in glance; the eyes of a mentor and a judge, but softened by the love of a father who gazes on a son needing counsel and guidance. He was so grand a man, so imbued with the majesty of moral strength, so luminously spiritual, so evidently above average humanity, that I felt abashed in his presence, and bowed my head and bent my knee as one does before a god or a god-like personage. A hand was lightly laid on my head, a sweet though strong voice bade me be seated, and when I raised my eyes, the Presence was seated in the other chair beyond the table.

He told me he had come at the crisis when I needed him; that my actions had brought me to this point; that it lay with me alone whether he and I should meet often in this life as co-workers for the good of mankind; that a great work was to be done for humanity, and I had the right to share in it if I wished; that a mysterious tie, not now to be explained to me, had drawn my colleague and myself together; a tie which could not be broken, however strained it might be at times. He told me things about HPB that I may not repeat, as well as things about myself, that do not concern third parties. How long he was there I cannot tell: it might have been a half-hour or an hour; it seemed but a minute, so little did I take note of the flight of time.

At last he rose, I wondering at his great height and observing the sort of splendour in his countenance—not an external shining, but the soft gleam, as it were, of an inner light—that of the spirit. Suddenly the thought came into my mind: "What if this be but hallucination; what if HPB has cast a hypnotic glamour over me? I wish I had some tangible object to prove to me that he has really been here; something that I might handle after he is gone!" The Master smiled kindly as if reading my thought, untwisted the *fehta* from his head, benignantly saluted me in farewell and—was gone: his chair was empty; I was alone with my emotions! Not quite alone, though, for on the table lay the embroidered head-cloth; a tangible and enduring proof that I had not been "overlooked," or psychically befooled, but had been face to face with one of the Elder Brothers of Humanity, one of the Masters of our dull pupil-race.[157]

Olcott's experience, he said, was the chief factor in his decision to go to India with HPB. How important that decision turned out to be, for both the West and the East, will become clear in Part V, "Mission to India."

Chapter 13

Last Days in America

On July 8, 1878, HPB became an American citizen, the waiting period having expired. "The next day's American papers," recalls Olcott, "were full of accounts of the event, and reporters were sent to interview the new citizen, who made them all laugh with her naive opinions upon politics and politicians."[158] The reporter from the *Daily Graphic* was informed:

> Yes, I have become a citizen of the United States, and I must say that I feel proud of the title. You ask why I renounce my allegiance to my country? I answer because I love liberty. There is but little liberty in Russia today. Here it is the reverse. There I have been subjected to great annoyances and have been fined so often that I can safely compute the sum at $10,000, and for trivial offenses, too. This is indeed a great country, but then you have one great drawback. The people are so shrewd, and there is much corruption.[159]

HPB spoke again of her citizenship when the *Bombay Gazette* referred to her as a Russian baroness and *The Times of India* said she claimed to be a princess. She wrote the *Gazette:*

> My present business is to take the *Gazette* to task for thrusting upon my unwilling republican head the Baronial coronet. Know please, once for all, that I am neither "Countess," "Princess," nor even a modest "Baroness," whatever I may have been before last July. At that time I became a plain citizen of the U.S. of America—a title I value far more than any that could be conferred on me by King or Emperor . . . my experience of things in general, and peacock's feathers in particular, has led me to acquire a positive contempt for titles, since it appears that outside the boundaries of their own Fatherlands, Russian princes, Polish counts, Italian marquises and German barons are far more plentiful *inside* than *outside* the police precincts. . . . I have never styled myself aught but what I can prove myself to be—namely, an *honest* woman, now a citizen of America, my adopted country, and the only land of *true* freedom in the whole world.[160]

Why, then, did she leave her adopted land? According to Judge:

It has been said by her detractors she merely left a barren field here, by sudden impulse and without a purpose. But the contrary is the fact. . . . She always said she would have to go to India as soon as the Society was under way here and *Isis* should be finished. And when she had been in India some time, her many letters to me expressed her intention to [go] to England so as to open the movement actively and outwardly there in order that the three great points on the world's surface—India, England, and America—should have active centers of Theosophical work.

As to leaving America for India, of this I speak with knowledge, for . . . I, at her request, drew up the contract for [*Isis*'s] publication between her and her New York publishers. . . . When that document was signed, she said to me in the street, "Now I must go to India."[161]

As with the founding of the TS, HPB did not initiate the active move to the Orient but waited for Olcott to suggest it. Here, he says, is how the way opened up:

[At the Lamasery] one evening in 1877, an American traveler who had recently been in India, called. He happened to sit so that, in looking that way I noticed on the wall above him the framed photograph of two Hindu gentlemen with whom I had made the Atlantic passage in 1870. I took it down, showed it to him, and asked if he knew either of the two. He did know Moolji Thackersey and had quite recently met him in Bombay. I got the address, and by the next mail wrote to Moolji about our Society, our love for India and what caused it. In due course he replied in quite enthusiastic terms, accepted the offered diploma of membership, and told me about a great Hindu pandit and reformer [Swami Dayanand Saraswati] who had begun a powerful movement called the "Arya Samaj," for the resuscitation of pure Vedic religion.

At the same time he introduced to my notice, in complimentary terms, one Hurrychund Chintamon, President of the Bombay Arya Samaj, with whom I chiefly corresponded thereafter; and whose evil treatment of us on arrival at Bombay is a matter of history. . . . Mr. Hurrychund wrote me, on reading my explanations of our views as to the impersonality of God—an Eternal and Omnipresent Principle which, under many different names was the same in all religions—that the principles of the Arya Samaj were identical with our own, and [he] suggested that, in that case, it was useless to keep up two societies, when by amalgamating we would increase our powers and usefulness and our chances of success. . . . So, the matter being explained to my colleagues in New York, our Council, in May, 1878, passed a vote to unite the two societies and change the title of ours to "The Theosophical Society of the Arya Samaj.". . .

So far all went well, but, in due course, I received from India an English translation of the rules and doctrines of the Arya Samaj . . . which gave us a great shock—gave me, at least. . . . It was evident that the Samaj was not identical in character with our Society, but rather a new sect of Hinduism—a Vedic sect accepting Swami Dayanand's authority as supreme judge as to which portions of the Vedas and Shastras were and were not infallible. The impossibility of carrying out the intended amalgamation became manifest, and we immediately reported that fact to our Indian colleagues . . .[162]

The Theosophical Society resumed its original status, and a new society was established for those who wanted to link up with the Arya Samaj. The association with the Arya Samaj, despite its drawbacks, provided an excuse for going to India. Prior to departure, HPB used the opportunity to counteract the widespread view circulated by soul-saving missionaries that the Hindus and other Orientals were ignorant savages.

It was this year of departure, 1878, that Thomas Edison became a member of the Theosophical Society. Olcott recalls:

On the 5th April, T. A. Edison sent me his signed application for membership. I had had to see him about exhibiting his electrical inventions at the Paris Exposition of that year; I being the honorary secretary to a Citizens' National Committee which was formed at the request of the French Government, to induce the United States Congress to pass a bill providing for our country taking part in the first international exposition of the world's industries since the fall of [their] Empire and the foundation of the French Republic.† Edison and I got to talking about occult forces, and he interested me greatly by the remark that he had done some experimenting in that direction. His aim was to try whether a pendulum, suspended on the wall of his private laboratory could be made to move by will-force.[163]

† In 1979, at the hundredth anniversary of the light bulb, the Edison archives in Madison, New Jersey displayed among other mementos of 1879 an official receipt from the Theosophical Society acknowledging Edison had paid his membership dues for that year.

In those days a promise of secrecy was exacted from prospective members, because, as indicated earlier, the Society had been compromised by the publication of false stories about its proceedings. Here is Edison's pledge.[164]

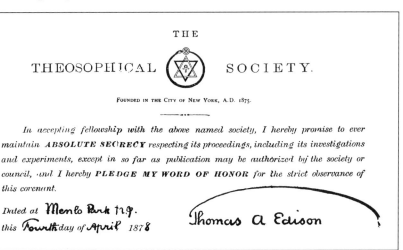

11. *Facsimile of Thomas Edison's pledge upon joining the Theosophical Society in 1878.* (The Theosophist, *August 1931, 657, Theosophical Society, Adyar Archives*)

HPB had spoken to Nadya about Edison's membership and on July third wrote her:

Of course Edison has kept all the promises and will keep them. Foolish Dobrovolsky has omitted a good deal from my article [on Edison in *Pravda*[165]] and the most interesting part of it to be sure. [Edison] accomplishes real miracles. Krishnavarma has taught him two more things, so that with a small, almost invisible mechanical contrivance on their neck the deaf will hear quite well.

Krishnavarma, a Hindu from the Punjab who had been staying at the Lamasery, had also accompanied Blavatsky and Olcott to Minneapolis on a business trip. While there, HPB continues:

All the ladies walked in procession by the windows of our hotel and the terrace where we were sitting, in order to stare at Krishnavarma. He is remarkably handsome . . . though swarthy like the color of coffee. In long, white, muslin garment and a white, narrow turban on his head, with diamonds on his neck and barefooted, he is really a curious sight among the Americans in black coats and white ties. Photographers came to ask me to allow them to take his picture, but he refused all of them, and everyone wondered at his good and pure English. The Lord knows how old he is. When one sees him for the first time he seems not more than 25, but there are moments when he looks like an old man of 100 years.[166]

As to the influence of Theosophy on Edison's philosophy, thirty years later he discussed his metaphysical views in an interview reported in the *Scientific American*. Archibald Keightley, MD, made an in-depth comparison with *The Secret Doctrine* and outlined nine points of similarity.[167] Just before Edison died, reporters inquired whether he believed in survival after death. He replied: "The only survival I can conceive is to start a new earth [life] cycle again."[168]

In April 1878, when Edison became a Fellow of the Theosophical Society, HPB had a strange experience. She wrote Vera:

I have not written to you for a month, and could you guess the cause of it? One beautiful Tuesday morning in April I got up as usual, and as usual sat down at my writing table to write to my Californian correspondents. Suddenly, hardly a second later, as it seemed to me, I realized that for some mysterious reason I was in my bedroom and lying on my bed; it being evening and not morning anymore. Around me I saw some of our Theosophists and Doctors looking at me with the most puzzled faces, and Olcott and his sister Mrs. Mitchell—the best friend I have here—both of them pale, sour, wrinkled, as if they had just been boiled in a saucepan.

"What's the matter? What's gone and happened?" I asked them. Instead of answering, they heaped questions upon me: What was the matter with me? And how could I tell—nothing was the matter with me. I did not remember anything, but it certainly was strange that only the other moment it was Tuesday morning, and now they said it was Saturday evening; and as to me, these four days of unconsciousness seemed only the twinkling of an eye. There's a pretty pair of shoes! Just fancy, they all thought I was dead and were about to burn this dismantled temple of mine. But at this, Master telegraphed from Bombay to Olcott: "Don't be afraid. She is not ill but resting. She has overworked herself. Her body wanted rest, but now she will be well." Master was right. . . . But it is simply awful to think about the work that has accumulated.[169]

It was in May that orders were received to begin preparations for the eventual departure for India.[170] When Blavatsky and Olcott finally left in December, it was intended at first that the move would be only exploratory. They were accompanied by two Britons: Rosa Bates, a teacher, and Edward Wimbridge, an artist and architect, appointed as a "committee of the Theosophical Society to visit foreign lands."[171]

Olcott appointed Major General Abner Doubleday president *ad interim,* to serve in his absence. The son of a U.S. congressman, Doubleday was born in New York State in 1819. When the Civil War broke out he was second in command at Fort Sumter, and he aimed the first gunfire in its defense. He served honorably in many campaigns, and a bronze statue of him was erected at the battlefield at Gettysburg for his heroism there. A distinguished engineer, Doubleday was originator of the grip and cable car system used in hilly San Francisco.

In addition to appointing Doubleday as President of the TS, Olcott selected William Q. Judge as temporary treasurer and corresponding secretary.[172] He had been scheduled to go to India with the others and it was a heart-wrenching decision to say no. He wrote Damodar: "My word of honor bars the path; and as HPB or M once said, 'The word of honor is inconvenient.'" The problem concerned his wife: "Does it not seem to you mean for me to run off leaving debts behind me unpaid and a woman unprovided for who through my solicitation left a good paying position as a teacher to marry me? She cannot recover it. It does not look like justice, and I fail to see that it would be just." His wife, "a Christian of decided beliefs . . . hates the TS and HPB, and does not want to converse on any religious subject."[173] Later, however, she helped her husband in his Theosophical work and in 1915, some years after his death, she joined the United Lodge of Theosophists.[174]

As the time for departure approached, the household at Forty-seventh Street was the scene of tumultuous activity. On December ninth the furnishings were auctioned off for very little. Reporters kept coming and going. On December tenth the New York *Herald* wrote: "To this parlor came strangers from all parts of the world, and some of the best citizens of New York were frequent visitors." The *Daily Graphic* reporter asked HPB whether she really planned to leave. "Yes," she said, "and the Lamasery where I have spent so many happy, happy hours. . . . How glad I shall be to see my dear Indian home again."[175]

Before leaving, Olcott visited Edison in Menlo Park and the following day returned with a phonograph weighing one hundred pounds. At the farewell reception at the Lamasery on the fifteenth, Olcott recalls, "quite a number of our members and friends, among them a Mr. Johnston, whom Edison had sent as his personal representative (he being unavoidably absent), talked into the voice-receiver messages to our then known and unknown brothers in India. . . . Among the voices kept are those of HPB—a very sharp and clear record,—myself, Mr. Judge and his brother John, Prof. Alex. Wilder," and a long list of others, "some very well known as authors, journalists, painters, sculptors, musicians, and in other ways." The recording, unfortunately, did not survive the passage of time.

"The 17th December was our last day on American soil," wrote Olcott. HPB's entry in his daily diary reports: "Great day! Olcott packed up. . . . What next? All dark—but tranquil." "And then," says the colonel, "comes written in large letters, the heart-cry of joy, CONSUMMATUM EST!"[176] The words, from *John* 19:30, were supposedly the last words of Christ on the cross: "It is finished."

HPB's closing paragraph reads: "Olcott returned at 7 P.M. with the tickets for the British Steamboat, the *Canada,* and wrote letters until 11:30. Curtis and Judge passed the evening. . . . At near 12, midnight, HSO and HPB took leave of the chandelier" under which so much work had been accomplished, "and drove off in a carriage to the steamer."

In all, five and a half years had elapsed since Blavatsky, an unknown Russian immigrant, came to these shores. Now she was leaving, never to return. In retrospect it seems remarkable that so much had been accomplished in so short a span of time.

Part **5**

Mission to India

Chapter 1

The Awakening of the East

D r. Edward Conze, who shared with Giuseppe Tucci the honor of being the two leading Buddhist scholars of our time, made a startling admission in his book *Buddhism: Its Essence and Development:*

The year 1875 marks an event of great importance.[1] Madame Blavatsky and Colonel Olcott founded the Theosophical Society. Its activities accelerated the influx of knowledge about Asiatic religions and restored self-confidence in the wavering minds of the Asiatics themselves. At that period, European civilization, a blend of science and commerce, of Christianity and militarism, seemed immensely strong. . . . A growing number of educated men in India and Sri Lanka felt, as the Japanese did about the same time, that they had no alternative but to adopt the Western system with all that it entails. The Christian missionaries looked forward to speedy mass conversions.

But then the tide turned, rather suddenly and unexpectedly. A few members of the dominant race, white men and women from Russia, America, and England, Theosophists, appeared among the Hindus and Ceylonese to proclaim their admiration for the ancient wisdom of the East. Madame Blavatsky spoke about Buddhism [and Hinduism] in terms of the highest praise, Colonel Olcott wrote a "Buddhist Catechism," and A. P. Sinnett published a very successful book in which all kinds of mysterious but fascinating ideas were presented as "Esoteric Buddhism". . . . By its timely intervention, the Theosophical Society has done a great service to the Buddhist cause.[2]

In *Oriental Religions and American Thought,* Professor Carl Jackson writes similarly:

Weakened by inner decay and overwhelmed by foreign rule and missionary attacks, both Hinduism and Buddhism were at a low point by the late nineteenth century, with educated youth rapidly breaking away. One of the period's most dramatic developments was an astonishing resurgence by both [in which] the Theosophical Society played a considerable role in sparking the desire for renewal.[3]

In the 1940's, India's renowned philosopher-president S. Radhakrishnan, expressed the same view:

When, with all kinds of political failures and economic breakdowns we (Indians) were suspecting the values and vitality of our culture, when everything round about us and secular education happened to discredit the value of Indian culture, the Theosophical Movement rendered great service by vindicating those values and ideas. The influence of the Theosophical Movement on general Indian society is incalculable.[4]

In appreciation for what the Theosophical movement had done in India, the government issued a special stamp in 1975 commemorating the one hundredth anniversary of the founding of the TS. The stamp displays the seal of the society and its motto, "There is no religion higher than truth."

12. Indian Commemorative stamp issued in 1975 showing the seal of the Theosophical Society. (Sylvia Cranston Archives, Santa Barbara, California)

If the Hindus in India and Buddhists in Sri Lanka, Burma, and Japan— in all of which countries Theosophists worked for revival—had lost faith in their heritage at that time and succumbed to foreign influences, might they not also have fallen easy prey when communism later overran Asia? Britain was always fearful that this would happen in India.

Americans are unaware that it was one of their own compatriots, Colonel Olcott, collaborating with HPB and their adept teachers, who played a decisive part in the resurgence in those countries. An article in the *New York Herald Tribune* (February 18, 1962), by Martin G. Berck of the United Nations, tells of a similar resurgence in Sri Lanka.

> Throughout the island of Ceylon [Sri Lanka], from the ancient capital of Anuradhapura to the venerated peak of Shri Pada, polished brass lamps were lit yesterday as Buddhists paused to do religious honor to an American. . . . With such homage, Ceylonese Buddhists marked the death on February 17, 1907, of Col. Henry Steel Olcott, whom they regard as a key and sainted figure in the renaissance of their religion and their national culture.

In 1968, Sri Lanka issued a stamp commemorating Olcott's work in promoting education and Buddhism there. Only two Buddhist schools existed in Ceylon in 1880 when HPB and Olcott visited; all the rest were missionary- or church-operated schools that had almost extinguished Buddhism on the island. By 1900, largely through Olcott's efforts, the Buddhist schools numbered two hundred.[5] In addition to Olcott's picture, the stamp depicts the Buddhist flag he designed. Blavatsky explained that hitherto the Buddhists "had no such symbol as the cross affords to the Christians, and consequently have lacked that essential sign of their common relation to each other." The flag was but one of many examples, she said, of the fraternal force the Theosophical movement was trying to evoke among all peoples.[6]

Olcott had been so successful in reviving Buddhism there, and also in Burma, that in 1888 a national committee of Japanese Buddhist priests invited him to do the same for Japan and sent a representative to India to escort him to their country. In an address to the Theosophists, the delegate pleaded that Olcott should "put courage in the hearts of our young men to prove to the graduates of our colleges and universities and to those who have been sent to America and Europe for education, that Western science is not infallible, and not a substitute but the natural sister of religion." Under the joint auspices of the nine main Japanese Buddhist sects, Olcott made a four-month lecture tour of the entire island. It stimulated such interest that it became a national event.[7]

As to India, in a June 27, 1885 address celebrating the third anniversary of the Bengal Theosophical Society, at which seven hundred were present, Olcott surveyed conditions before and after the Theosophists arrived in that country. He reminded them that the ancient schools of the Brahman gurus had been closed, the precious scriptures "mouldering upon the shelves for want of buyers . . . and, to complete the picture of national desolation, the crowded Pantheon of Hindu Theology became a mere quarry of old stone images, lifeless, meaningless, jeered at by even the callowest youths of the modern schools and colleges. . . . Is it so now? Look through the land, examine the native newspapers and other literature of the day, and answer. . . . The old books find buyers, and new editions are being demanded; Sanskrit schools are reopening. . . . There is the beginning of a conviction in the Hindu mind that their forefathers were wise and good, and their motherland the 'cradle of arts and creeds.'"[8]

This same year saw the birth of the Indian National Congress, which under Mohandas Gandhi's guidance became the dominant power leading to the historic hour when India gained her freedom. "In the beginning," Gandhi told his biographer Louis Fischer, the "top congressmen were theosophists."[9] In fact, one of them, Allan O. Hume, was hailed as the Father of the Congress. In *Hind Swaraj,* Gandhi's book on Indian Home Rule, the latter wrote: "How can we forget what Mr. Hume has written, how he lashed us into action, and with what effort he has awakened us, in order to achieve the objects of the Congress."[10]

As to Theosophy, Gandhi explained to his biographer Louis Fischer:

Theosophy is the teaching of Madame Blavatsky. It is Hinduism at its best. Theosophy is the Brotherhood of Man. . . . Jinnah and other Moslem leaders were once members of the Congress. They left it because they felt the pinch of Hinduism patronizing. . . . They did not find the Brotherhood of Man among the Hindus. They say Islam is the Brotherhood of Man. As a matter of fact, it is the Brotherhood of Moslems. Theosophy is the Brotherhood of Man.[11]

As the Theosophical Society takes no part in politics, whatever members accomplished in the Congress was performed by them as private citizens. HPB writes:

This remarkable political body was planned by certain of our Anglo-Indian and Hindu members after the model and on the lines of the Theosophical Society, and has from the first been directed by our own colleagues; men among the most influential in the Indian Empire. . . . We aroused the dormant spirit . . . of the Hindus, and one vent the new life made for itself was this Congress.[12]

Blavatsky believed that India's hour of freedom was still a long way off, for in a letter to Sinnett she remarked: ". . . Master says that the hour for the retirement of you English has not struck nor will it—*till next century* and that 'late enough to see even Dennie an old, old man' as KH said some time ago."[13] Dennie was Sinnett's son, born in 1868; he would have been seventy-nine had he lived until 1947, when India became self-governed.

Gandhi's first contact with the Theosophists came in 1889, when he was in London studying law. Up to then, as Professor James Hunt remarks in *Gandhi in London,* he was more interested in fashion than in becoming a lawyer. He was "suffering under the colonial mentality which led him to turn from Indian ways to adopt those of the West." During this period he learned to dance, became interested in Western music, took elocution lessons and studied French,[14] and he whole-heartedly believed that Indians should become like Englishmen. "It was through theosophy," Hunt continues, "that Gandhi was induced to study his own heritage. This effect was generated in many Indians . . . ."[15]

In Gandhi's *Autobiography,* he relates that "toward the end of my second year in England I came across two theosophists, brothers. . . .[16] They talked to me about the *Gita.* . . . They invited me to read the original with them. I felt ashamed, as I had read the divine poem neither in Sanskrit nor in Gujarati. . . . I began reading the *Gita* with them."[17] The *Bhagavad Gita* became the most important book in his life,[18] influencing all his decisions in the long struggle of India to become freed from British rule. He affirmed that his philosophy of *Ahimsā* (harmless-ness; peaceful nonresistance) was rooted in that scripture.[19]

Gandhi reports further that the two Theosophists who introduced him to the *Gita* also took him on one occasion to the Blavatsky Lodge and introduced him to Madame Blavatsky and Mrs. Besant.[†] He said, "I recall having read, at the brothers' [direction] Madame Blavatsky's *Key to Theosophy.*[‡] This book stimulated in me the desire to read books on Hinduism, and disabused me of the notion fostered by the missionaries that Hinduism was rife with superstition."[20]

It was in November 1889 that Gandhi met HPB. At that time, he said, he did not join the TS, because "with my meagre knowledge of my own religion, I did not want to belong to any religious body." However, a year and a half later, on March 26, 1891, he became an associate member of the Blavatsky Lodge.[21] Three months later, on June twelfth, he returned to India.

When Gandhi went to South Africa, in 1893, he came in close contact with the Theosophists at the Johannesburg TS: "I had religious

---

† Annie Besant was the famous Fabian Socialist who became associated with the Theosophists after reviewing in a London journal HPB's *The Secret Doctrine.* See Part VI, Chapter 9.

‡ Pyarelal on page 259 of *Mahatma Gandhi Volume I: The Early Phase* states: "Towards the close of 1890 he was introduced to Mme. Blavatsky and Mrs. Besant. He read Mme. Blavatsky's *Secret Doctrine,* and on March 26, 1891, was enrolled as an associate member of the Blavatsky Lodge."

discussions with them every day. There used to be readings from theosophical books, and sometimes I had occasion to address their meetings."[22] In 1895, he wrote, "I intend to spread as much as possible information about Theosophy."[23]

Jawaharlal Nehru became a member of the TS and, like Gandhi, first became interested in India's great scriptures through Theosophical contacts. In his autobiography, *Toward Freedom,* he relates that when he was eleven years old his new tutor, Ferdinand Brooks, took him in his charge:

> He brought a new influence to bear upon me which affected me powerfully for awhile. This was theosophy. He used to have weekly meetings of theosophists in his rooms, and I attended them and gradually imbibed theosophical phraseology and ideas. There were metaphysical arguments, and discussion about reincarnation and the astral and other supernatural bodies, and auras, and the doctrine of karma, and references not only to big books by Madame Blavatsky and other theosophists but to the Hindu scriptures, the Buddhist *Dhammapada,* Pythagoras, Apollonius [of] Tyanaeus, and various philosophers and mystics. I did not understand much that was said, but it all sounded very mysterious and fascinating, and I felt that here was the key to the secrets of the universe. For the first time I began to think, consciously and deliberately, of religion and other worlds. The Hindu religion especially went up in my estimation; not the ritual or ceremonial part, but its great books, the *Upanishads* and the *Bhagavad-Gita.* . . . I became a member of the Theosophical Society at thirteen, and Mrs. Besant herself performed the ceremony of initiation. . . . I have no doubt that those years with F. T. Brooks left a deep impress upon me, and I feel that I owe a debt to him and to theosophy.[24]

In 1983, Nehru's daughter, Prime Minister Indira Gandhi, gave the Besant lecture at the Adyar TS. She remarked:

> The Theosophical Society is a fellowship of seekers. Its contribution to India's cultural and political rebirth is well known. The gentle strength of the quest for truth enabled it to withstand opposition and misrepresentation in its early years. Perhaps that is what attracted my father to it . . . and probably the message of theosophy had much to do with his universalism, his reverence for different faiths and his repugnance for any kind of fanaticism.[25]

The feeling of universalism, which Theosophy cultivates, is in furtherance of the movement's first object, universal brotherhood. In

HPB's article "Our Three Objects" (*Lucifer,* September 1889), she reviews what had thus far been accomplished in India respecting this objective:

> When we arrived in India, in February, 1879, there was no unity between the races and sects of the Peninsula, no sense of a common public interest, no disposition to find the mutual relation between the several sects of ancient Hinduism, or that between them and the creeds of Islam, Jainism, Buddhism and Zoroastrianism. . . .
>
> Ten years have passed and what do we see? . . . One hundred and twenty-five branches of our Society have sprung up in India alone, each a nucleus of our idea of fraternity, a center of religious and social unity. . . . The growth of this kindly feeling has been proven in a variety of ways: first, in the unprecedented gathering of races, castes and sects in the annual conventions of the Theosophical Society;[†] second, in the rapid growth of a theosophical literature advocating our altruistic views, in the founding of various journals and magazines in several [native] languages, and in the rapid cessation of sectarian controversies.

In India, the work of the Theosophical movement overcame to some degree the prejudices between the British Raj and the natives. Olcott gives this example:

> On 4th March [1880], a European lady of northern India, wife of a high military officer, was admitted into the Society, and I mention the fact merely to recall a circumstance which shows the utter lack of social relations between the two races. After the ceremony of admission of the candidate was concluded, I called on several of our cleverest Parsi and Hindu members to express any sentiments of goodwill and fellowship they would wish the new lady member to convey to our colleagues in London. Short speeches were made . . . in excellent taste and perfect English. Mrs. M was astonished and delighted—she said—to find so much intelligence among the natives. In her eighteen years of residence in India she

---

† An Englishman who was present at the TS convention in Adyar in December 1885 wrote to a friend in London: "There were about eighty delegates present, men who had travelled some of them thousands of miles to get here. I was very much struck with the representative character of the men. There were several judges, pleaders, professors, and vice-presidents of colleges, and there were comparatively few who had not graduated at universities, modelled after the University of London. Nearly all the delegates keep their caste, and paint their foreheads accordingly. When we consider that these different castes would never have met on any platform before Theosophy came there, we can appreciate the fact that the Society is doing something in India." (Sinnett, *Incidents,* 10.)

had never even spoken to any Hindu but her servants! And she, the wife of a high officer.[26]

It is interesting to note that in the nineteenth century the Theosophical Society was not the first to hold aloft in India the idea of universal brotherhood. An experiment along these lines was begun in 1867 by a celebrated yogi in southern India, Ramalingam. He attracted thousands of followers, but they were more interested in the purported miracles he produced. One of his disciples, Pandit Vellayu, of Presidency College in Madras, in a witnessed statement made in 1882, reported that his teacher repeatedly told his followers before he died in 1874:

> You are not fit to become members of this Society of Universal Brotherhood. *The real members of that Brotherhood are living far away, towards the North of India.* You do not listen to me. You do not follow the principles of my teachings. You seem to be determined not to be convinced by me. YET THE TIME IS NOT FAR OFF, WHEN PERSONS FROM RUSSIA, AMERICA (these two countries were always named), and other foreign lands WILL COME TO INDIA AND PREACH TO YOU THIS SAME DOCTRINE OF UNIVERSAL BROTHERHOOD. Then only, will you know and appreciate the grand truths that I am now vainly trying to make you accept. You will soon find that THE BROTHERS WHO LIVE IN THE FAR NORTH will work a great many wonders in India, and thus confer incalculable benefits upon this our country.

Pandit Vellayu adds: "This prophecy has, in my opinion, just been literally fulfilled. The fact that the Mahatmas in the North exist is no new idea to us Hindus; and the strange fact that the advent of Madame Blavatsky and Colonel Olcott from Russia and America was foretold several [in 1874, five] years before they came to India, is an incontrovertible proof that my Guru was in communication with those Mahatmas under whose directions the Theosophical Society was subsequently founded."[27]

Chapter 2

Arrival in Bombay

HPB and Olcott arrived in Bombay on February 16, 1879. Two months had elapsed since leaving New York. After a very busy two weeks with the Theosophists in London, they boarded ship for India. The voyage was so rough that even HPB, who seldom was seasick, was bedridden for a few days.

The evening after their ship dropped anchor in Bombay Harbor, a reception was held with three hundred natives present. Professor of Oriental Religion Robert Ellwood, in *Alternative Altars,* quotes Olcott on these "wonderful first days in the Asian lands":

Every evening we held an impromptu durbar, when the knottiest problems of philosophy, metaphysics, and science were discussed. We lived and breathed in an atmosphere of mind, amid the highest spiritual ideals. . . . Visitors kept on crowding our bungalow, and stopping until late every evening to discuss religious questions. Old and young, it was all the same; and thus did we come, so early in our connection with the Hindus, to know the difference between Western and Eastern ideals of life, and the greater dignity of the latter. Questions of wealth, color, business, or politics scarcely ever crossed our threshold; the Soul was the burning topic of debate. . . .

Fanatics, if you please; crazy enthusiasts; dreamers of unpractical dreams . . . yet our dreams were of human perfectibility, our yearnings after divine wisdom, our sole hope to help mankind to higher thinking and nobler living. And, under those umbrageous palms, we were visited in person by Mahatmas; and their inspiring presence made us strong to proceed in the path we were treading.[28]

Soon after arrival came a period of settling in, and HPB and Olcott moved to their new home on Girgaum Backroad, in the Indian section of Bombay, where white people seldom set foot. For the next two years this became the headquarters of the TS. A servant named Babula was found who remained with Blavatsky throughout her stay in India. A Gujarati boy of fifteen, he knew a number of languages, and HPB is said to have taught him French.[29]

A series of strange adventures during this period involving HPB,

Moolji Thackersey, and Olcott are recorded in *Old Diary Leaves*, from which this one is taken:

> [On March 25th, HPB] told Moolji to fetch a buggy, and, when it came, mounted into it with him. She refused to answer his questions as to whither she was going, simply telling him to order the driver to turn to right or left or go straight ahead, as she might direct. What happened Moolji told us on their return in the evening. She had directed the course [through] numerous windings of streets and country roads, until they found themselves at a suburb of Bombay, eight or ten miles distant, in a grove of coniferae. . . . Moolji knew the place, because he had cremated his mother's body in that neighborhood. Roads and paths crossed each other confusedly in the wood, but HPB never faltered as to her course, and bade the driver turn and turn until they came to the seashore. Finally, to Moolji's amazement, they were brought up by the gate of a private estate, with a magnificent rose garden in front and a fine bungalow with spacious Eastern verandahs in the background.
>
> HPB climbed down and told Moolji to await her there, and not for his life to dare come to the house. So there he waited in a complete puzzle; for such a property he, a life-long resident of Bombay, had never heard of before. He called one of several gardeners who were hoeing the flowers, but the man would tell him nothing as to his master's name, how long he had lived there, or when the bungalow was built: a most unusual thing among Hindus. HPB had walked straight up to the house, had been received cordially at the door by a tall Hindu of striking and distinguished appearance, clad entirely in white, and had gone inside. After some time the two reappeared, the mysterious stranger bade her farewell, and handed her a great bunch of roses which one of the gardeners brought to his master for the purpose, and HPB rejoined her escort, re-entered the buggy, and ordered the driver to return home. All that Moolji could draw out of HPB was that the stranger was an occultist with whom she was in relationship and had business to transact that day. . . . The strangest part of this story to us was that, so far as we knew, there was no possibility of HPB's having learnt anything about this suburb and the way to it, at any rate since our arrival at Bombay, for she had never left the house alone, yet she had shown the completest familiarity with both. Whether any such bungalow existed or not, we had no means of knowing save on Moolji's testimony.
>
> He was so amazed with his experience [he kept repeating it] to his friends in the town, which led one, who professed to know the sub-

urb in question perfectly, to lay a wager of Rs. 100 that there was no such bungalow by the seashore and that he could not guide anyone to it. When HPB heard this, she offered to bet Moolji that he would lose the wager; whereupon he, declaring that he could retrace every foot of the way by which they had gone, closed with the offer, and I had a carriage called at once, and we three entered it. . . . We offered to give him as much time as he liked to pursue his search, but he felt completely baffled and [after several hours of circling around and around] gave in as beaten. So we drove home.

HPB told all of us that Moolji would have found the mystical bungalow if a glamor had not been brought to bear on his sight, and moreover, that the bungalow, like all other spots inhabited by Adepts, was always protected from the intrusion of strangers by a circle of illusion formed about it and guarded and kept potent by elemental servitors [or nature spirits]. This particular bungalow was in the constant keeping of an agent who could be relied upon, and used as an occasional resting and meeting place by Gurus and Chelas when traveling. [She said further:] "All the buried ancient libraries, and those vast hoards of treasure which must be kept hidden until its karma requires its restoration to human use, are protected from discovery by the profane, by illusory pictures of solid rocks, unbroken solid ground, a yawning chasm, or some such obstacle. . . ."[30]

In the weeks that followed, HPB and her entourage traveled to the famous Karli Caves; then, going north, they visited Rajputana, Allahabad, Benares, and many other places.[31] From Agra, HPB wrote Professor Wilder in the United States:

Agra, April 28, 1879.

My dear Doctor, my very dear friend:

How I do regret that you are not with us! How often I think of you, and wonder whether the whole of your archaeological and poetical soul would not jump out in fits of rapture were you but to travel with us . . . Here we are travelling for this last month by rail, bullock-cart, elephant, camel and bunder boat, stopping from one to three days in every town, village and port; seeing subterranean India, not the upper one, . . . True, ever since the beginning of March we are being toasted, baked and roasted. . . . But oh! for the ineffable coolness and glory of the mornings and after sunset here. The moon of America, is at best, when compared with that of India, like a smokey olive-oil lamp. We get up at four and go to bed at nine. We travel more by night and in the morning and afternoons. . . .[32]

Chapter **3**

Resistance to Change

I n early May 1879, the party returned to Bombay. From Olcott's enthusiastic description of all that transpired, one would hardly suspect that rankling inside was the thought that he had made a big mistake in coming to India. A letter at this time, received from his mahatmic teacher, reveals this:

> Since you have arrived at the conclusion that it was an "act of lunatics" to leave your country and come here in the way you did, presumably upon the representations of Mr. Hurrychund Chintamon and Mooljee Thackersey whereas you know it to be untrue, the sooner we come to an understanding the better for all of us. To begin with, it was your own most fervent desire to go to India. . . .
>
> Do not imagine that which cannot be; do not hope that at the last moment you will be helped. If you are unfit to pass your first probation and assert your rights of a future Adept by forcing circumstances to bow before you—you are as totally unfit for any further trials. . . .
>
> Your . . . son's picture [in Olcott's room] will ever draw you back to America.[33]

A major cause for despair was the stubborn refusal of the natives to cooperate in restoring their own culture. The phenomenal successes recorded in the last chapters did not come about overnight. Thus, in 1881, HPB had good reason to write:

> For six years now [since 1875], we have been publicly asserting that Indian Yoga† was and is a true science, endorsed and confirmed by

† The Yoga above referred to is Raja Yoga, as taught in such scriptures as *The Bhagavad-Gita* and the *Upanishads*. HPB defines it in her *Theosophical Glossary* (p. 225) as "[t]he true system of developing psychic and spiritual powers and union with one's *Higher Self*—or the Supreme Spirit, as the profane express it." "Raja Yoga," she adds, "is opposed to Hatha Yoga, the physical or psycho-physiological training in asceticism," which relies largely on bodily postures and breathing exercises.

202

thousands of experimental proofs; and that, though few in number, the true Indian Yogis may still be found when the right person seeks in the right way. That these affirmations should be challenged by Europeans was only to be expected . . . but that the Hindus . . . the heirs of the ancient philosophers, should also deny and scoff was a bitter draught to swallow. Nevertheless, we uttered our message, and not in a whisper, but boldly. Our voice came back to us almost echoless from the great Indian void. Hardly a brave soul stood up to say we were right, that yoga was true, and that the real Yogis still existed. We were told that India was dead; that all spiritual light had long since flickered out of her torch; that modern science had proved antiquity fools. . . . But when it was seen that we were not to be silenced by counter-proof, and that no such proof could be given, the first signs appeared of a change of the current of opinion.[34]

Also discouraging was the fact that for eighteen months since arriving, HPB was under surveillance by the British secret service as a possible Russian spy. Even Olcott was suspect. Their every move was watched; incoming letters and telegrams were read and outgoing letters often confiscated. Russiaphobia was at its height, owing to the success of Russian arms in the Trans-Caspian region with the fate of Afghanistan in the balance.[35] HPB wrote Miss Burr in the United States, who had complained about missing correspondence: "Hurrah for powerful, strong, fearless and unconquerable old England! The idea of the mere shadow of the Russian bear, the threatening outlines of which this king of animals, the British Lion, discovers even in the folds of the dress of an old Russian woman, and pricks up its ears and wags its powerful tail, and roars—this must fill every perspicacious mind with an overpowering sense of British strength."[36] Many of the natives, influenced by such suspicions, deferred affiliating with the Theosophists.[37]

During her entire stay in India, HPB was also the target of the slanderous abuse of missionaries, who viewed her activities as encroaching on their "god-given" rights to save the heathen. She once remarked:

The test of [one's] philosophy is always best made under circumstances which "try men's souls"; one can be charmingly serene when far away from the field of battle. Let anyone, who aspires to the martyr's crown, come to India and Ceylon, and help us in trying to establish a society on the basis of Tolerance and Brotherhood. He would then find of what stuff the average Christian is made.[38]

A recipient of a letter from a master once expressed surprise to him that he should refer to the work of the Theosophical Movement as "a Forlorn Hope." He replied: "What I meant by the 'Forlorn Hope' was that when one regards the magnitude of the task to be undertaken by our theosophical volunteers, and especially the multitudinous agencies arrayed, and to be arrayed, in opposition, we may well compare it to one of those desperate efforts against overwhelming odds, that the true soldier glories to attempt."[39]

Olcott having successfully resisted the temptation to return to America, the founders soon mobilized their forces and took positive action by publishing a monthly magazine, *The Theosophist,* with HPB as editor. The magazine had an international circulation, attracting many readers in the West who had never heard of Theosophy before. The first issue appeared in October 1879.

The reasons for publishing were various. "Since our arrival here," HPB wrote Major-General Doubleday (July 16, 1879), "we were gradually shut out of the local papers, and smothered by calculated neglect and indifference."[40] The opening editorial indicates other reasons:

The rapid expansion of the Theosophical Society from America to various European and Asiatic countries; the increasing difficulty and expense in maintaining correspondence by letter with members so widely scattered; the necessity for an organ through which the native scholars of the East could communicate their learning to the Western world, and, especially, through which the sublimity of [Indian], Buddhistic, Parsi, and other religions might be expounded by their own priests or pandits, the only competent interpreters; and finally, to the need of a repository for the facts—especially such as relate to occultism—gathered by the Society's fellows among different nations. . . .

It is designed that our journal shall be read with as much interest by those who are not deep philosophers as by those who are. Some will delight to follow the pandits through the mazes of metaphysical subtleties and the translations of ancient manuscripts, others to be instructed through the medium of legends and tales of mystical import. Our pages will be like the many viands at a feast, where each appetite may be satisifed and none are sent away hungry. The practical wants of life are to many readers more urgent than the spiritual, and that it is not our purpose to neglect them our pages will amply show.

HPB's own contributions to *The Theosophist* during the six years of her editorship were considerable, and five volumes of her *Collected Writings* are devoted to them. However, Beatrice Hastings, a noted British literary critic, was of the opinion that the complete magazine should be accessible:

> Surely there never was a more fascinating journal than the *Theosophist* under the editorship of H.P.B.! If literary folk wish to know what she was about *Between the Plots,* they may read this [journal]. It ought to be re-published verbatim, down to the advts. and with nobody's cuts of the supposed impermanent; it is all permanent, the life of the Society was lived in it.[41]

Mrs. Hastings would be happy to know that volumes 1 and 2 have been reproduced in paperback editions.[42]

In the second issue of *The Theosophist* (November 1879) HPB introduced an article on what today is called ecology, the need for which was rarely supported in her time. The article, by "Forester," is titled "The Indian Forest." Quoting from her introduction, "The Ruin of India":

> Our love for our adopted country moves us to give this subject of forest conservancy much consideration in these columns from time to time. Our trip northward last April, through 2,000 miles of scorched fields, through whose quivering air the dazzled eye was only refreshed here and there with the sight of a green tree, was a most painful experience. It required no poet's fancy, but only the trained forecast of the statistician to see in this treeless, sun-parched waste, the presage of doom unless the necessary steps were at once taken to aid lavish Nature to reclothe the mountain tops with vegetation. . . .
>
> In America, where our observations have been chiefly made, the wanton destruction of forests has been appalling. Whole districts have been denuded of larger timber, through the agency of fire, merely to obtain cleared land for tillage. The 90,000 miles of railway and 80,000 of telegraph lines have caused the denudation of vast tracts to procure their supplies of ties and poles. . . .
>
> While every patriot Hindu bewails the decadence of his country, few realize the real cause. It is neither in foreign rule, excessive taxation, nor crude and exhaustive husbandry, so much as in the destruction of its forests. The stripping of the hills and the drainage slopes of their vegetation [are] a positive crime against the nation,

and will decimate the population more effectually than could the sword of any foreign conqueror. . . .

We need only glance at the pages of history to see that the ruin and ultimate extinction of national power follow the extirpation of forests as surely as night follows day. Nature has provided the means for human development; and her laws can never be violated without disaster. A great native patriot wrote us, some months ago, "this poor nation is slowly dying for lack of food-grain." This is alas! too true; and he who would learn one great secret why food-grains fail, poverty increases, water courses dry up, and famine and disease ravage the land in many parts, should read the communication of "Forester" in this number.

The manager of *The Theosophist,* and a frequent contributor to its pages, was Damodar K. Mavalankar, who had only recently joined the TS. Having read *Isis Unveiled,* he was so impressed that he visited the Bombay headquarters to pay respects to its author. The son of a wealthy Brahman, Damodar was soon to renounce caste and, later, also his 50,000-rupee income when his family insisted he give up Theosophy.[43]

Olcott writes:

When Damodar joined the TS it was the rainy season and the dear boy used to come to see us of evenings, clad in a white rubber waterproof and leggings, a cap with flaps to match, a lantern in his hand, and the water streaming from the end of his long nose. He was as thin as Sarah Bernhardt, with lantern jaws, and legs—as HPB used to say—like two lead pencils. So far as appearances went, he seemed as little likely as any man in the Society to become a Mahatma or get within a thousand miles of a real ashrama. But appearances were as false in this case as they have been in those of other members who seemed infinitely his spiritual superiors, but proved otherwise. . . .

When a lad, brought near to death by fever and tossing in delirium, he had had a vision of a benignant sage, who came and took his hand and told him he should not die but should live for useful work. After meeting HPB, his interior vision gradually opened, and in him whom we know as Master KH, Damodar saw revealed the visitor of his youthful crisis. That sealed his devotion to our cause. . . .[44]

After reading *Isis* and joining the TS, Damodar wrote:

It is no exaggeration to say that I have been a really living man only these few months; for between life as it appears to me now and life as

I comprehended it before, there is an unfathomable abyss. . . . My aspirations were only for more Zamindaries,† social position, and the gratification of whims and appetites. . . .

The study of theosophy has thrown a light over me in regard to my country, my religion, my duty. I have become a better [Hindu] than I ever was. I have similarly heard my Parsi brothers say that they have been better Zoroastrians since they joined the Theosophical Society. I have also seen the Buddhists write often to the Society that the study of theosophy has enabled them to appreciate their religion the more. And thus this study makes every man respect his religion the more. It furnishes to him a sight that can pierce through the dead letter and see clearly the spirit. . . . If we view all the religions in their popular sense, they appear strongly antagonistic to each other in various details. None agrees with the other. . . . There must . . . be one common ground on which all the religious systems are built. And this ground which lies at the bottom of all, is truth.[45]

Damodar was the first to introduce into theosophical terminology the term *mahatma* as applied to the Himalayan adepts. Previously they had been referred to as the Brothers. However, *mahatma* was not newly coined; it had been used in ancient India for wise beings.[46] In HPB's article, "Mahatmas and Chelas" (*The Theosophist*, July 1884), she gives this definition:

A Mahatma is a personage, who by special training and education, has evolved those higher faculties and has attained that spiritual knowledge which ordinary humanity will acquire after passing through numberless series of reincarnations during the process of cosmic evolution, provided, of course, that they do not go in the meanwhile, against the purposes of Nature and thus bring on their own annihilation.

† Acquisition of more lands.

Chapter 4

Travels Northward

Damodar joined the household at the Bombay head-quarters and lived from then on with HPB and Olcott. In December 1879 he accompanied them on their second journey north, during which time they first visited Alfred Percy Sinnett and his wife, Patience, both of whom were to play important roles in the work of the Movement during the next few years. Sinnett was editor of *The Pioneer,* one of the leading influential papers in India, generally regarded as the mouthpiece of the government.

"Nine days after our landing at Bombay," reports Olcott, Sinnett had written expressing "to me the desire of becoming acquainted with HPB and myself, in case we should be coming up country, and his willingness to publish any interesting facts about our mission to India. In common with the whole Indian press, *The Pioneer* had noted our arrival." Sinnett added that his interest in the occult lay in discovering the laws underlying the remarkable phenomena he had once witnessed in London. The explanations then offered were "a confusing jumble of assertions and theories."[47]

The Sinnetts were now in their home in Allahabad, the winter capital of the viceroy and his government. The party of Theosophists arrived there on December fourth and remained almost two weeks. It was their first real contact with the British Raj. Olcott writes:

> Mrs. Sinnett's reception of us was most charming, and before she had spoken a dozen sentences we knew that we had won a friend beyond price. A Judge of the High Court and the Director of Public Instruction were among the callers that day. Mrs. Alice Gordon made her appearance on the 7th, having traveled a long distance to see HPB, and little by little we got to know most of the Anglo-Indians of the Station who were worth knowing by reason of their intelligence and breadth of mind. Some of them were very prepossessing, but to none were we so attracted as to the Sinnetts and Mrs. Gordon, then in the prime of her beauty and sparkling with intelligence. . . . It is strict etiquette in Anglo-India for the newcomer to call on the residents, but as HPB would call on nobody,

those who cared to know her had to ignore custom and visit her as often as they liked.[48]

During her stay HPB met Allan Hume, retired secretary of the government, who became for several years another friend of the Movement. Hume later became the father of the Indian National Congress.

≈

The next stop was Benares, where Olcott was honored by the pandits of that city for his work in reviving interest in Sanskrit literature and Indian philosophy. "From this meeting," he reports, "I went to pay my respects to Professor G. Thibaut, Ph.D., Principal of Benares College, and an old pupil and protégé of Professor Max Müller. I found him a most agreeable man, deeply versed in Sanskrit, yet without pretense or pomposity. . . ."[49]

The professor met HPB that evening at a small gathering. By Olcott's account, when the subject of Yoga arose, he said to her in his strong German accent:

"Madame Blavatsky, these pandits [in Benares] tell me that, undoubtedly, in the ancient times there were Yogis who had actually developed the Siddhis† described in the Shastras; that they could do wonderful things; for instance, they could make fall in a room like this, a shower of roses; but now nobody can do that. . . ." He had no sooner pronounced the last word than HPB started up in her chair, looked scornfully at him, and burst out: "Oh, they say that, do they? They say no one can do it now? Well, I'll show them; and you may tell them from me that if the modern Hindus were less sycophantic to their Western masters, less in love with their vices, and more like their ancestors in many ways they would not have to make such a humiliating confession, nor get an old Western hippopotamus of a woman to prove the truth of their Shastras!" Then, setting her lips together and muttering something, she swept her right hand through the air with an imperious gesture, and bang! on the heads of the company fell about a dozen roses. . . .[50]

Then the discussion proceeded with renewed vivacity. The Sankhya [school of Indian philosophy] was the topic and Thibaut put many searching questions to HPB, which she answered so

† In a footnote in *The Voice of the Silence* (p. 1), HPB defines the Sanskrit word *Siddhis* as "psychic faculties, the abnormal powers in man." "There are two kinds of *Siddhis*," she explains. "One group embraces the lower, coarse, psychic and mental energies; the other is one which exacts the highest training of Spiritual powers."

satisfactorily that the doctor said that neither Max Müller nor any other orientalist had made so clear to him the *real* meaning of the Sankhya philosophy as she had, and he thanked her very much.

Towards the end of the evening, in a pause in the conversation, he turned to HPB . . . and said that, as he had not been so fortunate as to get one of the roses that had so unexpectedly fallen, might he be favored with one "as a souvenir of this very delightful evening"? . . . His secret thought probably was, that if the first floral rain had been a trick, she would not be ready for a second, if taken unawares! "Oh yes, certainly," she said, "as many as you like." And, making another of her sweeping gestures, down fell another shower of flowers; one rose actually hitting the doctor on the top of his head.[51]

≈

The main reason for going to Benares at this time was to see Swami Dayanand Saraswati, head of the Arya Samaj, with whom the Theosophists were still associated. Damodar had arrived in Benares before HPB and Olcott and visited the Swami.

All that follows is recorded in a letter of Damodar to William Q. Judge, dated January 24, 1880. In the course of conversation, Damodar inquired whether Dayanand had ever heard of an Asiatic woman named Maji. The reason for this query was that several months previous to Damodar's visit a disciple of this woman, Pandit M. V. Pandea, had written HPB concerning her. The Swami denied any knowledge of Maji.

Now, when HPB visited the Swami, she asked the same question. Damodar was amazed to hear him say that he knew her well and would escort HPB and her party to her ashram, a mile or two distant on the banks of the Ganges. When the time came for the group to visit Maji, HPB could not go because she was ill. When Maji was informed of this, she glanced sympathetically at Olcott, because they both felt her presence. Maji then said that though she had never visited Europeans, she herself would see HPB once or twice before the Theosophists left Benares.

On the first visit, Maji inquired of HPB whether she knew that they both had the same guru. HPB asked for proofs. According to Damodar, "She said that Madam's Guru was born in Punjab but generally lives in the Southern part of India and especially in Ceylon. He is about 300 years old[52] and has a companion of about the same age, though both do not appear even forty."

When Maji departed, she promised to come again before the Theosophists left Benares. On the second visit, HPB did not join the party at first. Damodar relates to Judge that "Col. Olcott then asked Maji some questions about Madam. And Maji said that Madam was not what she seems to be. Her interior man had already been twice in a Hindu body and was now in his third."† Maji also revealed that up to now she, herself, "had never seen a European but, having got the information from her Guru, about Madam, she had come to see her. I then asked her if the real HPB was still in the body, but she refused to answer that question, and only added that she herself—Maji—was inferior to Madam."

Conversing alone with Maji, Damodar wrote to Judge:

She first tried to tempt me, trying to make me relinquish my object; but when all this failed, she told me that if I wanted to make any spiritual progress and see any of our Brothers, I must depend entirely for that upon Madam. None else was competent to take me through the right path. If I were to go alone anywhere, I may wander about here and there for years to gurus, but that will be quite use-less. . . . You will thus have seen of what a great consequence it is for me to be always with Madam. From the beginning I felt all that Maji had told me. Only two or three days after I applied for admis-sion into the Society I said to HPB, what I really felt, that I regarded her as my benefactor, revered her as my Guru and loved her more than a mother. . . . I afterwards consulted Swamiji [Dayanand] in regard to myself, [and] he, without my telling him a word of what Maji had said to me, urged me to do the very same thing, that is to say, to put my faith in HPB.[53]

Damodar later had a good occasion to refer to Maji when writing an article in *The Theosophist* (October 1883), "Can Females Become Adepts?" Among others mentioned was "a high female Adept" in Nepal and a third great female initiate, in southern India, named Ouvaiyar. Subba Row confirms this with other examples and then, going beyond adeptship, states that "there is one woman who still stands in the list of the Maha Chohans [one of the greatest sages]. . . . She has made many original discoveries."[54]

From Benares the Theosophists returned for another week with the Sinnetts, who became members of the TS on December twenty-sixth.

† "Her interior man" has been explained in the chapter "A Psycho-Physiological Change" (Part 4, ch. 8).

On the thirtieth, the party returned to Bombay, arriving on New Year's Day 1880.

In January, HPB received news from Russia that her first letter in the *Caves and Jungles of Hindostan* series had just been published and had created a sensation.[55] The series continued for a number of years and Olcott reports that, in Europe, in 1884 he met two young wealthy Russian noblemen who had been enticed to India after reading them. The stories charmed and bewildered all of Russia, they said.[56]

Chapter 5

Among the Buddhists

From the time that HPB and Olcott landed in Bombay they had been urged by the Sri Lankans to visit their country. This was not possible until May of 1880. The Theosophical party remained there for three months, the population turning out en masse to acclaim them as they went from city to city.

Surprisingly, the island people had heard of Blavatsky and Olcott before they came to India. The noted British Buddhist Dennis Lingwood tells the engaging story.

> In the 1870s the greatest orator in Sri Lanka's history, Megethuvatte Gunananda, sought in his lectures to undermine the missionary influence there. The Christians organized a huge public meeting at Panadura, determined to silence once and for all this formidable antagonist. Gunananda was challenged to meet in open debate the most learned in their ranks. Alone, but undaunted, he faced the united forces of Christian orthodoxy, and so impressive was his eloquence, so powerful his reasoning, his opponents were shamefully defeated. The repercussions of this historic debate were felt even in America, and a few years later, he received a letter from an American colonel and a Russian lady of noble birth expressing satisfaction at his victory and acquainting him with the formation of the Theosophical Society at New York in 1875. With the letter came two bulky volumes entitled *Isis Unveiled*. Gunananda immediately entered into a regular correspondence with the two foreign sympathizers, and started translating their letters and extracts from *Isis Unveiled* into Singhalese.† These translations circulated all over the island, and before long the names of H. S. Olcott and H. P. Blavatsky were repeated with wonder and delight in every Buddhist home.[57]

† *Isis Unveiled* is usually thought of as a book introducing Westerners to the Theosophical philosophy. It seems especially interesting that not only Gunananda was attracted to the volume, but Damodar also, and later the learned Brahman scholar T. Subba Row and his colleagues in Madras, who became Theosophists as a result.

It was on the occasion of their first visit to Sri Lanka that HPB and Olcott "took *pansil*" (formally became Buddhists). This action later led to some misunderstanding, although HPB carefully clarified her position:

> It is true that I regard the philosophy of Gautama Buddha as the most sublime system; the purest, and, above all, the most *logical* of all. But the system has been distorted during the centuries by the ambition and fanaticism of the priests and has become a popular religion. . . . I much prefer to hold to the *mother* source rather than to depend upon any of the numerous streams that flow from it. . . . Gautama in his reform and protest against the abuses of the wily Brahmans based himself entirely upon the esoteric meaning of the grand primitive Scriptures.[58]

During the present visit to Sri Lanka a number of branches of the TS were formed and many Singhalese joined the Theosophical Society. One of these was a sixteen-year-old boy who became the leading Buddhist missionary of our time, Anagarika Dharmapala—a towering figure in the work for the spiritual resurgence of Asia. Writing in *Asia* magazine (September 1927), he speaks of his second meeting with HPB.

> In December, 1884, Madame Blavatsky and Colonel Olcott again visited Colombo on their way to Madras. I went to my father and told him I wanted to go to Madras and work with them. At first he consented. But, on the day set for my departure, he announced solemnly that he had had a bad dream and could not allow me to go. The high priest, the other priests I had known from childhood, my grandparents, all opposed me. Though I did not know what to do, my heart was determined on the journey, which I felt would lead to a new life for me. Madame Blavatsky faced the priests and my united family. She was a wonderful woman, with energy and willpower that pushed aside all obstacles. . . . So the family were won over. . . .
>
> At one time she had told me that, since I was physically and mentally pure, I could come in contact with the Himalayan adepts. So in my nineteenth year I had decided to spend a lifetime in the study of occult science. But in Madras Madame Blavatsky opposed my plan. "It will be much wiser for you to dedicate your life to the service of humanity," she said. "And, first of all, learn Pali, the sacred language of the Buddha." At that time the Pali writings were little known.

Dharmapala furnished further details of contact with the Theosophists and HPB in a letter written in 1924, when he became a member of the Blavatsky Association in London:

I read the *Theosophist* from its first issue, and I made up my mind to dedicate my life to the study of the Arhat doctrine . . . to follow the life of self-abnegation as proclaimed by the Lord Buddha. I read HPB's article, "Chelas and Lay Chelas," in the *Theosophist,* which gave me strength to follow the higher life. The Masters about whom Sinnett wrote in the *Occult World* were to me real living beings, and I surrendered my life to them and silently pledged to lead the chela life. HPB helped me much in my effort. . . . Until the day of her departure [from Adyar] HPB took care of me. She wrote to me to follow the light that is within me. I have strictly followed her advice, and am glad to testify to her wonderful powers of mystic illumination. . . .

Love to all living beings, small and great, the desire to renounce sensual pleasures that impede the progress in the realm of spirituality and the strenuous effort to do meritorious deeds for the betterment of humanity, forgetting self, have been to me a kind of spiritual pabulum which I have partaken since I came in touch with the wonderful personality of HPB.[59]

Chapter 6

Simla—Summer Capital of the British Raj

O n several occasions during the next few years, HPB was in Simla visiting the Sinnetts or the Humes. Edward Buck, in *Simla, Past and Present,* asserts that Hume, former Secretary to the Government and later the founder of the Indian National Congress, was "a remarkable character of exceptional ability and brainpower," although "not free from the eccentricity which sometimes accompanies genius." Hume's home, Rothney Castle, high up on Jakko Hill, was one of the two finest dwellings in Simla and could be reached only by a troublesome climb that was worth making, as it "commanded an uninterrupted view of the snowy peaks of Tibet." Hume was a noted ornithologist, says Buck: "Many birds new to science were discovered by himself or by his agents. The specimens were all brought to 'Rothney Castle' and arranged there in classified order in cabinets which lined the walls of the room utilized as a museum." However, Buck notes, when Hume became a Theosophist "telegrams were sent to the collectors to stop work and shoot no more birds . . . one of the tenets of that creed being to take no life. . . ."[60]

Hume became president of the Eclectic Theosophical Society at Simla. In reply to a letter inquiring about the existence of the theosophical adepts and what good they were doing, he wrote:

That the Brothers exist I now know, but the proofs that I have had have been purely subjective and therefore useless to any but myself—unless indeed you consider it a proof of their existence that I here, at Simla, receive letters from one of them, my immediate teacher, dropped upon my table, I, living alone in my house and Madame Blavatsky, Col. Olcott and all their chelas, etc., being thousands of miles distant. . . .

As to what good the Brothers have done either to myself or others . . . if you consider the establishment of the Theosophical Society a good thing, then this is one *at any rate of the good things done by the Brothers for* others, *and if you think it a good thing for me that I have turned away*

*altogether from all worldly objects of desire and am devoting myself entirely
to trying to do good for others, then I suppose we may say this is a good thing
which the Brothers have helped to do for me.*[61]

When London's *Saturday Review* described HPB as "an unscrupu-
lous adventuress," Hume wrote, in a lengthy letter in her defense that
the periodical refused to print:

Can you rightly call people adventurers who not only make no
money out of the cause they espouse, but, on the contrary, spend on
it every farthing that they can spare from their private means? If not,
then assuredly Colonel Olcott and Madame Blavatsky are not
adventurers, for to my certain knowledge they have spent on the
Theosophical Society over £2,000 more than its total receipts. The
accounts have been regularly audited, printed and published, so that
any one may satisfy themselves on this head.[62]

HPB first visited Simla in the fall of 1880, when she spent six weeks
with the Sinnetts in their home, Brightland. Much of the phenomena
credited to her at this time is described by Sinnett in his first book, *The
Occult World,* which created a great stir in England. The descriptions of
two of the phenomena that follow were recorded by Olcott on October fourth, the day after their occurrence. The report was then mailed
to Damodar in Bombay, who privately circulated it among the workers
there. Somehow, *The Times of India* secured a copy and published it, to
the great discomfiture of the parties involved:

Great day yesterday for Madame's phenomena. In the morning she,
with Mr. and Mrs. Sinnett, Major Henderson, Mr. Syed Mahmood
(District Judge, Rai Bareilly), Mrs. Reed of Ajmere, and myself
went on a picnic [in the woods near Brightland, to which they
walked three or four miles]. Although she [HPB] had never been at
Simla before, she directed us where to go, describing a certain small
mill which the Sinnetts, Major Henderson, and even the jampanis
(palkiwallahs) affirmed, did not exist. She also mentioned a small
Tibetan temple as being near it. We reached the spot she had
described and found the mill—at about 10 A.M.; and sat in the shade
and had the servants spread a collation. Mr. Mahmood had joined
our party after the baskets were packed and so when we wanted to
have tea we found we were one cup and saucer short. Somebody
asked Madame Blavatsky to produce one by magic. She consented;
and, looking about the ground here and there, finally called Major

Henderson to bring a knife and dig in a spot she pointed to. He found the ground hard and full of small roots of a young cedar tree nearby. These he cut through and pulled up to a depth of say six inches, when something white was seen in the black soil; it was dug out, and lo! a cup decorated in green and gold, exactly matching the others Mrs. Sinnett's servants had brought. Madame told the Major to dig more; he did so; and at last found a saucer to match the cup! They were embedded in the ground like stones naturally there, and the cedar roots grew all around them like a network, and one root as large as your little finger had to be cut away to get at the saucer.

Then Major Henderson asked her to explain the science of it, but she said she could not, as he was not yet a Theosophist. He said he meant to be one. "When?" said she. "Tomorrow" he replied. Mrs. Sinnett said "Why not today?" "So I will," said the Major, "come Madame produce me a diploma on the spot!" "If I do, will you really join us" "I will." "Then you shall have it." She looked here and there and walked about near us a few moments, then sat down on the edge of a little bank. "If you want the diploma, you must hunt for it yourself; the 'Brother' who is helping me says it is rolled up, tied with about 50 feet of blue twine and covered with creeping vines," she said to the Major. The party all went to search and presently Major Henderson, raising the low branches of a deodar shrub and parting the grass said "I have it!" He really had— one of our diplomas filled out to Major Philip D. Henderson as Corresponding Fellow, and an official letter in my headquarter's letter paper, WRITTEN IN MY OWN HANDWRITING and signed "Faithfully yours—(the name in Tibetan characters) for H. S. Olcott, President of the Theosophical Society"! Fancy my astonishment! The letter was dated October 2/3—that is at the point (or night) between the two days and it referred to a conversation that had taken place between Major Henderson and Madame Blavatsky on the preceding evening.[63]

In *Old Diary Leaves,* Olcott relates:

To complete this part of my narrative, I will state that Mrs. Sinnett and I, reaching the house first, on the return of our party, went straight to the butler's pantry and found the three other cups of the nine which she had left of the original dozen, put away on an upper shelf with their handles broken, and otherwise dilapidated. The seventh cup produced at the picnic had, therefore, not formed part of her broken set.[64]

There were now thirteen cups, ten intact and three broken. The duplicate one and its saucer still exist, and were on display in New York City with other HPB momentos at the Statler Hilton Hotel in November 1975, when the hundredth anniversary of the founding of the Theosophical Society was celebrated in the place of its birth.

In *The Occult World*, Sinnett discusses a possible alternate explanation to the cup and saucer phenomena:

> If they were not deposited by occult agency, they must have been buried beforehand. Now, I have described the character of the ground from which they were dug up; assuredly that had been undisturbed for years by the character of the vegetation upon it. But it may be urged that from some other part of the sloping ground a sort of tunnel may have been excavated in the first instance through which the cup and saucer could have been thrust into the place where they were found. Now this theory is barely tenable as regards its physical possibility. If the tunnel had been big enough for the purpose it would have left traces which were not perceptible on the ground—which were not even discoverable when the ground was searched shortly afterwards with a view to that hypothesis. But the truth is that the theory of previous burial is morally untenable in view of the fact that the demand for the cup and saucer—of all the myriad things that might have been asked for—could never have been foreseen. It arose out of circumstances themselves the sport of the moment. If no extra person had joined us at the last moment the number of cups and saucers packed up by the servants would have been sufficient for our needs, and no attention would have been drawn to them. [Furthermore] it was by the servants, without the knowledge of any guests, that the cups taken were chosen from others that might just as easily have been taken.[65]

As to the official letter accompanying Major Henderson's diploma, and which so amazed Olcott when he saw his own handwriting replicated, HPB was once asked in India how such precipitations were possible. This was in 1882, when she visited Baroda with Olcott. The questioners were two high officials there, Judge Gadgil and a Mr. Kirtane.

Reports Olcott:

> She explained that inasmuch as the images of all objects and incidents are stored in the astral light, it did not require that she should have seen the person or known the writing, the image of which she

wished to precipitate; she had only to be put on the trace and could find and see them for herself and then objectivate them. They urgently begged her to do the thing for them. "Well, then," she finally said, "tell me the name of some man or woman most unfriendly to the Theosophical Society, one whom neither Olcott nor I could have ever [personally] known." At once, they mentioned Mr. . . . , the British resident, who held us and our Society in especial hatred, who never missed the chance of saying unkind things of us. . . .

[Then] taking a sheet of paper from the table, [she] told the gentlemen to mark it for identification. Receiving it back, she said: "Now turn me in the direction of his residence." They did so. She then laid the paper between her palms (held horizontally), remained quiet a moment, then held it toward us and went and sat down. Cries of amazement broke from the two Durbaris on seeing on the just before clean sheet of paper, a letter addressed to me in the handwriting and bearing the signature of the then British Resident at that Court. It was a most peculiar, small calligraphy, and the signature more like a tiny tangle of twine than a man's name. . . .

I thought [Gadgil and Kirtane] would explode with laughter when they read the contents of the note. It was addressed to "My dear Colonel Olcott," begged my pardon for the malicious things he had said against us, asked me to enter him as a subscriber to our "world renowned magazine, the *Theosophist*," and said he wished to become a member of the Theosophical Society: it was signed "Yours sincerely" and with his name. She had never seen a line of the gentleman's writing nor his signature, never met him in the flesh, and the note was precipitated on that sheet of paper held between her hands, as she stood in the middle of the room, in broad daylight, with us three witnesses looking on.[66]

During the Simla visit, Olcott found it opportune to open correspondence with the Viceroy's government, requesting a withdrawal of the secret service agents who dogged their every step. Not only did the government agree to do this, but taking advantage of HPB's presence, asked her to translate some Russian documents and letters into English.[67]

HPB's life in Simla at this time was a continuous round of visits, picnics, dining out, and being lionized generally. The attraction, of course, was the hope of witnessing the display of her occult powers, and few went away disappointed.

Chapter 7

What of Phenomena?

Of all the phenomena produced by HPB during the Simla visit, the one that outweighed all others in Sinnett's estimation was the opening up of correspondence between himself and the Himalayan adepts. Thirteen hundred pages of these letters now repose in the rare manuscript department of the British Library. In *The Occult World,* Sinnett reports how the correspondence was initiated:

> One day I asked Madame Blavatsky whether if I wrote a letter to one of the Brothers explaining my views, she could get it delivered for me. I hardly thought this was probable, as I knew how very unapproachable the Brothers generally are; but as she said that at any rate she would try, I wrote a letter, addressing it "to the Unknown Brother," and gave it to her to see if any result would ensue. . . . The idea I had specially in my mind was that of all test phenomena one could wish for, the best would be the production in our presence in India of a copy of the London *Times* of that day's date. . . .
>
> A day or two elapsed before I heard anything of the fate of my letter, but Madame Blavatsky then informed me that I was to have an answer. I afterwards learned that she had not been able at first to find a Brother willing to receive the communication.[68] Those whom she first applied to declined to be troubled with the matter. At last her psychological telegraph brought her a favorable answer from one of the Brothers with whom she had not for some time been in communication. He would take the letter and reply to it.[69]

This Brother was the Master KH. He replied:

> *Precisely because the test of the London newspaper would close the mouths of skeptics—it is unthinkable. . . . Were we to accede to your desires know you really what consequences would follow in the trail of success? The inexorable shadow which follows all human innovations moves on, yet few are they who are ever conscious of its approach and dangers. What are they to expect, they who would offer the world an innovation which, owing to hu-*

man ignorance, if believed in, will surely be attributed to those dark agencies two-thirds of humanity believe in and dread as yet? You say—half London would be converted if you could deliver them a Pioneer *on its day of publication. I beg to say that if the people believed the thing true they would kill you before you could make the round of Hyde Park; if it were not believed true, the least that could happen would be the loss of your reputation and good name—for propagating such ideas. . . .*

And without a thorough knowledge of Akas[a], its combinations and properties, how can Science hope to account for such phenomena? We doubt not but the men of your science are open to conviction; yet facts must be first demonstrated to them, they must first have become their own property, have proved amenable to their own modes of investigation, before you find them ready to admit them as facts. *Test after test would be required and would have to be furnished; every subsequent phenomenon expected to be more marvelous than the preceding one. Your daily remark is, that one cannot be expected to believe unless he becomes an eye-witness. Would the lifetime of a man suffice to satisfy the whole world of skeptics? . . .*

In common with many, you blame us for our great secrecy. Yet we know something of human nature, for the experience of long centuries—aye, ages—has taught us. . . . The world's prejudices have to be conquered step by step, not at a rush. As hoary antiquity had more than one Socrates so the dim future will give birth to more than one martyr. . . . And we have but to bear in mind the recent persecutions of mediums in England, the burning of supposed witches and sorcerers in South America, Russia and the frontiers of Spain to assure ourselves that the only salvation of the genuine proficients in occult sciences lies in the skepticism of the public: the charlatans and the jugglers are the natural shields of the "adepts." The public safety is only ensured by our keeping secret the terrible weapons which might otherwise be used against it, and which, as you have been told, became deadly in the hands of the wicked and selfish.[70]

In reply, Hume asked KH, "[W]hat good, then, is to be attained for my fellows and myself by these occult sciences?" The answer was:

When the natives see that an interest is taken by the English, and even by some high officials in India, in their ancestral science and philosophies, they will themselves take openly to their study. And when they come to realize that the old "divine" phenomena were not miracles, but scientific effects, superstition will abate. Thus, the greatest evil that now oppresses and retards the revival of Indian civilization will in time disappear.[71]

Good effects would also accrue among open-minded investigators in the West. Thus, when a Hindu correspondent to *The Theosophist* asserted that yogic powers are only of secondary importance, HPB answered: "For phenomenalistic purposes, yes—most assuredly. But our Indian brother must remember that the West knows nothing of the existence of such a power in man; and until it does know it there can be no truly scientific researches, especially in the department of Psychology."[72] It is important, she also argued, to demonstrate that occult phenomena can be produced "without dark rooms, spirits, mediums, or any of the usual paraphernalia."[73]

Besides, as HPB wrote Professor Corson in early 1875, if it appeared that Theosophists propounded "dogmas unsupported by vital proof . . . we should soon come into the present extremity of the denominational church." She continued:

> He who attains to the sublime heights of Wisdom and Intuition no more requires the buoyant support of these phenomena, than does the eaglet need to rest on its mother's back after his pinions are fairly spread; but the eagles of mind are few, and the twittering sparrows multitudinous, and it is not for those who can mount above the clouds of doubt to despise the needs of their weaker fellows . . . [The miracles of Jesus] heralded the birth of the Christian religion, clustered about its infancy, comforted, consoled, and armed its patristic propagandists. . . .[74]

Countess Wachtmeister relates that "many people have remarked to me, at different times, how foolish it was that 'phenomena' should ever have been connected with the Theosophical Society or that HPB should ever have wasted her time over such trivialities." To these remarks, she says:

> HPB has invariably given the same answer; namely, that at the time when the Theosophical Society was formed it was necessary to draw the attention of the public to the fact, and that phenomena served this object more effectually than anything else could have done. Had HPB given herself out in the first instance as simply a teacher of philosophy, very few students would have been drawn to her side. . . . But having once introduced this element of the marvelous, it was difficult to get rid of it when it had served its turn. All came eager to have their sense of wonder gratified, and, when disappointed, went away wrathful and indignant.[75]

That this was a well-understood, calculated risk known in advance seems quite evident. One critic contends, however, that after HPB's "supposed miracles had been exposed, largely thanks to the Society for Psychical Research, it was only then Blavatsky spoke contemptuously of them."[76] This is easy to refute simply by quoting statements made by Blavatsky and her teachers long before the SPR investigation, as will be seen.

From KH's first letter to Sinnett the strength of the latter's involvement in psychical research is apparent. HPB mentions in a letter written from Simla to Mrs. Hollis Billings (October 2, 1881) that Sinnett is "always craving for phenomena."[77] Mahatma M wrote him frankly in February 1882:

> *Try to break thro' that great* maya *against which occult students, the world over, having always been warned by their teachers—the hankering after phenomena. Like the thirst for drink and opium, it grows with gratification. The Spiritualists are drunken with it; they are thaumaturgic sots. If you cannot be happy without phenomena you will never learn our philosophy . . . but choose wisdom [and] all other things will be added unto it—in time. . . . Let us talk like sensible men. Why should we play with Jack-in-the-box; are not* our *beards grown?[78]*

In a letter to a Theosophist, HPB takes a similar tone:

> *Are you children, that you want marvels? Have you so little faith as to need constant stimulus, as a dying fire needs fuel! . . . Would you let the nucleus of a splendid Society die under your hands like a sick man under the hands of a quack? . . . You should never forget what a solemn thing it is for us to exert our powers and raise the dread sentinels that lie at the threshold. They cannot hurt us, but they can avenge themselves by precipitating themselves upon the unprotected neophyte. You are all like so many children playing with fire because it is pretty, when you ought to be men studying philosophy for its own sake. (The Path, August 1892, 161.)*

HPB herself wrote Sinnett (June 20, 1882) concerning his "obstinate, determined plan of taking the public in general and the Anglo-Indians in particular into the confidence of every phenomenon that takes place":

> *I most decidedly, emphatically and uncompromisingly kick against your eternal desire to do everything I do (in the way of stupid phenomena) with an eye to public enlightenment upon the subject. I DO NOT CARE ABOUT PUBLIC OPINION. I despise thoroughly and with all my heart Mrs. Grundy,[†] and do not care a snap of my finger whether the Wm. Beresfords and the Hon. "what d'ye call them" think well or bad of me as regards the*

---

† Mrs. Grundy was a character in Thomas Morton's play *Speed the Plough* (1798) and became a synonym for society in its imperious censorship of out-of-the-ordinary personal conduct.

phenomena produced. I refuse to proselytise them at the expense of the little self-respect and dignity that my duty to those beyond, and to the Cause have left in me. I rather not convert them, wherever the Brothers' names are mixed up with a phenomenon. Their names have been sufficiently dragged in the mud; they have been misused and blasphemed against by all the penny-a-liners of India. Nowadays people call their dogs and cats by the name of "Koot-hoomi". . . .[79]

In KH's second letter to Sinnett he endeavored to set his correspondent straight on the matter of priorities: ". . . you have ever discussed but to put down the idea of a universal Brotherhood, questioned its usefulness, and advised to remodel the TS on the principle of a college for the special study of occultism. This, my respected and esteemed friend and Brother—will never do!"[80] On this point the Maha Chohan,[81] the teacher of KH and M, was even stronger when addressing Hume and Sinnett:

Shall we devote ourselves to teaching a few Europeans, fed on the fat of the land, many of them loaded with the gifts of blind fortune, the rationale of bell-ringing, cup-growing, of the spiritual telephone and astral body formations, and leave the teeming millions of the ignorant, of the poor and despised, the lowly and the oppressed, to take care of themselves and of their hereafter as best they know how? Never. Rather perish the TS with both its hapless founders than that we should permit it to become no better than an academy of magic, a hall of occultism. . . . [Are we] expected to allow the TS to drop its noble title, that of Brotherhood of Humanity, to become a simple school of psychology? No, no, good brothers, you have been laboring under the mistake too long already.[82]

Our discussion is not complete without considering the place psychic powers have in the development of the human being. In a letter addressed by HPB to the 1891 annual convention of American Theosophists, she refers to the Americans as the forerunners of a coming new race:

Psychism, with all its allurements and all its dangers, is necessarily developing among you, and you must beware lest the Psychic outruns the manasic [mental] and Spiritual development. Psychic capacities held perfectly under control, checked and directed by the manasic [mind] principle, are valuable aids in development. But these capacities running riot, controlling instead of being controlled, using instead of being used, lead the student into the most dangerous delusions and the certainty of moral destruction.[83]

In what way are psychic powers valuable aids in development? Through their natural unfoldment and resulting expansion of consciousness, says HPB, "a person becomes gradually one with the UNIVERSAL ALL."[84] She also indicates that with "new senses and new powers . . . infinitely more good can be done than without them."[85] Thus, when Buddha attained enlightenment and commenced his work to redeem humanity, he is said to have received a number of supernormal gifts. Among these were the divine ear, or clairaudience; the divine eye, or a highly developed form of clairvoyance; telepathy, or the knowledge of the minds of other human beings; and, lastly, remembrance of former births.[86] He thereby could unerringly perceive the psychological and spiritual needs of each person he met, and of the human race as a whole.

Were these powers really *gifts?* "In days of old," answers Blavatsky, "men like Krishna, Gautama Buddha, Jesus, Paul, Apollonius of Tyana, Plotinus, Porphyry, and the like of them . . . by struggling their whole lives in purity, study, and self-sacrifice, through trials, privations, and self-discipline, attained divine illumination and seemingly superhuman powers."[87] Quite a contrast to the lack of training in these respects of modern mediums and channelers!

Arduous Journeys

A fter the visit to Simla in the fall of 1880, Blavatsky and Olcott traveled to a number of northern towns and cities, where the colonel lectured on Theosophy. Meanwhile the Sinnetts had returned home to Allahabad, and the founders joined them in early December and again at Christmas. During these journeys HPB contracted Punjab fever, and also Dengue fever, said to be more excruciating than the tortures of the Inquisition. The new year brought the founders back to Bombay. During their absence the TS headquarters had been moved to a suburb, Breach Candy. Their bungalow, called Crow's Nest [see Centerfold, photograph #29], was spacious, offering expansive views of sea and land, and afforded more peace than they had had in the thickly settled native quarters of the city, where they were constantly plagued by visitors.[88]

In March, Sinnett and his wife went to England for a holiday. There he completed *The Occult World,* which was published in June. Returning to India in July, he received a long letter from KH. It was the beginning of a lengthy correspondence on philosophical, scientific, and metaphysical subjects that ultimately enabled him to write *Esoteric Buddhism.*

It is not generally known that some of the metaphysical teachings given Sinnett did not commence with the letters received from KH, but came from HPB herself. In *The Early Days of Theosophy in Europe,* Sinnett mentions this instruction and gives examples of what she taught Hume and himself at Simla in the summer of 1881.[89] What is particularly interesting is that his notebook containing this and much more is reproduced in the appendix to *The Letters of H. P. Blavatsky to A. P. Sinnett,*[90] but the editor, apparently unaware that the teachings therein were given personally by HPB, attributed them directly to the Masters. Here the sevenfold constitution of man is delineated for the first time and in listing its divisions, HPB uses Tibetan and Sanskrit terminology as well as English equivalents. Sinnett relates that when

HPB taught Hume and himself, she was a stickler as to Tibetan words being correctly pronounced.

When *Esoteric Buddhism* was published, it opened a new world of ideas on human and cosmic evolution. A witness in London to this period, Francesca Arundale, reports that when the book was published, "It took the theological and scientific world by storm." She added: "the effect of *Esoteric Buddhism* and the later theosophical teachings on the theological and literary press can hardly be realized at the present day. Karma and Reincarnation, unknown terms almost before, were often spoken about in sermons and discourses by many leaders in the church. The newspapers were full of allusions critical or condemnatory of the new ideas, but these ideas had come to stay, and the seed thus sown has borne ample fruit."[91]

In KH's metaphysical correspondence with Sinnett, the latter was cautioned:

> *Knowledge can only be communicated gradually; and some of the highest secrets—if actually formulated even in your well prepared ear—might sound to you as insane gibberish. . . . The occult science is not one in which secrets can be communicated of a sudden, by a written or even verbal communication. If so, all the "Brothers" would have to do, would be to publish a* Handbook *of the art which might be taught in schools as grammar is. It is the common mistake of people that we willingly wrap ourselves and our powers in mystery—that we wish to keep our knowledge to ourselves, and of our own will refuse— "wantonly and deliberately" to communicate it. The truth is that till the neophyte attains to the condition necessary for that degree of Illumination to which, and for which, he is entitled and fitted, most if not all of the secrets are* incommunicable. *The receptivity must be equal to the desire to instruct. The illumination* must come from within.[92]

In the late summer and early fall of 1881, HPB was at Simla with the Humes, at Rothney Castle, for several months, and around the end of October she went to Lahore, where it is said she saw Master M. Thereafter she began an extensive tour of northern India at the orders of her teacher. As Olcott at this time was in Sri Lanka, this was the first time HPB was on her own in visiting towns and establishing TS lodges.

After further travels, HPB returned to the Bombay headquarters at the end of November. On March 31, 1882, she left for Allahabad, after which she went to Calcutta. Here she was invited to stay at the maharajah's palace, where, that very evening, the Bengal Theosophical Society was organized. Olcott had preceded HPB to Calcutta and had lectured the day before on "Theosophy, the Scientific Basis of Religion."

On April nineteenth Blavatsky and Olcott sailed for Madras, a trip that led to important developments since Madras was soon to become the headquarters of the TS. On this visit the Madras TS was founded and T. Subba Row met HPB for the first time.

To get some idea how arduous it was traveling around India to form branches of the TS, it may be instructive to focus on a trip in May from Nellore to Guntur. HPB's party had to first take a houseboat on the Buckingham Canal, then travel fifty-five miles along terrain so dangerous that Blavatsky and Olcott had to be carried in palanquins† through cobra-infested regions. Deep streams were forded with the aid of six coolies precariously balancing each of the palanquins on poles resting on the natives' heads in order to keep the occupants dry. Arriving at Guntur, the entire population—save children and the infirm—greeted the travelers. When retracing their way to Buckingham Canal and Nellore, they traveled seventy-eight miles in carriages drawn by bullocks on rough, bumpy roads to the nearest railway station, only to find that no train to Madras—their next destination—was expected for twelve hours.[93]

The members of the new Madras TS urged the founders to move their headquarters from Bombay to their city. This was eventually decided upon and property was purchased in the suburb of Adyar on November 17, 1882, exactly seven years after the founding of the TS in New York on November 17, 1875. Prior to moving to Madras, HPB became very ill in Bombay with Bright's disease. To her relatives she wrote:

My blood is transformed into water; it oozes out and forms bags a la kangaroo. All this is the result of, primo, *Bombay heat and humidity; and* secundo, *my constant irritations, disturbances, and troubles. I have become so nervous that the light step of Babula's naked feet causes palpitation of the heart. I have forced [Dr.] Dudley to acknowledge that I may die any moment as a result of any excitement; without such, I may last another year or two. Is this possible with the kind of life I live? . . . M wants me to [go away] at the end of September . . . where to I do not know! Probably somewhere in the Himalayas.*[94]

When well enough to travel, she left Bombay for Sikkim. In a letter to Prince Dondoukov in Russia she furnishes details:

† Covered or boxlike litters borne by means of poles resting on men's shoulders.

Sikkim, Ghum,
October 1, [1882]
13,000 feet under the clouds

. . . *As you see, . . . I am in the solitude of Ghum.*† *And what is Ghum? It is a mountain in Sikkim and a monastery where Lamas stay on their way to Tibet. . . . The doctors sent me away from Bombay, for I was dying at the beginning of September of a liver and kidney disease, and I went to the mountains. Passing through Benares I took your bronze things and having had them packed, sent the box to Allahabad. Then I went via Calcutta and Chandernagore to Cooch-Behar (the Raja is a Theosophist). There I was ill of fever for three days, because of the sudden change—a terrible heat succeeded by cold, rain and fog. A dozen Babu-Theosophists from Calcutta accompanied me, together with three Buddhists from Ceylon and Burma. All this crowd of naked feet and bare chests coming from the tropical valleys of Hindostan fell ill with the cold. I alone, being Russian, pulled myself together and got well. But instead of fifteen people, only the four Buddhist-Theosophists and one from Nepal followed me to Sikkim—all the others were laid up. As you know, Sikkim is an independent state between Tibet, Cooch-Behar and Bhutan. . . . I had asked the Foreign Office for a pass to Sikkim. It was refused. Grant, the secretary, writes: "We have no objection to your going to Tibet and crossing the British territory thither, but beyond our territory we do not answer for your safety. . . ." I then said: "You have not given me a pass—well, to the devil with you. I will go just the same."*

It was too late to go to Shigatse, the capital of the Tashi Lama, so I decided to go to the Lamasery four days from Darjeeling (a second Simla), situated on the border of Tibet itself. I went there on foot, because it is impossible to go in a carriage, unless it be astride a yak, and we climbed and crawled not four but eight whole days. At times they carried me in a "dandy," a kind of palanquin armchair, and several times nearly dumped me into the abyss; but we arrived all the same, even though not into Tibet proper, but on its border.

But here comes the funny part. The frontier is a fast-flowing stream with a swinging bamboo bridge; on the other side, military barracks with frontier guards, a Lamasery and a village. It is a narrow gorge where hardly ten men would pass side to side. We found on the Bhutan side two Englishmen, disguised as beggar-monks. I immediately recognized them and a few Hindu natives of the Survey Department—quite a caravan. We learnt that for a

---

† "Not in Sikkim, but in British India, the station before Darjeeling on the hill train. There is a Tibetan monastery at Ghum, and tourists from Darjeeling now visit the monastery." (*H.P.B. Speaks* 2:102 fn.)

week they had been waiting in vain to be allowed to pass over to the other side. . . .

Somebody said to me: "It is useless to have come, they will not let you pass." "We will see," I replied. I sent my Burmese Theosophist with a letter from Pha Luen Ugan Yatcha, the Lama of the Monastery of Pamionchi, addressed to the Superior of the Lamasery in front of us (called Pe-ma-in), and they let him pass. In an hour the chief Lama himself, looking as a dried up skeleton, came to me and Gelungs brought me tea with butter and all kinds of delicacies as a present. After this drink and warm reception, they led me across the bridge to their home with honors, together with the three Singhalese; but the Englishmen had to remain where they were! I was only afraid they would not let me go back. I stayed there three days, lived in a small house at the foot of the walls of the monastery and talked day and night with the Gelungs and the Superior (an incarnation of Sakya-Buddha); I spent hours in their library where no woman is allowed to enter—a touching testimony to my beauty and its perfect harmlessness, and the Superior pub-licly recognized in me a feminine incarnation of one of the Bodhisattvas, of which I am very proud. Then came a letter from Koot Hoomi, and the guides carried me back by another road to the bridge . . . and took me to Sikkim and across it, where I find myself at present, staying in another Lamasery, 23 miles from Darjeeling.[95]

At one point in her travels in Sikkim, HPB stayed at the ashram of her teachers. When she returned to Darjeeling—where for health reasons she was advised to stay two months—she wrote Sinnett on October ninth:

Oh the blessed, blessed two days! It was like the old times . . . the same kind of wooden hut, a box divided into three compartments for rooms, and standing in a jungle on four pelican's legs; the same yellow chelas gliding noiselessly; the same eternal "gul-gul-gul" sound of my Boss' inextinguish-able chelum pipe; the old familiar sweet voice of your KH (whose voice is still sweeter and face still thinner and more transparent); the same entourage for furniture—skins, and yak-tail stuffed pillows and dishes for salt, tea, etc. Well, when I went to Darjeeling sent away by them— "out of reach of the chelas, who might fall in love with my beauty" said my polite boss—on the following day I received the note I enclose from the Deputy Commissioner warning me not to go to Tibet!! He locked the stable door after the horse had been already out.[96]

Darjeeling, a British hill station, was a summer residence for civil servants and a resort town for their families. One of the attractions was the magnificent view afforded of the Himalayan mountains to the north some forty miles away. While there, HPB lived with some Theosophists who had recently arrived from the south. One of these, Mohini Chatterjee, a lawyer from Calcutta and a descendant of the Great Hindu reformer Raja Rammohun Roy, was one of the most brilliant of the early Theosophists in India. In an article, "The Himalayan Brothers—Do They Exist?" (*The Theosophist,* December 1883, 83–85), Mohini records his experiences at this time:

> During my visit to Darjeeling I lived in the same house with several theosophists . . . most of them as doubtful with regard to the Himalayan Mahatmas as I was myself at that time. I [had already] met at Darjeeling persons who claimed to be chelas of the Himalayan Brothers and to have seen and lived with them for years. They laughed at our perplexity. One of them showed us an admirably executed portrait of a man who appeared to be an eminently holy person, and who, I was told, was the Mahatma Koothoomi (now my revered master) to whom Mr. Sinnett's *Occult World* is dedicated.
>
> A few days after my arrival, a Tibetan pedlar of the name of Sundook accidently came to our house to sell his things. Sundook was for years well known in Darjeeling and the neighborhood as an itinerant trader in Tibetan knick-knacks, who visited the country every year in the exercise of his profession. He came to the house several times during our stay there, and seemed to us, from his simplicity, dignity of bearing and pleasant manners, to be one of Nature's own gentlemen. No man could discover in him any trait of character even remotely allied to the uncivilized savages, as the Tibetans are held in the estimation of Europeans.

As HPB was away from Darjeeling at this time, it seemed an excellent opportunity to obtain independent evidence through Sundook as to the possible existence of mahatmas in Tibet. Mohini continues:

> On the first day we put him some general questions about Tibet and the Gelugpa sect, to which he said he belonged, and his answers corroborated the statements of Bogle, Turnour, and other travelers. On the second day we asked him if he had heard of any persons in Tibet who possessed extraordinary powers besides the great lamas. He said there were such men. That they were not regular lamas but far higher than they, generally lived in the mountains, beyond Tchigatze and also near the city of Lhasa. These men, he said, produce many and very wonderful phenomena or "miracles," and some of their *chelas,* or lotoos, as they are called in Tibet, cure the sick by

giving them to eat the rice which they crush out of the paddy with their own hands, etc.

Then one of us had a glorious idea. Without saying one word, the above-mentioned portrait of the Mahatma KH was shown to him. He looked at it for a few seconds, and then as though suddenly recognizing it, he made a profound reverence to the portrait, and said it was the likeness of a Chohan (Mahatma) whom he had seen. . . .

He said he had seen the Mahatma in question, accompanied by a numerous body of gylungs, about that time of the previous year (beginning of October 1881) at a place called Giansi, two days' journey southward of Tchigatze, and whither the narrator had gone to make purchases for his trade. On being asked the name of the Mahatma, he said to our unbounded surprise, "*They* are called Koothum-pa." Being cross-examined and asked what he meant by "they," and whether he was naming one man or many, he replied that the Koothum-pas were many, but there was only one man or chief over them of that name; the disciples being always called after the names of their guru. Hence the name of the latter being Koot-hum, that of his disciples was "Koot-hum-pa." Light was shed upon this explanation by a Tibetan dictionary, where we found the word "pa" means "man"; "Bod-pa" is a "man of Bod or Tibet," etc. Similarly Koothum-pa means man or disciple of Koothoom or Koothoomi.

On being told [by the Theosophists] that people in India refused to believe that there were such men as the "Brothers" in Tibet, Sundook offered to take any voluntary witness to that country and convince us through him as to the genuineness of their existence. . . .

On being shown a peculiar rosary of beads belonging to Madame Blavatsky, the pedlar said that such things could only be received by those to whom the Tesschu [or Panchen] Lama presented them, as they could be got for no amount of money elsewhere.[97]

The question has been asked why is it that when Tibet was opened up to the Chinese who invaded the country in 1950, the Masters were nowhere to be found. Even in the 1920s, Alexandra David-Neel reported that she never saw these Hindu mahatmas during her travels there.

Nicholas Roerich, who also traveled in Tibet in the 1920s, did not find them either, though he did meet a wandering lama who told him many things about the real Tibet. One day Roerich asked, "Lama, have you met Azaras and Kuthumpas?"

The lama replied:

Many of our people during their lives have encountered the Azaras and Kuthumpas and the snow people who serve them. Only recently have the Azaras ceased to be seen in cities. They are all gathered in the mountains. Very tall, with long hair and beards, they appear outwardly like Hindus. . . .

The Kuthumpas are no longer seen now. Previously they appeared quite openly in the Tsang district [Shigatse] and at Manasarowar, when the pilgrims went to holy Kailasa. Even the snow people are rarely seen now. The ordinary person, in his ignorance, mistakes them for apparitions. There are profound reasons why, just now, the Great Ones do not appear so openly. My old teacher told me much of the wisdom of the Azaras. We know several places where these Great Ones dwelt, but for the moment these places are deserted. Some great reason, great mystery.

Roerich then asked, "Lama, then it is true that the Ashrams have been moved from the vicinity of Shigatse?"

"This mystery must not be uttered," the lama responded. "I already said that the Azaras may no longer be found in Tsang."

It became clear from the lama's remarks that Tibet was now in a descending cycle. He states: "Many lamas wear the lamaistic garment, but their inner life is far worse than that of a layman. Often among many thousands of lamas, you can find only a few isolated individuals, with whom you can converse about exalted matters and expect a worthy response. But is it not thus in your own religion?"[98]

In the middle of November, after returning to Darjeeling, HPB left for Allahabad to stay with the Sinnetts and then returned to Bombay. Soon thereafter, however, she made Madras her permanent residence.

Chapter 9

Move to Madras

Although most of the year Madras is insufferably hot and humid, in December it is at its best. It was on December 19, in 1882 that Blavatsky and Olcott arrived at the new Theosophical Society headquarters. HPB wrote Nadya in Russia:

It is just wonderful here. What air! What nights! And what marvelous quiet! There is none of the city bustle and street yells. I am sitting down and writing, and gaze over the ocean, sparkling and shoreless, as if alive. . . . When it is quiet and gentle, there is no more enchanting beauty in the world, especially on a moonlit night. Against the deep dark-blue sky, the moon appears here to be twice its size and ten times brighter than your European little mother-of-pearl ball.[99]

13. *William Quan Judge's drawing of the Theosophical Society's headquarters in 1884, Adyar.* (The Path, *June 1892, 75*)

During his visit in 1884,[100] Judge drew the above picture of the TS headquarters at Adyar in Madras when HPB lived there. Her bedroom is on the second floor. Later the building was altered to accommodate the TS library until it had a building of its own.

Today the Adyar TS is especially noted for this library. HPB referred to it in her article "Recent Progress in Theosophy" (*North American Review,* August 1890):

> It is our Adyar Library, founded by the loving labor of our president, Colonel H. S. Olcott, which is the crown and glory of the Theosophical Society. Though only three years old, it has already acquired a large collection of Oriental works of the greatest value— 3,046 volumes—besides over 2,000 works in European languages, and a number of rare palm-leaf manuscripts.

Almost one hundred years later, in 1982, Professor Harold Coward, head of the department of religious studies at the University of Calgary, in Canada, visited the library and reported that it then contained "a large and well-organized collection of some 17,300 manuscripts and 160,000 books," and the distinguished Harvard Sanskritist, Daniel Ingalls, refers to the library as "one of the chief repositories of Sanskrit manuscripts in the world."[101] Olcott's aim was "a revival of the original Hindu and Buddhist traditions in India and Ceylon. . . . In this way importance was given to Buddhist and Hindu texts at a time when traditional material was being downplayed under the impact of British culture."[102]

It is interesting that Subba Row, who undoubtedly was the most brilliant and erudite of the Hindu theosophists, had no knowledge of Sanskrit literature until he contacted HPB and Olcott. As a student he was awarded the Lord Elphinstone Scholarship at the Presidency College in Madras, and he later received the Elphinstone prize for English essay writing and still another award in psychology,[103] but he showed no interest in mysticism, metaphysics, or India's religious classics. After Subba Row's death at the early age of thirty-four, Olcott questioned his mother (herself a learned Brahman lady[104]) on these points:

> She told me that her son first talked metaphysics after forming a connection with the Founders of the Theosophical Society; a connection which began with a correspondence between himself and HPB and Damodar, and became personal after [the Founders met] him, in 1882, at Madras. It was as though a storehouse of occult experience, long forgotten, had been suddenly opened to him; recollection of his last preceding birth came in upon him; he recognized his Guru, and thenceforward held intercourse with him and other Mahatmas; with some personally at our Headquarters, with

others elsewhere and by correspondence. He told his mother that HPB was a great Yogi, and that he had seen many strange phenomena in her presence.[105]

Subba Row wrote to a personal friend:

The Occult Fraternities in every part of the world have now made a rule that admission into their ranks must be sought through the "Theosophical Society." I mistake no confidence when I inform you that I know personally of many instances in which those who were Chelas—a very high Chela one of them . . . were compelled by their Gurus to join the Society on pain of their being forsaken by them.[106]

This is in line with what one of the Masters wrote Sinnett: "There is more to this movement than you have yet had an inkling of, and the work of the TS is linked in with similar work that is secretly going on in all parts of the world."[107]

As to Subba Row, he became less and less helpful to the Theosophical cause owing to the ascendancy in his mind of feelings of Brahmanic exclusiveness. At the time of the adverse report of Hodgson and the SPR regarding HPB's phenomena, Subba Row told her:

You have been guilty of the most terrible of crimes. You have given out secrets of Occultism—the most sacred and the most hidden. Rather *that you should be sacrificed* than that which was never meant for European minds [be taught them]. People *had too much faith in you.* It was time to throw doubt into their minds. Otherwise they should have pumped *out of you all that you know.*[108]

At a happier time around New Year's 1883, Subba Row was present when a stranger visited HPB at headquarters. From the man's background one would think him unlikely to cross the threshold of a Theosophical center of work. His name was R. Jagannathia, and he himself tells of what occurred:

I was first introduced to HPB by Mr. Damodar K. Mavalankar, in the hall of the Theosophical Society building, as "R.J." and "Veritas" of *The Philosophic Inquirer.* She was seated in a chair, and surrounded by a small group of her admirers. The first impression she made on me was that she was not of this earth, as she had a pair of glowing but terrible eyes, under the arch of strongly-marked eyebrows. She was a woman in body, a man in speech, earthly in appearance, celestial in reality. . . .

"Ah!" exclaimed she, "I expected that you would come to me some day." I asked her how she could expect me, since she was a Theosophist and I am an atheist. She asked Mr. Damodar to fetch her scrapbook, and showed me some cuttings from my lectures on "Kapila, Buddha and Shankara," and said that she was carefully reading my contributions to *The Philosophic Inquirer,* which she appreciated, as they breathed a spirit of enquiry after Truth. As secularism was insufficient to satisfy my higher aspirations, she reasonably concluded that I would go to her for further light on the problem of problems—the mystery of life and death.

Then HPB asked me what I wanted to know. I questioned her on some points to all outward appearance difficult, each of which had been very carefully formulated by me overnight. As a member of the National Secular Society of England, I consoled myself with the idea that the problems I proposed were insoluble, and that they would tax her fine and philosophic intellect.

To my great astonishment she took up question after question, and answered each most elaborately and satisfactorily. She occupied nearly three hours [that day] in solving my questions. The array of facts she cited in support of her forcible and incontrovertible arguments, historical, philosophical and scientific, confused my poor intellect.

The whole audience was spellbound. And one peculiar point in her answering I cannot afford to omit. Her mastery of the various subjects was such that in her answer all the side-questions were anticipated and disposed of once for all. On the second and third day we were thus occupied for hours in the presence of the same audience; as the interest daily increased in proportion to my more and more difficult questions and her most able and satisfactory answers. . . .

On the third day, after answering the questions, on which I spent much thought and care, mustering all the force of my atheistic knowledge and learning, she cheerfully asked me if I had anything more to say. Readily and unreservedly I answered that "my stock was exhausted," and this afforded food for laughter for a few minutes to the whole company.

My idea was that Theosophy was something like the many religions of the world, and that HPB's knowledge and ingenuity might be a little more than those of the ordinary student. Emboldened by this hasty idea, I "went to shear but returned shorn." Glad was I to be defeated by her, for my defeat was an immense gain to me, as she opened my eyes to the slippery ground on which I then stood. In three days she shattered my seven years' knowledge of atheistic theories. . . .

This giant of intellect, wisdom and might, asked me what I thought of Theosophy, and if I would join the Theosophical Society and help the movement, if I were convinced of the truth of Theosophy. She founded the Theosophical Society, she said, under the orders of her guru, an Indian Mahatma, a Rishi, and came to disseminate a knowledge of Brahma-Vidya, the Wisdom-Religion. But to her regret many an intelligent and learned Hindu kept aloof from the movement and looked with some suspicion on her for her western origin and alien race.

I readily responded that I would join, and work and die for the sacred Cause, so long as a spark of life existed in this body. . . . I have been working for the Theosophical Society ever since, always alive to the sacredness of my promise to HPB [who] opened my eyes and enlightened my ignorance. She turned my attention to the precious and lustrous gems of knowledge lying deep in the oriental mines of wisdom. Very kindly and motherly advice she gave me in bidding me read the Upanishads, which were Schopenhauer's "solace in life and solace in death."[109]

In contrast to the previous years of travel, 1883 marked a period when HPB remained at headquarters most of the year. This provided more time to devote to *The Theosophist,* and she penned almost seven hundred pages in her *Collected Writings* that year. The wide variety of subjects covered can be gleaned from the titles of some of her articles, which include "The Religion of the Future," "The Bugbears of Science," "The Power to Heal," "Karma," "Chelas and Lay Chelas," "Is Foeticide a Crime?," "Transmigration of Life Atoms," "The Septenary Principle in Esotericism," "Zoroastrianism in the Light of Occult Philosophy," "Projection of the Double," "The Essentials of Religion," "The Sacred Tree of Kumbum," "The Rationale of Fasts," and "The Soul of Things."

"The Septenary Principle in Esotericism" relates to the sevenfold nature of humanity and the cosmos, a basic teaching in Theosophy. As applied to human beings, it is technically referred to as their seven principles. The following table is adapted from HPB's *Key to Theosophy,* the italicized words being Sanskrit equivalents for the English terms.[110]

THE PERISHABLE QUATERNARY

1. Physical Body (*Rupa*)
2. Astral Body (*Linga Sarira*)
3. Life or Vital Principle (*Prana*)
4. Animal Desires and Passions (*Kama Rupa*)

THE IMPERISHABLE TRIAD

5. Mind (*Manas*)
6. Spiritual Soul (*Buddhi*)
7. Spirit (*Atma*)

Manas, or mind, is said to become dual during incarnation; that part which is linked to the quaternary is called Lower Manas, or the brain mind; that which is united with Buddhi and Atma is called Higher Manas, or the intuitive mind. Quoting HPB: "The future state and the karmic destiny of man depend on whether Manas gravitates more downward to Kama rupa, the Seat of the animal principle or upwards to Buddhi, the Spiritual Ego," from which the voice of conscience and feelings of love and universal compassion flow. She defines *ATMA* as being "one with the Absolute, as its radiation."[111]

These seven principles were featured in Sinnett's book on theosophy, *Esoteric Buddhism* (1883). Readers were astonished. The twofold division of body and soul was all they were told about in the Protestant and Catholic church, and even then it was not clear whether man *is* a soul and *has* a body or the reverse. Most people were convinced they were their bodies because the church taught that to reach Heaven, their flesh and bones must be resurrected! Consequently the soul became a vague something that floats around, exerting little power on their lives.

It is held in Theosophy that the sevenfold division is not unique to human beings but applies to all the other kingdoms, including mineral. The differences in the kingdoms depend on how many of the seven principles are latent and how many are active. Only in the perfected individual are all principles fully awake. What is common to all is that everything is alive and is evolving, and has the power to record and reflect impressions.

It is owing to the latter power that the science of psychometry can be understood. The *Theosophist* article "The Soul of Things" treats the psychometric researches of the American geologist Professor William Denton as reported in his three-volume work of that title. In a letter to Nadya, HPB describes another example of this fascinating power:

I received your bundle of Novoye Vremyas *and went to bed a little after ten (you know I get up at five). Having taken up one of the newspapers, without choosing, just the nearest one, I stretched myself and went deep into thought about a certain Sanskrit book which I thought would help me to make good fun of Max Müller in my magazine. So you see it was by no means about you that I was thinking. And the newspaper lay all the time behind my head on the pillow, partly covering my forehead. When all of a sudden I felt myself transported into some strange and yet familiar house. The room I saw was new to me, but the table in the middle of it an old acquaintance. And there, sitting at the table, I saw you—you, my darling comrade, sitting smoking your cigarette and deeply thinking. The supper was laid on the table, but there was no one else in the room. Only it seemed to me that I caught a glimpse of Aunt [Catherine] going away through the door. Then you raised your hand and, taking a newspaper from the table, put it aside. I had just time to read its heading,* Herald of Odessa, *after which everything disappeared. To all seeming there was nothing strange in this occurrence, but here is something strange:*

I was perfectly sure that it was a number of the Novoye Vremya *that I had taken up, and having noticed in my vision some slices of black bread beside you, I was suddenly seized with such a desire to taste some of it—even a wee crumb—that I felt its taste in my mouth. I thought to myself, what does it all mean? What can be the cause of such a fancy? And in order to get rid of a desire that could not be gratified, I unfolded the newspaper and began to read. When lo! it actually was the* Herald of Odessa, *and not at all the* Novoye Vremya *in my hands. And, moreover, crumbs of my longed-for rye bread were sticking to it!*

And so these fragments on touching my forehead transmitted to my consciousness the whole scene as it probably happened at the precise moment of their sticking to the newspaper. In this case, the crumbs of rye bread have taken the place of a photographic apparatus. These dry pieces of bread gave me such intense delight, having transported me for a brief moment to you. I was quite filled with the atmosphere of home, and in my joy I licked up the biggest crumb, and as to the small ones—here they are, I have cut them out as they stuck to the paper and sent them back to you. Let them return home with some of my own soul.[112]

Nadya's interest in Theosophy matured over the years, and in August 1883 she was instrumental in forming a branch of the TS in Odessa, of which she became president.[113]

Chapter 10

A Need for Change

D uring 1883, the London TS gave HPB and Olcott much cause for concern owing to conflicts of opinions among its members. The Sinnetts were now living there, for in November 1882 Mr. Sinnett was notified by the owner of the *Pioneer* that his services were no longer required as editor. The family sailed from India for Europe in March of 1883 and after visiting Italy they arrived in England in the middle of May.

In January the London Branch had elected a new president, Mrs. Anna Bonus Kingsford, who, along with her close colleague Edward Maitland, was more sympathetic to gnostic Christian and Egyptian hermetic philosophies than the Eastern teachings the Sinnetts and many other members preferred. The Masters upheld her presidency and interest in Western esoteric teachings[114] even though she doubted the existence of such Masters. Kingsford's books on esoteric Christianity were very popular, particularly *The Perfect Way or the Finding of Christ,* published in 1882. The Masters also applauded her courageous work in antivivisection.[115] In her youth she had taken part in a fox hunt, but the sight of a victim's mangled body turned her against all forms of cruelty, a feeling that was intensified when studying medicine in Paris, where she was obliged to witness the excruciating torture of animals.

The London Lodge was not the only one in Europe having troubles at that time, as revealed in the letter that follows from HPB to Emilie de Morsier, who had complained to HPB about the opposing factions in the Lodge, in Paris (May 17, 1883):

> *My dear Sister and Friend, yes, you are too impressionable and too enthusiastic, but the excesses of others do not influence me, and nothing can make me falter on the path, once I have started on a journey. Do you want to know why? Because some twenty years ago I had lost faith in humanity as individuals, and love it collectively, and work universally instead of working for it individually. To do so I have my own way. I do not believe any longer in perfection; I do not believe any longer in infallibility, nor in immaculate characters.*

Each one of us is a piece of charcoal, more or less black and, excuse me, stinking. But there is hardly any piece so vile and dirty that it has not atoms wherein lie the germ of a future diamond. And I keep my eyes fixed on these atoms, and do not see the rest, and do not want to see. As I work for others and not for myself, I permit myself to use these atoms for the common cause.† *Thus I do not see, nor did I see, in Mr. Fortin anything but his talents and his practical ability for the demonstration of truth. He has incontestable scientific knowledge, and his wife is an unusual subject; and I do not see why, were he a thousand times worse than he is, I could not use him for the common cause, the good of humanity in general. . . . Everything has its good and its bad side. Let us take the good and use only that which is useful, and let us leave what is bad to break its own neck. . . .*

Our society preaches universal fraternity and love, but it leaves its branches free either to embrace each other or not. . . . Why could you not, you who are at loggerheads with Leymarie and Dr. Fortin, . . . make an effort to establish a separate branch which you might call, for instance, in contradistinction to the "Spiritist Group of the Theosophical Society" of Leymarie, and to the "Scientific Group of the Theosophical Society" of Dr. Fortin—the "Noological‡ Group of the Theosophical Society" or something of the kind? We need such independent centers of research and experimentation. . . . There is room for everybody. Set to work without worrying about the others. . . . The Chamber of Deputies is one, and yet how many parties does it contain! They are all working or believe they are working (which is the same thing) for France and have the glory of their native country more or less in view. Work therefore for Truth. Not an atom of your work will be lost.[116]

In December, HPB became ill, and during the annual convention of the TS in Adyar that month she appeared on crutches. Her condition worsened and in early 1884 her doctors warned that unless she changed climate for a while, she would die in three months. An arrangement was therefore made for Olcott to accompany her to France. He had business in London with the British government on behalf of the Sri Lankans [then Ceylon] to secure the religious freedom denied them for several centuries. Also while in London, he planned to arbitrate a peaceful settlement of the problems in the London TS.

† We may have in the above an answer to the frequently raised question of why HPB, with her supposed occult powers, gave friendship to individuals who later became her enemies. She once quoted Seneca: "It is another's fault if he be ungrateful; but it is mine if I do not give. To find one thankful man, I will oblige many who are not." ("The Theosophical Society: Its Mission and Future," *Lucifer*, August 1888, 421.)

‡ Noological is derived from the Greek *nous*, meaning "soul-mind" (Buddhi-Manas); in Theosophy, it refers to the higher soul or Buddhic nature.

T. Subba Row was chosen manager of *The Theosophist* in HPB's absence, and a Board of Control was set up to handle the affairs of the Society during the founders' absence. Prominent on the board was Franz Hartmann, MD, who had arrived in Madras in December from the United States and remained at Adyar for a little over a year.

Born in 1838 in Bavaria, Hartmann emigrated to the United States as a young doctor and became an American citizen. At about this time Spiritualism was the rage, but Hartmann, convinced it was a fraud, took no interest until he was witness to a series of remarkable séances. In his autobiography he writes:

> While my perplexity was at its highest and I despaired of the possibility of knowing anything certain about these manifestations, a number of *The Theosophist* . . . fell into my hands. It contained an article describing the seven-fold constitution of man [often referred to in Theosophy as man's principles]. This came to me like a revelation, and seemed to furnish the key to those mysteries whose explanation I had sought so long in vain. I was delighted with this discovery, and my greatest desire now was to become personally acquainted with Madame Blavatsky and to learn from her more of the secrets of life and death.[117] [Having written her, he received a letter from Olcott inviting him to Adyar.]
>
> On the first day after my arrival at Adyar, I received through Madame Blavatsky an unsought and unexpected test. I went to her room and found her writing. Not wishing to disturb her, I sat down near the window and thought of a lady friend of mine who had died at Galveston some years ago, wondering what had become of her "principles." I noticed that Madame Blavatsky turned her paper and seemed to play with her pencil in a state of absent-mindedness with a far-away look. She then handed me the paper. It contained the answer to my question in a drawing representing the corpse of my friend extended upon the ground and an elemental standing by its side watching for the escape of the astral soul, while the passage of her spirit to higher spheres was indicated by a rainbow.
>
> [Hartmann adds that] similar evidences of occult power I often received through H. P. Blavatsky[118] . . . but the [most] surprising of all phenomena was to me the fact that I found myself able to write articles on occult subjects for *The Theosophist* and to deliver, without any previous preparation, public lectures which found interested and appreciative audiences in India and afterwards in America, Germany, and Italy, although I had never spoken in public lectures before I arrived in India.

In later years Hartmann wrote scholarly works on metaphysical subjects, and he is especially noted for his *Life of Paracelsus*.[119]

One of the functions of the Board of Control was to supervise the activities of two employees—a married couple, Emma and Alexis Coulomb—who lived at the TS, first at Bombay and now in Madras. Emma was housekeeper and Alexis, a skilled carpenter and all-around handyman. Prior to coming to India they had lived for awhile in Sri Lanka, became poverty stricken, and appealed to HPB for help. She had known Emma from Cairo days, when she herself was in difficult straits, after the shipwreck off the coast of Greece. As Madame Coulomb, then Miss Cutting, had kindly befriended her, it was only natural HPB should reciprocate.

In 1884, while HPB and Olcott were in Europe, the Board of Control at Adyar dismissed the couple for dishonorable conduct, one charge being misuse of the Society's funds. Fuming with rage, the Coulombs took refuge with the Christian missionaries at Madras. In due time the missionaries announced that the Coulombs confessed that they assisted HPB in the production of fraudulent phenomena. Madame Coulomb also declared that when she knew HPB in Cairo, she discovered her to be a woman of low morals. Yet, when living in Sri Lanka in 1879, in response to an attack on HPB appearing in the news media, Madame Coulomb wrote this spirited defense of her in the Anglo-Indian Ceylon *Times* (June 5, 1879):

> I am not acquainted with any of the members of the [Theosophical] Society, except with Madame Blavatsky. I have known this lady for these last eight years, and I must say the truth, that there is nothing against her character. We lived in the same town, and on the contrary she was considered one of the cleverest ladies of the age. Madame B. is a musician, a painter, a linguist, an author, and I may say that very few ladies and indeed few gentlemen have a knowledge of things in general as Madame Blavatsky.[120]

As Blavatsky and Olcott made preparations for their journey to Europe, intimations of trouble with the Coulombs were far from their minds. They left India on February 20, 1884, accompanied by HPB's servant, Babula, and several other Hindus, including Mohini. Sailing from Bombay, they arrived in Marseilles on March twelfth.

Chapter 11

Visit to Europe

The seven months HPB and Olcott remained in Europe in 1884 were not a time of rest and quiet as her doctor had ordered, but rather of intense activity, during which Theosophy gained a respectable foothold and even became fashionable in intellectual circles. The two founders were sought after everywhere they went. The third founder, William Q. Judge, had come from America en route to India and spent several months in France with HPB, "ordered by the Master," she said, "to stop here and help me in writing *The Secret Doctrine.*"[121]

After landing at Marseilles, Blavatsky and Olcott spent a week in Nice as guests of Lady Caithness (Duchesse de Pomar) at Palace Tiranty, one of her residences. Spanish by birth, she first married the Duc de Pomar and after his death, the Earl of Caithness. When the latter died she settled in Paris, where she founded the Société Théosophique d'Orient et d'Occident.

From Nice, HPB and Olcott went to Paris and were met by Judge and Mohini. The four stayed at 46 rue Notre-Dame des Champs, provided by Lady Caithness, and this was HPB's headquarters during the entire period she remained in Paris.

"The mission of the theosophists in Europe received considerable attention in the major press," reports Michael Gomes. "On April 1, Victor Hugo's paper, *Le Rappel,* carried an article of three columns on the spread of Theosophy, and *Le Temps* followed the next day. *Le Matin* on April 21 carried a half-column article on the arrival of theosophists from all parts to meet in Paris."

The same day, the *English Morning News,* in Paris, interviewed HPB and announced that a grand *conversazione* in her honor was to be held in May [tenth] at Lady Caithness's sumptuous and "luxurious" home in the Faubourg St. Germain quarter of Paris.[122]

Judge wrote Olcott, who had left Paris soon after his arrival for London:

The U.S. will soon be full of you and her again. Th. Child, who gives the N.Y. *Sun* a column every week, has got a special appointment for tonight, and the correspondent of *Chicago Tribune* has asked for another.[123]

HPB held discussions at various homes in Paris, the substance of which was later embodied in Lady Caithness's book *The Mystery of the Ages*.[124]

In London, Olcott scheduled a TS meeting for April seventh to elect new officers and resolve the dispute between the Kingsford and Sinnett factions. HPB had been invited to attend, but refused.[125] The evening before, in Paris, HPB and Judge were reminiscing about New York days. The next day Judge wrote to Laura Holloway, a friend in New York:

> As we sat, I felt the old signal of a message from the Master and saw that she [HPB] was listening. She said: "Judge, the Master asks me to try and guess what would be the most extraordinary thing he could order now?" I said, "that Mrs. Kingsford should be made the President of the London Lodge." "Try again" [HPB said]. "That HPB should be ordered to go to London." That was right and he ordered her to take the 7:45 express, giving the exact hours it would arrive at the different stations and in London. All of which was correct, and we had no time table in the house. She disliked the order awfully and I can tell you, knowing her ill health and present unwieldy size, it was an awful journey. But last night I took her to the station and saw her go off in the train with a little hand bag. There is some peculiar object in this, as she might have gone with Olcott. . . .
>
> All the time she confessed her inability to see why she was ordered, as the Londoners will think it done for effect after her refusal to go then, and Olcott when he sees her will certainly feel like swearing. But the London situation is serious and [it] may be they intend to work some phenomena there for some good end. So I am left here alone in this house and am going to work a little on the book [*The Secret Doctrine*].[126]

Before HPB arrived at the London meeting, elections had already taken place; Mrs. Kingsford had become angered to find herself no longer president and a Mr. Finch in her place, with Sinnett as vice president and secretary and Francesca Arundale, treasurer. The atmosphere had become charged with conflict. A recent TS member, British clergyman Charles Leadbeater, records what followed:

> . . . Suddenly and sharply the door opposite us opened and a stout lady in black came quickly in and seated herself at the outer end of

our bench. She sat listening to the wrangling on the platform for a few minutes, and then began to exhibit distinct signs of impatience. As there seemed to be no improvement in sight, she jumped up from her seat, shouted in a tone of military command the one word "Mohini," and then walked straight out of the door into the passage. The stately and dignified Mohini came rushing down that long room at his highest speed, and as soon as he reached the passage he threw himself incontinently flat on his face on the floor at the feet of the lady in black.

Many people arose in confusion, not knowing what was happening; but a moment later Mr. Sinnett himself came running to the door, and went out and exchanged a few words and then, re-entering the room, he stood up at the end of our bench and spoke in a ringing voice the fateful words: "Let me introduce to the London Lodge—Madame Blavatsky." The scene was indescribable; the members wildly delighted and yet half-awed at the same time, clustered round our great Founder, some kissing her hand, several kneeling before her, and two or three weeping hysterically.[127]

HPB took over the meeting, demanding an explanation as to the unbecoming state of affairs. She then privately conferred with the officers, and it was agreed that Mrs. Kingsford should form a new group, calling itself The Hermetic Lodge, and the London Lodge continue as formerly.

Mary Gebhard of Elberfeld, Germany, who was present at the meeting, later attested:

On the 7th of April last, being at a meeting of the Theosophical Society at Mr. Finch's rooms, Lincoln's Inn, I had a vision in which I saw the Mahatma M. At the moment I was listening attentively to Colonel Olcott's opening speech to the Society. I saw standing on my right side, a little in front, a very tall, majestic-looking person whom I immediately recognized to be the Mahatma, from a picture I had seen of him in Mr. Sinnett's possession. He was not clad in white, but it seemed to me to be some dark material with colored stripes, which was wound round his form. The vision lasted only a few seconds. As far as I could learn, the only persons besides myself who had seen the Mahatma [present at the meeting] were Colonel Olcott, Mr. Mohini, and, of course, Madame Blavatsky.

Mrs. Gebhard adds that it was before this personage that Mohini prostrated himself, not HPB.[128]

HPB remained in London for a week, staying at the Sinnetts' home in Ladbroke Gardens, where she met many of the London theosophists.[129] She also visited Sir William Crookes's laboratory. When leaving for Paris, she was accompanied across the channel by Mary Gebhard and her son Arthur.[130]

Back in Paris, HPB felt impelled one day to go to the Russian church. She wrote her family:

> I stood there, with my mouth wide open, as if standing before my own dear mother, whom I have not seen for years and who could not recognize me! . . . I do not believe in any dogmas, I dislike every ritual, but my feelings towards our own church service are quite different. I am driven to think that my brains lack their seventh stopper. Probably it is in my blood. . . . I certainly will always say: a thousand times rather Buddhism, a pure moral teaching, in perfect harmony with the teachings of Christ, than modern Catholicism or Protestantism. But with the faith of the Russian church I will not even compare Buddhism. I can't help it. Such is my silly, inconsistent nature.[131]

After the *conversazione* at the home of Lady Caithness on May tenth, HPB went with Mohini and Judge to a beautiful French estate in Enghien, not far from Paris, where they remained for about three weeks. While there she wrote to her relatives, whom she had not seen in twelve years, urging them to visit her in Paris and Enghien:

> I have run away from my cosmopolitan friends and interviewers, and other prying torturers, leaving Paris for a few days for Enghien, Villa Croisac, belonging to my dear friends Count and Countess d'Adhémar. They are real friends, caring for me not only for the sake of phenomena—which be bothered. Here I have a whole *enfilade* of rooms at my own and at your service. . . . The Countess is a charming woman: She is a very rich American [from Kentucky], so nice and unpretentious. Her husband also, though a great aristocrat and a crusted legitimist, is very simple in his ways.[132]

Little has been recorded of HPB's stay at Enghien, except in an article by Judge, from which a few extracts are taken:

> Every convenience was given to our beloved friend, and there she continued her writing, while I at her request carefully read over, sitting in the same room, *Isis Unveiled,* making indices [as to subject matter] at the foot of each page, as she intended to use it in preparing the *Secret Doctrine.* . . .

Every evening it was the custom to spend some time in the drawing room in conversation, and there, as well as in the dining room, took place some phenomena which indeed were no more interesting than the words of HPB whether those were witty, grave or gay. Very often Countess d'Adhémar's sister played the piano in a manner to delight even HPB who was no mean judge. I remember well one melody, just then brought out in the world of Paris, which pleased her immensely, so that she often asked for its repetition. It was one suggestive of high aspiration and grandiose conceptions of nature. Many lively discussions with the Count on one side and HPB on the other had taken place there, and often in the very midst of these she would suddenly turn to Mohini and myself, who were sitting listening, to repeat to us the very thoughts then passing in our brains. . . .

[One] evening after we had all been in the drawing room for some time, sitting without lights, the moon shining over the lake and all nature being hushed, HPB fell into a thoughtful state. Shortly she rose and stood at the corner window looking over the water and in a moment a flash of soft light shot into the room and she quietly smiled. Reminding me of this evening the Countess d'Adhémar wrote after HPB died:

> HPB seemed wrapped in thought, when suddenly she rose from her chair, advanced to the open window, and raising her arm with a commanding gesture, faint music was heard in the distance, which advancing nearer and nearer broke into lovely strains and filled the drawing room where we were all sitting. Mohini threw himself at HPB's feet and kissed the hem of her robe, which action seemed the appropriate outcoming of the profound admiration and respect we all felt toward the wonderful being whose loss we will never cease to mourn.

This astral music was very plain to us all, and the Count especially remarked upon its beauty and the faintness of it as it sank away into the unknown distance.[133]

It was not until after HPB returned to Paris that Vera and Nadya arrived from Russia, remaining with her until the end of June. Vera was the precipitating factor in an experiment privately conducted by HPB that was publicized in England and Russia. A testimonial from witnesses appeared in the British periodical *Light* (July 12, 1884), from which the following is taken:

The undersigned attest the following phenomena:

On the morning of the 11th of June, instant, we were present in the reception room of the Theosophical Society at Paris, 46 Rue Notre Dame des Champs, when a letter was delivered by the postman. The door of the room in which we were sitting was open, so that we could see into the hall; and the servant who answered the bell was seen to take the letter from the postman and bring it to us at once, placing it in the hands of Mme. Jelihovsky [HPB's sister, Vera], who threw it before her on the table round which we were sitting. The letter was addressed to a lady, a relative of Mme. Blavatsky's [her Aunt Nadya], who was then visiting here, and came from another relative in Russia [Aunt Catherine]. There were present in the room, Mme. de Morsier, secretary-general of the Société Théosophique d'Orient et d'Occident; M. Solovyov, son of the distinguished Russian historian, and attaché of the Imperial Court, himself well-known as a writer; Colonel Olcott, Mr. W. Q. Judge, Mohini, Babu, and several other persons. Mme. Blavatsky was also sitting at the table. Mme. Jelihovsky asked [HPB], on the spur of the moment, to read its contents before its seal was broken. . . .

Thus challenged, Mme. Blavatsky at once took up the closed letter, held it against her forehead, and read aloud what she professed to be its contents. These alleged contents she further wrote down on a blank page of an old letter that lay on the table. Then she said she would give those present, since her sister still laughed at and challenged her power, even a clearer proof that she was able to exercise her psychic power *within* the closed envelope. Remarking that her own name occurred in the course of the letter, she said she would underline this through the envelope in red crayon. In order to effect this she wrote her name on the old letter (on which the alleged copy of the contents of the sealed letter had been written), together with an interlaced double triangle or "Solomon's seal" below the signature, which she had copied as well in the body of the letter. This was done in spite of her sister's remarking that her correspondent hardly ever signed her name in full when writing to relatives, and that in this at least Mme. Blavatsky would find herself mistaken. "Nevertheless," [HPB] replied, "I will cause these two red marks to appear in the corresponding places within the letter."

She next laid the closed letter beside the open one upon the table, and placed her hand upon both, so as to make (as she said) a bridge, along which a current of psychic force might pass. Then *with her features settled into an expression of intense mental concentration,* she kept her hand quietly thus for a few moments, after which, tossing the closed letter across the table to her sister, she said, "Tiens, c'est fait. The experiment is successfully finished." . . . Upon the envelope being opened by the lady to whom it was addressed, it was found *that Mme. Blavatsky had actually written out its contents; that her name was there; that she had really underlined it in red, as she had promised; and that the double triangle was reproduced below the writer's signature, which was in full, as Mme. Blavatsky had described it.*

Another fact of exceptional interest we noted. *A slight defect in formation of one of the two interlaced triangles, as drawn by Mme. Blavatsky, had been faithfully reproduced within the closed letter.* [Names of attesting witnesses are listed.]

Vera inquired from Olcott how HPB managed to transfer the red lead in her pencil to the letter in the sealed envelope. He replied:

To analyze such a phenomenon, we have to understand that, among the hidden, virtually unknown and uninvestigated human powers is the power to attract, displace, and move atoms. Thus, in this case, Mme. Blavatsky drew, without splitting them, the atoms of her red pencil, absorbed them into her nervous life force, made them circulate through her body like an electric current, from the right hand to the fingers of the left, then made them pass through the microscopic openings that are found in all paper, and fixed them on the spots she had indicated in advance by her concentrated will.

The above appeared in Vera's report on the Paris phenomena sent to a Russian periodical and reprinted in *Rebus*.[134] This is the first time it has been published in English, as is also the case respecting the following from the same source:

We were all sitting together a few days ago when one, Mr. Judge, the secretary of the Society, received in his mail a letter from America, which he *immediately* opened. The first thing attracting his attention was not the contents of the letter but the fact that several words were underlined in red ink, and a sentence written diagonally across the sheet in the same ink, signed by the familiar name of the Master. . . . That this could have been done by the writer in New York was the first thought that came into my mind, but I soon changed my opinion.

About two days later Mme. Blavatsky was listening to a young guest . . . , Mr. Bertram Keightley, bitterly complaining about his mother who was insisting that he either return home to Liverpool, or continue on his journey through the Continent, undertaken for health reasons. "Mother is terribly afraid that I might leave everything and follow you to Madras," he said. . . . It was then that the postman rang, and among other letters, there was one from Mrs. Keightley to her son. He opened it without much urgency, but suddenly his face reddened, and he looked both stunned and frightened. In the letter, his mother's words concerning the respect and obedience that children owe their parents were *underlined in red ink, with a familiar signature.* . . .

Mme. de M[orsier], secretary of the Society's Paris chapter . . . told me that a timely letter from the Master, which she found, together with its peculiar envelope, enclosed in an unrelated letter, had *prevented her from committing suicide* and made her a devout Theosophist.[135]

In earlier contributions to a Russian periodical, Vera recorded a conversation with her sister on the possibility of creating objects by means of psychical power. When Vera expressed strong disbelief in such phenomena, HPB replied: "Well, then do not believe. I am very little concerned about faith in such nonsense." Vera, who had five children to support and was often in dire financial straits, notes:

I argued angrily that this was by no means nonsense. That if she so easily created gold and gems, then she should enrich me. My sister laughed, saying this would be sorcery, resulting in harm to all concerned. "Your karma and mine is to be poor and we must carry it. If I tried to enrich you or myself by such means, then I would ruin us both, not necessarily in the present life but in centuries to come." To the question: "Why, then, did you give others such ruinous gifts if they bring harm?" She assured me that these absurd things which she was permitted to do were for convincing thick-headed materialists—who never understood anything unless their i's were dotted for them—that immense powers reside in man.[136]

In her article "Is Creation Possible for Man?" (*The Theosophist,* December 1881) HPB remarked that objects psychically produced do not appear out of nothing, but from preexisting matter in a sublimated state. Their objectification is no more miraculous than vaporous clouds condensing into rain and then becoming ice or carbon in its liquid state crystallizing as a diamond. Sometimes the matter drawn upon in the creation of objects was already in solidified form, as when HPB, for the delight of a child, displaced the atoms in a bunch of keys to make a whistle. Olcott's sister, Belle Mitchell, reported a number of such experiments made in New York days when the Mitchells lived in the same apartment building as did HPB.[137]

At the end of June, HPB left Paris for London. The day before departure, she wrote to a Russian acquaintance: "Tomorrow I go to London shaking from my feet the dust of Paris. . . . I am ill and not in the best of spirits. At such moments it is only *Theosophy* which enables me to carry on."[138]

Nadya, Vera, and Madame de Morsier were at the station to send her off. HPB later wrote her aunt:

My dear, my precious Nadejda Andreyevna! For many years I have not cried, but now I have cried out all my tears on losing sight of you two. I thought my heart would burst, I felt so faint. Happily, some kindly French people in the same compartment as myself brought me some water at the next station and took care of me as best they could. At Boulogne Olcott came to meet me, and was nearly ready to cry himself on seeing how ill I was. He was also greatly put out by the thought that you and Vera might think him heartless for not having come to fetch me in Paris. But the poor old body never knew I was so unwell. You know I am always shaky.

I spent a night in Boulogne, and next morning five more of our theosophists came from England to look after me. . . . I was nearly carried to the steamer and off it again, and triumphantly brought to London. I can hardly breathe, but all the same we have a reception this evening, to which probably about fifty of our old acquaintances will come. English people in their totality are not fickle; they have lots of constancy and loyalty. At Charing Cross, Mohini and Keightley nearly frightened to death all kinds of English people by falling down before me as if I had been an idol. It made me positively angry, this tempting of providence.[139]

Mohini had a private reason for prostrating himself. In March of 1884, he received the letter that follows from his Master:

To Mohini *alone*.

Appearances go a long way with the "Pelings" [Europeans]. One has to impress them externally before a regular, lasting, interior impression is made. Remember and try to understand why I expect you to do the following:

When Upāsika† [HPB] arrives, you will meet and receive her *as though you were in India, and she your own mother.* You must not mind the crowd of Frenchmen and others. You have *to stun them;* and if Colonel asks you why, you will answer him that it is the interior man, the *indweller* you salute, not HPB, for you were notified to that effect by us. And know for your own edification that One far greater than myself [the Maha Chohan] has kindly consented to survey the whole situation under her guise, and then to visit, through the same channel, occasionally, Paris and other places where foreign members may reside. You will thus salute her on seeing and taking leave of her the whole time you are in Paris.‡—regardless of comments and *her own surprise.* This is a test.140

In May, after his return from London to Paris, another letter from the same source was received by Mohini, now in Paris:

Your bearing towards, and about, Upāsika is so very *childish* that it is indeed calculated to create a worse impression than even her own flippant attitude when left entirely to herself.††† Do not forget that all the good results that are in store for our India . . . are all due to her individual efforts. You can hardly show her enough respect and gratitude, or more than she is entitled to. It is better to let the English know all the good she is morally achieving than [to] be ever entertaining them with stories [about her] that can show her only in a childish, whimsical light and make them laugh or even smile at her expense. . . . You are *the* representative of India to be *regenerated.* You have, therefore, to show the bearing of a philosopher if you would be a chela, not that of a laughing youth.141

In London, HPB stayed for six weeks at 77 Elgin Crescent, Notting Hill, the home of Francesca Arundale and her elderly mother. An intimate portrait of that period is given in the daughter's volume *My Guest—H. P. Blavatsky* and in her "In Memorium" tribute at the time of HPB's death. From both sources, the following has been collated:

---

† *Upāsika* signifies a female disciple.

‡ This would be very difficult for HPB to endure. Judge Khandalavala once said of her. "She was very adverse to flattery, and any kind of reverence that was attempted to be paid to her. Once a Hindu member went up to her to touch her feet and make obeisance, when she suddenly got up from her chair and rebuked him: 'I am not a saint: do not think of worshipping me.'" (*The Theosophist,* July 1929.)

††† On the flyleaf of Blavatsky's copy of *The Voice of the Silence* she inscribed the words: "From H.P.B. to H.P. Blavatsky, with *no* kind regards." (*The Theosophist,* August 1931, 560)

It was her custom while with us to devote the earlier part of the day to writing; she usually began at seven o'clock, but often earlier, and continued with a slight interval for lunch till about three or four o'clock in the afternoon. Then it was that the reception time began, and from early afternoon to late evening, one constant succession of visitors arrived. Many, of course, drawn by the fame of her great powers, merely came from curiosity. In those days the Psychical Research Society had not issued its famous report, and some of its members were often present seeking the signs and wonders they so much desired to behold.

The most pleasant time I had was always in the early morning; she always seemed more get-at-able then, her mouth settled in pleasant curves, her eyes kind and brilliant, and she always seemed to understand and sympathize not only with what one said but also with what one did not say. I never felt afraid of HPB, in spite of the very strong language she sometimes used. One always somehow felt it was *surface* strong language.

I might multiply instance after instance of phenomena [she performed] but knowing the small value that Madame Blavatsky herself put upon these things, it would be but a poor tribute to her memory to put that forward which is but the least part of her work. But the phenomena hunters, and those who only came to see and wonder, were but one portion of the great crowd. Many earnest minds engaged in scientific or philosophic study would come again and again, attracted by the power of an intellect that showed its vast strength in the way in which she dealt with the many subjects put before her. Grave professors from Cambridge came and spent an occasional afternoon in her company, and I can see before me now the bulky form in the loose robe in the big armchair, with the tobacco basket by her side, answering deep and learned questions on theories of cosmogony and the laws governing matter.

[Francesca relates] a very good description of these daily gatherings is given by Mrs. Campbell Praed in her book *Affinities*.[142] Very often Mohini Chatterji would answer questions on Indian philosophy. I have rarely met with anyone who could give such clear and forcible explanations clothed in such beautiful language. His lectures were much sought after, and we rarely closed our doors till one or two o'clock in the morning.[143]

It may be that Mohini was influenced at times by one greater than himself. In a letter to Sinnett written before the Theosophical party left India for Europe, HPB intimated this would occur: "Do not make the mistake, my dear boss, of taking the *Mohini you knew* for the Mohini who will come. . . . The ambassador will be invested with an *inner* as well as with an *outer* clothing."[144]

Mohini collaborated with Mrs. Laura Holloway in writing *Man: Fragments of Forgotten History.*[145] Holloway had recently come from New York to meet the Theosophists in London and for a while lived with HPB at the Arundales'. Judge knew her in the States and was enthusiastic about her possibilities as a future worker for the movement. In advance of her arrival, he wrote to Olcott of her "literary work, as well as psychical abilities of a kind that make HPB so remarkable." When HPB learned of her coming, she said: "*Oh my God, if I shall only find in her* A SUCCESSOR, *how gladly I will* PEG OUT!"[146]

Mrs. Holloway, however, did not measure up to expectations. In a letter to Francesca Arundale from one of the Masters, he wrote:

First about your friend—Mrs. H. Poor child! By placing so constantly her personality over and above her inner and better Self—tho' she knows it not—she has done all she could for the last week to sever herself from us forever. . . . As she says her ways are not *our* ways, nor can she comprehend them. Her personality coming in so strongly in her ideas of the fitness of things, she cannot certainly understand our acts on our plane of life. Tell her in all kindness, that if H.P.B. (as an example) was wrong last night—as she always is, from the Western point of view, in her everlasting natural impulses apparently so rude and indelicate—*she did it after all at her* Master's direct order. She never stops one moment to consider the propriety of things when concerned in carrying out such orders. In the eyes of you, the civilized and cultured portion of mankind, [to disclose one's real feelings at a social gathering] is the one unpardonable sin; in our sight—*i.e.*, uncultured Asiatics—it is the greatest virtue; before it became with her a habit, she used to suffer in *her* Western nature and perform it as a self-sacrifice of her personal reputation.[147]

While HPB was busily engaged in Paris and London, Olcott was often away on missions of his own, giving lectures and seeking to interest notable people in Theosophy. As recorded in his diary, between April ninth and twentieth [1884], he met Sir Edwin Arnold; Camille Flammarion, the astronomer; Oscar Wilde; Professor John Couch Adams, discoverer of the planet Neptune; Sir William Crookes;

Robert Browning; Sir Oliver Lodge; Matthew Arnold; and Lord and Lady Borthwick. Olcott later visited the Borthwicks at their home in Scotland and organized a branch of the TS in Edinburgh.[148] In May, at the invitation of Lord John Francis Russell, the elder brother of the noted mathematician and philosopher Bertrand Russell, he gave a talk at Oxford before his host's college friends.[149]

In the middle of April, an American member of the Society for Psychical Research (SPR) gave a dinner for Olcott at the Junior Athenaeum Club, inviting leading members of that society to meet him.[150] Among them was noted essayist and poet Frederic Myers, author of *Human Personality and Its Survival after Bodily Death,* a classic in its field. Myers had joined the TS the previous year. In May, Olcott was present at a meeting of the SPR in Cambridge, where he met its president, Henry Sidgwick, Knightsbridge Professor of Moral Philosophy at the university. Later in the month Olcott expressed to the SPR his willingness to be examined as a witness to the phenomena produced in America and in India through the agency of HPB or her teachers. A series of hearings were then held by a special committee formed for this purpose. Mohini and Sinnett were also examined.

In one interview Myers asked Olcott whether he could persuade HPB to perform some psychic phenomena in the presence of their committee. When the hearings were published, a footnote gave her reply: "No one could persuade me to do so unless Master commanded me to sacrifice myself once more—H. P. Blavatsky."[151]

Why did she refrain? The following experience related by Francesca Arundale perhaps provides the answer. The occasion was a visit to her home by Myers when HPB was present:

[She] and her visitor began talking about the phenomena in which Mr. Myers was so interested. "I wish you would show me a proof of your occult power," said he; "will you not do something that will prove that there are these occult forces of which you speak?" "What would be the good?" said Madame Blavatsky. "Even if you saw and heard, you would not be convinced." "Try me," he said. She looked at him for a moment or so in that strange, penetrating manner she had, and turning to me said: "Bring me a finger bowl and some water in it." They were sitting in the full light of a summer's afternoon; she was to the right of Mr. Myers who was seated in a small chair about three feet away. I brought the glass bowl of water and she told me to place it on a stool just in front of Mr. Myers and a fairly long distance from her, which I did. We sat for a few moments in quiet expectation, and then from the glass there seemed to come four or five notes, such as we have called the "astral bells." It was evident that Mr. Myers was astonished; he looked at HPB and her folded hands in her lap, and then again at the glass bowl; there was no visible connection between the two. Again the notes of the astral bell sounded, clear and silvery, and no movement on the part of Madame Blavatsky.

He turned to me, and one could see that he was quite confused as to how the sounds could have been produced. HPB smiled, and said: "Nothing very wonderful, only a little knowledge of how to direct some of the forces of nature." As Mr. Myers left he turned to me and said: "Miss Arundale, I shall *never* doubt again." But alas for the fickle, doubting mind; before a fortnight had passed he wrote to say he was not convinced, and that the sounds might have been produced in this way or that. HPB was not one whit disturbed; in fact she said: "I knew it, but I thought I would give him what he asked for."[152]

Alternate explanations for phenomena are always available, and that is why it is so difficult to prove the reality of occult forces. Official science, however, often has the same problem when endeavoring to prove *physical* phenomena. In fact, according to the distinguished scientist Gregory Bateson: *"Science probes; it does not prove."* It is always limited by the instruments used. Invent a more powerful telescope or microscope, or build a longer cyclotron and objects hitherto undetected will be disclosed, and current theories may require alteration, sometimes radically.[153] In *The Secret Doctrine* (1:477–78), HPB observes:

Science cannot, owing to the very nature of things, unveil the mystery of the universe around us. Science can, it is true, collect, classify, and generalize upon phenomena; but the occultists, arguing from admitted metaphysical data, declare that the daring explorer, who would probe the inmost secrets of Nature, must transcend the narrow limitations of sense, and transfer his consciousness into the region of noumena and the sphere of primal causes. To effect this he must develop faculties which are absolutely dormant—save in a few rare exceptional cases—in the constitution of our Race.

In contrasting Western and Eastern science, Dr. Walt Anderson remarks: "We are, in the West, so in awe of our machines that we believe they alone are capable of discovering the truth. It does not seem to have occurred to many physicists that the reality unfolded in their research and theory might be *experienced*." In the West, he adds, "the cosmos is explored by the cyclotrons and lasers and telescopes," while Eastern science "has been largely non-technical, relying on the apparatus of the disciplined human body and mind," as in practices of deep meditation.[154]

In the great Hindu classic Patanjali's *Yoga Aphorisms,* there is this instruction: "By concentrating his mind upon minute, concealed or distant objects, in every department of nature, the ascetic acquires thorough knowledge concerning them." The commentator states that "the term 'knowledge' as used here has a greater meaning than we are accustomed to giving it. It implies full identification of the mind, for any length of time, with whatever object or subject it is directed to."[155]

Can we imagine any modern scientist would engage in such a practice? *Science Digest* (July 1982) reports that "no world famous physicist takes the claims of Eastern mystical philosophy more seriously than Cambridge University's Brian Josephson, winner of the 1978 Nobel prize in physics," adding that Josephson "has staked his enormous scientific reputation on the possibility that he can gain insights into objective reality by practicing traditional Eastern meditational techniques."

Training and perfecting the human instrument as a receptor of truth is not an easy task, but, writes one of the mahatmas:

> Believe me, there comes a moment in the life of an adept when the hardships he has passed through are a thousand-fold rewarded. In order to acquire further knowledge, he has no more to go through a minute and slow process of investigation and comparison of various objects, but is accorded an instantaneous, implicit insight into every first truth. . . . The adept sees and feels and lives in the very source of all fundamental truths. . . .[156]

Meanwhile, flashes of intuition can solve many of the lesser problems, checked by the logic of reason and available evidences.

On July twenty-first, Blavatsky and Olcott were honored by the London TS in a brilliant reception at Prince's Hall in Piccadilly. The report appearing in the *Theosophist* (October 1884) states:

> Invitations to this "open meeting" or conversazione were issued by the officers of our London Branch, and so great was the pressure of applications for them that the edition of 500 tickets was speedily exhausted, and others had to be prepared. So large a gathering of eminent men and women never attended a theosophical meeting before. Among those present were their Excellencies the Russian

Ambassador, the Chief Secretary to the French Embassy, the Dutch Ambassador, the Roumanian Ambassador, the Russian Consul-General in Egypt, the Under Secretary of State for India, gentlemen from the Colonial Office, the office of the Chancellor of the Exchequer, the India Office and other departments of Government, a number of British Peers and Peeresses, of foreign nobles, of Members of Parliament, representatives of Science and Literature—among them, Dr. Ginsberg of the British Museum, who exposed the fraud of the Shapira MSS.; Prof. William Crookes, FTS.

Then follows a list of other notables, including Oscar Wilde.

The opening address was delivered by Olcott and "comprised a brief historical review of the origin and progress of the Theosophical Society and of the ideas it represents, together with a statement of what has actually been accomplished to date in each of the three departments of work contemplated in the three declared objects of the Society." The second talk was by Mohini, who explained the relationship India bears to the Theosophical movement and why Europe should take an interest in it. Sinnett gave the final speech, choosing as his theme "The Esoteric Philosophy of the East."

HPB wrote Nadya after the event:

I shall never get well even here. It's not life, but a sort of mad turmoil from morning till night. Visitors, dinners, evening callers, and meetings every day. The Russian authoress, Olga Alexandrovna de Novikoff alone has brought over the whole of Official London, except [Prime] Minister Gladstone, who according to the St. James' Gazette, "fears as much as he admires me." What do you know? It's some sort of glamour!

On August ninth, at the invitation of the SPR, HPB, accompanied by Francesca Arundale and Mohini, went to Cambridge for several days. Professor Sidgwick wrote in his journal:

Our favorable impression of Madame Blavatsky was maintained; if personal sensibilities can be trusted, she is a genuine being, with a vigorous nature intellectual as well as emotional, and a real desire for the good of mankind. This impression is all the more noteworthy as she is externally unattractive.[157]

On this occasion Blavatsky met SPR member Richard Hodgson, a young teacher and graduate of Cambridge. He was soon to be selected as the SPR's investigator in India of the phenomena produced by HPB and her teachers.[158] Olcott had invited this investigation, but HPB was very dubious as to the wisdom of his decision.[159]

In the middle of August, HPB left England for Elberfeld, Germany, where Olcott had formed a German TS just prior to her arrival. She was a guest of Gustav and Mary Gebhard for seven weeks. Accompanying her were Laura Holloway, Mohini, Bertram Keightley, and the Arundales.

The Gebhards played an important role in the history of the Theosophical movement. Gustav Gebhard was a wealthy banker and silk manufacturer. He was known as Consul Gebhard, as he had been the German consul to Iran. A noted linguist, he spoke flawless French and English. On his first business trip to New York he met his future wife, the present Mary Gebhard, the daughter of a British major and his Irish wife. Mary had an inborn inclination towards philosophy and occultism, and in Elberfeld she studied Hebrew with a clergyman to facilitate research into the Kabbalah. She became a pupil of the celebrated Kabbalist Eliphas Levi, until his death in 1875. Having learned of the existence of the TS, she corresponded with Olcott, and joined the Society. The Gebhards had seven children, most of whom became Theosophists.[160]

Miss Arundale paints a charming picture of the journey from London to Elberfeld:

No words can express the kindness of our host; he franked the whole party, and at some of the principal stations on the road we were served with baskets of fruit and dainty sandwiches and lemonade. We were a merry party. HPB was in her wittiest and most genial mood, and the large saloon carriage echoed with pleasant laughter and bright speech. That time at Elberfeld was a bright page to look back on. . . .[161]

During HPB's stay with the Gebhards, Solovyov visited for several days. Professor Elliott Coues of the Smithsonian Institute in Washington, D.C. did likewise. He had met Olcott in London, in June, and joined the TS in July. Nadya, with a friend, Gustav Zorn—secretary of the TS in Odessa[162]—came for almost a month, as did the Sinnetts.

At the end of August, Frederic Myers arrived when HPB was gravely ill. James Webb, who researched Myers's papers, discovered that "on 9 September Myers informed Massey that he had spent five and a half days cross-examining the bed-ridden H.P.B., and that his confidence in her had increased immeasurably."[163]

A few days later a bomb dropped. News arrived that a missionary organ, the *Madras Christian College Magazine,* published on September eleventh an article, "The Collapse of Koot Hoomi," based on correspondence released to the editor by the Coulombs, who several months earlier had been expelled from Adyar. The correspondence consisted of letters purportedly written to them by Blavatsky, while traveling in India, ordering the performance of fraudulent phenomena at Adyar. Advance proofs of the article were sent to leading Anglo-Indian papers in India and created a sensation. In some cities hundreds of placards were displayed announcing "The Fall of Madame Blavatsky; Her Intrigues and Deceits Uncovered."[164]

The *Times* of London published the story on September twentieth, and HPB's reply was published on October ninth:

> Sir,—*With reference to the alleged exposure at Madras of a dishonorable conspiracy between myself and two persons of the name of Coulomb to deceive the public with occult phenomena, I have to say that the letters purporting to have been written by me are certainly not mine. Sentences here and there I recognize, taken from old notes of mine on different matters, but they are mingled with interpolations that entirely pervert their meaning. With these exceptions the whole of the letters are a fabrication.*
>
> *The fabricators must have been grossly ignorant of Indian affairs, since they make me speak of a "Maharajah of Lahore," when every Indian schoolboy knows that no such person exists.*
>
> *With regard to the [Coulombs'] suggestion that I attempted to promote "the financial prosperity" of the Theosophical Society by means of occult phenomena, I say that I have never at any time received, or attempted to obtain, from any person any money either for myself or for the Society by any such means. I defy anyone to come forward and prove the contrary. Such money as I have received has been earned by literary work of my own, and these earnings, and what remained of my inherited property when I went to India, have been devoted to the Theosophical Society. I am a poorer woman today than I was when, with others, I founded the society.*—*Your obedient Servant,*
>
> H. P. Blavatsky
> *77 Elgin Crescent, Notting Hill, W.,*
> *October 7.*[165]

It should be mentioned at this point that earlier in May, while HPB was still in Paris, she had been warned that Madame Coulomb in Adyar was circulating stories that Blavatsky had written her incriminating letters. HPB tells of this in a letter to Sinnett:

> . . . when Subba Row wrote to me in Paris to collect my recollections well, to remember and tell whether I had ever written to her [Madame Coulomb] any compromising letter, for if so it was better

to buy them of her at any price, than to allow her to ruin my character and perhaps the TS—I answered him (May 1884) that I *had never written her anything* that I should fear to see published; that *she lied,* and could do what she pleased.[166]

She also wrote Olcott "Had I been such an ass" to compose such letters to the Coulombs, "I would never have gone to Europe; I would have turned heaven and hell [over] to prevent the Board of Control from turning them out; I would have returned home at the first intimation of danger."[167]

Miss Arundale recalls:

It was at the end of September that Madame Blavatsky again came to us for a short time before going to Mr. and Mrs. Oakley, previous to their all leaving for India. She was very depressed and unwell, almost worn out with the trouble that she had gone through. In a letter that she wrote me at that time, just before leaving Elberfeld, she says: "I have resigned my corresponding secretaryship in the Society: I have disconnected myself with it publicly; for I think that so long as I am in and at the head of the Society I will be the target shot at, and that the Society will be affected by it. . . . My heart—if I have any left—is broken by this step. But I had to sacrifice myself to the good of the Society. The *cause* before persons and personalities."[168]

Chapter 12

The Coulomb-
Hodgson Affair

A lthough the Hodgson report for the Society for Psychical Research was not released until December
1885, it is largely supportive of the 1884 Coulomb charges, and so
both require consideration together. Detailed consideration appears
no longer essential, however, since one hundred years later—in
1986—the SPR issued a press release stating that "the 'exposure' of the
Russian-born occultist, Madame H. P. Blavatsky by the SPR in 1885,
is in serious doubt, with the publication in the SPR *Journal* (vol. 53
April 1986) of a forceful critique of the 1885 report," by Dr. Vernon
Harrison, "a long-standing member of the SPR."

According to the press-release:

> Central to the case were two sets of disputed letters. One set,
> provided by two dismissed employees of The Theosophical Society
> at its headquarters in India, were supposedly in the handwriting of
> Madame Blavatsky and implicated her in fraudulent psychic phe-
> nomena. The other set, were ostensibly written in support of The
> Theosophical Society by members of an oriental fraternity, popu-
> larly called Mahatmas. Dr. Hodgson accepted the genuineness of
> the first set [but] argued that the Mahatma Letters were spurious
> productions by Madame Blavatsky and occasional confederates. Dr.
> Harrison,† on the contrary, suggests that it is the incriminating let-
> ters that are forgeries, concocted by the ex-employees for revenge;
> while the bulk of the Mahatma Letters, now preserved in the Brit-
> ish Library, are not in Madame Blavatsky's handwriting, disguised or
> otherwise.

For Dr. Harrison's detailed analysis of the handwriting evidence one
must read his lengthy report. Hodgson's evidence on handwriting,
Harrison found, was "so weak, partisan, and confused, that it might

---

† Dr. Harrison is an expert on handwriting and forgery, and for ten years was Research
Manager at Thomas De La Rue, printers of bank notes, passports, stamps, etc., for the British
government.

just as easily show that Madame Blavatsky wrote *Huckleberry Finn*—or that President Eisenhower wrote the *Mahatma Letters* [*The Secret Doctrine*]."[169]

Harrison's conclusion that HPB did not write the Mahatma letters is independently supported in three other investigations by experts. What follows are some highlights of the Coulomb-Hodgson affair.

≈

In early 1884, when HPB was preparing to leave India for her European visit, she paid a visit to Prince Harisinghji, in Varel. She was accompanied by Mohini, Dr. Hartmann, and Emma Coulomb, who had made a special request to be included. On previous occasions Coulomb had sought in vain to obtain two thousand rupees from this wealthy rajah and hoped this time to be successful. When HPB discovered this latest attempt and reprimanded her, Coulomb was furious and vowed vengeance: "I will never forgive her for the rest of my life, and will injure her as much as I can."[170]

It was no surprise to HPB that Coulomb nourished unkind feelings toward her. To Sinnett, she wrote:

> She began building her plan of treachery in 1880, from the first day she landed at Bombay [TS headquarters] with her husband, both shoeless, penniless and starving. She offered to sell *my secrets* to the Rev. Bowen of the *Bombay Guardian,* in July 1880, and she sold them actually to the Rev. Patterson in May 1885. . . . Why should I complain? Has not Master left it to my choice to either follow the dictates of Lord Buddha, who enjoins us not to fail to feed *even a starving serpent,* scorning all fear lest it should turn round and bite the hand that feeds it—or to face *karma* which is sure to punish him who turns away from the sight of sin and misery, or fails to relieve the sinner and the sufferer.[171]

Before HPB left for Europe, Coulomb requested that she and her husband have exclusive access to Blavatsky's rooms on the second floor in order to protect them from harm. When HPB protested that she had already granted permission to Dr. Hartmann to use her library, Emma became very excited and insisted that if he or anyone else could enter, she could "answer for nothing" as to what might happen. HPB then acceded to her wishes.[172]

Of all those at Adyar, Olcott was least suspicious of the Coulombs, who were very friendly to him. They worked hard and did their work well. On April fifth, when he was traveling by train with Mohini from

Paris to London, he received phenomenally this letter from one of the Masters:

Do not be surprised at anything you may hear from Adyar. Nor discouraged. It is possible—tho' we try to prevent it within the limits of karma—that you may have great domestic annoyances to pass thro'. You have harbored a traitor and an enemy under your roof for years, and the missionary party are more than ready to avail of any help she may be induced to give. A regular conspiracy is on foot. She is maddened by the appearance of Mr. Lane Fox and the powers you have given to the Board of Control.[173]

Back in India, on April twenty-sixth, another phenomenally delivered letter was addressed to Dr. Hartmann, as head of the Board of Control:

For some time already the woman has opened communication—a regular diplomatic *pourparler* with enemies of the cause, certain [missionaries]. She hopes for more than 2,000 rupees from them, if she helps them by ruining or at least injuring the Society by injuring the reputation of the founders. Hence hints as to "trap doors" and tricks. Moreover when *needed* trap doors *will be found,* as they have been forthcoming for sometime. . . . Keep all said above in strictest confidence, if you would be strongest. Let her not suspect you know it, but if you would have my advice, be prudent. Yet act without delay.[174]

The Board did not act immediately, but when they did, they took extreme measures. On May fourteenth a trial was conducted and the Coulombs were charged with a number of misdemeanors, including extortion, blackmail, slanders, and misuse of the Society's funds. The charges being uncontested, the couple were expelled.[175] The Board was gleeful at finally ridding themselves of the troublesome pair, but, humiliated and burning with desire for revenge, the Coulombs went straight into the welcoming arms of the Christian missionaries.

Writes R.A.V. Morris:

The missionaries had had things all their own way. With the prestige of the governing race behind them, they could persuade themselves that Brahmanism, being the creed of an "inferior" race, was necessarily an inferior religion, inevitably doomed in the course of time to be replaced by Christianity. Accordingly, when *The Theosophist* was started and an active movement for the revival of the native religions in their primitive purity was set on foot by a group of Europeans [and one American] the missionaries recognized the danger to their racial and religious dominance, and adopted the time dishonored tactics of blackening the reputation of their leading opponent as a preliminary to driving her and her society out of the field.[176]

The Board of Control had in fact been on the verge of expelling the Coulombs several weeks before but refrained when they received this letter from KH:

> So long as one has not developed a perfect sense of justice, he should prefer to err rather on the side of mercy than commit the slightest act of injustice. Madame Coulomb is a medium and as such irresponsible for many things she may say or do. At the same time she is kind and charitable. One must know how to act towards her to make of her a very good friend. She has her own weaknesses but their bad effects can be minimized by exercising on her mind a moral influence by a friendly and kindly feeling. Her mediumistic nature is a help in this direction, if proper advantage be taken of the same. It is my wish therefore that she shall continue in charge of the household business, the Board of Control, of course, exercising a proper supervisory control and seeing, in consultation with her, that no unnecessary expenditure is incurred. A good deal of reform is necessary and can be made rather with the help than the antagonism of Madame Coulomb. . . . Show this to Madame C. so that she may cooperate with you.[177]

When the Board ordered the Coulombs to leave, the couple refused to budge until HPB returned. The Board then cabled her in Paris for her consent. She apparently gave a reluctant permission, for she cabled the Coulombs: "Sorry you go. Prosper."[178]

Once the Coulombs were evicted, the Board took immediate possession of the second floor at headquarters and were aghast at what Alexis Coulomb had done while in possession of the room.[†] When Judge arrived from London with full authority from Olcott and Blavatsky to take charge, he made a full investigation. Entering HPB's bedroom he found an unfinished hole in the wall separating the bedroom from the private meeting room and library next door, the latter room having

---

† As Coulomb in the course of his job at headquarters was always hammering away fixing something, the Board had taken no notice of noises heard. A leaking roof, they knew, had to be repaired.

been added a year before. On the side in the meeting room was a cabinet called the shrine, which housed pictures of HPB's Indian teachers and some mementos of her stay with them in Tibet. It was the scene of various apports (a word frequently used in psychical research for objects phenomenally carried from one place to another). Coulomb had obviously intended that the hole he made would open up just behind the cabinet, for when the Coulombs confessed being partners with HPB in producing fraudulent phenomena, they claimed one of them would stand in this hole and place objects or letters in the shrine.

Coulomb had not had time to complete the hole. Judge said it was so new that its edges were ragged with the ends of laths sticking out, and the plaster was still on the floor. In the bedroom, Coulomb placed a cupboard with a false panel in the back that hid the hole in the wall. Judge writes:

> But the panel was too new to work and had to be violently kicked in to show that it was there. It was all unplaned, unoiled, and not rubbed down. He had been dismissed before he had time to finish. In the hall that opened on the stairs he had made a cunning panel. . . . This was not finished and force had to be used to make it open, and then only by using a mallet. Another movable panel he also made in the front room. . . . I had to use a mallet and file to open it. All these things were discovered and examined in the presence of many people, who then and there wrote their opinions in a book I provided for the purpose, and which is now at headquarters.
>
> The whole arrangement was evidently made up after the facts, to fit them on the theory of fraud. That it was done for money was admitted, for a few days after we had completed our examination the principal of the Christian College came to the place—a thing he had never done before—and asked that he and his friends be allowed to see the room and the shrine. He almost implored us to let him go up, but we would not, as we saw he merely desired to finish what he called his "exposure." He was then asked in my presence by Dr. Hartmann what he had paid to Coulomb for his work, and replied, somewhat off his guard, that he had paid him somewhere about one hundred rupees. This supports the statement by Dr. Hartmann[179] that Coulomb came to him [after he had been evicted] and said that ten thousand rupees were at his disposal if he would ruin the Society. He merely exaggerated the amount to see if we would give him more to be silent.[180]

Judge's testimony was published in two Boston periodicals[181] and was apparently unknown to Hodgson and later investigators. Hodgson

came on the scene six months after the Coulombs left. By this time
the mess left by Alexis Coulomb was cleaned up and the hole in the
wall closed up.

≈

Turning now to the reputed correspondence between HPB and
Madame Coulomb, Dr. Vernon Harrison discovered a remarkable
similarity between the handwritings of Alexis Coulomb and Madame
Blavatsky. Consequently, it would not have been difficult for him to
forge the incriminating portions of these letters.[182] When Harrison
was making his independent investigations, he appears not to have
known that the Theosophists living at Adyar when HPB lived there
were well aware of this similarity. HPB once wrote Sinnett:

> Alex Coulomb's handwriting is naturally like mine. We know all
> how Damodar was once deceived by an order written *in my hand-
> writing* to go upstairs and seek for me in my bedroom in Bombay
> when I was at Allahabad. It was a trick of Coulomb, who thought it
> good fun to deceive him, "a chela"—and had prepared a semblance
> of myself lying on my bed, and having startled Damodar—laughed
> at him for three days. Unfortunately that bit of a note was not pre-
> served. It was not intended for any phenomenon but simply a "good
> farce" (*une bonne farce*) by Coulomb, who indulged in many. And if
> he could imitate so well my handwriting in a note why could he not
> copy (he had four years to study and do it) every scrap and note of
> mine to Mme. Coulomb on identical paper and make any interpola-
> tions he liked? The fact that she was preparing for treachery ever
> since 1880 is a proof of it. . . . I have seen Coulomb copying one of
> such scraps of mine, at his table, in a scene shown to me by Master in
> the astral light. Shall my statement be believed, you think? Then
> what's the use![183]

Dr. Harrison points out that "it is a gross error of procedure that
Hodgson appears never to have examined the writings of either Mr. or
Mme. Coulomb, and that he has omitted specimens . . . in his report
of the letters supposedly incriminating HPB." "From this point on,"
Harrison declares, "he forfeits all claim to be an impartial investigator.
He becomes instead a hostile witness and must be treated as such."[184]

To make matters worse, the Blavatsky–Coulomb correspondence
has now completely vanished. The last person known to have seen the
letters was the Smithsonian scientist Elliott Coues, who died in 1899.
Michael Gomes tells of this in his three-part series "The Coulomb
Case" (1884–1984) published in *The Theosophist*:

William Emmette Coleman, an ardent spiritualist, in his "Critical Historical Review of the Theosophical Society" mentions that Elliott Coues, a former member of the TS who was expelled in 1889, "procured from the editor of the Christian College Magazine the original letters of HPB and other documents obtained by him from Mme. Coulomb, including very important letters of Mme. Blavatsky which until recently have never been published."[185]

Coues had good reason for wishing to obtain these, for Madame Blavatsky had sued him for libel because of his statements in the 20 July 1890 New York *Sun*. . . . A checque for twenty-five pounds sterling endorsed to W. E. Coleman on 21 November 1890 is among Coues' papers at the State Historical Society of Wisconsin, but not the letters. On the back of it Coues wrote, "*Price of the original Blavatsky letters bought by me of Mr. George Patterson through Mr. W. E. Coleman.*"[186]

Dr. Harrison observes that the fact that the Blavatsky–Coulomb letters were never used by Coues in his defense, and are now missing from his papers, is strong evidence "that the letters were indeed forgeries—and that in consequence the testimony of the Coulombs was quite unreliable. . . . Hodgson accepts the Coulombs' testimony almost without question, and if this is to be discounted, much of his case collapses."[187]

This testimony included not only the supposed Blavatsky–Coulomb letters but concerned numerous phenomena produced in India by HPB or her teachers. In these the Coulombs claimed a conspiratorial part. Both the letters and a description of the phenomena are recorded in Madame Coulomb's *Some Account of My Association with Madame Blavatsky from 1872–1884*. A detailed analysis thereof has been made by Beatrice Hastings (a non-Theosophist and noted literary critic) in her one-hundred-page booklet "The Coulomb Pamphlet," from which the following is taken:

What Mme. Coulomb lacked was the skill to make a judicially complete story of a mixture of already published and well-known facts,[188] of half-truths, lies and slander with a series of letters partly genuine and partly invented. But then, nobody could do that; the facts and the genuine parts would defeat the most hardy cunning. Mme. C. had to fit in a false side to well-known circumstances; and the result is a muddle, [leaving the reader] finally wondering how anyone ever came to accept this document as evidence.[189]

Perhaps that is why Madame Coulomb's story was never reprinted and was rarely referred to by Hodgson in his two-hundred-page report, although she was his chief witness. Walter Carrithers, who spent many years researching the Coulomb–Hodgson case, and under the pen name Adlai Waterman wrote *Obituary, the Hodgson Report,*[190] revealed in a private letter that in his early investigations he was not convinced by anything the Theosophists said in HPB's defense until he read Madame Coulomb's booklet, at which point he knew Coulomb was lying.[191]

One thing that Hastings overlooked, and which has apparently escaped the attention of everyone else until recently, is a peculiarity of some of the words in the letters. Before touching on this, it should be explained that HPB's purported correspondence with Madame Coulomb was largely in French—and bad French, as many have observed, while HPB's French is noted for its elegance and purity. An example of this poor French is that the words *au revoir,* so universally known, are each time spelled *a revoir.*[192] What has hitherto been overlooked is that another language keeps creeping in: Italian. Jean Overton Fuller first noticed this when researching her recent biography of HPB. In the following example, every word except *de* is Italian (although *Juiseppe* should be spelled with a "G"): *"Per l'amore de San Juiseppe fatte l'affare bene"* (For the love of St. Joseph, do the thing well). It is unimaginable that HPB would have appealed to St. Joseph for help.

Fuller writes: "We do not need to ask whether either of the Coulombs had a past in which the Italian language had some part. In her pamphlet Madame Coulomb obligingly lets slip that they did not go direct from Cairo to Ceylon, but went first to Calcutta, where she gave Italian lessons to Lady Temple."[193]

As to where Madame Coulomb *first* learned Italian seems a mystery. Fuller thought it was perhaps on the French Riviera, where Italians often go. But fifty years earlier, as an incidental bit of information unearthed, Hastings wrote: "She was of Levantine extraction, spoke Italian, but knew some English and French."[194]

Hodgson brought some of the Blavatsky–Coulomb letters to London for examination by handwriting experts,[195] who declared them genuine. Blavatsky's comment to Mrs. Sinnett was:

Ah, they must be famous, these experts. . . . The whole world may bow before their decisions and acuteness; but there is one person, at least, whom they can never convince . . . and it is H. P. Blavatsky. Were the GOD of Israel and Moses, Mahomet and all the prophets, with Jesus and the Virgin Mary to boot, [to] come and tell me that I have written one line of the infamous instructions to Coulomb—I would say to their faces—"fiddlesticks—*I have not.*" . . . *To this day* I have never been allowed to see one of those letters.[196]

In answer to Mrs. Sinnett's follow-up letter, HPB replied:

. . . while thanking you, and appreciating fully the great kindness of your heart that dictated you such words as—"were I convinced tomorrow that you had written those wretched letters I *should love you still"*—I answer—I *hope you would not,* and this for your own sake. . . . had I been guilty *once only*—of a deliberate, purposely concocted fraud, especially when those deceived were my best, my *truest* friends—no "love" for such one as I! At best—*pity* or eternal contempt. . . .

I would not have cared one brass pin for my *personal* reputation, only that every bullet of mud shot at, and passing *through* me, splatters the unfortunate T.S. with odoriferous ingredients.[197]

The other accusation to be considered is that HPB wrote the Mahatma letters. Two handwriting experts, F. G. Netherclift and Richard Sims, were used by Hodgson in comparing the writing of HPB with the purported letters of KH. Dr. Harrison writes that those experts "reached the conclusion that these documents were NOT written by Madame Blavatsky. . . . [But] Hodgson would have none of this. . . ." He said that after an investigation of KH writings in India he had concluded that, with a few exceptions, they were written by Madame Blavatsky. "On my arrival in England," wrote Hodgson, "I was surprised to find that Mr. Netherclift was of a different opinion concerning the KH writings submitted to him."

"The final report," Harrison says, "was held up while more specimens were obtained, and (I quote): 'the result was that Mr. Netherclift came to the conclusion that the whole of the documents were without doubt written by Madame Blavatsky.' Mr. Sims of the British Museum changed his position to suit." He comments: "I find Hodgson's blatant, and successful efforts to influence the judgment of his experts highly improper. No English court would accept a report known to have been made in such circumstances."[198]

In his twenty-five-page report, Harrison made a fresh examination of the various writings involved and provided plates to illustrate. His opinion reads: "I can find no clear evidence that HPB wrote" the KH letters, "and I find significant [evidence] that she did not. I do not know who wrote the Mahatma Letters, but I do not find it plausible to assume that Madame Blavatsky wrote them—the great bulk of them at any rate. That is my professional opinion."[199]

Two other handwriting experts—one in the nineteenth century, the other in the twentieth—had analyzed the handwriting of KH and HPB, and their conclusions both support Harrison's findings. The first was Dr. Ernst Shutze, calligrapher to the Court of His Majesty Wilhelm I, Emperor of Germany. In 1886, Gustav Gebhard submitted two letters, one from HPB and the other from KH, received by him in 1884 when HPB was visiting his family. In the letter accompanying his opinion, Dr. Shutze emphatically states *"If you have believed that both letters had come from one and the same hand, you have labored under a tremendous error."* In Shutze's opinion, he demonstrates that the "difference between the two are so glaring that I absolutely cannot come to the conclusion that they were written by the same hand."[200]

The second calligrapher was Dr. Paul L. Kirk of the criminological department at the University of California, one of the best-known handwriting experts in the United States. In 1963, three handwriting samples were submitted, one from HPB, another from KH, and a third from Damodar, whom Hodgson accused of writing some of the Mahatma letters. (The samples were taken from Hodgson's own report, but the names of the authors were withheld.) Dr. Kirk reported in a letter, dated February 17, 1964, that the material submitted was written by three different persons.[201]

Results of another kind of investigation were presented by Charles Marshall, in a paper read at the international Modern Language Teachers Institute Conference in Leningrad in January 1980. His paper, which strongly supports the findings that HPB was *not* the author of the Mahatma letters, is titled "The Mahatma Letters—A Syntactic Investigation Into the Possibility of Forgery† by Helena Petrovna Blavatsky, a 19th Century Occultist."[202] Marshall explained that this investigation utilized "a computer analysis of samples of writings by H. P. Blavatsky, the Mahatmas K. H. and M., plus a control group of other writings dating to the mid-1880s." He went on to say that "comparisons were made of several parameters, including the number of syllables in words, and words in sentences; and the frequency of appearance of groups of prepositions and conjunctions." This technique, or a similar one, says Marshall, has been applied in the past to test

---

† HPB amusingly points out that when her critics refer to the Mahatma letters as *forgeries,* they tacitly acknowledge that Masters exist, because how could she forge the handwritings of nonexistent beings?

the authenticity of the authorship of certain epistles attributed to St. Paul and a play attributed to Shakespeare.[203]

Hodgson's discussion of the motive behind HPB's alleged impostorship is particularly illuminating. Was it egotism? he asked. A knowledge of her character would suggest this supposition to be untenable. Was she a plain, unvarnished fraud? "She is, indeed, a rare psychological study, almost as rare as a 'Mahatma'!" he writes. "She was terrible exceedingly when she expressed her over-powering thought that perhaps her 'twenty years' work might be spoiled through Madame Coulomb." Was it religious mania, a morbid yearning for notoriety? he continued. To this, he responds:

> I must confess that the problem of her motives . . . caused me no little perplexity. . . . The sordid motive of pecuniary gain would be a solution still less satisfactory than the hypothesis of religious mania. . . . But even this hypothesis I was unable to adopt, and reconcile with my understanding of her character.
>
> At last a casual conversation opened my eyes. . . . I cannot profess, myself, after my personal experiences with Madame Blavatsky, to feel much doubt that her real object has been the furtherance of Russian interests.[204]

What was the casual conversation with HPB that opened Hodgson's eyes? He had been relaying to her the news of the recent movement of Russian troops in Afghanistan, which threatened a possible invasion of India. She expressed alarm: "That would be the death blow of the [Theosophical] Society." Hodgson regarded this "uncalled for vituperation" against her own country as a coverup of her real sympathies.[205] He could not imagine that her reaction was one of genuine concern for the welfare of the Theosophical Movement. She wrote to Sinnett: ". . . bad as I think the English government in India is in some respects—by reason of its unsympathetic character—the Russians would be a thousand times worse."[206]

Although Hodgson raised the question of HPB's motives, nobody appears to have inquired as to *his* motives in writing a report that the SPR news release (quoting Dr. Harrison) said was "riddled with slanted statements, conjectures advanced as fact or probable fact, uncorroborated testimony of unnamed witnesses, selections of evidence and *downright falsity*." (Italics added.) Yet, according to HPB, when Hodgson first came to Adyar, he was a "most excellent truthful young man,"[207] and we can presume at that time he sincerely sought to uncover the facts behind the phenomena produced in India. Could his motive have been the very one he ascribed to HPB—namely, love of country? The saying goes, "all's fair in love and war." A cold war between Russia and England regarding access to India's frontiers had been raging for years. Hodgson admits that prior to the "casual conversation with HPB," when "his eyes were opened," he had taken "no interest in political maneuvers in Central Asia." But now he was certain HPB was engaged in espionage work for the czar and, as a spy is a dangerous person, that she must be unmasked.

Cooper-Oakley, who at this time in India attended a dinner when Hodgson was present, is quoted as saying of him: "He is gone mad, behaved like one crazy. He fulminated against HPB insisting she was a Russian spy . . . capable of every and any crime."[208]

It seems significant that in the first public disclosure of the outcome of his investigations, Hodgson featured the spy theory. As an Australian, he chose the *Melbourne Age* (September 12, 1885) for his announcement, which was headed "The Theosophical Society, Russian Intrigue or Religious Evolution?" Russian politics was given as the motive behind the "huge fraudulent system worked by Madame Blavatsky with the assistance of the Coulombs and several others."[209]

Olcott broke the news to HPB—then in Europe—and she wrote Sinnett:

> Either this charge of being a *spy* has to be officially, *legally* disproved—or I have to quit all and say goodbye to all. . . . I *cannot stand* this any longer, Mr. Sinnett, there are limits to all and my long-suffering back refuses to carry any heavier burden. And *you* know that in my opinion a *spy* is hundred times worse than a thief. . . . [This charge] exiles me forever from India . . . it compromises all the Hindus—all those who were nearest and most devoted to me.[210]

This was written in November 1885, just a month before Hodgson's report was issued by the SPR. In July of 1886 she wrote Olcott:

> Now as to my coming back to India. . . . If you want me back you have to consent to my first bringing Hodgson before a Court of Law for his charge of [my] being a Russian spy. The attitude I will take as to other things liable to be brought in (Mahatmas and phenomena) is to refuse all discussion upon these matters. My complaint is on political and slanderous not metaphysical grounds. One has nothing to do with the other. . . . Sinnett says there are lawyers ready to take the case on *speculation,* my case is *so good and sure.* They are all astonished at our not bringing a case against Hodgson and the SPR. And the lawyers say *I need not even be in London* for that. I can give a

power of attorney. But if I fail to do so, the moment I return to India there will be some new conspiracy and scandal.[211]

Olcott, himself a lawyer, reasoned otherwise and no legal remedy was taken. Today, few believe HPB was a spy. The important issue now is how Hodgson's views on the subject may have influenced the kind of report he wrote.

In all fairness to Hodgson, it should be repeated that when he arrived in India to commence his investigations at the TS headquarters in Adyar, his attitude was one of friendliness, not skepticism and suspicion. British friends who knew him just before he came to India said he carried around in his bag Sinnett's *Occult World* and spoke with enthusiasm as to its Theosophical teachings.[212]

In closing this discussion of the Hodgson report, a few additional excerpts are offered from Dr. Vernon Harrison's paper in the *Journal* for the SPR:

For years Hodgson has been presented as an example of a perfect psychical researcher, and his report a model of what a report on psychical research should be. . . . On the contrary, the Hodgson Report is a highly partisan document forfeiting all claim to scientific impartiality. It is the address of a Counsel for the Prosecution who does not hesitate to select evidence to suit his case, ignoring and suppressing everything that tends to contradict his thesis. The Counsel for the Defence was never heard.

I cannot exonerate the SPR committee from blame for publishing this thoroughly bad report. They seem to have done little more than rubber-stamp Hodgson's opinions; and no serious attempt was made to check his findings or even to read his report critically. If they had done so, its errors of procedure, its inconsistencies, its faulty reasoning and bias, its hostility towards the subject and its contempt for the "native" and other witnesses, would have become apparent; and the case would have been referred back for further study. . . .

It is a thing most wonderful that Hodgson was able so completely to bamboozle, not only Netherclift and Mr. Sims of the British Museum, but also men and women of the caliber of Myers, Gurney and Mrs. Sidgwick—not to mention several generations of psychical researchers since the 1885 Report was published.

Chapter 13

Farewell to India

Despite the predictions that she dared not return and face her accusers, HPB prepared to leave for India from London. In an interview reported in the *Pall Mall Gazette* (October 23, 1884), she said: "I am returning to India to prosecute these traducers of my character, these fabricators of letters." To her family in Russia she wrote:

> Everything has changed. A hostile wind is blowing on us. What cure, what health is possible for me? I have to go back quickly to the climate that is fatal to me. It can't be helped. Were I to pay for it with death, I must clear up these schemes and calumnies because it is not me alone they harm; they shake the confidence of people in our work, and in the Society, to which I have given the whole of my soul. So how can I care for my life? . . . More than a thousand people have arisen in my defence. Not letters alone, but telegrams costing thousands of rupees have been sent to the *Times* of London. As to India, the war there is more than a newspaper war. About two hundred native students have crossed out their names from the registers of this Christian College whose journal has printed these wonderful letters of mine. . . .
>
> Madame Novikov brought Mackenzie Wallace to see me; he has lived in Russia, and has written such an excellent book about Russia and speaks Russian so well. He is going to be sent as a Secretary to the Viceroy, Lord Dufferin. He gave me a letter of introduction to Nubar Pasha of Cairo, requesting him to help me in finding information about the Coulombs.[213]

It was in Cairo, it will be recalled, that HPB first met Madame Coulomb. Nubar Pasha was a distinguished Egyptologist, prime minister of Egypt at the time of HPB's introduction.

HPB took passage to India on October thirty-first via Alexandria, Port Said, Cairo, and Sri Lanka. She was accompanied by the Cooper-Oakleys and at Port Said was joined by the British clergyman Charles Leadbeater, who planned to live and work at Adyar. In Cairo, where she spent ten days, Blavatsky was entertained royally by "the cream of society."[214] Nubar Pasha and a number of others joined the TS, the prime minister being enrolled as an Honorable Member.[215] Mrs. Isabel Cooper-Oakley later recalled:

HPB was a most interesting fellow-traveler, her varied information about every part of Egypt was both extensive and extraordinary. Would that I had space to go into the details of that time in Cairo, the drives through the quaint and picturesque bazaars, and her descriptions of the people and their ways. Especially interesting was one long afternoon spent at the Boulak Museum on the borders of the Nile, where HPB astonished Maspero, the well-known Egyptologist, with her knowledge, and as he went through the museum she pointed out to him the grades of the Initiate kings, and how they were to be known from the esoteric side.[216]

As to the investigation of the Coulombs, HPB cabled Olcott on November 24: "Success complete. Outlaws. Legal proofs." A followup letter recounted their fraudulent activities.[217]

Writes Mrs. Cooper-Oakley:

On leaving Cairo, HPB and I went straight to Suez. Mr. Oakley remained at Cairo to get the documents from the police about the Coulombs; Mr. Leadbeater joined us at Suez. After waiting two days for the steamer we started for Madras. I am not often thoroughly ashamed of my countrymen and women; but I confess I had reason to be so during that fortnight; the first pamphlets written by the missionaries were being circulated on board ship, and every insulting remark that could be made about HPB was heard.

The welcome received when the boat arrived in India was quite a contrast, she continues: "A deputation, accompanied by a brass band, came off in boats to meet us. . . . On landing at the pier head there were hundreds to meet HPB and we were literally towed by enthusiastic members down the pier in a truck, wildly decorated with paper roses, etc., and then surrounded by masses of smiling dark faces."[218]

They were then driven off to Pacheappah's Hall, where an address was delivered to HPB signed by three hundred students of Madras's Christian College that had published the Coulomb charges. The statement read, in part:

You have dedicated your life to the disinterested services of disseminating the truths of Occult Philosophy. Upon the sacred mysteries of our hoary Religion and Philosophies you have thrown a flood of light by sending into the world that marvelous production of yours, the "Isis Unveiled." By your exposition, has our beloved Colonel been induced to undertake that gigantic labor of love—the vivifying on the altars of Aryavarta† the dying flames of religion and spirituality.[219]

Olcott recalls:

She kept urging me to take her to a judge, or solicitor, or barrister, no matter which, for her to file her affidavit and begin our action, but I positively refused. I told her that within the next few days the Convention would meet, and that our paramount duty was to lay her case before the Delegates, have a special committee formed, of our ablest lawyers, and let them decide what steps she should take; that she and I had so merged our personalities into the Society, that we ought not to move until we should know the wish of our colleagues. She fretted and stormed and insisted, but I would not stir from my position, and when she threatened to go by herself and "wipe this stain off her character," I said that I should, in any case, resign my office and let the Convention decide between us: I knew too much about legal practice to do any such foolish thing. She then yielded.[220]

At the convention a special committee of fourteen of the Society's lawyers, judges, and statesmen was formed to determine the course to pursue. Their report to the convention resolved that "Madame Blavatsky should not prosecute her defamers in a court of law."[221] In the discussion that followed, the chief arguments offered for inaction were, first, that in the course of a trial ridicule would be heaped upon the sacred names of the Masters,[222] and second, that the validity of occult phenomena could not be proved in a court of law. The committee's report was received with acclamation. Olcott adds that on HPB's appearance the next evening before the audience of fifteen hundred persons who attended the celebration of the Society's ninth anniversary, she was cheered to the echo, and every allusion to her in the speeches of the several speakers aroused great enthusiasm.[223]

However, HPB was far from enthusiastic about the decision not to have her bring suit. Her visit to Cairo was now in vain. She feared that in the opinion of the world, her refusal to prosecute would henceforth

---

† Aryavarta is the ancient name of India.

be interpreted as a confession of guilt and that this would reflect on the integrity of the TS.

At the end of January 1885, HPB became ill—so seriously that Olcott, who had just gone to Burma, was called home. Mrs. Cooper-Oakley reports:

Very anxious were the hours and days of nursing that I went through those three weeks, as she grew worse and worse and was finally given up in a state of coma by the doctors. It proves how wonderful was the protective influence of HPB, ill or well; for though I was completely isolated with her near the roof of the house . . . yet night after night I wandered up and down the flat roof, to get a breath of fresh air between 3 and 4 A.M., and wondered as I watched the daylight break over the Bay of Bengal, why I felt so fearless even with her lying apparently at the point of death; I never could imagine a sense of fear coming near HPB. Finally came the anxious night when the doctors gave her up, and said that nothing could be done, it was impossible. She was then in a state of coma and had been so for some hours. The doctors said that she would pass away in that condition, and I knew, humanly speaking, that night's watch must be the last. [Oakley's husband had already gone to Madras to obtain a permit for cremation.[224]]

I cannot here go into what happened, an experience I can never forget; but towards 8 A.M. HPB suddenly opened her eyes and asked for her breakfast, the first time she had spoken naturally for two days. I went to meet the doctor, whose amazement at the change was very great. HPB said, "Ah! doctor, you do not believe in our great Masters."[225]

The following experience of Mrs. Cooper-Oakley, which she refrained from mentioning, was witnessed by others. During the evening,

in the outer room there sat whispering the two Cooper-Oakleys, Damodar Mavalanker, Bawaji D. Nath and Dr. Franz Hartmann, waiting for any call from HPB. Suddenly there appeared on the verandah the Master M. fully materialized; he passed quickly through the outer room into HPB's room. Meanwhile, those in the outer room withdrew. . . . When HPB recovered, she told her intimate friends how her Master had come and given her two choices—the first, to die and pass on into peace, with the end of her martyrdom, and the second, to live on a few years more to begin *The Secret Doctrine* . . .[226]

A century later, in discussing the decision of the delegates to the TS Convention of 1885, Dr. Harrison remarks that he cannot exonerate them from failing "to allow their founder a fair defence, they seemed concerned only with saving their own reputations. Whether she was impostor or not, HPB was entitled to a fair hearing. She never had it. Had she been allowed the legal and expert help she begged for, both Hodgson and the Society for Psychical Research would have been in dire trouble," and the Coulombs too.[227]

On March 21, 1885 HPB addressed the following letter to the General Counsel of the Theosophical Society:

Gentlemen,

The resignation of office, which I handed in on September the 27th, 1884, and which I withdrew at the urgent request and solicitation of Society friends, I must now unconditionally renew. My present illness is pronounced by my medical attendants mortal; I am not promised even one certain year of life. Under these circumstances it would be an irony to profess to perform the duty of Corresponding Secretary; and I must insist upon your allowing me to retire. I wish to devote my remaining few days to other thoughts, and to be free to seek changes of climate should such be thought likely to do me good.

I leave with you, one and all, and to every one of my friends and sympathizers, my loving farewell. Should this be my last word, I would implore you all, as you have regard for the welfare of mankind and your own Karma, to be true to the Society and not to permit it to be overthrown by the enemy.

Fraternally and ever yours—in life or death.

H. P. Blavatsky[228]

When the resignation was publicized in *The Theosophist*, it was followed by this certificate of her doctor:

I hereby certify that Madame Blavatsky is quite unfit for the constant excitement and worry to which she is exposed in Madras. The condition of her heart renders perfect quiet and a suitable climate essential. I therefore recommend that she should at once proceed to Europe, and remain in a temperate climate—in some quiet spot.

Mary Scharlieb MD and B.S., London

The decision to leave Adyar was *not* made by HPB; in fact, it was made under protest, as she would not willingly desert the work for Theosophy in India. The decision came from those who were concerned about her health, as well as from others who had lost faith in her mission and regarded her continued presence at Adyar as an embarrassment.[229]

One of the chief causes of this was Hodgson himself. Beyond his assignment as an SPR investigator, he went out of his way to instill in the minds of Theosophists everywhere he went that he had proved "all was fraud" as far as HPB was concerned.[230] He must have been a very persuasive fellow, for before he left India at the end of March 1885, he had even influenced the authorities at Adyar to withdraw two of the TS publications on the Coulomb case that in every way supported HPB. He himself relates this accomplishment.[231]

On March thirty-first, HPB left India, never to return. She sailed for Naples, accompanied by Mary Flynn; a Hindu chela, Bawaji; and Dr. Hartmann.

In June, Olcott wrote to Miss Arundale in London:

A subscription is started here [at Adyar] to defray the cost of poor HPB's illness (over £70) and her present change of residence, including her support until she gets money due her and becoming due at Moscow, for literary work. But with her gouty fingers, and weak heart, and albuminaria, I doubt if she will ever be able to do much henceforth. We must regard her as our Pensioner, and see that she is kindly cared for. Poor woman—after slaving so hard for the world, that she should under such circumstances be driven away from home, perhaps to die with a stigma of disgrace fastened upon her brilliant name![232]

It was not until the close of 1885 that the Hodgson report was issued. The aftermath was surprising, as Dr. Hartmann reports in his autobiography. The scandal "made the existence of the TS and the theosophical teachings known all over the world, and the consequence was that thousands procured and read the books of Madame Blavatsky, and made themselves acquainted with her views, while otherwise they might have remained in ignorance of these things all their life."[233] Especially in the United States the movement took on new life.[234] Only four months after Hodgson had his say, the first issue of W. Q. Judge's *Path* magazine was published in New York. A resurgence followed the next year in England, where HPB's magazine, *Lucifer,* commenced publication. In later years, Francesca Arundale observed: ". . . in the early days when one untoward event after another seemed to threaten the very existence of the Movement, and we exclaimed 'this surely will be the death of the Society,' we have seen later that,

phoenix-like, it has risen to new life from its very wounds, and becomes stronger from the blows it has endured."[235] These observations
were supported by statistics in Blavatsky's 1890 article "Recent Progress in Theosophy" in the *North American Review.* She wrote:

> To avoid prolixity we may begin with the year 1884, when the raid
> upon us was made by the London Society for Psychical Research.
> From the official report of that year it appears that on the 31st of De-
> cember, 1884, there were in existence, in all parts of the world, 104
> chartered branches of the Theosophical Society. In the year 1885, as
> an answer to our calumniators, seventeen new charters were issued;
> in 1886, fifteen; in 1887, twenty-two; in 1888, twenty-one. . . . Up
> to June, 1890, we find in our books upward of 200 branches. . . .
>
> And if no conspiracy, no attack, could ever seriously shake the
> society or impede its movement, nothing ever will. We can only
> thankfully repeat, slightly paraphrasing it, the Christian adage now
> so applicable to our movement, "*The blood of the martyrs is the seed of
> theosophy.*" Its society has done too much good work, the good grain
> is much too evident even in the piles of admitted chaff, not to have
> built a secure foundation for the temple of truth in the immediate, as
> in the distant, future.[236]

All this, however, was not apparent when HPB bade farewell to
India in 1885, and the next year was to be one of heartbreaking trials for
her personally.

Part 6

Horizons Open in the West

First Year on the Continent

H PB had no definite plans as to where she would permanently settle when she left India for Naples in March of 1885. Indifferent to places, her everyday concern was the writing of *The Secret Doctrine*. Ill though she was, she worked on the manuscript even on board the ship. Dr. Hartmann, who accompanied her on the voyage with Mary Flynn and Bawaji, reports that "frequently piles of sheets with notes" referring to the book "were found in the morning upon her table" before she set to work.[1]

After their arrival in Naples on April twenty-third, the travelers moved to nearby Torre del Greco and stayed at the Hotel del Vesuvio, named after the famous mountain that towers in the distance. Close by were the ruins of Pompeii, a tragic victim of the volcano's spewing in Roman days.

The three months spent in Italy were trying. In the rush to get HPB out of India, many needed possessions were left behind, including her precious glasses. Owing to dampness she suffered frequent attacks of rheumatism, and writing conditions were poor, so she decided to move to Würzburg in northern Bavaria. She wrote Patience Sinnett:

I do not want to live in any of the large centres of Europe. But I must have a warm and dry room, however cold outside, . . . I like Würzburg. It is near Heidleberg and Nürenberg, and all the centres one of the Masters [KH] lived in,[2] and it is He who advised my Master to send me there. Fortunately I have received from Russia a few thousand francs [from her writings], and some benefactors "sent me Rs. 500 and 400 from India". . . . I intend to take a nice set of rooms and happy will be the day I see you at my samovar, . . .[3]

En route HPB spent a week in Rome and another with Solovyov and Madame de Morsier in Cergues, Switzerland. Around the middle of August she arrived in Würzburg, accompanied only by Bawaji, Dr. Hartmann and Miss Flynn having left the party earlier. Soon thereafter she wrote Percy Sinnett:

For myself—I am resolved to remain sub rosa. *I can do far more by remaining in the shadow than by becoming prominent once more in the movement. Let me hide in unknown places and write, write, write, and teach whoever wants to learn. Since Master forced me to live, let me live and die now in relative peace. It is evident He wants me still to work for the T.S. since He does not allow me to make a contract with Katkov—one that would put yearly 40,000 francs at least in my pocket—to write exclusively for his journal and paper. He would not permit me to sign such a contract last year in Paris when proposed, and does not sanction it now for—He says—my time "shall have to be occupied otherwise."* [4]

Despite HPB's desire for retirement, news of her whereabouts soon spread. In August, Solovyov and his sister-in-law came for several weeks; in September, Francesca Arundale and Mohini visited; and HPB's Aunt Nadya was also a visitor during this period. They were followed by Dr. Hartmann, Professor Sellin, Arthur Gebhard, and several others.

The president of the Theosophical Society in Germany, Dr. William Hübbe-Schleiden, paid five visits. Handsome and jovial, he was a welcome guest wherever he went. Hübbe-Schleiden was a learned scholar and author who had studied law and political economics as a young man and traveled widely in geographical explorations. He had also been attaché to the German consulate general in London. In 1886 he founded a metaphysical magazine, *The Sphinx,* which he edited for twenty-two volumes. [5]

Several years after his visits to HPB, Hübbe-Schleiden was asked to record his observations as to how HPB wrote *The Secret Doctrine.* Here, in part, is what he wrote:

When I visited her in October, 1885 . . . she had scarcely any books, not half a dozen. . . . I saw her write down sentences as if she were copying them from something before her, where, however, I saw nothing. . . .

I saw a good deal of the well-known blue KH handwriting as corrections and annotations on her manuscripts as well as in books that lay occasionally on her desk. And I noticed this principally in the morning before she had commenced to work. I slept on the couch in her study after she had withdrawn for the night, and the couch stood only a few feet from her desk. I remember well my astonishment one morning when I got up to find a great many pages of foolscap covered with that blue pencil handwriting lying on her own manuscript, at her place on the desk. How these pages got there

I do not know, but I did not see them before I went to sleep and no person had been bodily in the room during the night, for I am a light sleeper.

I must say though that the view I took then was the same that I hold now. I never did and never shall judge of the value or the origin of any mental product from the way and manner in which it is produced. And for this reason I withheld my opinion then, thinking and saying: "I shall wait until *The Secret Doctrine* is finished and then I can read it quietly; that will be the test for me, the only one that will be any good."[6]

Hübbe-Schleiden also mentions being present when HPB was writing her article "Have Animals Souls?," published in three installments in *The Theosophist* (January–March 1886).[7] Although for centuries the Catholic Church had taught that animals were soulless, Blavatsky revealed that St. Paul and the early Church Fathers had affirmed otherwise. This is no mere theological debate. When the later Church denied soul life and immortality to the lower creatures, Christians felt little compunction about overworking animals on the farm, hunting them in sport, or trapping them for women's adornment. In today's technological society chickens are inhumanely confined as egg-laying machines, while other animals are subject to excruciating torture and miserable deaths in the laboratory. On December 31, 1979, The *New York Times Magazine* revealed the annual rate of animal experimentation in the United States to be 64 million, including 400,000 dogs, 200,000 cats, and thousands of horses and ponies.

AV, the journal of the American Anti-Vivisection Society, featured in its October 1982 issue Blavatsky's hundred-year-old paper "Have Animals Souls?" This was in an article by Dr. Liam Brophy, a Dublin-based scholar and frequent contributor to the journal. Of HPB's monograph, he says:

> [It is] one of the most erudite and convincing pronouncements on the subject of animal spirits ever published, [ranging] through the Bible, the Fathers of the Church, the Sacred Books of the East, Scholastic philosophy and modern literature. . . . That some of the highest Christian authorities, such as Saints Paul and John Chrysostom, also believed in the resurrection of the souls of animals was proved by Helena Blavatsky. . . . She cites several other Pauline texts as evidence that the Apostle to the Gentiles believed in an afterlife for animals, and held that man and animal are on a par on earth as to suffering ("the whole creation *omnis creatura* groaneth")

in their evolutionary efforts towards the goal. . . . It may surprise some that the eminent theosophist produced evidence to show that Pope Benedict XIV believed in the miracles of the specific resurrection of animals, and held them to be as well authenticated as "the Resurrection of Christ."

The present writer had occasion to use the foregoing in a previous book and sent Brophy a courtesy copy. In his acknowledgment (February 25, 1985), Brophy remarked:

> I am convinced that H. P. Blavatsky's long and scholarly article was inspired from beyond. It shows a knowledge of scholastic philosophy alone which is stupendous and almost impossible to one who had led such a wandering busy life as hers.

As to the antivivisection movement, Theosophists over the years have played an influential role. One such was Lord Hugh Dowding, the famed air chief marshal during the Battle of Britain in World War II, who helped save England from invasion by the Nazis. He carried his fight for animal rights even to the House of Lords, where on July 18, 1957 he delivered a much publicized speech, "Painful Experiments on Animals." In its conclusion he applied his Theosophically-based reincarnational philosophy:

> I firmly believe that painful experiments on animals are morally wrong, and that it is basically immoral to do evil in order that good may come—even if it were proved that mankind benefits from the suffering inflicted on animals. . . . I cannot leave this subject without some reference to its esoteric side—to the place of the animal kingdom in the scheme of things, to man's responsibility to animals, and to the results of man's failure to meet this responsibility. . . . All life is one, and all its manifestations with which we have contact are climbing the ladder of evolution. The animals are our younger brothers and sisters, and also on the ladder but a few rungs lower down than we are. It is an important part of our responsibilities to help them in their ascent, and not to retard their development by cruel exploitation of their helplessness.

The Lord Dowding Fund for Humane Research has granted 400,000 dollars to dozens of scientists to investigate alternate methods of experimentation that do not involve using animal life.[8]

Lord Dowding's wife, Lady Muriel, also a Theosophist, founded the widespread movement "Beauty Without Cruelty," aimed at eliminating experiments on animals to test cosmetics and outlawing the yearly trapping of animals—a torturous experience that causes slow, lingering deaths. In her autobiography, *Beauty—Not the Beast,* she tells of her work.[9]

Liam Brophy's article in the *AV* journal concludes with this selection from HPB's "Do Animals Have Souls?": "When the world feels convinced that animals are creatures as eternal as ourselves, vivisection and other tortures daily inflicted on the poor brutes [will cease, for governments will be forced] to put an end to those barbarous and shameful practices."

HPB's situation in Würzburg proved far from satisfactory. Although Louisa took care of the household, Bawaji was of little help in answering correspondence, attending to the needs of visitors, securing medical assistance, and handling the innumerable details a personal secretary and companion would naturally fulfill. Freedom from distractions was imperative in writing *The Secret Doctrine.*

It was at this juncture that Countess Constance Wachtmeister entered the picture. The countess descended from an ancient French family, her father being the Marquis de Bourbel. In 1863 she married a cousin, Count Carl Wachtmeister, then stationed in London as the Swedish and Norwegian minister at the Court of St. James. He later became minister of foreign affairs, and the king of Sweden honored his wife as "State Lady of the Land." After her husband's death in 1871, the countess investigated spiritualism but found it unsatisfactory. Upon reading *Isis Unveiled* in 1881 she joined the Theosophical Society in London, where she met HPB in 1884 at the time of the latter's surprise visit from Paris.[10] At Enghien, HPB told her "many things that I thought were known only to myself, and ended by saying that before two years had passed, I would devote my life wholly to theosophy. At the time I had reason to regard this as an utter impossibility, . . ."[11]

In the pages that follow, the story of the countess's relationship with HPB is taken from her book *Reminiscences of H. P. Blavatsky and The Secret Doctrine,* first published in 1893.

When the countess left Sweden in the fall of 1885, she had no intention of visiting Blavatsky in Würzburg. Her destination was Italy, where she had arranged to spend the winter with friends. En route to Italy, the countess paid a visit to the Gebhards in Elberfeld. Mrs. Gebhard asked her to delay her trip to Italy and visit HPB, as she had received a depressing letter concerning her difficult circumstances. The countess wrote offering to spend a month with "the Old Lady," as

HPB's intimates called her. Blavatsky politely refused, explaining that she had no room for a visitor and was occupied with writing *The Secret Doctrine*. As the countess was preparing to leave Elberfeld, with a cab waiting for her at the door, the following telegram arrived: "Come to Würzburg at once, wanted immediately. Blavatsky." Upon the arrival of the countess, HPB said, "I have to apologize for behaving so strangely. . . . I have only one bedroom here and I thought you might be a fine lady and not care to share it with me . . . but after my letter was posted, Master spoke to me and said that I must tell you to come."

The countess gave up her holiday and slept in HPB's single bedroom, divided by a large screen for privacy. Thus began a relationship that continued for several years, and except for a business trip or two on the part of the countess, the two lived in the same household until Blavatsky died.

The countess describes the circumstances under which *The Secret Doctrine* was written:

The circumstance which, perhaps, more than any other attracted my attention and excited my wonder when I began to help Madame Blavatsky as her amanuensis, and thus got some glimpses of the nature of her work upon *The Secret Doctrine,* was the poverty of her traveling library. Her manuscripts were full to overflowing with references, quotations, allusions, from a mass of rare and recondite works on subjects of the most varied kinds. . . .

Shortly after my arrival in Würzburg she took occasion to ask me if I knew anyone who could go for her to the Bodleian library [at Oxford]. It happened that I did know someone I could ask, so my friend verified a passage that HPB had seen in the astral light, with the title of the book, the chapter, page and figures all correctly noted. . . .

Once a very difficult task was assigned to me, namely, to verify a passage taken from a manuscript in the Vatican. Having made the acquaintance of a gentleman who had a relative in the Vatican, I with some difficulty succeeded in verifying the passage. Two words were wrong, but all the remainder correct, and, strangely enough, I was told that these words, being considerably blurred, were difficult to decipher.

These are but a few instances out of many. If ever HPB wanted definite information on any subject which came uppermost in her writing, that information was sure to reach her in one way or another, either in a communication from a friend at a distance, in a newspaper or a magazine, or in the course of our casual reading of books; and this happened with a frequency and appositeness that took it quite out of the region of mere coincidence. She would, however, use normal means in preference to the abnormal when possible, so as not to exhaust her power unnecessarily.[12]

As the days progressed and visitors came and went, the countess discovered that "to everybody she was different," explaining:

I have never seen her treat two persons alike. The weak traits in everyone's character were known to her at once, and the extraordinary way in which she would probe them was surprising. By those who lived in daily contact with her the knowledge of *Self* was gradually acquired, and by those who chose to benefit by her practical way of teaching progress could be made. But to many of her pupils the process was unpalatable, for it is never pleasant to be brought face to face with one's own weaknesses; and so many turned from her, but those who could stand the test, and remain true to her, would recognize within themselves the inner development which alone leads to occultism.

As to how this method operated in her own case, Wachtmeister revealed:

When I first went to her I was a woman of the world, one who had been a petted child of fortune. Through my husband's political position I occupied a prominent place in society; it therefore took me a long time to realize the hollowness of what I had hitherto looked upon as being the most desirable objects in life, and it required much training and many a hard battle with myself before I could conquer the satisfaction in self which a life of idleness, ease, and high position is sure to engender. So much had to be "knocked out of me," to use one of HPB's own phrases.[13]

Towards the close of December 1885, when the countess had been living with HPB only a month, the Hodgson Report was issued. Professor Sellin brought HPB a copy on New Year's eve.[14] An unfavorable report had been expected, but what arrived was devastating: two hundred pages of "evidence" of HPB's fraudulent phenomena. "Go, before you are defiled by my shame," she told the countess. "You cannot stop here with a ruined woman . . . who will be pointed at everywhere as a trickster and imposter."[15]

"One thing is a consolation," HPB wrote to a Theosophist in the United States, "the whole burden falls upon me, as the Masters are made out *myths*. So much the better. Their names have been dese-crated too long and too much."[16]

On January 6, 1886, a few days after HPB received the SPR report, a letter was received from Hübbe-Schleiden. He was very disturbed by Hodgson's evidence that certain expressions used by KH in his letters were also used in Blavatsky's writings, which would suggest she was the author of those letters. Strangely—as she wrote Sinnett that same day—the very night before she had relived in dream a scene from Tibetan days when KH was daily teaching her English. When the letter from the distinguished doctor was received that morning, the purport of the dream became plain. It was natural that some of her expressions were like KH's; he taught them to her![17]

Hübbe-Schleiden was soon to visit HPB in Würzburg. After leav-ing, he was startled to find the following precipitated certificates in his copy of the Hodgson proceedings:

If this can be of any use or help to Dr. Hübbe-Schleiden—though I doubt it—I, the humble undersigned Fakir, certify that the "Secret Doctrine" is dictated to Upāsika [HPB] partly by myself & partly by my Brother KH.

M∴

I wonder if this note of mine is worthy of occupying a select spot with the documents reproduced [by Hodgson] and which of the peculiarities of the "Blavatskian" style of writing[18] it will be found to most resemble? The present is simply to satisfy the Dr. that—"the more proof given the less believed." Let him take my advice and not make these two documents public. It is for his own satisfaction that the undersigned is happy to assure him that The Secret Doctrine *when ready, will be the triple production of M∴, Upasika, and the Doctor's most humble servant.*

K. H.[19]

Seven years later the certificates were published in *The Path* magazine (April 1893).

After Hodgson's report appeared, Wachtmeister recalled:

It seemed as if the Society had received its death blow; day after day came in resignations from those who had hitherto been looked upon as shining lights in the Society, or else insulting letters from men and women who until then had worn the mask of friendship. The remainder of the members of the TS were more or less para-

1. *Helena Andreyevna Fadeyev von Hahn,*
   HPB's mother (1814–1842).

2. *HPB as a young woman. (Theosophical*
Society, Pasadena Archives)

3. *Nadyezhda (Nadya) Fadeyev, HPB's aunt (1829–1919).*

4. *Vera Petrovna de Zhelihovsky, HPB's sister (1835–1896). (Theosophical Society, Pasadena Archives)*

5. Photograph of HPB inscribed to Professor Hiram Corson of Cornell University, around 1875.

6. Henry Steel Olcott, President-Founder of the Theosophical Society (1832–1907).

7. *William Quan Judge, Co-Founder, Theosophical Society (1851–1896). (Theosophical Society, Pasadena Archives)*

8. *William Quan Judge, Ceylon (Sri Lanka), 1884. The photograph, taken in the very year that Solovyov met Judge, negates Solovyov's description of him. August Lindstrom, a sculptor who had never seen Judge, observed this of him while making the death mask: "This is the remarkable combination I found—a tremendous willpower, with an equal development of gentleness; thorough practicability and adaptability conjoined to a highly idealistic nature, and a gigantic intellect in hand with selflessness and modesty."* (Letters That Have Helped Me, *Theosophy Company, 299–300). (Photograph given by Mrs. Alice Judge, William Q. Judge's wife, to Eloise Ives, United Lodge of Theosophists, New York City)*

9. *HPB en route from New York to India, 1878.*

10. Patience Sinnett (?–1908).

11. Alfred Percy Sinnett (1840–1921).

12. Damodar K. Mavalankar (1857–?).

13. Madame Blavatsky, Ceylon (Sri Lanka), 1880. (Theosophical Society, Adyar Archives)

14. *Anagarika H. Dharmapala, Buddhist missionary (1864–1933). (Theosophical Society, Wheaton, Illinois Archives)*

15. *Portrait of HPB by Hermann Schmiechen, 1885. (A. P. Sinnett, Incidents in the Life of Madame Blavatsky)*

16. *Countess Constance Wachtmeister (1839–1910).*

17. *HPB at "Maycot," Upper Norwood, London, England, 1887.*

18. *Dr. Anna Bonus Kingsford (1846–1888). (Edward Maitland,* Anna Kingsford—Her Life, Letters, Diary and Work*)*

19. *Archibald Keightley (1859–1930). (Theosophical Society, Pasadena Archives)*

20. *Bertram Keightley (1860–1945). (*The Theosophist, *September 1909)*

21. *General Abner Doubleday (1819–1893).*

22. *William Butler Yeats (1865–1939).*
(Photograph by Beresford, circa 1905)

23. *Æ, pseudonym of George William Russell*
(1867–1935).

24. *Annie Besant (1847–1933).*
(Theosophical Society, Wheaton,
Illinois Archives)

25. *Isabel Cooper-Oakley (1854–1914).*
*(*The Path, *July 1894, 122)*

26. *HPB in her perambulator at 19 Avenue Road, London, England.*

27. *Besant, Olcott, and Judge in the Garden at the TS Headquarters, London, England. (H. S. Olcott,* Old Diary Leaves, *4:412)*

28. The famous "Sphinx" photograph by Resta, 1889. (Theosophical Society, Pasadena Archives)

29. The "Crow's Nest," Bombay, India. (Theosophical Society, Adyar, Madras, India Archives)

30. HPB's residence and T.S. Headquarters: 17 Lansdowne Road, London, England; taken in 1957.

31. "The Messenger," painted in 1931 by Nicholas Roerich. Description: The person opening the door represents "Humanity," while the visitor entering the doorway is Helena Petrovna Blavatsky. HPB is clothed in blue robes, while the majestic purple-blue sky and golden horizon are portrayed behind her. The mountains and snow-covered ground reflect the beautiful blue hue of the sky. (In the private collection of the Theosophical Society, Adyar, Madras, India)

lyzed, and all they wanted to do was to keep quiet and out of sight, so that no mud should be thrown at them. But a few bright stars shone through the darkness, jewels of friends who kept staunch and true through all, and it was really their expressions of sympathy and love which kept HPB alive.[20]

One such was this February fifth letter to HPB from William Q. Judge in New York, on the SPR report:

So they have reported you. You are a corpse. You are squelched, you are a mere Mahatma fabrication. But they praise you too, for you must ever remain the chief, the most interesting, the hugest, the most marvelous and the most able impostor and organizer of great movements, who has appeared in any age either to bless or to curse it. Not Cagliostro had such honor as this! Well, you deserve honor; I only wish it were not accompanied by such vile lies and trash as they put on you. . . .

I shall have written before you get this, a letter to the Boston Index *which reprinted the report. You must have observed that Hodgson has left me out. And yet I am an important factor. I was there. I examined all, I had all in charge, and* I say there was no aperture *behind the shrine. Then as to letters from* ∴ *you know I have many that came to me which* resemble my writing. *How will they explain that? Did I delude myself? And so on.*

You can rely on me at this point for all the help that may be thought necessary. *You will remember that I was at Enghien with you the day of one of the phenomena. They did not get those times when I got letters from the postman with messages inside. . . .*

But people here are not distressed by this report. They see the truth runs through our whole movement and they are not so hidebound by reports and authority as in other places. . . . [I]n Boston and Cincinnati great interest is growing. They find me back from India still a believer and still explaining away what they call your "imposture."[21]

How rare it was for HPB to receive at this time such a vote of confidence becomes evident from the following letter, dated February 18, from the countess to Sinnett, enclosing the letter of Judge:

This morning's post took you some nasty letters as usual, but Heaven be blessed at last I can send you a real good one which did the Old Lady's heart good, after all the dirt and stones which have been recently thrown at her. Mr. Judge has had ten years' experience of her phenomena and yet he does not cry out FRAUD *like Bawaji. Mme. B. wants you to read this letter to him and Mohini.*[22]

Both Bawaji and Mohini were then living in London and were among those who turned against HPB during this period.

Wachtmeister notes that, "it is little to be wondered at that the progress of *The Secret Doctrine* was brought to a standstill during these stormy days," and that when, at last, the work was resumed, the necessary detachment and tranquility of mind were hard to attain. She continues:

> HPB said to me one evening: "You cannot imagine what it is to feel so many adverse thoughts and currents directed against you; it is like the prickings of a thousand needles, and I have continually to be erecting a wall of protection around me." I asked her whether she knew from whom these unfriendly thoughts came; she answered: "Yes, unfortunately I do, and I am always trying to shut my eyes so as not to see and know"; and to prove to me that this was the case, she would tell me of letters that had been written, quoting passages from them, and these actually arrived a day or two afterwards, I being able to verify the correctness of the sentences.
>
> One day at this time, when I walked into HPB's writing room, I found the floor strewn with sheets of discarded manuscript. I asked the meaning of this scene of confusion, and she replied: "Yes, I have tried twelve times to write this one page correctly, and each time Master says it is wrong. I think I shall go mad, writing it so often; but leave me alone; I will not pause until I have conquered it, even if I have to go on all night."
>
> I brought a cup of coffee to refresh and sustain her, and then left her to prosecute her weary task. An hour later I heard her voice calling me, and on entering found that, at last, the passage was completed to satisfaction, but the labor had been terrible, and the results were often at this time small and uncertain.
>
> As she leaned back enjoying her cigarette and the sense of relief from arduous effort, I rested on the arm of her great chair and asked her how it was she could make mistakes in setting down what was given to her. She said: "Well, you see, what I do is this. I make what I can only describe as a sort of vacuum in the air before me, and fix my sight and my will upon it, and scene after scene passes before me like the successive pictures of a diorama, or, if I need a reference of information from some book, I fix my mind intently, and the astral counterpart of the book appears, and from it I take what I need. The more perfectly my mind is freed from distractions and mortifications, the more energy and intentness it possesses, the more easily I can do this; but today, after all the vexations I have undergone in consequence of the letter from X., I could not concentrate properly, and each time I tried I got the quotations all wrong. Master says it is right now, so let us go in and have some tea." [23]

Teatime at seven marked the end of the day's work. After this, the countess recalls:

We would spend a pleasant evening together. Comfortably seated in her big armchair, HPB used to arrange her cards for a game of Patience, as she said, to rest her mind. It seems as if the mechanical process of laying her cards enables her mind to free itself from the pressure of concentrated labor during the day's work. She never cared to talk of theosophy in the evenings. The mental tension during the day was so severe that she needed above all things rest, and so I procured as many journals and magazines as I could, and from these I would read the articles and passages that I thought most likely to interest and amuse her. At nine o'clock she went to bed, where she would surround herself with her Russian newspapers and read them until late.[24]

It is difficult to picture HPB in these lighter moments, as her photographs reveal only the serious side of her nature.[25] Often at such times, the countess says, "a bright childish nature seemed to beam around her, and a spirit of joyous fun would sparkle in her whole countenance, and cause the most winning expression that I have ever seen on a human face."[26] Nor do the photographs portray the side of her character etched by Walter Old:

She was a charming conversationalist and had a spontaneity of manner that was exceedingly attractive. Indeed, I have heard it said that the most beautiful woman in England was like a faded wallflower in the presence of this remarkable personality. . . . When she laughed, she opened her mouth and her eyes wide with the abandon of a child. I had never seen a woman of mature years laugh with such child-like naturalness as she.[27]

Chapter 2

"The Iago of Theosophy"

T he Würzburg story is not complete without going into more particulars as to the visit of Solovyov in August and September of 1885 and what led to his appearing on the scene at that time.

He first met Blavatsky in Paris in the spring of 1884. Some weeks later she wrote to an acquaintance:

> *You had a call from a gentleman unknown to you, but very well known in Russia. He is a friend and comrade of mine in Theosophy. His name is Vsevolod Sergueyevich Solovyov and he is the author of many historical novels. He is a genuine* Theosophist—*not merely a member of the Theosophical Society. And I make a great distinction between the two.*[28]

Yet two years later, in a letter to Sinnett (March 3, 1886) HPB referred to him as "The Iago of Theosophy"—in reference, of course, to the Shakespearean scoundrel whose lies to Othello led him to strangle his beautiful chaste wife, Desdemona, and similarly drove to madness everyone in the drama who stood in the way of his ambitions.

Solovyov's version of his association with HPB was first recorded in a series of articles in *Russky Vyestnik* in 1892 and was published as a book the following year. In 1895 an edited English translation by Walter Leaf was published on behalf of the Society for Psychical Research in London under the title *A Modern Priestess of Isis.*[29] As the translation has been regarded ever since by HPB's critics as a major source of information concerning her life, her biographers are obliged to investigate its validity.

Professor Sidgwick, in a prefatory note, explains why the SPR sponsored the book. At first, he says, only certain portions relating to psychical research were to be printed in the Proceedings of the Society, but, he continues:

> On further consideration it seemed to us clearly desirable, if possible, that the greater part of Mr. Solovyov's entertaining narrative should be made accessible to English readers. For such English readers as were likely to be interested in learning anything more

about Madame Blavatsky would not so much desire additional proof that she was a charlatan—a question already judged and decided—but rather some explanation of the remarkable success of her imposture; and Mr. Solovyov's vivid description of the mingled qualities of the woman's nature—her supple craft and reckless audacity, her intellectual vigor and elastic vitality, her genuine bonhomie, affectionateness and (on occasion) persuasive pathos—afforded an important element of the required explanation, such as probably no one but a compatriot could have supplied. Whether the Theosophical Society is likely to last much longer, I am not in a position to say; but even if it were to expire next year, its twenty years' existence would be a phenomenon of some interest for the historian of European society in the nineteenth century; and it is not likely that any book will be written throwing more light on its origin than *A Modern Priestess of Isis*.

Inasmuch as Sidgwick believed that Solovyov's story should be especially valuable as coming from HPB's own countryman, it should also prove interesting how two of his fellow Russians viewed Solovyov's book and the subject thereof, Helena Blavatsky.

The first was the noted mathematician P. D. Ouspensky, a leading disciple of Gurdjieff. Quoting from Ouspensky's book *The Fourth Dimension,* published in Russia in 1918:

The several "exposures" of Blavatsky now in print remind one of sparrows who, having gathered around grapes painted on a wall, then shout they have been cheated, the grapes are uneatable, it's all a fraud, etc. Vsevolod Solovyov's book *A Modern Priestess of Isis,* which has been for many people the only source of information about Blavatsky, brims over with petty spite and consists of nothing but detective-like descriptions of spying, eavesdropping, questioning housemaids, in short, endless trivial details the reader cannot verify. And, meanwhile, the author does not say a single word about *what is most important,* Blavatsky's books, her life and her ideas.

H. P. Blavatsky was an outstanding personality, one that a great artist only could depict in its fullness and complexity. . . . As to the Theosophical Movement, its positive aspects are certainly very important. It has united and brought to light many studies which had previously been separate and fragmentary. It provides people a way out of the blind alley of materialism. It introduces many new words and concepts that open our minds to eternal questions, the mysteries of death, the riddles of being, and keeps us aware of them, never allowing us to forget. It summons man to live in the Eternal and not to be satisfied with the temporal. . . . These are bold insights that cannot be denied.[30]

The second Russian to be considered is Victor Bourenine, a noted publicist and cynic of the 1890s. His review of Solovyov's articles in *Russky Vyestnik,* from which the following is excerpted, appeared in the St. Petersburg *Novoye Vremya (New Times)* for December 30, 1892:

There are two Solovyovs in modern Russian literature. Mr. Vladimir Solovyov, otherwise the "philosopher," and Mr. Vsevolod Solovyov, otherwise the "philosopher's brother." The words "the philosopher's brother" alone are suggestive of Mr. Vsevolod Solovyov's having no literary name of his own, or at least, of his name being nothing in particular. Nevertheless this romancer has worked for the same number of years as his brother, the philosopher, that is to say, if I am not mistaken, for about twenty years, and what is more, he has worked most diligently. Mr. Vsevolod Solovyov, as is well known, has put forth a lot of historical novels, in which he has painted Russia's manners and Russia's life in all epochs. . . .

As the literary talent of the late Mme. Blavatsky did not rank with common talents, which is proven by her articles under the pseudonym Radda Bai in the *Russian Herald* under the editorship of Katkov; articles, which to my mind, were hundredfold more interesting and talented than all the quasi-historical novels of Vsevolod Solovyov and all his phantastical and non-phantastical writings.[†]

It is very possible that I am a victim of a wrong impression, but while reading Mr. Solovyov's [*Modern Priestess*] revelations, I often came to the following conclusion: either that Mr. Vsevolod Sollovyov is not quite exact in his narrations about his intercourse with Mme. Blavatsky, distorting the facts a bit and in general "being partial to fibs," to use the expression of a certain comedy, or that during his acquaintance with the priestess of Isis—I wish I could hunt up a refined expression—his health was not quite what it ought to be. Let the reader judge for himself.

Then follow selections from letters written by Solovyov to Blavatsky, which he forgot he ever wrote and clearly demonstrate his story to

---

[†] In 1991 Vsevolod Solovyov was nearly forgotten in Russia, although his distinguished brother Vladimir is well remembered. When Blavatsky's *Key to Theosophy* was published in 1889, the latter accorded it a lengthy review in *Russkoye Obozreniye (Russian Review,* August 1890, 881–86). (See Blavatsky, *Collected Writings* 7:334.) In 1994, Vsevolod Solovyov's *Collected Writings* were republished.

be a fabrication. Bourenine said he obtained copies of these letters from a relative of HPB. The relative was her sister, Vera Zhelihovsky, and the letters were subsequently published by her in a reply to Solovyov's accusations.

Now we turn to *A Modern Priestess of Isis*. If Solovyov had hoped to write a work that would go down in history as an accurate portrayal of his relationship with HPB and the Theosophists, it could hardly have had a more unfortunate beginning.

He tells of living in Paris in May 1884, a time when he was occupied with, among other things, mysticism and occult literature. He recalled the interesting narratives of Radda Bai (HPB) in the *Russky Vyestnik* and wondered whether he should seek her out in India, where she had gone to live. Just then, according to his account, a friend showed him a copy of *Le Matin* announcing Blavatsky had arrived from Nice a few days previously and had settled in Rue Notre-Dame-des-Champs, where people were flocking to visit the celebrity. Several times Solovyov reminds his readers that this was really a puffed-up ad prepared by Blavatsky to attract attention to her presence in Paris and that it never paid off, because when he visited her he found no crowds knocking at her door.[31]

Most of Solovyov's facts turned out to be fiction. First, it is not true that HPB arrived in Paris in May; she had come on March 28, many weeks earlier. Second, there was no need for paid announcements: the April first edition of *Le Rappel* carried a three-column report on the Theosophists, followed by *Le Temps* on the second and *Le Matin* on the twenty-first. Reporter Gil Blis interviewed HPB on May sixth, and on May eleventh the Paris correspondent of the *London World* covered the *conversazione* held by the Duchesse de Pomar.[32] HPB did not welcome all this attention; she had gone to Europe on her doctor's urgent advice to obtain a desperately needed rest.

Solovyov claims that the apartment HPB rented on Rue Notre-Dame-des-Champs was in a run-down neighborhood and the house unsightly to behold. However, these quarters had been graciously provided by the Duchesse de Pomar for her honored guests during their entire stay in Paris and could hardly fit this description.

At the top of a "dark, dark staircase" Solovyov met a slovenly figure in an Oriental turban who conducted him into "a tiny, dark lobby." This was Babula, HPB's servant. Solovyov later described this slovenly figure with an "ugly, roguish face" as "a most consummate rascal; a glance at his face was enough to convince one of this."[33] The fact is the Duchesse de Pomar delighted to parade Babula next to her coachman when driving through Paris. At Enghien the Countess d'Adhémar recruited him to serve guests in her drawing room, while Francesca Arundale, in writing of HPB's stay in her home in London a few months later, mentions: "There was also a very important member of the Indian contingent, namely Babula, HPB's servant; in his picturesque turban and white dress, he created quite a little sensation in the Crescent; and on the afternoons when tea was served and HPB's Russian samovar glistened and shone on the table, and Babula bore cups of tea and sweet cakes to the visitors, we were certainly a unique house in suburban London."[34]

It may be recalled that Judge was staying with Blavatsky at this time in Paris before leaving for India. Literary critic Beatrice Hastings, author of *Solovyov's Fraud,* thought it odd that Solovyov made no mention of him.[35] It turns out that he did, but Walter Leaf saw fit to expunge it from his translation.

Solovyov relates that one day while he was visiting HPB, "there was a bell at the door and a gentleman entered—however, there was nothing of the gentleman in him. Middle-aged man, with reddish hair, poorly dressed, with a coarse figure and an ugly repulsive face—he produced on me a most unpleasant impression."† After HPB introduced him as Mr. Judge, she privately asked Solovyov what he thought of him. "I wouldn't like to be alone with him in a desolate place," he replied. He then puts these words into HPB's mouth:

"He was the greatest scoundrel and swindler; on his soul there is probably more than one serious crime, and still, from the time he became a theosophist a complete change has taken place in him; now he is a saint."

"Then why has he such a repulsive face?" Solovyov reportedly asked.

"Very understandably; all his life left its imprint in his features. The face is a mirror of the soul, and this is not just a saying, but reality, and of course he needs lots of time to efface from his features this curse!"

Could HPB purportedly have said any of this? We must remember that Judge was only twenty-four when he became a Theosophist. He

---

† August Lindstrom, the sculptor who made Judge's death mask, observed: "I consider the nose as giving the best index to character of any feature. His nose was his most distinguishing feature, and shows great power and at the same time complete control over every thought and act, and although strong, it is of the delicate and sensitive type. His mouth showed tenderness and firmness present in equal proportion. His cheek bones also gave evidence of will strength. His hair was soft and showed refinement and gentleness. Taken altogether there was harmonious development, with no defects present, and careful examination of his head from every aspect proves that he was a great and noble man. If such a man as he would devote his life to the Theosophical Society, I think it must have a great mission and I shall ask to be admitted as a member." (William Q. Judge, *Letters That Have Helped Me,* Los Angeles, California, The Theosophy Company, 299–300)

came from Ireland at thirteen; worked hard as a clerk; studied law, and was admitted to the bar at twenty-one. Now he was thirty-three.[36] There is a picture taken of him in Sri Lanka (Ceylon) in 1884—the very year Solovyov is writing about (see Centerfold, photograph #8).

Judge did not have reddish hair, but from the photograph it is evident it was prematurely graying. The American architect Claude Bragdon, in *Episodes from an Unwritten History,* mentions the "engaging presence" of this "handsome Irish-American," and well-known Irish author George Russell (whose pen name was Æ), in a letter to Carrie Rea, spoke of Judge as "the wisest and sweetest [person] I have ever met. . . . I have more reverence for him than [for] any other human being I know of."[37]

From Solovyov's portrait of Judge and other characters in his book, one can appreciate a joint letter by Vera Johnston (HPB's niece) and her husband, Charles, printed in the *Pall Mall Gazette* (February 18, 1895), when the SPR first sponsored the publishing of Solovyov's book. Solovyov, they observed, had published many *novels* in Russian, but the only one translated into English was *A Modern Priestess of Isis.* Professor Sidgwick was right; it was entertaining indeed!

It was in Paris that Solovyov first met HPB's sister, Vera, and a close relationship developed that continued for a few years. Numerous letters were exchanged. When he wrote *A Modern Priestess,* Solovyov had apparently forgotten all about this six- to eight-year-old correspondence. Vera preserved all of his letters and also some he had written to HPB, which she had turned over to Vera. In addition, after Blavatsky's death, Vera received from Adyar Archives more of Solovyov's correspondence to HPB. When his articles on her sister were published in 1892 in *Russky Vyestnik,* Vera wrote a lengthy reply. No one would publish it even though she was a well-known author, so she published it herself in a booklet under the title *H. P. Blavatsky and a Modern Priest of Truth* in 1893.

When Solovyov's articles were published as a book he could hardly ignore Vera's booklet, so he included selections therefrom in Appendix A and in Appendix B gave his reply. However, some of the most compromising letters he wrote HPB, as well as other vital information, were not included. This became evident when Cathy Young translated into English the whole of Vera's booklet. The translation runs to 110 typewritten pages, and even this does not include the whole record, as other material from HPB's relatives is also evidential.

For an essential background, it is needful to quickly review Solovyov's professed feelings regarding Theosophy and HPB. He states right at the start of his book that he was wary of her credentials. When she spoke of her Master, he says, he "immediately felt something, a sort of intangible falsehood." Fascinated though he was by her wonderful eyes, "I was thoroughly dissatisfied." When soon thereafter he joined the Theosophical Society, his "'initiation' seemed like a silly joke of my own, which left behind it a sort of feeling of shame and even of repugnance. . . . I only felt a longing to get out at once into a purer atmosphere."[38]

This professed attitude should be compared with Solovyov's letter to HPB and to Vera and also HPB's correspondence with the various parties concerned.

"It's not long since I have come to London," HPB wrote Nadya, "but I have already got two such pitiful letters from Solovyov. The only thing he asks of me is to care for him and not forget him. He says he had never loved anyone outside of his family as he loves poor old me."[39]

After reading the French translation of *Isis,* Solovyov wrote to Vera (July 19, 1884), "I have read the second part of *Isis Unveiled* and am now convinced that it is a true prodigy." Vera claims he often said to her that it seemed unnecessary to speak of other of her sister's "miracles" after that which she had accomplished in writing the book.[40]

Solovyov spent a week at Elberfeld. After his return to Paris he received a long letter from Blavatsky, at the end of which was a precipitated note from KH "in his usual blue pencil." Both are quoted in *Modern Priestess.* In his comments that follow we have the novelist at his dramatic best:

I was so irritated by Koot Hoomi's "astral postscript" that at the first moment I was inclined to appeal at once to Madame Blavatsky to forget all about my existence. But I should have repented if I had followed this first impulse; that very day, at Madame de Morsier's, I met the most convinced and honest of the French theosophists; and they in spite of all the obviousness of the deception, admitted the postscript to be the authentic work not of "Madame's" hand but of Koot Hoomi's.

This absolute blindness on the part of people who were perfectly rational in everything but the question of "Madame's" impeccability, forced me finally to adhere to my original plan. Whatever came I would collect such proofs of all these deceptions as should be sufficient not only for me but for all these blind dupes. I would no longer give way to the involuntary sympathy and pity, which in spite of everything, still attracted me to Helena Petrovna. I would in the first place deal only with Madame Blavatsky, the thief of souls, who was trying to steal my soul too. She was duping me under the veil of personal friendship and devotion; she was trying to entangle and exploit me; and so my hands were free.[41]

How fickle is human memory! Here is the beginning of Solovyov's letter to HPB in response to her letter and KH's postscript:

Dear Helena Petrovna,

I have just received your letter. Believe it or not, neither the letter itself nor even Koot Hoomi's postscript came as a surprise to me. I shall create a sensation with it through Madame de Morsier. . . .

When HPB received the first news of the Coulomb scandal during her stay in Elberfeld and decided to return immediately to India, Solovyov wrote Vera (October 30): "Tomorrow HP leaves for Liverpool, then will go to Egypt and to India. That she is still living and, moreover, able to travel, to go such distances and at this time of the year, seems to me a miracle! Or rather, *another proof that the Mahatmas exist!* . . ."[42]

Now comes the period when HPB moved back to Europe. In *Modern Priestess,* Solovyov states that at Würzburg he soon forced out of Blavatsky a confession of her fraudulent activities over the years. Olcott was an accomplice, she said, as well as Damodar, Mohini, and even Subba Row! One thing HPB's critics almost always quote appeared in an article in *Newsweek* (November 24, 1975) on the occasion of the one hundredth anniversary of the founding of the Theosophical Society in New York:

Lions and eagles in every quarter of the globe have turned into asses at my whistle, and obediently wagged their great ears as I piped the tune!

Thoroughly disgusted, Solovyov left Würzburg early in September. He vowed he would have nothing more to do with HPB and never write her again. He added: "I still received letters from Madame Blavatsky, first in Paris and afterwards in St. Petersburg. She would on no account admit that our relations had come to an end, and that I had said goodbye to her forever."[43]

"Forever" turned out to be three or four weeks. Solovyov wrote HPB from Paris on October 8, 1885:

Dear Helena Petrovna,

. . . I have made friends with Madame [Juliette] Adam, and talked a great deal to her about you; I have greatly interested her, and she has told me that her Revue *is open not only to theosophy but to a defence of yourself personally if necessary. . . .*

Today I passed the morning with Richet,[†] and again talked a great deal about you, in connection with Myers and the Psychical Research Society. I can say positively that I convinced Richet of the reality of your personal power and of the phenomena which proceed from you. *He put to me three questions categorically. To the first two I answered affirmatively; with respect to the third I said that I should be in a position to answer affirmatively, without any trouble, in two or three months. But I do not doubt that I shall answer affirmatively, and then, you will see! There will be such a triumph that all the psychists will be wiped out. . . .*

> *Your cordially devoted*
> *Vs. Solovyov[44]*

Walter Leaf, in the preface to Solovyov's book, admits that the foregoing letter raises the most serious questions in his mind:

This does, so far as I can judge, imply a real inconsistency with Mr. Solovyov's narrative; it implies that he has not correctly represented the mental attitude in which he found himself after the Würzburg conversations. I confess that I am not satisfied with his own explanation that the whole letter is merely bantering. In fact under the circumstances, the "bantering tone" itself requires explanation.[45]

That the October eighth letter was not a teasing joke of Solovyov's is oddly revealed in *Modern Priestess* itself, where, in another connection, he quotes a letter in French from Charles Richet. Translated, it reads:

When I met you, you said to me: "Do not make your judgment in a hurry; she has demonstrated things that seem quite amazing to me, my opinion is not yet final, but I think she is an extraordinary woman, gifted with exceptional power. Wait, and I shall give you a fuller explanation."[46]

Now it is evident that at some point Solovyov did, in fact, turn against HPB. What precipitated the turning?

† Charles Richet (1850–1933), noted French physiologist and psychical researcher, awarded the Nobel prize for physiology and medicine in 1913.

It will be noted in his October eighth letter that he was expecting something to happen in the next few months that "will be such a triumph that all the psychists [SPR people] will be wiped out." In that letter he boasts to HPB how important he is to her in being able to influence such important people as Adam and Richet to take an interest in her. It is as if he were saying that now that he was doing so much for her, she should do something for him. What did he want? Why did he run after her and spend weeks with her in Würzberg?

In July 1885, HPB wrote Vera: "I am traveling with [Solovyov] in Switzerland. I really cannot understand what makes him so attached to me. As a matter of fact, I cannot help him in the least. I can hardly help him to realize any of his hopes. Poor man, I am so sorry for him." This was published in *The Path* (July 1895), with a note by the editor, who states that Solovyov "became her bitter enemy, as all his prayers to be taken as a Chela were utterly rejected."

In her booklet on Solovyov's *Modern Priestess,* Vera writes:

It is recorded in my diary that no one begged my sister for "secret audiences" as often and as persistently as he did—which he does not mention at all. . . . We, H. P. Blavatsky's intimates, knew very well not only the substance of these conversations, but even many details, from her and partly from himself, for, in his talks with me, he often was frank and sincere. He would beseech her, over and over again, to share with him her knowledge of purely demonstrative phenomena; his ambition was to return to Russia as a prototype of the "Prince Magus" in his novel "the Magi.". . .

Helena said to us: "Why, I'm just at a loss—what shall I do about Solovyov? He never leaves me alone, begs me to teach him phenomena—how can those things ever be taught?! 'How do you make this music sound in the air?' Well, what can I say to him? 'Well,' I say 'just what you see: I wave my hand in the air, and music comes. . . .'[47] What else can I tell him? Let him go through the things that I have gone through in India, then, perhaps he will achieve those powers too! As it is, he just wastes my time and his own." . . .

Another time, I remember, HP [Helena Petrovna] was even angry, and said to us, after Solovyov had left: "What an amazing man he is! Now he says, 'why have you taught Olcott, and you won't teach *me*!' I have never taught Olcott anything, it is just that he is a born magnetizer." That the Colonel was, indeed, a very powerful magnetizer, is true; we saw him cure many people. He cured my rheumatism, for instance, and he also cured Mr. Solovyov himself, as the latter then claimed.[48]

In India, he is said to have cured hundreds of natives.[49]

After Solovyov left Würzburg, he said he was inundated by letters from HPB. The fact seems to be he received nothing and that he realized his October eighth letter had not impressed her after all.

Solovyov then sought to make trouble for HPB in her own family. It began with inoculating Vera with the idea that Theosophy was antagonistic to Christianity. Vera introduces this by explaining:

> When Mr. Solovyov came to St. Petersburg in the autumn of 1885, we received him as a devoted friend and he came to us every day. His constant correspondence with myself and my eldest daughters had been most interesting; his lively conversation, his original views, and his sincerity greatly interested us. . . . It was then that we first heard unfriendly expressions about my sister and her cause.[50]

HPB advised Sinnett in February 1886 that Vera had written her "a thundering letter calling me a *renegade,* a 'sacrilegious Julian the Apostate,' and a 'Judas' to Christ."[51] Blavatsky replied: "It is evident that [Solovyov] is quite furious because he did not succeed in getting from me what he expected, and he has invented the excuse of anti-Christianity. . . . As for my anti-Christianity, you know what it is; I am an enemy of the ecclesiastical excesses of Protestants and Catholics; *the ideal of Christ crucified shines for me every day clearer and purer. . . .*" (Italics added.)[52]

Solovyov now took further steps to arouse to fever pitch the hatred of Vera and her daughters for HPB. Vera explains that although Solovyov in *Modern Priestess* speaks of herself as being at odds with her sister at this time, "he doesn't tell who was responsible for that, who had for his own purposes created this tension between us and then maintained it with lies and calumnies, going as far as to assert that my sister and a close friend of mine had accused [Vera] of having concealed the money of our deceased father." She adds, "Such was my confusion, it did not even occur to me that neither my sister nor any one of my friends could have ever said this, for they know that, at the time of his death, my father was residing with his other children in Stravropol, a thousand miles from Tiflis, which I, at that time, never left."[53]

Helena endeavored to heal relations with her sister and in one letter said: "There is one thing I can tell you, Vera, and this I can prophesy and foretell: you will bitterly regret your trust in Solovyov and your friendship with him, but it will be too late! . . . I, too, loved him as a brother!" Vera comments: "Oh! how many times have I remembered since, and with what bitterness I remember this prophecy of hers! . . . now when I have seen what this 'wretched' man is capable of."[54]

Not satisfied with alienating the sisters, Solovyov went further and destroyed the confidence of Madame de Morsier as well as most of the members of the Paris TS, in HPB and Theosophy.

During this period HPB also had serious problems with Mohini and Bawaji. Flattered by the adulation showered upon them by Theosophists in Europe, they had set themselves up as gurus on their own. Everywhere they went, students hitherto loyal to the Theosophical cause turned against it. HPB's correspondence at this time reveals to what length they went in causing confusion in the movement and in the personal lives of its members.

HPB wrote a year later to Julia Campbell Ver Planck, a promising new American Theosophist:

Yes, the work has brought upon me contumely, ignominy of all kinds, hatred, malice and slander. Were it only from the outsiders I would mind very little. But, sad to say, it is the "Theosophists" chiefly who tear me to pieces. Our mystic birds are so wise as to soil their own nest instead of leaving it and choosing another. True, "there are many mansions" in our Father's house, but for the world we are one. And it does seem hard that I should have created a "Frankenstein" only to turn round and try to rend me in pieces! Well, so be it, for it is my karma. "Barkis is willing" even to become the manure for the theosophical fields, provided it does bring crops some day.

The foregoing letter appeared in *The Irish Theosophist* (February 1895) with this comment: "The expression 'Barkis is willing,' HPB once said was a mantram unconsciously made by Dickens [in *David Copperfield*]. She used it upon occasion to certain persons on meeting (or writing) them for the first time. Spoken, it had such peculiar force as to [arouse] one who thus heard it from her lips and as she used it."

After Solovyov left Paris for Russia, all contact with him ceased. Coward that he was, he waited six years to write *A Modern Priestess*, when HPB was no longer alive to refute his story.

As to what befell Vera after HPB died, Boris de Zirkoff reports that "the mental suffering she experienced" after Solovyov published *A Modern Priestess of Isis,* in 1892 and 1893 "broke down her health and hastened her death."[55] She died in 1896, a year after *Modern Priestess* was published in English. On the positive side, Vera reported that in Russia, Solovyov's book stirred much interest in HPB's work in Theosophy and she had received many inquiries as to where her sister's writings could be obtained. "Occult Literature in Russia," an article in a recent book on modern art, asserts that as a result of Vera's "impassioned response" to Solovyov's articles, "Blavatsky's popularity grew."[56]

From the bibliography in the present volume, under "Zhelihovsky," the enormity of the debt owed to Vera for recording so much of the life of HPB becomes evident. Without this witness on the scene, much of Blavatsky's early life and many phases of her later life would have been lost to history.

Chapter 3

Moving Westward

In the spring of 1886 we find HPB on the eve of a major change of residence; at the time, however, it was only a temporary escape from the hot Würzburg summer. She had decided to spend the summer with Vera and her eldest daughter, both now joyfully reconciled with HPB. The plan was to go to the seaside town of Ostend on the Belgian coast. As Countess Wachtmeister was in Sweden on a business trip, HPB was accompanied by a recent visitor, Emily Kislingbury, an old British friend who was in New York at the time the TS was founded. Mr. Gebhard met the party at Cologne and persuaded them to visit his home in Elberfeld. HPB had intended to stay only a few days, but she sprained her ankle and was laid up for two months with various ailments. Vera and her daughter arrived in the middle of May and remained until July, when they traveled with her to Ostend. The niece, also named Vera, later recorded an incident that occurred at the Gebhards':

> Generally on coming down in the morning . . . I found my aunt deep in her work. So far as I know, she never wrote at that time in the morning, but carefully went over what was written the previous night. One day I saw evident traces of perplexity written on her face. Not wishing to disturb her, I sat down quietly and waited for her to speak. . . . At last she called out to me. "Vera," she said, "do you think you could tell me what is a pi?" Rather astonished at such a question, I said I thought a pie was some kind of an English dish. "Please don't make a fool of yourself," she said, rather impatiently, "don't you understand I address you in your capacity of a mathematical pundit? Come and see this."
>
> I looked at the page that lay before her on the table, and saw it was covered with figures and calculations, and soon became aware that the formula $\pi = 3'14159$ was put down wrongly throughout them all. It was written $\pi = 31'4159$. With great joy and triumph I hastened to inform her of her mistake. "That's it!" she exclaimed. "This confounded comma ['] bothered me all the morning. I was rather in a hurry yesterday to put down what I saw, and today at the

first glance at the page I intensely but vaguely felt there was some-thing wrong, and do what I could I could not remember where the comma actually was when I saw this number."

Knowing very little of Theosophy in general and my aunt's ways of writing in particular at that time, I of course was greatly struck with her not being able to correct such a slight mistake in the very intricate calculations she had written down with her own hand.

"You are very green," she said, "if you think that I actually know and understand all the things I write. How many times am I to repeat to you and your mother that the things I write are dictated to me, [and] that sometimes I see manuscripts, numbers and words before my eyes of which I never knew anything." On reading *The Secret Doctrine* several years later I recognized the page. It was one of the pages which discusses Hindu astronomy.[57]

The three arrived in Ostend at the height of the summer, when ac-commodations were expensive and scarce. After Vera and her daughter returned to Russia, and until the countess arrived sometime in August, HPB was alone with her maid—except for a visit from Mr. Sinnett.[58] She wrote her sister: "I shall take myself to task now that I am alone; and instead of a restless wandering Jew I shall turn myself into a 'her-mit crab,' into a petrified sea monster, stranded on the shore. I shall write and write,—my only consolation! Alas, happy are the people who can walk. What a life to be always ill—and without legs, into the bargain."[59]

A year and a half later her health was not much better. To Judge Khandalavala, she wrote: "My life to live yet is not very long, and I have learnt patience these three years. My health is better, but in gen-eral it is ruined for life. I am well only when I *sit and write*. I can neither walk nor stand for more than a minute." She had chronic kidney problems, which caused swollen legs, and her knees were so arthritic that one step caused excruciating pain.[60]

It may be puzzling to some why HPB, who had vigorous health during her world travels as a young woman, should be so frequently ill and for the last five years of her life practically confined to the chair in which she wrote. Malcolm W. Browne, science essayist for the *New York Times,* pondered this problem as related to a number of famous people in his March 10, 1981 article "Does Sickness Have Its Virtue?" He wrote:

In one of the letters written some time in the 1940's to his old friend and physician Rudolf Ehrmann, Einstein described his latest bout of acute abdominal pain. The complaint had intermittently plagued

Einstein for 30 years, and although it was presumed to be gall bladder trouble, it was never cured. . . . "When I suffer such an attack," Einstein said, "I can often work very successfully. It does not seem to be very favorable for the imagination if one feels too well. At least the gods seem well intentioned toward me when they squeeze the gall bladder. . . ."

Sigmund Freud, another chronic sufferer of abdominal pain, wrote: "I have long known that I can't be industrious when I am in good health; on the contrary, I need a degree of discomfort which I want to get rid of."

Browne reports further that in the book *Creative Malady,* Sir George Pickering, an eminent British professor of medicine, presented a striking analysis of the illness that invalided Charles Darwin for most of his adult life:

During Darwin's five years cruising the coasts of South America aboard the Beagle, he was apparently in such robust health he withstood the rigors of the voyage better than many of the professional crew members. But when the time came for him to settle down in England, marry, and begin work on his epochal theory of evolution, Darwin fell ill. From age 33 until his death 40 years later, he suffered attacks of nausea, shivering and faintness, needing constant rest and working only a few hours a day. [It provided him] the isolation and freedom from distraction that allowed him to think of the universe.

Summing up his thesis, Browne remarks: "In fact, sickness of one form or another seems to be fairly common at the pinnacle of scientific creativity, as it has been for such artistic luminaries as Dostoevsky, Proust, Van Gogh, and Berlioz."

Countess Wachtmeister rejoined HPB when the summer was nearly over and it was time to return to Würzburg. They decided, however, to remain in Ostend, which was close to London and the Theosophists there. Several of them visited, including Anna Kingsford and her friend Edward Maitland. The countess writes:

. . . they spent a fortnight with us. [Both Mrs. Kingsford and HPB] were usually occupied with their respective work during the daytime, but in the evenings delightful conversations ensued, and it was interesting to me to hear different points of *The Secret Doctrine* discussed from the Eastern and Western standpoints of occultism.

The powerful intellects of these two gifted women would be engaged in animated discussions, starting from apparently two opposite poles. Gradually the threads of their conversation would seem to approach each other, until at last they would merge in one unity. Fresh topics would then arise which would be grappled with in the same masterly way.[61]

During this same period, Sinnett's *Incidents in the Life of Madame Blavatsky* was published. In reviewing the volume, one writer observes:

The common sense and pervading sincerity of this book helped the reading public to see HPB as an extraordinary person, but exceedingly human and warmly sympathetic, steadily giving herself, soul, mind, and heart, to the cause that was sacred to her. She appears, in its pages, as a good natured, unrevengeful fighter, undismayed by the mountains of hatred and calumny heaped upon her, and one whose personal life was filled with astonishing phenomena and ever-present elements of the mysterious. The *Incidents* created a profound impression far and wide, turning to good account the curiosity aroused by the adverse report of the SPR and bringing many into the ranks of the Society.[62]

The work on *The Secret Doctrine* proceeded rapidly, but HPB was not satisfied with the ink available in Ostend, so she procured an improved formula and manufactured her own—just as she once had before in Russia.† As the virtues of this new ink spread, it became necessary to manufacture more of it, and soon HPB's ink-making became a small business. Dr. J. D. Buck, an American Theosophist, learned of this story from the countess herself in 1894 when she was on a U.S. lecture tour.[63] According to his account, an impoverished woman once came to HPB's door asking for assistance. He relates: "Deeply moved by the poor woman's story, HPB thrust her hand into the large pocket of the loose gown she wore while at work and found it empty; pulling out the drawer of her writing table with the same result. She then remembered the ink factory and called out, 'Here, Constance! give her the ink factory; that will relieve her,'—and it was done."[64]

Dr. Buck, who was a prominent medical practitioner of his day as

---

† Blavatsky was fussy about her writing materials. Well might she be when we consider that when the manuscript of *The Secret Doctrine* was completed, it was three feet high, and *all* handwritten! Miss Francesca Arundale reports that she once received an urgent letter from HPB, then in France: "I can get no paper of the kind I require, in Paris; please go to Oxford Street, and send me over a ream." (*My Guest,* 29).

well as a noted Theosophist, tells another story that relates to the Ostend period:

> A friend of mine who has probably made more discoveries in the
> ancient Kabbalah than anyone known to modern times, and who
> had devoted more than twenty years to this special line of work,
> raised once certain enquiries concerning his own researches, and
> expressed the doubt that any man then living could or would answer
> his enquiries. I suggested that he should write to HPB in regard to
> the matter, and after some delay he did so. The result was nearly
> forty pages of very closely-written MSS. answering every question
> he had raised, and adding a fund of information that astonished the
> recipient beyond all measure. This gentleman is not and never has
> been a member of the TS, but to the present time he declares his
> conviction that HPB was the most profound and wonderful woman
> of this or of any age. He, a specialist for half a lifetime in an obscure
> and unknown field, found HPB perfectly familiar with all his
> work.[65]

The man was J. Ralston Skinner, author of *A Key to the Hebrew-
Egyptian Mystery in the Source of Measures,* published in 1875, a work
frequently quoted in *The Secret Doctrine* and in print today.[66] For a century, Theosophical historians searched for HPB's correspondence with
him. Recently it was located in the archives of the Andover-Harvard
Theological Library at Harvard University. The letters were all written
from Ostend during the period under consideration. The credit for the
discovery belongs to Dr. Ananda Wickremeratne from Sri Lanka, an
Oxford graduate who had received a grant from the Harvard Center in
the Study of World Religions to investigate records at Harvard on the
influence of the Theosophical movement in Southeast Asia.

Dr. John Carman, director of the Center, writes:

> It seems clear to me from speaking with Dr. Wickremeratne and
> others that important work in this area remains to be done. It is my
> hope that Dr. Wickremeratne will during his time here lay some of
> the groundwork for that work, especially in surveying resources in
> Harvard and the Boston area of materials relevant to the history of
> theosophy.[67]

In his letter, Carman mentions a talk Dr. Wickremeratne gave at
their biweekly colloquium. The flyer describing the event speaks of
the key role the Theosophists played in "earning for themselves a
permanent, almost hallowed, niche in South Asian historiography."[68]

When HPB's letters to Skinner were being copied for the present writer, they were found in such fragile condition that they soon would fall apart. The library engaged professional help to restore them, and the completion of this task was announced in *The Harvard Divinity Bulletin* (December 1983–January 1984) in an article "Letter Perfect: Skinner Collection Restored." A photograph of one letter before and after restoration was shown.

In a letter dated February 17, 1887, HPB remarks to Skinner regarding his book the *Source of Measures:*

> *You have discovered* a *key to the universal language [of the esoteric philosophy]. You have done more than any living man in this direction . . . but it is only* one of the seven keys *I mention in* Isis Unveiled . . . *but you seem to scorn entirely its* first *key—the one which opens the earliest, metaphysical and abstract portion of the philosophy, the* paradigms *of all things, the Divine and Spiritual Models of its physiological and astronomical aspects. [Interesting she used the word* paradigm, *so frequently introduced in* avantgarde *thinking today.]*

After providing examples of how esoteric keys can open locked doors, she refers to Skinner's view that she herself, rather than the Masters, is the source of this wisdom:

> *Say, why did you labour under the impression that I was* lying *about the Masters? Can one lie about* living *men? And why should I have* invented *them or still support the "invention" since for 12 years and especially for the last three, I am made a* martyr *for the truths I told? Ah, Dear Sir, no woman in her right senses, nor a man either, would go willingly into such* hell, *as I have and persisted in having Spiritualists, Christians, Materialists, Scientists and the whole world, with two thirds of our own theosophists to boot against me, if I had not been forced by my oath and vows to do so. I have lost friends, country, money & health, to serve only as manure for the fields of* future theosophy.

Skinner wrote a Part Three to *The Source of Measures,* comprising some 350 pages of manuscript. It concludes with these words: "I, Ralston Skinner, January 10, 1887, shall send this original MSS [manuscript] to Madame Blavatsky, Ostend." This was done, and it is now in the Adyar archives and contains many annotations by her. Skinner said HPB could use the work as her own, but in her February seventeenth letter she refused, saying: "How can I quote without quotation marks? . . . How can I quote and let out your name?" *The Secret Doctrine* includes several long quotations from this work.[69]

Among the Skinner letters at Harvard is a photograph of HPB, on the back of which appear these words:

*To her new acquaintance and correspondent—but very, very old friend,
Mr. Ralston Skinner with ever growing feelings of sympathy and admiration, appreciation and the warmest friendship.*

H. P. Blavatsky ∴
London, May *1887*

Early in January 1887, HPB shared with Sinnett some intriguing
news just received:

> The Russian papers are again full of me. It appears that "my hand"
> saved from a death peril a gentleman while he was occupied with
> abusing me and calling all my writings LIES. [The news item] is called
> "The Mysterious Hand." . . . My aunt . . . writes to me to enquire
> whether it is I, or the *Chozain* (Master) who did it. The incident
> described took place in the fall of 1886.[70]

The original article "The Mysterious Hand" first appeared in Russia
in the St. Petersburg *Listok,* was reprinted in the *Rebus,* and made the
rounds of the Russian press. The people in the story were all well
known in St. Petersburg. The following is a translation:

> We were comfortably seated on the vast veranda of our summer
> residence near St. Petersburg. It was a little after noon, when after an
> early lunch we were enjoying our *siesta,* smoking cigars and ciga-
> rettes in the open air. There was storm in the air; the atmosphere
> hung heavily around us . . . all was motionless and silent. Our dear
> hostess, Marya Nikolaevne, had brought a book and began reading
> aloud a narrative by "Radda Bai" [HPB] on the "Blue Hills of
> Nilgiri." We all listened with pleasure. . . . Putting aside the vol-
> ume, she glanced at us all and then pronounced softly: "How won-
> derful!"
>   "But surely all that Radda Bai tells us . . . is bosh and fairy tales!"
> coolly said a gentleman present . . . Piotre Petrovitch, an indefatig-
> able and fascinating orator . . . "that which is truth for her is in my
> sight but a cock-and-bull story."
>   We were looking in surprise at the speaker, when suddenly, as he
> was uttering his last sentence, we saw him throw a nervous look at
> his right arm, which was resting on the railing of the veranda. Then,
> to our great amazement, he jumped from his chair as if he had been
> bitten by a viper; ran down the steps, examined nervously every
> corner in the little front garden, looked under the veranda and on
> the roof, and finally returned to the terrace looking very pale and as
> if he had seen a ghost.

"What is the matter?" exclaimed Marya Nikolaevne, much alarmed. Instead of replying, Piotre Petrovitch went on silently with his search. He examined once more the ground under the steps, then looked away into the forest, and finally began moving about the chairs, and looking under them. . . . "Did you see no one?" he asked. We looked at each other quite taken aback, and answered in one voice: "No one at all!"

"But I saw some one . . . and—a hand also," he said in the same tremulous tones. . . . "undeniably a woman's hand, white, half transparent, crossed with blue veins. It seemed to me as if some one had approached me from the front garden here, had seized me above the elbow, just in this place, and having pressed my arm thrice had tried to drag me down from the veranda into the garden." While saying all this, Piotre Petrovitch was breathing heavily and his pallor was as ghastly as ever. . . .

"Now you will be more cautious, perhaps, about denying the Indian cock-and-bull stories! It is the astral form of 'Radda Bai' who pulled your arm, to hint that you should not be slandering people!". . .

He heeded us not, but kept silent and gloomy, now and then examining suspiciously the right sleeve of his coat, at the place where he had seen the mysterious hand. Very soon he could endure it no longer; and, leaving his armchair once more, went again into the little garden, where, with something like his habitual animation, he began telling us the story over again. We all followed, laughing merrily at the skeptic.

Meanwhile the atmosphere had thickened and was now full of electricity. A large black thunder-cloud was overhanging our heads, dark and threatening, from which a flash of forked lightning suddenly sprang and fell on the house we had just left. We were startled and amazed; for right before our eyes the huge chimney on the roof fell to pieces and disappeared, bricks and mortar rolling with a thundering noise from the top of the house down on our terrace. More terrible still, the pillar on which Piotre Petrovitch had leaned while sitting in his armchair suddenly bent and gave way with a sinister creaking sound, and the whole large and heavy roof collapsed and fell down with an awful crash on our veranda. . . . We were struck dumb with horror and amazement!

"The hand, *her* hand . . . I say! That hand was pulling me away from the veranda, you know!" he repeated again and again to each of us, with a face white with terror, and widely opened eyes. We were, "too deeply appalled to make any remark," for they too had just been saved when they followed Piotre into the garden.[71]

HPB was alone as the Old Year passed into 1887. She had sent the Countess Wachtmeister to London on some private business. While there, the countess received a letter from HPB concerning the future of the TS. It opened by revealing that Blavatsky had had "a long conversation with the Master—the first for a long, long time," and had been told:

> . . . the whole Society (Europe and America) is under cruel proba-tion. Those who come out of it unscathed will have their reward. Those who will remain inactive or passive, even as those who will turn their backs, will have theirs also. It is a final and supreme trial. But there is news. Either I have to return to India to die this autumn, or I have to form between this and November next a nucleus of true theosophists, a school of my own, with no secretary, only myself alone, with as many mystics as I can get to teach them. I can stop here, or go to England, or whatever I like.[72]

It seems significant that not long after this Bertram Keightley from the London TS visited HPB in Ostend. He reports:

> I had gone over to urge upon HPB the advisability of coming to settle in London for the purpose of forming a center for active work in the cause of Theosophy. There were six of us in all who felt profoundly dissatisfied with the deadness which seemed to pervade the Society in England, and we had come to the conclusion that only HPB could give efficient aid in restoring the suspended animation of the movement, and initiating active and wisely directed work.[73]

This small group of young Theosophists had been meeting regularly on their own, and having reached an impasse in their Theosophical studies felt that HPB alone could solve their perplexities. A second visit was made, this time by Dr. Archibald Keightley, to exert further pressure upon HPB to come to London. Sinnett strongly disapproved of the move.[74] Blavatsky had written to him earlier:

> You ask my advice in the London Lodge business. Now that you have put the question to me you may like to hear, perhaps, what Master remarked several times about the L. L. I cannot repeat to you his words but you may find the spirit of it in the text of *Revelation,* 3:15 and 16.[†] You may judge, and I may leave you to draw your own inferences. So anything to give a fresh impetus is better than inertia.

† "He that hath an ear, let him hear what the Spirit saith unto the churches. . . . I know thy works, that thou art neither cold nor hot: I would thou wert cold or hot. So then because thou art lukewarm, and neither cold nor hot, I will spew thee out of my mouth." (*Rev.* 3:13, 15–16.)

If you remain for a while longer in your present state of lethargy, your L. L. will be before another year is over—covered with moss and slime. . . .[75]

Another problem with Sinnett's management, Bert Keightley points out, was that he believed "theosophy should be reserved entirely for what was technically known in England as 'Society'; that is to say, for what Mr. Gladstone would call the 'classes' as opposed to the 'masses,' or for kid gloves and swallow-tail coats." In contrast, he says, the younger members of the London Lodge "believed that if theosophy was ever destined to fulfill its mission in the world, it must appeal to the masses of the people, to the working men and to clerks, who, however much they were lacking in metaphysical study, were fully capable of comprehending the fundamental principles of theosophy. . . ."[76]

As a last measure to induce HPB to move to London, a number of the London Lodge members wrote her with individual entreaties. In reply she wrote a long collective letter, in the course of which she said: "If I can prop up [your Lodge,] let me be used as the meanest pillar, or mortar on your trowels to cement and mend the cracked walls of the luckless London Lodge. But if the masons do not put first in order their material and prepare the bricks, what can the cement do?"[77]

Having agreed to come, her first plan was to go to London on March twenty-seventh and remain for the summer. The countess would then be in Sweden to sell her property and henceforth would live with HPB permanently.

Ten days before leaving Ostend, HPB lost consciousness while sitting in her chair. This happened repeatedly, and the doctor diagnosed a serious malfunction of the kidneys. Mary Gebhard came from Elberfeld and took turns with the countess in attending the patient. As the local doctor believed the case was hopeless, the countess telegraphed a London Theosophist, Dr. Ashton Ellis, who came at once and for three days massaged Blavatsky's paralyzed organs. Temporary benefit resulted, but it soon became evident that HPB was dying. Madame Gebhard recommended a will be drawn up, for to die intestate in a foreign country would cause unending complications. So the American consul, together with a lawyer and the Belgian doctor, were to come the next day.

During the night watch the countess was horrified to detect the peculiar faint odor of death that sometimes precedes dissolution. She could hardly expect HPB would live through the night. From sheer exhaustion, the sentinel fell asleep at her post. In the morning she was astounded to find HPB sitting up in bed and asking for her breakfast.

During the night, she said, a choice had been offered: to die and take the easy way out, or to go on with the work at the risk of facing even greater difficulties than those hitherto encountered.[78]

When the lawyer, doctor, and the consul arrived, they found a joyous party. The doctor kept repeating, "But she should be dead, . . . she should be dead." He had never known a case in which a person in such condition recovered. The drawing of the will went smoothly until the lawyer learned HPB had left all her worldly goods to the countess and nothing to her relatives. Fearing the countess had exercised undue influence on her mind, he objected, but HPB vehemently opposed. Madame Gebhard, to avoid a scene, gently informed the lawyer, "perhaps when you know the amount which Madame Blavatsky has to will away, you will have no further objections to making the will as she desires, for had Madame Blavatsky died, there would not have been sufficient money to pay for her funeral expenses."

The party broke up several hours later. Departing, the American consul laughingly said: "Well, I think this is enough fatigue for a dying woman!"[79]

As to how these seemingly miraculous recoveries took place, HPB once gave a clue in *The Secret Doctrine* (1:555):

We say and maintain that SOUND, for one thing, is a tremendous Occult power; that it is a stupendous force, of which the electricity generated by a million of Niagaras could never counteract the smallest potentiality when directed with *occult knowledge*. Sound may be produced of such a nature that the pyramid of Cheops would be raised in the air, or that a dying man, nay, one at his last breath, would be revived and filled with new energy and vigor.

For Sound generates, or rather attracts together, the elements that produce an *ozone,* the fabrication of which is beyond chemistry, but within the limits of Alchemy. It may even *resurrect* a man or an animal whose astral "vital body" has not been irreparably separated from the physical body by the severance of the magnetic or odic chord. *As one saved thrice from death* by that power, the writer ought to be credited with knowing personally something about it.

This, adds HPB, may appear "too *unscientific* to be even noticed."[80] Yet recently in this century the levitation of objects by sound has been demonstrated by science. The National Aeronautics and Space Administration (NASA) has been using sound to levitate, spin, and move objects in space since August 1979. It has published more than twenty technical papers describing its successful research in this area, among them "Stabilized Acoustic Levitation of Dense Materials Using High-

Powered Siren," which includes photographs of objects such as steel balls suspended in empty space.[81] The research is being conducted by the Jet Propulsion Laboratory, California Institute of Technology, at Pasadena, under contract with NASA.

On May 1, 1887, HPB left Ostend for London. Her destination was a small cottage called Maycott in Upper Norwood, which became the center for Theosophical activities for several months before larger quarters were acquired. Thus began a new era of active work for Theosophy in the Western world.

Chapter 4

First Months in London

Bertram Keightley, in his account of the writing of *The Secret Doctrine,* tells of the last days in Ostend and the first at Maycott:

The move was effected, without any untoward event, though the packing up of her books, papers, MSS., etc., was a truly terrible undertaking, for she went on writing till the very last moment, and as sure as any book, paper, or portion of MSS. had been carefully packed away at the bottom of some box, so surely would she urgently need it, and insist upon its being disinterred at all costs. However, we did get packed at last, reached Maycott, and before we had been two hours in the house, HPB had her writing materials out and was hard at work again. Her power of work was amazing; from early morning till late in the evening she sat at her desk, and even when so ill that most people would have been lying helpless in bed, she toiled resolutely away at the task she had undertaken.[82]

Three weeks after HPB's arrival in London a new Theosophical lodge was born. Olcott relates that "a party of fourteen of the younger persons joined to form the since world-famous Blavatsky Lodge, the choice of the title being meant as a public protest of loyalty to her whose name had been so tarnished in the Coulomb-Missionary plot."[83] The minute book of the Blavatsky Lodge, in recording the first formal meeting on May nineteenth, declared *"that the aim of the lodge be active work."*[84]

The next meeting was on May twenty-fifth, at which resolutions were passed to start a magazine and to form a publishing company. Bertram Keightley, in his *Reminiscences,* tells why the magazine was decided upon:

[HPB] saw that it would take at least a year or more to get *The Secret Doctrine* ready for the press; [therefore, she] urged that in the meantime some sort of public propaganda or outward action was indispensable; and the only way we could hit upon was to start a

magazine under HPB's editorship. So we decided to start a magazine under the title of *Lucifer: the Light-bringer,* and we began to get to
work on the business preliminaries.[85]

Lucifer had a co-editor, the novelist Mabel Collins, recorder of the
Theosophical classic *Light on the Path.* It was in her home, Maycott,
that the new venture began.

Although Sinnett did not approve of HPB's return to London, he
later saw things differently. In *The Review of Reviews* (June 1891), at the
time of her death, he observed:

> . . . the few remaining years of her life have seen her personal
> ascendancy and influence with all around her constantly increasing.
> Her receptions have been crowded, her spirits and energy . . . have
> recovered their old vigor, schemes of all kinds have been set on foot
> around her for pushing on the Theosophical movement, and a prac-
> tical answer had been afforded to critics who suppose that the
> interest Mme. Blavatsky excites turns on the "phenomena," genu-
> ine or otherwise . . . by the fact that in these last few years her public
> energies have been entirely bent on teaching Theosophical philoso-
> phy and ethics, and no casual frequenter of her receptions or lecture
> room has ever been encouraged to expect the smallest manifestation
> of occult mysteries.

HPB explained this new policy in *Lucifer* (February 1888):

> "Occult phenomena" . . . failed to produce the desired effect. . . .
> It was supposed that intelligent people, especially men of science,
> would, at least, have recognized the existence of a new and deeply
> interesting field of inquiry and research when they witnessed physi-
> cal effects produced at will, for which they were not able to account.
> It was supposed that theologians would have welcomed the proof,
> of which they stand so sadly in need in these agnostic days, that the
> soul and the spirit are not mere creations of their fancy . . . but
> entities quite as real as the body, and much more important. These
> expectations were not realized. The phenomena were misun-
> derstood and misrepresented, both as regards their nature and their
> purpose. . . .
>   That the phenomena did excite curiosity in the minds of those
> who witnessed them, is certainly true, but it was, unfortunately, for
> the most part of an idle kind. The greater number of the witnesses
> developed an insatiable appetite for phenomena for their own sake,
> without any thought of studying the philosophy or the science of

whose truth and power the phenomena were merely trivial and, so to say, accidental illustrations. . . . Except in a few isolated and honorable instances, never [were they] received in any other character than as would-be miracles, or as works of the Devil, or as vulgar tricks, or as amusing gape-seed, or as the performances of those dangerous "spooks" that masquerade in séance rooms, and feed on the vital energies of the mediums and sitters. . . .

An occultist can produce phenomena, but he cannot supply the world with brains, nor with the intelligence and good faith necessary to understand and appreciate them. Therefore, it is hardly to be wondered at, that *word* came to abandon phenomena and let the ideas of Theosophy stand on their own intrinsic merits.

Soon after HPB moved to Maycott, she turned over the three-foot-high manuscript of *The Secret Doctrine* to the Keightleys, both of whom were Cambridge graduates, for analysis. After spending much time with the manuscript they concluded it was an extraordinary work but that the presentation was "without plan, structure, or arrangement." This HPB commissioned them to remedy. Not wishing to change her manuscript in its original form, they had it professionally typed and worked with that copy.[86]

In 1889, when Dr. Keightley attended a TS convention in the United States, he was interviewed by the *New York Times*. The subject of *The Secret Doctrine* arose when the reporter asked whether HPB "now ever produced any of the phenomena of manifestation of occult potencies with which she has been credited in the past?" Keightley answered:

Very rarely, except as they occur in a practical matter-of-fact way in the course of work. . . . While working upon her *Secret Doctrine,* Mme. Blavatsky [when she first came from India] had not a single book of reference or authority about her, yet would frequently make long quotations of two or three hundred words from various works, giving author, volume, and page as precisely as if by immediate reference. I became a little uneasy about it and said to her, "Do you not think I had better verify the accuracy of some of these quotations?"

"Certainly, if you wish to," she replied. So I took a lot of them and went to the British Museum, the only place where the books were, to my knowledge, accessible. There I found them accurate to the minutest degree, except that in one or perhaps two instances I did not find the passage quoted upon the page she had given. Say for instance, the page specified was 307. It was not there. But acting upon an idea that occurred to me, I turned to 703, and there found it word for word. The cause for the transposition of the figures was in their reversal in the astral light, which presents things exactly as if shown in a mirror. She did not always, when physically very weary, take the trouble to carefully reverse the process. . . .

The quotations referred to were mainly from the Journal of the Asiatic Society at Calcutta, many of them from Col. Wilford's papers, works not more than fifty or sixty years old and not exceedingly rare, but in the possession of very few private individuals, and certainly not in hers, nor consulted by her in the process of her work otherwise than in the astral light in the manner I have indicated.[87]

Many other subjects were discussed, but when the *Times*'s readers opened their papers the following day, they found the interview headed:

THE USEFUL ASTRAL LIGHT

By Which One Can Quote
What He Has Not Read

Among the visitors during the summer of 1887 was Alexander Fullerton, from the United States. An active worker at the New York TS and Judge's right-hand man in getting out *The Path,* he gave up his career as an Episcopal clergyman to work full time for Theosophy.[88] He recalled:

I well remember my first words with [HPB] in August, 1887. I remarked that I naturally felt some trepidation at being in the presence of one who could read every thought. She replied that such an act would be dishonest. I said that I should not exactly call it "dishonest," though it might be unkind or intrusive. She answered, No, that it would be dishonest; that she had no more right to possess herself of another person's secrets without his consent than of his purse; and that she never used the power unless either the person himself requested it, or the circumstances were of a kind to make it imperative.[89]

Chapter 5

A Meeting with HPB

Charles Johnston, a young Irishman, visited HPB while she lived at Maycott. He was one of the founders of the Dublin Theosophical Society, to which William Butler Yeats and other Irish authors belonged. Today Johnston is best known for his inspired translations of some of the Hindu classics.[90] He had learned Sanskrit while preparing for assignment to the Indian Civil Service, and after returning from India he taught it in London. His book on this ancient language won the praise of Orientalist Max Müller. At the turn of the century, and for many years thereafter, Johnston lived in New York City, where he worked actively in the Theosophical movement and taught history at Columbia University. His interview with HPB, which follows, is in condensed form:

I first met dear old "HPB," as she made all her friends call her, in the spring of 1887. Some of her disciples had taken a pretty house in Norwood, where the huge glass nave and twin towers of the Crystal Palace glint above a labyrinth of streets and terraces. London was at its grimy best.

HPB was just finishing her day's work. My first impression was of her rippled hair as she turned, then her marvelously potent eyes, as she welcomed me: "My dear fellow! I am so glad to see you! Come in and talk! You are just in time to have some tea!" Then a piercing call for "Louise," and her Swiss maid appeared, to receive a voluble torrent of directions in French.

When we were comfortably alone, she told me a charming tale of Louise's devotion. HPB had got away from her base of supplies somewhere, in Belgium I think, and things were rather tight for a while. A wealthy gentleman called to see the famous Russian witch, and tipped her maid munificently. As soon as he was gone, Louise appeared, blushing and apologizing: "Perhaps Madame will not be offended," she stammered, "but I do not need money"; and she tried to transfer the *douceur* to her mistress.

Louise's entry cut short the story, and HPB turned with a quizzically humorous smile to another theme: "Of course you have read the SPR Report?—The Spookical Research Society—and know that I am a Russian spy, and the champion imposter of the age?"

Yes, I read the Report. But I knew its contents already. I was at the meeting when it was first read, two years ago. But as far as I could see, [Hodgson] had never really investigated any occult phenomena at all; he simply investigated dim and confused memories about them in the minds of indifferent witnesses. [Myers] came down among us after the meeting, and smilingly asked me what I thought of the Report. I answered that it was the most unfair and one-sided thing I had ever heard of, and that if I had not already been a member of your Society, I should have joined on the strength of that attack. He smiled a kind of sickly smile, and passed on.

"The funny thing about the Psychical Researchers," I said, "is that they have proved for themselves that most of these magical powers are just what you say they are, and they seem to have bodily-adopted, not to say, stolen, your teaching of the Astral Light. Take the thing that has been most made fun of: the journeys of adepts and their pupils in the astral body; you know how severe they are about poor Damodar and his journeys in his astral body from one part of India to another, and even from India over to London. Well, they themselves have perfectly sound evidence of the very same thing. I know one of their committee, a professor of physics, who discovered thought-transference and made all the first experiments in it. He showed me a number of their unpublished papers, and among them was an account of just such astral journeys made quite consciously. I think the astral traveler was a young doctor, but that is a detail. The point is, that he kept a diary of his visits, and a note of them was also kept by the person he visited, and the two perfectly coincide. They have the whole thing authenticated and in print, and yet when you make the very same claim, they call you a fraud. Why?"

"They will never do much. They go too [far] on material lines," said HPB, "and they are far too timid. That was the secret motive that turned them against me. They were afraid of raising a storm if they said our phenomena were true. Fancy what it would have meant! Why it would practically have committed modern science to our mahatmas and all I have taught about the inhabitants of the occult world and their tremendous powers."

If ever I saw genuine awe and reverence in a human face, it was in hers, when she spoke of her own Master. I asked her something about his age. She answered: "My dear, I cannot tell you exactly, for I do not know. But this I will tell you. I met him first when I was twenty—in 1851. He was in the very prime of manhood then. I am an old woman now, but he has not aged a day. That is all I can say. You may draw your own conclusions."

Then she told me something about other Masters and adepts she had known—for she made a difference, as though the adepts were the captains of the occult world, and the Masters were the generals. She had known adepts of many races, from Northern and Southern India, Tibet, Persia, China, Egypt; of various European nations, Greek, Hungarian, Italian, English; of certain races in South America, where she said there was a Lodge of adepts.

"It is the tradition of this which the Spanish Conquistadors found," she said, "the golden city of Manoah or El Dorado. The race is allied to the ancient Egyptians, and the adepts have still preserved the secret of their dwelling place inviolable. There are certain members of the Lodges who pass from centre to centre, keeping the lines of connection between them unbroken. But they are always connected in other ways."

"In their astral bodies?" "Yes," she answered, "and in other ways still higher. They have a common life and power. As they rise in spirituality, they rise above difference of race, to our common humanity. The series is unbroken. Adepts are a necessity in nature and in super-nature. They are the links between men and the gods; these 'gods' being the souls of great adepts and Masters of bygone races and ages, and so on, up to the threshold of Nirvana. The continuity is unbroken."

"What do they do?"

"You would hardly understand, unless you were an adept. But they keep alive the spiritual life of mankind."

"How do the adepts guide the souls of men?"

"In many ways, but chiefly by teaching their souls direct, in the spiritual world. That is difficult for you to understand. But this is quite intelligible: At certain regular periods, they try to give the world at large a right understanding of spiritual things. One of their number comes forth to teach the masses, and is handed down to tradition as the founder of a religion. Krishna was such a Master; so was Zoroaster; so were Buddha and Sankaracharya, the great sage of Southern India. So also was the Nazarene [Jesus]."

"Have the adepts any secret records of his life?"

"They must have," she answered, "for they have records of the lives of all Initiates. Once I was in a great cave-temple in the Himalayan mountains, with my Master. There were many statues of adepts there; pointing to one of them, he said: 'This is he whom you call Jesus. We count him to be one of the greatest among us.'

"But that is not the only work of the adepts. At much shorter periods, they send forth a messenger to try to teach the world. Such a period comes in the last quarter of each century, and the Theosophical Society represents their work for this epoch."

"How does it benefit mankind?"

"How does it benefit you to know the laws of life? Does it not help you to escape sickness and death? Well, there is a soul-sickness, and a soul-death. Only the true teaching of Life can cure them. The dogmatic churches, with their hell and damnation, their metal[†] heaven and their fire and brimstone, have made it almost impossible for thinking people to believe in the immortality of the soul. And if they do not believe in a life after death, then they have no life after death. That is the law."

"How can what people believe possibly affect them? Either it is or it isn't, whatever they may believe."

"Their belief affects them in this way. Their life after death is made by their aspirations and spiritual development unfolding in the spiritual world. According to the growth of each [in our world] so is his life after death. It is the complement of his life here. All unsatisfied spiritual longings, all desires for higher life, all aspirations and dreams of noble things, come to flower in the spiritual life, and the soul has its day, for life on earth is its night. But if you have no aspirations, no higher longings, no beliefs in any life after death, then there is nothing for your spiritual life to be made up of; your soul is a blank."

"What becomes of you then?"

"You reincarnate immediately, almost without an interval, and without regaining consciousness in the other world."

"What else do you teach, as theosophists?"

"Well, Sir! I am being cross-examined this evening, it would seem," she answered with a smile. "We teach something very old, and yet which needs to be taught. We teach universal brotherhood."

"Don't let us get vague and general. Tell me exactly what you mean by that."

"Let me take a concrete case," she said. "Take the English. How cruel they are! How badly they treat my poor Hindus!"

"I have always understood that they had done a good deal for India in a material way," I objected.

"But what is the use of material benefits, if you are despised and trampled down morally all the time? If your ideals of national honor and glory are crushed in the mud, and you are made to feel all

---

† [Streets paved with gold.]

the time that you are an inferior race—a lower order of mortals—pigs, the English call them, and sincerely believe it. Well, just the reverse of that would be universal brotherhood. No amount of material benefit can compensate for hurting their souls and crushing out their ideals. Besides there is another side of all that, which we as theosophists always point out. *There are really no 'inferior races,' for all are one in our common humanity;* and as we have all had incarnations in each of these races, we ought to be more brotherly to them. They are our wards, entrusted to us; and what do we do? We invade their lands, and shoot them down in sight of their own homes; we outrage their women, and rob their goods, and then with smooth-faced hypocrisy we turn round and say we are doing it for their good. But there is a just law, 'the false tongue dooms its lie; the spoiler robs to render. Ye shall not come forth, until ye have paid the uttermost farthing.'"

"So that is what the adepts sent you forth to teach?"

"Yes, that and other things—things which are very important, and will soon be far more important. There is the danger of black magic, into which all the world, and especially America, is rushing as fast as it can go. Only a wide knowledge of the real psychic and spiritual nature of man can save humanity from grave dangers."

"Witch-stories in this so-called nineteenth century, in this enlightened age?"

"Yes, Sir! Witch-tales in this enlightened age! And mark my words! You will have such witch-tales as the Middle Ages never dreamt of. Whole nations will drift insensibly into black magic,† with good intentions, no doubt, but paving the road to hell none the less for that! Do you not see the tremendous evils that lie concealed in hypnotism? Hypnotism and suggestion are great and dangerous powers, for the very reason that the victim never knows when he is being subjected to them; his will is stolen from him. These things may be begun with good motives, and for right purposes. But I am an old woman, and have seen much of human life in many countries and I wish with all my heart I could believe that these powers would be used only for good! If you could foresee what I foresee, you would begin heart and soul to spread the teaching of universal brotherhood. It is the only safeguard!"

"How is it going to guard people against hypnotism?"

"By purifying the hearts of people who would misuse it. And

† [Hitler and his leading Nazis used the black arts, it is said, in carrying out the policies of the Third Reich, as did the Chinese Communists. Hypnotic brainwashing is a common practice.]

universal brotherhood rests upon the common soul. It is because there is one soul common to all men, that brotherhood, or even common understanding, is possible. Bring men to rest on that, and they will be safe. There is a divine power in every man which is to rule his life, and which no one can influence for evil, not even the greatest magician. Let men bring their lives under its guidance, and they have nothing to fear from man or devil.

"And now, my dear, it is getting late, and I am getting sleepy. So I must bid you goodnight!"

And the Old Lady dismissed me with that grand air of hers which never left her, because it was a part of herself. She was the most perfect aristocrat I have ever known.[91]

Chapter 6

17 *Lansdowne Road*

After four months at "Maycott," the Blavatsky Lodge required larger quarters more centrally located in London. The Keightleys found just the right place at 17 Lansdowne Road, a three-story building surrounded by lovely gardens.[92] (See Centerfold, photograph #30.)

The move to new headquarters in September 1887 occurred simultaneously with a gala event, the publication of the first edition of the handsome new magazine *Lucifer*. The magazine's format and design drew a sharp contrast to *The Theosophist*'s crowded pages, small type, and dull white paper.

The title of the magazine shocked many people, including HPB's relatives, because of the popular association of Lucifer with the devil, or with the fallen angels. She gave a full explanation of the word in the magazine's opening editorial; "What's in a Name?" But she expressed it best in a letter to her family:

> *Why should you assail me for having called my journal* Lucifer? *It's a splendid name! Lux, Lucis,—light; ferre—to carry; "the carrier of light"—what can be better? . . . it is only owing to Milton's* Paradise Lost *that* Lucifer *has become a synonym of fallen spirits. The first honest objective of my journal will be to remove the stain of misunderstanding from this name, which was used by the early Christians for Christ. . . .*
>
> Eosphoros *of the Greeks,* Lucifer *of the Romans—these are the titles of [Venus] the morning star, the herald of the bright sunlight. . . . Did not Christ say of himself: "I, Jesus . . . am the bright, the Morning Star"? (Revelation, 22:16) . . . let our journal also, like the pale, pure star of dawn, foretell the bright daybreak of truth—the blending of all disharmonies, of all interpretations by the letter, in the one light of truth by the spirit.*[93]

To avoid dogmatism, the magazine opened its pages to theosophists and non-theosophists alike, as HPB indicates in her article "What is Truth?" (*Lucifer*, February 1888): "The rankest materialists will find hospitality in our journal; aye, even those who have not scrupled to fill pages of it with sneers and personal remarks upon ourselves, and abuse of the doctrines of theosophy so dear to us." In a fifteen-part serial, *Lucifer* published a novel satirizing leading Theosophists, with Blavatsky portrayed as "a kind of *mediumistic* poll-parrot," to use her own words.[94] *The Talking Image of URUR,* as it is called, was written by Franz Hartmann and subsequently appeared as a book.[95]

Countess Wachtmeister returned from Sweden in September 1887 to assume new responsibilities as head of the newly formed Theosophical Publishing Company, to be located on Duke Street. Just before her return, HPB received a letter from the countess's son Carl Axel asking advice on a personal problem bearing on his health. On September eleventh she replied:

> *My dear Count,*
>
> *I answer only today because I did not like to answer* from my own head. *The advice is this: Lead the most regular life you can lead—going to bed rather early than late. Enter the Conservatory at Leipzig trying to make some preliminary arrangements for the privilege of* less hours *of study on account of health. If you take bodily exercise in the morning or in the evening it is quite enough . . . if you can manage to keep your thoughts centered and all engrossed in music—*harmony *rather. For* harmony, *mental, psychic and spiritual, your very soul bathed in it, will have a strong influence on the physiological portion of the system. It is when the man is tossed about mentally or can center his thoughts on nothing in particular that disharmony and hence a diseased condition, is produced in his body. Hold fast to music and its philosophy and all other philosophies will come to you naturally.*
>
> *I hope you have understood me, but if your mother is with you she will explain to you the Master's words.*
>
> *Wishing you success and health and thanking you for your confidence* believe me *ever yours fraternally,*
>
> H. P. Blavatsky[96]

The count's musical career brought him prominence as a composer. He wrote several symphonies and two operas, including an opera oratorio on the life of Buddha. One of his teachers is said to have been Vincent d'Indy. The count died at the age of eighty-two.[97]

Blavatsky spoke at another time of the influence of harmony, or the lack of it, on the physiological system: "Half, if not two-thirds of our ailings and diseases are the fruit of our imagination and fears. Destroy the latter and give another bent to the former, and nature will do the rest."† She adds, however, that one should not become too arrogant in willing away "such diseases as need, if they are not [to be] fatal, the immediate help of expert surgeons and physicians."[98]

One of the Theosophical adepts, while admitting that in our age "there are great triumphs of science . . . in cure of diseases," observes that these efforts "are nearly all directed to *effects* and do not take away the *causes* of the evils. . . . [I]n the future, as the flower of our civilization unfolds, new diseases will arise and more strange disorders will be known, springing from causes that lie deep in the minds of men and which can only be eradicated by spiritual living."[99]

HPB never professed to have the power to cure diseases, but there is evidence that she had knowledge along these lines. Alice Cleather tells of this in her book *H. P. Blavatsky As I Knew Her.* Shortly after Blavatsky's death, Mrs. Cleather had occasion to consult Dr. Z. Mennell, HPB's London physician, and noted:

It was a memorable visit, lasting nearly two hours (he kept a roomful of patients waiting while we talked). Very little was said about my own health. . . . But we talked much about HPB. He told me what an inspiration she had been to him in his medical work; how much she had taught him about the nature of the body and its powers—*particularly the brain.* Some of the things which she had demonstrated with her own organism, were so far beyond anything then known to medical science that it would have been useless to lay them before the College of Physicians, of which I believe he was a distinguished member. He told me that he *had* brought one instance before them, but was met with such hopeless and determined scepticism that he never repeated the attempt.[100]

As to HPB's healing power, one example is related by Archibald Keightley in his "Reminiscences of H. P. Blavatsky." He tells of becoming ill with a form of erysipelas, accompanied by high fever, after a strenuous schedule of Theosophical work:

† It is only in the past thirty or forty years that the medical profession has acknowledged the psychosomatic causes of many of our ailments. If it seems HPB exaggerated when she indicated that one-half or two-thirds of our diseases are caused by imagination and fears, note the following from Edward B. Kitfield, MD, who in 1989 was chosen by physicians "family doctor of the year" in Maine: "Three-quarters of what comes in the door of the doctor's office is based on psychology. If you take good care of yourself physically and emotionally, you don't need us. . . . Emotions regulate the immune system." Negative feelings inhibit its action. (Bangor *Daily News,* July 8, 1989.)

It so happened that Mme. Blavatsky's physician was calling and he looked in on me. What was said I do not know, but as I lay in a kind of stupor I found that Mme. Blavatsky had made a progress up two flights of fairly steep stairs (she who never went up a step if it could be helped, on account of the pain so caused) and had arrived to judge for herself of her doctor's report of me. She sat and looked at me, and then she talked while she held a glass of water between her hands, and this water I afterwards drank; then she went downstairs again bidding me to follow. Down I went and was made to lie on the couch in her room and covered up. I lay there half asleep while she worked away at her writing, sitting at her table in her big chair, with her back towards me. How long I was there I do not know, but suddenly just past my head went a flash of deep crimson lightning. I started, not unnaturally, and was saluted through the back of the chair with "Lie down, what for do you take any notice?" I did so and went to sleep and, after I had been sent upstairs to bed, I again went to sleep and next morning was quite well, if a little shaky. Then I was packed off to Richmond and forbidden to return till I was strong.[101]

In the same reminiscences, Keightley gives an intriguing report of the meetings at the Blavatsky Lodge when located at Lansdowne Road:

The discussions were informal and all sat around and asked questions of Mme. Blavatsky. . . . One part of our delight was for Mme. Blavatsky to reply by the Socratic method—ask another question and seek information on her own account. It was a very effective method and frequently confounded the setter of the conundrum. If it was a genuine search for information which dictated the question, she would spare no pains to give all information in her power. But if the matter was put forward to annoy her or puzzle, the business resulted badly for the questioner. The meetings took up a lot of time, but Mme. Blavatsky enjoyed the contest of wits.

All nations would be represented in those rooms on Thursday nights, and one could never tell who would be present. Sometimes there would be unseen visitors, seen by some but not by others of us. Results were curious; Mme. Blavatsky felt the cold very much and her room was therefore kept very warm, so much so that at the meetings it was unpleasantly hot very often. One night before the meeting time, I came downstairs to find the room like an ice-house, though fire and lights were fully on. I called HPB's attention to this, but was greeted with a laugh and "Oh, I have had a friend of mine here to see me and he forgot to remove his atmosphere."

Another time I remember that the rooms gradually filled until there was no vacant seat. On the sofa sat a distinguished Hindu, in full panoply of turban and dress. The discussion proceeded and apparently our distinguished guest was much interested, for he seemed to follow intelligently the remarks of each speaker. The president of the Lodge arrived that night very late, and coming in looked around for a seat. He walked up to the sofa and sat down— right in the middle of the distinguished Hindu, who promptly, and with some surprise, fizzled and vanished![102]

In between meetings and during the day, the Blavatsky Lodge was a hive of activity, reports a resident worker, the Irish Theosophist Claude Falls Wright. In addition to the stream of visitors there were always a number of volunteer helpers around, who assisted with various jobs. One day a group of workers were huddled together discussing what they considered an urgent problem. Having come to an impasse, one of the younger volunteers knocked on HPB's door and asked her to resolve the matter:

> "Madame," she said, "what is the most important thing necessary in the study of Theosophy?"
> "Common sense, my dear."
> "And Madame, what would you place second?"
> "A sense of humour."
> "And third, Madame?"
> At this point, patience must have been wearing thin.
> "Oh, just MORE common sense!"[103]

During this period HPB seldom went out, but in early January 1889, the Countess Wachtmeister and the American artist Edmund Russell[104] prevailed upon her to visit the studio of the noted London photographer Enrico Resta to have some pictures taken. One of them is the famous photo called the Sphinx. Years later Resta himself told the story of the visit in this letter to John Coats, then president of the London TS:

> *One morning (January 8, 1889) . . . I was in my studio . . . very busy taking photographs when an assistant whispered to me that a lady wanted to be photographed at once if possible, having very little time to spare. . . . In came Madame Blavatsky with Countess Wachtmeister. The first lady immediately sat down by a small table and I noticed she put her right hand into*

her pocket and rolled a cigarette, which you will see in the photos. . . . Without any "studio arrangement" Madame Blavatsky expressed the wish to face the camera in that natural position, and being tremendously impressed with the personality and expression, I took six plates, which to my delight were successful. Madame Blavatsky arose, thanked me for favouring her so quickly, saying some artist had recommended my work. The proofs were dispatched to be returned with a letter expressing pleasure at the results, and, as you know, many thousands have been printed for the Theosophical Society. . . . Occasionally I received a simple invitation to pay an informal visit to this great lady, where the conversation ranged over life in all its aspects, perhaps the limitless power of good, or a kindly interest in my own work which I loved. Some years later I gave up the studio, and the only negatives I chose to keep were these six [enclosed]. They have been deeply treasured by me, and are in perfect condition, but now that I am an old man of 85 I feel that these realistic emblems of a great personage should no longer be retained by me.[105]

One of HPB's visitors during the London years was a wealthy aristocrat from Spain, José Xifré, who was a close friend of Queen Isabella II and King Alphonse XII. It is reported that the king on his deathbed acknowledged Xifré as the only disinterested friend he had ever had.[106] As to his first meeting with HPB, Xifré said a glance from her eyes "penetrated and destroyed the personality that I had been up to that moment" and that "its ideas, tendencies and prejudices, more or less engraved, disappeared. . . . I shall not try to explain this seemingly startling fact, [but this] like all others, is based on the great law of karma. . . . To her I owe all that I know. . . . Both gentle tranquility and moral equilibrium were attained on making her acquaintance."[107]

On another occasion he asserted that HPB had twice saved his life. One of these incidents occurred when he was leaving London for the continent. She said: "You are not going to leave today." Xifré replied he had to leave. When Blavatsky insisted that he must not, he responded, "But, I *must* go, it is absolutely necessary for me to go, I cannot put off my departure." "You shall not go, you must stay overnight in London," she ordered. Reluctantly he obeyed. The following day the newspapers reported that the evening mail train Xifré would have taken was in a dreadful smash-up.[108]

Despite the opposition of the Catholic Church, Xifré, with several associates, actively promulgated Theosophy in Spain. By the end of 1889, a Spanish translation had been completed of *Isis Unveiled, Esoteric Buddhism, Light on the Path,* and *The Key to Theosophy.*[109] A pamphlet entitled "What Is Theosophy?" was distributed to universities, libraries, and clubs throughout Spain. In May 1893, the Theosophist journal *Sophia* was started in Madrid, which continued through seventeen volumes. De Zirkoff observes that "perhaps the greatest and most lasting result of José Xifré's indefatigable work, in close collaboration with a few trusted friends and co-workers, was the publication of a superb Spanish translation of *The Secret Doctrine,* the first volume of which appeared in 1895."[110] Xifré's Theosophical work was eventually silenced when he lost his fortune, an event he believed was engineered by the Church.[111]

In England the Anglican Church was instrumental in having *Lucifer* banned wherever magazines were sold. Particularly offensive to the Church, no doubt, was the editorial in the December 1887 issue, "'*Lucifer*' to the Archbishop of Canterbury, Greetings!" in which evidence was given that "in almost every point the doctrines of the Church are *in direct opposition to the teachings of Jesus.*" It concludes thus:

And now, my Lord Primate, we have very respectfully laid before you the principal points of difference and disagreement between Theosophy and the Christian Churches, and told you of the oneness of Theosophy and the teachings of Jesus. You have heard our profession of faith, and learned the grievances and plaints which we lay at the door of dogmatic Christianity. We, a handful of humble individuals, possessed of neither riches nor worldly influence, but strong in our knowledge, have united in the hope of doing the work which you say that your MASTER has allotted to you, but which is so sadly neglected by that wealthy and domineering colossus—the Christian Church.

Will you call this presumption, we wonder? Will you, in this land of free opinion, free speech, and free effort, venture to accord us no other recognition than the usual *anathema,* which the Church keeps in store for the reformer? Or may we hope that the bitter lessons of experience, which that policy has afforded the Churches in the past, will have altered the hearts and cleared the understandings of her rulers; and that the coming year, 1888, will witness the stretching out to us of the hand of Christians in fellowship and goodwill? This would only be a just recognition that the comparatively small body called the Theosophical Society is no pioneer of the Anti-Christ, no brood of the Evil one as the Church viewed it, but the practical helper, perchance the saviour, of Christianity, and that it is only endeavoring to do the work that Jesus, like Buddha, and the other "sons of God" who preceded him, has commanded all his followers to undertake, but which the Churches, having become dogmatic, are entirely unable to accomplish.

And now, if your Grace can prove that we do injustice to the Church of which you are the Head, or to popular Theology, we promise to acknowledge our error publicly. But—"SILENCE GIVES CONSENT."[112]

The archbishop remained silent. Letters received by *Lucifer* evinced widespread approval of this daring editorial. The magazine circulated fifteen thousand reprints as a further challenge to the Church to reform itself.

≈

Also in the December issue of *Lucifer* was the second of three installments of HPB's "The Esoteric Character of the Gospels"— another cause for opposition to Theosophy from those who literalized the teachings of Jesus.[113]

HPB points out that the Gospels themselves reveal that Jesus taught his disciples an esoteric or secret doctrine: "Unto you it is given to know the mystery of the Kingdom of God; but unto them that are without, all these things are done in parables" (*Mark* 4:11). "And when they were alone" Jesus "expounded all things to his disciples," but "without a parable spoke he not" to the others (*Mark* 4:34). In the New Testament we have the parables, but who knows their inner meanings?

Blavatsky said the esoteric teaching was preserved and taught by the Christian Gnostics, who in turn received it from the disciples of Jesus. One can well imagine how such a statement would shock the orthodox Christians of her day, for they had been taught that gnosticism was a dangerous heresy that had sprung up within the Catholic Church in the second century. The early Church fathers, over a period of several centuries, destroyed every Gnostic text that could be found. The death penalty was often enacted for being a Gnostic, and all one could learn about this religion was from the distorted accounts of Christian writers. The very name *Gnostic* came down to future generations as plague-infested.

Impartial historians, such as Gibbon, thought otherwise. HPB quoted him as stating that the Gnostics were "the most learned of the Christian name" and that they were not content to be mere believers. Nor were they content with mere learning, but sought direct, personal experience of the Gnosis.[114] The word *Gnostic* comes from a Greek word meaning "knowledge."

Since HPB's time, unbiased scholars have become more and more aware of the value of the Gnostic literature. One such scholar, the Reverend A. A. F. Lamplugh, wrote in the introduction to his translation of the Gnostic *Codex Brucisnus,* published in 1918 as *The Gnosis of the Light:* "Recent investigations have challenged . . . the traditional 'facts.' With some today, and with many more tomorrow, the burning question is, or will be—not how did a peculiarly silly and licentious heresy rise within the Church—but how did the Church rise out of the Great Gnostic Movement, how did the dynamic ideas of the Gnosis become crystallized into Dogmas?"[115] Similarly, Carl Jung was convinced that "the central ideas of Christianity are rooted in Gnostic philosophy."[116] Those acquainted with his writings know how deeply he studied Gnostic teachings and symbols.

In *Isis* (2:205), HPB mentions that in the New Testament the Gospel of St. John and the Acts of St. Paul teem with Gnostic expressions, as scholars admit today. It is of interest that two entries in the minutes book of the Blavatsky Lodge for the year 1889 record that on October twelfth, HPB addressed the Lodge on the Gospel of St. John and that on October twenty-fourth, she spoke on the subject of Jesus and St. John.

The most dramatic confirmation of the Theosophical view that the secret teachings of Jesus were studied and cherished by the earliest Gnostics came in the middle of the twentieth century. In 1945, on a cliff near Nag Hammadi, a town on the Nile about three hundred miles from Cairo, an Arab farmer named Muhammad Ali, accompanied by his brothers, made an astonishing discovery. Dismounting from their camels, they sought to obtain special soil to fertilize their crops and, digging around a massive boulder in an old Coptic cemetery, hit a red earthenware jar almost three feet high. Muhammad hesitated to break the jar, imagining a *jinn,* or spirit, might reside therein. But, thinking it might contain gold, he smashed it, only to be disappointed to find thirteen books bound in leather plus a mass of loose papyrus manuscript sheets. Returning home, he dumped it all by the oven, and his mother used many of the loose sheets to kindle the fire.

How the book finally came to the attention of the authorities in Egypt—and of scholars around the globe—is a story of high drama, excitement, intrigue, and, in the Christian academic world, jealous battles for who would be first to translate the documents.[117] The general public was largely unaware of the discovery until 1979, when Elaine Pagels's *The Gnostic Gospels* was published. Having learned Coptic at Harvard University, Pagels had been sent by the university to Egypt to study the Nag Hammadi documents. Her widely acclaimed book received the National Book Critics Circle Award and was a

Book-of-the-Month-Club selection. *The New Yorker* called it "an intellectually elegant, concise study. . . . The economy with which she evokes the world of early Christianity is a marvel."

"Those who circulated and revered the [Nag Hammadi] writings," Pagels states, "did not regard themselves as heretics, but as Gnostics— that is Christians who possess knowledge (gnosis) of Jesus' secret teaching—knowledge hidden from the majority of believers, until they have proven themselves to be spiritually mature." She cites the verse previously quoted from the Gospel of St. Mark, wherein Jesus said to his disciples, "To you has been given the secret of the kingdom of God, but for those outside everything is parables" (*Mark* 4:11).

In *The Gnostic Gospels,* Pagels remarks that "ideas that we associate with Eastern religions emerged in the first century through the Gnostic movement, in the West, but they were suppressed and condemned by polemicists like Irenaeus." Prominent among these ideas was reincarnation, although the source was not Eastern religions but, according to the Gnostics, original Christianity itself. Professor Geddes MacGregor, in his book *Reincarnation in Christianity,* states that "reincarnational views were commonplace in the Gnostic climate in which Christianity developed."[118] As to the Nag Hammadi texts, French Egyptologist Jean Doresse disclosed that they teach that "man has to pass through successive births before reaching the goal."[119]

Another Coptic work, which Pagels cites in other connections, is the *Pistis Sophia.* Discovered in the mid-eighteenth century, it contains many pages in which Christ himself instructs his disciples on various aspects of reincarnation[120] [and other post-resurrection mystery teachings]. HPB's scholarly secretary, G. R. S. Mead, was the first to render the *Pistis Sophia* into English from the Latin translation. Prior to its publication as a book, about half of it was serialized in *Lucifer,* and HPB made comments equal to forty pages in this magazine.[121]

Theosophy's work in the field of esoteric Christianity is not without recognition in the *Encyclopaedia Britannica's* article on Christianity by church historian Ernst Wilhelm Benz. In the section "Modern Currents of Esoteric Christianity" Benz includes theosophy, which he defines as "characterized mainly by a combination of Christian traditions and teachings, and Asian higher religions." He concludes the section with a surprising comment: ". . . Many scholars are convinced that an esoteric Christianity in the 20th century is needed to fulfill a positive task as a counter-movement to a loss of spiritual substance in a dogmatically, institutionally, and socially static church organization."[122]

One closing thought on the discoveries of the *Pistis Sophia* and the

Nag Hammadi scriptures. From outer appearances it was entirely accidental that the *Pistis Sophia* and the Nag Hammadi scriptures came to light. So it was with the Dead Sea Scrolls, which have caused such a stir among scholars. In *Isis Unveiled* (2:26), HPB quotes Max Müller, who observed in the 1860s:

> The science of religion is only just beginning. . . . During the last fifty years the authentic documents of the most important religions in the world *have been recovered in a most unexpected and almost miraculous manner.* We have now before us the Canonical books of Buddhism; the *Zend-Avesta* of Zoroaster is no longer a sealed book; and the hymns of the *Rig-Veda* have revealed a state of religions anterior to the first beginnings of that mythology which in Homer and Hesiod stands before us as a mouldering ruin.

HPB adds in a footnote:

> One of the most surprising facts that have come under our observation, is that students of profound research should not couple the frequent recurrence of these "unexpected and almost miraculous" discoveries of important documents, at the most opportune moments, with a premeditated design. Is it so strange that the custodians of "Pagan" lore, seeing that the proper moment had arrived, should cause the needed document, book, or relic to fall as if by accident in the right man's way?

One wonders how many other documents, books, or relics lie hidden from view, awaiting the right moment for their appearances.

Chapter 7

Prevision of the World Wars?

Discussing Carl Jung's dream prophecy of World War I,[123] Lewis Mumford wrote in *The New Yorker* (May 23, 1964): "This dream, uncanny in retrospect because it was soon verified by events, may be placed in the same category as Madame Blavatsky's much earlier and even more realistic vision of the destruction of whole cities by nuclear blasts." This vision is to be found in HPB's story "Karmic Visions" (*Lucifer,* June 1888).

At the time the story was written there had been no major wars in Europe for two decades, and this peace would continue for another twenty-five years. European observers were encouraged to predict a millennium of peace, prosperity, and scientific progress. It is in this setting that HPB's story foretells the onslaught of World War I and the time period subsequent, when armies would have weapons to destroy millions of people instantaneously.

Part One of "Karmic Visions" focuses on Clovis, the fifth-century ruler and founder of the Frankish kingdom, who made Paris his capital; Part Two focuses on Clovis reborn as a monarch, who, although unnamed in the story, strongly resembles the ill-fated and much loved Frederick III. After a reign of only ninety-nine days, Frederick died of throat cancer in June 1888, the very month that "Karmic Visions" was published. His father, Wilhelm I, had died earlier that year. *Lucifer's* editorial for the New Year, 1889, comments:

A year ago it was stated that 1888 was a dark combination of numbers; it has proved so since. . . . Almost every nation was visited by some dire calamity. Prominent among other countries was Germany. It was in 1888 that the Empire reached, virtually, the 18th year of its unification. It was during the fatal combination of the four numbers 8 that it lost two of its Emperors, and planted the seeds of many dire Karmic results.

One dire result was that when the reborn Clovis, Frederick III, died, the heir to the throne was his eldest son, Kaiser Wilhelm II of World

War I fame, a prime mover in that ghastly conflict. (Wilhelm II was half British, for his mother, Frederick's queen, was the eldest daughter of Queen Victoria.)

"Karmic Visions" opens in a war camp of Clovis, who recently was baptized a Christian at Rheims. He has just inflicted a brutal defeat on a German tribe, the Alemanni, and prisoners have been brought before him to be disposed of as he sees fit. One is a pagan seeress who fearlessly recounts the many crimes he committed to achieve lordship over the Franks. As to the German tribe he has just slaughtered, she predicts: "You shall be reborn among your present enemies, and suffer the tortures you have inflicted upon your victims. All the combined power and glory you have deprived them of shall be yours in prospect, yet you shalt never reach it!" The king hurls her to the ground, and as he lifts his murderous spear, the prophetess cries out: "I curse you! May my agony be tenfold yours!" The spear pierces the victim's throat, nailing her head to the ground. Blood spurts out, covering Clovis and his friends.

Next we find Clovis reborn in Germany as Frederick. The opening selections come from the happy period of his youth and manhood, followed by glimpses of him battling his fatal disease—the tracheotomy operation on his throat having left him permanently speechless. At this period he was the only heir to the throne. His father had been king of Prussia, but after the Franco-Prussian War, and owing to Bismarck's nationalistic policies, was now the first emperor of a combined Germany. The story that follows, using HPB's words, is given in condensed form:

Among millions of other Souls, a Soul-Ego is reborn; for weal or for woe, who knows! Captive in its new human form, it grows with it, and together they become, at last, conscious of their existence. Happy are the years of their blooming youth.

One day an arrogant and boisterous enemy threatens the father's kingdom, and the savage instincts of the warrior of old awaken in the Soul-Ego and cause its Ego of clay to draw the soldier's blade, assuring him it is in defense of his country. They make a footstool of the fallen enemy and transform their sire's little kingdom into a great empire. Satisfied they could achieve no more for the present, they return to the seclusion and to the dreamland of their sweet home.

But an evil day comes to all in the drama of being. The strong body is found stretched one day on the thorny bed of pain. Even in sleep the Soul-Ego finds no rest. Hot and feverish its body tosses about in restless agony. Through the mental agony of the soul, there lies a transformed man.

[He now has a vision of the Franco-Prussian War in which he led his country's army against France.] He sees thousands of mangled corpses covering the ground, torn and cut to shreds by the murderous weapons devised by science and civilization, blessed to success by the servants of his God. He sees the old mothers who have lost the light of their souls; families, the hand that fed them. He beholds widowed young wives thrown on the wide, cold world, and beggared orphans wailing in the streets by the thousands. He finds the young daughters of his bravest old soldiers exchanging their mourning garments for the gaudy frippery of prostitution, and the Soul-Ego shudders in the sleeping form. His heart is rent by the groans of the famished; his eyes blinded by the smoke of burning hamlets, of homes destroyed, of towns and cities in smouldering ruins.

And in his terrible dream, he remembers that moment of insanity in his soldier's life, when standing over a heap of the dead and the dying, waving in his right hand a naked sword, red to its hilt with smoking blood, and in his left, the colors rent from the hand of the warrior expiring at his feet, he had sent in a stentorian voice praises to the throne of the Almighty, thanksgiving for the victory just obtained!

"What have they brought thee or to thy fatherland, those bloody victories!" whispers the Soul in him. "A population clad in iron armor," it replies. What is thy future Kingdom, now? A legion of war-puppets, a great wild beast in their collectivity. A beast that, like the sea yonder, slumbers gloomily now, but to fall with the more fury on the first enemy that is indicated to it. Indicated, by whom? *It is as though a heartless, proud Fiend, assuming sudden authority, incarnate Ambition and Power, had clutched with iron hand the minds of a whole country.*[124] [italics added.]

The whole world is hushed in breathless expectation. Not a wife or mother, but is haunted in her dreams by the black and ominous storm-cloud that overhangs the whole of Europe. The cloud is approaching. It comes nearer and nearer. Oh woe and horror! I foresee once more for earth the suffering I have already witnessed. I read the fatal destiny upon the brow of the flower of Europe's youth! But if I live and have the power, never, oh never shall my country take part in it again!

And now the hand of Fate is upon the couch of pain. The hour for the fulfillment of nature's law has struck at last. The old [king] is no more; the younger man is henceforth a monarch. Voiceless and helpless, he is nevertheless a potentate, the autocratic master of millions of subjects. Cruel Fate has erected a throne for him over an open grave, and beckons him to glory and to power. Devoured by suffering, he finds himself suddenly crowned. The wasted form is whirled from the balmy south to the frozen north, whither he speeds to reign and—speeds to die. In the moving palace [of the train] the luxurious vehicle is full of exotic plants. Its swinging monotonous motion lulls the worn-out occupant to sleep. It travels through aeons of time, and lives, and feels, and breathes under the most contrasted forms and personages. Thus "Death" becomes but a meaningless word for it, a vain sound.

"What is my Past? Why do I suffer?" enquires the Soul-Ego. A long parchment is unrolled, and reveals a long series of mortal beings, in each of whom the Soul-Ego recognizes one of its dwellings. When it comes to the last but one, it sees a blood-stained hand doing endless deeds of cruelty and treachery, and it shudders.

"What is my Future?" asks the Soul-Ego despairingly. "Is it to be forever with tears, and bereaved of Hope?"

No answer is received. But the Dreamer feels whirled through space. The Soul-Ego finds himself as strong and as healthy as he ever was. Yes, it is no longer the tall, noble form with which he is familiar, but the body of somebody else, of whom he as yet knows nothing. [He learns of the destruction by pneumo-dynovril[125] of the last two million soldiers in the field in the western portion of the globe.]

All around seems strangely changed. Ambition, grasping greediness or envy—miscalled *Patriotism*—exist no longer. Cruel selfishness has made room for just altruism. No more wars are possible, for the armies are abolished. Soldiers have turned into diligent, hardworking tillers of the ground, and the whole globe echoes his song in rapturous joy. Kingdoms and countries around him live like brothers. The great, the glorious hour has come at last! That which he hardly dared to hope and think about in the stillness of his long, suffering nights, is now realized. The great curse is taken off, and the world stands absolved and redeemed in its regeneration!

He makes a strong effort and—is himself again. Prompted by the Soul-Ego to REMEMBER and ACT in conformity, he lifts his arms to Heaven and swears in the face of all nature to preserve peace to the end of his days—in his own country, at least.

A distant beating of drums and long cries of what he fancies in his dream are the rapturous thanksgivings, for the pledge just taken.

An abrupt shock, loud clatter, and, as the eyes open, the Soul-Ego looks through them in amazement. The heavy gaze meets the respectful and solemn face of the physician offering the usual draught. The train stops. He rises from his couch weaker and wearier than ever, to see around him [honoring the new monarch] endless lines of troops armed with a new and yet more murderous weapon of destruction—ready for the battlefield.[126]

Chapter 8

The Secret Doctrine

Volume One of *The Secret Doctrine* was published on November 1, 1888 and Volume Two December 28, 1888.† The subtitle reads: "The Synthesis of Science, Religion, and Philosophy." The first volume, "Cosmogenesis," describes how worlds originate—or rather, are reborn after their periodic time of rest—and also how our particular globe and its lower kingdoms evolved up to the time the human form is being developed. "Anthropogenesis," the second volume, discusses the further evolution of that form; the lighting up of mind by the incarnation of human souls from prior worlds; the subsequent evolution of the early races up to the present period; and the future development projected for those races if the original grand design is carried out. Each volume is divided into three parts: The Stanzas of Dzyan; The Evolution of Symbolism; and Science and The Secret Doctrine Contrasted.

HPB writes:

These truths are in no sense put forward as a *revelation,* nor does the author claim the position of a revealer of mystic lore, now made public for the first time in the world's history. For what is contained in this work is to be found scattered throughout thousands of volumes embodying the scriptures of the great Asiatic and early European religions, hidden under glyph and symbol, and hitherto left unnoticed because of this veil. What is now attempted is to gather the oldest tenets together and to make of them one harmonious and unbroken whole. The sole advantage which the writer has over her predecessors, is that she need not resort to personal speculations and theories. For this work is a partial statement of what she herself has been taught by more advanced students, supplemented, in a few details only, by the results of her own study and observation. . . .[127]

It is useless to say that the system [of occult science] is no fancy of one or several isolated individuals. That it is the uninterrupted

---

† Although Volume I was in HPB's hands on October 20, 1888. Kirby Van Mater, *Secret Doctrine Centenary: Report of Proceedings,* Theosophical University Press, California, 1989, 84.

record covering thousands of generations of Seers whose respective experiences were made to test and to verify the traditions passed orally by one early race to another, of the teachings of higher and exalted beings, who watched over the childhood of Humanity. That for long ages, the "Wise Men" of [our present race], of the stock saved and rescued from the last cataclysm and shifting of continents, had passed their lives *in learning, not teaching*.

How did they do so? . . . by checking, testing, and verifying in every department of nature the traditions of old by the independent visions of great adepts; *i.e.,* men who have developed and perfected their physical, mental, psychic, and spiritual organisations to the utmost possible degree. No vision of one adept was accepted till it was checked and confirmed by the visions—so obtained as to stand as independent evidence—of other adepts, and by centuries of experiences. . . . The flashing gaze of those seers has penetrated into the very kernel of matter, and recorded the soul of things there, where an ordinary profane, however learned, would have perceived but the external work of form. But modern science believes not in the "soul of things," and hence will reject the whole system of ancient cosmogony. . . . [It believes] that the Universe and all in it has been gradually built up by blind forces inherent in matter.[128]

In the introductory section to *The Secret Doctrine,* HPB establishes the three fundamental propositions upon which the whole work is based:

(a) An Omnipresent, Eternal, Boundless, and Immutable PRINCIPLE on which all speculation is impossible, since it transcends the power of human conception and could only be dwarfed by any human expression or similitude. . . . To render these ideas clearer to the general reader, let him set out with the postulate that there is one absolute Reality which antecedes all manifested, conditioned being. This Infinite and Eternal Cause . . . is the rootless root of "all that was, is, or ever shall be.". . .

(b) The Eternity of the Universe *in toto* as a boundless plane; periodically "the playground of numberless Universes incessantly manifesting and disappearing," called "the manifesting stars," and the "sparks of Eternity." [The Secret Doctrine also affirms] "the Eternity of the Pilgrim." . . . "Pilgrim" is the appellation given to our *Monad* . . . during its cycle of incarnations. It is the only immortal and eternal principle in us, being an indivisible part of the integral whole—the Universal Spirit, from which it emanates, and into which it is absorbed at the end of the cycle. . . .

This second assertion of the Secret Doctrine is the absolute universality of the law of periodicity, of flux and reflux, ebb and flow, which physical science has observed and recorded in all departments of nature. An alternation such as that of Day and Night, Life and Death, Sleeping and Waking, is a fact so common, so perfectly universal and without exception, that it is easy to comprehend that in it we see one of the absolutely fundamental laws of the universe. . . .

(c) The fundamental identity of all Souls with the Universal Over-Soul, the latter being itself an aspect of the Unknown Root; and the obligatory pilgrimage for every Soul—a spark of the former—through the Cycle of Incarnation (or "Necessity") in accordance with Cyclic and Karmic law, during the whole term. In other words, no . . . divine Soul can have an independent (conscious) existence before the spark which issued from the pure Essence of the . . . OVER-SOUL, has (a) passed through every elemental form of the phenomenal world . . . and (b) acquired individuality, first by natural impulse, and then by self-induced and self-devised efforts (checked by its Karma), thus ascending through all the degrees of intelligence, from the lowest to the highest Manas [or Mind], from mineral and plant, up to the holiest archangel (Dhyani-Buddha). The pivotal doctrine of the Esoteric philosophy admits no privileges or special gifts in man, save those won by his own Ego through personal effort and merit throughout a long series of metempsychoses and reincarnations. . . .

Such are the basic conceptions on which the Secret Doctrine rests. . . . Once the reader has gained a clear comprehension of them and realised the light which they throw on every problem of life, they will need no further justification in his eyes, because their truth will be to him as evident as the sun in heaven.[129]

In the third proposition, the subjects of karma and reincarnation are introduced. Here is what HPB says elsewhere in *The Secret Doctrine:*

The reincarnationists and believers in Karma alone dimly perceive that the whole secret of Life is in the unbroken series of its manifestations. . . . Those who believe in *Karma* have to believe in *destiny,* which from birth to death, every man is weaving thread by thread around himself, as a spider does his cobweb. . . . This law, whether Conscious or Unconscious—predestines nothing and no one. . . . Karma creates nothing, nor does it design. It is man who plans and creates causes, and Karmic law adjusts the effects; which adjustment is not an act but universal harmony, tending ever to resume its original position, like a bough, which, bent down too forcibly, rebounds with corresponding vigor. If it happens to dislocate the arm that tried to bend it out of its natural position, shall we say that it is the bough which broke our arm, or that our own folly has brought us to grief?[130]

Karma has never sought to destroy intellectual and individual liberty. . . . It has not involved its decrees in darkness purposely to perplex man, nor shall it punish him who dares to scrutinize its mysteries. On the contrary, he who unveils through study and meditation its intricate paths, and throws light on those dark ways, in the windings of which so many men perish owing to their ignorance of the labyrinth of life, is working for the good of his fellow-men. . . .[131]

Believers in Karma cannot be regarded as Atheists or materialists—still less as fatalists. . . . It is a doctrine which explains the origin of Evil, and ennobles our conceptions of what divine immutable Justice ought to be, instead of degrading the unknown and unknowable Deity by making it the whimsical, cruel tyrant, which we call Providence.[132]

An Occultist or a philosopher will not speak of the goodness or cruelty of Providence; but, identifying it with Karma-Nemesis, he will teach that nevertheless it guards the good and watches over them in this, as in future lives; and that it punishes the evil-doer—aye, even to his seventh rebirth. So long, in short, as the effect of his having thrown into perturbation even the smallest atom in the Infinite World of Harmony, has not been finally readjusted. For the only decree of Karma—an eternal and immutable decree—is absolute Harmony in the world of matter as it is in the world of Spirit. It is not, therefore, Karma that rewards or punishes, but it is we, who reward or punish ourselves according to whether we work with, through and along with nature, abiding by the laws on which that Harmony depends, or—break them.[133]

[Connected with the workings of karma are] the invisible tablets of the Astral Light, "the great picture-gallery of eternity"—a faithful record of every act, and even thought of man. . . . As said in "*Isis*," this divine and unseen canvas is the BOOK OF LIFE. . . . The Eternal Record is no fantastic dream, for we meet with the same records in the world of gross matter. "A shadow never falls upon a wall without leaving thereupon a permanent trace which might be made visible by resorting to the proper processes," says Dr. Draper. . . . "Upon the walls of our most private apartments," [he continues,] "where we think the eye of intrusion is altogether shut out, and our retirement can never be profaned, there exist the vestiges of our acts, silhouettes of whatever we have done." Drs. Jevons and Babbage believe that every thought, displacing the particles of the brain and setting them in motion, scatters them throughout the Universe, and they think that "each particle of the existing matter must be a register of all that has happened." (*Principles of Science*, 2:455)[134]

Thus, says HPB, "the ancient doctrine has begun to acquire rights of citizenship in the speculations of the scientific world."[135]

It is a law of occult dynamics that "a given amount of energy expended on the spiritual or astral plane, is productive of far greater results than the same amount expended on the physical objective plane of existence." [Thus] the suppression of one single bad cause will suppress not one, but a variety of bad effects. And if a Brotherhood or even a number of Brotherhoods may not be able to prevent nations [in the future] from occasionally cutting each other's throats—still unity in thought and action, and philosophical research into the mysteries of being, will always prevent some . . . from creating additional causes in a world already so full of woe and evil. . . . This state will last . . . until we begin acting from *within,* instead of ever following impulses from *without.* . . . The closer the union between the mortal reflection MAN, and his [inner Divine Self], the less dangerous the external conditions and subsequent reincarnations.[136]

Intimately, or rather indissolubly, connected with Karma, then, is the law of rebirth, or of the reincarnation of the same spiritual individuality in a long, almost interminable, series of personalities. The latter are like the various costumes and characters played by the same actor, with each of which that actor identifies himself and is identified by the public, for the space of a few hours. The *inner,* or real man, who personates those characters, knows the whole time that he is Hamlet for the brief space of a few acts, which represent, however, on the plane of human illusion the whole life of Hamlet. And he knows that he was, the night before, King Lear, the transformation in his turn of the Othello of a still earlier preceding night; but the outer, visible character is supposed to be ignorant of the fact.

In actual life that ignorance is, unfortunately, but too real. Nevertheless, the *permanent* individuality is fully aware of the fact, though, through the atrophy of the "spiritual" eye in the physical body, that knowledge is unable to impress itself on the consciousness of the false [or illusionary] personality. . . . "That which is part of our souls is eternal," says Thackeray . . . and though "the book and volume" of the *physical* brain may forget events within the scope of one terrestrial life, the bulk of collective recollections can never desert the divine soul within us. Its whispers may be too soft, the sound of its words too far off the plane perceived by our physical senses; yet the shadow of events *that were,* just as much as the shadow of the events *that are to come,* is within its perceptive powers, and is ever present before its mind's eye. . . .[137]

In the second proposition of *The Secret Doctrine* it is stated that the immortal monad or soul within us is absorbed into the Universal Spirit at the end of our world. In Oriental teachings this absorption is referred to as entering into nirvana and poses the old question as to whether it means individual annihilation. Western Orientalists in the nineteenth century believed it did. *The Secret Doctrine* replies:

> To see in Nirvana annihilation amounts to saying of a man plunged in a sound *dreamless* sleep . . . that he, too, is annihilated. . . . Reabsorption is by no means such a "dreamless sleep," but, on the contrary, *absolute* existence, an unconditioned unity, or a state, to describe which human language is absolutely and hopelessly inadequate. . . . The human mind cannot in its present stage of development . . . reach this plane of thought. It totters here, on the brink of incomprehensible Absoluteness and Eternity. . . .
>
> Nor is the individuality . . . lost because reabsorbed. For, however limitless—from a human standpoint—the paranirvanic state, it has yet a limit in Eternity. Once reached, the same monad will reemerge therefrom as a still higher being, on a far higher plane, to recommence its cycle of perfected activity. . . . For it is said in the Sacred Slokas: *"The thread of radiance which is imperishable and dissolves only in Nirvana re-emerges from it in its integrity on the day when the Great Law calls all things back into action."*
>
> In each of us that golden thread of continuous life is the *Sutratma,* the luminous thread of immortal, *impersonal* monadship, on which [the spiritual harvests] of all our earthly lives . . . are strung as so many beads—according to the beautiful expression of Vedantic philosophy.[138]

HPB makes it clear that even when the human monad is *absorbed* in nirvana, its individuality is not necessarily totally absorbed. In her *Transactions of the Blavatsky Lodge,* for example, she says of Nirvana: "Then everything becomes one, all individualities are merged into one, yet each knowing itself, a mysterious teaching indeed."[139] *The Secret Doctrine* explains:

Sooner or later, all that now seemingly exists, will be in reality and actually in the state of [Paranirvana†]. But there is a great difference between *conscious* and *unconscious* "being." The condition of [paranirvana] without Paramartha, the Self-analysing consciousness . . . is no bliss, but simply extinction (for Seven Eternities). Thus, an iron ball placed under the scorching rays of the sun will get heated through, but will not feel or appreciate the warmth, while a man will. It is only "with a mind clear and undarkened by personality, and an assimilation of the merit of manifold existences devoted to being in its collectivity (the whole living and sentient Universe)," that one gets rid of personal existence, merging into, becoming one with, the Absolute, and continuing in full possession of Paramartha [Self-consciousness].[140]

If such fruitage of past lives were not preserved, then each new universe when reborn would have to start from scratch, with no prior experience to draw upon. Elsewhere HPB says that when great souls receive their final initiation "every Ego has to remember all the cycles of his past incarnations for Manvantaras[‡]. . . . It sees the stream of its past incarnations by a certain divine light. It sees all humanity at once, but still there is ever, as it were, a stream which is always the 'I.'"[141]

In a remarkable scientific experiment it has been demonstrated that what we have been discussing could really be true. An article in *The New Scientist* (November 11, 1982) discusses the experiments of Dr. David Bohm, former professor of theoretical physics at Birbeck College, University of London. He earned his PhD at the University of California under the celebrated Robert Oppenheimer. When Bohm was assistant professor at Princeton, his discourses with Einstein became a turning point in his life. Quoting from *The New Scientist*:

Bohm's latest book, and certainly his most interesting, is *Wholeness and the Implicate Order* (Routledge, 1980). . . . The central idea is the "enfolded order" [an idea that struck Bohm in the 1960s as he was watching a television program].

A specially-designed jar at the Royal Institution has a rotating cylinder inside; between the cylinder and glass jar itself is a narrow space filled with glycerine. The cylinder is turned by a handle at the top, and some ink is dropped into the glycerine from above. As Bohm watched the handle turning the cylinder, he saw the dark ink become "enfolded" into the light-colored viscous glycerine and

---

† *"Paranirvana"* means "beyond nirvana," or the highest nirvanic state.

‡ In this context *"Manvantara"* means past cycles involving other worlds.

smear away almost to nothing. Then, the handle was turned back the other way and as if by a miracle, the original drop of ink reappeared; it was "unfolded" from the glycerine, and reconstituted itself and regained its original coherence.[†] Bohm exclaimed: "Well, that's what I want!". . .

Bohm now believes that forms "explicate" themselves similarly from the Universe as a whole, and then "fold back in again," only to re-emerge again, in ceaseless succession. . . . There is no doubt at all that Bohm regards himself and every one of us as also being momentarily explicated or precipitated forms which have emerged in the Universe and will return into it, like drops of ink. The implication of this "implication" is that our "disappearance" need not be the end of us.

Such a view of human evolution has perhaps still further implications when linked with the idea that self-conscious beings from prior worlds return with the knowledge acquired in those worlds. This, if true, would utterly transform the idea of evolution taught in scientific textbooks that the first humans were simply cavemen just a little more evolved than animals. Perhaps the Theosophical view can be better understood by using these analogies: A school is begun by teachers, not pupils, and a family is started by parents, not children, a pattern that applies to the human family as a whole. Those who incarnated first from prior worlds were the greatest and wisest.

According to *The Secret Doctrine,* in the early days of the human race, while it was still in its purity, a Great Being appeared among men, and after him a group of semidivine, semihuman beings:

> "*Set apart*" in Archaic *genesis* for certain purposes, they are those in whom are said to have incarnated the highest Dhyanis, "Munis and Rishis from previous [worlds]"—*to form the nursery for future human adepts,* on this earth and during the present cycle.

It is under the direct, silent guidance of this MAHA—(great)—GURU that all the other less divine Teachers and instructors of mankind became, from the first awakening of human consciousness, the guides of early Humanity. It is through these "sons of God" that infant humanity got its first notions of all the arts and sciences, as well as of spiritual knowledge; and it is they who have laid the first foundation-stone of those ancient civilizations that puzzle so sorely

---

† When several drops of ink were successively added to the liquid, the same result occurred; each drop reappeared when the motion of the handle of the cylinder was reversed. (Bohm, *Wholeness,* 149.)

our modern generation of students and scholars. Let those who doubt this statement explain the mystery of the extraordinary knowledge possessed by the ancients—alleged to have developed from lower and animal-like savages . . . on any other equally reasonable grounds. . . . No man descended from a Palaeolithic cave-dweller could ever evolve such a science unaided, even in millenniums of thought and intellectual evolution.[142]

Such "extraordinary knowledge" includes not only advanced knowledge of mathematics and astronomy but the ability to create architectural marvels and exquisite works of art, such as the 16,000-year-old cave paintings discovered near Lascaux, France, in 1940 and the Tassili frescoes found in 1933 in a canyon of the Sahara Desert, which Maurice Dolbier describes as "one of the greatest treasures left by our pre-historic ancestors." Paintings were discovered that were identified as representing "sixteen different art phases and at least thirty different styles." Some by their "superb rendering of the human form" are comparable to "the sculptures of ancient Greece or the works of the Renaissance artists."[143]

If, as just indicated, Theosophy teaches that human development on this planet began with the highest and best from prior worlds, it should not be surprising to learn that it also teaches that the awakening of life in general began not in matter, but in spirit. Professor Theodore Roszak speaks of this in his book *Unfinished Animal,* published by Harper & Row in 1975. In the section "Madame Blavatsky's *Secret Doctrine,*" he writes:

The Darwinians, HPB contended, begin at the "midpoint" of the total evolutionary progression. Lacking a spiritual dimension to their thought, their approach can only treat the later, biological phases of our physical development. But even the full meaning of this phase cannot be grasped until it is paralleled by the cosmic transformations of spirit that preceded it and continue to influence it. For matter exists, in HPB's system, only to be the receptacle of spirit; it responds to the unfolding needs of spirit as part of the grand redemptive cycle. "Our physical planet," as she puts it, "is but the handmaiden of the spirit, its master." This, the Hidden Wisdom's traditional conception of evolution, stands in HPB's work as "the secret doctrine," the "primeval revelation" which she was convinced lay at the core of all religions and philosophies.

At this point Roszak inserts a quote from *Isis* (1:285):

Our "ignorant" ancestors traced the law of evolution throughout the whole universe. . . . From the universal ether to the incarnate human spirit, they traced one uninterrupted series of entities. These evolutions were from the world of spirit into the world of gross matter; and through that back again to the source of all things. The "descent of species" was to them a descent from the spirit, the primal source of all, to the "degradation of matter."

He then continues:

Yet, though this immersion of spirit in matter is, from one point of view, a "degradation" it [is] for the purpose of vastly enriching our consciousness. By our collective evolutionary course, and by innumerable personal incarnations, we make our way through all the realms of being: mineral, plant, animal, human, divine. And it is by virtue of this hard-won "harvest of experience" that each human being becomes a microcosm of the universe. As with Pico della Mirandola's conception of a chameleon-natured humanity, our goal is to make human consciousness the compendium of all possible forms of existence. We are, in this way, the agents who elevate plant and animal life, inert and mindless matter, to self-awareness. It is exactly to achieve this cosmic heightening of consciousness that spirit sacrifices itself by its initial descent. In the words of the Kabbalistic formula several times quoted by HPB: "a stone becomes a plant; a plant, a beast; a beast, a man; a man, a spirit; and the spirit, a God."

HPB located our era at the pivot point of this progression, where spirit, having reached the human phase of its journey, is ripe to recapture the memory of its origins and to gain the leverage necessary to raise itself and physical nature to the level of divinity. This task would still take thousands of years of purification and enlightenment in HPB's cosmological system; but its end was clear in her view: a Mahayana vision of universal salvation. It is one of her best moments.[144]

In 1935, fifty years after *The Secret Doctrine* was published, George Russell, in a letter to the Irish author Seán O'Faoláin, indicates some of the interest in literary and scholarly circles aroused by the appearance of that book:

You dismiss H. P. Blavatsky rather too easily as "hocus pocus." Nobody ever affected the thought of so many able men and women by "hocus pocus." The real source of her influence is to be found in *The Secret Doctrine,* a book on the religions of the world suggesting or disclosing an underlying unity between all great religions. . . . it is one of the most exciting and stimulating books written for the last hundred years. It is paying a poor compliment to men like Yeats, Maeterlinck, and others, to men like Sir William Crookes, the greatest chemist of modern times, who was a member of her society, to Carter Blake, F.R.S., the anthropologist, and the scholars and scientists in many countries who read H. P. Blavatsky's books, to assume that they were attracted by "hocus pocus." If you are ever in the National Library, Kildare Street, and have a couple of hours to spare, you might dip into "The Proem" to *The Secret Doctrine,* and you will understand the secret of the influence of that extraordinary woman on her contemporaries. . . . You should not be misled by popular catch-words . . . but try to find out the real secret of H. P. Blavatsky's influence, which still persists strong as ever, as I have found over here [in London] among many intellectuals and well-known writers.[145]

The aforementioned scientist Dr. C. Carter Blake contributed a paper regarding his contacts with HPB for inclusion in the appendix of Countess Wachtmeister's *Reminiscences of H. P. Blavatsky and The Secret Doctrine.* Quoting from his statement:

On ordinary lines it is strange that an old, sickly woman, not consulting a library and having no books of her own of consequence, should possess the unusual knowledge that Madame Blavatsky undoubtedly did. Indeed, it is incomprehensible, unless she were of an extraordinary mental capacity, and had spent her whole life in study. On the contrary, from many sources we gain undoubted evidence that Madame Blavatsky's education had not even been carried as far as that of a High School student of the present day.

But it is a fact that she knew more than I did on my own particular lines of anthropology, etc. For instance, her information was superior to my own on the subject of the Naulette Jaw. Page 744 in the second vol. of *The Secret Doctrine* refers to facts which she could not easily have gathered from any published book.

On page 754, also of the second vol. [of *The*] *Secret Doctrine,* the sentence beginning: "If we turn to the new world," and speaking of the existence of "pliocene mammalia and the occurrence of pliocene raised beaches." I remember in conversation with her in 1888, in Lansdowne Road, at the time she was engaged on *The Secret Doctrine,* how Madame Blavatsky, to my great astonishment, sprung upon me the fact that the raised beaches of Tarija were pliocene. I had always thought them pleistocene—following the line of reasoning of Darwin and Spotswood Wilson.

The fact that these beaches are pliocene has been proven to me since from the works of Gay, *Istoria Fiscia de Chile,* Castlenaw's book on Chile, and other works, though these out-of-the-way books had never then come into my hands, in spite of the fact that I had made a *specialty* of the subject; and not until Madame Blavatsky put me on the track of the pliocene did I hear of them.

On page 755, II, *Secret Doctrine,* her mention of the fossil footprints from Carson, Indiana, U.S.A., is again interesting as a proof that she did not obtain her information by thought-reading. When Madame Blavatsky spoke of the footprints to me I did not know of their existence, and Mr. G. W. Bloxam, Assistant Secretary of the Anthropological Institute, afterwards told me that a pamphlet on the subject in their library had never been out.

Madame Blavatsky certainly had original sources of information (I don't say what) transcending the knowledge of experts on their own lines.[146]

In the chapter "Science and the Secret Doctrine," in Part VII of this biography, other scientists, including Einstein, will be considered who have evinced an interest in this book. HPB believed, however, that scientists in general would ignore her writings for some time to come: "They will be driven out of their position not by spiritual, theosophical, or any physical or even mental phenomena, but simply by the enormous *gaps* and *chasms* that open daily and will still be opening before them, as one discovery follows another, until they are finally knocked off their feet by the ninth wave of simple common sense."[147]

Do such "gaps and chasms" exist today in modern science? "The only solid piece of scientific truth about which I feel totally confident," writes the distinguished physician and author Dr. Lewis Thomas, "is that we are profoundly ignorant about nature. Indeed, I regard this as the major discovery of the past hundred years of biology."[148] He is not alone in his observation. In 1977, *The Encyclopaedia of Ignorance* was published at Oxford, in which the world's eminent scientists surveyed the unsolved problems in their fields.[149] A similar work, involving astronomical research, was published in 1979: *Mysterious Universe: A Handbook of Astronomical Anomalies,* by William R. Corliss.[150] The reviewer in the *New York Times* (October 2, 1979) remarks that the volume is composed "almost entirely of articles published by professional scientific journals" and is "a remarkably full compilation of scientific head-scratching regarding the heavens surrounding our planet." Corliss is a specialist in anomalous science, and each of his many books thus far published covers a different branch of science.

Chapter 9

A New Recruit

The first edition of Volume I of *The Secret Doctrine* was soon sold out, necessitating a new printing. W. T. Stead, the famed editor of the *Pall Mall Gazette,* and *The Review of Reviews,* received his copy from HPB herself. He replied on December 8, 1888:

> You are a very great woman and I do not think that anyone but yourself (either man or woman) could have written *The Secret Doctrine,* nor do I feel competent, from the depths of my ignorance, even to express an opinion upon its extraordinary contents—but I think so learned and so gifted a lady should not bear false witness against her neighbor even when that neighbor is such a far away little person as myself. You say you know I hold you in small estimation. Believe me when I say that therein you calumniate me. I do not profess to understand you, for you inhabit space of more dimensions than I can even conceive, but I am not so great a fool as to be unable to see that you have a genius quite transcendent, and an extraordinary aptitude for both literature and propagandism, which the rest of your fellow-creatures may well envy. I have to thank you very much for your book. I have read only your preface and the chapter on Keely, in whose discoveries I am much interested,[151] but I promise myself the pleasure of reading much more as time goes on. Thank you much for the promise of your second volume.[152]

When Volume II arrived, Stead had a problem in having both volumes reviewed, as his regular reviewers refused to tackle it. He then thought of Annie Besant, and she agreed.[153] Born in London in 1847, Besant was all Irish on her mother's side and half Irish on her father's. In her youth she was a devout Christian and married a clergyman. When her faith in church dogmas wavered, her husband threatened that she must accept them or leave her home, and she chose to leave.

Writes her biographer, Professor Arthur Nethercot:

> Mrs. Annie Besant was known all over the English-speaking world, and by many people on the continent, as one of the most remarkable

women of her day. She was a Freethinker; a consorter with materialists like Charles Bradlaugh; an agitator in radical political circles . . . a feminist; an early convert to Fabian Socialism, through
the agency of Bernard Shaw; a teacher of science; an author-editor-
publisher . . . a social and educational reformer; and an orator
whose power was so compelling and whose charm was so potent
that Shaw was only one among thousands who extolled her as the
greatest woman speaker of the century. [Then she became] still
more notorious as a strike leader and union organizer—anathema to
the conventional and conservative in both church and state.[154]

In her 1893 autobiography, Mrs. Besant recalls the stages of her development that led to the moment when she received the two volumes
of *The Secret Doctrine:*

Ever more and more had been growing on me the feeling that something more than I had was needed for the cure of social ills. The Socialist position sufficed on the economic side, but where to gain the
inspiration, the motive, which should lead to the realization of the
Brotherhood of Man? Our efforts to organize bands of unselfish
workers had failed. Much indeed had been done, but there was not a
real movement of self-sacrificing devotion, in which men worked
for Love's sake only, and asked but to give, not to take. Where was
the material for a nobler Social Order, where the hewn stones for the
building of the Temple of Man? A great despair would oppress me as
I sought for such a movement and found it not.
   Not only so; but since 1886 there had been slowly growing up
a conviction that my philosophy was not sufficient; that life and
mind were other than, more than, I had dreamed. Psychology was
advancing with rapid strides; hypnotic experiments were revealing
unlooked-for complexities in human consciousness, strange riddles
of multiplex personalities, and, most startling of all, vivid inten-
sities of mental action when the brain, that should be the generator
of thought, was reduced to a comatose state. Fact after fact came
hurtling in upon me. . . . Into the darkness shot a ray of light—
A. P. Sinnett's *Occult World,* with its wonderfully suggestive letters,
expounding not the supernatural but a nature under law, wider than
I had dared to conceive. I added Spiritualism to my studies, experimenting privately, finding the phenomena indubitable, but the
spiritualistic explanation of them incredible.[155]

It was not until the early spring of 1889 that Mr. Stead had asked
Besant to review *The Secret Doctrine.* "As I turned over page after

page," she relates, "the interest became absorbing; but how familiar it seemed; how my mind leapt forward to presage the conclusions, how natural it was, how coherent, how subtle, and yet how intelligible. I was dazzled, blinded by the light in which disjointed facts were seen as parts of a mighty whole, and all my puzzles, riddles, problems, seemed to disappear." "The effect was partially illusory," she added, for later "the brain has to gradually assimilate that which the swift intuition had grasped as truth." "But the light had been seen," she added, "and in that flash of illumination I knew that the weary search was over and the very Truth was found. I wrote the review[156] and asked Mr. Stead for an introduction to the writer, and then sent a note asking to be allowed to call."[157]

HPB replied:

I too have long been wishing to make your acquaintance, as there is nothing in the world that I admire more than pluck and the rare courage to come out and state one's opinions boldly in the face of all the world—including Mrs. Grundy. I am at home every evening from our tea time at seven till eleven o'clock; and I shall be delighted to see you whenever you come. . . . This invitation includes of course also Mr. Burrows or anyone whom you may choose to bring with you.[158]

Herbert Burrows was a prominent socialist of the time and a close collaborator with Besant in her work. When one spring evening they finally met HPB, Besant recalls:

She talked of travels, of various countries, easy brilliant talk, her eyes veiled, her exquisitely molded fingers rolling cigarettes incessantly. Nothing special to record, no word of Occultism, nothing mysterious, a woman of the world chatting with her evening visitors.[159]

Once again I went, and asked about the Theosophical Society, wishing to join, but [inwardly] fighting against it. For I saw, distinct and clear . . . what that joining would mean. I had largely conquered public prejudice against me by my work on the London School Board, and a smoother road stretched before me, whereon effort to help should be praised not blamed. Was I to plunge into a new vortex of strife, and make myself a mark for ridicule and fight again, the weary fight for an unpopular truth? Must I turn against materialism, and face the shame of publicly confessing that I had been wrong, misled by intellect to ignore the Soul? . . .

[She conquered her fears and decided to join.]

[Madame Blavatsky] looked at me piercingly for a moment.

"Have you read the report about me of the Society for Psychical Research?" "No; I never heard of it, so far as I know." "Go and read it, and if, after reading it, you come back—well."

I borrowed a copy of the Report, read and re-read it. Quickly I saw how slender was the foundation on which the imposing structure was built. The continual assumptions on which conclusions were based; the incredible character of the allegations; and—most damning fact of all—the foul source from which the evidence was derived. Everything turned on the veracity of the Coulombs, and they were self-stamped as partners in the alleged frauds.[160]

Mrs. Besant became a member of the TS together with Herbert Burrows on May 21, 1889. She publicly announced in *The Star* the fact of her joining. Throughout England the news was received with astonishment. To explain her reasons she gave two lectures at the Hall of Science, in August, one on the fourth and the other on the twelfth. The second, titled "Why I Became a Theosophist," was circulated in pamphlet form. Besant repeated the speech several times elsewhere. Gandhi recalls hearing it at the Queen's Hall at the People's Palace, the great community center for working people in Whitechapel.[161] The talk included Theosophical teachings, such as karma, reincarnation, and the masters of wisdom.

HPB relayed the news of Mrs. Besant's joining the TS to her relatives and added:

> My war with the materialists and atheists is worse than ever! All the Freethinkers, the godless liberals, all the friends of Bradlaugh are up in arms against me because I am supposed to have lured their beloved Annie Besant from the path of truth. . . . Church people became so elated *over her recantation of godlessness* that they even forgot their personal hatred of me and praise *Theosophy*!!! . . .
>
> What a wholehearted, noble, and wonderful woman she is! . . . A regular Demosthenes in skirts! . . . It was precisely an eloquent orator that we lacked. I myself cannot speak at all; and others also, while they know it, yet they cannot tell it.[162]

When Besant joined the TS, to her deep regret, the Freethinkers for whom she had won so many battles asked her to resign on the ground that membership in both bodies was incompatible. Olcott recalled that several years earlier Bradlaugh and Besant ruled similarly when a Secularist in India wanted to link up with the Theosophists. Who could have then dreamed that one day she would be in the same dilemma![163]

Chapter 10

The Esoteric Section

In the fall of 1888, *Lucifer* carried an announcement of the formation of an Esoteric Section of the Theosophical Society. As head of the TS, Col. Olcott explained the purpose and structure of the new section:

I. To promote the esoteric interests of the Theosophical Society by the deeper study of esoteric philosophy, there is hereby organized a body, to be known as the "Esoteric Section of the Theosophical Society."

II. The constitution and sole direction of the same is vested in Madame H. P. Blavatsky, as its Head; she is solely responsible to the members for results; and the Section has no official corporate connection with the Exoteric Society save in the person of the President-Founder.

III. Persons wishing to join the Section, and willing to abide by its rules, should communicate directly with:—Mme. H. P. Blavatsky, 17 Lansdowne Road, Holland Park, London, W.

At the time of HPB's death, he reports that there were one to two thousand enthusiastic members of the ES.

A letter from HPB to Dr. J. D. Buck in the United States, dated December 1, 1888, indicates the purpose and nature of the inner section:

The need of it was very much felt everywhere. Unable to give out a great many things publicly (either in Lucifer, *or in* The Secret Doctrine*), and old and tried members being entitled to learn certain things in occultism—more than simple outsiders, the formation of such a section—while I am alive and can be useful to people—was very much clamored for from all sides. There is no room for* despotism *or ruling . . . in it . . . no glory for me, but a series of misconceptions, slanders, suspicion and ingratitude in almost an immediate future; but if out of the hundred (109) theosophists who have already pledged themselves, I can place on the right and true path half a dozen or so—I will die happy. Many are called, few chosen. . . . I can only show the way to those whose eyes are open to the truth, whose souls* *are full of altruism, charity and love for the whole creation and who think of themselves* last. . . .

. . . *the Esoteric Section is not of the earth earthy; it does not interfere with the exoteric administration of the Lodges. . . . It requires neither subscription, fees nor money, for as I have not so received it, I* shall not *so impart it and that I would rather starve in the gutter than take one penny for my teaching the sacred truths. Postage and stationery are the only expenses, and this the Council of the Blavatsky Lodge will provide for, if my "Secret Doctrine" does not bring me enough to cover these expenses. . . . He who would have his inheritance before I die—for mighty little shall they have once I am gone—let him ask for it. What I have, or rather what I am permitted to give—I am willing to give though it is not much.*[164]

Her refusal to make grandiose promises as to the wonderful things that would occur if members joined the ES forms quite a contrast to the enticements offered by the so-called occult media today and the fabulous fees they often exact.

Before joining the ES, prospective members frequently wrote to HPB to ascertain what their commitments would involve. One such inquirer wished to know whether a soldier could become a member. She replied: "What is this about 'the soldier not being free?' Of course, no soldier can be free to move about in his physical body wherever he likes. But what has the esoteric teaching to do with the outward man? A soldier may be stuck to his sentry box like a barnacle to its ship, and the soldier's Ego be free to go where it likes and think what it likes best." However, she adds:

No man is required to carry a burden heavier than he can bear; nor do more than it is possible for him to do. . . . a man tied by his duty to one place has no right to desert it in order to fulfill another duty, let it be however much greater; for the first *duty* taught in occultism is to do one's duty unflinchingly *by every duty*. Pardon these seemingly absurd paradoxes and Irish Bulls; but I have had to repeat this *ad nauseam usque* for the last month. "Shall I risk to be ordered to leave my wife, desert my children and home if I pledge myself?" asks one. "No," I say, "because he who plays truant in one thing will be faithless in another. No real, genuine MASTER will accept a chela who sacrifices *anyone* except himself to go to that Master." If one cannot owing to circumstances or his position in life, become a full adept in this existence, let him prepare his mental luggage for the next, so as to be ready at the first call when he is once more reborn.[165]

In the Esoteric Section, members were not taught practical occultism or how to perform psychic phenomena. That ruled out also what is called ceremonial magic, so popular today. In one of her letters to Ralston Skinner in the Harvard collection, HPB indicates that such ceremonies can be dangerous:

I have read and re-read your Hebrew Egyptian Mystery *twenty times over and recommend it to all our Kabbalists such as Rev. A. W. Ayton . . . and Mathers,† a very good Kabbalist, only one who loses too much his head with ceremonial magic which I detest. [Certain] geometrical diagrams and figures especially have a power in them of reacting on the awakening to activity [of] the half blind and brainless creatures of the elements, which power and creatures you may deny. . . . We of the esoteric Vedanta philosophy of Hinduism . . . know the power certain circles and diagrams have on the Elements. This is why I believe in but hate and* dread *ceremonial magic. Beware of certain figures and combinations thereof, Mr. Skinner. . . .*[166]

Observes one writer:

With the formation of the Esoteric Section, a new influence began to make itself felt in Theosophical history. While little was printed in the Theosophical journals concerning the Section—all its activities being carried on under strict pledge of secrecy‡—the effect of this new organization was to consolidate the energies and devotion of the most ardent members of the Society, with obvious benefits to the work of the Movement. As head of this Section, HPB was freed of organizational procedures in her relation with esoteric students, whom she regarded as her pupils, and she gave such private teachings to them as would serve the cycle of inner development they were undergoing.[167]

As the circulation of the teachings was private, no commercial printer could be used. HPB mentions what she terms the primitive method used for reproducing esoteric documents in a letter to Vera,

---

† S. L. McGregor Mathers, who a few years later became one of the founders of the Golden Dawn.

‡ HPB was once accused of deception for maintaining silence as to information given her under a pledge. She responded: "If I am to be held in this matter a *deceiver,* then so is every Mason, every Oddfellow, every statesman, every priest who receives confession, every physician who takes the Hippocratic oath, and every lawyer, one." (Blavatsky: *Collected Writings,* 6:289.)

who had been complaining at not having heard from her sister for so long:

> Do take the trouble to count my occupations, you heartless Zoilas. Every month I write from forty to fifty pages of "Esoteric Instructions," instructions in secret sciences, which must not be printed. Five or six wretched voluntary martyrs among my esotericists have to draw, write and lithograph during the nights, some 320 copies of them, which I have to superintend, to rectify, to compare and to correct, so that there may be no mistakes and my occult information may not be put to shame.

Then follows a long list of other jobs she had to perform.[168]

James Pryse describes how the problem of reproducing the esoteric teachings was finally solved. The story opens in Los Angeles in the spring of 1888:

> In those days many Theosophists were ambitious to become "chelas" or "lay chelas" by getting into communication with the Masters whom HPB represented. Having no doubt that the Masters were being pestered by so many applicants, I refrained from any attempt to reach HPB or her Master, or to attract their attention to my unimportant self. . . .
>
> One evening while I was meditating [on Paracelsus], the face of HPB flashed before me. I recognized it from her portrait in *Isis,* though it appeared much older. Thinking that the astral picture, as I took it to be, was due to some vagary of fancy, I tried to exclude it; but at that the face showed a look of impatience, and instantly I was drawn out of my body and immediately was standing "in the astral" beside HPB in London. It was along toward morning there, but she was still seated at her writing desk. While she was speaking to me, very kindly, I could not help thinking how odd it was that an apparently fleshy old lady should be an Adept. I tried to put that impolite thought out of my mind, but she read it, and as if in answer to it her physical body became translucent, revealing a marvelous inner body that looked as if it were formed of molten gold.
>
> Then suddenly the Master M. appeared before us in his mayavi-rupa. To him I made profound obeisance, for he seemed to me more like a God than a man. Somehow I knew who he was, though this was the first time I had seen him. He spoke to me graciously and said, "I shall have work for you in six months." He walked to the further side of the room, waved his hand in farewell and departed. . . .

Six months afterward, the Master's promise was made good. My brother John and I, returning from a trip to South America, landed in New York City. We found Mr. Judge perplexed by a difficult problem: HPB had directed him to send her instructions to all American members of the ES, but had sent him only one copy, and he had no facilities for making the many copies needed. We solved that problem for him by establishing [a press] and printing the instructions in book-form.

Both brothers were excellent printers and had been publishers of a number of small-town newspapers in the United States. After helping Judge out, word was received from HPB in London for James to start the H.P.B. Press there, where not only the ES instructions were thenceforth printed but the Society's books and other literature as well.[169]

Chapter **11**

A Conspiracy Underway

I n June of 1889, HPB wrote:

A *curious prophecy was made to me, in 1879*, in India, by a mystic who said that every letter in the alphabet had either a beneficent or a maleficent influence on the life and work of every man. Persons whose names began with an initial of which the sound was adverse to some other person had to be avoided by the latter. "What is the letter most adverse to me?" I enquired. "Beware of the letter C," he replied, "I see three capital C's shining ominously over your head. You have to beware of them especially for the next ten years and shield your Society from their influence. They are the initials of three persons who will belong to the Theosophical body, only to turn its greatest enemies." I had forgotten the warning till 1884, when the Coulombs appeared on the stage. Are Dr. Coues and Miss [Mabel] Collins [Cook] preparing to close the list—I wonder?[170]

What is also interesting about these three individuals is that their names share not only the letter "C" but "Co" at the beginning of their last names. Even Mabel Collins's married name, Cook, does likewise. After choosing the title for this chapter, the present writer noticed *conspiracy* also began with these letters!

Upon returning to the States from Europe, where he had met Olcott and Blavatsky in 1884 and then joined the TS, Coues founded the TS in Washington, D.C. and later became president of the American Board of Control of the Society.[†] As to his professional career, he had been an anatomist, a historian, a naturalist, and an ornithologist. Peter Brooks, a distinguished conservationist, says of Coues: "Among the professionals who established ornithology as a science, none is remembered with such respect—almost awe—than Elliott Coues."[171]

The conspiracy to be discussed in this chapter began with an alliance between Coues in America and Mabel Collins in London and received

† The American Board of Control was set up by Olcott to manage the Society's affairs in the United States.

370

public attention in two letters of Coues published in the *Religio-Philosophical Journal,* on May 11 and June 1, 1889. In his first letter Coues writes that "about four years ago" (in 1885), being interested in *Light on the Path,* he "wrote Mrs. Collins a letter, praising it and asking her about its real source." This was because *Light on the Path,* said Coues, "was supposed to have been dictated to Mrs. Collins by 'Koot Hoomi,' or some other Hindu adept who held the Theosophical Society in the hollow of his masterly hand." Miss Collins promptly replied, in her own handwriting, that *Light on the Path* "was inspired or dictated from the source above indicated." Coues goes on to say that since that time "nothing passed between Mrs. Collins and myself until yesterday [May 2, 1889], when I unexpectedly received the following letter" [Miss Collins's letter is dated April 18, 1889]:

I feel I have a duty to write you on a difficult and (to me) painful subject, and that I must not delay it any longer. You will remember writing to ask me who was the inspirer of "Light on the Path." . . . At that time I was both studying Madame Blavatsky and studying under her. I knew nothing then of the mysteries of the Theosophical Society, and I was puzzled why you should write me in such a way. I took the letter to her; the result was that I wrote the answer at her dictation. . . . I wish to ease my conscience now by saying that I wrote this letter from no knowledge of my own and merely to please her; and that I now see that I was wrong in doing so. I ought further to state that "Light on the Path" was not to my knowledge inspired by anyone; but that I saw it written on the walls of a place I visit spiritually . . . there I read it and wrote it down. I have myself never received proof of the existence of any Master; though I believe (as always) that the mahatmic force must exist.

In the second letter to the *Religio-Philosophical Journal,* Coues states that in his first communication he did not give the original letter from Collins because "I could not conveniently lay my hands on it." He says he now gives it "word for word," adding, "It is in Mrs. Cook's handwriting, undated and unsigned.". . .

The writer of *The Gates of Gold* is Mabel Collins, who had it as well as *Light on the Path* and the *Idyll of the White Lotus* dictated to her by one of the adepts of the group which through Madame Blavatsky first communicated with the Western world. The name of this inspirer cannot be given, as the personal names of the Masters have already been sufficiently desecrated.

Coues continues: "This is exactly, word for word, what Mrs. Cook now says she wrongly wrote to me because Madame Blavatsky 'begged and implored' her to do so, and which she also wrote at her dictation. It certainly has the genuine Blavatskian ring about it."

This 1885 letter that Mabel Collins wrote to Coues was concocted by him. *Through the Gates of Gold* was not published until 1887! Furthermore, in 1885, when she claims she was studying under HPB and the latter dictated the reply, Blavatsky was in India, thousands of miles away.[172] The first time HPB saw a copy of *Light on the Path* was in 1886, when Arthur Gebhard gave her a copy in Germany.[173]

Mabel Collins had frequently disclaimed authorship of the three books mentioned, stating that they had been dictated to her by one of the adepts.[174] HPB identified him as Hilarion, a Greek teacher, and one who collaborated with her in her own stories. That Mabel Collins, a novelist, was incapable of producing such works appears evident from an item appearing in the London *Star*, quoted by HPB in "Literary Jottings" (*Lucifer*, December 1888):

Miss Mabel Collins' *Light on the Path* has been translated into Sanskrit, and will be placed by the Hindoo Pundits as one of the Sanskrit classics. Translation into Sanskrit is a thing which has not been done for at least 100 years past; but the book is sufficiently Buddhistic and occult to satisfy even the learned Hindoos.

"This little book"—a true jewel, HPB comments, "belongs to, and emanates from the same school of Indo-Aryan and Buddhist thought and learning as the teachings of *The Secret Doctrine*."

What Coues fails to mention in his letters to the *Religio-Philosophical Journal* was that Mabel Collins had just been expelled from the Esoteric Section of the TS. According to HPB, she "broke her vows, becoming guilty of the blackest treachery and disloyalty to her HIGHER SELF. And when I could no longer keep in the ES either herself or her friend [Michael Angelo Lane], the two convulsed the whole Society with their calumnies and falsehoods."[175] Collins sued HPB, but when the case opened in July 1890, Blavatsky's counsel showed a letter of Collins to her own attorney and he immediately asked the court to terminate the case.[176] The contents of this letter have never been revealed.

Coues's dissatisfaction with the TS began when the Board of Control, over which he had ruled despotically for two years, was abolished. In October 1886, the twelve American lodges organized themselves into an American section of the Theosophical Society and elected William Q. Judge as general-secretary.[177] HPB tells what happened thereafter in a letter to Charles Johnston's unmarried sister, in Ireland:

[Coues] for some time past [has] been writing to me requesting among other things that the TS in America should be placed under his control. He has endeavoured to incite me against Judge and Olcott, and has actually gone so far as to suggest that I should join in a conspiracy to *deceive* them! Just previous to the last convention at Chicago, he wrote me suggesting that there was time yet for him to be elected president, and requested that I should telegraph the Convention with an order to that effect.

That I should deliberately deceive the whole body of the TS in America by saying it was the Master's wish that he should be elected president, was the real import of his request. Needless to say, his plan failed! And now, as a result of this, he turns round upon the Society and upon me, threatening all manner of evil.[178]

Coues's ambitions to dominate the Society were unmasked in two pamphlets quoting the scientist's letters to HPB.[179] HPB's replies were recently discovered in the Coues collection in the State Historical Society of Wisconsin, and have since been published in a six-part series edited by Michael Gomes in *The Canadian Theosophist* (September–October 1984 through January–February 1986).

As a result of Coues's machinations, the charter of his Gnostic TS was revoked on June 22, 1889 and he was expelled from the Society.[180] After his expulsion, Coues continued his attack on HPB in an even more virulent form in the *Religio-Philosophical Journal*. "Keep silence," she told Theosophists, "if ye are wise. He who stoops to analyze or even notice such indescribable and nauseating filth, only risks dirtying his hands."[181] In maintaining silence, HPB remarked a few months later, she was only following Coues's advice to herself four years earlier (November 22, 1885):

You are a grand and wonderful woman, whom I admire as much as I appreciate. . . . I admire your fortitude and endurance in bearing burdens enough to kill anybody but *the Blavatsky* whose like has not before been seen, nor will be ever. . . . Never mind your enemies! They will get a spurious and vicarious reputation by attacking you, which you can afford to let them have, though you don't want to confer upon them the immortality they would get by your condescending to fight them. When history comes to be written they will appear, if at all, hanging on to your skirts. Shake them off, and let them go!

(signed) Elliott Coues

HPB responded, "And so I do."

In the late spring of 1890, Coues changed his tactics in his campaign against Blavatsky. As his biographers Cutright and Brodhead put it, he decided to take the advice he had given a friend, Mr. J. A. Allen, several years previously: "*While you are in a controversy,* no matter what are the merits of the case, or who is right—strike for the great dailies and weeklies."[182] Coues chose the *Sun,* one of New York's leading newspapers, which was quoted throughout the country and edited by the famous journalist Charles Dana. The attack began with a preliminary editorial in the *Sun* for June 1, 1890. Theosophy was referred to as a humbug religion, and the public was informed that Professor Coues "showed up the lying and trickery of the Blavatsky woman after having been one of her dupes for several years." Then, on July twentieth, a long "interview" with Coues was featured in the *Sun's* Sunday supplement—seven columns of fine print in the giant papers of those days. As one veteran newspaperman remembered it, it brought together "every calumny that could be imagined or raked up from the ends of the earth." The "interview" was sensationally headed "Blavatsky Unveiled; The Tartar Termagant Tamed by Smithsonian Scientist!" In preparation, Coues had engaged in a vast "fact-finding" correspondence with all of HPB's enemies.[183] Henceforth, most hostile biographers would draw upon the so-called interview for their stock-in-trade.

"Every age has its bogus prophets," said Coues. "This being a feminine age, it is only natural that its greatest charlatan should be a sort of she Cagliostro."

Both the *Sun* and Coues deceived the public by calling the article an interview, as he wrote both parts. Thus the imagined reporter asked all the right questions, for which Coues had prewritten answers. The Coues collection in Wisconsin contains the original typed "interview." In the left-hand margin of the first page, in Coues's handwriting, are these words: "Original copy of article as *prepared* for the *Sun* making nine or ten columns but cut to about six columns of print." It was signed by Elliott Coues. This inked-in statement appears to have been added later to identify the document, and Coues himself forgot it was supposed to be an interview. Three of his suggested subheadings were apparently too risky for the *Sun* to print:

The Cossack's Career of Crime
Darker Doings Disclosed
Will Inspector Byrnes or Anthony Comstock†
Raid the Ring in New York?

HPB's most prominent American disciples, Olcott and Judge, were labeled as both dupes and willing accomplices. Coues even tried to convey the impression that he himself had never been a member of the cult: "I confess to a natural irritation at the way I found my name associated in public opinion with her clap-trap, and the use made of it as a foil to the fraudulent schemes of a pack of scoundrelly vulgarians would be enough to excite any honest man's indignation."[184] As purported proof of Blavatsky's sexual promiscuity, Coues referred to a letter from Richard Hodgson (now secretary of the American SPR) concerning her life in Cairo in 1871-72. He also quoted an 1885 letter from Emma Coulomb to Colonel John C. Bundy, now editor of the *Religio-Philosophical Journal*. "The first definite information I have" as to her immorality, writes Coues, "is in an extract from a letter of the late D. D. Home, the noted English spiritualistic medium, written to Mr. W. E. Coleman of San Francisco. This locates her in Paris in 1857 or '58 as a demi-monde in liaison with the Prince Emile de Wittgenstein, by whom she had a deformed son, who died in Kieff in 1868." This last accusation finally stirred HPB to take action. She wrote a letter, printed in *The Path* (September 1890), under the heading "Madame Blavatsky Appeals to the Law":

To the Editor of the Path:

While I fully agree to the proposition that we should forgive our enemies, yet I do not thereby lose "my appeal unto Caesar," and in that appeal, which is now made to the Law and not to the Emperor, I may keep the command to forgive, while for the protection of the name of a dead friend and the security in the future of Theosophists, I hale into the Courts of the land those who, having no sense of what is right or just, see fit to publish broadcast wicked and unfounded slanders.

For some fifteen years I have calmly stood by and seen my good name assailed by newspaper gossips who delight to dwell upon the personal peculiarities of those who are well known. . . . But now a great metropolitan daily paper in New York, with no knowledge of the facts in the case, throws broadcast before the public many charges against me, the most of which meet their refutation in my life for over a decade. But as one of them reflects

† Comstock was a famous exposer of frauds in those days.

strongly upon my moral character and brings into disrepute the honorable name of a dead man, an old family friend, it is impossible for me to remain silent, and so I have directed my lawyers in New York to bring an action against the N.Y. Sun for libel.

This daily paper accuses me of being a member of the demi-monde *in [1857 or 1858] and of having improper relations with Prince Emile-Wittgenstein, by whom the paper says I had an illegitimate son. The first part of the charge is so ridiculous as to arouse laughter, but the second and third hold others up to reprobation. Prince Wittgenstein, now dead, was an old friend of my family, whom I saw for the last time when I was eighteen years old, and he and his wife remained until his death in close correspondence with me. He was a cousin of the late Empress of Russia, and little thought that upon his grave would be thrown the filth of a modern New York newspaper. This insult to him and to me I am bound by all the dictates of my duty to repel, and am also obliged to protect the honor of all Theosophists who guide their lives by the teachings of Theosophy; hence my appeal to the Law and to a jury of my fellow Americans. I gave up my allegiance to the Czar of Russia in the hope that America would protect her citizens; may that hope not prove vain.*

Two suits against Coues and the *Sun* were brought by Judge, one on behalf of Blavatsky, the other for the New York TS. Both were confined to charges of immorality; 50,000 and 60,000 dollars respectively were asked for damages. Owing to a crowded calendar, the cases dragged on into 1891.

In March a notice appeared in the *Path* that in a pre-trial hearing before Judge Beach in the Supreme Court, the lawyer for the *Sun* confessed his client's inability to prove the charge of immorality. The notice continues: "The case now looks merely like one in which the only question will be the amount of damages, and everything must now stand until the case is reached in the trial term."[185]

The confession of inability to prove the case was a considerable victory. Subsequently, in a motion made by HPB's attorney on April 27, 1891 (a photostatic copy of which the present writer possesses, certified by the County Clerk of the Supreme Court, New York County), it is attested that "certificates of medical experts" are available to prove that the libelous charges made by Coues "are absolutely without foundation."[186] More specifically, the records also reveal, according to evidence unearthed by Walter Carrithers, that the "attorney for the plaintiff informed the Court during the proceedings that there was being held in readiness the testimony of two gynecology experts who would swear to the fact that Madame Blavatsky had not, as charged by the *Sun,* borne a child."[187]

The editor of the *Sun,* Charles Dana, was not a man to admit defeat easily and was known to pursue ruthlessly the objects of his wrath to the bitter end. HPB described him as having "sat for years on the late Henry Ward Beecher" and "harassed to death the 'truly good man,' Deacon Smith of Cincinnati."[188]

HPB died before her case came to trial, and her death automatically terminated the suit. Judge's suit against the *Sun* continued, but was dropped when the *Sun* agreed to print an editorial retraction, which appeared on September 26, 1892.[†] It is of some importance that it is not limited to the charge of immorality but includes other accusations made by Coues. It reads:

> We print on another page an article in which Mr. WILLIAM Q. JUDGE deals with the romantic and extraordinary career of the late Madame HELENA P. BLAVATSKY. We take occasion to observe that on July 20, 1890, we were misled into admitting into *THE SUN*'s columns an article by Dr. E. F. COUES of Washington, in which allegations were made against Madame BLAVATSKY's character, and also against her followers, which appear to have been without solid foundation. Mr. JUDGE's article disposes of all questions relating to Madame BLAVATSKY as presented by Dr. COUES, and we desire to say that his allegations respecting the Theosophical Society and Mr. JUDGE personally are not sustained by evidence, and should not have been printed.[189]

A few extracts from Judge's long article, titled by the *Sun* "The Esoteric She," follow:

> The aim and object of her life were to strike off the shackles forged by priestcraft for the mind of man. She wished all men to know they must bear the burden of their own sins, for no one else can do it. Hence she brought forward to the West the old Eastern doctrines of karma and reincarnation. Under the first, the law of justice, she said each must answer for himself, and under the second make answer on the earth where all his acts were done. . . .
>
> Her life since 1875 was spent in the unremitting endeavor to draw within the Theosophical Society those who could work unselfishly to propagate an ethics and philosophy tending to realize the brother-

---

† Michael Gomes, *Witness for the Prosecution: Annie Besant's Testimony on Behalf of H. P. Blavatsky in the N.Y. Sun/Coues Law Case,* Occasional Papers, Vol. I, Fullerton, California, Theosophical History, pp. 7–11

hood of man by showing the real unity and essential non-separateness of every being. And her books were written with the declared object of furnishing the material for intellectual and scientific progress on those lines. The theory of man's origin, powers, and destiny brought forward by her, drawn from ancient Indian sources, places us upon a higher pedestal than that given by either [Western] religion or science, for it gives to each the possibility of developing the godlike powers within and of at last becoming a co-worker with nature. . . .

As every one must die at last, we will not say that her demise was a loss; but if she had not lived and done what she did, humanity would not have had the impulse and ideas toward the good which it was her mission to give and proclaim. And there are today scores, nay hundreds, of devout, earnest men and women intent on purifying their own lives and sweetening the lives of others, who trace their hopes and aspirations to the wisdom-religion revived in the West through her efforts, and who gratefully avow that their dearest possessions are the result of her toilsome and self-sacrificing life. If they, in turn, live aright and do good, they will be but illustrating the doctrine which she daily taught and hourly practiced.[190]

Chapter 12

Was She a Plagiarist?

In 1890, when the *Sun* published Coues's professed exposure of HPB, another assault on her character was being silently prepared by a man named William Emmette Coleman, who was soon to spread far and wide the accusation that in all her writings Blavatsky plagiarized on a grand scale. It is impossible to calculate how many people have refused to read Blavatsky's writings as a result of this charge. Incidentally, it seems rather amazing that we now have another "Co" to add to Coulomb, Coues, and Collins!

Coleman was involved in both the Coulomb and the Coues-Collins cases. It was he who journeyed from the United States to London to obtain from the Scottish missionary Patterson the purportedly original HPB-Coulomb letters that Coues had hoped to use in defending himself in HPB's libel suit; it was also he who supplied Coues with the information circulated in a *Sun* "interview" that HPB's supposed illegitimate child was fathered by Wittgenstein. Coleman's letter on this subject, dated March 31, 1889, is in the Coues collection.

Why did Coleman thus involve himself? And why did he circulate the charges of plagiarism? Was he a disinterested person in pursuit of truth? One might think so when reading his credentials provided in a footnote to his research paper on the source of HPB's writings. Yet where was this paper printed? Of all places, it appeared as Appendix C in Solovyov's *A Modern Priestess of Isis,* published in 1895 on behalf of the Society for Psychical Research; (Chapter 2 of the present section). In Solovyov's book, it achieved an immortality it was not otherwise likely to receive. Coleman's credentials in the footnote include memberships in the American Oriental Society, the Royal Asiatic Society of Great Britain and Ireland, the Pali Text Society, and the Egyptian Exploration Fund. One would hardly imagine he was a clerk in the Quartermaster Department of the U.S. Army, first at Fort Leavenworth in Kansas and later in San Francisco. But more importantly, what the SPR carefully concealed—which ever since HPB's detractors have refrained from mentioning—is that Coleman was a leading spiritualist of his day who wrote scathing denunciations of Theosophy and HPB in the spiritualists' journals.

Nothing can be clearer on this than what Coleman himself wrote to Coues on July 8, 1890, on the letterhead of the Chief Quartermaster office: "I emphatically denounced and ridiculed the theory of occultism, of elementary spirits, etc., before the Theosophical Society was organized [in 1875], and from that time to this I have strenuously opposed Theosophy all the time."[191]

HPB's article "My Books" speaks of the "libelous matter emanating from America" and that "it has all come from one and the same source, well known to all Theosophists, a person [Coleman] most indefatigable in attacking me personally for the last twelve years."[192]

As to the plagiarism charges, it should be understood that as applied to HPB, Coleman's use of the term extends far beyond its dictionary definition: "To steal and pass off (the ideas or words of another) as one's own."[193] This Blavatsky did not do.† But surely she must have been guilty of something dreadful, for reading Coleman's opening paragraph in his paper of August, 1893, we find

> During the past three years I have made a more or less exhaustive analysis of the contents of the writings of Madame H. P. Blavatsky; and I have traced the sources whence she derived—and mostly without credit being given—*nearly the whole of their subject matter.*[194]

HPB's so-called plagiarism is a practice followed by practically every author who publishes the fruits of his research—even by Coleman himself. To understand the foregoing, one must be able to distinguish between primary sources and secondary sources. If you were to quote from an Emerson essay, for example, that essay would be your primary source. If, however, you quote Emerson quoting Shakespeare, that portion of Emerson's essay would be called your secondary source. In Coleman's view, you must credit right then and there—in a footnote or endnote—not only Shakespeare, but the secondary plagiarism, for you are misleading your readers into thinking you yourself found the reference in the works of Shakespeare. However, citing only primary sources is a legitimate practice that most authors of scholarship follow all the time. In *Isis Unveiled,* HPB frequently gave credit to the original author but not to the secondary source.

Writers today acknowledge indebtedness to secondary sources indi-

---

† When Ralston Skinner gave HPB, as a gift, his manuscript of Part Three of *Source of Measures,* he said she could use it as her own work. She refused, saying, "How can I quote without quotation marks? . . . How can I quote and let out your name?" (Feb. 17, 1886, Ralston Collection, Andover-Harvard Theological Library, Harvard University.)

rectly by including in their bibliographies the names of books they drew upon in their research. To list all would be unwise, for among the numerous volumes researched only a few may be considered worthy of mentioning. If Coleman were to apply to these hundreds of thousands of authors the rules† he demanded HPB abide by, he would call them all plagiarists.

As was common in books of her day, HPB's works had no bibliographies. However, her secondary sources were often referred to in the text when quoting primary material; thus the reader became aware of the book as a worthy source of information. To illustrate, Coleman accuses HPB of using forty-four passages—he should say quotations—from C. W. King's book *The Gnostics and Their Remains* in *Isis* without acknowledgment. Yet, when using *Gnostics* as a primary source, she credits it and its author on thirty-two occasions.

It is interesting to note that the immortal Goethe confessed to obtaining his material in the same way other writers do, but you would not know this unless you happened to read an obscure reference his biographer Emil Ludwig discovered:

> I owe my achievements . . . to thousands of things and persons outside myself, which constituted my material . . . and all I had to do was to catch hold of it, and reap what others had sown for me. . . . The main thing is to have a great desire, and skill and perseverance to accomplish it. My work is that of a composite being and happens to be signed Goethe.[195]

Coleman himself did not always practice what he preached concerning giving credit to secondary sources. In his essay "Sunday Not Being the Real Sabbath," he borrowed without credit numerous quotations from a paper on the subject by William Henry Burr. In a sixteen-page pamphlet, Burr, complaining against Coleman, wrote:

> The facts are as follows: W. E. C. has borrowed from my little work all that he has quoted or summarized from Justin, Irenaeus, Clement, Tertullian, Victorinus, Origen, Eusebius, Jerome, Luther, Melanchthon, Baxter, Ileylin, Milton, Paley, and Neander. Every reference given by him to the aforesaid authorities is borrowed from

---

† With all of Coleman's screaming about Blavatsky's supposed plagiarism in his printed articles in the spiritualists' journals, he convinced even her that she must have broken some important "literary rules," and so she explains in "My Books" that when she wrote *Isis* she was ignorant of these rules. The article of Coleman's that, in particular, she was answering was the one in *The Golden Way* for April 1891. Her lengthy article in reply, written eleven days before she died, was the last one she wrote in this incarnation. Considering the state of her health at that time, it is amazing that she could muster up the energy to do this.

me, and he has added nothing from their works which he did not find in my work. [Burr's publication: 1881, Washington, D.C.]

Nor did Coleman acknowledge that Burr's booklet existed. Burr also cites which parts Coleman had plagiarized.

≈

Coleman claims that HPB's purpose in quoting so many authorities of the past and present was to show herself off as "an enormous reader possessed of vast erudition," when actually "her ignorance was profound in all branches of knowledge." One wonders, then, how she could understand the heavy tomes she researched and select just the right material for her purpose. Beatrice Hastings observes:

> [Coleman] took no account of the fact that HPB was engaged precisely in citing "authorities" to support her in her quest for the thread of occult science stretching from the most ancient to modern times. She would quote indifferently from an old book or from a New York newspaper so long as the matter served her purpose. Mr. Coleman found it very convenient to brush over her constant citation of names and authorities. The truth is that there is scarcely a page of the book without a name; one is whirled from authority to authority and left in no doubt whatever that she is compiling and means to show that she is not inventing her subjects. She could hardly have cited names more often without wearying the reader. To know where to stop, as she did, requires literary tact. . . . What could be better done with a vast library of scattered information than to assemble the essentials in one book?[196]

It would be a mistake, however, to imagine that Blavatsky's works were largely anthologies. Coleman would have us believe that *Isis,* in particular, was little more than borrowings from other people's writings. It is easy to prove otherwise: A line-by-line count reveals that only 22 percent is quoted material and 78 percent, HPB speaking. Furthermore, the quotations are not of primary value, but merely supportive of her main thesis. Today when her books are quoted it is not her selections from other authors that are presented, but her own originally worded offerings or, as she would claim, that of her teachers.

≈

Thus far Coleman's plagiarism hunting as described in his paper has been focused chiefly on *Isis Unveiled.* Next he turns to *The Secret Doctrine* and other works of Helena Blavatsky. Here, it seems, he overreaches himself and loses all rights to credibility as an honest researcher.

In discussing *Isis,* Coleman gave the page numbers and books copied from, and sometimes parallel passages as well; from here onwards he provides no such information. However, he professes that "the detailed proofs and evidence of every assertion . . . will be embodied in full in a work I am preparing for publication—an exposé of theosophy as a whole." This promise was reiterated many times in the paper, as if to assure the readers that all the proofs, without doubt, would soon be forthcoming. However, from the date of his paper, August 1893, until his death in 1909, sixteen years elapsed without the book appearing. Coleman provided neither news concerning its publication nor apologies for its delay.

Coleman says that *The Secret Doctrine* "is of a piece with *Isis*" in that it is "permeated with plagiarisms, and is in all its parts a rehash of other books." He lists twenty-one books as some of those from which HPB plagiarized [did not name secondary sources]. Of these, only five mention the number of "borrowed passages":

Wilson's translation of the *Vishnu Purana*	130
Professor Alexander Winchell's *World-Life*	70
Dowson's *Hindu Classical Dictionary*	123
Decharme's *Mythologie de la Grece Antique*	60
Myers's *Qabbala*	34

The Secret Doctrine runs to 1,570 pages; the source books, too, are large. How can one locate parallel passages in this work and the secondary source named, with no pagination given for either? Unless one were to set up an elaborate computer program, it seems an impossible job. Nevertheless, a test case was decided upon. Among the five books just listed, Coleman points to two as very largely forming the basis of *The Secret Doctrine*: Wilson's translation of the *Vishnu Purana,* and *World-Life* by Alexander Winchell, professor of geology and paleontology at the University of Michigan. The latter work was chosen because, being on science, it has well-delineated subject matter (such as chapters on the sun and the moon) and might be checked against the text of *The Secret Doctrine,* using the huge 396-page index to the *SD* in the Blavatsky *Collected Writings* edition. A research assistant, who modestly requested to remain anonymous, volunteered to undertake this tedious assignment and spent two to three hours daily on the work for six months. Halfway through she complained that "it was very discouraging to keep looking for something you can't find." However, she did find a few unacknowledged borrowings from secondary sources—not Coleman's boasted seventy passages, but six (see end-note[197]). No wonder Coleman never wrote his book! He calculated well; people would believe his claimed research without the promised proofs.

One discovery Coleman took pride in announcing was that he had located the sources of the *Stanzas of Dzyan,* upon which, HPB says, *The Secret Doctrine* and *The Voice of the Silence* were based. The *Stanzas,* says Coleman, were "the work of Madame Blavatsky—a compilation in her own language, from a variety of sources." Coleman's evidences were to be given in his promised book, which never appeared.

Many besides Coleman have claimed to identify the source of the *Stanzas.* HPB's scholarly secretary, G. R. S. Mead, once had an exchange of correspondence with Max Müller on this subject. George Mead, who had received his BA and MA with honors at Cambridge, where he majored in Greek and Latin, and also studied philosophy at Oxford, later wrote books on gnosticism, hermetic philosophy, and the origins of Christianity.[198] Mead's report of his correspondence with Max Müller appeared in *The Theosophical Review* (April 1904, 139–41), of which Mead was editor, and reads as follows:

Some ten years ago or more the late Professor Max Müller, to whom all lovers of the Sacred Books of the East owe so deep a debt of gratitude, published his most instructive set of Gifford Lectures, entitled *Theosophy or Psychological Religion.* These I reviewed in much detail in a series of three articles in this *Review.* The aged Professor wrote to me a kindly note on the subject, taking exception to one or two points, and we exchanged several letters.

He then expressed himself as surprised that I should waste, as he thought, what he was good enough to call my abilities on "Theosophy," when the whole field of Oriental studies lay before me, in which he was kind enough to think I could do useful work. Above all, he was puzzled to understand why I treated seriously that charlatan, Mme. Blavatsky, who had done so much harm to the cause of genuine Oriental studies by her parodies of Buddhism and Vedanta which she had mixed up with Western ideas. Her whole Theosophy was a *réchauffé* of misunderstood translations of Sanskrit and Pâli texts.

To this I replied that as I had no object to serve but the cause of truth, if he could convince me that Mme. Blavatsky's Theosophy was merely a clever or ignorant manipulation of Sanskrit and Pâli texts, I would do everything in my power to make the facts known to the Theosophic world; . . . I therefore asked him to be so good as to point out what in his opinion were the original texts in Sanskrit or Pâli, or any other language, on which were based either the "Stanzas of Dzyan" and their commentaries in *The Secret Doctrine,* or any of the three treatises contained in *The Voice of the Silence.* I had myself for years been searching for any trace of the originals or of fragments resembling them, and had so far found nothing. If we could get the originals, we asked nothing better; it was the material we wanted.

To this Professor Max Müller replied in a short note, pointing to two verses in *The Voice of the Silence,* which he said were quite Western in thought, and therefore betrayed their ungenuineness.

I answered that I was extremely sorry he had not pointed out the texts on which any sentence of the "Precepts" or any stanza of the "Book of Dzyan" was based; nevertheless, I should like to publish his criticism, reserving to myself the right of commenting on it.

To this Professor Max Müller hastily rejoined that he begged I would not do so, but that I would return his letter at once, as he wished to write something more worthy of the [*Theosophical*] *Review.* I, of course, returned his letter, but I have been waiting from that day to this for the promised proof that HPB was in these marvelous literary creations nothing but a sorry centonist who out of rags of misunderstood translations patched together a fantastic motley for fools to wear. And I may add the offer is still open for any and every Orientalist who desires to make good the, to me, ludicrous contention of the late Nestor of Orientalism.

I advisedly call these passages enshrined in her works marvelous literary creations, not from the point of view of an enthusiast who knows nothing of Oriental literature, or the great cosmogonical systems of the past, or the Theosophy of the world faiths, but as the mature judgment of one who has been for some twenty years studying just such subjects. . . .

The Stanzas [of Dzyan in *The Secret Doctrine*] set forth a cosmogenesis and anthropogenesis which in their sweep and detail leave far behind any existing record of such things from the past; they cannot be explained as the clever piecing together of the disconnected archaic fragments still preserved in sacred books and classical authors; they have an individuality of their own and yet they bear the hall mark of an antiquity and the warrant of an economy which the Western world thinks to have long passed away. Further, they are set in an atmosphere of commentary apparently translated or paraphrased from Far Eastern tongues, producing a general impression of genuineness that is difficult for a scholar who has sufficiently overcome his initial prejudices to study them, to withstand.

In the introduction to *The Secret Doctrine* (1:xlv), HPB speaks of those who would discredit her writings on grounds of their being plagiarized from such writers as Eliphas Levi and Paracelsus, and from Buddhism and Brahmanism.† She replies:

> As well charge Renan with having stolen his *Vie de Jesus* from the Gospels, and Max Müller his "Sacred Books of the East" . . . from the philosophies of the Brahmins and Gautama, the Buddha.
> But to the public in general and the readers of the "Secret Doctrine" I may repeat what I have stated all along, and which I now clothe in the words of Montaigne:

> I HAVE HERE MADE ONLY A NOSEGAY OF CULLED FLOWERS,
> AND HAVE BROUGHT NOTHING OF MY OWN
> BUT THE STRING THAT TIES THEM.

In her last article, "My Books," HPB repeats Montaigne's words and asks whether anyone can say that she has "not paid the full price for the string."

As to the source of the Stanzas of Dzyan, startling news was published in 1983—that the mystery is now solved by Tibetologist David Reigle. He writes in his seventy-page booklet *The Books of Kiu-te* (Wizards Bookshelf, San Diego, CA, 1983):

> The Books of Kiu-te are described in H. P. Blavatsky's monumental work, *The Secret Doctrine,* as a series of highly occult works, some of which are public, and others secret. The former are said to be found in the possession of any Tibetan Gelugpa monastery. The latter include the *Book of Dzyan,* from which a number of stanzas were translated to form the nucleus of *The Secret Doctrine.* The *Book of Dzyan* is said to be the first volume of the commentaries on the secret Books of Kiu-te, and at the same time a glossary of the public Books of Kiu-te.
> Although the above information was made known at the end of last century, until now the actual identity of the public Books of Kiu-te has remained a mystery. Neither learned Tibetans nor Western scholars knew of any books by that name. They were therefore labeled as figments of H. P. Blavatsky's imagination, along with

---

† The person who made this claim turned out to be Coleman himself. It appeared in his article "The Splendid Fraud," published in the San Francisco *Daily Examiner* (July 8, 1888).

everything else in *The Secret Doctrine*. But by simply tracing the reference she gave when referring to these books, they have now been positively identified. As she said, they are indeed found in the library of any Tibetan Gelugpa monastery, as also in those of the other sects (Kargyudpa, Nyingmapa, and Sakyapa), and they are indeed highly occult works, being regarded by the entire Tibetan Buddhist tradition as embodying the Buddha's secret teachings. As will be seen, only the spelling of the term foiled previous attempts to identify them.

HPB at times spelled the books "Kiu-te" as used by the Capuchin monk Horace della Penna in the early 1700s. Today the "public Books of Kiu-te" are known as one of the main sections of the Kanjur, a major portion of the Tibetan Canon. Reigle's persistent research has led to further discoveries which he reports in his book.

Chapter 13

New Books and New Places

In the late spring of 1889, when the Coues-Collins case reared its head, other events—happily, of a different nature—were taking place. HPB wrote French friends: "My physician demands that I take a rest, at least for a fortnight. I need a change of air."[199] She had received an invitation to go to Fontainebleau, not far from Paris. The offer came from an American friend from Boston, wife of a U.S. senator, Mrs. Ida Candler, who was staying there with her daughter. HPB remained there for three weeks.

Soon after arrival she wrote two delightful letters to Nadya as to the benefits the change had wrought. When they were published in *The Path* (November 1895), the editor commented that the letters revealed "how very open Madame Blavatsky was to new impressions, even in her old age." HPB wrote:

Delicious air, all impregnated with the resin of the pine forest and warmed by the sun, to which I am exposed whole days, driving in the lovely park—has revived me, has given me back my long lost strength. Just fancy, several theosophists came yesterday from London to see me, and so we all went to see the castle. Out of the fifty-eight state rooms of the palace I have done forty-five with my *own unborrowed legs*!! It is more than five years since I have walked so much!

I have ascended the entrance steps, from which Napoleon I took leave of his guardsmen; I have examined the apartments of poor Marie Antoinette, her bedroom and the pillows on which rested her doomed head; I have seen the dancing hall, *galerie de François I,* and the rooms of the "young ladies" Gabrielle d'Estrée and Diane de Poitiers, and the rooms of Madame de Maintenon herself, and the satin cradle of *le petit roi de Rome* all eaten up by moths, and lots of others things. The Gobelins, the Sèvres china and some of the pictures are perfect marvels! . . . I have also put my fingers on the table on which the great Napoleon signed his resignation. But best of all I liked the pictures embroidered with silk *par les demoiselles de St. Cyr* for Madame de Maintenon. I am awfully proud of having walked all around the palace all by myself. Think of it, since your stay in Würzburg I have nearly lost my legs; and now, you see, I can walk all right. . . .

But what trees in this *doyen des forêts!* I shall never forget this lively forest. Gigantic oaks and Scotch firs, and all of them bearing historical names. Here one sees oaks of Molière, of Richelieu, of Montesquieu, of Mazarin, of Béranger. Also an oak of Henri III, and two huge seven hundred year old trees *des deux frères Faramonds.* I have simply lived in the forest during whole days. They took me there in a bath chair or drove me in a landau. It is so lovely here, I did not feel any desire to go to see the Exhibition.

Recently a French Theosophist, Jean-Paul Guignette, went to Fontainebleau to investigate old records to see what he could find concerning HPB's visit. He located an item in *L'Abeille de Fontainebleau,* which listed arrivals at the hotel: Mrs. Candler and daughter arrived on June 7, 1889, at the Hôtel de la Ville de Lyons et de Londres; Madame Blavatsky on July fifth, and Annie Besant on July fifteenth. He also located lovely old pictures of the hotel and gardens.[200]

However, the visit to Fontainebleau was notable in Theosophical history not because HPB went there for a change of air, slept in a certain hotel, or visited the famous palace, but rather because it was there that she wrote most of *The Voice of the Silence.* Perhaps escape from London's foggy, polluted atmosphere was conducive to setting down this precious work.

Mrs. Besant recorded her visit to Fontainebleau in her autobiography, where she describes the writing of the *Voice:*

I was called away to Paris to attend, with Herbert Burrows, the great Labor Congress held there from July 15th to July 20th, and spent a day or two at Fontainebleau with H. P. Blavatsky, who had gone abroad for a few weeks' rest. There I found her translating the wonderful fragments from "The Book of the Golden Precepts," now so widely known under the name of *The Voice of the Silence.* She wrote it swiftly, without any material copy before her, and in the evening made me read it aloud to see if the "English was decent." Herbert Burrows was there, and Mrs. Candler, a staunch American theosophist, and we sat round HPB while I read. The translation was in perfect and beautiful English, flowing and musical; only a word or two could we find to alter, and she looked at us like a startled child, wondering at our praises—praises that anyone with the literary sense would endorse if they read that exquisite poem.[201]

In the chapters on Tibet in the present biography, Eastern scholars testified as to the genuineness of *The Voice of the Silence*. Notables in the West have also valued this book. Alfred, Lord Tennyson, Poet Laureate of England, is said to have been reading this poem at the time he approached death.[202] HPB, commenting on one of Tennyson's last poems, observed: "This looks as if Lord Tennyson had been reading Theosophical books, or is inspired by the same grand truths as we are."[203]

William James, in his celebrated Gifford Lectures, *The Varieties of Religious Experience,* quotes a number of passages from *The Voice of the Silence* and suggests, "There is a verge of the mind which these things haunt; and whispers therefrom mingle with the operations of our understanding, even as the waters of the infinite ocean send their waves to break among the pebbles that lie upon our shores." Here are the passages:

> He who would hear the voice of *Nada,* "the Soundless Sound," and comprehend it, he has to learn the nature of *Dhâranâ.*† . . . When to himself his form appears unreal, as do on waking all the forms he sees in dreams; When he has ceased to hear the many, he may discern the *ONE*—the inner sound which kills the outer. . . . For then the soul will hear, and will remember. And then to the inner ear will speak—THE VOICE OF THE SILENCE. . . . And now thy *Self* is lost in SELF, *thyself* unto THYSELF, merged in THAT SELF from which thou first didst radiate. . . . Behold! thou hast become the Light, thou hast become the Sound, thou art thy Master and thy God. Thou art THYSELF the object of thy search: The VOICE unbroken, that resounds throughout eternities, exempt from change, from sin exempt, the seven sounds in one, THE VOICE OF THE SILENCE.

Preceding the words "Behold! thou hast become the Light," James omitted the following sentence, which would have helped in understanding the remainder of his selection:

> And now, rest 'neath the Bodhi tree, which is perfection of all knowledge, for, know, thou art the Master of SAMÂDHI—the state of faultless vision.[204]

One passage that appears to have especially appealed to James is this one addressed to a disciple: "Learn to part thy body from thy

---

† "*Dhâranâ* is the intense and perfect concentration of the mind upon some one interior object, accompanied by complete abstraction from everything pertaining to the external Universe, or the world of the senses." (HPB.)

mind . . . and to *live in the eternal,*"[205] for in the paragraph following his selections from *The Voice,* he observes (Italics added.):

That doctrine . . . that eternity is timeless, that our "immortality," if we *live in the eternal,* is not so much future as already now and here, which we find so often expressed today in certain philosophic circles, finds its support in a "hear, hear!" or an "amen," which floats up from that mysteriously deeper level. We recognize the passwords to the mystical region as we hear them, but we cannot use them ourselves; it alone has the keeping of "the password primeval."[206]

Another Westerner who evinced interest in the *Voice* is a leading British Buddhist, Dennis Lingwood, best known as Bhikshu Sangharakshita. He studied Pali and was well versed in both Theravada and Mahayana Buddhism. In the 1950s, Lingwood gave a lecture on *The Voice of the Silence* at the Indian Institute of World Culture, one of five he delivered there. The first four were published as *A Survey of Buddhism,* one reviewer hailing it as the principal event of the twenty-five hundredth Buddha Jayanti Year. The fifth, *Paradox and Poetry in The Voice of the Silence,* was published as a booklet. It reads, in part:

The Voice of the Silence, though it does not claim to be the utterance of a Buddha, is nevertheless akin to the *sutra* rather than to the *sastra* group of texts. . . . It seeks more to inspire than to instruct, appeals to the heart rather than to the head. To make use of De Quincey's classification, it belongs not to the literature of information, the purpose of which is to augment knowledge, but to the literature of power, the aim of which is to move. So important is a clear understanding of the difference not merely between the kinds of effect they are calculated to produce and the organs upon which they are intended to act, that, according to *The Voice of the Silence* itself, the disciple at the very outset of his quest is admonished, "Learn above all to separate Head-learning from Soul-wisdom, the 'Eye' from the 'Heart' doctrine. . . ."

We should [however] be on our guard against the very common error of assuming that by the mystical is meant anything irrational and illogical. As T. S. Eliot sardonically remarks, before one can go beyond the intellect one must have an intellect.

But meanwhile the problem of communication remains. How is it possible to convey the nature of *samadhi* to one who has no personal experience of it when language, the main vehicle of communication, is derived from those very levels of experience which *samadhi* transcends? Certain Zen masters, of course, solve the problem in their own way by endeavoring to dispense with language altogether. The traditional Buddhist solution of the problem is much less drastic. One group of *sutras* . . . places its reliance mainly on the method of systematic paradox. Another group . . . has recourse to poetry, especially in the highly developed form of cosmic myth. *The Voice of the Silence* is probably unique in making use of a combination of both methods, a procedure which no doubt has much to do with the extraordinary effectiveness of this little treatise in awakening the dormant Soul-wisdom of the qualified disciple.[207]

≈

After leaving Fontainebleau, HPB was prevailed upon by Ida Candler to get some sea air, so they spent two weeks on the island of Jersey off the French coast. HPB wrote Nadya: "Well, my old comrade, I have seized a short little minute in the interval of work, which is simply smothering me after my inertia and laziness at Fontainebleau, and write to you in bed, in spite of being perfectly well. The doctor has put me there for precaution's sake, as lately my knees have been aching a little."[208]

The work to which she refers includes editing the next issue of *Lucifer.* As George Mead reports, "It was not until the beginning of August, 1889, that I came to work permanently with HPB. She was away in Jersey then, and the copy and proofs of *Lucifer* were being busily transmitted backwards and forwards to the accompaniment of an infinity of characteristic notes and telegrams. I had only time to review two books before a pressing telegram came from HPB and I started for Jersey."

One of the jobs she gave Mead was to read over the manuscript of *The Voice,* which until then he had not known was being prepared. He reports:

> I told her it was the grandest thing in all our theosophical literature, and tried, contrary to my habit, to convey in words some of the enthusiasm that I felt. . . . HPB was not content with her work, and expressed the greatest apprehension that she had failed to do justice to the original in her translation. . . . This was one of her chief characteristics. Never was she confident of her own literary work, and cheerfully listened to all criticisms, even from persons who should have remained silent. Strangely enough she was always most timorous of her best articles and works and most confident of her polemical writings.[209] . . . the fresh atmosphere of life and reality

with which she surrounded her great expositions—all this I claim for her enduring reputation. She was a titan among mortals; . . . our titan was elemental, as indeed are all titans, but in laying foundations it is necessary to have giants, and giants when they move about cannot but knock over the idols in the shrines of the dwarfs.

While HPB was away from London, her *Key to Theosophy* was published. Upon returning she sent a copy to William Stead. "I do not ask you to review, *but to read it,*" she told him, "for this work, at least you will understand [as] metaphysics is absent from it. Mr. Oscar Wilde gave me his *word of honor* to review it but—this does not go far, nor do I care for it. What I do care for is that you should read it; for then you will know the whole truth about it."[210]

The *Key* is in the form of a dialogue between an enquirer and a Theosophist. In the preface it is explained:

The purpose of this book is exactly expressed in its title. . . . It is not a complete or exhaustive text book of Theosophy, but only a key to unlock the door that leads to the deeper study. It traces the broad outlines of the Wisdom Religion, and explains its fundamental principles; meeting, at the same time, the various objections raised by the average Western enquirer, and endeavouring to present unfamiliar concepts in a form as simple and in language as clear as possible.

That it should succeed in making Theosophy intelligible without mental effort on the part of the reader, would be too much to expect. . . . To the mentally lazy or obtuse, Theosophy must remain a riddle; for in the world mental as in the world spiritual each man must progress by his own efforts. The writer cannot do the reader's thinking for him, nor would the latter be any the better off if such vicarious thoughts were possible.

Among the subjects covered are the nature of the after-death states; the mystery of mind; the sevenfold nature of man and of the cosmos; and reincarnation and karma. Several sections discuss the social problems of our time and the solutions offered in Theosophical philosophy. One such section concerns the education of children and young adults. The subject is introduced when the enquirer comments:

One of your strongest arguments for the inadequacy of the existing forms of religion in the West, as also to some extent the materialistic philosophy which is now so popular, but which you seem to consider as an abomination of desolation, is the large amount of misery and wretchedness which undeniably exists, especially in our great cities. But surely you must recognize how much has been, and is being done to remedy this state of things by the spread of education and the diffusion of intelligence.

The Theosophist replies:

You have opened a subject on which we theosophists feel deeply, and I must have my say. I quite agree that there is a great advantage to a small child bred in the slums, having the gutter for playground, and living amid continued coarseness of gesture and word, in being placed daily in a bright, clean school-room hung with pictures, and often gay with flowers. There it is taught to be clean, gentle, orderly; there it learns to sing and to play; has toys that awaken its intelligence; learns to use its fingers deftly; is spoken to with a smile instead of a frown; is gently rebuked or coaxed instead of cursed. All this humanizes the children, arouses their brains, and renders them susceptible to intellectual and moral influences. The schools are not all they might be and ought to be; but, compared with the homes, they are paradises; and they slowly are re-acting on the homes. But while this is true of many of the Board schools, your system deserves the worst one can say of it. . . .

In response to the question "What is the *real* object of modern education?" HPB asks:

Is it to cultivate and develop the mind in the right direction; to teach the disinherited and hapless people to carry with fortitude the burden of life (allotted them by Karma); to strengthen their will; to inculcate in them the love of one's neighbor and the feeling of mutual interdependence and brotherhood; and thus to train and form the character for practical life? Not a bit of it. . . . Every young man and boy, nay, everyone of the younger generation of schoolmasters will answer: "The object of modern education is to pass examinations," a system not to develop right emulation, but to generate and breed jealousy, envy, hatred almost, in young people for one another, and thus train them for a life of ferocious selfishness and struggle for honors and emoluments instead of kindly feeling.

And what are these examinations—the terror of modern boyhood and youth? They are simply a method of classification by which the results of your school teaching are tabulated. Now "science" teaches that intellect is a result of the mechanical interaction of the brain-stuff: therefore, it is only logical that modern education should be almost entirely mechanical—a sort of automatic machine for the fabrication of intellect by the ton. Very little experience of examinations is enough to show that the education they produce is simply a training of the physical memory, and, sooner or later, all your schools will sink to this level. As to any real, sound cultivation of the thinking and reasoning power, it is simply impossible while everything has to be judged by the results as tested by competitive examinations. . . .

When further asked, "What would you have, then?" HPB responds:

If we had money, we would found schools where children should above all be taught self-reliance, love for all men, altruism, mutual charity, and more than anything else, to think and reason for themselves. We would reduce the purely mechanical work of memory to an absolute minimum and devote the time to the development and training of the inner faculties and latent capacities. We would endeavor to deal with each child as a unit, and to educate it so as to produce the most harmonious and equal unfoldment of its powers, in order that its special aptitudes should find their full natural development. We should aim at creating *free* men and women, free intellectually, free morally, unprejudiced in all respects, and, above all things, *unselfish*. And we believe that much if not all of this could be obtained by *proper and truly theosophical education.*[211]

Having drawn attention in *The Key to Theosophy* to various social needs of the time, Blavatsky enlarged the scope of her surveillance in her editorials in *Lucifer* and in such articles as "The Tidal Wave," "The Fall of Ideals," "The Cycle Moveth," "Progress and Culture," and "Civilization the Death of Art and Beauty."

Chapter 14

Move to Avenue Road

E arly in 1890, HPB's literary activities were suspended
for a time. She wrote two French Theosophists: "I
have been so sick—complete nervous prostration—that it was impossible for me to write a single word on any other theory than transcendental philosophy. For this does not call for any cerebral action, nor any
thought, and all I have to do is to open one or another drawer in one of
the chests of my memory and then—to copy."[212] In February she
wrote Vera:

As you see, I am in Brighton, on the seashore, where I was sent by
the doctors, to inhale the oceanic evaporations of the Gulf Stream,
to get rid of a complete nervous prostration. I do not feel any pains,
but palpitations of the heart, a ringing in the ears—I am nearly
deaf—and weakness too, such weakness that I can hardly lift my
hand. I am forbidden to write or read or even to think, but must
spend whole days in the open air—"sit by the sea and wait for fair
weather." My doctor got frightened, himself, and frightened all the
staff. It is an awfully expensive place; and my money—alas! So my
esotericists put their money together immediately and persuaded
me to go. And now subsidies fly to me from all points of the
compass, for my care; some of them even unsigned, simply to my
address. America especially is so generous that, upon my word I feel
ashamed. . . .

Two or three theosophists at a time take turns at my side, coming
from London; watching my every movement like Cerberuses. Now
one of them is putting his head in with a tearful request to stop
writing, but I must let you know that I am still alive. You have been
to Brighton, have you? We have splendid spring weather here; the
sun is simply Italian, the air is rich; the sea is like a looking-glass, and
during whole days I am pushed to and fro on the esplanade, in an
invalid chair. It is lovely. I think I am already strong enough. My
brain moves much less, but before I was simply afraid for my head.
My doctor said . . . "You have overworked yourself"; he says,

"you must give yourself a rest." That's it! And with all this work on my hands! "You have written your fill," he says, "now drive about."

It is easy for him to speak, but all the same I must put the third volume of the *[Secret] Doctrine* in order, and the fourth—hardly begun yet, too. . . . don't be afraid. There is no more danger. Take consolation from the enclosed newspaper cuttings. You see how the nations magnify your sister! My *Key to Theosophy* will bring many new proselytes, and *The Voice of the Silence,* tiny book though it is, is simply becoming the Theosophists' bible.

They are grand aphorisms, indeed. I may say so, because you know I did not invent them! I only translated them from Telugu, the oldest South-Indian dialect. There are three treatises, about morals and the moral principles of the Mongolian and Dravidian mystics. Some of the aphorisms are wonderfully deep and beautiful. Here they have created a perfect *furore,* and I think they would attract attention in Russia, too. Won't you translate them? It will be a fine thing to do.[213]

When the foregoing appeared in *The Path* (December 1895), the editor commented: "The sea air did her good, but she did not keep her strength long. Not later than April she was again forbidden to work, abstaining from which was a real torture for her, as with her failing strength the activity of her thought seemed only to increase."

In the *Theosophist Supplement* for June 1890, Olcott reports news of HPB's condition:

Latest advices from Mr. Mead about HPB's health are of a disquieting nature. She was so ill as to be unable to even write her editorial leader for the May *Lucifer.* Her devoted and most able physician Dr. Z. Mennell, sends me word that it will be impossible, without danger to life, for her to come here [to India] in December, as she and I had fully arranged that she should. She is just now passing—he tells me—through a grave crisis, upon the issue of which hangs life or death. Every grateful Asiatic heart will fervently pray the scale may turn in the right direction. There is no other "HPB."

HPB had good reason for getting well. The movement was expanding, and the headquarters of the British section of the TS was soon to move from Lansdowne Road to larger quarters on Avenue Road on the other side of London, close to Regent's Park. For many months preparations had been underway to be ready for occupancy in July. Part of the property had been the home of Annie Besant, who made it available to the Society. In April 1890, HPB wrote Vera:

I am forbidden to work now, but all the same I am awfully busy changing from one end of London to the other. We have taken three separate houses, joined by a garden, for several years; 19 Avenue Road, with building-right. I am building a lecture hall, to hold 300 people; the hall is to be in Eastern style, made of polished wood, in a brick shell, to keep the cold out; and no ceiling inside, the roof being supported by beams and made also of polished wood. And one of our theosophists who is a painter is going to paint allegorical signs and pictures over it. Oh, it will be lovely![214]

Olcott reports that "R. Machell, artist, had covered the two sloping halves of the ceiling with a symbolical representation of the six great religions and of the zodiacal signs."[215] Today, on Christmas cards one often finds the six great religions thus united; in those days, however, it was unheard of.

The inaugural meeting took place on July third. HPB wrote her sister:

At one end of the hall they placed a huge armchair for me and I sat as if enthroned. I sat there hardly able to keep myself together, so ill was I, my doctor near at hand in case I should faint. . . . About 500 people had assembled, nearly twice as many as it would hold. . . . And imagine my astonishment; in the first row I was shown Mrs. Benson, the wife of the Archbishop of Canterbury, to whom my *Lucifer* addressed a "brotherly message." I am sure you remember it? What are we coming to!

The speeches were by Sinnett and others, but, needless to say, no one spoke so well as Annie Besant. Heavens, how this woman speaks! I hope you will hear her yourself. She is now my coeditor of *Lucifer* and the president of the Blavatsky Lodge. Sinnett is to remain the president of the London Lodge alone. As for me, I have become a regular theosophical pope now: I have been unanimously elected president of all the European theosophical branches.[216] But what is the use of all this to me? . . . If I could get some more health—that would be business. But honors and titles are altogether out of my line.[217]

Most of the staff at Avenue Road lived on the premises. Besant writes of this period:

The rules of the house were—and are—very simple, but HPB insisted on great regularity of life; we breakfasted at 8 A.M., worked till lunch at 1, then again till dinner at 7. After dinner the outer work for the Society was put aside, and we gathered in HPB's room where we would sit talking over plans, receiving instructions, listening to her explanations of knotty points. By 12 midnight all the lights had to be extinguished.

She herself wrote incessantly; always suffering, but of indomitable will, she drove her body through its tasks. . . . As a teacher she was marvelously patient, explaining a thing over and over again in different fashions, until sometimes after prolonged failure she would throw herself back in her chair: "My God" (the easy "Mon Dieu" of the foreigner) "am I a fool that you can't understand? Here so-and-so"—to someone on whose countenance a faint gleam of comprehension was discernible—"tell these flapdoodles of the ages what I mean."

With vanity, conceit, pretence of knowledge, she was merciless, if the pupil were a promising one; keen shafts of irony would pierce the sham. With some she would get very angry, lashing them out of their lethargy with fiery scorn; and in truth she made herself a mere instrument for the training of her pupils, careless what they, or anyone else thought of her, providing that the resulting benefit to them was secured.[218]

George Mead tells how HPB's method of training her pupils worked with him: "One thing she was always impressing upon me was to develop a sense of the 'fitness of things,' and she was merciless if this law of harmony were broken, leaving no loop-hole of escape, and listening to no excuse, although, indeed, the minute afterward, she was again the affectionate friend and elder brother, shall I even say, comrade, as she alone knew how to be."[219]

As far as the record goes, there appears to have been only one occasion on which HPB emerged from her life at 19 Avenue Road, and that was in August 1890, when she traveled to East London to open a residence club for underpaid working girls. Early in the year she had been given a thousand pounds to be used at her discretion for human service, preferably for women, and the present project was decided upon. Professor Nethercot, who researched the story, reports:

When it was thrown open in the middle of August, the *Star* [reporter] found no dreary, whitewashed, forbidding-looking place, but rather a private home, with bright and prettily furnished rooms, the beds in the sleeping rooms even being separated from each other by gaily colored Japanese screens. The club also contained a library, a workroom, sitting rooms . . . and a dining room. . . . The club could accommodate about a dozen roomers and take care of several score more for meals and meetings. By the end of December, Mrs. Besant was able to announce that the membership had reached over one hundred and fifty names and that Mrs. Kitty Lloyd, the matron (of course a devoted theosophist), had her hands full serving about the same number of meals every day. . . . At the August opening, attended by about fifty girls, Madame [Blavatsky] had recovered sufficiently from her chronic illness to be present with her whole staff. There were tea, cakes, and even some dancing and singing, climaxed by speeches from Mrs. Besant and Herbert Burrows. Madame merely beamed happily.[220]

In advance of the opening, HPB was deeply concerned regarding one of the rules of the Women's Club and wrote to Annie Besant:

Mr. H. Burrows stated last night *authoritatively* and as one having power in the administration of this *"Women's* Club" that no girl would be received in it whether as inmate or member *who did not belong to the Trade Union. Now what RIGHT* had he to say this? . . . Mr. K's desire was as expressly stated to me in letters and orally, that every girl and woman tempted by poverty to resort to the streets should, irrespective of creed (whether religious or political), class, trade, and opinion, be made to benefit by this club in the limits of its rooms and resources. [Mr. Burrows's order] goes against the fundamental principle of the TS, i.e., brotherhood, irrespective of creed, views, class, race or color and therefore it is untheosophical.

More than that: it is to drag the TS and all those who founded it into a determined groove of action; it is to pin them forcibly and as *unexpectedly,* to one definite and narrow sectarian view of theosophy and philanthropy; to connect us all before the public (as there were two editors there and reporters) with Trades' Unions, strikes, public demonstrations, etc. . . . And if we, of the TS, and the TS itself, live to this day and nothing could crush us it is just because of the wise policy of our Society as a body, of absolute non-interference with such political movements, and keeping always within the limits of law . . . which rioters and rebels, however worthy their cause, do not.[221]

Vera, who was with HPB at this time in London, recalls:

During my stay there were many conditions which disturbed me concerning my sister. Though all who worked there obviously respected, loved, and valued her, they were all *new* people, who were fearfully busy, and in addition, accustomed to a Spartan mode of life. Not one knew how to relieve her of the annoyances and inconveniences of daily living and to furnish her the proper daily care and attention which she sorely needed. . . .

Only Countess Wachtmeister, who took care of her so well at Würzburg and pulled her through at Ostend, in my opinion, could have saved her. I told my sister that many times. But from early morning till evening the countess was at the office in the city, several miles away. Helena Petrovna ardently protested against my suggestions, assuring me that the countess *was needed for the work* and could not neglect it. Self-interest was not a distinguishing trait of my sister's. Thus she sent away to India that very summer, for the same reason, Bertram Keightley—a man devoted to her as if she were his own mother and more. She maintained that he was needed *there.* And more important, that his removal from London was necessary *for him* and would serve his welfare.

During our last evenings together, her greatest pleasure was to listen to simple Russian songs. She would turn first to one then another of my daughters, "Sing something, my heart! Well, possibly 'Nochenky,' (Dear Little Night) or 'Travooshky,' (The Blade of Grass). . . . Sing any of our native songs. . . ." The last evening my daughters sang until midnight such songs as "Sredi Dolini Rovniya" (Amid Level Valleys) and "Vniz po Matushke po Volge" (Down the Mother Volga), our Russian hymn, and Russian Lenten prayers. She listened with such feeling and happiness as though she knew she would never hear them again.[222]

In the late summer of 1890, HPB was engaged in writing "Psychic and Noetic Action," one of her major contributions in the field of Theosophical psychology. The article appeared in two parts in *Lucifer,* in October and November. In it, she examines the shortcomings of the then prevailing "physiological psychology" and contrasts the latter with the psychology of modern and ancient Theosophy. As indicated before, "Noetic" is an adjective of *Nous,* which HPB defines in her *Theosophical Glossary* as "a Platonic term for the Higher Mind or Soul. . . . It means Spirit as distinct from animal Soul—*psyche.*" HPB also terms it the "divine consciousness or mind in man."

In the 1930s, much of the material in "Psychic and Noetic Action" was discussed in an article called "What is the Soul?" by the British philosopher and agnostic C. E. M. Joad, who, until his death in 1953, was widely known for his lucid analyses of modern culture and philosophy. He wrote:

Madame Blavatsky . . . postulates two souls or selves which are broadly defined as follows: The first is body-dependent, that is to say, the events in it are determined by prior events taking place in the body; it is known as the "Lower Self," or as "psychic activity." It manifests itself, through our organic system. . . .

The second self, known as the "Higher Self" [which], instead of being a mere bundle of psychological events, like the first self . . . is a unity, or rather, it is a unifying principle. It has no special organ as its counterpart in the body—for how can there be a specific organ to determine the motions of that which unifies all organs? . . . It is not, therefore, located in the brain. . . . Its activity, described as "Noetic" as opposed to the "psychic" activity of the first self, derives from the "Universal Mind." . . . Finally, the Higher Self is identical and continuing in and through different lives. It is the permanent element which runs like a thread through the different existences which are strung like beads along its length.

The distinction between the two selves is applied by Madame Blavatsky, with great ingenuity, to counter some of the difficulties raised for any spiritualized philosophy by scientific materialism. . . . It is impossible not to feel the greatest respect for Madame Blavatsky's writings on this subject, respect, and if the word may be permitted, admiration. Writing when she did, she anticipated many ideas which, familiar today, were in the highest degree novel fifty years ago.[223]

In March of 1890, the Theosophical Publishing Society in London published Part One of a two-part work called *Transactions of the Blavatsky Lodge*. The second part, which came out in January 1891, was bound together with the first as a book and is still in print.[224] From the title one would hardly suspect that the volume concerned *The Secret Doctrine* and contains HPB's own answers to questions put to her at meetings of the Blavatsky Lodge from January 10 to March 14 of 1889. Her responses were stenographically reported and afterward revised by her for publication.

Similar meetings were held when the Lodge moved to Avenue Road. A record remains of HPB's active participation. The recorder was Robert Bowen, a retired naval commander, whose son, Captain P. G. Bowen, published this remarkable testament years later in *Theosophy in Ireland* (January–March 1932), under the title "The 'Secret Doctrine' and Its Study." It has since been reprinted in various Theosophical magazines and also in booklet form.[225] The document is dated April 19, 1891, just twenty days before HPB died.

The major portions of the paper, too long to include here, present HPB's suggestions as to how the serious student can best study the *SD*. A few extracts from other portions of the pamphlet are here given.

Robert Bowen records:

HPB was specially interesting upon the matter of *The Secret Doctrine* during the past week. I had better try to sort it all out and get it safely down on paper while it is fresh in my mind. As she said herself, it may be useful to someone thirty or forty years hence.

First of all then, *The Secret Doctrine* . . . contains, she says, just as much as can be received by the world during this coming century. This raised a question—which she explained in the following way:—

"The World" means Man living in the Personal Nature. This "World" will find in the two volumes of the *SD* all its utmost comprehension can grasp, but no more. But this was not to say that the Disciple who is not living in "The World" cannot find any more in the book than the "World" finds. Every form, no matter how crude, contains the image of its "creator" concealed within it. So likewise does an author's work, no matter how obscure, contain the concealed image of the author's knowledge. From this saying I take it that the *SD* must contain all that HPB knows herself, and a great deal more than that, seeing that much of it comes from men whose knowledge is immensely wider than hers. *Furthermore, she implies unmistakably that another may well find knowledge in it which she does not possess herself.* It is a stimulating thought to consider that it is possible that I myself may find in HPB's words knowledge of which she herself is unconscious. She dwelt on this idea a good deal. X said afterwards: "HPB must be losing her grip" meaning, I suppose, confidence in her own knowledge. But Y and Z and myself also, see her meaning better, I think. She is telling us without a doubt not to anchor ourselves to her as the final authority, nor to anyone else, but to depend altogether upon our own widening perceptions.

Later note on above: I was right. I put it to her direct and she nodded and smiled. It is worth something to get her approving smile! . . .

She has changed much since I met her two years ago. It is marvelous how she holds up in the face of dire illness. If one knew nothing and believed nothing, HPB would convince one that she is something away and beyond body and brain. I feel, especially during these last meetings since she has become so helpless bodily, that we are getting teachings from another and higher sphere. We seem to feel and KNOW what she says rather than hear it with our bodily ears. X said much the same thing last night.

Last Days of HPB

Georc Mead wrote of this period:

When we moved to our present headquarters, many things were changed. Looking back it now seems almost as if she had got us in training for leaving at any moment. . . . Ever since she went to Brighton in the early part of last year she has suffered most cruelly in her physical body, and been unable to work as she used to. But we always lived in great expectations of restitution to at any rate her normal state of health. At Lansdowne Road she used always to be pleased to receive visitors, and nearly every evening they came in to see her. But in Avenue Road she gradually began to isolate herself more and more, so that often she would not receive even the members of the household in the evening unless she especially sent for them. Then again, she was strangely quiet latterly, rarely showing the great energy that was her particular characteristic. Still the same indomitable will was there, though her body was worn out, for she worked on at her desk even when she ought to have been in bed, or in her coffin.[226]

In a letter to a friend, dated May 25, 1891, Countess Wachtmeister expressed similar feelings:

We have indeed had a terrible time, and it seems hardly possible even now to realize that HPB is gone. We all felt so sure that she would live to the end of the century; so that though all this winter we have seen her continually failing and decreasing in strength, we were not really alarmed. HPB did very little work this winter and, as I wrote you before, [she] gradually separated herself from us. I believe now that she knew that the end was coming soon, and did this to accustom us to her absence, and also to watch us and see how we should get on alone without her; and now we have to work alone and do the best we can.[227]

During the last few months of her life, HPB was busy preparing her *Theosophical Glossary.* It was not published until 1892, a year after she died. She was also occupied with rewriting some of her occult stories, which were published in the same year under the title *Nightmare Tales*,[228] although they were much more than that. Originally they appeared in various journals, among them the New York *Sun*, the *Banner of Light*, *Lucifer*, and *The Theosophist*.[229] Today they have all been reprinted in a book, *The Tell-tale Picture Gallery*.[230] Four of the eight stories concern events in HPB's own life or were in some way witnessed by her. One of these, the longest and probably the most important, is called "A Bewitched Life as Narrated by a Quill Pen." It dates back to the time HPB was visiting Europe and was staying at the Gebhards' home in Elberfeld, on the eve of the Coulomb scandal.

HPB's annual letter to the convention of American Theosophists, this time held in Boston, was dated April fifteenth, three weeks before she died. Her representative was Annie Besant, who made her first trip to the United States on this occasion. In view of subsequent events in the Theosophical Society,[231] the letter seems rather prophetic:

For the third time since my return to Europe in 1885, I am able to send to my brethren in Theosophy and fellow citizens of the United States a delegate from England to attend the annual Theosophical Convention and speak by word of mouth my greeting and warm congratulations. Suffering in body as I am continually, the only consolation that remains to me is to hear of the progress of the Holy Cause to which my health and strength have been given; but to which, now that these are going, I can offer only my passionate devotion and never-weakening good wishes for its success and welfare. The news therefore that comes from America, mail after mail, telling of new branches and of well-considered and patiently worked-out plans for the advancement of Theosophy cheers and gladdens me with its evidences of growth, more than words can tell. . . .

Let me remind you all once more that such work is now more than ever needed. The period which we have now reached in the cycle that will close between 1897–8 is, and will continue to be, one of great conflict and continued strain. If the TS can hold through it, good; if not, while Theosophy will remain unscathed, the Society will perish—perchance most ingloriously— and the world will suffer. . . . No opportunity will be lost of sowing dissension, of taking advantage of mistaken and false moves, of instilling doubt, of augmenting difficulties, of breathing suspicions, so that by any and every means the unity of the Society may be broken and the ranks of our Fellows thinned and thrown into disarray. Never has it been more necessary for the members of the TS to lay to heart the old parable of the bundle of sticks, than it is at the present time: divided, they will inevitably be broken, one by one; united, there is no force on earth able to destroy our Brotherhood.

Now I have marked with pain, a tendency among you, as among the Theosophists in Europe and India, to quarrel over trifles, and to allow your very devotion to the cause of Theosophy to lead you into disunion. Believe me, that apart from such natural tendency, owing to the inherent imperfections of human nature, advantage is often taken by our ever-watchful enemies of your noblest qualities to betray and to mislead you. . . . Self-watchfulness is never more necessary than when a personal wish to lead, and wounded vanity, dress themselves in the peacock's feathers of devotion and altruistic work; but at the present crisis of the Society a lack of self-control and watchfulness may become fatal in every case. . . . If every Fellow in the Society were content to be an impersonal force for good, careless of praise or blame so long as he subserved the purposes of the Brotherhood, the progress made would astonish the World and place the Ark of the TS out of danger. . . .

My own span of life may not be long, and if any of you have learned aught from my teachings, or have gained by my help a glimpse of the True Light, I ask you in return, to strengthen the cause by the triumph of which, that True Light, made still brighter and more glorious through your individual and collective efforts, will lighten the world. . . .

May the blessings of the past and present great Teachers rest upon you. From myself accept collectively, the assurance of my true, never-wavering fraternal feelings, and the sincere heart-felt thanks for the work done by all the workers,

> *From their Servant to the Last,*
> *H. P. BLAVATSKY*

It was on the first day of the convention, April twenty-sixth, in the afternoon session, that the foregoing letter was read by Mrs. Besant to those assembled. She then followed with another letter from HPB:

Brother Theosophists:

I have purposely omitted any mention of my oldest friend and fellow-worker, W. Q. Judge, in my general address to you, because I think that his unflagging and self-sacrificing efforts for the building up of Theosophy in America deserve special mention.

Had it not been for W. Q. Judge, Theosophy would not be where it is today in the United States. It is he who has mainly built up the movement among you, and he who has proved in a thousand ways his entire loyalty to the best interests of Theosophy and the Society.

Mutual admiration should play no part in a Theosophical Convention,

but honor should be given where honor is due, and I gladly take this oppor-
tunity of stating in public, by the mouth of my friend and colleague, Annie
Besant, my deep appreciation of the work of your General Secretary and of
publicly tendering him my most sincere thanks and deeply-felt gratitude, in
the name of Theosophy, for the noble work he is doing and has done.[232]

Yours fraternally,
H. P. Blavatsky ∴

On Saturday, April twenth-fifth, HPB came down with influenza;
an epidemic of the disease was raging in London at the time. Several
times during the next two weeks she told Dr. Mennell she was dying,
but as she had cheated death so often, neither he nor anyone in the
household believed it.

HPB's "last message" for the Society was given to Mrs. Cooper-
Oakley two nights before she died. At three A.M. she suddenly looked
up and said, "Isabel, Isabel, keep the link unbroken; do not let my last
incarnation be a failure" (*The Path*, July 1894).

By "last" she apparently did not mean her *final* incarnation, as that
would be contrary to one of the basic teachings in *The Voice of the Silence,* epitomized in the "Pledge of Kwan Yin," the Buddhist Goddess
of Mercy:

> Never will I seek nor receive private individual salvation; never
> will I enter into final peace alone; but forever and everywhere
> will I live and strive for the redemption of every creature
> throughout the world.[233]

On May seventh, the night before HPB died, she experienced intense suffering. Laura Cooper, the sister of Isabel Cooper-Oakley,
writes:

> Owing to the increased difficulty in breathing, HPB could not rest
> in any position; every remedy was tried without avail, and finally
> she was obliged to remain seated in her chair propped with pillows.
> The cough almost ceased, owing to her great exhaustion. . . .
> About 4 A.M. [on the eighth] HPB seemed easier, and her pulse was
> fairly strong, and from that time until I left her at 7 o'clock all went
> quietly and well. My sister then took my place, while I went for a
> few hours' rest, leaving word for Dr. Mennell to give me his opin-
> ion of HPB when he called. This he did shortly after nine, and his
> report was satisfactory; the stimulant was having a good effect and
> the pulse stronger; he saw no cause for immediate anxiety, advised

me to rest a few hours, and told my sister she could go to her business. About 11:30 I was aroused by Mr. Wright, who told me to come at once as HPB had changed for the worse, and the nurse did not think she could live many hours.

[But] suddenly there was a further change, and when I tried to moisten her lips I saw the dear eyes were already becoming dim, though she retained full consciousness to the last. In life HPB had a habit of moving one foot when she was thinking intently, and she continued that movement almost to the moment she ceased to breathe. When all hope was over the nurse left the room, leaving C. F. Wright, W. R. Old and myself with our beloved HPB; the two former knelt in front, each holding one of her hands, and I, at her side with one arm around her supported her head; thus we remained motionless for many minutes, and so quietly did HPB pass away that we hardly knew the second she ceased to breathe; a great sense of peace filled the room. . . .[234]

During the week preceding, strange things had been occurring in the home of HPB's aunts Nadya and Catherine in Russia. On May 4, 1891 Nadya reported them to Vera. Later a copy was sent to Olcott, which he published in *The Theosophist* (April 1893, 430–31):

I had a warning, but at first I did not understand it. You know the ring she sent me from India? A plain, large ring with an agate; the stone is oval, flat, of a light yellowish colour, quite transparent, and with a minute sprig of moss embedded in the middle of the crystal. I have worn it some twelve years, and its color never changed—it was always clear as glass. But since about a month [the date of this letter was 4(o.s.)/16th, May 1891] I perceived that it was darkening, and had lost its brilliancy. Finally it became black as coal, so that the sprig of moss could no more be seen. I could not imagine how a quartz stone like this could darken. I washed and cleaned and rubbed it, but to no effect. The stone remained black until Helen's death, gradually cleared, and after some days returned to its natural transparency. . . .

On Easter Monday we heard in the very middle of the dining-table, a knock so loud that everyone was startled. She was alive then; but all those subsequent days we heard strange sounds, as of the breaking of glass and snappings and blows in the furniture, night and day. When I received Countess Wachtmeister's letter that things were going worse, she (Helen) was no more, but we were not aware of her death. I was busy reading it in the drawing-room to my sister (Mdme. Witte) who, after listening to my reading, said "I am sure she will recover." At the same moment there was a crash; we jumped to our feet in affright and ran to look what had happened, for the noise, which came from one corner of the room, was as if the wall had crumbled into pieces. Then we thought, perhaps, the dining-table with all the glasses and porcelain on it were smashed. Not at all: all was in order and unharmed. After I received Vera's letter and your telegram, all noises ceased.

Dr. Franz Hartmann relates a similar case in which a man died far from home. Such loud noises were heard by his family that all the neighbors woke up. Hartmann comments: "This may have been brought about by the intense thought-forms of the dying man. The physical body is a storehouse of a great deal of energy which becomes liberated at the time of death and by which such noises can be produced. Paracelsus says this is produced by Evestrum, or the astral body."

But beautiful sounds were also heard when HPB died, as Vera learned later from Nadya: "Several times during the night, and once during the day . . . the organ near her large portrait began to play suddenly. It was closed and had been touched by no one. Also, bells sounded forth without cause or reason."[235]

Two days after HPB died, and before the aunts had learned of her passing, the relatives were

in their large drawing room as usual in the evenings, trying to read but really thinking intently about their distant dear niece. Suddenly Mme. de Witte [Catherine], gazing fixedly into the same dark and distant corner of the room [where the loud noises had come from] whispered: "I see her! There she is!" She described the wraith as clad in white, and with great white flowers on her head, exactly as she was laid out in her coffin. This was her farewell to earth.[236]

HPB's body was cremated in Woking, England, on May tenth. Among those who attended was William Stewart Ross, editor of the *Agnostic Journal,* wherein he often wrote under the pen name Saladin. In the May sixteenth issue, he describes the funeral. (His report is condensed.):

From stale, grey London we were whirled out among the green fields and through masses of fruit trees white as the vesture of Soracte's hill, that day we followed to the furnace the mortal remains of Helena Petrovna Blavatsky. We bore no warrior to the pyre. We were accompanying to the flames an oracle, a sphinx, or a sibyl, rather than anything that the world commonly produces in its ordinary villages and towns.

One in a wagon-load of uncapped mourners, I reached the crematorium. The Theosophists crowded round a boiler-looking object with anxious but decorous curiosity, to gratify which one of the attendants opened up a circular orifice about the size of a crown piece. Those present looked in succession into this opening; most, I noticed, gave one quick glance, and turned away with an involuntary shudder. When it came to my turn to peep in I wondered not that my predecessors had shuddered. If Virgil or Milton or Dante had ever seen such an Inferno, they would never have written about the Inferno at all, relinquishing the theme as utterly ineffable.

As I was so contemplating, the hearse arrived. Into the chapel the coffin was borne and laid upon an oaken tressel, and we all stood up and uncovered. Mr. G. R. S. Mead, a young gentleman of refined features, stepped forward to the head of the coffin and read an impressive address. The door from the crematorium into the chapel opened, and four employees moved off with [the coffin] through the doorway. Four Theosophists who had known and loved Madame Blavatsky, and had, like myself, found the grandest and the worst-abused woman in the world identical followed her remains through that wide doorway down to the furnace, and the great doorway was slammed and bolted.

Her demise falls heavily upon me who was of her brotherhood, but who do not share in the stoical consolations of her creed. To her followers she is still alive. The Madame Blavatsky I knew can in the mind of no Theosophist be confounded with the mere physical instrument which served it for but one brief incarnation. But I lay not firm enough hold upon this doctrine for it to give consolation to me. Her followers are gnostic on grave issues of teleology on which I am only agnostic. To me Madame Blavatsky is dead, and another shadow has fallen athwart my life.

Any discriminating person who came in contact with [HPB] could easily understand why she was so dearly loved, and no less easily conjecture why she was so bitterly hated. She wore her heart upon her sleeve. Unfortunately for anyone who hopes to "get on" in this world, she did not possess even a single rag of the cloak of hypocrisy. *She declined to place her feet in the very marks in which Mrs. Grundy trod, even as an eagle could not be made to walk for leagues on the hoofprints of an ass.*

She did not call those who reviled and wronged her by a more bitter epithet than "flapdoodles." Such assailants as the Coulombs and Dr. Coues she referred to with expressions equivalent to "Father forgive them, for they know not what they do," even when these assailants were doing their best to cut her, soul and body, with numerous and ghastly wounds, and to fill them with salt and salve them with vitriol. She hath that overflow of soul which falls to the lot of the few.[237]

Editorials on Her Passing

From India, England, and the United States, three expressions of appreciation for HPB's work are here offered. The first, dated May 15, 1891, came from the *Indian Mirror,* one of the leading native papers:

Helena Petrovna Blavatsky has ceased to exist on this earthly plane. . . . She was not of this nation or that. The wide earth was her home, and all mankind were her brothers . . . the whole of her life was simply extraordinary. There is no existing human standard by which to judge her. She will always stand out alone. . . .

For ourselves . . . it is impossible to realize the enormity of this loss. Our affection for Madame Blavatsky was so personal, we were so longing to see her in the flesh once more in India . . . that now that this desire has been cruelly crushed by death, a stupor has crept over all our senses, and we are writing as if it were mechanically. We recall the features of the dear lady . . . her quick movements, the rapid flow of words, those light, glowing eyes, which saw through you and, at a glance, turned you inside out. Anon we behold her, kind and gentle as a mother, and wise as a father, pouring faith, hope, and consolation into your ears, as you mention to her your doubts and your anxieties. . . .

The Theosophical Society was founded [to disseminate, among other objects,] the religious and philosophic truths of Vedanta and Buddhism among the Western nations. But those truths were known very partially in this country itself. Madame Blavatsky was accordingly required to transfer her labors among us, and for several years she became a living sacrifice for the sake of the Hindus, who, however, turned away most ungratefully from her, when she most needed their support. But now they have been rightly punished. Their land is not made sacred, as English ground has been, by her tomb or cenotaph.† And English Theosophists have been certainly

---

† [At that time it had not been decided what to do with HPB's ashes. Eventually one-third was given to Adyar, one-third to the TS European headquarters in London, and the remaining third to the U.S. headquarters in New York.]

much more faithful to her than we in India have been. Theirs is and will be the exceeding great reward. But shall we not endeavor to wipe away the reproach and the shame? It can only be by raising such a memorial to Helena Petrovna Blavatsky's memory as shall show the strength and extent of our repentance, and our appreciation of all that she ever did for India.[238]

In London, W. T. Stead, editor of *The Review of Reviews,* wrote in its June 1891 issue:

Among the many and varied spiritual teachers at whose feet I have sat in the course of a very eclectic journalistic career, Madame Blavatsky was one of the most original. There are those who, because they can crack a joke about a teacup, imagine they have disposed of Theosophy. . . . What Madame Blavatsky did was an immeasurably greater thing than the doubling of teacups. She made it possible for the most cultivated and skeptical men and women of this generation to believe, and to believe ardently, to an extent that made them proof against ridicule and disdainful of persecution—that not only does the invisible world that encompasses us contain intelligences vastly superior to our own knowledge of the truth, but that it is possible for man to enter into communion with these hidden and silent ones, and to be taught of them the Divine mysteries of Time and Eternity. . . . That is a great achievement, and one which *a priori* could have been laughed at as impossible. Yet she performed that miracle.

Madame Blavatsky, a Russian, . . . converted leading Anglo-Indians to a passionate belief in her Theosophy mission, even when the Jingo fever was hottest, and in her declining years she succeeded in winning over to the new-old religion Annie Besant, who had for years fought in the forefront of the van of militant atheism. A woman who could achieve these two things is a woman indeed. . . .

Madame Blavatsky, in the midst of a generation that is materialistic and mechanical [succeeded] in compelling a race of inquirers and economists to admit at least the existence of the conception that all material things are but a passing illusion and that the spiritual alone is. Madame Blavatsky also reinforced and almost recreated in many minds the sense of this life being a mere probation. In this respect her teaching was much more in accord with the spirit of the New Testament than much of the pseudo-Christian teaching of our day. She widened the horizon of the mind, and she brought something of the infinite sense of the vast, illimitable mystery which characterizes some of the Eastern religions into the very heart of Europe in the nineteenth century.

In a subsequent editorial Stead added:

Reincarnation may or may not be true. Whether true or false, it has, until the last decade, been almost unthinkable by the average Westerner. This is no longer the case. Multitudes who still reject it as unproved have learned to recognize its value as a hypothesis explaining many of the mysteries of human life . . . it is indisputable that the sympathetic recognition of the possibility of reincarnation has widened the range of popular thought. . . . And this, which is unquestionably a great achievement, will ever be associated with the name of Madame Blavatsky.[239]

≈

The following editorial appeared in the May 10, 1891 issue of the *New-York Daily Tribune:*

Few women in our time have been more persistently misrepresented, slandered, and defamed than Madame Blavatsky, but though malice and ignorance did their worst upon her there are abundant indications that her life-work will vindicate itself, that it will endure, and that it will operate for good. . . .

The life of Madame Blavatsky was a remarkable one, but this is not the place or time to speak of its vicissitudes. It must suffice to say that for nearly twenty years she had devoted herself to the dissemination of doctrines, the fundamental principles of which are of the loftiest ethical character. However Utopian may appear to some minds an attempt in the nineteenth century to break down the barriers of race, nationality, caste, and class prejudice and to inculcate that spirit of brotherly love which the greatest of all Teachers enjoined in the first century, the nobility of the aim can only be impeached by those who repudiate Christianity. Madame Blavatsky held that the regeneration of mankind must be based upon the development of altruism. In this she was at one with the greatest thinkers, not alone of the present day, but of all time. . . . This alone would entitle her teachings to the candid and serious consideration of all who respect the influences that make for righteousness.

In another direction . . . she did important work. No one in the present generation, it may be said, has done more toward reopening the long sealed treasures of Eastern thought, wisdom, and philoso-phy. No one certainly has done so much toward elucidating that profound wisdom religion wrought out by the ever-cogitating Ori-ent, and bringing into the light those ancient literary works whose scope and depth have so astonished the Western world, brought up in the insular belief that the East had produced only crudities and puerilities in the domain of speculative thought.

Her own knowledge of Oriental philosophy and esotericism was comprehensive. No candid mind can doubt this after reading her two principal works. Her steps often led, indeed, where only a few initiates could follow, but the tone and tendency of all her writings were healthful, bracing, and stimulating. The lesson which was constantly impressed by her was assuredly that which the world most needs, and has always needed, namely, the necessity of subduing self and of working for others. Doubtless such a doctrine is distasteful to the ego-worshippers, and perhaps it has little chance of anything like general acceptance, to say nothing of general application. But the man or woman who deliberately renounces all personal aims and ambitions in order to forward such beliefs is certainly entitled to respect, even from such as feel least capable of obeying the call to a higher life.

The work of Madame Blavatsky has already borne fruit, and is destined apparently, to produce still more marked and salutary ef-fects in the future. Careful observers of the time long since dis-cerned that the tone of current thought in many directions was being affected by it. A broader humanity, a more liberal speculation, a disposition to investigate ancient philosophies from a higher point of view, have no indirect association with the teachings referred to. Thus Madame Blavatsky has made her mark upon the time. Thus, too, her works will follow her . . . and some day, if not at once, the loftiness and purity of her aims, the wisdom and scope of her teachings, will be recognized more fully, and her memory will be accorded the honor to which it is justly entitled.[240]

"Did You Ever Meet Madame Blavatsky?"

The American artist Edmund Russell knew HPB in London in the late 1880s. In *Lucifer* she refers to him as "'our mutual friend' the very popular Edmund Russell." Yeats wrote of Russell to Katherine Tynan in a September 1888 letter: "The other day I met [at Madame Blavatsky's] a most curious and interesting man—I do not wish to say as yet whether he be of interest in himself but his opinions are. . . . He is the most interesting person I have met at Madame's lately. . . ."[241] What now follows is a composite of four of Russell's five character sketches of HPB:[242]

I have read many articles about Helena Petrovna-Hahn-Blavatsky and from most of them would never dream the writers had so much as seen her. They write with as little appreciation of personal qualities as the African hunter for the quarry he slaughters, mad in the endeavor to trap the beast. Everything suppressed in the effort to prove her a charlatan. Which emphatically she was not. Or a divinity which as emphatically she refused to be. She was indeed big game.

It was in the last years of her life at Lansdowne Road, Holland Park, that I had opportunity to observe her under every circumstance. I never belonged to the working associates, but was a member of her Esoteric-Circle. As an outsider, an artist, the youngest of her followers, I suppose I amused her, and she talked very frankly to me. She had long retired absolutely from Society. People who wanted to see her came to see her. The woman who drew back on the doorstep:—"I'm afraid to go in." "I tremble at the thought of meeting her"—was soon at her feet.

SHE HELD BY LOVE, NOT FEAR

The Ganges of her guests was an ethnological congress—Italian and Russian officers—Bengali—Brahmins—Patriarchs of the

Greek Church—mystics from every land. All felt her penetration and her power. Each fell to the charm of her universality. She lifted people to the expression of their best at once. It gave men new force to feel they had met one who could look right through to their real selves, uninfluenced by the littleness of which others make so much. Naturally, the creedbound, the literal Jonah-swallowing-the-whale order who were frightened at symbolic interpretation, were uncomfortable in the light of her logic and deep-dredged knowledge and went away calling her "a dreadful woman." Sometimes their wives confessed, "We don't approve of her—but love her just the same."

I remember well her sister Madame Zhelihowsky who used to visit her for long periods. *Tres grande dame,* a grey-haired woman of aristocratic poise and dignity well known to the highest Russian society. Madame herself could be most elegant of manner when she chose, but seldom gave herself the trouble. She had the simplicity of those who knowing they are royal do as they please.

When she wanted to draw anyone on in argument, she pretended not to know English very well, but her knowledge and command increased as she swept into discussion. It was amusing to watch her parry with a journalist—lean, mental, cross-examining—who had come to trap her. At such times she would put on that stupid look Loie Fuller[†] uses so effectively, as if only a *little* brighter she might be called half-witted; lead him on to play out all his rope, then, regaining her trenches step by step, drop her bombs; till finally she wiped up the floor with him. Then with hearty laugh she would grasp his hand.

"YOU ARE A SPLENDID FELLOW—COME
OFTEN—COME ALWAYS!"

I have seen her in an argument suddenly strike her forehead with her clenched fist: "What an idiot I am! My dear friend, forgive me—you are right, and I am wrong." How many will do this?

A review saying that no such thing as theosophy ever existed, the great secret doctrine being her own invention, Madame replied: "If I thought so, I would take off my hat to HPB. I am only the scribe; they would make me the creator! That is being greater than I claim!" Utterly indifferent to gossip, she never bothered to deny. She once

† [Loie Fuller (1862–1928) was a noted American dancer.]

said to me:—"Mud has rained down so long on me I do not attempt even to open an umbrella."

Samadhi or god-consciousness was her ideal. She was the bar of iron heated red-hot which becomes as fire, forgetting its own nature. Most people occupy themselves with the needs or pleasures of the lower all the time. She seemed not to have needs or pleasures of her own. Often she did not go out of the house for half a year. Not even for a walk in her garden. The influence of such example was the secret of the astonishing growth and expansion of the Theosophical Society. She lived in great truth, yet was called a liar; in great generosity, and was called a fraud; in a detestation of all shams, and yet—was crowned the Queen of Humbugs.

She knew her Bible well, though to her it was only one of many sacred books, all sacred to her; for through her theosophy—god-wisdom or good-wisdom—she taught us to drop the final *s* from religions, and that little letter seems at last to be losing its grip. A deep student of universal analogies, some of her interpretations were electrical. The last words of Christ, "Eli! Eli! Lama Sabachthani" [God! Why hast thou forsaken me?], a sorrow to many and which some make, with George Moore, a renunciation of his mission, she turned into a joy: "My God! My God! How Thou hast glorified me!"

She was the last of the mammoths. Only the cave-temples of India can describe her. She was *Elephanta* or *Ajunta* domed with faded frescoes of golden glory.

I have known many near in stature to the gods—Salvini, Gladstone, Robert Browning, William Morris, Rodin, Sarah Bernhardt—none had her cosmic sweep of power, though all carried the same infantine charm when away from the treadmill. The great always remain children and occasionally let themselves out of the cage.

She was certainly the greatest personality I ever met. Even her enemies—and she had many—acknowledged this. Those of consistent conventionality could not understand her absence of pose. Her instantaneous change from laughing childhood to grave old age. It was indecent. They never dropped the mask.

She looked like a man—a woman—a lion—an eagle—a turtle—a toad—cosmic—all things. Outwardly she suggested the *monsterism* of those strange forms Blake drew; whose clothes, hair, gestures, seem part of the rocks and trees which surround them; who walk girdled with the Zodiac and hold converse with the gods. Her Cossack face showed sometimes in repose the sadness of being great and living, but it usually reflected the joy. Nothing could embitter her. She was not tragic in the Greek sense. Shakespeare's saving grace of humor shone a golden thread through her darkest gloom.

In America, that remarkable lady Mary A. Livermore[†] and I happened to be speaking in the same city. A dinner was given in our joint-honor to which most of the clergymen of the town were invited. Of course, Mrs. Livermore went in on the arm of the host. I with the hostess. The table was very long. We were very far apart. The reverend ones were of different denominations. It was dreadfully dull. The only way to make a big dinner a success is for the conversation to shoot across the table. I let things drift till the middle of the repast, then in a lull:—

"Mrs. Livermore! Did you ever meet Madame Blavatsky?"

The effect was magical. All awoke. Everyone was brilliant from that moment in attack or defence and I marveled to find how deeply the leaders of the church had studied her thought. How familiar they were with her work. Though disapproving *en bloc* her doctrines, her light had penetrated to their very sanctuaries and her [magazine *Lucifer's*] "Letter to the Archbishop of Canterbury" had struck home.

I occasionally hear of someone who "didn't like" her or was jealous of her. As well not like the Elgin Marbles or be jealous of the Sphinx. She was yet as sweet and radiant in spirit as William Blake, who, when a very old man after endless privation and unappreciation, said to a little girl: "My dear, I can only hope that your life may be as beautiful and happy as mine."

---

† [Mary Ashton Livermore (1820–1905), an American suffragette and reformer, was founder and editor of *The Agitator* and, later, *The Woman's Journal*.]

Part 7

The Century After

Chapter 1

Scope of Enquiry

At the time of Helena Blavatsky's death, her colleague William Q. Judge recalled:

In London I once asked her what was the chance of drawing the people into the Theosophical Society in view of the enormous disproportion between the numbers of members and the millions of Europe and America who neither knew of nor cared for it. Leaning back in her chair, in which she was sitting before her writing desk, she said: "When you consider and remember those days in 1875 and after, in which you could not find any people interested in your thoughts, and now look at the widespreading influence of theosophical ideas—however labelled—it is not so bad. We are not working merely that people may call themselves *theosophists,* but that the doctrines we cherish may affect and leaven the whole mind of this century."[1]

Some of these influences have been discussed. The chapters ahead will examine the hundred-year period after HPB's death for evidences of a similar kind in the realms of science, religion, the arts, psychology, and other areas of human interest.

These chapters will also include evidences that in *The Secret Doctrine,* HPB anticipated future discoveries made by science. She did not, however, make claim to firstmanship, as she considered herself simply a transmitter of wisdom known by the ancients that she learned from her teachers. Nor did she claim always to be correct in her transmissions—neither she nor her teachers ever pretended infallibility.

One would naturally suppose that HPB's influence in the twentieth century manifested with greatest efficacy among theosophists in the various theosophical associations during these hundred years.† However, that is too big a story to attempt to chronicle here.

† The names and addresses of the three principal associations having sections, branches, or Lodges in various parts of the world are: The Theosophical Society, Adyar [Madras], Chennai, 600 020, India; The Theosophical Society, P. O. Box C, Pasadena, California 91109; and United Lodge of Theosophists, 245 West 33rd Street, Los Angeles, California, 90007.

That HPB's influence reached into least expected places seems evident in the letter that follows from the Right Reverend Eric Bloy, bishop of the Episcopal Diocese of Los Angeles, now retired. The letter, dated November 18, 1971, and on his official stationery, is addressed to Boris de Zirkoff:

> *How thoughtful of you to send me a copy of "H.P.B. and* The Secret Doctrine*." I am enjoying reading it. Many years ago* The Secret Doctrine *opened up for me many expanding horizons, as I believe I once told you, and I shall be eternally grateful. The concepts expressed in the* Secret Doctrine, *when even but partially grasped, deliver one from any despair, to which the present world malaise can so easily give rise. "The best is yet to be," says Browning, and we who are privileged to serve mankind under the direction of the great Teachers know this for sure. The day of Brahma has not yet blazed forth in all its glory.*

Another case is that of Rabbi Joshua Lieberman, who was renowned in the 1940s and 1950s for his radio talk broadcast over many networks in the United States. On one occasion he named several books that had been an inspiration to him in his life's work, one of which was Robert Crosbie's *The Friendly Philosopher*. Lieberman's audience would have been surprised to learn that the subtitle read "Letters and Talks on Theosophy and the Theosophical Life." Crosbie was founder in 1909 of the United Lodge of Theosophists.

In speaking of Blavatsky's public work from 1875 to her death, Crosbie once drew attention to the fact that around this period three important cycles intersected:

> The first five thousand year period of *Kaliyuga,* which began at the death of Krishna, the Teacher of the "Bhagavad-Gita," was completed in this time. The hundred year cycle, when in the last twenty-five years of every century an effort is made by the Great Lodge [of Masters], through Teachers or their disciples, to place better ideas before mankind was also in operation.[†] The sun, during this period, passed from Pisces into Aquarius, and there, too, was a sign.[2]

Remarkable events were occurring at this time in the field of religion and science, all connected, it appears, with the influence of HPB and her teachers.

---

† See Blavatsky, *Key to Theosophy,* pp. 306–307.

Chapter 2

The World Parliament of Religions

An unprecedented event took place in September 1893, as part of the Columbian Exposition in Chicago in celebration of the four hundredth anniversary of the discovery of America by Christopher Columbus. This was the World Parliament of Religions. Reports leading American Buddhist writer, Rick Fields:

> To house the exposition as a whole, an entire city had been built along the shores of Lake Michigan. The gleaming palaces of the "white city" recalled the great empires of the past—Greece, Rome, Egypt, renaissance Italy. . . . The response to the more than ten thousand letters the organizers had sent throughout the world [inviting attendance] overwhelmed even the most optimistic of them.

At the opening of the World Parliament of Religions, the chairman, Dr. John Henry Barrows, remarked: "Religion, like the white light of Heaven, has been broken into many colored fragments by the prisms of men. One of the objects of the Parliament of Religions has been to change the many-colored radiance back into the white light of heavenly truth."[3]

The numerous Christian sects had hitherto never gathered together, while the major Oriental faiths had never previously been invited to the West. HPB, who had worked so hard to accomplish such a reconciliation, would have rejoiced to be present.

Not surprisingly, some Christian groups refused to attend. The head of the Anglican Church in England, the Archbishop of Canterbury, wrote: "The Christian religion is the one religion," adding that he did not see "how that religion can be regarded as a member of a Parliament of Religions without assuming the equality of the other intended members and the parity of their position and claims."[4]

Seated on the platform at the opening session to welcome the gathering were Protestant leaders, a Catholic cardinal from New York, Jewish rabbis, and holy men, or scholars, from the East. Professor Carl Jackson, in *Oriental Religions and American Thought,* notes:

> A number of the Asian representatives had been theosophists, including Kinza Hirai and Dharmapala, the chief exponents of Buddhism at the congress. [Hirai's] Parliament address on "Synthetic Religion," in which he envisioned the merging of all religions, definitely suggests the influence of theosophy. Dharmapala . . . had even closer theosophical ties: he had served as Olcott's loyal assistant and personal secretary in the Sri Lanka work.

Originally, it may be recalled, Dharmapala was under HPB's tutelage and it was she who recommended he become a Buddhist Pali scholar and missionary.

Jackson continues:

> The most controversial delegate at the Parliament, Alexander Russell Webb—or "Mohammed" Webb as he now preferred—had also been a theosophist. . . . Olcott, who had interviewed Webb in 1892 shortly after his resignation as American consul in Manila, declares that Webb had been a "strenuous advocate of Buddhism" up to a "few months of his acceptance of Islam." Asked about his change of allegiance, Webb had informed Olcott that "although he had become a Muslim he had not ceased to be an ardent theosophist," that "Islam, as he understood it," was "distinctly in accord" with theosophy. Webb's unflinching defense of Islam at the Parliament created a sensation. Finally, there is professor G. N. Chakravarti [also a Theosophist] who joined Vivekananda in presenting Hinduism at the Parliament. . . .[5]

Dharmapala and Chakravarti were also delegates on behalf of the Theosophical Society. Other Theosophical delegates included W. Q. Judge and J. D. Buck from the United States and Annie Besant and Isabel Cooper-Oakley from England.

At one point it seemed as if the Theosophical Society would be denied representation [per report of the Theosophical Congress]. It was assigned at first to the Psychic Committee for placement, but Elliott Coues was chairman and an adverse decision, of course, was inevitable. Then the TS was referred to the Committee of Moral and Social Reform, which was headed by Coues's sister! Six months went by without its representation.

Then, in April of 1893, George Wright, the TS representative in Chicago, was called to the office of the president of the Parliament.

Wright relates: "He took my breath away by informing me that the Religions Committee had unanimously agreed to grant the TS a separate congress of its own, to take place during the great Parliament of Religions and that I had been appointed chairman of the Committee of Organization."[6]

William Q. Judge, as international vice president of the TS and principal organizer of the Theosophical Congress, was appointed its chairman [per report of the Theosophical Congress]. It was accorded two days for its meetings, September fifteenth and sixteenth. So many of the public jammed the congress that the managers of the Parliament accorded it two special weekend meetings before the general Parliament itself, and one at prime time, eight P.M. Although four thousand could be seated at the final meeting, hundreds stood in the aisles and by the walls. Two of Annie Besant's lectures highlighted karma and rebirth in relation to social problems, and several other Theosophical speakers gave prominence to these ideas. Judge delivered before the main Parliament a lengthy presentation on "the lost chord of Christianity," as he often called reincarnation. The next night, also before the Parliament, he discussed rebirth from the viewpoint of the universal law of cycles. His speech, however, was abruptly interrupted by one of the Parliament managers—a Presbyterian minister—who explained to the crowd that as there was no one at the Presbyterian meeting, it was believed that many members had wandered into the present hall by mistake owing to a confusion in the notifications and so would they please leave immediately. Not a person in that vast audience stirred![7] At the close of the historic gathering, Dr. Barrows announced:

> The Parliament has shown that Christianity is still the great quickener of humanity . . . that there is no teacher to be compared with Christ, and no Saviour excepting Christ. . . . I doubt if any Orientals who were present misinterpreted the courtesy with which they were received into a readiness on the part of the American people to accept Oriental faiths in place of their own.[8]

Historian Carl Jackson, however, discovered that the impressions of other witnesses had quite a different tone:

> Observers at the sessions repeatedly noted the positive impression that the Asian lecturers made. Affirming that the Parliament had become a "fact" whose "principles and lessons" could "never again be eliminated" from the American Christian consciousness, Florence Winslow ascribed much of the impact to the "strong personalities" of the men who had represented Hinduism, Buddhism,

Confucianism, and Shintoism at the congress. Their "seriousness, earnestness, devoutness and spirituality" precluded any thought that the Oriental religions would "fall or melt into mist" before a triumphant Christianity. She lauded Dharmapala as the "gentlest of men, almost Christian in his reverence for Christ" and eulogized Vivekananda as "one of the most thoroughly and broadly educated men" of the day as well as a "magnificent orator."

Lucy Monroe, who provided a running coverage of the sessions in *The Critic,* was also deeply struck by Dharmapala and Vivekananda, whom she proclaimed the "most impressive figures of the Parliament." She suggested that perhaps the "most tangible result" of the Parliament had been the "feeling it aroused in regard to foreign missions." "The impertinence of sending half-educated theological students to instruct these wise and erudite Orientals was never brought home to an English-speaking audience more forcibly."[9]

This seems a far cry from the prevailing view in Western lands eighteen years previously, when HPB commenced her public work to counteract the notion that Asians were ignorant savages and their religion a motley of superstitious beliefs. But her efforts were not the first in this direction. The American transcendentalists Emerson, Thoreau, and Whitman spoke freely of their admiration of the East. Among others, there was also Sir Edward Arnold, famous for his *The Light of Asia* on the life of Buddha and for his translation of *The Bhagavad-Gita,* under the title of *The Song Celestial*—Gandhi's favorite rendition into English of this Hindu classic. In 1888 Queen Victoria, in recognition of Arnold's work, made him Knight Commander of the Indian Empire. When Tennyson died in 1892, Arnold was her choice for poet laureate of England. Prime Minister Gladstone, however, wanted a fundamentalist.

Sir Edwin, when interviewed, was once asked if he had ever met HPB. He replied:

I knew Madame Blavatsky very well and am acquainted with Col. Olcott and A. P. Sinnett and I believe there is no doubt that the theosophical movement has had an excellent effect upon humanity. It has made a large number of people understand what all India always understood, and that is the importance of invisible things. The real universe is that which you do not see, and the commonest Indian peasant knows that to be true by inheritance. The theosophists have impressed upon the present generation the necessity of admitting the existence of the invisible. The senses are very limited, and everybody ought to know that behind them lies an illimitable field of development.[10]

In the chapter "An Evening with Sir Edwin Arnold" in the Very Reverend E. C. Paget's *A Year Under the Shadow of St. Paul's,* he wrote: "On Madame Blavatsky's name being mentioned Sir Edwin spoke of his acquaintance with her and of her extraordinary mental attainments. As an illustration, he said that he had once quite casually referred to her for the date of a celebrated Sanscrit grammarian which she at once gave with perfect exactness and with the utmost readiness."[11]

In turn, HPB's appreciation of Arnold is evident, for in her will she asked that her friends gather together each year on the anniversary of her death day and read from Arnold's *The Light of Asia* and from *The Bhagavad-Gita,* no specified edition. White Lotus Day is now celebrated around the world by Theosophists. It was named such by Colonel Olcott because at Adyar, India, on the first anniversary of HPB's passing, lotuses grew with unusual profusion.

Chapter 3

Science and The Secret Doctrine

In 1988, the time of the centenary anniversary of the publication of *The Secret Doctrine,* a number of symposia on the work were held in the United States, Europe, and India. At one presentation at Culver City, California, leading American Theosophist, Jerry Hejka-Ekins observed:

> It is unlikely that a book reviewer receiving *The Secret Doctrine* back in 1888 would judge the work as one that would last beyond a few reprintings. It is a ponderous work of some 1500 pages, filled with Far Eastern philosophical and religious terms contrasted with nineteenth-century science and its now discarded theories. But somehow, after a hundred years, *The Secret Doctrine* remains in print and is still being studied. . . .
>
> What is it about *The Secret Doctrine* that makes it endure and continue to influence today's thinking where other works have been long forgotten? Perhaps it is that the book is really a twentieth-century work, written 100 years before its time. . . . Unless the writer of *The Secret Doctrine* had been able to anticipate future discoveries, the book would have quickly become dated in the light of an advancing science. Yet HPB made the prophecy that "it is only in the twentieth-century that portions, if not the whole, of the present work will be vindicated" (2:442).[12]

Prophecies are rarely made in *The Secret Doctrine.* The one that follows is particularly arresting because specific dates were given as to its fulfillment (1:611):

> The exact extent, depth, breadth, and length of the mysteries of Nature are to be found only in Eastern esoteric sciences. So vast and so profound are these that hardly a few, a very few of the highest Initiates—those *whose very existence is known but to a small number of*

Adepts—are capable of assimilating the knowledge. Yet it is all there, and one by one facts and processes in Nature's workshops are permitted to find their way into the exact sciences while mysterious help is given to rare individuals in unraveling its arcana.

It is at the close of great cycles, in connection with racial development, that such [disclosures] generally take place. We are at the very close of the cycle of 5,000 years of the present Aryan Kaliyuga; and between this time [1888] and 1897 there will be a large rent made in the Veil of Nature, and materialistic science will receive a death-blow.[13]

There are two parts to the prophecy. The first raises the question as to whether there were any remarkable discoveries unveiled to science in the nine-year period just mentioned. David Deitz, in his work *The New Outline of Science,* gives a helpful overview:

The history of civilization discloses few contrasts greater than that furnished by the difference in viewpoint of the nineteenth-century physicists and their successors in the twentieth century. As the nineteenth century drew near its close, physicists felt that they had completed their tasks. One eminent scientist of the time, making an address in 1893, said that it was probable that all the great discoveries in the field of physics had been made. He sketched the history and development of the science, finally summarizing the well-knit, and as he thought, all-sufficient theories of the nineteenth century. The physicist of the future, he said sadly, would have nothing to do but repeat and refine the experiments of the past, determining some atomic weight or constant of nature to an additional decimal place or two.[†]

And then, two years later, on December 28, 1895, Wilhelm Conrad Roentgen presented the secretary of the Physical Medical Society of Würzburg with his first written report of his [accidental] discovery of x-rays. On the first day of 1896 he mailed copies of the printed article to scientific friends in Berlin and elsewhere. With them he sent some prints of the first x-ray photographs he had taken . . . the most spectacular of all showed the bones of the human hand. Here was exactly what the speaker of 1893 had said could not happen: a new discovery had been made. . . . Roentgen had found some mysterious rays which penetrated opaque objects as easily as sunlight poured through window glass. There was nothing

† ["The chairman of the physics department at Harvard discouraged graduate study because so few important matters remained unsolved." (Gary Zukav, *The Dancing Wu Li Masters,* New York, Bantam, 1980, 311.)]

in nineteenth-century physics to explain this startling phenomenon. . . . Not only the scientists but people everywhere were
excited by the news. Roentgen found himself world famous overnight. [He was awarded the first Nobel Prize for physics in 1901.]

The next major discovery in the realm of atomic physics was that
of radioactivity, made [in 1896] a few weeks after Roentgen's announcement, by Antoine Henri Becquerel in Paris. Becquerel's
father, also a physicist, had investigated fluorescence, the fact that
many substances when exposed to sunlight subsequently glowed in
the dark. Becquerel recalled his father's work and wondered if there
was any similarity between fluorescence and x-rays. Accordingly, he
wrapped a photographic plate in black paper and placed upon it a
crystal of a uranium salt which his father had used. He exposed the
arrangement to sunlight. Upon developing the plate he found it
fogged or darkened, proving that some ray had indeed penetrated
the black paper. He supposed that the action of the sunlight had
caused the uranium to give off x-rays.[14]

In preparation for further experiments, Becquerel accidentally discovered not the x-rays he was looking for but radioactivity. Remarked the
eminent physicist Robert Millikan:

Radioactivity was revolutionary to human thought, for it meant
that some, even of the "eternal atoms," namely, those of uranium
and thorium, are unstable and are spontaneously throwing off with
great energy pieces of themselves, thus transforming themselves
into other atoms. . . . Of all the new discoveries it was the most
startling to human thought and the most stirring to human imagination, for it destroyed the idea of the immutability of the elements
and showed that the dreams of the alchemists might yet come
true.[15]

The next "unveiling" to come within the time period predicted
in *The Secret Doctrine* was the most important of all, the discovery of
the electron in 1897 by Sir J. J. Thomson. Dr. Karl Compton, former
president of the Massachusetts Institute of Technology, made this
comment in his 1936 address as retiring president of the American
Association for the Advancement of Science:

The history of science abounds with instances where a new concept
or discovery has led to tremendous advances into vast new fields . . .
whose very existence has hitherto been unsuspected. . . . But to my
notion, no such instance has been so dramatic as the discovery of the

electron, the tiniest thing in the universe, which within one generation has transformed a stagnant science of physics, a descriptive
science of chemistry and a sterile science of astronomy into dynam-
ically developing sciences fraught with intellectual adventure, inter-
relating interpretations and practical values.[16]

Thomson's discovery was the culmination of a series of experiments initiated earlier by Sir William Crookes, who had been engaged
in the study of electrical discharges in a high vacuum in a Crookes'
tube, invented by him. The tube became the prototype for the television tubes and fluorescent lighting in use today. Crookes' experiments
implied a fourth state of matter, which he called radiant matter and
which twenty years later turned out to be electrons! It is interesting that
in 1888, in *The Secret Doctrine* (1:621), HPB predicted that Crookes'
"discovery of radiant matter will have resulted in a further elucidation
with regard to the true source of light, and revolutionize all the present
speculations."

The discovery of the electron, remarks renowned American physicist, Robert Millikan, was "the most useful to mankind, with its myriad of extensions and applications to radio, to communications of all
kinds, to motion pictures, and to a score of other industries. . . ." Discoveries in the sciences have been greatly accelerated by use of electronic instruments.

The Secret Doctrine itself has been used for practical purposes. Major
Hubert S. Turner, the inventor of the coaxial telephone cable, which
was laid across the United States in the late 1940s, used in connection
with the invention some key passages in *The Secret Doctrine* (1:129–32)
regarding the "Ring Pass-Not"† and applied their profound occult
ideas to the world of physical force.[17]

The prophecy in *The Secret Doctrine* under consideration affirmed that
as a result of the "large rent made in the veil of nature . . . materialistic science will receive a death blow." In *Time, Matter and Values,* Millikan concluded after recounting the new discoveries in physics:
"Result, dogmatic materialism in physics is dead."[18] Raymond F.
Yates, in *These Amazing Electrons,* asserts: "The old school was in full
retreat. Physics was totally at sea. It was momentarily stunned by an
avalanche of ponderous questions. The last solid brick had fallen from
the edifice of materialism and the neat little system of categories and

† The "Ring Pass-Not" is that which divides the world of form from the formless world.

pigeon-holes it had so laboriously arranged had fallen with a sickening thud."[19]

According to David Deitz, as the nineteenth century closed, it was apparent that "a major revolution had occurred in the realm of physics." He continues:

> Four significant discoveries—x-rays, radioactivity, radium, and the electron—convinced scientists that their task was only beginning, not ending. The time had come to invade the interior of the atom. It is doubtful, however, if anyone foresaw, at the dawn of the twentieth century, the major advances that would be made in theoretical understanding or the spectacular applications that would arise from this new knowledge.[20]

The cycle of scientific awakening that accompanied the discovery of the electron continued to evolve with two additional discoveries, further undermining the foundation of materialistic doctrines:

> 1900—*Quantum Physics.* Max Planck laid the foundations of quantum theory by observing that matter emits and absorbs radiation in discrete packets or quanta, later called photons by Einstein, showing that light is therefore corpuscular as well as wavelike. (More than two decades later Louis de Broglie showed that matter, too, displays wave-particle duality.) In 1913, Niels Bohr posited that electrons jump from one orbit to another around an atomic nucleus by absorbing or emitting quanta of energy, without passing through the intervening space (in other words, made a quantum leap, an expression frequently used today in many contexts). This was a large step away from mechanistic doctrine.

> 1905—*Einstein's Equation $E=mc^2$.* Einstein's theory "added recognition that mass or substance is equivalent to energy and that time and space are integral parts of the substance-energy continuum make-up of the universe."[21]

As indicated in the preface to the present work, a number of scientists have been interested in *The Secret Doctrine.* According to his niece, Einstein always had a copy of it on his desk. Details as to her testimony are given in Preface endnote 11.[†] Evidence is also provided concerning the two persons who could have interested Einstein in the volumes.[22] *The Secret Doctrine* contains many teachings that were denied by the science of HPB's day but were subsequently proved

---

† See also Joy Mills comment, *Secret Doctrine Centenary: Report of Proceedings*, Pasadena, California, The Theosophical Society, 1988, 70.

true, and it is entirely possible that it contains hints of other truths that have yet to be accepted. Here are three examples in which it prefigured discoveries made in the field of physics.

1. *Atoms are divisible.* Sir Isaac Newton wrote in *Optics* that "God in the beginning formed matter in solid massy, hard, impenetrable moving particles, of such sizes and figures, and with such properties, and in such proportion to space, as most conduced to the end for which he formed them."[23] Scientists later eliminated the theology in this statement but retained the "hard, impenetrable particles" or atoms as the building blocks of the universe. When the electron was discovered in 1897, the blocks began to crumble. The atom is divisible.

Here is what HPB said in *The Secret Doctrine* (1:519–20):

> The atom *is* divisible, and must consist of particles, or of sub-atoms. . . . It is on the doctrine of the illusive nature of matter, and the infinite divisibility of the atom, that the whole science of Occultism is built.

As to infinite divisibility, a scientist friend wrote to the present author: "science has proceeded in this direction only step by step— finding first electrons, then protons, then neutrons, then quarks and other particles—each time thinking it had at last found the ultimate particle. Now it has finally reached pure waves as in string theory which corresponds to the science of the *SD*."†

When quarks were first theorized, Werner Heisenberg commented:

> Even if quarks could be found, for all we know they could again be divided into two quarks and one antiquark, etc., and thus they would not be more elementary than a proton. . . . We will have to abandon the philosophy of Democritus and the concept of fundamental elementary particles. We should accept instead the concept of fundamental symmetries, which is a concept out of the philosophy of Plato.[24]

2. *Atoms are perpetually in motion.* The scientists of HPB's day not only believed atoms were indivisible, they also believed they were mo-

---

† "In 1984," writes Stephen Hawking, "there was a remarkable change of opinion in favor of what are called string theories. . . . What were previously thought of as particles are now pictured as waves traveling down the string, like waves on a vibrating kite string." (Hawking, *A Brief History of Time,* 158, 160.)

tionless, except in the gaseous state. *The Secret Doctrine* (1:507–8 fn) states:

> Occultism says that in all cases where matter *appears* inert, it is the most active. A wooden or a stone block is motionless and impenetrable to all intents and purposes. Nevertheless and *de facto* its particles are in ceaseless eternal vibration which is so rapid that to the physical eye the body seems absolutely devoid of motion; and the spatial distance between those particles in their vibratory motion is—considered from another plane of being and perception—as great as that which separates snow flakes or drops of rain. But to physical science this will be an absurdity. . . .

Today it is difficult to believe this was ever thought to be an absurdity.

According to *The Secret Doctrine* the ceaseless motion of atoms in what we regard to be a solid object conforms to a universal law underlying the cosmos, "that there is no rest or cessation of motion in nature."[25] This accords with Einstein's views, as discussed in *The Theory of Relativity,* by Garrett Service:

> Scientific investigations show that in infinitely little, as well as infinitely great things, *all is motion . . .* we find *nothing at rest.* This being so, says Einstein in effect, motion must be regarded as the natural, as well as the actual condition of matter, a state of things that needs no explanation from us, for it arises out of the very constitution of the universe. It is the very essence of existence.[26]

In *The Secret Doctrine* (1:14), HPB affirms that "absolute abstract motion" is a symbol for the Absolute itself.

3. Matter and energy are convertible. The opposite was believed by nineteenth century science which Einstein disproved in 1905 in his famous equation $E = mc^2$. Millikan translates the equation thus:

> . . . m is mass in grams, c is the speed of light in centimeters (30,000,000,000 cm. per sec.) and E is energy in absolute energy units, namely ergs. Stated in common engineering language, Einstein's equation says that if one gram of mass is transformed into heat each second, 90 billion kilowatts of power are continuously produced.

"The conception here," adds Millikan, is *"the exceedingly important one that matter is itself convertible into radiant energy."*[27] A more general way of explaining this now proven fact is to say that matter is energy condensed, whereas energy is matter spread out.

In *The Secret Doctrine* (1:623), HPB quotes from W. Q. Judge's *Path* magazine (January 1887, 297):

> As declared by an American theosophist, "The Monads (of Leibnitz) may from one point of view be called *force,* from another *matter.* To occult Science, *force* and *matter* are *only two sides of the same* SUBSTANCE."

That substance she called *prakriti,* which emanates from primordial matter, or *mūlaprakriti* (root-matter).

In *Isis Unveiled* (1:198), HPB directly asserts the convertibility of force and matter:

> Every objective manifestation, whether it be the motion of a living limb, or the movement of some inorganic body, requires two conditions: will and force—plus *matter,* or that which makes the object so moved visible to our eye; and these three are all convertible forces. . . .

The reference that follows (*SD* 2:672) is especially interesting not only because the words *atomic energy* indicate that atoms have energy, but because HPB appears to have been the first to use this expression so common today:

> "The wave motion of living particles" becomes comprehensible on the theory of a spiritual . . . universal Vital Principle, independent of *our* matter, and manifesting as *atomic energy* only on *our* plane of consciousness.

In view of all the foregoing, it is not surprising to learn from the current publishers of *The Secret Doctrine* that orders frequently come from professors at colleges and universities. One professor at the California Institute of Technology ordered the book every few years. Upon friendly inquiry it was learned that whenever a copy was marked up too much for clear reading, he obtained a new one.

The present writer learned during a 1982 visit to Boston and Cambridge that chemistry teachers and students at the Massachusetts Institute of Technology were formulating plans to investigate teachings in *The Secret Doctrine* as related to their specialties. In 1988, it was learned from Dr. Philip Perchion, a scientist who had worked on the

atomic bomb, that teachers and students at MIT had formed an alchemical society and regularly studied *The Secret Doctrine*. He also said
that he and several chemistry teachers, mostly retired MIT professors,
meet periodically to discuss the *SD* at the Harvard Club in New York.

≈

We turn now from physics to the biological sciences, beginning
with genetics.

The scientific world hailed the deciphering of the genetic code by
James Watson and Francis Crick as solving all the major mysteries in
cell biology. Watson and Crick were awarded the Nobel Prize in physiology. Today, however, biologists are keenly aware that the puzzles are
more perplexing than ever.

The source of the genetic code is a total enigma; scientists do not
know how nature produced it. Sir Fred Hoyle points out that, within
the genetic material in the nucleus of each cell, there are 200,000 chains
of amino acids arranged in a very special, intricate pattern (diagrammed by Watson and Crick in their double helix model). The
odds against arriving at this arrangement by a series of accidents via
natural selection and random mutations, says Hoyle, is similar to the
odds against throwing five million consecutive sixes on a single die.[28]

Another mystery involves the switching on and off mechanisms in
the genes. Every cell in our body carries in its nucleus a complete set of
genes and contains all the information to reproduce a new human
being. In any one cell, however, only a few of the genes are functional.
In a skin cell, for instance, or a liver cell, or the cell of an eye lens, only
those genes that can produce that kind of cell are "turned on." All the
other genes are "turned off." If all the genes operated simultaneously,
disorganized, undifferentiated growth—cancer—would occur. So
now the biologists talk about the yet-to-be-discovered *operator* genes,
whose functions are switched on by *activator* genes and then switched
off by *regulator* genes. Among geneticists, the gene trigger is the most
hotly sought clue to the puzzle of life.[29]

To emphasize the dilemmas in cellular biology and genetics, Dr.
Lewis Thomas draws attention to the problem concerning the birth of
the human brain:

The real amazement is this: [a baby starts] out as a single cell; this
divides into two, then four, then eight, and so on, and at a certain
stage, as the cells differentiate, there emerges one cluster of cells
which will have as its progeny the human brain.

The mere existence of those special cells should be one of the great astonishments of the Earth. One group of cells is switched on to become the whole trillion-cell massive apparatus for thinking and imagining. All the information needed for learning to read and write, playing the piano, or the marvelous act of putting out one hand and leaning against a tree, is contained in that first cell. All of grammar, all arithmetic, all music.

It is not known how the switching-on occurs. . . . No one has the ghost of an idea how some of [the embryonic cells] suddenly assume the special quality of brainness.[30]

Furthermore, the brain itself is so astonishingly complex, notes *Fortune* science editor Tom Alexander, that "a long-standing puzzle is how a structure so elaborate and highly organized gets wired together." He notes: "Elementary calculations suggest that there simply cannot be enough information encoded in the DNA molecules that constitute the body's genetic blueprint to specify how two neurons—the most primitive of the brain's computers—are connected."[31] Scientists report that "the brain each day uses more connections than all the world's telephone systems" and "in a split second it has the ability to use millions of interconnections."[32]

Now in *The Secret Doctrine* (2:149), HPB states: "*The whole issue of the quarrel between the profane and the esoteric sciences depends upon the belief in, and demonstration of, the existence of an astral body within the physical,* the former independent of the latter." She indicates that the "inner soul of the physical cell—the 'spiritual plasm' that dominates the germinal plasm" is to be found therein and that this is "the key that must open one day the gates of the terra incognita of the biologist now called the dark mysteries of embryology" (1:219).

The subject is considered so important in *The Secret Doctrine* that, of the three fundamental propositions underlying Volume 2, one is "the birth of the *astral,* before the physical body, the former being a model for the latter." In *The Ocean of Theosophy,* W. Q. Judge writes:

The astral body is made of matter of very fine texture as compared with the visible body, and has a great tensile strength, so that it changes but little during a lifetime, while the physical alters every moment. . . . [The astral] is flexible, plastic, extensible, and strong. The matter of which it is composed is electrical and magnetic in its essence, and is just what the whole world was composed of in the dim past when the processes of evolution had not yet arrived at the point of producing the material body for man.[33]

According to this teaching, this design body is not separate from the physical one but permeates and sustains the physical. Without the design body, the physical body could not cohere. The design body is said to grow apace with the physical; thus at conception it would be microscopic in size but perfect in shape.

Among evidences brought forward as to the existence of the astral body is the familiar phenomenon of the phantom limb in cases where an arm or leg has been amputated. In such cases, says Judge, "the astral member has not been interfered with and hence the man feels as if it were still on his person, for knives or acid will not injure the astral model. . . ."[34]

Dr. Oliver Sacks, the neurologist who wrote the bestseller *The Man Who Mistook His Wife for a Hat,* says of phantom limbs:

> All amputees, and all who work with them, know that a phantom limb is essential if an artificial limb is to be used. Dr. Michael Kremer writes: "Its value to the amputee is enormous. I am quite certain that no amputee with an artificial lower limb can walk on it satisfactorily until the body-image, in other words the phantom, is incorporated into it.". . . One such patient, under my care, describes how he must "wake up" his phantom in the mornings: first he flexes the thigh-stump towards him, and then he slaps it sharply—"like a baby's bottom"—several times. On the fifth or sixth slap the phantom suddenly shoots forth, rekindled, *fulgurated,* by the peripheral stimulus. Only then can he put on his prosthesis and walk.

The literature on phantoms is confusing, Dr. Sacks says, as to whether they are pathological or whether they are real. But patients are not confused. One of them says:

> There's this *thing,* this ghost-foot, which sometimes hurts like hell—and the toes curl up, or go into spasm. This is worse at night, or with the prosthesis off, or when I'm not doing anything. It goes away when I strap the prosthesis on and walk. I still feel the leg then, vividly, but it's a *good* phantom, different—it animates the prosthesis, and allows me to walk.[35]

In June of 1981 the publication in England of Rupert Sheldrake's *A New Science of Life: The Hypothesis of Formative Causation* set the fires of controversy raging. *Nature,* one of Britain's leading scientific magazines, called it "the best candidate for burning there has been for many years," while the equally distinguished *New Scientist* stated: "It is quite clear that one is dealing here with an important scientific inquiry into the nature of biological and physical reality." Arthur Koestler called Sheldrake's theory ". . . an immensely challenging and stimulating hypothesis, soberly presented, which proposes an unorthodox approach to evolution."

In the United States it attracted such attention that Sheldrake was invited to speak in Washington before the Congressional Committee for the Future. As to his educational background, Sheldrake was a scholar of Clare College, Cambridge, where he read Natural Sciences. After spending a year as a Frank Knox Fellow at Harvard University studying philosophy and the history of science, he returned to Cambridge and took a Ph.D. in biochemistry. He was a Fellow of Clare College and Director of Studies in biochemistry and cell biology from 1967 to 1973, and as a Rosenheim Research Fellow of the Royal Society, carried out research at Cambridge on the development of plants and on the aging of cells. He is also a member of the Theosophical Society in Britain. On October 6, 1984, he gave a one-day seminar at the Theosophical Society in Wheaton, Illinois. A report was written up by Professor Ralph H. Hannon (*American Theosophist,* Dec. 1984). Dr. Hannon reports:

After being introduced by Dr. Renée Weber, Professor of Philosophy at Rutgers University, to an audience of over 130, including many scholars and scientists, Dr. Sheldrake began by explaining the basic concept of his theory. Besides the already known fields of science, such as gravitational fields, Sheldrake has hypothesized morphogenetic fields, or M-fields. He says these are invisible organizing structures that mold or shape things like crystals, plants, and animals, and also have an organizing effect on behavior. In other words, this field becomes a kind of blueprint that regulates and forms subsequent units of the same type. These new units "tune" into (or "resonate" with) and then repeat the previously created "archetype," which can operate across time and space. Stated another way, as each new unit is formed and shaped, it reinforces the M-field and the "habit" is established. This theory extends all the way from molecular crystals to complex living organisms. An important point is that it becomes progressively easier and faster for subsequent units of whatever species we are discussing to adopt the structure. Eventually, the structure appears inherent and virtually changeless.

Sheldrake first discussed the conventional genetics programming and DNA doctrine. According to this, the way in which organisms develop is somehow "programmed" into their DNA. He then argued that DNA indeed codes the sequence for amino acids, which form protein. But from the M-fields standpoint, the form and organization of cells, tissues, organs and organisms as a whole are governed by a hierarchy of morphogenetic fields that are not inherited chemically but are, instead, given directly by "morphic resonance" from past organisms of the same species.

To clarify this idea, Dr. Sheldrake used the analogy of a television set. Imagine a person who knows nothing about electricity. He is shown a television set for the first time. He might at first think that the set actually contains little people, whose images appear on the screen. But after looking inside and finding only wires and transistors, he might hypothesize that the images somehow arise from complicated interactions among the components of the set. This theory would seem particularly plausible in light of the fact that the images become distorted or disappear when components are removed. If it were then suggested that the images in fact depend upon invisible influences entering the set from far away, he might reject it. His theory that nothing comes into the set from the outside would be reinforced by the discovery that the set weighs the same whether turned "on" or "off."

This point of view may resemble the conventional approach to biology, where wires, transistors, etc., correspond to DNA, protein molecules, etc. Sheldrake agrees that genetic changes can affect the inheritance of form or instinct by altering the "tuning" or by introducing distortions into the "reception." But genetic factors by themselves cannot fully account for the inheritance of form and instinct, any more than the particular pictures on the screen of a TV set can be explained in terms of its wiring diagram alone.

The public itself was so fascinated by Sheldrake's work that the *New Scientist,* in its October 28, 1982, issue, announced a prize of £250 (about $400) to be awarded to the individual who would devise the test "that will most critically explore" Sheldrake's idea. The Tarrytown Group is encouraging more ambitious endeavors. It will award a prize of $10,000 to the person who performs the "best test" that either confirms or refutes Sheldrake's hypothesis.

Professor Hannon continues:

Sheldrake indicated that this theory was first proposed to the scientific community in the 1920's by the renowned Harvard psychologist William McDougall. It was discovered that successive generations of rats [even stupid rats] significantly improved their ability to escape from a tank of water containing a maze. When the experiments were repeated in Scotland and Australia with unrelated strains of rats as controls, it was found that it made no difference which rats were used, all improved their performance.

Because, in Sheldrake's view, the human nervous system is also governed by M-fields, the same principle would hold true for human beings. This would have great implications for our understanding of how and why people learn. Learning of this kind would thus be a kind of basic species inheritance, more or less automatically "remembered." It would not be located in the individual brain at all, but given directly from species structure through morphic resonance. The cumulative experiences of humankind would thus indeed include the archetypical forms described by Jung.

Sheldrake's article in the special fall 1983 issue of *The American Theosophist* concludes:

Some aspects of the hypothesis of formative causation recall elements of various traditional and occult systems, for example, the concept of the etheric body, the idea of group souls of animal species, and the doctrine of the akashic records. However, it is put forward as a strictly scientific hypothesis, and as such will have to be judged by empirical test. But if the experimental evidence supports it, then it should provide a basis for a new science of life which will go far beyond the limited mechanistic biology of today.

According to the jacket of Sheldrake's book:

The reverberations of the hypothesis of formative causation could overturn many of our fundamental concepts about nature, brain function, and consciousness. For example, Sheldrake proposes that memory may not be stored in the brain but may be "given directly from its past states by morphic resonance." In psychology, he reframes a number of longstanding problems, such as the collective unconscious and psi. Sheldrake's hypothesis may also explain parallel inventions; the intuitive "knowing" of psychomotor skills, such as tennis or drawing; the apparent "body memory" of old traumas; feeding and mating behaviors; the power of ritual and symbol; accelerated learning and reinforcement; the accumulative effect of an idea held by a number of individuals; behavioral conditioning; holographic reality.

Elsewhere (*The American Theosophist,* Special Fall 1983 issue) Sheldrake suggests:

M-fields can be thought of by analogy with magnetic fields, which have a shape, even though they are invisible. [In the case of a magnet, this shape can be revealed by the patterns taken up by iron filings scattered around it.] Morphogenetic fields, through their own structure, mold developing cells, tissues, and organisms. Thus, for example, in a human embryo a developing ear is molded by an ear-shaped morphogenetic field, and a developing leg by a leg-shaped field.

But what are these fields, and where do they come from? For over fifty years, their nature and even their existence has remained obscure. However, I believed that these fields are just as real as the electromagnetic and gravitational fields of physics, but that they are a new kind of field with very remarkable properties. Like the known fields of physics, they connect together similar things across space, with seemingly nothing in between, but in addition, they connect things together across *time.*

The idea is that the morphogenetic fields which shape a growing animal or plant are derived from the forms of previous organisms of the same species. The embryo as it were "tunes in" to the forms of past members of the species. The process by which this happens is called *morphic resonance.* Similarly, the fields which organize the activities of an animal's nervous system are derived from past animals of the same kind; in their instinctive behavior, animals draw on a sort of species "memory bank" or "pooled memory."

It appears, then, that there may be a tendency in nature to share knowledge once learned. Even crystals do this. As Hannon points out: "New chemicals synthesized for the first time are indeed usually difficult to crystallize, and do in fact tend to form crystals more readily as time goes on."

One hundred years ago Theosophists were teaching of the multiple uses to which the astral world could be put. A useful chapter in W. Q. Judge's booklet *Echoes from the Orient* (chapter 21, page 59) states:

Probably in the whole field of Theosophic study there is nothing so interesting as the astral light. Among the Hindus it is known as Akasa, which can also be translated as ether. Through a knowledge of its properties they say that all the wonderful phenomena of the Oriental Yogis are accomplished. It is also claimed that clairvoyance, clairaudience, mediumship, and seership as known to the

Western world are possible only through its means. It is the register of our deeds and thoughts, the great picture gallery of the earth, where the seer can always gaze upon any event that has ever happened, as well as those to come. . . . [It] permeates every atom of the globe and each molecule upon it. Obeying the laws of attraction and repulsion, it vibrates to and fro, making itself now positive, and now negative. This gives it a circular motion which is symbolized by the serpent. It is the great final agent, or prime mover, cosmically speaking, which not only makes the plant grow but also keeps up the diastole and systole of the human heart.

Very like the action of the sensitive photographic plate is this light. It takes, as Flammarion says, the pictures of every moment and holds them in its grasp. For this reason the Egyptians knew it as the Recorder; it is the Recording Angel of the Christian, and in one aspect is Yama, the judge of the dead in the Hindu pantheon, for it is by the pictures we impress therein that we are judged by Karma. . . .

As it preserves the pictures of all past events and things, and as there is nothing new under the sun, the appliances, the ideas, the philosophy, the arts and sciences of long-buried civilizations are continually being projected in pictures out of the astral into the brains of living men. This gives a meaning not only to the oft-recurring "coincidence" of two or more inventors or scientists hitting upon the same ideas or inventions at about the same time and independently of each other, but also to other events and curious happenings.

Some self-styled scientists have spoken learnedly of telepathy, and other phenomena, but give no sufficient reason in nature for thought-transference or apparitions or clairvoyance or the hundred and one varieties of occurrences of an occult character noticed from day to day among all conditions of men. It is well to admit that thought may be transferred without speech directly from one brain to another, but how can the transference be effected without a medium? That medium is the astral light. The moment the thought takes shape in the brain it is pictured in this light, and from there is taken out again by any other brain sensitive enough to receive it intact. . . .

Yet all I have referred to here are only instances of a few of the various properties of the astral light. So far as concerns our world it may be said that astral light is everywhere, interpenetrating all things; to have a photographic power by which it grasps pictures of thoughts, deeds, events, tones, sounds, colors, and all things. . . .

The astral light is a powerful factor, unrecognized by science, in the phenomenon of hypnotism. Its action will explain many of the problems raised by Binet, Charcot and others, and especially that class in which two or more distinct personalities seem to be assumed by the subject, who can remember in each only those things and peculiarities of expression which belong to that particular stratum of their experience. These strange things are due to the currents in the astral light. In each current will be found a definite series of reflections, and they are taken up by the inner man, who reports them through speech and action on this plane as if they were his own. By the use of these currents too, but unconsciously, the clairvoyants and clairaudients seem to read in the hidden pages of life.

This light can therefore be impressed with evil or good pictures, and these are reflected into the subconscious mind of every human being. If we fill the astral light with bad pictures . . . it will be our devil and destroyer, but if by the example of even a few good men and women a new and purer sort of events are limned upon this eternal canvas, it will become our Divine Uplifter.

[According to *Theosophy* magazine, November 1988]:

In his new book, *The Presence of the Past—Morphic Resonance and the Habits of Nature* (Times Books, 1988), Sheldrake explores the implications of formative causation in the areas of psychology, sociology, and culture . . . Fortunately, morphic resonance is a function that can be tested over a period of years. . . . While the tests involving new skills have no reported results as yet, it is of interest to see what has occurred with the experiments involving long-established skills. All of them indicate the effect of something like morphic resonance. For instance, groups in America and Britain were asked to learn three short Japanese nursery rhymes, one well known to generations of Japanese children. The other rhymes were composed to resemble the first, but unknown in Japan. The traditional rhyme was easier to learn. Other tests using foreign words, half real and half scrambled, were given to people who did not know the language. Again, the real words were easier to learn. Similar experiments were made with the Morse code and the keyboard of the typewriter, patterns that have been generally accepted for over a hundred years. In both cases the established correlations and sequences were easier to learn than any others they were able to devise. . . .

Speaking of Sheldrake's work, David Spangler, in his book *Emergence* (page 103) comments:

[It] has tremendous implications for the transmission of knowledge and behavior.[†] It and other similar theories coming out of the fields of chemistry and biology suggest that a cultural transformation and the adoption of a new paradigm could come about very swiftly— out of the learning and embodiment of the essentials of that new vision by only a few members of our species.

The images emerging out of science have similar characteristics and implications. They all indicate the holistic nature of the universe. They also all indicate the power and influence of each part of that universe: no single individual is too unimportant to be able to make a contribution. From this flows other values of the new paradigm: its humanistic orientation, its commitment to ecology, its encouragement of a transcendental world view, its support of community and the arts of connectedness and ways of empowering the individual, such as greater decentralization in the political and economic realms.

The most arresting evidence for the astral design body comes from two Yale scientists, Harold Saxton Burr and S. C. Northrop, who discovered in the body of all creatures what they call an *electric architect*—a construct that recalls Judge's description of the astral body as "electrical and magnetic" in nature. Their paper on this was presented before the National Academy of Science after four years' study of the organic development of salamanders and mice. The professors describe the electrical phenomena accompanying their growth, the patterns of which were recorded on electrocardiographs and electroencephalographs, revealing definite characteristics for each species. In a *New York Times* report (April 25, 1939), the science editor provides this nontechnical statement of the significance of the experiments:

There exists in the bodies of living things an electrical architect who molds and fashions the individual after a specific predetermined pattern, and remains within the body from the pre-embryonic stages until death. All else in the body undergoes constant change; the individual myriads of cells of which the body is made, excepting the brain cells, grow old and die, to be replaced by other cells, but the electrical architect remains the only constant throughout life, building the new cells and organizing them after the same pattern of the original cells, and thus, in a literal sense, constantly recreating the

† Gallup poll for 1982 (George Gallup, Jr., *Adventures in Immortality,* New York, MacGraw-Hill, 198–200) states that eight million people in the United States have had some kind of near-death experience!

body. Death comes to the individual after the electrical architect within him ceases to function.

The electrical architect promises a new approach to the understanding of the nature of life and the living processes. It indicates that each living organism possesses an electrodynamic field, just as a magnet emanates all around it a magnetic field of force. Similarly, the experimental evidence shows, according to Dr. Burr, that each species of animals and very likely also the individuals within the species have their characteristic electric field, analogous to the lines of force of the magnet.

This electric field, then, having its own pattern, fashions all the protoplasmic clay of life that comes within its sphere of influence after its image, thus personifying itself in the living flesh as the sculptor personifies his idea in stone.

Thirty-three years later, Burr published his *Blue-print for Immortality: The Electric Patterns of Life*. He reported that "for nearly half a century the logical consequences of this theory have been subjected to rigorously controlled experimental conditions and met with no contradictions."[36]

A writer in *New Scientist* (January 26, 1982), reviewing recent experiments in "electrophysiology," asks: "Why has the work been pursued by only a handful of researchers when earlier results had been so promising?" He concludes that "the answer may have to do with trends and fashions that shape every field of science." The new experiments taking advantage of the latest electronic equipment available have revealed previously undetected electric fields associated with the growth of fertilized egg cells into embryos. The writer continues:

Hitherto mysterious events in morphogenesis (the origin of forms) now invite re-investigation, with electrical studies the starting point. . . . One of the most spectacular of these mysteries is the formation of the nervous system. The questing migratory tips of nerve cells—growth cones—creep throughout the body, often for distances that are immense compared with the size of the nerve cell, to innervate their various target organs. What tells the growth cone where to go?

Perhaps it simply traveled on the appropriate lines of magnetic force in the astral pattern body. As to the solution of the puzzle of the switching on and off of the genes, an experiment conducted by Burr and Northrop would provide an answer. They transplanted the eye-making cells of a salamander to its tail. In the new electromagnetic environment, the genes became tail-making ones.

A more fundamental problem now arises as to the astral design body. Who or what are the designers? This opens up the whole subject of the Theosophical view of evolution and its prime movers, described in both volumes of *The Secret Doctrine*. Basically, the teaching is: "The Universe is worked and *guided from within* outward. . . . The whole Kosmos is guided, controlled, and animated by an endless series of Hierarchies of sentient beings, each having a mission to perform. . . . They vary infinitely in their respective degrees of consciousness and intelligence."[37] The most advanced might be called the architects of the universe, beings who were once human and are now godlike in powers and duties.

Support for this theory came soon after HPB died and from an unexpected quarter, the celebrated biologist Thomas Huxley, leading Darwinist of the nineteenth century, and an arch skeptic most of his life. In *Some Essays on Controversial Subjects,* he wrote:

> Looking at the matter from the most rigidly scientific point of view, the assumption that, amidst the myriads of worlds scattered through endless space, there can be no intelligence, as much greater than man's as his is greater than a blackbeetle's, no being endowed *with powers of influencing the course of nature* as much greater than his, as his is greater than a snail's, seems to me not merely baseless, but impertinent. Without stepping beyond the analogy of that which is known, it is easy to people the cosmos with entities, in ascending scale until we reach something practically indistinguishable from omnipotence, omnipresence, and omniscience. (Italics added.)

Huxley also changed his views on consciousness:

> I understand the main tenet of Materialism to be that there is nothing in the universe but matter and force. . . . *Kraft und Stoff*—force and matter—are paraded as the Alpha and Omega of existence. . . . Whosoever does not hold it is condemned by the more zealous of the persuasion to the Inferno appointed for fools or hypocrites. But all this I heartily disbelieve. . . . There is a third thing in the universe, to wit, consciousness, which I cannot see to be matter or force, or any conceivable modification of either.[38]

Alfred Russel Wallace, who evolved the theory of natural selection independently of Darwin, freely admitted the limitations of the theory. He believed that the guiding action of "higher intelligences" is a "necessary part of the great laws which govern the material universe." He added that natural selection could not explain how artists and musical and other aesthetic talents arose, inasmuch as they gave no competitive advantage in the struggle for survival.[39]

In *The Secret Doctrine* (2:648–9), we find the following:

"Natural Selection" is no Entity; but a convenient phrase for describing the mode in which the survival of the fit and the elimination of the unfit among organisms is brought about in the struggle for existence. . . . But Natural Selection. . . . *as a Power,* is in reality a pure myth; especially when resorted to as an explanation of the origin of species. Of itself, "it" *can produce nothing,* and only operates on the rough material presented to "it."

The real question at issue is: what CAUSE—combined with other secondary causes—produces the "variations" in the organisms themselves. Many of these secondary causes are purely physical, climatic, dietary, etc., etc. Very well. But beyond the secondary aspects of organic evolution, a *deeper principle has to be sought for.* The materialist's "spontaneous variations," and "*accidental* divergencies" are . . . powerless to account for the stupendous complexities and marvels of the human body for instance. . . . The underlying [cause of] variation in species . . . is a sub-conscious intelligence pervading matter, ultimately traceable to a REFLECTION of the Divine and Dhyan-Chohanic Wisdom.

Wallace's views, as summarized by Professor Roszak, show natural selection in a similar light: "In his eyes adaptation was essentially conservative and unenterprising. It moves in a purely horizontal direction. . . . If evolution was merely a matter of survival by adaptation, we might still be a planet of hearty bacteria. . . . Overlaying it Wallace saw a more daring vertical movement which boosts evolution toward higher levels of complexity and consciousness." And this vertical movement had its impulse from a spiritual source.[40]

The Secret Doctrine indicates that the vertical movement comes chiefly at strategic points in the evolutionary journey. This would receive support from the recent theory of punctuated equilibria, which reveals that Darwin's theory of gradual changes is not borne out by the fossil records. As *Newsweek* (November 3, 1980) reports: "Increasingly, scientists now believe that species change little for millions of years, and then evolve quickly, in a kind of quantum leap. . . ." The distinguished anthropologist Loren Eiseley discusses this theory in relation to the human brain in his book *The Immense Journey:*

As one great student of paleoneurology, Dr. Tilly Edinger recently remarked, "If man passed through a Pithecanthropus phase, the evolution of his brain has been unique, not only in its result but also in its tempo. . . . Enlargement of the cerebral hemispheres by fifty percent seems to have taken place, speaking geologically, within an instant, and without having been accompanied by any major increase in body size."[41]

This might coincide with the period discussed in *The Secret Doctrine* of the "lighting up" of the mind by the incarnation of human souls from a prior world into hitherto mindless human forms.[42] Having reached the human stage in a prior world, there would be no need for the soul to go through the animal stage all over again.

Blavatsky's view that natural selection and accidental random mutations could not possibly produce a world as complex as ours is independently accepted by more and more scientists today, as is the case with Dr. Freeman Dyson, professor of physics at the Institute for Advanced Studies at Princeton. The following selection from his new book, *Infinite in All Directions,* was considered of sufficient importance for *Time* to quote in its April 1988 issue:

I don't think that this universe came together by accident. The mind, I believe, exists in some very real sense in the universe. But is it primary or an accidental consequence of something else? The prevailing view among biologists seems to be that the mind arose accidentally out of molecules of DNA or something. I find that very unlikely. It seems more reasonable to think that mind was a primary part of nature from the beginning and we are simply manifestations of it at the present stage of history. It's not so much that mind has a life of its own, but that mind is inherent in the way the universe is built, and life is nature's way to give mind opportunities it wouldn't otherwise have.[43]

In the book itself, Dyson quotes from a 1985 lecture, "Life and Mind in the Universe" by Dr. George Wald, emeritus professor of biology at Harvard and co-recipient of the 1967 Nobel Prize for physiology:

I and practically all biologists and most other people had supposed that consciousness or mind was a late product in the evolution of animals. The idea came to me that instead of that, the constant pervasive presence of mind guided matter in that direction. I realized that I was in the best of company; that ideas of this essential kind were millennia old in the Eastern philosophies. And numbers of people among the monumental group of physicists [of the first half of the twentieth century] had come to exactly that kind of thought. I found Eddington at one point saying the stuff of the world is mind stuff and giving it the primary place over matter. Von Weizsacker, a rather philosophical physicist, spoke of what he called the identity principle, that mind and matter are the twin aspects of all reality.[44]

Such speculation inevitably leads to consideration of not only life on earth, but elsewhere in the universe. They also concern such problems as whether evolutionary development on earth is wiped out when the planet and the solar system die.

A professor at Princeton once spoke to Einstein about the professor's son, a brilliant college student who was so dejected and depressed he refused to continue his studies or do anything else. He was worried not about his own death, but about the death of the solar system! Someday, he said, it would all go to pieces, and then everything accomplished on earth would go for naught. It would be as if nothing really happened here at all, so why bother to do anything now?

Darwin was concerned with the same problem. In a letter to his son, he spoke of the inevitable destruction of our solar system, when "the sun with all the planets will grow too cold for life. Believing as I do that man in the distant future will be a far more perfect creature than he now is, it is an intolerable thought that he and all other sentient things are doomed to complete annihilation after such long-continued progress. To those who fully admit the immortality of the human soul, the destruction of our world will not appear so dreadful."[45]

Darwin may not have been speaking of the ordinary view of immortality—that of permanent escape into a heavenly state after one brief sojourn here. He seems to intimate that evolution, as a process, might continue from world to world, if souls are in fact imperishable, which in this case would mean being reborn. The possibility that worlds—and even the galactic universes as a whole—reincarnate—is a subject currently engaging the serious attention of astronomers and physicists. *New York Times* essayist Malcolm Browne reported several years ago:

> Two rival theories about the ultimate fate of the universe are running neck and neck just now. The excitement of the race has spurred astronomers, mathematicians, particle physicists, chemists and theorists to search their specialties for clues that might contribute something to the outcome. The question is whether the universe is "open" and will continue forever its present apparent expansion, or whether it is "closed," destined one day to stop

expanding and fall back on itself, to be then reborn. If the universe is "open" and ever expanding, then, of course, the energy needed to sustain life would eventually become so dispersed as to be unusable, and everything would die.

Some scientists develop personal preferences for one kind of *Gotterdämmerung* or another. There are those who would prefer an open one-shot universe, considering it to be consistent with biblical scripture. Some others would prefer a closed, oscillating universe, esthetically akin to the Hindu wheel of death and rebirth.[46]

Sir Stephen Hawking, who holds the post at Cambridge once held by Sir Isaac Newton, is regarded by many as the leading physicist of recent times. He reveals in his widely acclaimed book *A Brief History of Time: From the Big Bang to Black Holes* that at first he believed in an "open universe," in which the cosmos was destined to permanent destruction. But now he and his colleagues view the universe as continually expanding and contracting, without beginning or end. Consequently, the Big Bang eruption was not the first of its kind. He comments: "It is an interesting reflection on the general climate of thought before the twentieth century that no one had suggested that the universe was expanding or contracting. It was generally accepted that either the universe had existed forever in an unchanging state, or that it had been created at a finite time in the past more or less as we observe it today."[47]

Understandably, Hawking never read the following in *Isis Unveiled* (2:264–5), which HPB thought of sufficient importance to repeat in *The Secret Doctrine* (1:3–4), with one minor correction:

The esoteric doctrine teaches, like Buddhism and Brahmanism, and even the Kabbalah, that the one infinite and unknown Essence exists from all eternity, and in regular and harmonious successions is either passive or active. In the poetical phraseology of Manu these conditions are called the "Days" and the "Nights" of Brahma. The latter is either "awake" or "asleep.". . .

Upon inaugurating an active period, says *The Secret Doctrine,*[†] an expansion of this Divine essence from without inwardly and from within outwardly, occurs in obedience to eternal and immutable law, and the phenomenal or visible universe is the ultimate result of the long chain of cosmical forces thus progressively set in motion. In like manner, when the passive condition is resumed, a contraction of the Divine essence takes place, and the previous work of

† Before *The Secret Doctrine* was produced, HPB often used this expression in her writings.

creation is gradually and progressively undone. The visible universe becomes disintegrated, its material dispersed; and "darkness" solitary and alone, broods once more over the face of the "deep." To use a metaphor from the Secret Books, which will convey the idea still more clearly, an outbreathing of the "unknown essence" produces the world; and an inhalation causes it to disappear. *This process has been going on from all eternity, and our present universe is but one of an infinite series, which had no beginning and will have no end.*

The central concept in the Big Bang theory is that the universe began with the explosion of a "small spark" of substance from which ultimately all the stars and galaxies emanated. In *The Secret Doctrine* (1:1–5), where the stages of development of the cosmos are symbolically diagrammed, there is an analogous statement, except that here the universe begins in spirit, not in matter:

> An Archaic Manuscript—a collection of palm leaves made impermeable to water, fire, and air, by some specific unknown process—is before the writer's eye. On the first page is an immaculate white disk within a dull black ground. On the following page, the same disk, but with a central point. The first, the student knows to represent Kosmos in Eternity, before the re-awakening of still slumbering Energy, the emanation of the Word in later systems. The point in the hitherto immaculate Disk . . . denotes the dawn of differentiation. It is the point in the Mundane Egg, the germ within the latter which will become the Universe, the ALL, the boundless, periodical Kosmos, this germ being latent and active, periodically and by turns.

Later, HPB quotes approvingly a French theorist who speculated that the entire cosmos can be concentrated "in a single point" (*SD* 1:489). Another *SD* reference (1:379) speaks of "the Universe evolving from the central Sun, the POINT, the ever-concealed germ." [The capitalization of "POINT" is hers].

Owing to recent discoveries, the Big Bang theory is being seriously questioned today. It was hitherto believed that the explosive matter was randomly spewed out in every direction. However, recently astronomers have found what they refer to as a grid of eight galaxies with equal light-years of space separating them. One of the discoverers of this grid was so discouraged that he said it looks as though we are totally ignorant of how the universe began and must start all over again from scratch.

Then, at the annual meeting of the American Astronomical Society on January 10, 1990, it was announced, as reported by the *New York*

Times (January 12) under the heading "Found: A Continent of Galaxies That Draws Others Toward It":

> Astronomers reported today that they had confirmed the existence of one of the largest concentrations of galaxies and matter ever found. . . . Called the "great attractor" and 150 million light-years from Earth, the huge structure exerts a steady gravitational pull on the Milky Way and millions of other galaxies. . . .
>
> The discovery confirms theories discussed in astronomy for the last several years that the basic objects in the universe are far larger and more complicated than astronomers had imagined. The objects are not simply galaxies or clusters of them, but huge "continents of galaxies" a hundred times larger.
>
> The galaxies in the attractor do not expand away from one another as those in the rest of the universe do, but instead are "falling" together into a region that is hundreds of millions of light-years wide. The speed of the movement, 400 miles a second, was also surprising. It suggested that these galaxies were being drawn toward something. . . . Most convincing, astronomers said, was that some galaxies studied were on the opposite side of the attractor from the Milky Way; they were found to be drawn toward the attractor as well. . . .
>
> Under the current descriptions of the history of the universe, it would take longer than the universe has existed for a structure this large to form. Dr. Schramm said theories must now be developed to create a new mechanism at the beginning of the universe that could account for the huge structures. . . . The great attractor is one of a number of huge structures whose existence has been theorized in the past few years, including the "great wall," which is thought to be a great "sheet" of galaxies stretching for a billion light years.
>
> [These structures are no longer *theorized* but appear to be facts.][48]

This discovery may be of immense importance. Until now, it has been only a speculation on the part of scientists that the present expansion of worlds and galaxies in the Big Bang universe might some day reverse itself, but the Great Attractor continent of galaxies gives weight to this theory.† The theory of periodical rebirth of the universe then could gain additional support.

† It may be proved later that these newly discovered enormous groupings of galaxies really belong to universes other than the so-called Big Bang universe. After all, it was only sixty-five years ago that galaxies were recognized to exist *outside* our Milky Way galaxy.

In light of such vast considerations, it may seem of small moment that some twenty years ago the first astronauts landed on the moon, even though it was one of the big moments in our history on earth. On the twentieth anniversary of the event, physician and biologist Dr. Lewis Thomas was asked to contribute some thoughts on the occasion. These were featured in the *New York Times* on July 15, 1989. Thomas first spoke of the moon walk and the varied impressions it evoked, continuing:

> But the moment that really mattered came later, after the equipment had been set up for taking pictures afield. There, before our eyes, causing a quick drawing in of breath the instant it appeared on television screens everywhere, was that photograph of the Earth.
>
> Suspended just above the moon's horizon, light and round and shimmering like a bubble, deep blue with pure white clouds scattered across its face, it was the loveliest object human beings had ever looked upon: home. Moreover, as anyone could plainly see in the photograph, it was *alive*. That astonishing and round thing, hanging there all alone . . . was a living thing, a being. That photograph, all by itself, was the single most important event in the whole technical episode, and it hangs in the mind 20 years later, still exploding in meaning.
>
> The notion that life on Earth resembles, in detail, the sort of coherent, connected life we attribute to an organism is now something more than a notion. Thanks in large part to the studies begun in the 1970's by James Lovelock, Lynn Margulis and their associates, we now know that planetary life, the "biosphere," regulates itself.
>
> It maintains in precision the salinity and acid-base balance of its oceans, holds constant over millions of years the exactly equilibrated components of its atmosphere with the levels of oxygen and carbon dioxide at just the optimal levels for respiration and photosynthesis. It lives off the sun, taking in the energy it requires for its life and reflecting away the rest into the unfillable sink of space. This is the "Gaia hypothesis," the new idea that the Earth itself is alive. . . .
>
> Finally, as something to think about, there is the strangest of all paradoxes: the notion that an organism so immense and complex, with so many interconnected and communicating central nervous systems at work, from crickets and fireflies to philosophers, should be itself mindless. I cannot believe it.

It was the picture of the earth from the moon as a "dappled sapphire" that inspired the chemist and biophysicist Dr. Lovelock to initiate the scientific studies described in his book *Gaia, A New Look at Life on Earth,* published in 1979 by Oxford University Press. [Lovelock holds degrees in chemistry, medicine, and biophysics.] Yet his "new idea" had been formulated by HPB and other Theosophists a century ago. Judge wrote a fascinating story, "The Skin of the Earth," on this subject. In his *Ocean of Theosophy* he speaks of the earth as an "entity and not a mere lump of gross matter."[49]

In *The Secret Doctrine* (1:49), HPB says:

> The idea of universal life is one of those ancient conceptions which are returning to the human mind in this century, as a consequence of its liberation from anthropomorphic theology. Science, it is true, contents itself with tracing or postulating the signs of universal life, and has not yet been bold enough even to whisper "Anima Mundi!" The idea of "crystalline life," now familiar to science, would have been scouted half a century ago. . . . It hardly seems possible that science can disguise from itself much longer, by the mere use of terms such as "force" and "energy," the fact that things that have life are living things, whether they be atoms or planets.

Nobel Prize-winning scientist Brian Josephson, professor of physics at Cambridge, appears to concur in much of the foregoing. He remarked in an interview:

> There may be elements of intelligence in every atom of matter and, like the world's biological forms, it may undergo evolution toward even higher levels. . . . Physicists tend to think of matter as something lifeless and mechanical and are conceptually on the wrong track. At the tiniest level, matter seems to behave much more like something biological and living. There may be an underlying life and intelligence below the phenomenon we ordinarily see and even beyond the phenomenon being studied by physics. . . . Similarly, there appears to be a mysterious wholeness or unity to all matter that scientists can't explain but which is frequently described in Eastern religions.[50]

It may come as a surprise to learn that Sir Isaac Newton also regarded the whole of nature as being alive. Malcolm Browne reports this in a *New York Times* article (April 10, 1990) on the new interest among scientists in the alchemists:

> The ranks of the alchemists included a few of the greatest scientists of all time, Isaac Newton and Robert Boyle among them. Although Newton's renown rests on his landmark discoveries in physics and

mathematics, about half of his career was devoted to alchemy, a fact that has disturbed some of his modern admirers. But Dr. Betty Jo Teeter Dobbs, a professor of history at Northwestern University who has studied Newton's work for many years, regards alchemy as central to his career, not just an aberration.

Dr. Dobbs argues in a new book[51] that Newton, a puritan, feared what he considered to be the rise of atheism.† She asserts that he embraced the alchemical notion of universal animation, an infusion by God of the divine spirit into all things.

Here we have an example of a great scientific mind who was also deeply religious. Newton was not unique in this connection. A 1984 volume, *Quantum Questions, Mystical Writings of the World's Great Physicists,* examines the writings of Heisenberg, Schroedinger, Einstein, de Broglie, Jeans, Planck, Pauli, and Eddington—"all of whom express a deep belief that physics and mysticism are somehow fraternal twins. . . . Each of these remarkable men, without exception, came to believe in a mystical or transcendental world view that embodies the world as a spiritual, rather than material, phenomenon."[52]

This would appear to support the underlying thesis of *The Secret Doctrine* that, as its subtitle indicates, a synthesis of science, religion, and philosophy is possible. The following selections from Einstein's writings suggest that, for the father of relativity, science and religion are far from incompatible:

The most beautiful and most profound emotion we can experience is the sensation of the mystical. It is the sower of all true science. He to whom this emotion is a stranger, who can no longer wonder and stand rapt in awe, is as good as dead. To know that what is impenetrable to us really exists, manifesting itself as the highest wisdom and the most radiant beauty which our dull faculties can comprehend only in their primitive forms—this knowledge, this feeling is at the center of true religiousness.[53]

I maintain that cosmic religious feeling is the strongest and noblest motive for scientific research. Only those who realize the immense efforts and, above all, the devotion without which pioneer work in theoretical science cannot be achieved are able to grasp the strength of the emotion out of which alone such work, remote as it

---

† "The innermost thoughts and ideas of Newton were perverted," writes HPB, "and of his great mathematical learning only the mere physical husk was turned to account. Had poor Sir Isaac foreseen to what use his successors and followers would apply his 'gravity,' that pious and religious man would surely have quietly eaten his apple, and never breathed a word about any mechanical ideas connected with its fall." (*SD* 1:484.)

is from the immediate realities of life, can issue. . . . It is cosmic religious feeling that gives a man such strength. A contemporary has said, not unjustly, that in this materialistic age of ours the serious scientific workers are the only profoundly religious people.[54]

The next selection from Einstein's thoughts is quoted in the *Autobiography of Robert A. Millikan:* "It is enough for me to contemplate the mystery of conscious life, perpetuating itself through all eternity—to reflect upon the marvelous structure of the universe, which we can dimly perceive—and to try humbly to comprehend even an infinitesimal part of the *intelligence* manifested in nature."[55]

The idea that nature manifests intelligence appears far removed from the concept that prevails today among many scientists that randomness, chance, and lawlessness reign in both the subatomic world and in the vast reaches of space where universes are born and die. In a June 1990 television program, "The Quantum Universe," in the series "Smithsonian World," a Russian scientist, Roger Rees, asserted that "quantum mechanics made everything finally random. A thing could go this way or that. The mathematics deny certainty; they reveal only probability and chance."[56]

In *The Emperor's New Mind,* English Physicist Dr. Penrose reveals himself as one of a growing number of physicists who think Einstein was not being stubborn when he said his "little finger told him that quantum mechanics is incomplete."[57] Penrose adds that "puzzles, in one guise or another, persist in *any* interpretation of quantum mechanics as the theory exists today."[58] He believes that in the future, quantum theory will "undergo some fundamental changes," at which time deeper laws may be discovered that will explain even the great mystery of human consciousness,[59] as well as what appears to be random action of atomic particles.

In the latter connection, a quote from HPB's article "Kosmic Mind" seems appropriate: ". . . every atom, like the monad of Leibnitz, is a little universe in itself [and manifests a degree of consciousness.]" She refers to the similar views of Thomas Edison: "I do not believe that matter is inert, acted upon by an outside force. To me it seems that every atom is possessed by a certain amount of primitive intelligence: look at the thousand ways in which atoms of hydrogen combine with those of other elements. . . . Do you mean to say they do this without intelligence?" HPB added that "Mr. Edison is a theosophist, though not a very active one. Still the very fact of his holding a diploma seems to inspire him with Theosophical truths."[60]

Applied in practice, and adapting Heisenberg's law of probabilities, one can predict what a mass of atoms or atomic particles will do but cannot predict what an *individual unit* will do. One can find examples of this so-called choice everywhere in nature.

HPB admits that her views concerning the presence of intelligent life throughout the cosmos will be regarded as reviving "the superstitions of *crazy* alchemists."[61] This is reminiscent of a story told by physicist Heinz Pagels in *Cosmic Code: Quantum Mechanics as the Language of Nature.*

According to this story Pauli once came to Pupin Laboratory at Columbia University to give a lecture upon Heisenberg's new nonlinear theory of elementary particles. Niels Bohr was in the audience, and after the lecture he remarked that the new theory couldn't be right because it wasn't crazy enough. Bohr and Pauli were soon standing on opposite ends of a table with Bohr saying, "It's not crazy enough" and Pauli responding with "It's crazy enough." It would have been hard for an outsider to realize what was at stake for those two great physicists and that it wasn't simply madness. Both Bohr and Pauli knew that the craziness of the quantum theory turns out to be right.

In Heinz Pagel's words:

All profound human creations are beautiful, and physical theories are no exception. An ugly theory has a kind of conceptual clumsiness which it is impossible to hold in the mind for too long. . . . The first time new ideas appear they are often bizarre and strange, and if the ideas are correct, beauty is seen later. . . . When physicists really understand the internal logic of the cosmos it will be beautiful.[62]

Could there be a more beautiful concept than that from galaxies to atom, conscious intelligent life is universal and there is no dead matter anywhere? If this is true, it would answer the great enigma as to whether other worlds are inhabited, for if minerals are alive, then of course all worlds are inhabited. In *The Secret Doctrine* (2:699) is the arresting statement that all globes "are, were, or will be 'man-bearing.'" HPB elsewhere quotes the Kabbalistic aphorism that "a stone becomes a plant, a plant a beast; the beast a man; a man a spirit; and the spirit a god."[63]

≈

The ancient view propounded in *The Secret Doctrine* that life is universal and in essence spiritual imposes a grave responsibility upon human beings to use that life beneficently. Man's frightful misuse and abuse of matter has threatened the survival of the earth.

In response to this threat more than a thousand religious, political, and scientific leaders from eighty-three nations attended a conference in Moscow in January 1990 sponsored by the Global Forum of Spiritual and Parliamentary Leaders on Human Survival. The twenty-three scientists present, including three Nobel laureates, issued an appeal for an alliance between religion and science. Besides recognizing the power of religion to shape behavior, the scientists said: "Many of us have had profound experiences of awe and reverence before the universe," adding that they believe "efforts to safeguard and cherish the environment need to be infused with a vision of the sacred."

What makes the appeal especially startling is that its author was astronomer Carl Sagan. In his popular television series "Cosmos" and in his best-selling book of the same name, he often evinced antagonism toward religion, and he was accused of regarding science as a monolithic repository of truth. When interviewed respecting the appeal, Sagan said he had become increasingly aware of the universality of religion and of its potential as "a force for good." Although other signers of his draft, he added, had sought to revise phrases about global warming or the ozone layer, not one had questioned the language about religion, reverence, and the sacred.[64] There was one note of dissent, however, which came from a clergyman. He said it was a mistake to regard nature or man as sacred—that only God is sacred.

Other religionists have expressed fear that if all life is regarded as holy, a return to primitive pantheism, when people worshipped stones and trees, is likely. *The Secret Doctrine* in its section "Summing Up" (1:279–80) has some passages on worship worth pondering:

(1) *The Secret Doctrine* teaches no *Atheism,* except in the Hindu sense of the word *nastika,* or the rejection of *idols,* including every anthropomorphic god. In this sense every Occultist is a *Nastika.*

(2) It admits a Logos or a collective "Creator" of the Universe; a *Demiurgos*—in the sense implied when one speaks of an "Architect" as the "Creator" of an edifice, whereas that Architect has never touched one stone of it, but, while furnishing the plan, left all the manual labour to the masons; in our case the plan was furnished by the Ideation of the Universe, and the constructive labour was left to the Hosts of intelligent Powers and Forces. But that *Demiurgos* is no *personal* deity—*i.e.,* an imperfect *extra-cosmic god*—but only the aggregate of the Dhyan-Chohans and the other forces.

As to the latter—

(3) They are dual in their character; being composed of *(a)* the irrational *brute energy,* inherent in matter, and *(b)* the intelligent soul

or cosmic consciousness which directs and guides that energy, and which is the *Dhyan-Chohanic thought reflecting the Ideation of the Universal mind.* . . . As that process is not always perfect; and since, however many proofs it may exhibit of a guiding intelligence behind the veil, it still shows gaps and flaws, and even results very often in evident failures—therefore, neither the collective Host (Demiurgos), nor any of the working powers individually, are proper subjects for divine honours or worship. All are entitled to the grateful reverence of Humanity, however, and man ought to be ever striving to help the divine evolution of *Ideas,* by becoming to the best of his ability a *co-worker with nature* in the cyclic task.

The ever unknowable and incognizable *Karana* alone, the *Causeless* Cause of all causes, should have its shrine and altar on the holy and ever untrodden ground of our heart—invisible, intangible, unmentioned, save through "the still small voice" of our spiritual consciousness. Those who worship before it, ought to do so in the silence and the sanctified solitude of their Souls; making their spirit the sole mediator between them and the *Universal Spirit,* their good actions the only priests, and their sinful intentions the only visible and objective sacrificial victims to the *Presence.*

The journey in the present chapter began with a consideration of the prophecy in *The Secret Doctrine* that a large rent would be made in the veil of science during the nine-year period 1888–97. A scientist friend who has gone into this prophesy and its fulfillment in greater depth than is possible here came to the conclusion, "The veil of nature was indeed rent asunder with a gash so unexpected, so staggering, so strange, with follow-on penetrations so unimaginably deep into the smallest and largest realms of nature, with such overwhelming consequences for science in all areas, and for man's daily way of living that there is no parallel in all of our recorded history."

Chapter 4

From Yeats to Thornton Wilder and Beyond

IRISH LITERARY RENAISSANCE

John Eglinton, in his 1937 biography of George Russell, *A Memoir of Æ,* observes:

> Probably there has never been in any country a period of literary activity which has not been preceded or accompanied by some stimulation of the religious interest. . . . Anyone in search of this in Ireland at this time will find it, unless he disdains to look in that direction, in the ferment caused in the minds of a group of young men by the early activities of the theosophical movement in Dublin. The proof is, not only that there was no other religious movement in Ireland at this time, but that Yeats and Russell, who were to be the principal leaders of the Literary Revival, were closely associated with this one.

In *Irish Literature and Drama,* Stephen Gwynn mentions that these two men "were to dominate the entire literary revival and affect the whole intellectual life of Ireland in their time."[65]

In 1896, Russell wrote to Yeats: "The gods are filling Ireland with fire; mystics are arriving from everywhere, as H. P. Blavatsky and W. Q. Judge prophesied. What Emerson did for America we can do now with even greater effect."[66]

In his book *Ireland's Literary Renaissance,* Ernest Boyd writes:

> The theosophical movement provided a literary, artistic and intellectual center from which radiated influences whose effect was felt even by those who did not belong to it. Further, it formed a rallying ground for all the keenest of the older and younger intellects, from John O'Leary and George Sigerson, to W. B. Yeats and Æ. It brought into contact the most diverse personalities, and definitely

widened the scope of the new literature, emphasizing its marked advance on all previous national movements. . . . It was an intellectual melting-pot from which the true and solid elements of nationality emerged strengthened, while the dross was lost.

Boyd tells how the Theosophical movement in Dublin originated one afternoon in 1885 in the house of Edward Dowden, author of *The Life of Shelley.* Yeats was present:

> Somebody mentioned a strange book which had recently appeared, *Esoteric Buddhism* by the theosophist A. P. Sinnett. Yeats procured a copy and recommended it to his boyhood companion Charles Johnston, who wanted to be a Christian missionary. After reading the book Johnston was converted to the author's views, and thereafter he and a few others joined with Yeats to regularly meet together to discuss such subjects. The *Dublin University Review* announced that "a Society has been started in Dublin to promote Oriental religions and theosophy generally. It has been called the Hermetic Society. . . ."[67]

In the next year, Johnston went to London to interview Blavatsky. Together with Claude Falls Wright[68] they helped form the Dublin Theosophical Lodge, which drew within its influence many other Irish writers of that period.

"These young enthusiasts," says Boyd, "created in time a regular center of intellectual activity, which was translated in part into some of the most interesting literature of the Irish Revivals. Their journals *The Irish Theosophist,* the *Internationalist,* and *The International Theosophist,* contained a great deal of matter which has since taken a high place in modern Anglo-Irish literature."[69] The most important one, *The Irish Theosophist,* ran through five volumes, beginning October 1892.

When HPB was living at 17 Lansdowne Road she wrote to Miss Georgie Johnston (sister of Charles):

> . . . *I am glad to see such a genuine sincere thirst for knowledge in the Irish Fellows. It is the Irish* invariably *who were, and are the best members of the TS and my best loved and trusted friends. When all the Anglo-Indians arose against me in India and several English fellows deserted me in 1884 it is Captain Bannon, Capt. O'Grady and five or six others who remained my staunch supporters and defended me through thick and thin. I trust in the Irish and I love the Irish ever since 1851 when Johnny O'Brien saved my life in Greece and got nearly killed himself.*[70]

William Butler Yeats (1865–1939)

T. S. Eliot viewed Yeats as "one of the few whose history is the history of their own time, who are a part of the conscience of an age which cannot be understood without them."[71]

One of the first contacts Yeats had with Theosophy was in 1884, when Mohini Chatterji came to Ireland with Olcott, during the period HPB visited Europe. One year later, when he was going to art school, he read Sinnett's *Occult World* and his *Esoteric Buddhism*. The experience was overwhelming, and he cut classes to continue these studies. He became an active member of the Dublin TS and its predecessor, the Hermetic Society, of which he was chairman. In 1887, the Yeats family moved to London. He first visited HPB when she was at Maycot and then later at Lansdowne Road, where he became a member of the Blavatsky Lodge. When the Esoteric Section was formed in 1888 he was one of the early members.

Professor William York Tindall, in a 1942 essay "Transcendentalism in Contemporary Literature," includes this analysis of Yeats's interest in Blavatsky:

> In her capacity of middleman between East and West, this extraordinary woman enlightened Yeats, who was ready to receive what she had to offer. For some years he had held the biologists and physicists responsible for the materialism of the West and for the spiritual limitation that accompanied it. Darwin, Huxley, and Tyndall, he complained in the early 1880's, had robbed him of the religion of his youth and had given him nothing with which to replace it. Forced by his intellect and their teachings to accept materialism, he was miserable under it and he longed for something to satisfy the persistent, irrational yearnings of his soul. The Church of Ireland would no longer do. . . . In this quandary he discovered theosophy, which . . . offered his soul, without apparent offense to his intellect, the expansion it desired.

Tindall believed that Yeats's experience was typical among a number of writers of his time: "For the literary man wandering in T. S. Eliot's wasteland or between [Matthew] Arnold's two worlds, theosophy has been a favorite resort. . . ."

That Yeats's interest in HPB was in earnest from its inception can be gathered from some of his letters of that period. To John O'Leary he wrote:

> Come to see her when you are in London. She is the most human person alive, is like an old peasant woman, and is wholly devoted,

all her life is but sitting in a great chair with a pen in her hand. For years she has written twelve hours a day.[72]

In one of his *Letters to the New Island* he reports:

H. P. Blavatsky . . . is certainly a woman of great learning and character. A London wit once described her as the low comedian of the world to come. This unkind phrase, anything but an accurate account of this strange woman, had this much truth, that she can always enjoy a joke even against herself.[73]

And in his "Occult Notes and Diaries" there is this entry:

I believe Madame Blavatsky's teachers are wholly righteous learned teachers and that I have in them all due confidence as from pupil to teacher.[74]

In these "Occult Diaries" Yeats also indicated his disappointment with the Esoteric Section because no occult experiments were conducted, and so he brought pressure on HPB to experiment. Knowing that she believed such investigations could be dangerous, he was surprised she agreed to his trying his hand at them. He reports:

I was always longing for evidence, but ashamed to admit my longing, and having read in Sibly's *Astrology* that if you burned a flower to ashes, and then put the ashes under a bellglass in the moonlight, the phantom of the flower would rise before you. I persuaded members of the section who lived more alone than I and so could experiment undisturbed to burn many flowers without cease.[75]

Such futile abuse of nature disturbed the members, and as Yeats was apparently unwilling to suspend his activities, he was politely asked to resign. He left the movement in 1889.

In Yeats's famous autobiography, the section "Four Years 1887–1891" treats of his relationship with HPB. It also speaks of his association with The Golden Dawn and with one of its chief founders, MacGregor Mathers, kabbalist and Theosophist, author of *The Kabbalah Unveiled.* When the 1922 edition of Yeats's autobiography was published under the title *The Trembling of the Veil,* Mathers's wife, Moira, sister of the noted French philosopher Henri Bergson, was disturbed by Yeats's analysis of her late husband and wrote the poet:

[Your] inaccuracies may be due to the fact that you have reported events and impressions of so many years ago and when you had become so completely out of touch with the original of your portrait. . . . I have noted also your study of HPB, another great Pioneer who has made the way easier for you and for me. You can never have seen the soul behind those eyes, though you have so admirably described the shell of her.[76]

Yet from the excerpts that follow, he did seem at times to catch a glimpse of the real HPB:

She sat nightly before a little table covered with green baize and on this green baize she scribbled constantly with a piece of white chalk. She would scribble symbols, sometimes humorously explainable, and sometimes unintelligible figures, but the chalk was intended to mark down her score when she played patience. One saw in the next room a large table where every night her followers and guests, often a great number, sat down to their vegetable meal, while she encouraged or mocked through the folding doors. A great passionate nature, a sort of female Dr. Johnson, impressive I think to every man or woman who had in themselves any richness, she seemed impatient of the formalism and the shrill abstract idealism of those about her, and this impatience broke out in railing and many nick-names: "Oh you are a flap-doodle, but then you are a theosophist and a brother.". . .

Besides the devotees who came to listen and to turn every doctrine into a new sanction for the puritanical convictions of their Victorian childhood, cranks came from half Europe and from all America, and they came that they might talk. One American said to me, "She has become the most famous woman in the world by sitting in a big chair and permitting us to talk." They talked and she played patience, and totted up her score on the green baize, and generally seemed to listen, but sometimes she would listen no more. There was a woman who talked perpetually of "the divine spark" within her, until Madame Blavatsky stopped her with—"Yes, my dear, you have a divine spark within you and if you are not very careful you will hear it snore!". . .

I found her almost always full of gaity that, unlike the occasional joking of those about her, was illogical and incalculable and yet always kindly and tolerant. I had called one evening to find her absent but expected every moment. She had been somewhere at the seaside for her health and arrived with a little suite of followers. She sat down at once in her big chair, and began unfolding a brown paper parcel while all looked on full of curiosity. It contained a large family Bible. "This is a present for my maid," she said. "What a Bible and not even annotated," said some shocked voice. "Well, my children," was the answer, "what is the good of giving lemons to those who want oranges?". . .

As to the Masters, recalls Yeats:

[All the members of HPB's household] seemed to feel their presence, and all spoke of them as if they were more important than any visible inhabitant of the house. When Madame Blavatsky was more silent, less vivid than usual, it was "because her Masters were angry"; they had rebuked her because of some error, and she professed constant error. Once I seemed in their presence, or that of some messenger of theirs. It was about nine at night, and half a dozen of us sat round her big tablecloth, when the room filled with the odor of incense. Somebody came from upstairs, but could smell nothing—had been outside the influence it seems—but to myself and the others, it was very strong. Madame Blavatsky said it was a common Indian incense, and that some pupil of her "Master's" was present; she seemed anxious to make light of the matter and turned the conversation to something else. Certainly it was a romantic house, and I did not separate myself from it by my own will.[77]

In the foregoing, as in his other writings, one can discover no acknowledgment on Yeats's part that Blavatsky in any way influenced his poetry or prose.[†] However, recent writers have found many evidences that she did. A sampling of these works is listed in endnote 78.

An overall picture of what Yeats owed to HPB is given by Richard Ellmann, the famed biographer of Joyce. Quoting from his biography *Yeats: The Man and the Mask:*

As to specific doctrines, Yeats accepted tacitly most of what the theosophists believed, though he understandably preferred to attribute the doctrines to Boehme, Swedenborg, and other reputable sources whom he was now inspired to read, rather than to Blavatsky. . . . Whether her ideas took immediate effect or remained latent in his mind, they gave his thought a basis, and the work in which he afterward embodied his philosophy and theology, *A Vision,* is full of connections with theosophy. . . .

[†] Privately, Yeats did admit to John Eglinton, in a general way, that the Theosophical Society "had done more for Irish literature than Trinity College in three centuries." (Eglinton, *Irish Literary Portraits,* 94.)

After providing examples of other possible borrowings, Ellmann continues:

> The occult and religious traditions compounded by theosophy contained much that was sensible, even profound. . . . What Yeats now hoped to do was to systemize his knowledge, to put his intuitions and those of the great poets and mystics together, to perform experiments and demonstrate the existence of an occult world, to describe that world more exactly and stylistically than Madame Blavatsky had done. . . . Theosophy had furnished him with shield and sword, and he went forth like Don Quixote, though with some hesitancy, to tilt at the windmills of modern life. . . . Notwithstanding his final excommunication, five or six years of theosophy, three of them years of active membership under the organization's founder, had left their mark on Yeats.[79]

Yeats's work brought him success and honor. In 1923 he received the Nobel Prize for literature. Upon addressing the Swedish Royal Academy, he said: "When your king gave me medal and diploma, two forms should have stood, one at either side of me, an old woman sinking into the infirmity of age and a young man's ghost." In the symbology of the Kabbalists' tree of life, these forms are Chocma [Hokhmah] and Binah, maternal love's understanding and bright intellect.[80] However, at the inception of his career there *was* an old woman standing at his side, protecting him as a beloved son, as the following instance reveals.

In the original manuscript of what became his autobiography, Yeats wrote of HPB: "I remember how careful she was that the young men about her should not overwork," and then added: "I overheard her saying to some rude stranger who had reproved me for talking too much, 'no, no, he is very sensitive.' "[81] At another time he said that perhaps one attraction he had for HPB was that in her presence he escaped "from the restlessness of my mind." She was "humorous, unfanatical, and displaying always, it seemed, a mind that seemed to pass all others in her honesty."

More than once HPB protected Yeats from involvement in psychic practices. Yeats wrote to Irish writer John O'Leary: "You need not be afraid of my going in for mesmerism. It interests me but slightly. No fear of Madame Blavatsky drawing me into such matters—she is very much against them and hates spiritualism vehemently—says mediumship and insanity are the same thing."[82]

Similarly, in his original autobiographical manuscript, Yeats wrote:

She often warned me against some excess of belief or practice. One night I was sitting silent among a talking group, and noticed that there was a curious red light falling on a picture in a room I could see through folding doors. I walked towards the picture, and as I came near it vanished. I came back to my place and she said, "What was it?" "It was a picture," I said, "Tell it to go away." "It is already gone." "That is right," she said, "I thought it was mediumship and it is only clairvoyance." "What is the difference?" I said. "If it were mediumship, it would stay in spite of you. Beware of that. . . ."[83]

Yeats owed a very different kind of learning experience to HPB. It is recorded in an entry dated November 3, 1925, in *Lady Gregory's Journals:*

Reading Trollope's *Phineas Finn* to Yeats in the evenings [Lady Gregory was reminded of Yeats's] first effort to speak in Parliament[†] that Birrell had said was so wonderful. . . . I asked Yeats how his speaking had begun, and he said he had become used to it in the little theosophical societies he belonged to. But his best lesson had been from Mme. Blavatsky. He had (like Phineas) prepared a speech with great care, had then written it out and read it to the assembly. It was received in dead silence and he felt that not a word of it had been understood. Mme. Blavatsky had called him over, said "Give me the manuscript. Now you go back and say your say about it." He did so with the greatest success.[84]

George W. Russell (Æ) (1867–1935)

The British scientist Raynor Johnson writes of George Russell in *The Light and the Gate:*

If it is greatness to become the embodiment of spirituality to many others, Æ may be counted probably the greatest Irishman of his day. . . . All who met him felt that he was "different"—in some way apart from them, as though he had strayed into this world from an older and wiser one with which he was more familiar. . . . He had an intense sympathy with man in his outcast state. . . . He [wrote]: "I remember the deep peace which came to me when I had the intuition that Christ, Prometheus, are in every heart, that we all took upon ourselves the burden of the world like the Christ, and

† When the Irish Free State was formed, Yeats was chosen to be one of the first senators.

were foreseers as Prometheus was, of the agony of the labor he undertook, until the chaos is subdued and wrought in some likeness to the image in the divine imagination." Much of his poetry speaks of man at this age-long task—the outcast from the "Ancestral Self"—the "fallen majesty"—making his slow way back again.[85]

As to how Æ contacted Theosophy, his biographer, Henry Summerfield, writes:

While Russell was studying art he began to write verse and shortly afterwards he was spellbound by a new student who arrived at the Metropolitan School in May 1884. This youth, two years older than himself, was slender, dark-haired, and carelessly dressed; he looked and talked like a poet, and it was not long before his conversation was full of stories about Madame Blavatsky and her centuries-old Himalayan Masters.

The young man was Yeats. A little later, while "waiting for a friend in a lodging house, he fell into conversation with a stranger, Charles Johnston, a recent school fellow of Yeats." Through this contact he was again drawn to Theosophy.[86]

A close friend of Æ wrote that at this time he was "a diffident and inarticulate youth," yet that he "assimilated theosophy with almost miraculous speed, just as though it were 'a familiar lesson temporarily forgotten, but now recalled with fuller understanding.' Within a week he was taking part in discussions with old students, and giving lectures on his new-old studies."[87]

He continues:

His grounding in theosophy was received from W. Q. Judge's articles in the *Path* and HPB's *Lucifer*. . . . Then came the great series by HPB: *The Secret Doctrine, The Voice of the Silence* and *The Key to Theosophy*. Having (to quote his own words) "bathed in these I marveled what I could have done to merit birth in an age wherein such wisdom was on offer to all who could beg, borrow or steal a copy of those works."[88]

In a letter to B. P. Wadia (October 17, 1922), a leading Theosophist in India, Russell spoke of Theosophists working in other movements besides an organized Theosophical society "and imparting to them a spiritual tendency." "I have tried to do this," he wrote, "in the economic and cultural movements I have been involved with in Ireland."[89]

Russell became an active supporter of Sir Horace Plunkett's Irish Agricultural Society. For eight years he traveled through every county of Ireland, talking to farmers about the advantage of cooperatives. For twenty years he edited the *Irish Homesteader* and for ten years the *Irish Statesman*. Owing to his vast experience in this field, he was consulted by two British prime ministers, and during the darkest days of the Depression he was invited to the United States by the Secretary of Agriculture, Henry Wallace, to undertake a lecture tour of the country to survey the work of the New Deal and to encourage the farmers in their fight against poverty.

While he was in New York, the Poetry Society held a dinner in his honor, during which each speaker in turn assured everyone that Æ was the most loved man in Ireland.[90] Honored for both his poetry and his prose, he was also an artist of note.

A question has arisen as to whether Æ ever met HPB. One witness attesting that he did is James Pryse, who reported that he first became acquainted with Russell during his frequent visits to the London Headquarters of the TS.[91] P. G. Bowen adds that these visits "were achieved through the good offices of Charles Johnston and Mrs. Johnston, whose aunt HPB was." When several people, in the presence of Æ and Yeats, questioned the genuineness of Blavatsky's phenomena, Russell reportedly turned to his friend on the way home and said: "They may say what they like, but I have seen her do some wonderful things."[92]

Yeats and Russell were the best of friends during the early period of their connection with Theosophy, but Colin Wilson remarks in his book *The Mysteries:*

Yeats and Russell drew apart after 1890. Yeats had become a member of The Golden Dawn, and Russell distrusted ritual magic. Although he accepted all the basic principles of magic—as his work reveals—Russell remained basically a mystic, absorbed in his vision of the fundamental oneness of the universe and his certainty that individual consciousness is only a tributary of the collective consciousness of humanity.

But the difference between Yeats and Russell was more fundamental than this. Russell's mystical and religious insights were deeper than anything Yeats ever experienced. Yeats remained hardheaded, consumed by intellectual curiosity, intent upon creating a bridge between the universe of the mystic and the universe of the ordinary man. The result is that Yeats is a major poet while Russell is a minor poet.[93]

Some authors speak of Æ's connection with Theosophy and the Dublin Theosophical Society as no more than a phase of Æ's early development. His own actions and words tell a different story, as indicated by Captain Bowen: "From 1898 down to 1933 when he left Ireland, Æ kept alive in Ireland a nucleus of genuine students under the name of the *Hermetic Society*." In an early letter to Bowen, Æ said:

Sometimes it had a big membership, sometimes a small. It waxed and waned, and waxed again, people coming and going here and there; and I felt inwardly satisfied that they all more or less passed through a bath of theo-sophical ideas. I had no private doctrine, nothing but HPB, W. Q. Judge, the Bhagavad Gita, Upanishads, Patanjali, *and one or two other scrip-tures. . . . I did my best to keep to the study HPB and WQJ initiated.*[94]

What endeared Russell to so many people was that he *lived* his philosophy. In 1935, at the time of his death, the *Irish Times* reported that a procession of mourners more than a mile long followed the casket to the cemetery. Summerfield writes:

A woman obviously of modest means placed an extravagant offer-ing of flowers on the grave. She had been a servant in his household during the early days of his marriage and had "got into trouble," but instead of being turned away had been cared for. On being ques-tioned about the costliness of her gift, she declared: "I would have died for him."[95]

James Joyce (1882–1941)

It would be difficult to find two people more different in temperament than Æ and James Joyce, yet when in 1902 the latter decided to make himself known in Dublin literary circles, he presented himself first to Russell. Richard Ellmann tells the story in his biography, *James Joyce*.

Russell was not home when Joyce knocked at his door at ten o'clock one night in early August. By Ellmann's account:

When his knock was not answered, he walked up and down the street until Russell returned. It was then midnight, but, unwilling to give up his idea, Joyce knocked at the door anyway and asked if it was too late to speak to him. "It's never too late," Russell coura-geously replied and brought him in. They sat down and Russell looked at Joyce inquiringly. Since Joyce seemed to experience some difficulty in explaining why he had come, Russell talked for a bit and then asked, "Has it emerged yet?" It had not.

Russell's life was divided, he told Joyce, into the three parts: economics, literature and mysticism. Was it the economics† that interested Joyce? No, it was not that. Joyce finally said shyly what he had prepared as part of his bold offensive in advance, that he thought it possible an avatar might be born in Ireland. He may have been referring to himself but his implication, as Russell understood it, was that the sight of his host comfortably smoking his pipe in an armchair had made Joyce think that the avatar was not in front of him. He remained, nevertheless, for hours, talking.

Joyce's main motive in seeking out Russell, says Ellmann, was that "he was full of useful information about Eastern philosophy and he was a means of access to other writers." They took up Theosophical subjects, "although Joyce was skeptical of theosophy as being a recourse for disaffected Protestants. . . . Nevertheless he was genuinely interested in such theosophical themes as cycles, reincarnation, the succession of gods, and the eternal motherfaith that underlies all transitory religions."

When they came to discuss the writers in Dublin, Ellmann continues:

[Joyce] allowed that Russell had written a lyric or two, but complained that Yeats had gone over to the rabblement. He spoke slightingly of everyone else, too. When pressed by Russell, he read his own poems, but not without first making clear that he didn't care what Russell's opinion of them might be. Russell thought they had merit but urged him to get away from traditional and classical forms.

This advice Joyce later accepted with a vengeance when writing his novels!

Russell ended by saying (as he afterwards remembered with great amusement), "you have not enough chaos in you to make a world."[96] However, by the time *Ulysses* was written, Joyce had enough chaos in him to change the whole world of Western writers, and it has never been the same since! Even those who detest Joyce cannot ignore him. "He made it impossible to be unaware of word choices," remarks Ted

---

† In other words, did he want money, or perhaps a job? At that time Russell was not yet involved in his work with the Irish farmers but was obliged to slave away at a job in Dublin at Pim's drapery shop.

Mooney.[97] Æ's opinion was: "I think with horror of that famous book, *Ulysses,* which is the *ultimate boundary of realism,* but I also think of it with *respect. If Joyce would write a Purgatorio and a Paradiso to the Inferno which is his 'Ulysses,'* there would be one of the greatest works in literature."[98]

In Stuart Gilbert's *James Joyce's Ulysses,* prepared by him in Paris with Joyce's constant help, he tells of Joyce's contact with Theosophy and the Irish Theosophists, and writes in the preface:

When we chanced to be discussing . . . Mme. Blavatsky's entertaining *Isis Unveiled,* [Joyce] asked me if I had read any of Sinnett's work. (A. P. Sinnett, a cultured and intelligent man, was a member of Mme. Blavatsky's circle in India, and her biographer.) Naturally I took the hint and procured his [volumes on Theosophy] *Esoteric Buddhism* and *Growth of the Soul,* well-written books from which Joyce certainly derived some of his material.[99]

In Russell M. Goldfarb's essays "Madame Blavatsky" in the *Journal of Popular Cultures* (Winter 1971), he contrasts Joyce's response to the work of HPB with that of Ernest Rhys, a friend of Yeats:

Madame Blavatsky did not tempt Ernest Rhys into becoming a convert, nor did what he read in her books strengthen his belief in her. His skepticism is echoed in James Joyce's *Ulysses* when J. J. O'Molloy says to Stephen Dedalus, "What do you think really of that hermetic crowd, the opal hush poets: Æ the master mystic? That Blavatsky woman started it. She was a nice old bag of tricks."

On the other hand whereas Rhys met and dismissed HPB, James Joyce read her works and drew upon them. In *James Joyce's Ulysses,* Stuart Gilbert constantly footnotes *Isis Unveiled* to explain Joycean references to the astral soul, reincarnation, Koot Hoomi, and HPB's elemental.

Gilbert reveals that Joyce's use of the idea of reincarnation is one of what he terms the directive themes in *Ulysses.* Gilbert has already alerted his readers to the fact that "it is impossible to grasp the meaning of *Ulysses,* its symbolism and the significance of its leitmotifs without an understanding of the esoteric theories which underly the work. . . . References to the eternal recurrence of personalities and things abound in *Ulysses* and many of the obscurer passages can be readily understood if this fact be borne in mind."[100]

Ellmann, who enumerated other directive themes derived from

Theosophy, commented that *Finnegans Wake* gathered all these up into a half-secret doctrine; one of the ideas was cycles. The American poet Eugene Jolas revealed that in the *Wake,* Joyce "painted the rotations of the wheel of life, and made a hero out of Time: incessant creation and return. He rebuilt the city across the ages in Finn's multiple metamorphoses."[101]

Leon Edel's book on Joyce asserts that "all of Joyce, from the sermons on Hell in *A Portrait of the Artist* to the last words of *Finnegans Wake,* echoes of Life, Death, and Resurrection; the cycles of history, which from the beginning measure the life of Man, were ever present in his mind."[102]

A Portrait of the Artist as a Young Man concludes with these memorable words of the hero Stephen Dedalus as he ventures forth into the world to embark upon his career: "I go to encounter for the millionth time the reality of experience and to forge in the smithy of my soul, the uncreated conscience of my race. . . . old father, old artificer, stand me now and ever in good stead."[103]

In M. J. C. Hodgert's study of *Ulysses* and *Finnegans Wake,* published in the *Cambridge Journal* (October 1952), he came to the conclusion that "Joyce considered occultism as a suitable framework for his most serious literary conceptions, as Yeats did."

BRITISH AND AMERICAN AUTHORS

Jack London (1876–1916)

London is celebrated for his novels of adventure, such as *The Call of the Wild,* his first book. One would hardly expect that one of his heroes would bring home from the library a copy of *The Secret Doctrine,* in response to a chance meeting with a Theosophist. This occurred in London's 1909 semi-autobiographical story *Martin Eden.* Another character, Stevens, is also a Theosophist. An analysis of *Martin Eden* in relation to London's career as a writer is provided in Chapter 9 of William Linville's doctoral dissertation, *Helena Petrovna Blavatsky, Theosophy and American Thought.*

Generally speaking, London's characters reveal themselves to be dominated by an enlightened selfishness, accompanied by a stubborn will to allow nothing to stand in the way of achieving their goals, while at the same time espousing the highest ethics. This position is addressed in the passages that follow from HPB's *Key to Theosophy:*

"No theosophist has the right to this name unless he is thoroughly imbued with the correctness of Carlyle's truism: 'The end of man is an *action* and not a thought, though it were the noblest'" (230).

London's "daemons of 'White Logic,'" concludes Linville, "was never to be incorporated with his theosophical impulses. He echoed HPB's ideas in many of his best works, but he never ceased to question whether or not her gentle optimism was not too 'unmanly' for Jack London to completely accept."

However, according to Linville, one idea in HPB's philosophy that London appears to have strongly accepted was reincarnation, especially in his *Before Adam* and *The Star Rover*. In the latter book we find:

All my life I have had an awareness of other times and places. I have been aware of other persons in me. . . . I, whose lips had never lisped the word "king," remembered that I had once been the son of a king. More—I remembered that once I had been a slave and a son of a slave, and worn an iron collar round my neck. . . . All my previous selves have their voices, echoes, promptings in me. . . . I am man born of woman. My days are few, but the stuff of me is indestructible. I have been woman born of woman. I have been a woman and borne my children. And I shall be born again. Oh, incalculable times again shall I be born.

This emphasis on reincarnation apparently inspired another author, James Jones, to write the passage that follows in *From Here to Eternity*:

[Prewitt] remembered one day for no good reason how Jack Malloy had always talked about Jack London all the time. . . . So he started to [read London's books] in earnest. Of them all, he liked *Before Adam* and *The Star Rover* the best because for the first time they gave him a clear picture of what Malloy had meant by reincarnation of souls.[104]

E. M. Forster (1879–1970)

Professor Russell Goldfarb observes:

One may speculate about how much Ezra Pound had to do with theosophists when he lived in Kensington about the turn of the century, or whether Dylan Thomas learned about the occult "third eye" from a few minutes with a book by HPB or from a profound study of esoteric doctrine. But there need be no speculation about E. M. Forster's interest in Madame Blavatsky, for the novelist is known to have paid continuing attention to both her and the theosophical movement.

In Forster's *Howards End,* Goldfarb points out, "Margaret Schlegel reads theosophy books, thinks about auras and astral planes, and ponders the 'endless levels beyond the grave.'" He continues, "*A Passage to India* is set in the spiritual home of theosophy, and Mrs. Moore, a leading character in the novel, may actually be modeled on Madame Blavatsky," for "that thesis is developed by Paul Fussell, who draws various parallels between Madame Blavatsky and Mrs. Moore." Goldfarb cites Fussell's article in the *Philosophical Quarterly* (October 1953) "E. M. Forster's Mrs. Moore: Some Suggestions." In it, Fussell writes:

It has for some time been a commonplace in the criticism of E. M. Forster's novels that each of his five works contains what Peter Burra has called an "elemental character." Gino, Stephen, George, Mrs. Wilcox and Mrs. Moore share certain "redemptive" characteristics, and Mrs. Moore in *A Passage to India* (1924) has been termed "the deepest of all Mr. Forster's redemptive characters." Now this somewhat spooky depth of Mrs. Moore has, I suspect, puzzled many readers who have had little trouble grasping the essential meaning of Mrs. Wilcox, of *Howards End* (1921). Mrs. Moore is, in one sense, a continuation into a new narrative context of the soul of Mrs. Wilcox, but I believe that something rare and strange has been added during the transmutation: I should like to suggest that what has been added is an infusion of certain elements of the character of Helena Petrovna Blavatsky (1831–1891). A simultaneous focus on the essential features of the two women can shed some much needed light on certain otherwise inexplicable tendencies in Mrs. Moore's character, and can help fix Forster's novel even more solidly than it has been in the spiritual and intellectual climate of its own time.

  Certain similarities between the clairvoyant Blavatsky and the grey-haired old lady who broods mysteriously over the events of *A Passage to India* can be pointed out at once: both were singularly fond of playing patience; and both are found to be strangely irritable while doing so; both visited India under rather similar circumstances, had interesting experiences in caves, and, while in India, engaged in a form of perception thought by some to have been telepathic; the two women took similar attitudes toward the British in India, and both left India ill and under like circumstances; both women felt impelled to make an effort to bring about a union of East and West, and so "solve" the problem of British India; and finally, both women, partly as a result of their attempts to help bridge the gap between the intuitive East and the more analytical West, were regarded by many in India as demigoddesses after their departure.[105]

D. H. Lawrence (1885–1930)

Present-day Asian critics, dealing with Lawrence as a key twentieth-century figure in the coming of age of the West, see him as a religious thinker in a style that is Hindu or Buddhist. As to any Theosophical influence in his writing, his earliest biographers appear totally ignorant. The first Westerner to document such influence was William York Tindall of Columbia University, in his *D. H. Lawrence and Susan His Cow,* published in 1939. Tindall interviewed Lawrence's wife, who informed him "that her husband read and delighted in all of Mme. Blavatsky's works, and that, as he read, he used to smile at the 'mundane egg,' an occult subject of which, judging by the number of allusions to it in their works, neither Mme. Blavatsky nor Lawrence ever tired."

Although Tindall discovered that Lawrence borrowed profusely from HPB, he was quick "to deny predecessors or rivals who appeared to impair his sense of his own originality," and hence downplayed their influence. Thus in 1919, when Lawrence wrote to a friend in spiritual distress, recommending Blavatsky's *Isis Unveiled* and *The Secret Doctrine,* "according to his habit," says Tindall, "he qualified his praise of what he found useful, saying that Mme. Blavatsky's books, while good, were 'not *very* much good.' " Yet, he adds, "symbolic clues to the past" given by her "were never more knowingly followed by the most orthodox theosophist."[106]

Lawrence's foreword to his *Fantasia of the Unconscious* (1922), says Tindall, "is perhaps the most important passage for the understanding of his later work" and "might have been written by Mme. Blavatsky herself." In it, he writes:

> I honestly think that the great pagan world of which Egypt and Greece were the last living terms, the great pagan world which preceded our own era once, had a vast and perhaps perfect science of its own, a science in terms of life. In our era this science crumbled into magic and charlatanry. But even wisdom crumbles.
>
> I believe that this great science previous to ours and quite different in constitution and nature from our science, once was universal, established all over the then-existing globe. I believe it was esoteric, invested in a large priesthood. Just as mathematics and

mechanics and physics are defined and expounded in the same way in the universities of China or Bolivia or London or Moscow today, so, it seems to me, in the great world previous to ours a great science and cosmology were taught esoterically in all countries of the globe, Asia, Polynesia, America, Atlantis and Europe. . . .

Then came the melting of the glaciers, and the world flood. The refugees from the drowned continents† fled to the high places of America, Europe, Asia, and the Pacific Isles. And some degenerated naturally into cave men, neolithic and palaeolithic creatures, and some retained their marvelous innate beauty and life-perfection, as the South Sea Islanders . . . and some, like Druids or Etruscans or Chaldeans or Amerindians or Chinese, refused to forget, but taught the old wisdom, only in its half-forgotten, symbolic forms. More or less forgotten, as knowledge: remembered as ritual, gesture, and myth-story. . . . And so it is that all the great symbols and myths which dominate the world when our history first begins are very much the same in every country.[107]

Tindall considers *The Plumed Serpent,* which focuses on the teachings of Quetzalcoatl, the prophet of the ancient Mexicans, to be Lawrence's most Theosophical novel. "The Great Breath of Lawrence's Quetzalcoatl," writes the biographer, "was exhaled by Mme. Blavatsky. The secret sun behind the sun, which is invoked throughout *The Plumed Serpent* is Mme. Blavatsky's central sun, the soul of all things, of which the apparent sun is only the symbol."[108]

Tindall also calls Lawrence's *Apocalypse* a Theosophical tract: "His quest of primitive truth through the symbols of the Book of Revelation, their meaning hidden beneath Christian corruptions from all but the esoteric eye, is one which Mme. Blavatsky had pursued before him in *The Secret Doctrine.*[109]

HPB, of course, was not the only source Lawrence used. His books often leaned toward primitive animism and in such cases he borrowed from scholars such as Frazer, Tylor, and Harrison.[110]

T. S. Eliot (1888–1965)

Eliot shared with Yeats the distinction of being viewed as the greatest poet of the twentieth century. Eliot's *The Waste Land* opened a new era

---

† [Lawrence mistakenly merges the sinking of the Polynesian continent (or what HPB called Lemuria) with the sinking of Atlantis. Lemuria, she said, belonged to the earlier period, when the Third Race flourished. It did not sink but was destroyed by fire or, perhaps, volcanic eruptions. The Atlanteans were Fourth Race people.]

in poetry, and the Madame Sosostris in that poem is believed to be none other than Blavatsky.[111]

> Madame Sosostris, famous clairvoyante,
> Had a bad cold, nevertheless
> Is known to be the wisest woman in Europe . . .[112]

A year or two prior to writing *The Waste Land* (1922), Eliot underwent severe nervous problems and, it is said, made a study of Theosophy. Much of the symbolism in the poem appears to reflect that study. Earlier, in 1920, his poem "A Cooking Egg" appeared, which contains these lines:

> I shall not want Pipit in Heaven:
> Madame Blavatsky will instruct me
> In the Seven Sacred Trances† . . .

Tom Gibbons's *Rooms in the Darwin Hotel* provides evidence that Eliot's works reveal "an occult correspondence between the structure of the human body and the structure of the universe." In HPB's writings, man is often shown to be the microcosm of the macrocosm. Gibbons believes "it is arguable that both 'The Waste Land' and [Joyce's] *Ulysses* are based upon different versions of the occult doctrine of correspondences between the human and divine worlds, and that they employ this doctrine in a similar vein of dramatic irony to suggest that the apparently random and pointless events of twentieth-century life are in fact part of the cosmic and spiritual pattern which unifies all creative things."[113]

Thornton Wilder (1897–1975)

Although in *Our Town* Wilder portrays the conventional Christian teaching of death, it was not necessarily his own view. His first novel, published in 1926, was titled *The Cabala,* indicating he was aware of Jewish mysticism. In his last novel, *The Eighth Day* (1967), there is evidence he looked into Theosophy as well.

In a scene from the latter book, two orderlies in a large hospital are conversing. One of them observes that "all people lead as many lives as

---

† HPB would probably prefer *meditations* to *trances,* as she viewed the latter as harmful to the human psyche at this stage of its evolution, when conscious awareness is required to reach godlike wisdom.

there are sands in the Ganges River." "What do you mean by that?" asks the other in astonishment. "We are born again and again," is the reply. "These three men here—look at them! . . . They will be dead in a few hours. . . . And they will be born again hundreds of thousands of times. . . ." "There's a mighty ladder," he continues. "In each new life a person may acquire merit that will permit him to step up a rung or two, or he may fall into error and slip back." Advanced souls, he says, will eventually "arrive at the threshold of supreme happiness. But— now mark my words—arrived at that threshold these individuals will not step over it. They will deny themselves supreme happiness. They will continue to be reborn. They will choose to wait until all others have reached that threshold."

The foregoing is taught in both Mahayana Buddhism and Theosophy. That Wilder was an admirer of Theosophy seems evident from his reference to Mrs. Besant below.

On the great ladder-of-being portrayed, which Wilder refers to as a mighty staircase, he says sometimes one can see a little further. Some, he states, have ascended not just one step *but four*: "Socrates or Mrs. Besant, or Tom Paine or Abraham Lincoln."[114]

CHILDREN'S STORIES

L. Frank Baum (1856–1919)

Baum is best known as the author of the beloved fantasy tale *The Wizard of Oz*. The book has been very popular with children ever since it was published in 1900, long before Judy Garland starred in the 1939 movie. In the article "A Notable Theosophist L. Frank Baum," Dr. John Algeo, professor of English at the University of Georgia and former editor of *American Speech,* reports that Baum became interested in Theosophy through his mother-in-law, Matilda Joslyn Gage, who joined the TS in March 1885. She was one of the leading figures in the women's rights movement in the United States, being active in it as early as the 1850s. Gage became president of the National Woman Suffrage Association and collaborated with Elizabeth Cady Stanton and Susan B. Anthony in writing the *History of Woman Suffrage.*

Baum joined the Theosophical Society in 1892. Two years before, in the opening issue of the *Aberdeen Saturday Pioneer,* of which he was editor, he had introduced his readers to Theosophy. HPB was then still alive. Baum first spoke of the insecurity many Christians felt about the challenge of other religions and the yearning of many people for knowledge outside the church:

> Among the various sects so numerous in America today who find their fundamental basis in occultism, the theosophists stand pre-eminent both in intelligence and point of numbers. . . . Theosophy is not a religion. Its followers are simply "searchers after Truth." Not for the ignorant are the tenets they hold, neither for the worldly in any sense. Enrolled within their ranks are some of the grandest intellects of the Eastern and Western worlds. . . . They accept the teachings of Christ, Buddha and Mohammed, acknowledging them as Masters or Mahatmas, true prophets each in his generation, and well versed in the secrets of nature. The theosophists, in fact, are the dissatisfied of the world, the dissenters from all creeds. . . .
>
> We have mentioned their high morality: they are also quiet and unobtrusive, seeking no notoriety, yet daily growing so numerous that even in America they may be counted by thousands. But, despite this, if Christianity is Truth, as our education has taught us to believe, there can be no menace to it in theosophy.[115]

In concluding his article Dr. Algeo writes: "Further evidence for Baum's involvement with theosophy is found in his children's books, especially *The Wizard of Oz*. . . . Theosophical ideas permeate his work and provided the inspiration for it." Indeed, *The Wizard of Oz* can be regarded as Theosophical allegory, pervaded by Theosophical ideas from beginning to end, as Algeo indicates in his follow-up article "The Wizard of Oz, The Perilous Journey."[116] The story came to Baum as an inspiration, and he accepted it with a certain awe as a gift from outside, or perhaps from deep within himself.

Owing to the popularity of this book upon its publication in 1900, Baum "converted it to the stage, and it became a highly successful musical play on Broadway, inspiring a number of similar works (such as Victor Herbert's *Babes in Toyland*)." He also wrote many other stories for children, including thirteen more Oz tales.[117]

Chapter 5

The World of Art

"**A** s theosophy moved into the twentieth century . . . spreading vigorously from country to country, it became for a time the dominant alternate culture. It was the 'school' toward which artists and seekers could look for a radically *other* description of the world and man." Thus wrote Roger Lipsey in a recent volume, *An Art of Our Own; The Spiritual in Modern Art.* Lipsey continues:

> Who among us hasn't seen and enjoyed the works of Piet Mondrian, an adherent of theosophy throughout his life? Kandinsky, long a "painter's painter" and an acquired taste, has come into his own in recent years through comprehensive exhibitions and studies. Never a proper theosophist and diverse in his interests, he was a lifetime seeker of truth who seems to have derived his basic understanding of what "truth" means from the scope and audacity of the theosophical world view.[118]

Kandinsky and Mondrian are considered the two chief founders of modern or abstract art.

Wassily Kandinsky (1866–1944)

At the centenary of Kandinsky's birth in 1866, the art critic for the *New York Times,* Hilton Kramer, contributed an article for the occasion. In tracing Kandinsky's development, Kramer discusses the crucial period when the artist studied theosophy, enabling him "to make his revolutionary leap into abstraction." He states that Kandinsky "needed a theoretical framework for carrying painting beyond the realm of representation," adding, "With a mind like his—at once intellectual and mystical, seeking 'laws' and principles before committing itself to practice—the idea must always precede its realization." According to Kramer, the artist's "commitment to theosophy guaranteed—to him, at least—that abstract art would attain a higher spiritual meaning."[119]

484

Kandinsky is especially noted for his little volume *Concerning the Spiritual in Art*. It was published in 1911 and was so timely and uplifting that avant-garde artists everywhere tuned into its message. Like all classics, it seems just as potent and beautiful today as when it first appeared. Early in the book he speaks of Blavatsky:

> Art is looking for help from the primitives [and is] turning to half-forgotten times in order to get help from their half-forgotten methods. *However, these very methods are still alive and in use* among nations whom we, from the height of our knowledge, have been accustomed to regard with pity and scorn. To such nations belong the Hindus, who from time to time confront those learned in our civilization with problems which we have either passed by unnoticed or brushed aside with superficial words and explanations.
>
> Mme. Blavatsky was the first person, after a life of many years in India, to see a connection between these "savages" and our "civilization." From that moment there began a tremendous spiritual movement which today includes a large number of people and has even assumed a material form in the *Theosophical Society*. This society consists of groups who seek to approach the problem of the spirit by way of the *inner* knowledge. The theory of theosophy which serves as the basis to this movement was set out by Blavatsky in the form of a [dialogue] in which the pupil receives definite answers to his questions from the theosophical point of view.[120]

In a footnote, Kandinsky names HPB's *Key to Theosophy* as the treatise just described. However, when it came to developing his own theories and actualizing them on canvas, he made abundant use of *The Secret Doctrine*.[121] Such is the documented conclusion of Dr. Laxmi Sihare in his doctoral thesis, *Oriental Influences on Wassily Kandinsky and Piet Mondrian, 1909–1917*. His six-year study thereof at New York University's Art School was made possible by scholarships and grants from the Rockefeller Foundation and the John D. Rockefeller 3rd Fund.†

Sihare indicates that Kandinsky was particularly interested in the following idea in *The Secret Doctrine* (1:520): "It is on the doctrine of the illusive nature of matter and the infinite divisibility of the atom that the whole science of occultism is built." The artist furthermore

† The above is mentioned in a printed notice, dated November 20, 1967, of the Division of Creative Arts of New York University, inviting the publicists to attend a series of illustrated lectures by Dr. Laxmi Sihare, sponsored by the Sperrin Foundation. It is further stated that Sihare was then "Research Consultant to the Division of Creative Arts" at NYU and formerly "Special Research Consultant to the International Council of the Museum of Modern Art."

kept abreast of scientific developments that substantiated this view, such as J. J. Thomson's discovery of the electron.[122] This was a decisive factor that led to eliminating material objects in the paintings of abstract artists. Kandinsky joyfully wrote in an early autobiography:

> The destruction of the atom to my soul was equal to the destruction of the world. Suddenly the heaviest walls broke down. Everything became uncertain, tottering and soft. I would not have been surprised if a stone had dissolved in the air in front of me and become invisible. Science seemed to me to have been destroyed; its most important basis was but an illusion, an error of the scientists, who did not build their celestial structures . . . with a steady hand, stone by stone, but were rather feeling for truth, unguided in the dark, and blindly misinterpreted one item as another.[123]

Besides Blavatsky's work, Kandinsky was interested in the writings of Annie Besant and Charles Leadbeater, especially their books *Thought Forms* and *Man Visible and Invisible*. He also drew upon the writings of Rudolf Steiner, who headed the Theosophical Society in Germany from 1902 to 1913.[124]

Piet Mondrian (1872–1944)

The most highly regarded of the founders of abstract art today is this Dutch artist. In his article "Mondrian: He Perfected Not a Style But a Vision" (*New York Times,* February 24, 1974), Hilton Kramer observed:

> Later abstractionists, particularly in America, carried the reduction of visual incident in painting to extremes Mondrian himself never dreamed of, yet his work has never been eclipsed by these later efforts. On the contrary, its stature has increased with the passage of time, and one of the reasons for this, I believe, is precisely the relation that obtains—and is seen to obtain—between his art and its metaphysical foundations. We do not feel, in the presence of a Mondrian, that we are being offered a "merely" esthetic delectation. We feel ourselves in the presence of a larger struggle—indeed, a larger world—in which mind grapples with eternal threats to its fragmentation and dissolution. . . . [Today, in art,] what were once problems of metaphysical debate and social redemption are reduced to problems of style and taste. Inevitably, the requisite tension—the inner drama of a protagonist perfecting not a style but a vision—is missing.

Frank Elgar, in his book *Mondrian,* states that the artist was "deeply concerned with matters of religion and always actively interested in theosophy," having joined the Theosophical Society as early as 1909.[125] Elgar quotes Martin James in *Art News,* in the yearly issue for 1957:

> Mondrian's theosophy was more than a personal quirk. Several artists around 1910 sought through it deeper and more universal values, meaning behind meaning, new dimensions to understanding. The thought that the ancient seers perceived and imparted a veiled wisdom, that behind the many guises of truth there is *one* truth, is partly based on Oriental and Neo-Platonic ideas; it easily links with the romantic and symbolist theory of illuminism, which gives the artist extraordinary, even occult power of insight into the nature of the world, the reality behind appearances—a new content for art.

In Sihare's 1967 doctoral thesis he was of the opinion that "among sources acknowledging Mondrian's debt to the Orient through theosophy, the views of Michel Seuphor, who has consistently written on Mondrian's works since the 1930s, should be given first priority. Brief but pithy passages from Seuphor's writings belonging to the 1950s precisely sum up his views." These include the following:

> Theosophy . . . was first of all a means of [Mondrian's] escaping the paternal influence. . . .

> It was in theosophy that he found liberation from his native Calvinism. . . .

> His investigation of theosophy was long and meticulous.[126]

Today, the leading Mondrian authority is Professor Robert Welsh. His article "Mondrian and Theosophy" was featured as the opening contribution in *Piet Mondrian Centennial Exhibition,* published by the Guggenheim Museum in New York in 1972, where the exhibition was held. Welsh explains that "the ideas relevant to [his] . . . discussion were proliferated in numerous texts, lectures, and discussions undertaken by Madame Blavatsky and her followers. . . . However, for the sake of convenience, and because its role as a source of other quotations often has been overlooked, her monumental, two-volume *Isis Unveiled* of 1877 will provide the exclusive text upon which our discussion is based;" a Dutch translation of *Isis* having been available to Mondrian.

In relating several of Mondrian's paintings to the Theosophical view of evolutionary growth through reincarnation, Welsh points particularly to one called *Metamorphosis,* and to another, the celebrated triptych *Evolution,* and comments:

> Evolution is no less than the basic tenet in the cosmological system predicted by Madame Blavatsky and, as such, replaces the Christian story of Creation as an explanation for how the world functions. This cosmology is analogous to Hindu and other mythologies which stress a perpetual cosmic cycle of creation, death and regeneration. It also has much in common with the Darwinian scientific theory of evolution. Darwin's only essential mistake, in Blavatsky's opinion, was to substitute matter for spirit as the motivating force in the universe. In her own world view, matter, though constituting a necessary vehicle through which the world of spirit was to be approached, clearly stands second in importance to the latter phenomenon.

This view of evolution, says Welsh, "pervades the art theoretical writings of Mondrian." In his *Sketchbooks* of 1912 to 1914, Welsh continues, "he specifically alludes to the Theosophical Doctrine of Evolution as a determining factor in the history of art. . . . In short, Mondrian could not have chosen as the theme of his monumental triptych a doctrine which was more central to theosophic teaching than this."

In assessing his own achievements, Mondrian wrote in a letter to Michel Seuphor: "It is in my work that I am something, but compared to the Great Initiates, I am nothing." By "the Great Initiates," he was referring to the flower of humankind, the perfected souls such as Christ and Buddha, who became such through many cycles of rebirth. However, Mondrian likely borrowed the expression from a book widely influential among artists, composers, and writers bearing that title. Published in 1889, the volume went through over two hundred printings in French alone and was translated into a number of European languages, including English. The author, Édouard Schuré,[†] was a noted journalist and a music critic, a friend of Wagner, Nietzsche, and other celebrities of the time. His name is frequently mentioned in works on the history of modern art. Schuré wrote *The Great Initiates* under the influence of a vision he experienced while residing in Florence: "In a flash I saw the Light that flows from one mighty founder of religion to another. These Great Initiates, those mighty figures whom

---

† Schuré was an early member of the Theosophical Society in Paris.

we call Rama, Krishna, Hermes, Moses, Orpheus, Pythagoras, Plato, and Jesus, appeared before me in a homogeneous group."[127]

When Mondrian was asked in 1918 whether the writings of a former Theosophist, Schoenmeeker, were of any use to him, he denied this, asserting, "I got everything from *The Secret Doctrine,* not from Schoenm,† although he says the same things."[128]

In his book *The Occult in Art,* the British art historian Fred Gettings describes Mondrian's workshops:

> Mondrian was notoriously exacting about the design of his studio. . . . From his early workshop in rue du Depart in Paris, through those in Holland, to his last studio in East 59th Street, New York, the interior design resembled the severe rectilinear compositions which predominate in the paintings which made him famous . . . ; he insisted that the antiques with which other artists tend to clutter up their working spaces, thereby making them into "museums of old art," actually prevented the artist from keeping close contact with present time.
>
> In view of this, it is remarkable that Mondrian should permit one large photograph to be placed on the wall of his geometrically arranged room, alongside the rectangles of pure hues. This was the larger-than-life portrait of the most influential occultist of the nineteenth century, H. P. Blavatsky.[129]

Paul Klee (1879–1940)

Paul Klee was another founder of modern art. In 1911, he was working with Kandinsky in Munich when the latter made his "leap into abstraction." Even before that (from about 1902) Klee developed an individual style of expressing the subconscious mind and fantasy in art. The selections that follow are from an article by Professor Robert Knotts, "Paul Klee and the Mystic Center," included in a 1987 compilation on modern art. He opens with a quote from Klee: "It is the artist's mission to penetrate as far as may be toward that secret place where primal power nurtures all evolution."

In one of his paintings, Klee used the human navel as a symbol of the sacred center. Professor Knotts explains:

> In the painting a mysterious figure is shown holding in his cupped hand a glowing navel, the internal divine light from which all

---

† An abbreviation for Schoenmeeker.

knowledge spreads. . . . The idea of the center is of great importance in all mysticism. The popular mystic Mme. H. P. Blavatsky,
who was well-known to Klee and others, wrote [in *Isis Unveiled*
1:xxxix]:

> The Ancients placed the astral soul of man, his self-con-
> sciousness, in the pit of the stomach. The Brahmans shared this
> belief with Plato and other philosophers. . . . The navel was
> regarded as "the circle of the sun," the seat of internal divine
> light. Among the Parsis there exists a belief up to the present day
> that their adepts have a flame in their navel which enlightens to
> them all darkness and discloses the spiritual world as well as things
> unseen.

Knotts adds that "certainly Blavatsky was of interest to Klee in
revealing the mysterious forces that speak on a different level of human
consciousness, a level for which Klee always felt a kinship. In his work
Klee almost always removes things from their immediate surroundings, placing them in ever-expanding realms which result in a close
correspondence between earth and cosmos, the living and the dead,
things past and present."[130]

Paul Gauguin (1848–1903)

The celebrated French artist Paul Gauguin, representative of the sym-
bolist school of painting, is another artist who came under Theosophical influence. Art historian Thomas Buser writes of this in an article
"Gauguin's Religion" appearing in *Art Journal* (Summer 1968):[131]

One of the many different things about Paul Gauguin was that he
painted religious pictures. Religious paintings by the major artists of
the late nineteenth century are undoubtedly few, and few of the
major artists, even in private, were concerned with religion. For
Gauguin, however, religion played an important role in his art and
in his life. . . . Gauguin was by no means a creative nor a systematic
theologian. Nevertheless . . . his faith was easily more mystical than
that prevalent in the Church at the time. Quite simply, Gauguin
seems to have been enamored of theosophy. . . .

At various moments, what Gauguin writes and, as we shall see,
what Gauguin paints closely parallel the theosophical doctrine of
Édouard Schuré's popular book, *Les Grands Initiés*. . . . What did
interest Gauguin in theosophy right from the start was its doctrine of
the initiate or visionary who can penetrate the *beyond*. . . .

Buser believes that undoubtedly Gauguin was acquainted with theosophy by 1889, when Schuré's book was published. Indeed, theosophy went hand in hand with the creation of Gauguin's mature styles. At the least, Gauguin's theosophy helps to explain how he could find so much compatibility in the styles of religious art of so many different civilizations: Javanese, Egyptian, Greek, and so on.

Much of Buser's article is concerned with an analysis of Gauguin's paintings, and he makes this comment on the artist's *Nirvana:*

> It must be more than mere coincidence that this painting seems to be almost an illustration for the following passages from Schuré's book:
>
>> Immense is the prospect opening out to one who stands on the threshold of theosophy. . . . On seeing it for the first time, one feels dazed; the sense of the infinite proves overpowering. Unconscious depths open within ourselves, showing us the abyss from which we are emerging and the giddy heights to which we aspire. Entranced by this sense of immensity, though terrified at the distance, we ask to be no more, we appeal to *Nirvana!* . . .
>>
>> It has been said that man was born in the hollow of a wave and knows nothing of the mighty ocean stretching before and behind him. This is true; but transcendental mysticism drives our barque on to the crest of a wave, and there, continually lashed by the furious tempest, we learn something of the sublimity of its rhythm; and the eye, compassing the vault of heaven, rests in its azure calm.

In conclusion Buser writes:

> Although the subjects in Gauguin's painting can thus never be completely "explained," there is something that can be said about them. To put it crudely: when it came time for Gauguin to think about a subject, he thought theosophically. His imagination was theosophical. Theosophy was his world view. Hopefully, this knowledge of ours does not explain away the paintings but deepens their meaning. . . . There is also some justification here for borrowing John Renald's general remark that Gauguin had "the fondness of the half-educated for intricate and high-sounding theories."

The air Gauguin breathed contained occultism; in many ways occultism formed the basis for all Symbolism. In Gauguin's case, however much theosophy fulfilled his religious needs, theosophical theory supplied him with the intellectual construction on which to deepen the commitment of his painting while his sensibilities transformed the construction into highly imaginative creations.

Gauguin's sympathy for Theosophical ideas included reincarnation, and he wrote thereon in his posthumous work *Modern Thought and Catholicism,* penned by the artist during his final years in Tahiti. It opens with the query "Whence do we come, what are we, where do we go?"—the title of the large canvas Gauguin finished in 1898—and continues:

> The parable of Jacob's ladder extending from earth to heaven, which the angels of God ascend and descend by steps, indeed resembles the ascent and descent by gradations from the lowest to the highest of life, according to the more or less active exercise of their qualities . . . degrading or elevating according to merit or demerit. [This is the] idea of metempsychosis, recognized in the Hindu religion, and which Pythagoras, deriving it from the Hindus, taught in Greece. . . . From what has preceded, [it follows that] it is the soul which has formed its organism; that it is the soul which has produced the evolution of living organisms constituting species. . . . God . . . as a symbol of the pure eternal spirit, the *general spirit* of the universe . . . becomes the principle of all harmonies, the end to be attained, presented by Christ, and before him by Buddha. And all men will become Buddhas.[132]

One may ask in conclusion whether the pioneers of modern art were successful in evoking a spiritual element in art and whether the inspiration they received from Blavatsky's writings permeated the profession as a whole. Roger Lipsey writes in *An Art of Our Own:*

> The century is now nearly complete, and there is an odd feeling of exhaustion in the visual arts. While there is no lack of gifted artists, astute critics, and well-endowed art institutions, the culture of the visual arts is nonetheless sad, as if we continue to produce art and think about it in the absence of some crucial inspiration or sense of direction. . . .
>
> We speak of Postmodernism now, as if we have drained Modernism, the predominant art movement of the twentieth century, of its possibilities and find ourselves moving into bleak terrain. . . . There was, however, a hidden side of Modernism, and this means, of course, a hidden side of modern artists. It may be that we have not only failed to "drain" this resource but have nearly overlooked its existence. Many of the universally respected artists whose works are altogether familiar and whom we feel we understand have in fact escaped understanding because we haven't yet penetrated the spiritual history of modern art. These were men and women who cared for "the things of the spirit." . . .

The culture at large has been amazingly unreceptive to the spiritual aspect of the artists' thought and work. [The] original aspiration to transcend personal psychology and explore a transpersonal world of meaning and energies . . . was largely forgotten, even denied.[133]

However, a change in direction may have been signaled in November 1986, with the opening of an exhibition in Los Angeles and the presentation of its accompanying catalog, *The Spiritual in Art and Abstract Painting 1890–1985*. The occasion was to celebrate the opening of the new wing of Los Angeles County Museum of Art. A number of the leading art historians in the Western world, such as Sixten Ringborn, Rose-Carol Washton Long, and Robert P. Welsh, helped organize the exhibition and its magnificent catalog. In large format, it included over four hundred paintings, many in color, and numerous articles on the various phases of modern art and its leading exponents.

The exhibition in Los Angeles remained open for three months, attracting a huge attendance; it then moved to the Museum of Contemporary Art in Chicago for another three months, after which it ended in the Hague.

John Dillenger, author of *A Theology of Artistic Sensibilities*, commented in the *Los Angeles Times* (February 22, 1987):

The exhibition has deservedly received major attention in the art world, both for its visual achievement and for the interesting questions it raises with respect to the spiritual, mystical and occult origins of abstract art. The documentation in the book will forever change how we understand those origins. Moreover, that one of the major museums in this country should inaugurate a new period in its life with the subject matter of the spiritual in art represents a major shift in contemporary sensibilities. Two decades ago this would have been unthinkable. . . . Scholars have generally known of the role of spiritual movements in the late 19th and early 20th centuries as a background ethos in the emergence of abstract art; art in which the traces of the visible world as we know it began to disappear. Never before has that role been documented so extensively as in this work.[134]

At the end of the catalog there is a large picture of HPB and a two-page article on Theosophy, stating categorically:

The Theosophical Society became the most widely influential organization for the public promotion of OCCULT teaching in modern times. . . . the society is historically important for popularizing ideas of reincarnation and karma, secret masters, and Tibet as the land of ageless wisdom; for fostering the revival of Buddhism in Ceylon (Sri Lanka) and Hinduism in India; for encouraging the comparative study of religion; and for persuading many that the essential teachings of the great religions are one.[135]

Chapter 6

Mahler, Sibelius, and Scriabin

Gustav Mahler (1860–1911)

Until his death in 1911, Mahler received little attention as a composer. It was as a conductor that he was renowned in Europe and later in America. His symphonies and other compositions were in advance of their time and were received with puzzlement rather than acclaim. He prophesied, "My time will come," and so it has. He is now regarded as a great master.

In 1895, Mahler began his third symphony. Although his earlier symphonies are tragic in character and disclose bitter disillusionment with life, the third was titled "The Joyful Knowledge," and according to noted Mahler authority Deryck Cook indicated "a new-found optimism, or rather a kind of mystical revelation of the validity and purpose of existence."

What was this joyful knowledge? In a biography of the composer, Mahler's close friend Richard Specht records a conversation with him in Hamburg in 1895. According to Specht, Mahler said with great conviction: "We all return; it is this certainty that gives meaning to life and it does not make the slightest difference whether or not in a later incarnation we remember the former life. What counts is not the individual and his comfort, but the great aspiration to the perfect and the pure which goes on in each incarnation."[136] The third symphony could be said to depict the reincarnation of life through the kingdoms to man and beyond.

Cook quotes a letter in which Mahler states that he wanted to express in the work an evolutionary development of nature that hides "within itself everything that is frightful, great, and also lovely." He notes that the composer added:

Of course, no one ever understands this. It always strikes me as odd that most people when they speak of "nature" think only of flowers, little birds, and woodsy smells. No one knows the god Dionysus, the great Pan. There now! You have a sort of program—that is, a sample of how I make music. Everywhere and always, it is only the voice of nature!

The vast first movement, says Cook, represents "nature in its totality . . . awakened from fathomless silence that it may ring and resound." The subsequent movements portray the stages of reincarnational ascension from vegetable and animal through mankind, back to the omniscient, omnipotent Divine Source.[137]

It was through another reincarnationist, the distinguished conductor Dr. Bruno Walter—a protégé and intimate friend of Mahler—that the present writer learned of the composer's belief in rebirth. This conviction, I was told, rose through association with some Theosophical acquaintances whom he met in the 1890s.[138] Dr. Walter was kind enough to direct me to the book, *Gustav Mahler,* which recorded Mahler's conversation with Richard Specht.

Jean Sibelius (1865–1957)

On the occasion of Sibelius's ninetieth birthday, the music critic for the *New York Times* (December 1955) wrote:

The interrelationship between life and art is one of Sibelius's chief concerns. . . . Sibelius's identification with the fields, the woods, the sea and the sky is so profound that it has always permeated his music. . . . As a boy, Sibelius wandered in the wilderness of his native province of Hame. Birds always fascinated him. "Millions of years ago, in my previous incarnations," he once told Jalas [his son-in-law], "I must have been related to swans or wild geese, because I can still feel that affinity."

A friend and neighbor of the Sibelius family, Mrs. Ida Sohlman, informed the writer that Sibelius spoke openly with intimate associates of his conviction in reincarnation and also of his previous lives. Independent confirmation of this came in January 1982, in a chance meeting with Harri Kallio in Santa Barbara, California, where Kallio teaches. The writer met him at the Institute of World Culture, with which he is actively associated. He told of spending some time in Fin-

land and of a special visit made to the Sibelius family and to Yryo Palo-
heimo, an archaeologist who lived next door to the composer. Kallio
learned from the latter that Sibelius and the circle of artists surrounding
him were much involved in the study of Theosophy, as well as
Rosicrucian teachings.

Alexander Scriabin (1872–1915)

In his foreword to Faubion Bowers' *The New Scriabin,* the noted
Russian pianist Vladimir Ashkenazy wrote:

> I consider Scriabin one of the greatest composers. . . . His music
> has a unique idealism. . . . The basis of his thought was an inde-
> structible faith and loyalty to Art as a means of elevating man's spirit
> and of showing light, goodness and truth. Although one cannot say
> that without understanding his philosophy one cannot understand
> the music, one penetrates deeper into his music if one studies what
> compelled Scriabin. One cannot separate the man-as-philosopher
> from the composer of such beautiful music.[139]

What, then, was Scriabin's philosophy? Boris de Schloezer, the
composer's Russian biographer, discloses that Theosophy was the only
very strong outside influence he ever received.[140] In Faubion Bowers's
two-volume biography of Scriabin, detailed information on this is
provided.

According to Bowers's account, early in the century Scriabin read a
French translation of Helena Blavatsky's *The Key to Theosophy* and
wrote at the time (May 5, 1905): "*La Clef de la Théosophie* is a remarkable book. You will be astonished at how close it is to my thinking."
Bowers writes that "from now on more and more of his friends and
adherents were drawn from the Theosophical Society." His colleagues
mention that "Scriabin's conversations were full of theosophy and the
personality of Blavatsky." A French translation of *The Secret Doctrine*
was one of his cherished possessions.

In 1922, Scriabin's apartment in Moscow was designated as a state
museum and restored to appear exactly as it had been in his lifetime.
His books, including *The Secret Doctrine,* were located and re-
purchased. This apartment, says Bowers, had a tremendous influence
on rising composers and was "a gathering place for youth."[141]

After his contact with theosophy, Scriabin's work became permeated with mystical undertones. Musicologist Gerald Abraham contrasts
the composer's first orchestral work, a piano concerto composed in

1896–97, with the composer's greatest composition, his symphonic tone poem, *Prométhée, le poème du feu*, written in 1909–10, and comments: "It seems hardly credible that in only thirteen years a composer could have evolved from the graceful, elegant, rather Chopinesque concerto to a work which was regarded in his day as in the very front of the avant-garde."[142]

Bowers observes:

> There have been few specifically mystical composers such as Scriabin. Scriabin's closest counterparts are found not in music but in poetry with William Blake, or in painting with Nicholas Roerich. . . . Scriabin's philosophy above all else wanted transubstantiation in music.

The composer wished to reawaken human beings to their essential selves. Scriabin wrote that "in the mysteries of antiquity there was real transfiguration, real secrets and sanctities," but *"all our little saints of today have forgotten their powers of old."*[143] When these "little saints" were trying to expose Blavatsky as a fraud, Scriabin defended her "by saying that all truly great people were subject to that kind of trumped-up 'ignominy.'"[144]

In 1987 de Schloezer's biography of Scriabin was published for the first time in an English translation. Among the many references to Theosophy and HPB that occur throughout the book de Schloezer writes:

> [Scriabin] felt greatly beholden to Mme. Blavatsky's *Secret Doctrine* in his own development; indeed he felt tremendous admiration for Mme. Blavatsky to the end of his life. He was particularly fascinated by her courage in essaying a grandiose synthesis and by the breadth and depth of her concepts, which he likened to the grandeur of Wagner's music dramas. . . . The theosophic vision of the world served as an incentive for his own work. "I will not discuss with you the truth of theosophy," he declared to [de Schloezer] in Moscow, "but I know that Mme. Blavatsky's ideas helped me in my work and gave me power to accomplish my task."†

† *Scriabin: Artist and Mystic* (Berkeley and Los Angeles: University of California Press, 1987), 68, 69

Chapter 7

Buddhism Moves West

U ntil the middle of the twentieth century, Buddhism was regarded as a fringe religion in Europe and America. A change began when a Penguin paperback titled *Buddhism* was published in 1951 in the United States and Britain. Since then over a million copies have been sold.[145] Christmas Humphreys (1901–1983), the author, was president and founder of the renowned Buddhist Society in London and for sixty years guided its fortunes.

Humphreys also distinguished himself as a member of the legal profession. He was Senior Prosecutor for the Crown and, later, Judge of the High Court Bench. His father, likewise a noted jurist, was called "The Hanging Judge." Humphreys was called "The Gentle Judge" and helped transform the lives of those who were tried before him.[146]

The paperback *Buddhism* often mentions Theosophy and quotes from HPB's writings. This is not strange, because Humphreys was a Theosophist as well as a Buddhist. On several occasions he said: "The theosophists complain because I am too Buddhist; the Buddhists complain because I'm too theosophist. I am always theosophist, but if I ever found a religion of more use to more people, I would change in a flash."[147]

Both his introduction to Buddhism and, later, to Theosophy came when Humphreys studied law at Cambridge. He once explained what occurred during this period of his life:

At the age of sixteen I was an enthusiastic Christian. . . . I had a brother four years older who in 1917 [during World War I] was killed at Ypres, and the bottom of my world fell out. I was filled, beyond my personal grief, with a furious sense of injustice. . . . There was no more sense in the world as there was no more happiness. I began to read widely in the field of comparative religion.

Then, in 1919, Humphreys came upon Coomaraswamy's *Buddha and the Gospel of Buddhism* and said to himself, "That is true, and it seems that I am a Buddhist!" His "real explosion of awareness," he says, came through understanding the ideas of karma and rebirth:

The first doctrine that seemed to me obvious was Rebirth. I was not re-learning this "Buddhism"; I was remembering it. I knew it almost without troubling to re-read the book, and in a short time I was writing and giving talks on Buddhism.

Although he was not completely satisfied with the philosophy as it is usually taught in the world, Humphreys had found a path to travel:

I saw the road but why is it there? Where was the map, or a section of it, in which I could see the beginning and a vision of its end? For even the next step can be dull when the very direction of the Way remains unknown. . . . Mrs. Rhys Davids said, "Buddhism is the long road between our imperfections now and the perfection which is latent in each human mind." But I wanted that Plan. I remember stopping in the street in Cambridge and demanding loudly, "It won't do, dammit, it won't do! Who am I and what am I, revolving on this speck of mud in this particular universe?"

I found my Plan in a commentary on what are called the Stanzas of Dzyan, a very old Tibetan scripture, in a book called *The Secret Doctrine,* by H. P. Blavatsky. This for the first time gave me what seemed to me then, and seems to me now, a clear exposition in outline of the coming into being of the universe and its ceasing to be, and within this the genesis and meaning of man. Here was a map of becoming.[148]

Humphreys joined the local lodge of Theosophists at the university and soon became president. After graduating from Cambridge in 1922, he became active in the TS in London. A few years later, he asked permission to form a Buddhist lodge within the TS. The request was granted.

One of Humphrey's pupils, Muriel Daw, reports that as her teacher studied *The Secret Doctrine* and became imbued with *The Voice of the Silence,* he came to love Helena Blavatsky with a deep devotion. His reverence for the spirit that shone through her and his gratitude for her life were unbounded. Her inspiration never left him, and her picture hung over the head of his bed until his death.[149]

Humphreys's activities in the Buddhist Lodge within the TS continued for two years. Then, he says, "In 1926 by common consent of all members we left the Theosophical Society, on the ground that in our view its activities were then encrusted with peripheral organizations to the exclusion of the great teaching given to Madame Blavatsky by her masters in Tibet."[150]

What was later called The Buddhist Society was then formed with the ardent support of, among others, a Theosophist named Aileen Faulkner, whom Humphreys married the following year. Their fruitful partnership endured for over fifty years. Another active worker in the new society was Edward Conze, whom Humphreys refers to as the leading authority in the field of Mahayana Buddhism. In a journal entry for January 15, 1964, Mircea Eliade wrote:

> Yesterday and today, almost the whole time with Ed Conze. He gave two lectures on Buddhism—amusing and extremely well attended. Long conversations between us. I learned that he was, and still is, a theosophist: he admires *The Secret Doctrine,* and believes that Mme. Blavatsky was the reincarnation of Tsonkapa[151] [the great reformer of Tibetan Buddhism in the fourteenth century and founder of the Gelugpa school, to which the Dalai and Panchen lamas belong].

After the Buddhist Society was formed, Humphreys continued to lecture and write on behalf of Theosophy. In *Exploring Buddhism,* he remarks that *The Secret Doctrine* "may yet be accepted as one of the greatest of religious works available to man."[152] In the introduction to *Karma and Rebirth,* he informs the readers that the book is "a humble attempt to reconsider the subject in the light of such 'authorities' as are available," mainly the scriptures of the Hindus and Buddhists. He continues: "When to these are added, by way of commentary, the writings of H. P. Blavatsky, who was herself trained in Tibetan monasteries, there is available a triple 'authority' which, taken as a whole, provides the basis for an all-embracing Law which guides and governs the evolution of mankind."[153]

In the struggle for survival, the Buddhist Society was greatly helped by a pupil of HPB, Dharmapala of Sri Lanka. He had come to England for two years to teach the Buddhist Society Buddhism, introducing himself in a letter to Humphreys from Switzerland by referring to "that pure Buddhist work" *The Voice of the Silence.* "Needless to say, we received him joyously, and after much searching helped him to find a house north of Regent's Park, where he founded the British Maha Bodhi Society, now housed in magnificent premises in Chiswick."

In 1927 the Japanese scholar Dr. D. T. Suzuki published his first series of *Essays in Zen Buddhism.* Humphreys remarks that "it told us far more than Zen Buddhism; it gave us a blazing vision of the immensity of Mahayana Buddhism when our knowledge so far was exclusively of the Theravada,"[154] excepting HPB's *Voice of the Silence.* In 1910, Suzuki had written concerning the *Voice* to his fiancée, Beatrice

Lane, at Columbia University: "Here is the real Mahayana Buddhism."

Humphreys met Dr. Suzuki in 1936 at The World Congress of Faiths, in London. "After a speech which none of us who heard it will forget," says Humphreys, "he came to the Lodge . . . and here was contact made . . . with the Master in the flesh," which continued until Suzuki's death in 1966.

It was not until the mid 1950s, when Suzuki was in the United States, that the Zen boom was born. This was the time when fifty U.S. psychologists and psychiatrists met with him in Mexico to learn about his ideas. Many other contacts were made with important thinkers in the West.

Besides Suzuki, the man who did most to popularize Zen in America was Alan Watts, who wrote thirty books on this and other subjects. *In My Own Way* he writes of Humphreys and his wife (using their nicknames):

Toby and Puck gave me an education which no money could possibly buy, and the depth of my gratitude to them is immeasurable. Even though I now remonstrate, mildly, against some of Toby's interpretations of Buddhism, I shall love him always as the man who really set my imagination going and put me on my whole way of life. It must be understood that Toby and Puck were, first of all, theosophists. . . . Thus it was through the work of Blavatsky that these traditions were delivered to Toby when he was a student at Cambridge, in company with the psychiatrist Henry Dicks, and Ronald Nicholson, who later became *sadhu* Sri Krishna Prem.[155]

(Prem is especially noted today for his book on *The Secret Doctrine* called *Man the Measure of All Things*.)[156]

During Watts's association with Humphreys in London, he edited the journal of the Buddhist Society for two years and thus received basic training in work for Buddhism. It was through Humphreys that he met Suzuki.

Humphreys's own contribution to the Zen explosion was considerable. Besides the books he wrote and the classes he conducted on Zen, he was largely responsible for making Dr. Suzuki's writings available to Western readers and was his agent in Europe.

Humphreys, however, was not interested in only one school of Buddhism. His primary interest was in World Buddhism, and he believed that only in a combination of all schools can the grandeur of Buddhism be discovered. In 1945 he expressed the consensus of such teachings in his famous "Twelve Principles of Buddhism," which was accepted by all the Buddhist sects and has been translated into fourteen languages.

Author Colin Wilson once asked Humphreys to contribute an article on HPB to a new volume he was compiling. Therein Humphreys wrote:

> What a woman! . . . misunderstood, vilified and abused, and yet with a brilliant, cultured and deeply learned mind; the very soul of generosity; a woman of direct speech and action, refusing to talk the pious platitudes and nonsense that we chatter under the guise of socially good manners, but offering the truth for anyone who wanted it. . . . She was never neutral, or the same to all. She made a great number of friends who would die for her, and enemies who would kill her if they could. . . . Those strong blue eyes could see into the character of every man and woman who came to her, and even see by whom she would later be betrayed. . . . She would help from her meager funds (and she was always poor), all those in need, even though she knew at the time that they were planning to smash the cause she had given her life to serve. . . .
>
> As a speaker she was magnetic; she never lectured but she would talk, and those who heard her could think of nothing else. In 1920, when I came into the movement, I knew a number of people who had known her well, and on this they were agreed, that after meeting her nothing was quite the same again.[157]

Chapter 8

Catalysts of the Reincarnation Renaissance

lthough, as indicated earlier, Helena Blavatsky is
A credited with reviving belief in reincarnation in
modern times, it was not until the middle of the twentieth century that
the number of reincarnationists accelerated at a rapid rate.

After she died, such beliefs progressively spread among Theosophical groups and their several offshoots. It was very popular in the
pervasive New Thought movement, the Religious Science churches,
and also the Unity School of Christianity, whose founders, Charles
and Myrtle Fillmore, were Theosophists.[158] Even the spiritualists were
teaching the doctrine and ceased "materializing" the dead.

The present chapter focuses on the phenomenal growth of reincarnational belief from the mid-1950s onwards. By 1969, when the first
Gallup poll was taken on the subject, 20 percent of the religious
population of the United States believed in reincarnation. By 1981 this
figure rose to 23 percent, and since then it has again risen spectacularly.

The 1981 poll was reported in George Gallup, Jr.'s *Adventures in
Immortality*. The census, he says, was the most comprehensive survey
on beliefs about the afterlife that has ever been undertaken. It was
addressed to adults eighteen years old and over. The question asked on
reincarnation was quite explicit: "Do you believe in reincarnation—
that is, the rebirth of the soul in a new body after death—or not?" It
was addressed not just to religious people, as the 1969 poll was, but to a
cross-section of the adult population in the United States. According
to Gallup, "Of those adults we polled, 23 percent, or nearly one-
quarter, said they believe in reincarnation."[159] This would mean there
were then over 38 million reincarnationists in the United States, using
as a base the 1981 population figures of 166 million who were eighteen
years old and over. Since by far most Americans have been born into
religions that do not presently teach reincarnation, this finding was
amazing.

Several people were largely catalysts for this arresting change, and it
can be traced to HPB's influence as each had a theosophical back-

ground, as we shall see. One was the psychologist Dr. Gina Cerminara, author of the best-selling *Many Mansions,* a 1950 volume that documents the story of the clairvoyant Edgar Cayce (1877–1945). Cayce as a young salesman suddenly lost his voice. He sought medical help frantically, but without success. On a friend's advice he turned to hypnosis, under which he was able to describe not only what was wrong but the method of cure. Encouraged to do the same for others, he continued in this career for twenty years with remarkable success. "In his early years," writes Cerminara, Cayce "was as startled as the next man to learn he had given medical counsel to an Italian in fluent and flawless Italian. Nor was the complicated medical terminology that rolled off his tongue any more intelligible to him in his waking state than was the fluent Italian."[160]

Then, one day in October 1923, a man named Arthur Lammers came to see Cayce. Lammers was not interested in being healed; he was a Theosophist in search of proof of its teaching. In *There is a River,* Thomas Sugrue tells what happened:

> Lammers . . . asked questions Edgar did not understand—what were the mechanics of the subconscious, what was the difference between spirit and soul, what were the reasons for personality and talent? He mentioned such things as the Kabbalah, the mystery religions of Egypt and Greece, the medieval alchemists, the mystics of Tibet, yoga, Madame Blavatsky and theosophy, the Great White Brotherhood, the Etheric World. Edgar was dazed.
>
> "You ought to find out about these things," Lammers said. ". . . There are hundreds of philosophic and thousands of theological systems. Which are right and which are wrong? . . . What is the real nature of the soul and what is the purpose of this experience on earth? Where do we go from here? . . . What were we doing before we came here? Haven't you asked any of those questions?"
>
> "No," Edgar said. He couldn't think of another word to say. He didn't dare tell the truth: that he had always considered such an idea sacrilegious, because God was revealed in the Bible, and to suppose that [Cayce through his readings] could answer the mysteries of the universe would be an open invitation for Satan to speak through him. That was what he had felt. Now, as he heard Lammers speak, he knew the feeling had passed.[161]

Lammers had recently become interested in astrology and asked Cayce for a horoscope while in trance. This came through in brief staccato sentences, but toward its close came the astounding words: "HE WAS A MONK!" This electrified those present, but the one who was most amazed—in fact, deeply disturbed—was Cayce, himself, when he awoke. Owing to his strong Christian upbringing, he underwent torturous doubts when such past-life readings continued to come through, and it was only after much study and searching of the Bible that he finally reconciled himself to reincarnation.[162]

Lammers later asked the sleeping Cayce, "Where was the information coming from that revealed the past lives of people?" The answer came that the first source was Cayce's subconscious mind, but at a deeper level than psychologists usually tap. The second source, as Cerminara reports it, had to do with what the readings called Akashic Records. As always, with unfamiliar words, the sleeping Cayce spelled out the term—*Akasha,* the noun, *Akashic,* the adjective. In brief, Cayce's explanation was this:

> *Akasha* is a Sanskrit word that refers to the fundamental etheric substance of the universe, electro-spiritual in composition. Upon this *Akasha* there remains impressed an indelible record of every sound, light, movement, or thought since the beginning of the manifest universe.
>
> The *Akasha* registers impressions like a sensitive plate, and can almost be regarded as a huge candid camera of the cosmos. The ability to read these vibratory records lies inherent within each of us, dependent upon the sensitivity of our organization, and consists in attuning to the proper degree of consciousness much like tuning a radio to the proper wavelength. . . . Frequently the readings indicated that the "*Akashic* Records" could also be called "The Universal Memory of Nature" or "The Book of Life."[163]

What may be still stranger is that if you consult a Sanskrit–English dictionary you will not receive such definitions as Cayce gave in trance, but you will find them in the writings of HPB and her colleagues.

The accuracy with which the records could be read would naturally depend upon the inner development of the seer. They can reach the conscious mind only by filtering through the subconscious, and consequently can become tinged or even distorted by its religious and philosophical outlook. In Cayce's case, the readings have a strong Christian coloring and are steeped in the language of the Bible, which he read through once a year.

Gina Cerminara spent several years going through carefully kept records of the more than fourteen thousand cases that came under Cayce's influence. Like Lammers, who had started Cayce on his reincarnational career, she too was a Theosophist. In an interview Cerminara revealed that her grandfather and mother were members of the

Theosophical Society, adding: "I am very grateful for the intellectual framework that theosophy gave me. When I went to study the Cayce readings, almost nothing that Cayce said was new to me or astonished me because, for the most part, it resonated to something in the theosophical literature."[164]

Cerminara's *Many Mansions* brought Cayce's work to worldwide attention, for her remarkably well-written, inspiring book, with its practical psychological application to daily living, has been published in many languages, including Icelandic and Japanese. When fairly soon after publication it came into the hands of Morey Bernstein, famed author of *The Search for Bridey Murphy,* interest in reincarnation rocketed to unprecedented heights. Bernstein had regressed under hypnosis[†] a young American woman who in six sessions appeared to recall in detail a life lived in Ireland.

The leading scientist on reincarnation, Dr. Ian Stevenson, viewed the Bridey Murphy case in a favorable light:

The majority of claimed memories of previous lives evoked in this way seem to me utterly worthless. Although skeptical about most "previous lives" elicited during hypnosis, I do not reject all experiments of this type as valueless. Indeed, I am quite convinced that in a small number something important and genuine has occurred. I think of the case of Bridey Murphy.[165]

In the wake of the Bridey Murphy case, numerous questions concerning reincarnation arose in the minds of people. One who responded was Professor C. J. Ducasse, who lectured on reincarnation in various schools and for many years was head of the Department of Philosophy at Brown University. In two of his books, *A Critical Examination of the Belief in a Life After Death* and *Nature, Mind and Death,* he discusses the philosophical evidence for reincarnation. His 1960 Garvin lecture "Life After Death Conceived as Reincarnation" is entirely on the subject.

Ducasse disclosed what led him to choose his career as teacher of philosophy in an article, "Philosophical Liberation," published in 1930

---

† H.P.B. was once asked: "Q. *What becomes of diseases cured by hypnotism; are they really cured or are they postponed, or do they appear in another form? Are diseases Karma; and, if so, is it right to attempt to cure them?*

"Ans. Hypnotic suggestion may cure for ever, and it may not. All depends on the degree of magnetic relations between the operator and the patient. *If* Karmic, they will be only postponed, and return in some other form, not necessarily of disease, but as a punitive evil of another sort. It is always 'right' to try and alleviate suffering whenever we can, and to do our best for it. Because a man suffers justly imprisonment, and catches cold in his damp cell, is it a reason why the prison-doctor should not try to cure him of it?" (Blavatsky, "Hypnotism and Its Relations to Other Modes of Fascination," *HPB on Psychical Phenomena,* HPB Pamphlet Series, The Theosophy Company, Los Angeles, California, 1938.)

in the scholarly review *Contemporary American Philosophy*. Born in France in 1881, he spent years traveling around the world working at odd jobs. He eventually settled in New York for three years (1903–1906) and worked as a steno-typist for an insurance company. While he was visiting his family in France, an acquaintance showed him a small book describing the views of Theosophists. Upon returning to New York, Ducasse joined the Theosophical Society, and in his free time he was in charge of its library. Among the volumes he read was *The Science of Peace* by Hindu Theosophist and scholar Bhagavan Das.[166] Das's discussion of fundamental ontological questions awakened Ducasse's interest in the same subjects. Having come into some money, he went to Seattle and there enrolled at the University of Washington, eventually receiving his PhD from Harvard. The many years of schooling and teaching, however, never diminished his interest in reincarnation but only challenged him to subject the idea to rigorous philosophical scrutiny.

Dr. Ian Stevenson (Carlson Professor of Psychiatry at the University of Virginia Medical School) is the leading scientist on reincarnation research. He specializes in cases in which children, both in the West and East, have spontaneous detailed memories of what they claim are former lives. Eight volumes of his case histories have thus far been published by the University Press of Virginia,[167] while the number of reincarnation cases now in his files totals over two thousand. Stevenson finds the past-life recall of the children he investigates—some of whom remember over fifty verified items, including names of people, places, and incidents—usually to be 90-percent accurate. Some children even remember a language they once knew. The ability is called xenoglossy, a subject on which Stevenson has written two volumes. In all cases he explores the possibility as to whether explanations other than reincarnation could apply.

In September 1977, the one hundred sixty-fifth volume of a distinguished psychiatric periodical, the *Journal of Nervous and Mental Disease (JNMD),* devoted almost the entire issue to Stevenson's research into survival after death—and more particularly into reincarnation as a means for such survival. This event had been preceded in May of that year by the publication of Stevenson's lengthy paper "The Explanatory Value of the Idea of Reincarnation" in the same journal. Dr. Eugene Brody, editor of the journal and a psychiatrist at the University of Maryland Medical School, said when interviewed, "I must have had three or four hundred requests for reprints from scientists in every discipline. It's pretty clear that there's a lot of interest in this topic."

In an interview in *Quest* (September/October 1978), Stevenson reveals what happened in his childhood that ultimately led him into full-time reincarnation research. The interviewer, Tom Buckley of the *New York Times,* begins by summarizing Stevenson's career. Not only was he head of the psychiatry department at the University of Virginia Medical School and chief psychiatrist at the university hospital, he had written scores of papers on psychiatry in the professional journals and two standard books on psychiatric interviewing and diagnosis. In addition, he saw private patients and taught at the university. In Buckley's words, "He is a fully qualified psychoanalyst. Beyond all that, he has been, ever since completing his own training, a member of the medical elite—a holder of fellowships at the New York Hospital and the Ochsner Clinic in New Orleans." He continues:

At the age of 48, Stevenson abandoned psychiatry to devote himself full-time to his reincarnation research. It was obvious that there had to be a powerful reason for a decision that many of his colleagues regarded as bizarre, to put it mildly, and yet I was not prepared for the answer Stevenson gave me when I asked him why he had done it. "Even while I was in medical school I told myself I was going to get into psychical research as soon as I could. But I knew that as a preliminary I'd have to build a satisfactorily medical career, and this I did."

But what, I asked, had led him to the study of reincarnation specifically? His answer to this question was inevitably less precise. . . . His mother was interested, he told me, in Eastern religions. She had a small library of books on the subject[†] and Stevenson, a bookish lad, recalls having curled up with them on many a rainy and snowy afternoon.

I would call myself prematurely grave as a child, he went on smiling at the odd echo of the word. I had a tendency to associate more with adults than with other children. This may undermine my credibility as a scientist—he smiled again—but I can remember an occasion around my ninth birthday on board the *Empress of Scotland* en route to Southampton when I was expounding the merits of reincarnation to two rather bemused older women.

A study of his cases reveals how emotionally detached he is from any form of bias. His peers have recognized this; several were quoted in an article in *Look* (October 20, 1970), "Is There Another Life After Death?" Dr. Albert J. Stunkard, then chairman of the department of

---

† In a letter to the present writer (March 30, 1977), Stevenson identifies these as Theosophical books: "The books on theosophy that I read as a child were in my mother's library, not my father's. Many years ago a newspaperman extracted from me the information that I read theosophical books in the library of our home when I was a child. This is true, but the library had been assembled by my mother, not my father."

psychiatry at the University of Pennsylvania in Philadelphia, remarks:

> Stevenson's present work seems queer to many conventional scientists. It is certainly controversial. But he is the most critical man I know of working in that sphere, and perhaps the most thoughtful, with a knack for building into his research appropriate investigative controls.

And Dr. Gertrude Schmeidler, former professor of psychology at the City College of the City University of New York, averred that "Stevenson is a most careful and conscientious person of great intellectual ability and high professional standards. He has a most painstaking approach to collection and analysis of raw data."

Stevenson has refused countless offers to appear on television or in other ways to sensationalize his research. Nevertheless, his painstaking work over three decades is becoming more and more widely known and is gradually contributing considerably to the present widescale interest in reincarnation.

In the scientist Stevenson and the actress Shirley MacLaine—our next reincarnation catalyst—we have two poles of research on the same subject.

MacLaine's 1983 book *Out on a Limb* sold over four million copies, and she appeared on numerous television programs to discuss it. The volume features, besides herself, a man named David, who was the moving power in her new role as a teacher of reincarnation. David, MacLaine says, is a composite character, representing several men who opened her mind to inner realities. Their identity has been something of a mystery, although the one responsible for her adventure in the Andes—the climax of her book—is now known to some. It is this person who informed MacLaine in Peru that she was destined to be a New Age teacher and write books on her newly acquired philosophy. The thought of the public humiliation that might result petrified her.[168]

In the fall of 1985, it was learned that MacLaine's mentor was Charles Silva when a circular announced that he as "confidant and guide to Shirley MacLaine in her best seller *Out on a Limb*" was giving a seminar at the Elizabeth Seton College in Yonkers, New York, on September twenty-eighth. The circular also identified him as author of the book *Date with the Gods*.[169]

The latter book describes Silva's adventures, occult and otherwise, during two visits to the Andes, in 1974 and 1975. It further relates that when he returned to the States in 1976 to write his book, he spent a week in research on Long Island with a friend named Myrna, "who spent many years of her life studying: the woman is a genius, she is into the secret doctrines of Madame Blavatsky and the lost continent Atlantis. She knows all about health foods, macrobiotics, zone therapy, theosophy, and is a fine artist."[170]

Upon querying Myrna[171] about Silva, it was learned that for one summer in 1969 he and the woman he lived with—a native of Long Island, but now a school teacher in Los Angeles—rented the top floor of a house she and her sister owned.

When Myrna first met Silva he was a confirmed materialist, but in due time he became enthusiastic about Theosophy and acquired a complete set of HPB's books. Silva subsequently shared these books with Shirley MacLaine at a time when she knew next to nothing about reincarnation and allied subjects. This was in 1976 and early 1977, before their trip together to the Andes later that year.

When a staff reporter for *TV Guide,* upon interviewing MacLaine in 1986 inquired whether she knew anything about Theosophy, she replied, "Oh, I know all about that."[172]

The hippie generation exerted considerable influence on the reincarnation renaissance. The Beatles, for example, were intrigued by eastern philosophy. What is perhaps not so well known is Elvis Presley's deep interest in these metaphysical themes. In *Elvis,* Albert Goldman lists some of the books he studied for a number of years: H. P. Blavatsky's *The Secret Doctrine* and *The Voice of the Silence,* Richard Maurice Bucke's *Cosmic Consciousness,* Krishnamurti—*The First and Last Freedom,* Nicholas Roerich—*Flame in Chalice,* Dane Rudhyar—*New Mansions for New Men,* and W. Y. Evans-Wentz's *Tibetan Book of the Dead.*[173]

Professor Goldman points out:

> The writings to which Elvis Presley devoted himself for the balance of his life were established in the 1870s in New York City by the notorious and fascinating Madame Blavatsky. Elvis always had on hand copies of Madame Blavatsky's writings. . . . In fact, one little volume purporting to be translations by Blavatsky of the most ancient runes of Tibet, *The Voice of [the] Silence,* was such a favorite of Elvis's that he sometimes read from it onstage and was inspired by it to name his own gospel group, Voice.[174]

This interest was aroused when he changed barbers. The new man was Larry Geller of New York who introduced him to the idea of masters. Elvis's immediate irreverent response was, "Who the hell are the masters?"[175] Priscilla, Elvis's wife, writes in her biography, *Elvis and Me:*

> Elvis discovered that there were many great masters besides Jesus.

There were Buddha, Muhammad, Moses, and others, each "chosen by God to serve a purpose." What I was now witnessing in Elvis was the emergence of that part of his nature that was thirsting for answers to all the fundamental questions of life.

He asked Larry why, out of all the people in the universe, he had been chosen to influence so many millions of souls. Granted this unique position, how could he contribute to save a world burdened with hunger, disease, and poverty? Why was there so much human suffering in the first place? And why wasn't he happy, when he had more than anyone could want? He felt he was missing something in life. Through Larry's insight, he hoped to find the path that would lead him to the answers.

He was eager for all of us—especially me—to absorb all the knowledge he was consuming. Happy to share everything, he read to us for hours and handed out books he thought would interest us.[176] [Goldman remarks:] That he did read these books with great care is evident even from the appearance of his copies, dog-eared, travel-stained, heavily underscored on almost every page. Elvis committed many of the key passages to memory and would recite them aloud while Larry Geller held the book like a stage prompter.[177]

How seriously he tried to apply these studies is reported by his wife: "We have to control our desires," he told her, "so they don't control us."

The final item in this chapter brings us to the work of Geddes Mac-Gregor who had a dual career: one as an Anglican priest, the other as a professor of philosophy both in Europe and in the United States.

Thus far in the chapter it has become evident that reincarnationists have appeared in the fields of science and philosophy. What about religion? Professor Geddes MacGregor indicates that the last two decades of his career have been engaged in such research in the area of Christianity. In a lecture he has stated: "I was interested in reincarnation when I was fifteen. I read all sorts of theosophical literature at that time and I have never really *not* been interested in it since."[178]

As to MacGregor's credentials, he is a professor of philosophy and also an Episcopalian priest. He received his doctorate in philosophy from Oxford, and also two post-doctorate degrees: the French State *grand doctorat,* awarded *summa cum laude* from the Sorbonne in Paris; and doctor of divinity from Oxford. Hebrew Union in the United States conferred the honorary degree of doctor of humanities. Presently he is emeritus distinguished professor of philosophy at the University of Southern California, where from 1960 to 1975, he taught the philosophy of religion. As an Anglican priest, among his various appointments was special preacher at St. Paul's Cathedral in England for 1969, and at Westminster Abbey for 1970. His numerous books on Christianity include two on reincarnation.[179]

In a 1982 lecture delivered at the Theosophical Society in Wheaton, Illinois, MacGregor's topic was "Christianity and the Ancient Wisdom," from which the following is taken:

> I well remember when, at the age of fifteen, I happened to come across some books by distinguished members of the Theosophical Society. I was immediately captivated, not so much by the books themselves as by that to which they seemed to be recalling me. . . . When I became about the same time committed to the Christian Way I at first mistakenly thought I must set aside such theosophical teachings. I never actually renounced them; nor could I. On the contrary, they have ever since illumined all my Christian thinking, although only in the last decade or so have I seen more clearly than ever before how close is the connection between the experience and the outlook of the great Christian mystics and the Ancient Wisdom to which I was providentially introduced so early in life. It lay germinating in my soul, affecting my spirituality at every point without coming to full fruition till comparatively late in life.
>
> No one who has read my writings with a perceptive eye can have failed to see (sometimes perhaps more clearly than myself) how deeply these theosophical ideas have affected my thought. Like the medieval cathedral builders I was building better than I knew. . . . I have always enjoyed a peculiarly sharp awareness of having been somehow catapulted at an early age into a very special mode of consciousness for an understanding and appreciation of which I needed to acquire a great deal of technical learning.[180]

MacGregor's first book on reincarnation, published in 1978, was *Reincarnation in Christianity: A New Vision of the Role of Rebirth in Christian Thought.*[181] The second, *Reincarnation as a Christian Hope,* was published in 1982 in London and later in the United States. He also wrote *The Christening of Karma: the Secret of Evolution.*[182] He has given courses on reincarnation at the University of California at Berkeley and at the University of Iowa.

Here, as told to the present writer, is his story of how he began lecturing and writing on Reincarnation. In 1976, he was asked to give the

Birks Lecture at McGill University in Montreal. He at first gave the school a choice of three topics for the lecture series. But then in the spirit of devilish fun, he threw in a fourth: "Is Reincarnation Compatible with Christianity?" The immediate response was "You left us no choice!"

In the volume itself, MacGregor writes:

> Reincarnation is one of the most fascinating ideas in the history of religion, as it is also one of the most recurrent themes in the literature of the world. It is widely assumed to be foreign to the Christian heritage, and especially alien to the Hebrew roots of biblical thought. That assumption is questionable. . . . It has persistently cropped up in various crannies along the Christian Way, from the earliest times down to the present. It has flourished in Judaism. Wherever western thinkers have learned to love the Christian Way well enough to strip off dead dogma without destroying living tissue, it has found a place in the Church's life.[183]

Chapter 9

Myths, Dreams, and the Collective Unconscious

S ymbols and myths are considered of sufficient importance in *The Secret Doctrine* to devote one-third of each
of its two volumes to their discussion. Volume One contains fifteen
chapters on the subject, and HPB opens with these words (1:303):

> The study of the hidden meaning in every religious and profane leg-
> end, of whatsoever nation, large or small—pre-eminently the tradi-
> tions of the East—has occupied the greater portion of the present
> writer's life.[†] She is one of those who feel convinced that no
> mythological story, no traditional event in the folk-lore of a people
> has ever been, at any time, pure fiction, but that every one of such
> narratives has an actual, historical lining to it. In this the writer
> disagrees with those symbologists, however great their reputation,
> who find in every myth nothing save additional proofs of the
> superstitious bent of mind of the ancients. . . . Such superficial
> thinkers were admirably disposed of by Mr. Gerald Massey, the poet
> and Egyptologist. . . . His pointed criticism is worthy of reproduc-
> tion in this part of this work, as it echoes so well our own feelings,
> expressed openly so far back as 1875, when "Isis Unveiled" was
> written. [Massey states:]

> > For thirty years past Professor Max Müller has been teaching in
> > his books and lectures, in the *Times* and various magazines, from
> > the platform of the Royal Institution, the pulpit of Westminster
> > Abbey, and his chair at Oxford, that mythology is a disease of
> > language, and that ancient symbolism was a result of something
> > like a primitive aberration. "We know," says Renouf . . . "that
> > mythology is the disease which springs up at a peculiar stage of
> > human culture."

† In Yeats's *Autobiography,* he says of Blavatsky: "I knew that her mind contained all the folklore of the world." (New York: Doubleday, 1958, 118).

[Massey's] reply is, 'Tis but a dream of the metaphysical theorist that mythology was a disease of language, or anything else except his own brain. The origin and meaning of mythology have been missed altogether by these solarites and weathermongers! Mythology was a primitive mode of *thinking* the early thought. It was founded on natural facts, and is still verifiable in phenomena. There is nothing insane, nothing irrational in it, when considered in the light of evolution, and when its mode of expression by sign-language is thoroughly understood. The insanity lies in mistaking it for human history or Divine Revelation. Mythology is the repository of man's most ancient science, and what concerns us chiefly is this—when truly interpreted once more, it is destined to be the death of those false theologies to which it has unwittingly given birth.

Sir James Frazer, the renowned author of *The Golden Bough* and its many volumes, entertained views similar to Müller's, as Professor Mircea Eliade reports: "In some 20,000 pages [he] had discovered how all the thoughts, imaginings and yearnings of archaic man, all his myths and rites, all his gods and religious experiences, are only a monstrous mass of beastliness, cruelty and superstition, happily abolished by scientific human progress."[184]

In the twentieth century the attitude toward myths and legends began to change, with the appearance of the works of Carl Jung and such volumes as Erich Fromm's *The Forgotten Language* and Joseph Campbell's *The Hero with a Thousand Faces*. In *The Forgotten Language,* Fromm writes:

The dreams of ancient and modern man are written in the same language as the myths whose authors lived in the dawn of history. . . . Yet this language has been forgotten by modern man. Not when he is asleep, but when he is awake. Is it important to understand this language also in our waking state? . . . I believe that symbolic language is the one foreign language that each of us must learn. Its understanding brings us in touch with one of the most significant sources of wisdom, that of the myth, and it brings us in touch with the deeper layers of our own personalities. . . .

In his *Hero with a Thousand Faces,* Joseph Campbell enlarged our concept of what a myth may be: "Myth is the secret opening through which the inexhaustible energies of the cosmos pour into human cultural manifestations. Religions, philosophies, arts, the social forms of primitive and historic man, prime discoveries in science and technology, the very dreams that blister sleep, boil up from the basic, magic ring of myth. . . . The symbols of mythology are not manufactured; they cannot be ordered, invented, or permanently suppressed. They are spontaneous productions of the psyche, and each bears within it, undamaged, the germ power of its source."[185]

With ideas like these, one wonders whether Campbell was ever interested in Theosophy? We learn from a biography of Campbell, *A Fire in the Mind* by Stephen and Robin Larsen, published in 1991, that Campbell had many contacts with Theosophists. The biographers state that in 1928 when Campbell was planning a world tour he was "tremendously excited with the natural way in which his Theosophical and Oriental contacts fitted into his developing travel and study plans; his sense of an inner center formerly so sorely missing, was beginning to emerge."[186]

In *The Power of Myth,* Campbell reminds us that "Freud and Jung both felt that myth is grounded in the unconscious."[187] Jung is famous for his theory of the collective unconscious. Here is his explanation of this intriguing subject:

A more or less superficial layer of the unconscious is undoubtedly personal . . . but this personal unconscious rests upon a deeper layer, which does not derive from personal experience . . . [it] is inborn. This deeper layer I call the *collective unconscious* . . . it has contents and modes of behavior that are more or less the same everywhere and in all individuals . . . and thus constitutes a common psychic substrate of a suprapersonal nature which is present in every one of us.[188]

One proof of its existence, says Jung, is the fact that "the myths and fairytales of world literature contain definite motifs which crop up everywhere," adding that they are "part of the inherited structure of the psyche and can therefore manifest . . . spontaneously anywhere, at any time."[189]

In a few lines in *The Secret Doctrine* (2:293) it is startling to find the same idea written some forty years earlier:

The imagination of the masses, disorderly and ill-regulated as it may be, could never have conceived and fabricated *ex nihilo* so many monstrous figures, such a wealth of extraordinary tales, had it not had, to serve it as a central nucleus, those floating reminiscences, obscure and vague, which unite the broken links of the chain of time to form with them the mysterious, dream foundation of our *collective consciousness.* [Italics added.]

Jung once wrote that when Indian philosophy was first discovered in the West it first "remained the preserve of Sanskrit scholars and philosphers," adding: "But it was not so very long before the Theosophical Movement, inaugurated by Madame Blavatsky, possessed itself of the Eastern traditions and promulgated them among the general public."[190]

By the turn of the century, Sigmund Freud had already posited his theory that within each individual lay an unconscious mind in which repressed or forgotten ideas were stored. This unconscious mind often reacted on the conscious mind in an unhealthy manner without the person being aware of it.

The published journal of Mircea Eliade contains this entry, dated June 6, 1964, relating to Freud's celebrated work on dreams:

> While Freud was preparing his *Traumdeutung,* the English Theosophists were talking about "akashic history" and "nature's memory." According to the latter, nothing of what happened has ever been forgotten by nature. The memory of these events—cosmic, historical, personal—is conserved in different natural objects. Certain men—those who possess a "proper psychically attuned mind"— succeed, upon contact with certain tangible objects, to capture the latent history that lies there.
>
> It's interesting to note that Freud also thinks that nothing of what happens to man in his childhood is lost; that is, really forgotten. Everything can be recovered (with the help of the psychoanalyst) from a basis not of "tangible objects" but of images. . . . The theory of akashic history of which the theosophists dreamed . . . corresponds in its structure to Freudian theory. Freud was fascinated with occultism. Could he have read the theosophical lucubrations in fashion after 1895, and very popular especially in 1898?[191]

Freud's biographer Ernest Jones, in the chapter "Occultism" in his three-volume *Sigmund Freud: Life and Work,* affirms it was a subject that "truly wracked" Freud and "perplexed him to distraction."[192]

It also can be said that ten years before Freud, HPB wrote of repressed or forgotten ideas being stored in the subconscious mind. This was in her article "Memory in the Dying,"† which appeared in *Lucifer* in 1889. HPB approvingly quotes Edgard Quinet, author of *Creation:*

"The thoughts we think, but are unable to define and formulate, once repelled, seek refuge in the very root of our being.". . . When chased by the persistent efforts of our will "they retreat before it, still further, still deeper into—who knows what—fibres, but wherein they remain to reign and impress us unbidden and un-known to ourselves." Yes, *unseen and eluding grasp, they yet work, and thus lay the foundations of our future actions and thoughts, and obtain mastery over us,* though we may never think of them and are often ignorant of their very being and presence. [Italics added.]

To ferret out these subconscious feelings, Freud recommended that psychiatrists and psychoanalysts study a patient's dream life. Such doc-tors, over the years, tabulated certain types of dreams as being evi-denced of sexual repression while ascribing different meanings to others. Dream books also often assign fixed meanings for specific dreams.

This method is not recommended by HPB. In her twenty-page study of dreams, contained in the appendix of *Transactions of the Blavatsky Lodge,* to the question "Are there any means of interpreting dreams—for instance, the interpretation given in dream books?" she replies, "None but the clairvoyant faculty and the spiritual intuition of the 'interpreter.' Every dreaming Ego differs from every other, as our physical bodies do."[193] By *clairvoyant faculty* she probably did not refer to consulting clairvoyants, as she seems to have a dim view of their reliability.

As an aid in classifying our dreams, HPB concluded her treatise on dreams with the following.

We may roughly divide dreams into seven classes:

1. Prophetic dreams. These are impressed on our memory by the Higher Self, and are generally plain and clear: either a voice heard or the coming event foreseen.

2. Allegorical dreams, or hazy glimpses of realities caught by the brain and distorted by our fancy. These are generally only half true.

---

† See the pamphlet by Jean-Louis Siémons, *A Nineteenth Century Explanatory Scheme for the Interpretation of Near-Death Experience: The Transpersonal Model of Death as Presented in Madame Blavatsky's Theosophy,* Paris, Institut National Agronomique, 16, rue Claude Bernard, 75005, Paris, France: Tel (1 46·66·0·8·41).

3. Dreams sent by adepts, good or bad, by mesmerizers, or by the thoughts of very powerful minds bent on making us do their will.

4. Retrospective; dreams of events belonging to past incarnations.

5. Warning dreams for others who are unable to be impressed themselves.

6. Confused dreams, the causes of which have been discussed above.

7. Dreams which are mere fancies and chaotic pictures, owing to digestion, some mental trouble, or such-like external cause.

Allegorical dreams would appear to be those that have their source in the collective unconscious but would have a special meaning to the individual experiencing them. *The Secret Doctrine* (2:22 fn) indicates that "as there are seven keys of interpretation to every symbol and allegory, that which may not fit a meaning, say from the psychological or astronomical aspect, will be found quite correct from the physical or the metaphysical."

Chapter 10

Mother of the New Age?

M*cCall's* March 1970 issue was devoted almost entirely to "The Occult Explosion." The editorial page refers to HPB as "The Founding Mother of the Occult in America." Attention was directed to a featured article by Kurt Vonnegut, Jr., entitled "The Mysterious Madame Blavatsky,"† from which the following is taken:

Many Americans, I find, are dimly aware that there was a Madame Blavatsky somewhere in our P. T. Barnum past. When I make them guess who she was and what she did, they commonly suppose that she was an outstanding quack among many quacks who pretended to talk to the dead. This response is ignorant and unfair. . . . She was forty-two when she arrived here in 1873, and her head was buzzing with occult theories, but she was squeamish about contacts with the dead. . . .

She claimed to have traveled around the world three times before stopping off here. "This lady," said the New York *Daily Graphic,* "has led a very eventful life, traveling in most of the lands of the Orient, searching for antiquities at the base of the Pyramids [and] witnessing the mysteries of Hindu temples. . . ."

She was so *brave,* to begin with, traveling so far alone. She was so brilliant, mastering language after language, to learn what local wise men knew. And she was so generous, wanting almost nothing for herself. . . . And she was scared to death that untrained, unworthy persons would tinker with magic and raise hell. She made enemies in America by saying that mediums were taking ghastly risks with forces they did not understand.

† The page facing the article, contains a large color portrait of Blavatsky, surrounded, as the legend reads, by "symbols of some of her most famous disciples . . . Thomas Edison's light bulb; an abstract painting by her Dutch follower Piet Mondrian; a baseball player for 'founder' Abner Doubleday; Belgian playwright Maurice Maeterlinck's 'Blue Bird'; a telescope representing the famous French astronomer Nicolas Flammarion. Other symbols refer to her interest in Indian religions, her Russian origins, and her endless wanderings around the world."

Vonnegut then quotes the following from one of HPB's articles on occultism:[194]

It is the motive, and the motive alone, which makes any exercise of power become black, malignant, or white, beneficent Magic. It is impossible to employ spiritual forces if there is the slightest tinge of selfishness remaining in the operator. For, unless the intention is entirely unalloyed, the spiritual will transform itself into the psychic, will act on the astral plane, and dire results may be produced by it. The powers and forces of animal nature [the psychic nature] can equally be used by the selfish and revengeful, as by the unselfish and the all-forgiving; the powers and forces of spirit lend themselves only to the perfectly pure in heart—and this is DIVINE MAGIC.[195]

He concludes his long article:

I have approached Madame Blavatsky from inside, so to speak, have listened to her and those who loved her. I might as easily have assumed that her life was a low comedy and have eagerly quoted her many enemies, who thought she was a graceless fraud. At a minimum, Madame Blavatsky brought America wisdom from the East which it very much needed, which it still very much needs. . . . So I say, "Peace and honor to Madame Blavatsky." I am charmed and amused that she was an American citizen. . . . Bizarre as she may have been, she was something quite lovely; she thought all human beings were her brothers and sisters—she was a citizen of the world. She said this among other things:

> Let not the fierce sun dry one tear of pain
> Before thyself has wiped it from the
> sufferer's eye.

Cheers.

If we compare HPB's views on true occultism, as Vonnegut quotes from her writings, with what is usually regarded as occultism, she would certainly disclaim being called "the Founding Mother of the Occult in America." As to the part that pseudo-occultism plays in the New Age movement, a leading spokesman for that movement, David Spangler, relegates it to the second of four levels at which the New Age can be met and explored.

Spangler, passionately interested in science, pursued scientific studies in college before turning to New Age interests. He was co-director of the famous Findhorn Community in northern Scotland and now directs the Lorian Association in the United States, teaches in various colleges, and lectures all over the United States and Canada. It is in his latest book, *Emergence, the Rebirth of the Sacred,* that he speaks of the four levels at which the New Age can be explored:

[The first level] is as a superficial label, usually in a commercial setting. A quick perusal of *New Age* magazine or *East West Journal,* both of which have national distribution, or of any of the many smaller new age-oriented publications will demonstrate this application: one can acquire new age shoes, wear new age clothes, use new age toothpaste, shop at new age businesses, and eat at new age restaurants where new age music is played softly in the background.

The second level is what I call the "new age as glamour." This is the context in which individuals and groups are living out their own fantasies of adventure and power, usually of an occult or millenarian form. Many UFO-oriented groups fall into this category. The principal characteristic of this level is attachment to a private world of ego fulfillment and a consequent (though not always apparent) withdrawal from the world. [On this level] the New Age has become populated with strange and exotic beings, such as extraterrestrials, with which channelers claim to communicate. It is a place of psychic powers and occult mysteries. It is in this context that one is most likely to find the words *New Age* used, unfortunately. . . .

The third level is the new age as an image of change. Here the distinguishing characteristic is the idea of transformation itself, usually expressed as a paradigm shift [or a change in the basic assumptions and values at the heart of a particular culture]. This image of the new age is the one most popularly presented to the public, in books such as Willis Harman's *An Incomplete Guide to the Future,* Marilyn Ferguson's *The Aquarian Conspiracy,* and physicist Fritjof Capra's *The Turning Point.* It is the level discussed in many international and regional conferences, debated by futurists and social theorists, and explored in government projects such as the Global 2000 report to President Jimmy Carter. In this context the idea of an emerging new culture is usually seen in social, economic, and technological terms rather than spiritual ones. . . .

On the fourth level, the new age is fundamentally a spiritual event, the birth of a new consciousness, a new awareness and experience of life. . . . It is the new age as a state of being, a mode of relationship with others that is mutually empowering and enriching. Rather than spiritual *experience,* which is the focus one is more apt to find in the second level—that of psychic and spiritual glamour—this level centers upon the spiritual *function,* which is service.[196]

Spangler quotes Lewis Mumford's *The Transformation of Man* (1956):

We live on the brink of a new age: the age of an open world and of a self capable of playing its part in that larger sphere. An age of renewal, when work and leisure and learning and love will unite to produce a fresh form for every stage of life, and a higher trajectory for life as a whole.[197]

Spangler provides as an example of the fourth level, in which "the idea of a new age as a spiritual phenomenon is discussed and prophesied," the work of metaphysical and esoteric groups such as the Theosophical Society.[198] In 1977, Spangler gave two talks on Theosophy. One was in Ferndale, Detroit, on October 15, 1977, from which the following is taken:

I heard of the Theosophical Society and theosophy itself when I was about 15 or 16, but I did not really get into reading any theosophical works until I was in my early twenties. Prior to that time I had various kinds of inner experiences which convinced me of the fact that we lived in a multi-dimensional universe. . . . When I began lecturing I needed some kind of deeper, more structured understanding that I could orient myself to. . . . Theosophy was what I was directed to. This was in 1965.

The speaker then reviewed Western history before modern Theosophy came on the scene. He began with the period when Roman Christianity won out over Celtic Christianity and the Vatican was the supreme ruler. Then followed the revolt of scientifically minded people, who limited their investigations to that which can be recognized by the five senses. They put all knowledge into little boxes, says Spangler, and regarded this knowledge alone as real, leaving out 90 percent of the universe—the unseen universe. This caused a separation among people and was a potential for tyranny.
Spangler continues:

So along comes something to rattle science's cages, to get it looking in new ways. Now what could possibly be big enough, strong enough, strange enough, to rattle science's cages in the depths of the materialism of the nineteenth century? A cigarette smoking woman, by the name of Madame Blavatsky. Here was a being who had the capacity to demonstrate that certain assumptions science was making were only that. And we owe a lot to her whether we are theosophists or not. . . . She is a true pioneer; a real Copernicus, if you wish.

And since most things are group efforts, along with Madame Blavatsky came the TM [the Theosophical Movement] and theosophy. Theosophy was part of the vehicle chosen to resurrect a knowledge that everything in the world that was meaningful but was not open to or obvious to the five senses, was esoteric knowledge, esoteric tradition in the deepest and highest sense—a study of essences. . . . Theosophy is an ideal vehicle, a fiery and passionate vehicle to bring a certain realization into western human consciousness. It is said that theosophy is inspired by the Brothers, or Masters of Compassion and Wisdom.[199]

Spangler gave another talk, "Theosophy, the Personal Adventure, the Planetary Opportunity," on October 11, 1977, at the headquarters of the Theosophical Society in America at Wheaton, Illinois. During the course of the lecture he considered two difficulties metaphysically inclined students face and must overcome.

The first is the danger of imbibing an overload of allegedly occult information, which, Spangler says, leads inevitably to mental indigestion, confusion, and a state of excited anticipation for more and more "esoteric rewards." The avalanche of occult literature that floods the market accentuates the problem. The second is that the student should recognize that all this literature, and the writers thereof, are not saying the same things; hence, the writings cannot in all respects be true. Respecting the latter, Spangler says:

Anyone who goes into the esoteric movement very deeply can understand this in view of the fact that there are several different esoteric traditions in our world. You have theosophy, you have the Arcane School and the writings of Alice Bailey, you have Rudolf Steiner and Anthroposophy, you have numerous transmissions through various individuals such as the Seth Material, for example. You have things like at Findhorn, and you have the work going on in parapsychological research, and in biofeedback. It would be nice if all these things said the same thing but they don't.

Now this isn't surprising if one thinks of the inner planes as having at least as much complexity as the physical world. It would be quite possible for someone to investigate life on earth and arrive in the Southwest of this country, someone else in the Midwest, someone in Africa or in Asia. The reports would not be the same. Earth is a hot place in which nothing lives. Or earth is nothing but a huge city also in which nothing seems to live. Or earth is a forest, or the living things of earth are all rooted. . . .

To me the Theosophical Society and theosophy as a recognizable concept was created a hundred years ago by the Masters of Wisdom to create an instrument, to weld together a fiery instrument, which could give us tools for dealing with extended perceptions in a richer universe so that we are not overwhelmed and we find greater patterns of synthesis and simplicity.

The Theosophical Society was created to be a system of energy that could help us move from levels of difference to perception of essence, and out of perception of essence to perceive and be able to act out of wholeness, the wholeness that unites us. This is clearly stated in the first objective of the Society which is to establish brotherhood amongst all beings in our world. So, you see, Findhorn is really an extension of the Theosophical movement. . . .

If we consider for a moment who the Masters of Compassion and Wisdom are, what they represent, this may become clearer to us. When I create something it is an extension of what I am—hopefully. The Theosophical Society was created by human beings but it was also a creation, an extension, or emergence out of that level or domain of life . . . which is the personification or the embodiment of the principles of synthesis and wholeness.

The speaker then describes the nature of the Masters of Wisdom and the Theosophical Movement as a manifestation of their work. "The Theosophical Movement," he adds, "is really the mother of the whole New Age movement, and as such has a tremendous role to play in the unfoldment of the New Age."

Findhorn, the New Age Community in Northern Scotland that Spangler regards as an extension of the Theosophical Movement, has been called "the archetypal New Age Center and Community" for hundreds of small communities that in the past few decades have sprung up in the Americas, in Europe, and in parts of the Orient. The present writer lectured there in the summer of 1978. It was interesting to note that although this community is nonsectarian, the religious/philosophical background of most of the resident members was either Alice Bailey's Arcane School, Rudolf Steiner's Anthroposophy, or Theosophy. Both Mrs. Bailey and Dr. Steiner had a prior history with the Theosophical Society. Bailey was active in the Society for a number of years in California, whereas Steiner headed the German Theosophical Society from 1902 to 1913.

While Mrs. Bailey freely acknowledged her debt to HPB and Theosophy, it was otherwise with Steiner. In his autobiography, written two years before his death in 1925, he is quite insistent (as have been his followers ever since) that before, during, and after his association with the TS he always pursued his own line of teaching and was not in any way influenced by Theosophy.[200] Even his sympathetic biographer, Colin Wilson, who refers to HPB as a "mixture of charlatanry and literary genius," admits that it "seems clear theosophy exerted a far greater influence than [Steiner] was willing to admit."[201]

A Dutch scholar, H. J. Spierenburg, thoroughly researched this influence. He examined all known letters of Steiner and surveyed the 350 volumes of his *Collected Writings*.[†] The result was published in a series of articles in a Dutch magazine and was subsequently translated into English by J. H. Molijn.[202] Selections are presented here under four categories, and taken mostly from lectures and letters:

1. A Prophecy of Nostradamus

In a lecture on June 10, 1904, Steiner spoke of this prophecy of Nostradamus:

> When the 19th century will have come to an end, one of the Brothers of Hermes will come from Asia to unite humanity again.

He commented: "The Theosophical Society is a fulfillment of this prophecy by Nostradamus." It may be recalled that in the preface to *Isis Unveiled* (1:vii), HPB states that her work "is a plea for the recognition of the Hermetic philosophy, the anciently universal Wisdom Religion, as the only possible key to the Absolute in science and theology."[203]

2. The Secret Doctrine

In a letter to Maria Sivers (August 20, 1902), Steiner wrote: "*The Secret Doctrine* has duly arrived and lies on my desk; it is very useful in my relevant studies, and I consult it continually."[204]

Then, in a letter to Gunther Wagner, he cites *The Secret Doctrine* (1:42) and quotes one of the Stanzas of Dzyan to the effect that our

† Steiner's *Collected Writings* are so huge because they include all editions of books and articles he wrote as well as his lectures.

planetary world is destined to receive Seven Truths. Four have already been received, because mankind is presently in the Fourth Stage or Round. Steiner comments: "Let me *for the time being* say that theosophy, i.e. that portion of theosophy which has been included in the esoteric sections of *The Secret Doctrine,* is composed of parts of the Fifth Truth."[205]

As late as June 21, 1909, Steiner wrote: ". . . the Stanzas of Dzyan and the Mahatma letters have still not been understood fully by a long way, and they should therefore be studied intensively, belonging as they do to the greatest wisdom revealed during the evolution of mankind."[206]

3. Masters of Wisdom and Compassion

In a letter to one Anna Wagner Steiner, dated January 2, 1905, Steiner wrote:

> You know that behind the whole Theosophical Movement are highly developed beings whom we call "Masters" or "Mahatmas." These exalted beings have already covered the way which humanity as such still has to go. They now work as the great "teachers of wisdom and harmony. . . ." At that moment they are active on the higher planes, to which the rest of humanity will advance in the course of the coming periods of development, the so-called rounds. On the physical plane they work through "messengers.". . .[207]

He wrote in a letter to Maria Von Sivers (January 9, 1905):

> My dearest, let us not lose courage: as long as we are in contact with the great Lodge, no evil can *actually* happen to us, whatever takes place *seemingly*. It is only by our courageous perseverence that we can be assured of the help of the exalted Masters.[208]

4. H. P. Blavatsky

Quoting from a lecture Steiner gave in Berlin on May 5, 1909:

> To understand the work of H. P. Blavatsky one must be able to judge and, what seems very strange, even much better than H. P. Blavatsky did herself! This she knew and it is the reason that she said: "These matters did not originate with me; they derive from those high individuals who stand behind our Movement. . . ." Let

us assume that she spoke the truth. Let us assume that there are indeed such great Masters of wisdom and harmony, and it is they who inspired her. On this assumption everything can be explained without the necessity of miracles coming into question. For in this case great, powerful individuals back her up and she was the instrument through which these grand secrets were communicated to the world. Then the question could at most be asked: "Why this Blavatsky?" But anyone who says this does not know the times. If someone else had been suitable to act as a channel for the words of the Masters of wisdom and harmony, . . . this one would have been chosen. . . . What was necessary was nobility of soul and a heart full of devotion capable of absorbing what had to be infused into humanity. And that she possessed! In this light everything can be explained.

[As her works] contain matter which belongs to the most imposing wisdom humanity has so far been offered, matter which is not to be found even with the greatest scholars, it cannot have been made up by her. It is this which the world will have to realize more and more every day.[209]

Stephan A. Hoeller, Ph.D., author of an article titled "H. P. Blavatsky: Woman of Mystery and Hero of Consciousness,"[†] is associate professor of comparative religions at the University of Oriental Studies in Los Angeles, a Gnostic and Jungian scholar. This article on H. P. Blavatsky was revised from an address delivered on the centenary anniversary of her passing, at the headquarters of the Theosophical Society in America, Wheaton, Illinois, on May 8, 1991. The article has been condensed.

In attempting to sketch a profile of the astonishing woman–magus Madame Blavatsky, and to give certain indications of the character of her work, it may be useful to first define the historical position into which this person and her mission may be made to fit for our understanding. Even though all informed persons would agree that "HPB," as she was and still is often known, partakes of many qualities of uniqueness, it is also true that she and her work belong to a particular and peculiar kind of tradition that has increasingly gained recognition in scholarship in recent decades, and became known as the *alternative reality tradition.*

Western (originally Mediterranean) culture possesses two realities, and around these there constellated themselves two traditions. The first tradition is exemplified by the worldview of the ancient

---

† Stephan A. Hoeller, "H.P. Blavatsky: Woman of Mystery and Hero of Consciousness," *The Quest,* Wheaton, Illinois, Autumn 1991, 70–77.

Hebrews and the Greeks of the Homeric era. One of its first features is that the human being is a body that may or may not have a tenuous appendage called a soul. In addition to the body, the most important part of the human being is reason, declares this reality tradition. With this reason the human being recognizes the will of God, or of the gods, and with the same reason the human subdues nature and bends her to his will. Psychologically expressed, this first reality orientation is based primarily upon the human ego. Reason, will, law, the unique position of individuals and of nations in the stream of history, these are the hallmarks of the first reality.

The second reality orientation is different from the first. It is rooted neither in the revelation of a monotheistic God, nor in the Aristotelian so-called clarity of reason. The second, or alternative reality, comes from ancient peoples as the Celts to the north and the Egyptians and the Babylonians to the south of the Mediterranean basin. The great representatives of this reality were Platonism, Neo-platonism, Pythagoreanism, Hermeticism and Gnosticism in antiquity. In addition to these we find numerous later representatives of this tradition throughout the history of Western spirituality.

What are the principal features of this alternative reality tradition? The alternative reality usually says that there is a body, a soul, and a spirit, and that the latter two are superior in a fundamental sense to the body. The nonphysical part of the human being is capable of virtually infinite degrees of expansion, and this expansion is accomplished by way of an initiatory growth of consciousness. The alternative reality tradition also asserts that rather than subduing nature by way of the intellectual will, the human being ought to establish a sympathetic rapport with nature. Such a rapport is envisioned as feasible because certain subtle spiritual connections are envisioned as joining human nature and nature in the external world. In another sense it might also be accurate to say that while the first reality enjoins upon the human to subdue the cosmos by way of reason and the will, the second, or alternative reality, holds out the promise that the human might overcome the cosmos through the process of an initiatory expansion of consciousness.

The worldview of the alternative reality is *magical*. Magic has been linguistically linked with the idea of greatness, as evidenced by such terms as magnitude, magnification, and even magnet, all of which contain the Indo-Aryan syllable *mag*. The magical worldview perceives in the inner recesses of the human being a concealed greatness, and it holds that by releasing this greatness into effective manifestation humans may overcome the limitation of embodied existence in the cosmos, indeed they may overcome the world entirely. Matter, nature, and the cosmic order are outgrown by the human being, who thus joins increasingly a realm of supernature, a world of transcendental reality. In view of certain contemporary emphases on nature, Gaia, creation spirituality, and the like, it is important to remember that the alternative reality and the tradition based thereon is founded on the human potential to transcend earth, nature, and cosmos, and not on a mere harmonious adjustment to them. The alternative reality is also non-tribal and even non-social in emphasis. It addresses itself not to how humans may live most profitably together in society, but rather and primarily to how the ineffable greatness may be discovered and released within the individual human soul. Thus we find that various embodiments of this tradition at once emphasize universal brotherhood as against tribal and national loyalties, and also affirm that society can be advanced not by collective means but by way of the internal transformation of individuals who comprise society. The values of tribe, nation, society and indeed of the entire cosmos are radically relativized by the discovery of the ineffable greatness that resides in the human spirit.

Enter now Madame Blavatsky, the great, perhaps indeed the greatest pioneering representative of the alternative reality tradition in the nineteenth and twentieth centuries. *Who was she?*

First of all, she was *a woman,* and that says a lot. She overcame the limitations her gender imposed on her in her time, and she became a fiercely independent, sovereign, and self-motivated person in her own right, never relinquishing these achievements in the course of her life. In her time, women and intellectual and spiritual callings were considered incompatible, indeed they appeared to many like fire and water; they were not supposed to mix. Along with a small handful of nineteenth-century women who became spiritual leaders, H. P. Blavatsky defied this mighty prejudice of her age.

Secondly, she was *a rebel*—against society as she found it, against religion as she experienced it, against conventionality and hypocrisy in all forms. Her rebellion, however, was never predominantly political or socioeconomic in thrust. She was caught up in the romantic fervor of the Italian *risorgimento* and may have even fought in Garibaldi's army for the freedom and unification of Italy. Also, there is much evidence that she actively opposed the racism, caste-consciousness, and oppression of women she encountered in late nineteenth-century India where she came to reside for a goodly period.

Thirdly, she was *not a formally educated scholar,* but an inspired person of knowledge. A talented writer, her essays, books, poetic-inspirational works, and short stories were written and published in several languages. She was a brilliant conversationalist, raconteur, and informal lecturer. She could be extremely formal, and totally informal. She was a versatile, fascinating companion. She painted, played the piano, and was conversant with the arts in general. While, like most women of her age, she did not attend an institution of higher learning, she showed an amazing knowledge of many disciplines, and held her own against many learned, formally schooled academicians. Many of her contemporaries and those of later generations dearly wished to possess even a fraction of the erudition combined with intuition she always manifested.

Fourth, she was *Russian.* Though she spent a good deal of her adult life away from Russia, and while she accepted and cherished her status as a naturalized citizen of the U.S., she was a true daughter of Mother Russia. Some feel that her life and character correspond strongly to the archetype of the traditional Russian wandering holy person, known as the *staretz* (literally "old one"), denoting a wandering, non-clerical ascetic, or pilgrim, who travels about the countryside, exhorting people concerning spiritual matters, sometimes in a decidedly unorthodox manner.

Her tragedy was that she lived among people who did not understand her. They wanted a *teacher*—nice, clean, scrubbed, mannerly, moral by their alienated standards of morality; learned, truthful, honest in myriads of inconsequential petty details. A schoolmistress, a schoolmarm who would teach them how to be wise, and above all, powerful in occult ways. She was a technician of the sacred. They wanted a prosaic teacher for their prosaic souls. They wanted somebody like themselves, who merely *knew* more than they did. She was a different species. She didn't just have knowledge that was different, but she *was* different. She was a stranger in a strange land—not only a Russian aristocratic bohemian of unconventional ways among rigid, alienated, repressed Victorian English and American middle class people, who didn't know the difference between appearance and substance. And with all that, with these great handicaps and obstacles in her way, she still managed to set hundreds and hundreds of their hearts on fire, so that no matter where they were their fire never died. Even when they turned against her, even when they called her a fraud, a charlatan, a plagiarist, and immoral woman, even then they secretly knew that she had given them life, energy, inspiration, creativity, meaning. Even her enemies bore unintentional testimony to her greatness and to her power.

But not all turned against her. Some sensed, knew who or what she was. Few if any understood her, but they came to her, and they received from her her unique charisma and they carried it forward. Henry Olcott, the American Civil War colonel and lawyer. He did not really understand her, but he became the president of her Theosophical Society, he traveled and worked relentlessly in her behalf.

And there were others: Judge, the Irish-American lawyer. He knew that he had met the greatest thing of his life, and he would never let go. Annie Besant, the rebel, the social revolutionary, the feminist and Fabian socialist, the greatest silver-tongued orator of her day. She took one look at the aging, sick, tormented Blavatsky in a London room, and dropped all her beliefs, friends, causes, involvements, threw herself at the feet of the old lioness from Russia. G. R. S. Mead; scholar, translator of Gnostic texts, unequaled authority on gnosticism and hermeticism of his time, who served her until her death, and delivered the last oration over her ashes in May of 1891 in England. And all the others, hundreds and indeed thousands: Poets, artists, scholars, journalists, clergy, politicians, statesmen and the humble folk from all walks of life. They all came, and many of them carried on what she began after her death. Blavatsky's influence both during her life and after her death was far larger than even her most fervent admirers realize. . . . What a woman! What a marvel, what a mystery. . . . She didn't give a tinker's damn for the sacred cows and conventions of Europe, America, or India—but she *was somebody*. She was herself; she was HPB. She followed her star, lived by her vision, died for her mission. She came from the aristocracy of imperial Russia, and she joined the nobles of the spirit. She was the grandmother of New Thought, and she is the greatgrandmother of the New Age . . . Hindus and Buddhists in India and Ceylon revered her, because she restored their self-esteem that had been damaged by colonial arrogance. She was disliked by many spiritualists, whom she reminded that they were spirits themselves, and therefore had no need to consort with the alleged spirits of the dead. Were she alive today, she would excoriate the modern mediums, called channelers, as so many "flap-doodles," her favorite term of derision.

Our discussion here chiefly concerned who she was. The reason for this is that what she did and accomplished were the natural outflow of who she was. Her many books, including *The Secret Doctrine;* the theosophical movement which she helped to found in 1875 and which is still thriving; the inspiration she has passed on to innumerable devoted hearts and strong minds; all of these were, and are, and will be, because of who she was. And who was she then? We don't know. We shall probably never know. She remains the noble mystery.

But there is something else we do know, and that is that those who are not grateful for what they received assuredly do not merit further blessings. And so it is incumbent upon us today to express gratitude for who she was and for what she gave us, for what she brought to us. No one returned from the magic circle of her company unchanged. Even today, those of us who have drawn near the flame she once helped kindle have been immeasurably aided by her inspiration. We must thank her today, and until the end of our days. Thank you, Helena Petrovna, thank you, thank you very much. . . .

The chapter that follows provides one more example of the timeliness of her writings.

Chapter 11

Near-Death Experiences and Cosmic Consciousness

The March 1992 *Life* magazine cover story is entitled "At the Edge of Eternity," by Verlyn Klinkenborg, with a subtitle "As Scientists Study the Meaning of Near-Death Experiences, Perhaps We Can Inch Closer to an Understanding of Life." *Life* reports:

All through history, people who have approached the border of death's kingdom have returned with eerily similar visions. But it was not until 1975 that knowledge of near-death experiences became a mass phenomenon, a subject of both scientific study and public controversy. In [November† of] that year psychiatrist Raymond Moody [published] *Life After Life,* [with a foreword by Elisabeth Kübler-Ross, M.D.‡ This was] the first commercially published book to compile anecdotes about near-death experiences, or NDEs. In the intervening years, *Life After Life* has sold seven million copies and given birth to an industry. Now the increasingly open discussion of these visions has begun to change the climate of dying in America.

Where once there were only a few researchers working on the subject, there are now dozens worldwide: physicians, psychologists, sociologists, anthropologists, biologists, philosophers, theologians, parapsychologists, mediums, shamans, yogis, lamas and not a few journalists. There is a *Journal of Near-Death Studies* and an International Association for Near-Death Studies. In 1975 Moody was able to interview in depth only about 50 persons who had had NDEs, but since then pollsters have estimated that some eight million Americans have had near-death experiences. Well over a thousand

---

† *Life After Life* was published in November 1975. It may be significant that November of 1975 was the 100th anniversary of the founding of the Theosophical Society.

‡ Elisabeth Kübler-Ross is a trailblazing pioneer in the field of NDEs; see her biography entitled *Quest,* by Derek Gill.

near-death stories have now been gathered, sorted and churned into statistics.

Two fascinating cases are presented by *Life*:

When she was 22, Kimberly Clark Sharp collapsed outside a motor vehicle bureau in Kansas and lay on the sidewalk, near death. "I found myself surrounded by dense, warm, foggy, gray material. In the fog I could see individual droplets of penetrating lightness and droplets of unfathomable darkness. Suddenly there was an explosion under me and reaching out to the farthest limits of my view was this light. It was absolutely alive, in a greater sense than we experience aliveness. It was so bright, the sun is not as bright, yet it didn't hurt my eyes. It filled up everything, and I was in the center of it. This light was all love, there was nothing there but love of the greatest intensity. I was being given information, in a communication between myself and the light, and I understood everything I was told. What is life, why we are born, universal kinds of knowledge. Profound, but there was a simplicity to it. It was like something I had known but had forgotten. It was heaven, more than ecstasy. It was a reunion of the highest order."

The second case reads:

I was deathly ill, shaking with fever, when I arrived at the hospital. My temperature was almost 106 and I was having cardiac arrhythmias. I felt an incredible pain. The wall of my uterus was ripping apart. I was in septic shock, going into labor. As I lost consciousness I heard a voice shouting, "I can't get her blood pressure!"

And then, within the tiniest fraction of an instant, I was out of my body and out of pain. I was up on the ceiling in a corner of the room, looking down, watching doctors and nurses rush around frantically as they worked to save my life . . . I was in a sort of a tunnel, a cloudlike enclosure, a grayish opalescence that I could partially see through. I felt wind brushing against my ears, except I didn't have ears. I was there, but my body wasn't.

I began to feel the most incredible, warm, golden, loving feeling, and the feeling was also a wonderful, warm, golden light. I was in this light, part of this light. There was a presence in the light, a wisdom, and that wisdom was the final word. The wisdom loved me and at the same time it knew everything about me. Everything I had ever done and felt was there for me to see. I wanted to proceed into the light and stay there forever, but I was shown that I had to go back and take care of my two children.

In that same fragment of a second, I was back in my body, back in all the pain. My son was being delivered, and I heard everybody screaming, "She's back!" I was so upset, so angry to be ripped away from the most wonderful peace in all the universe. And then they told me my son had been born dead.

I have kept this experience to myself, but I go over it in my mind every night, and it has taught me three things. First, I know that death is not painful. I will never be afraid to die. Second, I know that it's important to be true to myself and to others, because I will be accountable for my life when it's over. . . . And the third thing I know is that when you die you're not snuffed out. I know that I'm more than my body. There's a soul that's me. And I know that I, my soul, will always be there. I know for certain that there is life after death.

Among current research on NDEs is a study of HPB's views with this double title: *A Nineteenth Century Explanatory Scheme for the Interpretation of Near-Death Experiences: The Transpersonal Model of Death as Presented in Madame Blavatsky's Theosophy*. The author, Jean-Louis Siémons, a member of IANDS (International Association for Near-Death Studies) is professor of biophysics at the Institut National Agronomique, at Paris. In his 27-page paper Dr. Siémons asks: What did science know of NDEs a century ago? He answers: "Very few facts indeed, apart from accounts of people rescued from drowning (and other accidents), which Mme. Blavatsky duly mentioned in her earliest book in 1877. Also, the panoramic vision of life was known to occur in certain pathological conditions (epileptic aura)."[210]

Dr. Siémons uses as one of his sources HPB's article in *Lucifer* (October 1889) "Memory in the Dying"; quoting therefrom:

We find in a very old letter from a MASTER, written years ago to a member of the Theosophical Society, the following suggestive lines on the mental state of a dying man:

"At the last moment, the whole life is reflected in our memory and emerges from all the forgotten nooks and corners, picture after picture, one event after the other. The dying brain dislodges memory with a strong, supreme impulse; and memory restores faithfully every impression that has been entrusted to it during the period of the brain's activity . . . No man dies insane or unconscious, as some physiologists assert. Even a madman or one in a fit of *delirium tremens* will have his instant of perfect lucidity at the moment of death, though unable to say so to those present. The man may often appear dead. Yet from the last pulsation, and between the last throbbing of his heart and the moment when the last spark of animal heat leaves the body, *the brain thinks* and the Ego lives, in these few brief seconds, his whole life over again."

The above statement has been more than once strenuously opposed by materialists; Biology and (Scientific) Psychology, it was urged, were both against the idea, and while the latter had no well-demonstrated data to go upon in such a *hypothesis,* the former dismissed the idea as an empty "superstition." (Meanwhile, even biology is bound to progress, and this is what we learn of its latest achievements. Dr. Ferré has communicated quite recently to the Biological Society of Paris a very curious note on the mental state of dying *which corroborates marvelously the above lines.*) For, it is to the special phenomenon of life-reminiscences, and that sudden re-emerging on the blank walls of memory, from all its long neglected and forgotten "nooks and corners" of "picture after picture" that Dr. Ferré draws the special attention of biologists. [Italics added.]†

In *The Key to Theosophy,* HPB writes:

At the solemn moment of death every man, even when death is sudden, sees the whole of his past life marshalled before him, in its minutest details. . . . But this instant is enough to show him the whole chain of causes which have been at work during his life. He sees and now understands himself as he is, unadorned by flattery or self-deception. He reads his life, remaining as a spectator looking down into the arena he is quitting; he feels and knows the justice of all the suffering that has overtaken him.[211]

In the above is strong evidence that HPB had an intimate knowledge of the details of the NDEs, which only became known generally in the twentieth century. Comparison of her statements with modern cases is given by Dr. Siémons.

[HPB] "*He reads his life . . . as a spectator . . .*"[212]

"There was a certain detachment as I watched all this. I had the sensation that I was on the outside looking in and it seemed that this reoccurrence [sic] of my life was taking place in front of me and I was viewing it.

". . . I saw my whole life take place in many images, as though on a stage at some distance from me."[213]

---

† Cf. Hughlings Jackson, "On a particular variety of epilepsy" (*Brain,* part XLII, 179) quoted by Dr. Ch. Ferré in an article (dated Feb. 16, 1989): "Note pour servir à l'histoire de l'état mental des mourants" (*Mémoires de la Société de Biologie de Paris,* tome 1er, 9e série, 1989).

[HPB] *"As a spectator looking down into the arena he is quitting."*

"I acted out my life, as though I were an actor on a stage upon which I looked down from practically the highest gallery in the theater. Both hero and onlooker, I was as though doubled."[214]

[HPB] *"He sees and now understands himself as he is, unadorned by flattery or self-deception."*

"It was like I got to see some good things I had done and some mistakes I had made, you know, and try to understand them."[215]

"Some people characterize this as an educational effort on the part of the being of light."[216]

"The being would ask something like, 'What have you done with your life to show me?' What was expected in return was . . . a general self scrutiny, putting one's whole life in question."[217]

[HPB] *"But this instant is enough to show him the whole chain of causes which have been at work during his life."*

"It was like: 'Okay, here's why you had the accident. Here's why this happened. Because so and so and so . . . it all had meaning.' Definitely."[218]

The big problem in NDE research is to identify the "being of light." In Theosophy that Being is said to be one's own Higher Self. HPB says it is practically omniscient. Dr. Siémons remarks that:

Quite often, in their efforts of description, experiencers use different labels to identify this "presence"—God, Christ, Angel, Guide . . . Obviously, in their complete ignorance of deep (spiritual) psychology, they could hardly find better terms to translate, in an intelligible mode, this unexpected encounter with their own individual Ego-Self, which seems to "know all about them"; to bear them "a total love and acceptance" and to have with them a kind of intimate, "personal" exchange. *For very good reasons* indeed—in the light of Theosophy—if we remember that this Ego is not a stranger to its terrestrial personality, but remains closely "interested" in its destiny: from birth to death, the transpersonal individuality broods over . . . its earthly representative (or emanation), registering the latter's behavior and inspiring it with its own knowledge and energy, through the unspoken language of intuition, dreams, etc.

The theosophical interpretation is supported by Kenneth Ring, Professor of Psychology at the University of Connecticut (Storrs). Quoting from his book, *Life at Death:*[219]

Moody spoke of a "being of light" and though none of our respondents used this phrase some seemed to be aware of a "presence"
(or "voice") in association with the light . . . Here we must, I think,
make a speculative leap. I submit that this presence [or] voice is
actually—oneself! It is not merely a projection of one's personality,
however, but one's *total self,* or what in some traditions is called the
higher self. In this view, the individual personality is but a split-off
fragment of the total self with which it is reunited at the point of
death. During ordinary life, the individual personality functions in a
seemingly autonomous way, as though it were a separate entity. In
fact, however, it is invisibly tied to the larger self structure of which
it is a part.[220]

Dr. Ring also adds: "What has this to do with the light? The answer
is—or so I would say—that this higher self is so awesome, so overwhelming, so loving, and unconditionally accepting (like an all-
forgiving mother) and so *foreign* to one's individualized consciousness
that one perceives it as *separate* from oneself, as an unmistakable *other.* It
manifests itself as a brilliant golden light, but it actually is oneself, in a
higher form, that one is seeing."[221]

HPB's translation of *The Voice of the Silence* contains these pertinent
verses:

All is impermanent in man except the pure bright essence of Alaya
[the universal soul]. Man is its crystal ray; a *beam of light* immaculate
within, a form of clay material upon the lower surface. That beam is
thy life-guide and thy true Self, the Watcher and the silent
Thinker.[222] [Italics added.]

Doctors speak of two kinds of death: clinical death, when all vital
signs disappear, and irreversible biological death, when the organs have
deteriorated beyond function. Revival is then impossible.

From an occult standpoint, however, there may be other criteria for
determining real death, and this appears to be demonstrated in the case
shortly to be considered. What are such criteria? Helena Blavatsky
writes, (*Isis Unveiled* 1:481) that "a resuscitation, after the soul and spirit
have entirely separated from the body and the last electric thread is
severed, is impossible." In *The Secret Doctrine,* (1:555), she adds that a
person can still be revived "whose astral 'vital body' has not been irreparably separated from the physical body by the severance of the magnetic or odic cord." Interesting that in the Old Testament it is averred
that, when death occurs, "the silver cord is loosed." (*Ecclesiastes* 12:6).

There have been a number of reports of deathbed visions experienced by onlookers who claim to have actually seen this loosening or severing of the silver, magnetic cord. Dr. Kenneth Ring in his aforementioned *Life at Death* cites several and quotes the following remarkable description given by a physician, Dr. R. B. Hout, who witnessed the death of his aunt. During the experience he saw not only the silver cord but what Blavatsky called the severing of "the last electric thread." First, in his vision, the doctor describes:

[My attention] was called to something immediately above the physical body, suspended in the atmosphere about two feet above the bed. At first I could distinguish nothing more than a vague outline of a hazy, foglike substance. There seemed to be only a mist held there suspended, motionless. But, as I looked, very gradually there grew into my sight a denser, more solid, condensation of this inexplicable vapor. Then I was astonished to see definite outlines presenting themselves, and soon I saw this foglike substance was assuming a human form.

Soon I knew that the body I was seeing resembled that of the physical body of my aunt; the astral body hung suspended horizontally a few feet above the physical counterpart, I continued to watch and the Spirit Body now seemed complete to my sight. I saw the features plainly. They were very similar to the physical face, except that a glow of peace and vigor was expressed instead of age and pain. The eyes were closed as though in tranquil sleep, and a luminosity seemed to radiate from the Spirit Body.

As I watched the suspended Spirit Body, my attention was called to a silverlike substance that was streaming from the head of the physical body to the head of the spirit "double." Then I saw the connection-cord between the two bodies. As I watched, the thought, "The silver cord!" kept running through my mind. I knew, for the first time, the meaning of it. This "silver cord" was the connecting-link between the physical and the spirit bodies, even as the umbilical cord unites the child to its mother.

The cord was attached at the occipital protuberance immediately at the base of the skull. Just where it met the physical body it spread out, fanlike, and numerous little strands separated, and were attached separately, to the skull base. But other than at the attachments, the cord was round, being perhaps an inch in diameter. The color was a translucent luminous silver radiance.

The cord seemed alive with vibrant energy. I could see the pulsations of light stream along the course of it, from the direction of the physical body to the spirit "double." With each pulsation the Spirit Body became more alive and denser, whereas the physical body became quieter and more nearly lifeless. By this time the features were very distinct. The life was all in the astral body; the pulsations of the cord had stopped.

I looked at the various strands of the cord as they spread out, fan-like, at the base of the skull. Each strand snapped, the final severance was at hand. A twin process of death and birth was about to ensue. The last connecting strand of the silver cord snapped and the Spirit Body was free.

Then came the dramatic moment when the luminous body rose up from its reclining position. "The closed eyes opened and a smile broke from the radiant features. She gave me a smile of farewell, then vanished from my sight."

If it were suspected that such awesome events transpire when human beings die, how differently people would view the process and how differently they would react. They would soon realize emotional grief could disturb the departure of a beloved friend or relative.

The solemnity and transcendental nature of death is described in Isaac Bashevis Singer's novel *Shosha*. One of his characters relates a mystical experience of "universal oneness" that permeated his being years ago. "I had merged with eternity. At times I think it was like the state of passing over from life to what we call death. We may experience it in the final moments or perhaps immediately after. I say this because no matter how many dead people I have seen in my life, they have had the same expression on their faces: Aha, so that's what it is! If I had only known! What a shame I can't tell the others."[223]

In IANDS archives Ring reports:

More than a hundred letters from people who have written us to the effect, "Well, I was never actually close to death, but I also seem to have had what you call a near-death experience. . ." Then these correspondents typically relate an incident in their lives—during meditation, childbirth, a personal crisis, a church service, or, in many cases, seemingly spontaneously—in which they, too, seem to have been touched by much the same thing that NDErs come to know during a near-death crisis. . .

. . . A recent informal study conducted by a University of Connecticut graduate student, Pamela Rivard, can illustrate this thesis.

In brief, Rivard was interested in interviewing persons who claimed to have undergone a significant religious awakening in the recent past. Her findings demonstrate unequivocally that there are many points of obvious overlap between the religious experiences of her respondents and NDEs, both in phenomenology and transformative effects.

Such convergences serve to buttress a point that is often overlooked in discussion of NDEs but that is crucial to any attempt to explain them: *What occurs during an NDE has nothing inherently to do with death or with the transition into death.* In my opinion, this point cannot be emphasized too strongly, and the failure to do so has led to a serious distortion in our understanding of the NDE. What happens to an individual during an NDE is *not* unique to the moment of apparent imminent death. It is just that coming close to death is one of the very reliable triggers that sets off this kind of experience.

The reason that this has been lost on many professionals and the public alike is that the current wave of research has fastened on the NDEr as an exemplar of this variety of transcendental experience. In our collective fascination with the drama of death, we have come nearly to equate what we have called the NDE with the moment of death itself and have failed to recognize that dying is only one, albeit a common one, of the circumstances that tends to be conducive to this kind of experience.

Dr. Ring continues:

The NDE should be regarded as one of a family of related mystical experiences that have always been with us, rather than as a recent discovery of modern researchers who have come to investigate the phenomenology of dying.

To support further this claim of the generality of (what I will persist, for now, in labeling) the NDE, consider this summary, provided by psychiatrist Stanley Dean, of the characteristics of what he calls "ultraconsciousness" and its effects. "Ultraconsciousness" is a term coined by Dean, but it is virtually synonymous with an older, more familiar term, cosmic consciousness. Incidentally, Dean's summary was first published in 1974, before the explosion of interest in near-death phenomena. Here is Dean's list:

1. The onset is ushered in by an awareness of dazzling light that floods the brain and fills the mind. In the East it is called the "Brahmic Splendor." Walt Whitman speaks of it as ineffable

light—"light rare untellable, lighting the very light—beyond all signs, descriptions, languages." Dante writes that it is capable of "transhumanizing a man into a god . . ."

2. The individual is bathed in emotions of supercharged joy, rapture, triumph, grandeur, reverential awe, and wonder.

3. An intellectual illumination occurs that is quite impossible to describe. In an intuitive flash one has an awareness of the meaning and drift of the universe, an identification and merging with Creation, infinity, and immortality, a depth beyond depth of revealed meaning—in short, a conception of the Over-Self so omnipotent that religion has interpreted it as God . . .

4. There is a feeling of transcendental love and compassion for all living things.

5. Fear of death falls off like an old cloak; physical and mental suffering vanish. There is an enhancement of mental and physical vigor and activity, a rejuvenation and prolongation of life . . .

6. There is a reappraisal of the material things in life, an enhanced appreciation of beauty, a realization of the relative unimportance of riches and abundance compared to the treasures of the ultraconscious.

7. There is an extraordinary quickening of the intellect, an uncovering of latent genius. Far from being a passive, dreamlike state, however, it can endow an individual with powers so far-reaching as to influence the course of history.

8. There is a sense of mission. The revelation is so moving and profound that the individual cannot contain it within himself but is moved to share it with all fellowmen.

9. A charismatic change occurs in personality—an inner and outer radiance, as though charged with some divinely inspired power, a magnetic force that attracts and inspires others with unshakeable loyalty and faith.

10. There is a sudden or gradual development of extraordinary psychic gifts such as clairvoyance, extrasensory perception, telepathy, precognition, psychic healing, etc. . . .[224]

Dr. Ring informs:

According to George Gallup's figures, there may well be eight million adult Americans who have experienced NDEs. Of course, we have no idea how many people in the world may already have had this kind of experience, but it certainly does not seem unreasonable to assume that millions of individuals outside the United States must also have had NDEs. In any event, with resuscitation technology likely to improve and to spread in use around the globe, it appears highly likely that many millions *more* will come to know for themselves what the people described in this book already know.

But, of course, the point is not simply that many millions will know the NDE for themselves but also *how the NDE will transform them afterward.* We have already examined in depth how people's lives and consciousness are affected by NDEs and what values come to guide their behavior. Now, to begin to appreciate the planetary impact of these changes, we must imagine these same effects occurring in millions of lives throughout the world, regardless of race, religion, nationality, or culture.

From this perspective, we are now finally able to discern the larger meanings of NDEs. May it be that NDErs—and others who have had similar awakenings—*collectively represent an evolutionary thrust toward higher consciousness for humanity at large?* Could it be that the NDE itself is an evolutionary mechanism that has the effect of jump-stepping individuals into the next stage of human development by unlocking spiritual potentials previously dormant? Indeed, are we seeing in such people—as they mutate from their pre-NDE personalities into more loving and compassionate individuals—the prototype of a new more advanced strain of the human species striving to come into manifestation? No longer *Homo sapiens* perhaps, but tending toward what John White has called *Homo noeticus?*[225]

Does *The Secret Doctrine* say anything about a new human race? Here are some lines from Vol. II, pages 444–46:

. . . Occult philosophy teaches that even now, under our very eyes, the new Race and Races are preparing to be formed, and that it is in America that the transformation will take place, and has already silently commenced. Pure Anglo-Saxons hardly three hundred years ago, the Americans of the United States have already become a nation apart, and, owing to a strong admixture of various nationalities and inter-marriage, almost a race *sui generis,* not only mentally, but also physically . . . in short, the germs of the *Sixth* sub-race, and in some few hundred years more, will become most decidedly the pioneers of that race which must succeed to the present European or fifth sub-race, in all its new characteristics. After this, . . . they will launch into preparations for the seventh sub-race; until, in consequence of cataclysms—the first series of those which must one day destroy Europe, and still later the whole Aryan race (and thus affect both Americas), as also most of the lands directly connected with the confines of our continent and isles—the Sixth Root-Race will have appeared on the stage of our Round. When shall this be? Who knows save the great Masters of Wisdom, perchance, and they are as silent upon the subject as the snow-capped peaks that tower above them. All we know is, that it will silently come into existence; so silently, indeed, that for long millenniums shall its pioneers—the peculiar children who will grow into peculiar men and women—be regarded as anomalous *lusus naturæ,* abnormal oddities physically and mentally. Then, as they increase, and their numbers become with every age greater, one day they will awake to find themselves in a majority. It is the present men who will then begin to be regarded as exceptional mongrels, until these die out in their turn in civilised lands; surviving only in small groups on islands—the mountain peaks of to-day—where they will vegetate, degenerate, and finally die out . . .

. . . This process of preparation for the Sixth great Race must last throughout the whole sixth and seventh sub-races. . . . But the *last* remnants of the Fifth Continent will not disappear until some time after the birth of the *new* Race; when another and *new* dwelling, the sixth continent, will have appeared above the *new* waters on the face of the globe, so as to receive the new stranger . . . Yet the Fifth will not die, but survive for a while; overlapping the new Race . . . Thus it is the mankind of the New world . . . whose mission and Karma it is, to sow the seeds for a forthcoming, grander, and far more glorious Race than any of those we know at present. The Cycles of Matter will be succeeded by Cycles of Spirituality and a fully developed mind. On the law of parallel history and races, the majority of the future mankind will be composed of glorious Adepts.[226]

Chapter 12

Not Without Honor

In the United States, a group of two hundred Bible scholars, ministers, and lay persons known as the Jesus Seminar have discovered after six years' intensive research, using the latest test for historical reliability, that no more than 20 percent of the sayings attributed to Jesus in the New Testament were uttered by him. Among those he never uttered was "I am the way, the truth and the life. No one comes to the Father except through me."† Thus is undermined the chief dogma of orthodox Christianity that only through Jesus can anyone be saved.

Ari Goldman reports the foregoing in his column in the *New York Times* (February 8, 1991). He adds that: "Among the observations Jesus then [did make] was a comment found with slight variation in the Gospel of Matthew, Mark, and John, about a prophet having no honor in his own country." HPB's books were always banned in Russia. Her books were banned when the Soviets took over.‡ How astonishing then to learn from *The Theosophist,* August, 1990:

The motherland of Madame Blavatsky is now alive with interest in her life and work. This was brought into sharp focus during the visit of the International President [of The Theosophical Society (Adyar)], Mrs. Radha Burnier, to Moscow and Leningrad from 14 to 24 June 1990 at the invitation of the Soviet Writers Union and the Association "Peace Through Culture.". . .

There were two functions of importance in Moscow, the first of which took place on 18 June when an exhibition on HPB was opened in the imposing premises of the Writers Union. It displayed photographs of her, her books in Russian, extracts from her writings, statements by M. K. Gandhi, Jawaharlal Nehru, Nicholas Roerich, and others about her influence on their lives, and some theosophical books in English taken from Adyar. Moscow press and

† See *H. P. Blavatsky Collected Writings*, 13:55, 14:396 fn; *The Secret Doctrine,* 2:231 fn.

‡ During the decade following 1908 when the Czar's censor was fired, and a new liberal one was appointed, a new spirit existed in Russia, and Theosophy flourished.

television covered the event and several million viewers saw the opening on prime television time, when it was announced that 1991 would be celebrated as the International Year of Blavatsky, it being the 100th anniversary of her passing away.

On the following day, 19 June, there was a meeting to honour HPB in the hall of the Soviet Writers Union. Its five hundred seats were insufficient to hold those who came, not only from Moscow, but from other cities. A large portrait of HPB surrounded by flowers adorned the dais; Mr. Valentin M. Sidorov, [then] President of "Peace through Culture," outlined the life of HPB, explained the Objects of the Theosophical Society, and welcomed the International President, whose visit, he said, was an historical event, after more than seventy years when HPB's books were banned and the TS shut out of the country of her birth. This was followed by a talk by Mrs. Burnier. . . . After a short interval, poems by and about HPB were recited and folk songs dear to her were sung. Each artist made an offering of a rose to the memory of HPB.

The programme in Leningrad [now St. Petersburg] also included two meetings, one of which was in the premises of the Writers Union. After a brief introduction and talk by Mrs. Radha Burnier, questions were invited. The keen interest of the participants, numbering about two hundred, was evidenced by the variety and range of questions regarding the TS and theosophy. Members of the Roerich Foundation were much involved in the programmes and the relationship of the TS with the Roerichs was also discussed.

A number of private talks with enquirers and sympathizers took place both in Moscow and Leningrad [St. Petersburg]. In the discussion with the officers of "Peace Through Culture" it was proposed to request the city authorities of Dnepropetrovsk (formerly called Ekaterinoslav), the birthplace of HPB, to permit a suitable plaque to be put on the house where she was born, which is fortunately still intact. This was done on September 12, 1991, the date according to the present Russian calendar, when HPB was born. [Modern calendar birthday is August 12, old Russian calendar birthday is July 31.]

It is also part of the plan for the "Year of HPB" to reprint [5,000 copies of] the Russian translation of *The Secret Doctrine*. The President, Mrs. Radha Burnier, offered to print by offset the existing Russian translation on the Vasanta Press, Adyar, as paper shortage in Russia makes it impractical to publish such a work in Russia in time for distribution in 1991. It is proposed to provide libraries and other important institutions in Russia with *The Secret Doctrine*. . . .

A remarkable new beginning has thus been made for theosophy to become widely known in Eastern Europe. It is gratifying that the initiative has arisen from the people themselves† of this vast area, unfortunately so long benighted, who are thirsting for spiritual knowledge and the light needed to solve grave human problems.[227]

It may be of some significance that during the International Year of Blavatsky, the Russian people overthrew the shackles of communism in favor of a democratic form of government. In August 1991, at the time of the aborted coup of the Soviet hard-liners, this item appeared in the *New York Times* (August 24):

> George F. Kennan, one of the leading American historians and diplomatic experts on the Soviet Union [now Russia], has said he believes that the events surrounding the failed coup in Moscow eclipse the Russian Revolution in importance. "I find it difficult to find any other turning point in modern Russian history that is so significant as this one. . . . For the first time in their history they have turned their back on the manner in which they've been ruled—not just in the Soviet period but in the centuries before. They have demanded a voice in the designing of their own society."

"Peace Through Culture," the sponsor of the meetings in Moscow and Leningrad [St. Petersburg], is a nonpolitical and nongovernmental association. Its name was formulated by Nicholas Roerich, a Theosophist and noted Russian artist whose paintings are to be found in many museums. His original set designs for the operas of Wagner, Moussorgsky, and Rimsky-Korsakov and ballets such as Stravinsky's "Rite of Spring" are classics of the stage. Roerich wrote many books on art, culture, and philosophy. As an explorer and scientist he conducted extensive archaeological research in Russia and in Central Asia. He was nominated for the Nobel Peace Prize for his pact for the international protection in war and peace of monuments and other cultural treasures. The Roerich Pact was signed by thirty-six nations, and President Roosevelt, when signing it at the White House, in the presence of many world leaders, said: "It possesses a spiritual significance far greater than the text of the instrument itself."[228]

† That the initiative did indeed come from Russians themselves is evident from the fact that when Mrs. Burnier went to Moscow she had no idea of all that had been planned in advance of her visit. (*Adyar Newsletter,* May, 1990, 3.)

THE BANNER OF PEACE
THROUGH CULTURE

Since time immemorial, warriors have carried banners into war. This is a banner for peace.

This ancient universal symbol is one of the world's oldest. Its three spheres were designated by Nicholas Roerich, the designer of the Banner, as the synthesis of all arts, all sciences, and all religions within the circle of culture. He defined culture as the cultivation of the creative potential in man. He believed that the achievement of peace, through culture, is a goal to be realized through the positive effort of the human will.

Wherever the Banner is displayed, it recognizes the great achievements of the past, the present, and the future. It encourages the individual to strive to fulfill his highest potential, beautifying all aspects of life; it encourages each person to take responsibility for the evolution of the planet; it signifies the peace-builder; and it symbolizes the transformation of the individual and of society. It represents cooperation—the cornerstone of the emerging planetary culture—in all aspects of human activity.

Nicholas Roerich was a world-renowned artist, philosopher, archaeologist, and author. He created an international treaty, the Roerich Pact and Banner of Peace. It provided that the Banner fly over all historic monuments and educational, artistic, and scientific institutions to indicate special protection and respect in times of war and of peace. It acknowledged that cultural treasures are of lasting value to all people as the common heritage of humanity.

The Pact was introduced by Roerich in New York in 1929 and earned him a nomination for the Nobel Peace Prize. On April 15, 1935, President Franklin D. Roosevelt presided over ceremonies at the White House in Washington, D.C., in which twenty Latin American countries joined the U.S. in signing this historic document.

Nicholas Roerich said, "Positive creativeness is the fundamental quality of the human spirit. Let us welcome all those who, surmounting personal difficulties,...propel their spirits to the task of Peace-building, thus ensuring a radiant future."

"Where there is Peace, there is Culture;
Where there is Culture, there is Peace."
NICHOLAS ROERICH (1874-1947)

Roerich was a close friend of Vice President Henry Wallace and suggested to him that the time had come for the United States to use the hitherto uncut side of the Great Seal of this country. Wallace passed on the suggestion to Roosevelt,[229] and so today on the dollar bill is to be found the reverse side of the seal, with its portentous symbol of an unfinished pyramid and a mysterious eye in place of the capstone. The words *Novus Ordo Seclorum,* meaning "A New Order of Ages," appear under the pyramid.

The gift from the Theosophical Society-Adyar, of five thousand copies of *The Secret Doctrine* by H. P. Blavatsky, was made using the translated edition by Helena Roerich,[†] published in Riga in 1937, which Boris de Zirkoff called magnificent.[230] Daniel Entin, director of the Roerich Museum in New York, advises that the translation was actually a family project, Nicholas and the sons being involved too.

Three years ago, an item in New York *Newsday* (December 5, 1989) on the Roerich Museum and its director appears to have escaped notice elsewhere. Quoting therefrom:

Roerich, who died in 1947, is a hero in the Soviet Union, where even leader Mikhail Gorbachev has a fondness for him. Two years ago, Gorbachev invited Roerich's son to lunch at the Kremlin and told him that he would sponsor a Roerich center in Moscow. As a result, Roerich societies have sprung up in cities across that country and Raisa Gorbachev has been involved in the starting of a fund in his name.

Subsequently, Gorbachev provided a plane for the son, Svetoslav, to transfer his entire collection of Roerich paintings in Bangalore, India, where he lives, to Moscow, where it is now housed.

As to when the Roerichs first became interested in Theosophy, Entin advises that in the archives of the museum is a letter from the TS in London disclosing that the Roerichs joined in 1919. "I have no proof that they were members in Russia," Entin writes, "but they very well may have been. . . . But there's no doubt that they moved in circles of people who were deeply interested in the [Theosophical] teachings that were prevalent at that time."

During the last decades of Nicholas Roerich's career he lived in

---

† The *San Francisco Chronicle* (May 24, 1991), in reporting on new religious movements based on New Age "spiritual alternatives," comments:

About 50,000 copies of *The Secret Doctrine,* the founding text of the Theosophical movement, a century-old occult religion and one of the roots of New Age spirituality, are now being rushed into print by Russian publishers for Eastern Europe. . . .

India. In a letter to Annie Besant in Adyar (March 31, 1924), he wrote from Darjeeling, where he and his wife then lived:

> *The great Foundress of the Theosophical Society H. P. Blavatsky in her last article, pointed out the importance of Art. She foresaw the future significance of this great creative force, which will help to build the coming world, as Art is the nearest bridge between different nations. We should always remember this last thought of the great personality, and the simplest way to keep it always in mind would be to found at Adyar a Museum of Art, dedicated to the name of H. P. Blavatsky. Such an institution will attract the hearty [sic] of the representatives of every branch of Art, and gather new people around the place where originated so many lofty ideas. If the Society is willing to consider my proposal, I am ready to offer as a donation to the Blavatsky Museum, my painting "The Messenger" which was painted here, and is dedicated to the memory of this great woman.*[231]

The offer was accepted and on January 18, 1925, according to a Madras newspaper:

> [Roerich] unveiled the picture and said, "In this home of Light let me present this picture, dedicated to Helena Petrovna Blavatsky, as the nucleus of a future Blavatsky Museum whose motto will be, 'Beauty is the Garment of Truth.'"
>
> The picture, about 42 inches high by thirty-six, is a striking tempera work in a colour key of violet, depicting a woman in a Buddhist Temple, opening the door to admit a messenger in the early morning.

A beautiful reproduction in color is to be found in *The Theosophist* (May 1991). Mrs. Sina Fosdick, an official of the Roerich Museum, advised the present writer that the young woman in the painting represents humanity, while the messenger who enters the temple signifies HPB and the beginning of her public work in 1875 (see centerfold photograph #31).[232]

The Roerichs' last home was in the Kulu valley in the Punjab, and from there Nicholas wrote Boris de Zirkoff on July 7, 1939:

> Thank you for your letter of May the 20th, which only now reached our far off mountains. I am glad to be able to write you in Russian; glad also that you are a close relative of HPB, for whom we have such a profound reverence. There will come a time when her name will resound all over Russia, with dignity and respect. . . . Only too often have Russians themselves forgotten about their own

leaders of thought; it is time for us to learn how to value real treasures. . . .

Even as I write you these lines, there rise before my eyes, out there
in the distance, the snow-capped peaks and the lofty pass leading to
Tibet. They stand as silent witnesses to those enduring Truths in
which is hidden spiritual rejuvenation, and the ultimate perfectibility of the human race. The Great Ones are always ready to help,
but men so often turn away from that help.[233]

Today, it is the young Russians in particular who are so avidly inter-
ested in studying the teachings of Blavatsky. They are also interested in
locating the libraries' and universities' holdings of her long-lost letters.
That they once existed is indicated by the manuscript of Helen F.
Pissareff's *History of the Russian Theosophical Movement.* It relates that in
1909 she, together with a group of Russian Theosophists, attended the
Fifth International Congress of the TS in Budapest. In returning to
Russia they chose to go by boat via Athens, Constantinople, and
Odessa—the last because all of them wanted to meet two of HPB's
nieces, daughters of her sister, Vera. They were royally received and
were given photographs, portraits, and other valuable material, which
were deposited in the St. Petersburg Theosophical Center and placed
in a large album. In later years the gifts were confiscated by the
revolutionary authorities. What a treasure this would be if they could
be located![234]

Today the search to find HPB material in Russian libraries and archives goes on. To date about a hundred of her letters have been found.
The interest in Theosophy continues as well: Many Theosophical
study groups and a Theosophical Society have been formed. So it can
now be said that HPB is not without honor in her own country. But
what about her adopted country, the United States of America? There
are, of course, many Theosophists here and her books are in increasing
demand. However, it is sad to learn that when American reporters in
Russia passed on to their home editors the news that in Russia, 1991
was declared to be the International Year of Blavatsky, not one newspaper or periodical that I know of published the announcement.

Why was this? An 1898 article by James Pryse entitled "Helena
Petrovna Blavatsky," recently reprinted in *The Canadian Theosophist*
(May/June 1991), suggests an answer:

The truly great stand far in advance of their fellows, and are appreciated fully only by the generations that come after; they are understood by but few in their own times. Near scrutiny is only for small

things; that which is big has to be observed at a proportionate distance to be judged adequately. It is told that among the statues presented in competition to be placed on a temple in ancient Greece there was one that appeared rough, unfinished and angular, exciting the ridicule of the judges; but when each of the perfectly finished statues had in turn been placed aloft only to be taken down because its details were indistinguishable at so great a height, and the gleam from its polished surface only confused its outlines, the rejected one was finally elevated to the place, and all were lost in wonder at its beauty, for its rough surface kept the outlines clear, and distance softened its rough-hewn curves.

If H. P. Blavatsky appeared rough, crude and even uncouth to those about her, it was only because she had been cast in a titan mould. In this age of complaisant orthodoxies, conventionalized schools of thought, of commonplaces hackneyed and inane, she seemed strangely out of place; like an old-time prophet, boisterous as Elijah, grandiose as Isaiah, mysterious as Ezekiel, she hurled scathing Jeremiads at the puerilities and hypocrisies of the nineteenth century. She was a forerunner shouting loudly in the wilderness of beliefs. She did not belong to the present age. Her message came from the mighty past, and she delivered it not to the present but to the future. For the present was shrouded in the darkness of materialism, and in the far past was the only light by which the future could be illumined. . . . She proclaimed, to all those who had ears to hear, the long-forgotten truths of which humanity now has need. She bore witness of the Gnosis to an age that had become agnostic. She brought tidings of the great Lodge, which in times of old was the "good Shepherd" of mankind.

To conclude this story of the life and influence of Helena Blavatsky, here are a few lines from her own pen. They were discovered in her desk after her body died on May 8, 1891:

There is a road, steep and thorny, beset with perils of every kind— but yet a road; and it leads to the Heart of the Universe. I can tell you how to find Those who will show you the secret gateway that leads inward only. . . . For those who win onwards, there is reward past all telling: the power to bless and save humanity. For those who fail, there are other lives in which success may come.[235]

HPB

I

Appendix A

1885 Report of the Society for Psychical Research: Vernon Harrison's Professional Opinion

> He who hears an innocent person slandered, whether a brother
> theosophist or not, and does not undertake his defense as he would
> undertake his own—is no Theosophist.
>   — H. P. Blavatsky, *Lucifer*, November 1887

A SENIOR MEMBER OF THE SPR and a court-accepted expert on questioned documents, Vernon Harrison wrote a powerful critique of the Hodgson Report, published in the SPR's *Journal* in April 1986. Since then, Dr. Harrison has continued his research, including a line-by-line examination of 1,323 color slides of the Mahatma Letters from the British Library set. His findings are reported in his 1997 book, *H. P. Blavatsky and the SPR: An Examination of the Hodgson Report of 1885*[†]:

> The results of the present investigation, which has been extended over a fifteen-year period, are now presented in the hope that future biographers of Madame H. P. Blavatsky, the compilers of reference books, encyclopedias and dictionaries, as well as the general public, will come to realize that the Hodgson Report is not the model of impartial investigation so often claimed for it over the past century. It is flawed and untrustworthy; and Hodgson's observations and conclusions need to be taken with a considerable port of salt.
>
> The case of Helena Petrovna Blavatsky needs re-examination in this light. She deserves no less. (xii)

In Harrison's later analysis of the Hodgson Report, entitled "J'Accuse

---

[†] Theosophical University Press, Pasadena, California. Dr. Harrison received his Ph.D. in physics from the University of Birmingham, England, and subsequently worked as a research physicist for the Printing & Allied Trades Research Association in London. In 1967 he moved to Thos. De La Rue & Co., printer of banknotes and other security documents, as Research Manager. An important part of his work was to study the methods of counterfeiters and forgers. According to his Affidavit he is a Chartered Physicist and Chartered Engineer, Fellow of the Institute of Physics, Honorary Fellow and Past President of the Royal Photographic Society of Great Britain, Fellow of the Chartered Institution of Building Services Engineers, Fellow of the Royal Society of the Arts and for the past twenty years professional examiner of questioned documents.

d'autant plus" ("I Accuse all the more"), Harrison presents his professional Opinion and Affidavit. We reproduce here, with Dr. Harrison's permission, his Opinion in its entirety.

Opinion

On the basis of the Hodgson Report itself and of the primary evidence available to me, I give it as my OPINION that:

1) The Hodgson Report is not a scientific study. It reads like part of a judicial inquiry recording only the address of the Counsel for the Prosecution. There is no address of a Counsel for the Defense, no cross-examination of the Prosecution's chief witnesses, no recall of Defense witnesses rejected by the Prosecution, and no Judge's summing up.

2) Richard Hodgson was either ignorant or contemptuous of the basic principles of English Justice. No court would accept his testimony.

3) In cases where it has been possible to check Hodgson's statements against the direct testimony of original documents, his statements are found to be either false or to have no significance in the context. This applies in particular to *Three Cardinal Statements* on which hangs his whole contention that Madame Blavatsky wrote the Mahatma Letters herself in a disguised hand in order to deceive.

4) Having read the Mahatma Letters in the holographs, I am left with the strong impression that the writers KH and M were real and distinct human beings. They had their fair share of prejudice and were influenced by the viewpoint of their time.

5) Who KH was I do not know, but I am of the opinion that all letters in the British Library initialed KH originated from him. The basic characteristics of his handwriting are present from first to last, but in the earliest letters in particular there are variations in and distortions of some of the characters. These variations do not bear the hallmark of the apprentice forger.

I am satisfied that the Mahatma Letters were not dictated to *chelas* who wrote them in their own handwriting. However, it is stated in the letters themselves that many of them were transmitted in KH's handwriting by *chelas* using "precipitation" or what seems to be a human FAX process. If this suggestion is plausible, it could be that the *chelas* were having difficulty with the system at first, which had to be "debugged." Most of the "debugging" must have been done within a fortnight.

6) I draw attention to curious and unexplained features of the KH letters, namely the clear, regular striations of some of the writing apparently made with blue pencil, the small amount of ink penetration even when thin "rice" paper was used, the unexplained features of the erasures seemingly made with ink eradicator yet without staining or roughening of the paper, the variability of some (but not all) of the characters and the (at times) grossly exaggerated t-bars. These features suggest that the documents preserved in the British Library may be *copies*, made by some unknown process, of originals which we do not possess.

7) It is almost certain that the incriminating Blavatsky-Coulomb letters have been lost or destroyed, but there is strong circumstantial evidence that these letters were forgeries made by Alexis and Emma Coulomb, who had strong motives and ample means for doing so.

8) I have found no evidence that the Mahatma Letters were written by Helena Blavatsky consciously and deliberately in a disguised form of her own handwriting developed over a period of several years, as claimed by Richard Hodgson. That is, I find no evidence of common origin between the KH, M, and HPB scripts. In any ordinary legal case I would regard them as different scripts and attribute them to different authors.

9) If any of the KH and M scripts came through the hand of Madame Blavatsky while she was in a state of trance, sleep, or other altered states of consciouness known to psychologists and psychiatrists, KH and M might be considered sub-personalities of Helena Blavatsky. To what extent the sub-personalities are independent is a matter for debate; but in no case would conscious fraud or imposture be involved. Nor does this supposition circumvent the difficulty that there are KH letters which even Hodgson had to admit Madame Blavatsky could not possibly have written as she was too far away at the time and communications were bad.

10) I am unable to express an opinion about the "phenomena" described in the first part of the Hodgson Report. All eyewitnesses and items of firsthand evidence are gone, and I have no way of checking whether any of the reported "phenomena" were genuine; but having studied Hodgson's methods, I have come to distrust his account and explanation of the said "phenomena."

11) H. P. Blavatsky was known to be highly complex and hard to understand. There are still many unanswered questions concerning her life and work. However, I am of the opinion that in any future assessment of her, the "REPORT OF THE COMMITTEE APPOINTED TO INVESTIGATE PHENOMENA CONNECTED WITH THE THEOSOPHICAL SOCIETY," published in 1885 by the Society for Psychical Research, should be used with great caution, if not disregarded. It is badly flawed.

IN WITNESS WHEREOF I HAVE MADE MY AFFIDAVIT DATED THE 27th DAY OF FEBRUARY 1997, NOW LODGED WITH THE INTERNATIONAL HEADQUARTERS OF THE THEOSOPHICAL SOCIETY, PASADENA, CALIFORNIA, USA, A COPY OF WHICH HAS BEEN SENT TO THE SOCIETY FOR PSYCHICAL RESEARCH, LONDON, ENGLAND.

VERNON HARRISON

Appendix B

Sources for the Original Writings of HPB

The editions listed are printed and distributed by the following USA publishers. Catalogs are available upon request.

The Theosophy Company
United Lodge of Theosophists
245 West 33rd Street
Los Angeles, CA 90007-4108
213-748-7244
code: **ULT**

Theosophical University Press
The Theosophical Society
P. O. Box C
Pasadena, CA 91109-7107
626-798-3378
code: **TUP**

Theosophical Publishing House/Quest Books
Theosophical Society in America
P. O. Box 270
Wheaton, IL 60189-0270
630-665-0130
code: **TPH**

Published during Helena Blavatsky's Lifetime

ISIS UNVEILED (1877)
This book, totaling more than 1,300 pages, was the first to issue from the pen of HPB. *Isis Unveiled* unites a historical review of religious and scientific ideas with the spirit of the quest for truth. Of special interest to the West is the investigation of the origins of Christianity, including a study of the teachings of the Gnostic sects of the first centuries, and an explanation of the mystery of Jesus. The first truly scientific account of the vast subject of "Magic" is offered in this work. Its subtitle is: *A Master-Key to the Mysteries of Ancient and Modern Science and Theology*. **ULT, TUP, TPH**

THE SECRET DOCTRINE (1888)
Subtitled *The Synthesis of Science, Religion, and Philosophy*. The systematic character of this book is revealed by the subjects treated at length in its pages: Cosmogenesis, Cosmic Evolution, Anthropogenesis, the Evolution of Symbolism, the Archaic Symbolism of the World Religions, and Science and the Secret Doctrine Contrasted. *The Secret Doctrine* (*SD*) differs from *Isis* in that it deliberately unfolds specific teachings about the nature of things. In the introductory pages of Vol. 1, HPB wrote: "The SECRET DOCTRINE is not a treatise, or a series of vague theories, but contains all that can be given out to the world in this century." The *SD* remains the most comprehensive source book of theosophical teachings in this cycle. (1,537 pages) **ULT, TUP, TPH**

559

THE KEY TO THEOSOPHY (1889)
Deluged by questions on the *SD*, HPB afforded a general perspective on the theosophical teaching—and the theosophical movement. An invaluable reference text, the *Key* was published to trace, as its author said, the broad outlines of the Wisdom Religion. This book is in the form of questions and answers as a dialogue between an Inquirer and a Theosophist. It explains the fundamental principles while addressing the various objections raised by the average Western inquirer. (319 page) **ULT, TUP, TPH**

THE VOICE OF THE SILENCE (1889)
This rendition into English of selected passages from the *Book of the Golden Precepts* appeared with the inscription by HPB: "For the daily use of Lanoos (disciples)." Of surpassing beauty in expression, it is a manual of instruction which whispers to the intuition and thrills with the majestic purpose of the Saviors of mankind. (112 pages) **ULT, TUP, TPH**

GEMS FROM THE EAST: A Birthday Book of Precepts and Axioms (1890)
Compiled by H. P. Blavatsky
A precept or axiom, compiled chiefly from Oriental sources, is given for each day of the year, while more lengthy selections from poets and philosophers introduce the months. (224 pages) **TUP, TPH** (in *H. P. Blavatsky Collected Writings* [*BCW*])

TRANSACTIONS OF THE BLAVATSKY LODGE (1890-91)
In 1889 when HPB was in London, weekly meetings of the Blavatsky Lodge were devoted to the discussion of the archaic Stanzas on which the *SD* is based. *Transactions* provides HPB's answers to metaphysical and scientific questions, as stenographically reported and afterwards revised by her for publication. It also includes an extensive treatise on Dreams. (112 pages) **ULT, TUP** (title: *Secret Doctrine Commentary: Stanzas I–IV*), **TPH** (*BCW*)

Published Posthumously

THE THEOSOPHICAL GLOSSARY (1892)
Theosophical books contain many unfamiliar concepts, terms, and allusions without adequate definition or explanation in available dictionaries and encyclopedias. *The Theosophical Glossary* meets this need by providing definitions and brief philosophical essays by HPB and others on terms and subjects of theosophical teachings. (393 pages) **ULT**

FROM THE CAVES AND JUNGLES OF HINDOSTAN (1892)
HPB's philosophical and esoteric travelogue through India originally published in Russian newspapers. (725 pages) **TPH**

NIGHTMARE TALES (1892)

Occult stories by H. P. Blavatsky embodying esoteric truths. Now reprinted in *The Tell-Tale Picture Gallery* together with William Q. Judge's mystical stories of an ancient sacred lore. (226 pages) **ULT**

A MODERN PANARION (1895)

Published as a memorial of HPB's life and work, this book includes articles she wrote before the Society was formed which appeared in the press of the day and in spiritualistic journals. Students wishing to become better acquainted with the spirit of the opening years of the theosophical movement in the nineteenth century will appreciate this volume. (516 pages) **ULT**

STUDIES IN OCCULTISM (1895)

In this series of magazine articles, H. P. Blavatsky clarifies the "essential difference between theoretical and practical Occultism," and the gulf that separates the potentially harmful occult arts from genuine occultism, the path of altruism. Also included is a three-part article on the "The Esoteric Character of the Gospels" which casts revealing light on the mystery of Jesus—as man and as Christ—and also upon the succession of messianic ages. (218 pages) **TUP**

THE LETTERS OF H. P. BLAVATSKY TO A. P. SINNETT (1925)

Transcribed and compiled by A. Trevor Barker

A companion volume to *The Mahatma Letters to A. P. Sinnett*, this correspondence is a profoundly moving documentary of H. P. Blavatsky's life and character. (420 pages) **TUP**

H. P. BLAVATSKY COLLECTED WRITINGS

Compiled and edited by Boris de Zirkoff

The most comprehensive edition of HPB's articles and writings, presented in 14 volumes. This effort was initiated in the 1920s and is still in progress. (average 600 pages per volume) **TPH**

H. P. BLAVATSKY COLLECTED WRITINGS CUMULATIVE INDEX

Compiled by Boris de Zirkoff and edited by Dara Eklund — Volume 15

This is a complete index of the 14 volumes. (646 pages) **TPH**

THEOSOPHICAL ARTICLES

A set of three volumes of HPB's enlightening magazine articles. (1,542 pages) **ULT**

FIVE MESSAGES TO THE AMERICAN THEOSOPHISTS (1888–1891)

This pamphlet consists of H. P. Blavatsky's letters to several Theosophical Conventions held in the United States. These Messages are valuable statements of the general purposes of the Theosophical Movement. **ULT, TUP** (title: *H. P. Blavatsky to the American Conventions: 1888–1891*), **TPH** (*BCW*)

WHAT IS THEOSOPHY? — ITS NONSECTARIAN SPIRIT
This is a collation from the writings of H. P. Blavatsky, focusing on the purpose its statements were originally designed to serve—the establishment of "Theo-Sophia," Divine Wisdom. (20 pages) **ULT**

Additional HPB Compilations and Publishers

THE SECRET DOCTRINE — Electronic edition
Prepared by Vicente Hao-Chin, Jr.
Available on five floppy discs with built-in search engine. It runs on Windows 3.1/95/98. **Theosophical Publishing House–Philippines** [code: **TPH–Philippines**], 1 Iba Street, Quezon City, Philippines, +63 2 740 3751

AN INVITATION TO THE SECRET DOCTRINE
This is a succinct statement of the *SD*'s principal teachings in HPB's own words. Included are the Robert Bowen notes of HPB's study suggestions, photographs of HPB's manuscript, a historical account of "The Writing of *The Secret Doctrine*" by Kirby Van Mater, and a glossary of terms. (112 pages) **TUP**

THE SECRET DOCTRINE INDEX
Prepared by John P. Van Mater
Because the *SD* comprises a virtual encyclopedia of the "anciently universal wisdom-tradition," this volume is as much an index of *ideas* as it is of subjects, works, persons, and proper names. Main entries are cross-referenced; foreign terms are identified by language, often with a brief definition. Includes an appendix of foreign phrases with translation, and source references. (441 pages) **TUP**

BLAVATSKY REFERENCE BOOKS
Compiled and annotated by H. J. Spierenburg
Each volume collates HPB's statements and perspectives on a specific theme from her books, articles, and teachings. Published by **Point Loma Publications**, P. O. Box 6507, San Diego, CA 92166-6507; 619-222-9609.

THE BUDDHISM OF H. P. BLAVATSKY

H. P. BLAVATSKY ON THE GNOSTICS

THE NEW TESTAMENT COMMENTARIES OF H. P. BLAVATSKY

THE VEDA COMMENTARIES OF H. P. BLAVATSKY

THE VEDANTA COMMENTARIES OF H. P. BLAVATSKY

ASTROLOGY OF A LIVING UNIVERSE

Additional Resources

THE THEOSOPHIST, Volume 1 (1879)
A photographic facsimile of the first magazine issued by the Theosophical
Society, published by **Wizards Bookshelf**, P. O. Box 6600, San Diego, CA,
92166-6600; 619-258-0049.

FIVE YEARS OF THEOSOPHY
This is a collection of articles from the early years of *The Theosophist*. A
number of articles by HPB are included in this volume; others of interest are
by T. Subba Row, Mohini M. Chatterji, and Damodar K. Mavalankar. **ULT**

THEOSOPHICAL ARTICLES AND NOTES
The articles in this volume are compiled from a variety of sources. Included is
material taken by dictation from HPB to Countess Wachtmeister, notes from
Robert Bowen, and data from A. P. Sinnett's *The Occult World*. **ULT**

THE MAHATMA LETTERS TO A. P. SINNETT
Transcribed and compiled by A. Trevor Barker
These are letters on occultism, religion, and philosophy written by H. P. Bla-
vatsky's teachers. They yield a clearer understanding of HPB and of the
Mahatmas' mission in fostering a real universal fraternity. **TUP, TPH**

THE MAHATMA LETTERS TO A. P. SINNETT in Chronological Sequence
Arranged and edited by Vicente Hao-Chin, Jr.
This edition includes background notes by Virginia Hanson, and appendices
that include all the other known letters to A. P. Sinnett and A. O. Hume.
TPH–Philippines

H. P. BLAVATSKY AND THE SPR: An Examination of the
Hodgson Report of 1885 — *by Vernon Harrison, Ph.D.*
The Hodgson Report is best known for its denunciation of H. P. Blavatsky as
an "impostor," and is often quoted in encyclopedias, reference books, and
biographical works (see Appendix A). Harrison, a long-standing member of
the SPR, conducted an extensive examination of the report and found it
"riddled with slanted statements . . . and downright falsity." **TUP**

SECRET DOCTRINE REFERENCE SERIES
Several difficult-to-find titles, referenced by HPB in *The Secret Doctrine*, are
now published by **Wizards Bookshelf**, P. O. Box 6600, San Diego, CA,
92166-6600; 619-258-0049. Titles:

The Anugītā; The Book of Enoch the Prophet; Chaldean Account of Genesis; The
Divine Pymander of Hermes Trismegistus; Eleusinian & Bacchic Mysteries; Esoteric
Budhism; The Life and Teachings of Paracelsus; The Lost Fragments of Proclus; On

the Mysteries: Iamblichus; Mythical Monsters; New Platonism & Alchemy; The Origin and Significance of the Great Pyramid; Plato: Cratylus, Phaedo, Parmenides, Timaeus, and Critias; Posthumous Humanity; Qabbalah: The Philosophical Writings of Solomon Ben Yehuda Ibn Gebirol, and the Zohar; Sacred Mysteries Among the Mayas and Quiches; Sepher Yetzireh; Sod, The Son of Man; Theon of Smyrna: Mathematics Useful for Understanding Plato; The Theosophist, Volume 1; The Twelve Signs of the Zodiac; The Zohar. Other Books: *The Books of Kiu-Te, or The Tibetan Buddhist Tantras; Proceedings of the First International Symposium on H. P. Blavatsky's Secret Doctrine*

On the Internet:

Full text online versions of Helena Blavatsky's books are available at:

www.theosociety.org/pasadena/tup-onl.htm

This edition of *HPB: The Extraordinary Life of Helena Blavatsky* is published in cooperation with the Institute of Noetic Sciences, whose website contains additional theosophical and related subjects

www.noetic.org

Acknowledgments

Special mention and gratitude is due Carey Williams (nom de plume for Dr. Caren M. Elin) for her co-commitment and devotion to this effort since its inception over a decade ago. Without her sacrificial labor in the final years, the publication of this book may have never come to fruition.

Deep appreciation is given to Virginia Ross and Will Thackara for their graphics expertise.

Special recognition is made to the following individuals who helped to make this new revised edition a true labor of love on behalf of HPB: Inguna and Gvido Trepša for all their help in researching and verifying all documented quotations in the text as well as endnotes, for their Russian translation of *HPB*, which in turn has enhanced the accuracy of this new American edition; Will Thackara for his assistance in research and for preparing the text for publication; Raymond Rugland for his expertise in retypesetting the entire work; Dara Eklund, Nicholas Weeks, Vera Meyer, Thelma Pugliese, Nanette de Fuentes, and Cathy Dees for their proofreading skills and suggestions; and to Adolph Edgar Atkins for making this edition possible.

We are very much indebted to the following individuals for their valuable help in preparing this and earlier editions of *HPB*:

H. Clay Bailey III, Ina Belderis, Jim Belderis, Jules van Bergen, Peter Bernin, Kitty Bijl, Adella Bivins, J. P. Brakel, Radha Burnier, Daniel Caldwell, Walter Carrithers, Reed Carson, Gilda Cello, Prudence Ceppos, Arthur Ceppos, John Cooper, Armand Courtois, Sherry Craft, Kay Croissant, Leonid Danilov, Doris Davy, Ted Davy, Cathy Dees, Terry Dickinson, Doreen Domb, Alan Donant, Arie van Duerzen, Dara Eklund, Arlene Elin, Daniel Entin, Bernard Firth, Dorothy Frank, Nanette de Fuentes, Margaret Geiger, Michael Gomes, Dennis Gottschalk, Piet Hagedoorn, Karel Hillebregt, Aloyse Hume, David Hume, Georgia James, Helena Kerekhazi, Ruth Kinsburg, Boris Kinsburg, Joan Lange, Mary G. Langford, Micheline Leblois, Claude Leblois, Erica Lauber, Chi-Jen Lukacsik, H. Robert McOwen, Miriam Merrill, Vera Meyer, Joy Mills, Sandra Mirisch, Jerome Muratore, Pico Nazzaro, Christine Nolt, Bas Rijken van Olst, Harry Rijken van Olst, Sue Perley, David Pratt, Leslie Price, Fred Pruyn, Thelma Pugliese, Alice Rosenblatt, Arnold Rosenblatt, Barbara Savoury, Jean-Louis Siémons, W. Emmett Small, Reinout Spaink, H. J. Spierenburg, Elena

Starichonok, Dallas TenBroeck, Roderick Townley, Gvido Trepša, Inguna Trepša, Natalia Troitskaia, Eldon Tucker, Vonda Urban, James Voirol, Rochelle Voirol, Nicholas Weeks, Betty Willis, Margaret Winton, and Cathy Young.

Gratitude is given to the following libraries and archives:

Alexandria West Library and Archives, Turlock, CA, Archivist: Jerry Hejka-Ekins; The Blavatsky Foundation, Fresno, CA, Archivist: Walter Carrithers; now in Tuscon, Arizona, Archivist: Daniel Caldwell; The British Library, London, England; Columbia University Libraries, New York, NY; Concord Grove Press, United Lodge of Theosophists, Santa Barbara, CA, Archivist: Nandini Iyer; Andover-Harvard Divinity School Library, Archivist: Dr. Alan Seaburg; Eileen J. Garrett Library of Parapsychology Foundation, New York, NY; Harvard University Library, Cambridge, MA; Huntington Library, Pasadena, CA; Krotona Institute of Theosophy Library, Ojai, CA, Archivist: Lakshmi Narayan; Ligatma Publishing House and Archives, Riga, Latvia, Archivist: Gvido Trepša; New York Public Library: Reference Room, 42nd Street, New York, NY; The New York Society for Psychical Research, New York, NY; Nicholas Roerich Museum and Library, New York, NY, Archivist: Daniel Entin; Olcott Library and Research Center of The Theosophical Society in America, Wheaton, IL, Archivist: Lakshmi Narayan; Advisers: Dorothy Abbenhouse and Shirley Nicholson; The Theosophical Society Library and Archives, Adyar, Madras, India, Archivist: Paul Zwollo; The Theosophical Society Library and Archives, Pasadena, CA, Archivists: Kirby Van Mater and John Van Mater; Advisers: Grace F. Knoche and Will Thackara; Theosophical Society of New York Library, New York, NY, Archivist: Elizabeth Meller; United Lodge of Theosophists Library, New York, NY; United States Library of Congress, Washington, DC; and Yale University Beinicke Rare Books and Manuscripts Library, New Haven, CT, Adviser in Tibetan Literature: Dr. Wesley Needham.

Notes*

Preface

1. William Q. Judge, "The Esoteric She," *The Sun*, New York, September 26, 1892; reprinted in *H. P. Blavatsky* (booklet), Los Angeles, California, Theosophy Company

2. Charles Johnston, "A Memory of Madame Blavatsky," *Lucifer*, London, England, Theosophical Publishing Society, June 1891, 287–88

3. William Stewart Ross ("Saladin"), "Death of Madame Blavatsky," *Agnostic Journal*, May 16, 1891; reprinted as "How an Agnostic Saw Her," *Lucifer*, June 1891, 311–16

4. A. P. Sinnett, *The "Occult World Phenomena" and the Society for Psychical Research, with a Protest by Madame Blavatsky* (booklet), London, England, George Redway, 1886, 51

5. Vernon Harrison, "J'Accuse: An Examination of the Hodgson Report of 1885," *Journal of the Society for Psychical Research*, London, England, April 1986, 309–10; Vernon Harrison, *H. P. Blavatsky and the SPR: An Examination of the Hodgson Report of 1885*, Pasadena, California, Theosophical University Press, 1997, 33

6. H. G. Wells, *The Man Who Could Work Miracles: Twenty-Eight Science Fiction Stories of H. G. Wells*, New York, New York, Dover, 1942, 701

7. This was in New York City in the 1920s, when those named were residents of the newly built Shelton Hotel. Carolyn Swanton, "Claude Fayette Bragdon: A Theosophist," *American Theosophist*, Wheaton, Illinois, Theosophical Society in America, September 1983, 263

8. Blavatsky, letter to Vera Zhelihovsky, "Letters of H. P. Blavatsky XIII," *The Path*, New York, New York, William Q. Judge publisher, December 1895, 270

9. *Roget's International Thesaurus*, 4th edition, New York, New York, Thomas W. Crowell, 1977

10. Damodar Mavalankar, "Can Females Become Adepts?" *The Theosophist*, Adyar, Madras, India, The Theosophical Society, Oct. 1883, 23

11. Iverson Harris, *The Journal of San Diego History*, San Diego (California) Historical Society, Summer 1974, 16. In checking this information it

*Abbreviation used: EN means endnote.

567

was learned that a niece of Einstein's, in India during the 1960s, paid a special visit to the headquarters of the Theosophical Society at Adyar. She explained that she knew nothing of theosophy or the society, but had to see the place because her uncle always had a copy of Madame Blavatsky's *Secret Doctrine* on his desk. The individual to whom the niece spoke was Eunice Layton, a world-traveled theosophical lecturer who happened to be at the reception desk when she arrived. While in Ojai, California, in January 1982, Sylvia Cranston met Mrs. Eunice Layton, who confirmed the story.

12. *Ojai Valley News,* Ojai, California, September 28, 1983, 6–7

13. *Collected Letters of W. B. Yeats: Volume One,* edited by John Kelly, Oxford, England, Clarendon Press, 1986, 1:164

14. Cathy Young (Ekaterina Jung), *Growing Up in Moscow,* New York, New York, Ticknor & Fields, 1989

15. Theodore Roszak, *The Unfinished Animal,* New York, Harper & Row, 1975, 117–25

16. *The Theosophist,* August 1990, 448–49

17. Blavatsky, *H. P. Blavatsky to the American Conventions: 1888–1891,* Pasadena, California, Theosophical University Press, 1979, 9

18. Zinaida Vengerova, "Blavatsky," in *Critico-Biographical Encyclopedia of Russian Writers and Savants,* St. Petersburg, Russia, 1892, 3:301 footnote

Part 1. Life in Russia

1. Lydia P. Bobritsky, "Helena Andreevna Hahn," *The Theosophical Forum,* Covina, California, August 1948, 450

2. Vera Petrovna de Zhelihovsky, "Helena Petrovna Blavatskaya: Biografichesky ocherk," (Helena Petrovna Blavatsky: A Biographical Sketch), *Russkoye obozreniye* (Russian Review), November 1891, 246 footnote, privately translated by Mary G. Langford, San Gabriel, California, in the Sylvia Cranston Archives, Santa Barbara, California; A. V. Starchevskii, "Roman odnoi zabytoi romanistki" (The Romance of a Forgotten Novelist), *Istoricheskii vestnik* (Historical Messenger), St. Petersburg, Russia, September 1886, 530

3. Victor and Jennifer Louis, *The Complete Guide to the Soviet Union,* New York, New York, St. Martin's Press, 1976, 15

4. Blavatsky, *H. P. Blavatsky Collected Writings,* Wheaton, Illinois, The Theosophical Publishing House, 1966, 2:353

5. Bobritsky, "Helena Andreevna Hahn," 451–52

6. Blavatsky, *H. P. Blavatsky Collected Writings,* 1:xxviii

7. Marion Meade, *Madame Blavatsky: The Woman Behind the Myth,* New York, New York, G. P. Putnam's Sons, 1980, 16

8. Blavatsky, *H. P. Blavatsky Collected Writings*, 1:xxviii

9. Blavatsky, *H. P. Blavatsky Collected Writings*, 1:xxvi

10. Andrey Mihaylovich de Fadeyev, *Vospominaniya, 1790–1867* (Reminiscences, 1790–1867), part 1, Odessa, Russia, South Russian Society for printing, 1897, 5

11. Blavatsky, *H. P. Blavatsky Collected Writings*, 3:506–7

12. Bobritsky, "Helena Andreevna Hahn," 452

13. Vera Petrovna Zhelihovsky, *Kak ya bila malenkoy: Iz vospominaniy ranyago dyetstva Veri Petrovni Zhelihovsky* (When I Was Small: From the Reminiscences of the Early Childhood of Vera Petrovna Zhelihovsky), 2nd revised and enlarged edition, St. Petersburg, Russia, A. F. Devrient, 1894, 1:33–38, privately translated by Cathy Young, New Jersey, in the Sylvia Cranston Archives, Santa Barbara, California

14. Zhelihovsky, *Kak ya bila malenkoy*, 1:18

15. Catherine S. Nekrasova, "Helena Andreyevna Hahn, 1814–1842: Biographical Sketch," *Russkaya starina* (Russian Days of Yore), St. Petersburg, Russia, August 1886, volume 51, part 1, 339, privately translated by Mary G. Langford, in the Sylvia Cranston Archives, Santa Barbara, California

16. A. P. Sinnett, *Incidents in the Life of Madame Blavatsky*, New York, New York, J. W. Bouton, 1886, 97

17. Blavatsky, *H. P. Blavatsky Collected Writings*, 2:355

18. Zhelihovsky, *Kak ya bila malenkoy*, 1:60, 124, 149–50

19. Sinnett, *Incidents in the Life of Madame Blavatsky*, 14

20. Bobritsky, "Helena Andreevna Hahn," 449

21. Nekrasova, "Helena Andreyevna Hahn, 1814–1842," September 1886, volume 51, part 10, 570–71

22. Henry Steel Olcott, *Old Diary Leaves: The History of the Theosophical Society*, Adyar, Madras, India, The Theosophical Publishing House, 3rd printing, 1974, 3:378

23. H. P. Blavatsky, *The Voice of the Silence*, Los Angeles, California, The Theosophy Company, 1928, 12–13

24. Blavatsky, *The Voice of the Silence*, 13, 67

25. *National Geographic*, March 1985, 295

26. Sinnett, *Incidents in the Life of Madame Blavatsky*, 18–19

27. Sinnett, *Incidents in the Life of Madame Blavatsky*, 21

28. *The Bhagavad-Gita*, from the Sanskrit, by William Q. Judge, Los Angeles, California, The Theosophy Company, 1986

29. Nadyezhda Fadeyev, "Helena Pavlovna Fadeyev," *Russkaya starina* (Russian Days of Yore), St. Petersburg, Russia, December 1886, 749–51, privately translated by Cathy Young, New Jersey, in the Sylvia Cranston Archives, Santa Barbara, California

30. Blavatsky, *H. P. Blavatsky Collected Writings*, 1:xxx–xxxi

31. Nekrasova, "Helena Andreyevna Hahn, 1814–1842," August 1886, volume 51, part 4, 347–48

32. Bobritsky, "Helena Andreevna Hahn," 454

33. Nekrasova, "Helena Andreyevna Hahn, 1814–1842," August 1886, volume 51, part 5, 353

34. Nekrasova, "Helena Andreyevna Hahn, 1814–1842," August 1886, volume 51, part 5, 353

35. Nekrasova, "Helena Andreyevna Hahn, 1814–1842," August 1886, volume 51, part 5, 351

36. Zhelihovsky, *Kak ya bila malenkoy,* 1894 (used by author throughout)

37. Meade, *Madame Blavatsky: The Woman Behind the Myth,* 24–33

38. Bobritsky, "Helena Andreevna Hahn," 453

39. Bobritsky, "Helena Andreevna Hahn," 454

40. Nekrasova, "Helena Andreyevna Hahn, 1814–1842," August 1886, volume 51, part 5, 354

41. Ignace Hommaire-de-Hell, *Travels in the Steppes of the Caspian Sea, Crimea . . . ,* London, Chapman Hall, 1867, 165–68

42. Zhelihovsky, *Kak ya bila malenkoy,* 2:4

43. Zhelihovsky, "Neobyasnimoye ili neobyasnenneye: Iz lichnih i semeynih vospominaniy" (The Inexplicable or The Unexplained: From Personal and Family Reminiscences), *Rebus,* Moscow, Russia, volume 4, number 6 (1885), 60, privately translated by Cathy Young, New Jersey, in the Sylvia Cranston Archives, Santa Barbara, California

44. Zhelihovsky, "Yelene Petrovne Blavatskaya: Biografichesky ocherk" (Helena Petrovna Blavatsky: A Biographical Sketch), *Russkoye obozreniye* (Russian Review), November 1891, 243–45, privately translated by Cathy Young, New Jersey, in the Sylvia Cranston Archives, Santa Barbara, California

45. "Character Sketches," *Review of Reviews,* London, 1893, 659

46. Zhelihovsky, *Kak ya bila malenkoy,* 2:129–132

47. Nekrasova, "Helena Andreyevna Hahn, 1814–1842," Sept. 1886, part 8, 560, 562; Zhelihovsky, *Kak ya bila malenkoy,* 326, 115; Zhelihovsky, *Moyo otroschestvo* (My Adolescence), 3rd edition, 1900, part 1, section 12, 59, privately translated by Cathy Young, New Jersey, in the Sylvia Cranston Archives, Santa Barbara, California

48. Nekrasova, "Helena Andreyevna Hahn, 1814–1842," part 9, 565

49. Zhelihovsky, *Kak ya bila malenkoy*, chapters 1–23; Fadeyev, *Vospominaniya*, part 1, 148, 167

50. Sinnett, *Incidents in the Life of Madame Blavatsky*, 28

51. Sinnett, *Incidents in the Life of Madame Blavatsky*, 32–33

52. Vera Petrovna de Zhelihovsky, "Pravda o Yelene Petrovne Blavatsky," *Rebus*, November 1891, 245, 247, privately translated by Mary G. Langford, San Gabriel, California, in the Sylvia Cranston Archives, Santa Barbara, California

53. Zhelihovsky, "Pravda o Yelene Petrovne Blavatsky," 246

54. Zhelihovsky, *Kak ya bila malenkoy*, 117

55. Zhelihovsky, *Kak ya bila malenkoy*, 214–16

56. Zhelihovsky, *Kak ya bila malenkoy*, 217–20

57. Nekrasova, "Helena Andreyevna Hahn, 1814–1842," part 11, 573

58. Zhelihovsky, *Kak ya bila malenkoy*, chapters 35–37

59. Zhelihovsky, *Moyo otrochestvo*, part 1, chapter 1, 1–4

60. Zhelihovsky, "Pravda o Yelene Petrovne Blavatsky," 246 footnote

61. Nekrasova, "Helena Andreyevna Hahn, 1814–1842," part 11, 572

62. Zhelihovsky, "Pravda o Yelene Petrovne Blavatsky," 246

63. Mary K. Neff, *Personal Memoirs of H. P. Blavatsky*, Wheaton, Illinois, The Theosophical Publishing House, 1971, 17; Vera P. Jelihovsky, "Helena Petrovna Blavatsky," *Lucifer*, November 1894, 204

64. Bobritsky, "Helena Andreevna Hahn," 457

65. Nekrasova, "Helena Andreyevna Hahn, 1814–1842," part 8, 559

66. Nekrasova, "Helena Andreyevna Hahn, 1814–1842," part 9, 566

67. Sinnett, *Incidents in the Life of Madame Blavatsky*, 29

68. Sinnett, *Incidents in the Life of Madame Blavatsky*, 30–31, 41; Zhelihovsky, *Kak ya bila malenkoy*, chapters 24, 25

69. Sinnett, *Incidents in the Life of Madame Blavatsky*, 37–38

70. Sinnett, *Incidents in the Life of Madame Blavatsky*, 39–40

71. Olcott, *Old Diary Leaves*, 3:9–10

72. Sinnett, *Incidents in the Life of Madame Blavatsky*, 35

73. Sinnett, *Incidents in the Life of Madame Blavatsky*, 42–43

74. Sinnett, *Incidents in the Life of Madame Blavatsky*, 47–48; Countess Constance Wachtmeister, *Reminiscences of H. P. Blavatsky and The Secret Doctrine*, Wheaton, Illinois, Theosophical Publishing House, 1976, 56; Blavatsky, *The Letters of H. P. Blavatsky to A. P. Sinnett*, London, England, T. Fisher Unwin Ltd., 1925, 150

75. Sinnett, *Incidents in the Life of Madame Blavatsky,* 42

76. Sinnett, *Incidents in the Life of Madame Blavatsky,* 46–47

77. Blavatsky, *H.P.B. Speaks,* edited by C. Jinarajadasa, Adyar, Madras, India, The Theosophical Publishing House, 1951, 2:62–63

78. Blavatsky, *The Theosophical Glossary,* Los Angeles, California, The Theosophy Company, 1930 (facsimile of the original edition as first issued London, England, 1892) 197; Blavatsky, *Isis Unveiled,* Los Angeles, California, The Theosophy Company, 1968, centenary anniversary edition, 1:xxxiv

79. Blavatsky, *The Theosophical Glossary,* 196–98, 238; Blavatsky, "Practical Occultism," *Lucifer,* April 1888, 150–54; "Occultism versus the Occult Arts," May 1888, 173–81

80. Zhelihovsky, *Moyo otrochestvo,* part 2, 181–85

81. Louis, *The Complete Guide to the Soviet Union,* 520

82. Zhelihovsky, *Moyo otrochestvo,* part 1, chapters 28, 29; part 2, chapters 1, 2, 5

83. Zhelihovsky, *Moyo otrochestvo,* part 1, 54

84. Zhelihovsky, *Moyo otrochestvo,* part 2, chapter 11

85. Zhelihovsky, *Moyo otrochestvo,* part 2, 190–93

86. Zhelihovsky, *Moyo otrochestvo,* part 2, 277

87. Blavatsky, *H.P.B. Speaks,* Adyar, Madras, India, The Theosophical Publishing House, 1951, 2:61

88. Zhelihovsky, *Kak ya bila malenkoy,* 92; *Moyo otrochestvo,* part 1, 76, 96

89. Helene Pissareff, "Helena Petrovna Blavatsky," *The Theosophist,* January 1913, 500, 504

90. Blavatsky, *H. P. Blavatsky Collected Writings,* 1:xxxv; Zhelihovsky, *Moyo otrochestvo,* part 2, 271–72; A. L. Pogosky, "Helena Petrovna Blavatsky: a Chapter out of Her Past," *The Theosophist,* July 1913, 477 footnote

91. Sinnett, *Incidents in the Life of Madame Blavatsky,* 54

92. Blavatsky, *The Letters of H. P. Blavatsky to A. P. Sinnett,* 214, 217

93. Vera P. Zhelihovsky, "Helena Petrovna Blavatsky," *Lucifer,* November 1894, 204; "Radda-Bai: A Biographical Sketch," in *Enigmatical Tribes in the "Light Blue Mountains," Durbar at Lahore,* From the Caves and Jungles of India, St. Petersburg, Russia, V. I. Gubinsky, 1893, 2–3, privately translated by Mary G. Langford, San Gabriel, California, in the Sylvia Cranston Archives, Santa Barbara, California

94. Blavatsky, *H. P. Blavatsky Collected Writings,* 1:xxxvi

95. Zhelihovsky, *Moyo otrochestvo,* part 2, 216

96. Sinnett, *Incidents in the Life of Madame Blavatsky,* 54–55

97. Zhelihovsky, *Moyo otrochestvo*, part 2, 217

98. Sinnett, *Incidents in the Life of Madame Blavatsky*, 56–57

99. Zhelihovsky, *Moyo otrochestvo*, part 2, 303

100. Blavatsky, "Marvellous Spirit Manifestations," *Daily Graphic*, New York, New York, October 30, 1874, 873; *H. P. Blavatsky Collected Writings*, 1:32

101. Blavatsky, *H.P.B. Speaks*, 2:64

102. Sinnett, *Incidents in the Life of Madame Blavatsky*, 57–59

Part 2. World Search

1. Blavatsky, *H. P. Blavatsky Collected Writings*, 2:354 footnote; Hugh Seth Watson, *The Russian Empire, 1801–1917*, 499

2. Blavatsky, *H.P.B. Speaks*, 2:v–xvi

3. Blavatsky, *H.P.B. Speaks*, 2:61–63

4. C. G. Jung, *The Collected Works*, volume 13; *Alchemical Studies* (Bollingen Series 20), Princeton, New Jersey, Princeton University Press, 1967, jacket

5. C. G. Jung, *The Development of Personality* (Bollingen Series 20), London, England, Routledge and Kegan Paul, 1954, 28, 238

6. C. G. Jung, *The Collected Works*, volume 12, *Psychology and Alchemy* (Bollingen Series 20), London, England, Pantheon, 1953, jacket

7. H. P. Blavatsky, "Philosopher's Stone," in *The Theosophical Glossary*, 253; H. P. Blavatsky, *Isis Unveiled*, Los Angeles, California, The Theosophy Company, 1968, 1:309, (facsimile centenary anniversary edition, both volumes printed in one book; reproduction of the original edition, first published New York, New York, 1877); *H. P. Blavatsky, Collected Writings 1877, Isis Unveiled*, volumes 1 and 2, Wheaton, Illinois, The Theosophical Publishing House 1972

8. C. G. Jung, *Alchemical Studies*, 339

9. Blavatsky, *Lucifer*, December 1889, 272

10. C. G. Jung, *Psychology and Alchemy*, 120, note 41

11. Sinnett, *Incidents in the Life of Madame Blavatsky*, 60, 67; Blavatsky, letter to Sydney Coryn, November 2, 1889, Theosophical Society Archives, Pasadena, California

12. Blavatsky, *The Letters of H. P. Blavatsky to A. P. Sinnett*, 151, 177

13. A. L. Rawson, "Madame Blavatsky, A Theosophical Occult Apology," *Frank Leslie's Popular Magazine*, February 1892

14. Blavatsky, *H.P.B. Speaks*, 2:65–66

15. Charles Blech, *Contribution à l'histoire de la Société Théosophique en France*, Paris, France, Éditions Adyar, 1933, 140

16. Sinnett, *Incidents in the Life of Madame Blavatsky,* 51

17. Zhelihovsky, *Moyo otrochestvo,* 23, 117, 119, 120; Blavatsky, *H. P. Blavatsky Collected Writings,* 1:xxxiii

18. Olcott, *Old Diary Leaves,* 3rd printing, 1974, 1:458

19. Sinnett, *Incidents in the Life of Madame Blavatsky,* 61

20. Blavatsky, *Isis Unveiled,* 1:268–69

21. Blavatsky, *H.P.B. Speaks,* 2:66

22. Blavatsky, *H.P.B. Speaks,* 2:67

23. Blavatsky, *The Letters of H. P. Blavatsky to A. P. Sinnett,* 150–51

24. Wachtmeister, *Reminiscences of H. P. Blavatsky and The Secret Doctrine,* 1976, 44–45; Blavatsky, *H. P. Blavatsky Collected Writings,* 1:3

25. Wachtmeister, *Reminiscences of H. P. Blavatsky and The Secret Doctrine,* 1976, 44

26. Wachtmeister, *Reminiscences of H. P. Blavatsky and The Secret Doctrine,* 1976, 45

27. Blavatsky, *H. P. Blavatsky Collected Writings,* 8:399

28. Blavatsky, *The Letters of H. P. Blavatsky to A. P. Sinnett,* 150

29. Wachtmeister, *Reminiscences of H. P. Blavatsky and The Secret Doctrine,* 57

30. Sinnett, *Incidents in the Life of Madame Blavatsky,* 61–66

31. Blavatsky, *The Secret Doctrine,* 2:444–46

32. Sinnett, *Incidents in the Life of Madame Blavatsky,* 61–62

33. Blavatsky, *Isis Unveiled,* 2:474 footnote

34. Sinnett, *Incidents in the Life of Madame Blavatsky,* 62–63

35. Blavatsky, *Isis Unveiled,* 1:546, 547, 595–99; Sinnett, *Incidents,* 64

36. Sinnett, *Incidents in the Life of Madame Blavatsky,* 65–66

37. Blavatsky, *H.P.B. Speaks,* 2:20

38. Sinnett, *Incidents in the Life of Madame Blavatsky,* 66

39. H. S. Olcott, "Traces of H. P. B.," *The Theosophist,* India, April 1893, 429

40.

WHItehall #16XX 2323
Ext.:

Your reference   :
Please quote in reply :R.519/52

COMMONWEALTH RELATIONS OFFICE

KING CHARLES STREET

20^{d} LONDON S.W.1
February, 1952.

Dear Madam,

    In reply to your letter of the 11th February, the following
particulars relating to Major General Charles Murray (1826—1893)
have been extracted from the military records of this Office:-

    Charles Murray, born 17th March 1826, baptized 11th Feby.
1840 at St. Anne's, Westminster, was the son of James
and Catherine Murray of Soho Square, Captn. in the East
India Company's Service. (Cadet Papers, Vol: 95, No. 460).

    Cadet: Bengal Infantry, 1841/42.
Ensign   "   "   1842.
Lieut. 70th Regt. Native Infantry 1851.
Commandant, Sebundy Sappers and Miners, 1854-55.
Captain Staff Corps, 18 Feb. 1861.
Major   "   "   18 Feb. 1863.
Lieut Colonel   "   28 Dec. 1868.
Brevet Colonel, Retired 31 Dec. 1874 in India.
Major General, 25 January 1875.
Died at Monghyr, 30th Aug. 1893.

Yours faithfully,

JR Lloyd

Superintendent of Records.

Mrs M.L. Stanley,
    61, Westbourne Park Road,
        W.2.

41. Meade, *Madame Blavatsky: The Woman Behind the Myth,* 472

42. A. L. Rawson, "Two Madame Blavatskys—The Acquaintance of Madame H. P. Blavatsky with Eastern Countries," *The Spiritualist,* April 5, 1878, 70–71. This was written on March 18, 1878 by A. L. Rawson, 84 Bond St., New York; Blavatsky, *H. P. Blavatsky Collected Writings,* 1:357; 2:71–72

43. Blavatsky, *H.P.B. Speaks,* 2:20

44. Zhelihovsky, "Pravda o Yelene Petrovne Blavatsky" (The Truth About Helena Petrovna Blavatsky), *Rebus*, volume 2, number 40, 1883, 357

45. Radda-Bai (Blavatsky), *H. P. Blavatsky Collected Writings: From the Caves and Jungles of Hindostan,* Wheaton, Illinois, The Theosophical Publishing House, 1975, 272–273

46. Radda-Bai (Blavatsky), *H. P. Blavatsky Collected Writings: From the Caves and Jungles of Hindostan,* 273 footnote

47. Sinnett, *Incidents in the Life of Madame Blavatsky,* 66

48. Sinnett, *Incidents in the Life of Madame Blavatsky,* 66–67

49. Blavatsky, *H. P. Blavatsky Collected Writings,* 1:xli–xlii footnote; Florence Young, letter of January 14, Boris de Zirkoff Archives, The Theosophical Society, Wheaton, Illinois

50. John Unruh, Jr., *The Plains Across,* Chicago, Illinois, University of Chicago Press, 1978, 311

51. Unruh, *The Plains Across,* 401

52. Whitman, *Leaves of Grass,* New York, New York, Modern Library, 90, 91

53. Sinnett, *Incidents in the Life of Madame Blavatsky,* 67

54. Blavatsky, *Isis Unveiled,* 1:vi–vii

55. Blavatsky, *The Letters of H. P. Blavatsky to A. P. Sinnett,* 151

56. Radda-Bai (Blavatsky), *H. P. Blavatsky Collected Writings: From the Caves and Jungles of Hindostan*

57. Blavatsky, *H.P.B. Speaks,* 2:21

58. Blavatsky, *The Letters of H. P. Blavatsky to A. P. Sinnett,* 153; Blavatsky, *H. P. Blavatsky Collected Writings,* 13:210

59. Vengerov, *Kritico-biograficheskily slovar Russkin Pisately i uch evik*

60. Olcott, "Traces of H. P. B.," 429

61. Sinnett, *Incidents in the Life of Madame Blavatsky,* 67–72; Blavatsky, *The Letters of H. P. Blavatsky to A. P. Sinnett,* 151

62. Blavatsky, *Isis Unveiled,* 2:598, 626–28

63. Sinnett, *Incidents in the Life of Madame Blavatsky,* 72; Blavatsky, *The Letters of H. P. Blavatsky to A. P. Sinnett,* 151

Part 3. Maturing Years

1. Zhelihovsky, "Neobyasnimoye ili neobyasnenneye," *Rebus* 3:4, 41; Sinnett, *Incidents in the Life of Madame Blavatsky* 76–77, privately translated by Cathy Young, New Jersey, in the Sylvia Cranston Archives, Santa Barbara, California

2. "Letters from H.P.B.'s Husbands," *The Theosophist,* August 1959, 295–96; letter 1 from General Blavatsky to Madame N. A. Fedeev

3. Zhelihovsky, "Pravda o Yelene Petrovne Blavatsky," *Rebus*, volume 2, number 40 (1883), 357

4. Blavatsky, *The Letters of H. P. Blavatsky to A. P. Sinnett*, 154

5. Blavatsky, letter to the editor of *Light*, London, England, published July 27, 1889; Blavatsky, *H. P. Blavatsky Collected Writings*, 2:363. (The reference to meeting K. H. was omitted from *A Modern Panarion* reprint.)

6. Blavatsky, Letter to Sidney and Herbert Coryn, November 2, 1889, Theosophical Society Archives, Pasadena, California

7. Zhelihovsky, "Helena Petrovna Blavatskaya: Biografichesky ocherk" (Helena Petrovna Blavatsky: A Biographical Sketch), *Russkoye obozreniye*, volume 6 (November 1891), 250

8. William Q. Judge, "The Esoteric She," *The Sun*, New York, New York, September 26, 1892

9. Sinnett, *Incidents in the Life of Madame Blavatsky*, 78–79, 82–89; Zhelihovsky, "Pravda o Yelene Petrovne Blavatsky," *Rebus*, volume 2, number 40 (1883), 358

10. Sinnett, *Incidents in the Life of Madame Blavatsky*, 94; Zhelihovsky, "Pravda o Yelene Petrovne Blavatsky," *Rebus*, volume 2, number 41 (1883), 367

11. Sinnett, *Incidents in the Life of Madame Blavatsky*, 94–95; Blavatsky, *H. P. Blavatsky Collected Writings*, 14:477

12. Sinnett, *Incidents in the Life of Madame Blavatsky*, 85

13. Zhelihovsky, "Pravda o Yelene Petrovne Blavatsky," *Rebus*, volume 2, number 40, (1883), 358; Sinnett, *Incidents in the Life of Madame Blavatsky*, 80–81; Blavatsky, *The Letters of H. P. Blavatsky to A. P. Sinnett*, 154–55; Blavatsky, *H. P. Blavatsky Collected Writings*, 14:476, 479

14. Sinnett, *Incidents in the Life of Madame Blavatsky*, 87–91

15. Sinnett, *Incidents in the Life of Madame Blavatsky*, 91 footnote

16. Sinnett, *Incidents in the Life of Madame Blavatsky*, 91–96

17. Sinnett, *Incidents in the Life of Madame Blavatsky*, 91–97; Zhelihovsky, "Pravda o Yelene Petrovne Blavatsky," *Rebus*, volume 2, number 41 (1883), 367–68

18. Sinnett, *Incidents in the Life of Madame Blavatsky*, 92–97, 105, 107; Zhelihovsky, "Pravda o Yelene Petrovne Blavatsky," *Rebus*, volume 2, number 43 (1883), 389–90

19. Blavatsky, "Letters of H.P.B. to Dr. Hartmann," *The Path*, March 1896, 369

20. Zhelihovsky, "Neobyasnioye ili neobyasnenneye," *Rebus*, volume 4, number 5 (1885), 51–52

21. Sinnett, *Incidents in the Life of Madame Blavatsky*, 134–35; Zhelihovsky, "Pravda o Yelene Petrovne Blavatsky," *Rebus*, volume 2, number 44 (1883), 399–400; Olcott, *Old Diary Leaves*, 1:9

22. Sinnett, *Incidents in the Life of Madame Blavatsky,* 135–38

23. Zhelihovsky, "My Sister—H. P. Blavatsky," *The London Forum,* London, England, December 1934, 406–7

24. Nikolayeff, *Reminiscences of Prince A. I. Baryatinsky,* excerpts in *Istorichesky vestnik* (Historical Messenger), St. Petersburg, Russia, December 1885, 622–24; *Theosophia,* Los Angeles, California, May–June 1947, 15–16

25. Blavatsky, *H.P.B. Speaks,* 2:156

26. Sinnett, *Incidents in the Life of Madame Blavatsky,* 146; Blavatsky, *The Letters of H. P. Blavatsky to A. P. Sinnett,* 156

27. Sinnett, *Incidents in the Life of Madame Blavatsky,* 146 footnote; Blavatsky, *H. P. Blavatsky Collected Writings,* 14:484

28. Zhelihovsky, "Pravda o Yelene Petrovne Blavatsky," *Rebus* volume 2, number 46 (1883), 418; Sinnett, *Incidents in the Life of Madame Blavatsky,* 150

29. Sinnett, *Incidents in the Life of Madame Blavatsky,* 152–53

30. Blavatsky, *H.P.B. Speaks,* 2:116; Nadya, letter to H. P. Blavatsky, May 23, 1877 (old style), Adyar Archives, The Theosophical Society, Adyar, Madras, India; interview with HPB in *Morning News,* Paris, France, April 21, 1884

31. Blavatsky, *H. P. Blavatsky Collected Writings,* 1:xlvii, 11–25

32. Blavatsky, *The Letters of H. P. Blavatsky to A. P. Sinnett,* 144

33. Blavatsky, *The Letters of H. P. Blavatsky to A. P. Sinnett,* 144; *H. P. Blavatsky Collected Writings,* 1:54–55

34. H. P. Blavatsky, "Mr. A. Lillie's Delusions," *Light,* London, England, Aug. 9, 1884, 323–24; Blavatsky, *H. P. Blavatsky Collected Writings,* 4:277–78

35. René Guenon, *Le Théosophisme: Histoire d'une pseudo-religion,* Paris, France, 43

36. Olcott, *Old Diary Leaves,* 1:9, 264; Blavatsky, *The Letters of H. P. Blavatsky to A. P. Sinnett,* 151–52

37. Blavatsky, letter to *The Spiritualist,* London, England, August 12, 1881; Blavatsky, *H. P. Blavatsky Collected Writings,* 3:268

38. Mahayana Buddhism had its origin in India before Buddhism was eventually driven out by Brahmins and Muslims. HPB writes (in *The Secret Doctrine,* Los Angeles, California, The Theosophy Company, 1974, 1:xx–xxi [facsimile of original edition, of 1888]; and *H. P. Blavatsky Collected Writings 1888: The Secret Doctrine,* Adyar, Madras, India, The Theosophical Publishing House, 1978, 1:xx–xxi): "Time and human imagination made short work of the purity and philosophy of these teachings, once that they were transplanted from the secret and sacred circle of the Arhats, during the course of their work of proselytism, into a soil less prepared for metaphysical conceptions than India; i.e., once

they were transferred into China, Japan, Siam, and Burma. How the pristine purity of these grand revelations was dealt with may be seen in studying some of the so-called 'esoteric' Buddhist schools of antiquity in their modern garb, not only in China and other Buddhist countries in general, but even in not a few schools in Tibet, left to the care of uninitiated Lamas and Mongolian innovators."

39. Sylvia Cranston and Joseph Head, *Reincarnation: The Phoenix Fire Mystery,* Pasadena, California, Theosophical University Press, 1994, 60–67, 74–76, 83–84, 89–91, 92–93, 100

40. In answer to an inquiry, HPB wrote in *The Theosophist* of January 1886: "[I do not] believe in an individual, segregated spirit in me, as a something apart from the whole. . . . I maintain as an occultist, on the authority of the Secret Doctrine, that though merged entirely into Parabrahm, man's spirit while not individual *per se* yet preserves its distinct individuality in Paranirvana, owing to the accumulation in it of the aggregates, or *skandhas* that have survived after each death, from the highest faculties of Manas [or Mind]. The most spiritual, i.e. the highest and divinest aspirations of every personality . . . become part and parcel of the Monad [and are] preserved to the end of the great cycle (*Maha-Manvantara*) when each Ego enters Paranirvana, or is merged in Parabrahm. To our talpatic, or mole-like comprehension the human spirit is then lost in the One Spirit, as the drop of water thrown into the sea can no longer be traced out and recovered. But *de facto* it is not so in the world of immaterial thought. . . . That such Parabrahmic and Para-nirvanic 'spirits' or units, have and must preserve their divine (not human) individualities, is shown in the fact that, however long the 'night of Brahma' or even the Universal Pralaya . . . yet, when it ends, the same individual Divine Monad resumes its majestic path of evolution . . . and brings with it all the essence of compound spiritualities from previous countless rebirths." (See also the Theosophy Company booklet *Kabbalah and Kabbalism,* 33–34.)

41. Lobsang P. Lhalungpa, *Tibet the Sacred Realm: Photographs 1880–1950,* Philadelphia, Pennsylvania, Philadelphia Museum of Art/Aperture, 1983, 37

42. Heinrich Harrer, *Seven Years in Tibet,* New York, New York, E. P. Dutton, 1954, 221

43. Blavatsky, *The Letters of H. P. Blavatsky to A. P. Sinnett,* 4

44. "Echoes from the Past," *The Theosophist,* October 1907, 77

45. "Echoes from the Past," *The Theosophist,* October 1907, 77

46. Lobsang P. Lhalungpa, *Tibet the Sacred Realm,* 80

47. G. P. Malasekera, "Blavatsky," in *Encyclopedia of Buddhism,* volume 3, Colombo, Śri Lanka, 1971

48. D. T. Suzuki, *The Field of Zen,* edited by Christmas Humphreys, London, England, Buddhist Society, 1969, xiii

49. Rick Fields, *How the Swans Came to the Lake,* Boston, Massachusetts, Shambhala, 1981, 296

50. *Buddhist News,* August 1965, 90

51. De Zirkoff Archives, The Theosophical Society, Wheaton, Illinois

52. H. P. Blavatsky, *The Voice of the Silence,* Santa Barbara, California, Concord Grove Press, 1989; (Centenary Edition)

53. Blavatsky, *The Voice of the Silence,* Peking, China, Chinese Buddhist Research Society, 1927

54. Blavatsky, *The Voice of the Silence,* preface

55. Margaret Cousins, "A Pilgrimage in the Himalayas," *World Theosophy,* Los Angeles, California, volume 1, number 2 (February 1930), 156–59

56. "Travels of H.P.B.," *World Theosophy,* Los Angeles, California, August 1931, 591

57. Franz Hartman, "Psychometrical Experiments," *The Theosophist,* March 1887, 354–58

58. Blavatsky, "Letters of H.P.B. to Dr. Hartmann," *The Path,* volume 10, (January 1896), 297–98

59. Blavatsky, "Letters of H.P.B. to Dr. Hartmann," *The Path,* volume 10, (January 1896), 298–99

60. Blavatsky, *H. P. Blavatsky Collected Writings,* 14:422–25

61. Zhelihovsky, "Pravda o Yelena Petrovne Blavatsky," *Rebus,* 1883, 56

62. Sven Hedin, *A Conquest of Tibet,* New York, New York, E. P. Dutton 1934, 380; *Trans-Himalaya: Discoveries and Adventures in Tibet,* London, New York, The Macmillan Co., 1909, 1:317, 322–23, 325–26

63. Barbara M. Foster and Michael Foster, *Forbidden Journey: the Life of Alexandra David-Neel,* San Francisco, California, Harper & Row, 1989, 57

64. Alexandra David-Neel, *My Journey to Lhasa,* Boston, Massachusetts, Beacon Press, 1986, xi

65. Zhelihovsky, "Pravda o Yelene Petrovne Blavatsky," *Rebus,* 1883, 66–67

66. Blavatsky, "Letters of H.P.B. to Dr. Hartmann," *The Path,* volume 10, (March 1896), 370

67. Blavatsky, "Mr. A. Lillie's Delusions," *Light,* London, England, August 9, 1884; Blavatsky, *H. P. Blavatsky Collected Writings,* 4:269–80

68. *The Theosophical Forum,* Point Loma, California, May 1936, 343–46

69. Sven Eek, editor, *Damodar and the Pioneers of the Theosophical Movement,* Adyar, Madras, India, The Theosophical Publishing House, 1978, 60–62

70. Olcott, *Old Diary Leaves,* 3:54–55, 57

71. Blavatsky, *The Theosophical Glossary,* 295

72. Blavatsky, *The Voice of the Silence,* preface, i–ii

73. Mahatmas M. and K.H., *The Mahatma Letters to A. P. Sinnett,* transcribed and compiled by A. T. Barker, Adyar, Madras, India, The Theosophical Publishing House, 1962, appendix, 471–72

74. *The Eclectic Theosophist,* San Diego, California, January–February 1990, 3

75. C. Jinarajadasa, editor, *Letters from the Masters of the Wisdom,* Adyar, Madras, India, The Theosophical Publishing House, 1973, 1:84–85, 132–34; *First Report of the Committee of the Society for Psychical Research, Appointed to Investigate the Evidence for Marvellous Phenomena Offered by Certain Members of the Theosophical Society,* London, England, [1884], 113–14

76. Jinarajadasa, *Letters from the Masters of the Wisdom,* 1:84–85, 132–34; *Report of the Result of an Investigation into the Charges against Madame Blavatsky, brought by the Missionaries of the Scottish Free Church of Madras, and examined by a Committee appointed for that Purpose by the General Council of the Theosophical Society,* Madras, India, The Theosophical Society at Adyar, 1885, 96

77. Blavatsky, *H. P. Blavatsky Collected Writings,* 6:274–77

78. *Report of the Result of an Investigation into the Charges against Madame Blavatsky,* 1885, 96

79. *First Report of the Committee of the Society for Psychical Research,* [1884], 115

80. Blavatsky, letter to her family, *The Path,* January 1895, 299

81. Blavatsky, *The Letters of H. P. Blavatsky to A. P. Sinnett,* 153; Neff, *Personal Memoirs of H. P. Blavatsky,* 301

82. "Letters of H.P.B. to Dr. Hartmann," *The Path,* March 1896, 369–70

83. Rawson, "Two Madame Blavatskys," *The Spiritualist,* April 5, 1878

84. Blavatsky, *The Letters of H. P. Blavatsky to A. P. Sinnett,* 153, 215; Sinnett, *Incidents in the Life of Madame Blavatsky,* 153–54; Neff, *Personal Memoirs of H. P. Blavatsky,* 165

85. Boris de Zirkoff, *Theosophia,* Volume XI, No. 4, Spring 1955, 13

86. Sinnett, *Incidents in the Life of Madame Blavatsky,* 158–59

87. Blavatsky, *H. P. Blavatsky Collected Writings,* 14:487

88. Blavatsky, *H. P. Blavatsky Collected Writings,* 1:xlvi

89. Blavatsky, *H. P. Blavatsky Collected Writings,* 1:xlix–1

90. Blavatsky, *H.P.B. Speaks,* 1:192–93

91. Olcott, *Old Diary Leaves,* 1:27–28

92. Olcott, *Old Diary Leaves,* 1:20; Blavatsky, *The Letters of H. P. Blavatsky to A. P. Sinnett,* 153–54

93. Wachtmeister, *Reminiscences,* 146–47; Olcott, *Old Diary Leaves,* 1:28–29

94. Meade, *Madame Blavatsky: The Woman Behind the Myth,* 101

Part 4. America—Land of Beginnings

1. HPB's first naturalization papers are dated September 22, 1873; her citizenship papers are signed "Helen P. Blavatsky" (photocopy, National Archives, New York Branch)

2. Vera Zhelihovsky, "Radda-Bai," in Blavatsky, *Caves and Jungles of Hindostan,* St. Petersburg, Russia, V. I. Gubinsky, 1893, privately translated by Mary C. Langford, California, in the Sylvia Cranston Archives, Santa Barbara, California, 6

3. Olcott, *Old Diary Leaves,* 1:21–22

4. *World Theosophist,* Los Angeles, California, December 31, 1973

5. Olcott, *Old Diary Leaves,* 1:20

6. Blavatsky, *Some Unpublished Letters of Helena Petrovna Blavatsky,* edited by Eugene Rollin Corson, London, Rider & Company, 1929, 127–28

7. Arthur Conan Doyle, *The History of Spiritualism,* 1:77, 80

8. R. Laurence Moore, *In Search of White Crows,* New York, New York, Oxford University Press, 1977, 3–4

9. Doyle, *The History of Spiritualism,* 1:191

10. Zhelihovsky, "Neobyasnimoye ili neobyasnenneye," *Rebus,* 1885, 7, 13

11. Carl Sandburg, *Abraham Lincoln—The War Years,* New York, New York, Harcourt Brace & Co., 3:343–45

12. Nettie Colburn Maynard, *Was Abraham Lincoln a Spiritualist?,* Philadelphia, Pennsylvania, Hartranft, 1891, 70–74, 82–93, 129–32, 135, 153, 163–70, 181. Precious glimpses into Lincoln's character afforded the medium during those contacts are some of the rewarding highlights of her book

13. Maynard, *Was Abraham Lincoln a Spiritualist?,* 91–92

14. Helene Pissareff, "The World Mission of H. P. Blavatsky," *The Theosophist,* May 1911, 189

15. "Sir William Crookes," *Encyclopaedia Britannica,* 1959

16. Sir William Crookes, *Researches in Spiritualism,* Los Angeles, California, Austin Publishing Company, 1922, 84–98

17. Bertram Keightley, *Reminiscences of H.P.B.,* 20–21; C. Jinarajadasa, editor, *The Golden Book of the Theosophical Society,* Adyar, Madras, India, The Theosophical Publishing House, 1925, 68; Olcott, calendar diary 1884, April 28, May 18, May 27, June 15, June 24, July 1

18. Blavatsky, "Comment on the Mystery of Levitation," *H. P. Blavatsky Collected Writings,* 4:168

19. Blavatsky, "Letters of H.P.B. to Dr. Hartmann," *The Path*, volume 10, (March 1896), 369–70

20. Howard Murphet, *Hammer on the Mountain*, 1–20; Blavatsky, *H. P. Blavatsky Collected Writings*, 1:503–8

21. Murphet, *Hammer on the Mountain*, 5

22. Olcott, *Old Diary Leaves*, 1:1–3

23. Henry S. Olcott, *People from the Other World*, Hartford, Connecticut, American Publishing Company, 1875, 410–11; new edition, Rutland, Vermont, Charles E. Tuttle Company, 1972

24. Olcott, *Old Diary Leaves*, 1:3–6

25. Olcott, *People from the Other World*, 453

26. Olcott, *People from the Other World*, 298–307, 310–13, 317–23, 328–35, 355–61, 413 (see also Blavatsky's description of the apparition, *H. P. Blavatsky Collected Writings*, 1:32–33)

27. Olcott, *Old Diary Leaves*, 1:7–9

28. Blavatsky, *H. P. Blavatsky Collected Writings*, 1:53

29. Olcott, *Old Diary Leaves*, 1:9–10

30. Sinnett, *Incidents in the Life of Madame Blavatsky*, 132; Blavatsky, *H. P. Blavatsky Collected Writings*, 14:482

31. *Light*, October 11, 1884, 418–19; Blavatsky, *H. P. Blavatsky Collected Writings*, 6:291

32. Sinnett, *Incidents in the Life of Madame Blavatsky*, 177–79; H. P. Blavatsky, *The Key to Theosophy*, Los Angeles, California, The Theosophy Company, 1987 (facsimile of original edition, London, England, 1889); Zhelihovsky, "Helena Petrovna Blavatskaya," *Russkoye obozreniye*, volume 6 (November 1891), 253–55

33. Blavatsky, *H. P. Blavatsky Collected Writings*, 2:78–80; 6:108; Olcott, *Old Diary Leaves*, 1:304–05; William Q. Judge, *The Ocean of Theosophy*, Los Angeles, California, The Theosophy Company, 1971, 38, 146

34. Blavatsky, *The Key to Theosophy*, 29

35. Blavatsky, *The Key to Theosophy*, 145–47

36. Blavatsky, *The Key to Theosophy*, 150

37. Olcott, *Old Diary Leaves*, 1:69–73; Blavatsky, *H. P. Blavatsky Collected Writings*, 1:47, 74

38. Olcott, *Old Diary Leaves*, 1:32. HPB's interview by the *Graphic* contains fantastic claims, presumably made by her, of such a nature that de Zirkoff, the editor of *H. P. Blavatsky Collected Writings*, refused to include the interview in the series. It turns out he instinctively made the right choice. HPB included this interview in a gift of several volumes of *The Spiritual Scientist* to Emily Kislingbury, first secretary of the British

National Association of Spiritualists; these volumes may be found in her library. The interview in question is heavily annotated in HPB's handwriting, as being lies invented by the interviewer.

39. Olcott, *Old Diary Leaves,* 1:32–33

40. Michael Gomes, *The Dawning of the Theosophical Movement,* Wheaton, Illinois, The Theosophical Publishing House (a Quest Book), 1987, 235

41. Gomes, *The Dawning of the Theosophical Movement,* 45–61; Blavatsky, *H. P. Blavatsky Collected Writings,* 1:56–72, 75–83

42. Olcott, *People from the Other World,* 425–78

43. Olcott, *Old Diary Leaves,* 1:13–14; Blavatsky, *H. P. Blavatsky Collected Writings,* 1:73; photo of HPB's statement, 1:facing 80

44. Blavatsky, *H. P. Blavatsky Collected Writings,* 1:lvii

45. Olcott, *Old Diary Leaves,* 1:10–12, 17, 321–22; Blavatsky, *H. P. Blavatsky Collected Writings,* 6:271; Olcott, *People from the Other World* 453–55, 472

46. Blavatsky, *H.P.B. Speaks* 1:41

47. Olcott, *People from the Other World,* 305–7

48. Olcott, *Old Diary Leaves,* 1:55–58

49. Olcott, *Old Diary Leaves,* 1:58

50. Gomes, *The Dawning of the Theosophical Movement,* 76

51. Jinarajadasa, editor, *Letters from the Masters of the Wisdom,* 2nd series, Adyar, Madras, India, The Theosophical Publishing House, 1977, 27–29, 31–34

52. Blavatsky, *H. P. Blavatsky Collected Writings,* 1:101

53. Blavatsky, *H. P. Blavatsky Collected Writings,* 1:83–84

54. Blavatsky, *H. P. Blavatsky Collected Writings,* 1:2

55. Blavatsky, *H. P. Blavatsky Collected Writings,* 1:83–84

56. Charles R. Flint, *Memories of an Active Life,* New York, G. P. Putnam's Sons, 1923, 115–32

57. Blavatsky, *H. P. Blavatsky Collected Writings,* 1:99–100

58. Blavatsky, *H. P. Blavatsky Collected Writings,* 1:86–87; Olcott, *Old Diary Leaves,* 1:72–73; Blavatsky, *Some Unpublished Letters of Helena Petrovna Blavatsky,* 157–58

59. Blavatsky, "A Few Questions to 'Hiraf,' " *The Spiritual Scientist,* Boston, Massachusetts, July 15 and 22, 1875, 217–18, 224, 236–37; Blavatsky, *H. P. Blavatsky Collected Writings,* 1:101–3, 113

60. *The Theosophical Movement 1875–1950,* Los Angeles, California, The Cunningham Press, 1951, 36–7; Judge, *The Ocean of Theosophy,* 147–49

61. *The Word,* New York, New York, December 1915, 146−52

62. About the attitude of Spiritualist papers toward HPB, see Blavatsky, *H. P. Blavatsky Collected Writings,* 1:186−92; 3:364−65

63. Blavatsky, *Some Unpublished Letters of Helena Petrovna Blavatsky,* 192−93

64. John Eglinton, *A Memoir of Æ,* London, England, Macmillan, 1937, 1

65. James Joyce, *Ulysses,* New York, New York, Modern Library, 1961, 185

66. Eglinton, *A Memoir of Æ,* 13

67. W. Q. Judge, *Letters That Have Helped Me,* Los Angeles, California, Theosophy Company, 1946, 262−64; Eek, *Damodar and the Pioneers of the Theosophical Movement,* 5−6

68. Judge, *Letters That Have Helped Me,* 262−64

69. Judge, "Yours Till Death and After, H.P.B.," *Lucifer,* June 1891, 290−92

70. Laura C. Holloway, "William Quan Judge, A Reminiscence," *The Word,* New York, New York, volume 22, number 2 (November 1915), 77

71. Blavatsky, *H. P. Blavatsky Collected Writings,* 1:94; Gomes, *The Dawning of the Theosophical Movement,* 79

72. Blavatsky, *H. P. Blavatsky Collected Writings,* 1:463

73. Olcott, *Old Diary Leaves,* 1:118−19; Michael Gomes, "Studies in American Theosophical History," *The Canadian Theosophist,* September/October 1989, 76−78; July/August 1990, 63−64

74. William Brehon (WQJ) "Plain Theosophical Traces," *The Path,* August 1892, 133−36

75. Blavatsky, *The Key to Theosophy,* 1; Jean-Louis Siémons, "Theosophia in Neo-Platonic and Christian Literature," London, Theosophical History Centre, 1988. Dr. Siémons teaches physics in the field of molecular biology at the Institut National Agronomique, Paris, France

76. Professor Hannon, "Theosophy as a Koan," *American Theosophist,* October 1987

77. William Quan Judge, *Echoes of the Orient: The Writings of William Quan Judge,* compiled by Dara Eklund, San Diego, California, Point Loma Publications, 1980, 2:362

78. Blavatsky, *H. P. Blavatsky to the American Conventions: 1888−1891,* Pasadena, California, Theosophical University Press, 1979, 6

79. [Blavatsky], "Going To and Fro in the Earth," *Lucifer,* November 1889, 251−54

80. Blavatsky, *The Key to Theosophy,* 20

81. Blavatsky, *H. P. Blavatsky to the American Conventions: 1888−1891,* 7−8

82. Blavatsky, *The Key to Theosophy,* appendix, 309−10

83. Blavatsky, *H. P. Blavatsky Collected Writings,* 1:150

84. Olcott, *Old Diary Leaves,* 1:18

85. Nadya Fadeyev, letter to HPB, Odessa, Russia, August 28 (September 10), 1876, privately translated by Mary G. Langford, San Gabriel, California, in the Sylvia Cranston Archives, Santa Barbara, California

86. Blavatsky, "Letters of H. P. Blavatsky I," *The Path,* December 1894, 268–70

87. Blavatsky, "Letters of H. P. Blavatsky II," *The Path,* January 1895, 297

88. Blavatsky, "Letters of H. P. Blavatsky I," *The Path,* December 1894, 266

89. Zhelihovsky, "Yelena Petrovna Blavatskaya: Biografichesky ocherk," *Russkoye obozreniye,* volume 6, (November 1891), 256

90. Olcott, *Old Diary Leaves,* 1:103

91. Annie Besant, *H. P. Blavatsky and the Masters of Wisdom,* London, England, The Theosophical Publishing House Ltd., reprint 1962, 7

92. Blavatsky, *The Key to Theosophy,* 298–99, 301

93. Olcott, *Old Diary Leaves,* 1:202–3

94. Blavatsky, *Some Unpublished Letters of Helena Petrovna Blavatsky,* 150–1

95. Gomes, *The Dawning of the Theosophical Movement,* 110–115

96. Gomes, *The Dawning of the Theosophical Movement,* 111

97. Blavatsky, *Some Unpublished Letters of Helena Petrovna Blavatsky,* 118

98. Blavatsky, *Some Unpublished Letters of Helena Petrovna Blavatsky,* 27–28

99. Charles Lazenby, *"Isis Unveiled," The Path,* Hale, England, July 1910, 9

100. Gomes, *The Dawning of the Theosophical Movement,* 114, 220, note 14; interview with Mrs. Pauline Corson Coad, June 23, 1958, transcribed from the tape recording at the Department of Manuscripts, Cornell University Library, Ithaca, New York

101. Lazenby, *"Isis Unveiled," The Path,* Hale, England, July 1910, 9

102. Olcott, *Old Diary Leaves,* 1:207–8

103. Meade, *Madame Blavatsky: The Woman Behind the Myth,* 154; Blavatsky, *Some Unpublished Letters of Helena Petrovna Blavatsky,* 170

104. Lazenby, *"Isis Unveiled," The Path,* Hale, England, July 1910, 9

105. Nadya Fadeyev's letters to HPB from Odessa, Russia, letter 8 (May 11, 1877), page 2; letter 10 (June 9, 1877), page 3, Adyar Archives Microfilm, The Theosophical Society, Adyar, Madras, India

106. Blavatsky, *Isis Unveiled* 1:vii–viii

107. Blavatsky, *The Key to Theosophy,* 307

108. Blavatsky, *H. P. Blavatsky Collected Writings,* 1:531–33; Gomes, *The Dawning of the Theosophical Movement,* 119

109. *The Word,* New York, New York, May 1908, 78–80, 82–83

110. Blavatsky, "My Books," *Lucifer*, May 1891, 241–47

111. Olcott, *Old Diary Leaves*, 1:147–84; Gomes, *The Dawning of the Theosophical Movement*, 99–109; Blavatsky, *H. P. Blavatsky Collected Writings*, 14:560

112. *The Word*, New York, New York, June 1908, 153–55

113. Blavatsky, *H. P. Blavatsky Collected Writings*, 1:302

114. G. Hope, "The Kitchen—Waking Life Confirmation of Astral Work," *The Theosophist*, January 1931, 261

115. Blavatsky, *H. P. Blavatsky Collected Writings*, 1:302

116. Gomes, *The Dawning of the Theosophical Movement*, 225, note 74; Blavatsky, letter to Wallace, November 7, 1877, Wallace Papers, British Museum, London, England; reprinted with facsimile in *The Eclectic Theosophist*, January–February 1983, 78

117. *The Theosophist*, April 1906, 559

118. Olcott, *Old Diary Leaves*, 1:294–95 footnote; Blavatsky, "My Books," *Lucifer*, May 1891, 241–47

119. Olcott, *Old Diary Leaves*, 1:296

120. Blavatsky, *H. P. Blavatsky Collected Writings*, 1:323, 388

121. Introductory in Blavatsky's *Isis Unveiled*, *H. P. Blavatsky Collected Writings*, Boris de Zirkoff, editor, 1:[3] and footnote

122. Blavatsky, *H. P. Blavatsky Collected Writings*, 1:413

123. Olcott, *Old Diary Leaves*, 1:252–54; Gomes, *The Dawning of the Theosophical Movement*, 143

124. "Letters of H. P. Blavatsky, III," *The Path*, February 1895, 383

125. *Light*, October 10, 1891, 490; Gomes, *The Dawning of the Theosophical Movement*, 156–57; Blavatsky, *H. P. Blavatsky Collected Writings*, 1:308

126. Blavatsky, *Isis Unveiled*, 2:587–90

127. When HPB uses the word "reincarnation" in *Isis Unveiled*, "as distinct from metempsychosis" (1:351), she speaks negatively of the idea, for with that term French spiritualists implied immediate rebirth after death with no time for rest between incarnations; they also taught that the personality is reborn. Theosophy teaches that the personality (from *persona*, a mask)—called "Astral Monad" in *Isis Unveiled*—dies with the body, or soon thereafter, and only the individuality (higher mind, soul, and spirit) is immortal and is reborn. Unaware of this subtle but important distinction, many people have declared that when *Isis Unveiled* was written, HPB did not believe in reincarnation. Even Olcott was confused (*Old Diary Leaves*, 1:278–83; 289). HPB later clarified her *Isis* statements in *The Theosophist*, August 1882, 288–89; in *The Path*, November 1886, 232–45; in *Lucifer*, April 1889, 88–99; and in *The Key to Theosophy*, 191–92.

Regarding the passage in *Isis Unveiled* (1:346) where HPB appears to deny reincarnation on this earth, there is an interesting comment in a letter of Master M to Sinnett: "By-the-bye, I'll rewrite for you pages 345–57, Volume 1 *Isis*—much jumbled by Olcott, who thought he was improving it!" (*The Mahatma Letters to A. P. Sinnett*, 76 footnote).

W. Q. Judge writes that in the early days in New York "H.P.B. told me personally many times of the real doctrine of reincarnation, enforced by the case of the death of my own child, so I know what she thought and believed" (Judge, *Letters That Have Helped Me*, 19). See also *Theosophical Forum*, October 1893, 1–3; *Conversations on Occultism II* Judge Pamphlet Series 10, The Theosophy Company; *Echoes of the Orient* 2:317–19. This appears confirmed by HPB's statements in *Isis Unveiled* on metempsychosis, a term used for centuries in Europe as a synonym for what is now generally called reincarnation.

Rebirth was not featured in Theosophy until the 1880s, when the sevenfold constitution of man was taught and clearly delineated what part of human beings is reborn and what is not (*The Mahatma Letters to A. P. Sinnett*, 285). When *Isis Unveiled* was written, and for a long time after, American and British spiritualists bitterly opposed the idea of rebirth, as it would have destroyed elaborate structures erected by Andrew Jackson Davis and others regarding the blessed summerland after death.

128. Blavatsky, *Isis Unveiled*, 1:8–9, 12; 2:145

129. Blavatsky, *Isis Unveiled*, 1:8–9, 12, 345–46; 2:145

130. Olcott, *Old Diary Leaves*, 1:295 footnote

131. Blavatsky, *H. P. Blavatsky Collected Writings*, 4:252–53

132. Blavatsky, "My Books," *Lucifer*, May 1891, 241–42

133. Olcott, *Old Diary Leaves*, 1:330–31, 417

134. *The World*, New York, March 26, 1877; Gomes, *The Dawning of the Theosophical Movement*, 119–20

135. Olcott, *Old Diary Leaves*, 1:331

136. Philadelphia *Times*, April 22, 1888, reprinted in Gomes, *The Dawning of the Theosophical Movement*, 177–78

137. Olcott, *Old Diary Leaves*, 1:206

138. Gomes, *The Dawning of the Theosophical Movement*, 156

139. William Q. Judge, "Habitations of H.P.B., No. III," *The Path*, November 1893, 237–38

140. Judge, "Habitations of H.P.B., No. III," *The Path*, November 1893, 238–39

141. Isabella B. Mitchell, 1878 letter, in "Cuttings and Comments," *The Theosophist*, January 1901, 253–54; Gomes, *The Dawning of the Theosophical Movement*, 171–72

142. *The Word*, New York, New York, January 1905, 182–87

143. Olcott, *Old Diary Leaves*, 1:140

144. Vsevolod Sergyeevich Solovyoff, *A Modern Priestess of Isis*, translated by Walter Leaf, London, England, Longmans, Green and Co., 1895, 268–70

145. Theodore Besterman, *Mrs. Annie Besant: A Modern Prophet*, London, England, Kegan Paul, Trench, Trubner & Company, Ltd., 1934, 148–51

146. Henry Steel Olcott, "H.P.B.'s Departure," *H.P.B.: In Memory of Helena Petrovna Blavatsky 1831–1931*, London, England, The Blavatsky Association, 1931, 167

147. Besant, *H. P. Blavatsky and the Masters of the Wisdom*, London, England, Theosophical Publishing House, reprint 1962, 6–7

148. "Special Gotham Book Mart Issue," *Journal of Modern Literature*, Philadelphia, Pennsylvania, Temple University, volume 4, number 4 (April 1975), 777–78

149. Olcott, *Old Diary Leaves*, 1:37–38

150. Eek, *Damodar and the Pioneers of the Theosophical Movement*, 46–47

151. J. L. Davidge, reprinted in *Theosophy in Australia*, December 1959, 7–8

152. Judge, *The Ocean of Theosophy*, 137

153. Judge, *Occult Phenomena*, Los Angeles, California, The Theosophy Company (William Q. Judge Pamphlet Series number 19), 16–17

154. Olcott, *Old Diary Leaves*, 1:429–31

155. Olcott, *Old Diary Leaves*, 1:458–59

156. Blavatsky, *Some Unpublished Letters of Helena Petrovna Blavatsky*, 33

157. Olcott, *Old Diary Leaves*, 1:376–80

158. Olcott, *Old Diary Leaves*, 1:473

159. Gomes, *The Dawning of the Theosophical Movement*, 182–83

160. Blavatsky, *H. P. Blavatsky Collected Writings*, 2:40–41

161. William Q. Judge, "H.P.B.—A Lion-Hearted Colleague Passes," *The Path*, June 1891, 66–67

162. Olcott, *Old Diary Leaves*, 1:395–98

163. Olcott, *Old Diary Leaves*, 1:466–68

164. *The Theosophist*, August 1931, 657

165. Gomes, *The Dawning of the Theosophical Movement*, 191–92, 234, note 63

166. July 3, 1878, translation by Boris de Zirkoff, de Zirkoff Archives, The Theosophical Society, Wheaton, Illinois. Another translation in *H.P.B. Speaks*, 1:188–89, 202–3

167. A. Keightley, "The Secret Doctrine and Mr. Edison," *Theosophical Quarterly*, New York, New York, October 1921, 133–34

168. Head and Cranston, *Reincarnation: The Phoenix Fire Mystery*, 419

169. Blavatsky, "Letters of H. P. Blavatsky, IV" *The Path*, March 1895, 411–12; Josephine Ransom, *A Short History of the Theosophical Society, 1875–1937*, Adyar, Madras, India, Theosophical Publishing House, 1938, 314

170. Ransom, *A Short History of the Theosophical Society, 1875–1937*, 106

171. *The Path*, May 1885, 56–57

172. Henry Steel Olcott, A Historical Retrospect, *1875–1896, of the Theosophical Society*, Madras, India, 1896, 116; Ransom, *A Short History of the Theosophical Society, 1875–1937*, 106

173. Eek, *Damodar and the Pioneers of the Theosophical Movement*, 63–64, 76–77

174. Eek, *Damodar and the Pioneers of the Theosophical Movement*, 6 footnote

175. *Daily Graphic*, New York, New York, December 10, 1878, 266; Gomes, *The Dawning of the Theosophical Movement*, 190

176. Olcott, *Old Diary Leaves*, 1:480–81; Blavatsky, *H. P. Blavatsky Collected Writings*, 1:431–32

Part 5. Mission to India

1. Edward Conze, *Buddhism: Its Essence and Development*, New York, New York, Philosophical Library, 1951 (paperback, New York, New York, Harper Torchbook). The 1875 founding of the Theosophical Society is given a place in the appendix listing significant events in the history of Buddhism.

2. Edward Conze, *Buddhism: Its Essence and Development*, 210–11

3. Carl T. Jackson, *The Oriental Religions and American Thought: Nineteenth Century Explorations*, Connecticut, Greenwood Press, 1934, 163

4. John B. S. Coats, *The Theosophist*, June 1975, 151–52; Head and Cranston, *Reincarnation: The Phoenix Fire Mystery*, 477–79; "Death of Dr. S. Radhakrishnan," *The Eclectic Theosophist*, November 15, 1975

5. *The Middle Way*, May 1973, 44

6. Blavatsky, "Our Three Objects," *Lucifer*, September 1889, 1–7

7. Olcott, *Old Diary Leaves*, 4:81–95

8. *The Theosophist*, Supplement, Madras, India, August 1885, 279; condensed from *Indian Mirror*

9. Louis Fischer, *The Life of Mahatma Gandhi*, New York, New York, Harper & Row, 1950, 437

10. *The Theosophical Movement 1875–1950*, 71

11. Fischer, *The Life of Mahatma Gandhi*, 437

12. Blavatsky, "Our Three Objects," *Lucifer*, September 1889

13. Blavatsky, *The Letters of H. P. Blavatsky to A. P. Sinnett*, 206

14. James D. Hunt, *Gandhi in London,* New Delhi, India, Promilla & Company Publishers, 1978, 34; *The Collected Works of Mahatma Gandhi, volume 1: 1884–1896,* New Delhi, India, Publications Division, Ministry of Information and Broadcasting, Government of India, 1958, 354

15. Hunt, *Gandhi in London,* 31

16. M. K. Gandhi, *Autobiography,* translated by Mahadev Desai, Washington D.C., Public Press, 1948, 90–91

17. *Young India,* November 12, 1925. Gandhi enlarged on this incident: "My contact with two English friends made me read the *Gita,* I say 'made me read it,' because it was not my own desire that I read it. . . . I was ashamed of my ignorance. The knowledge of my total ignorance of my scriptures pained me. Pride I think was at the bottom of the feeling." The *Gita* became the most important book in his life.

18. M. K. Gandhi, *The Teachings of the Gita,* Bombay, India, Anand T. Hingorani, 1971, preface

19. Gandhi, *The Teachings of the Gita,* 7, 9

20. Cranston and Williams, *Reincarnation: A New Horizon in Science, Religion and Society,* 228, 229; M. K. Gandhi, *Gandhi's Autobiography: The Story of My Experiments with Truth,* 60, 90–91, 321

21. Gandhi, *The Collected Works of Mahatma Gandhi, volume 1: 1884–1896,* 355; Pyarelal Nair, *Mahatma Gandhi, volume 1: The Early Years,* Ahmedabad, India, Navajian Publishing House, 1965, 259

22. Gandhi, *Autobiography,* 321

23. *The Canadian Theosophist,* November–December 1983, 101

24. Jawaharlal Nehru, *Toward Freedom: The Autobiography of Jawaharlal Nehru,* The John Day Company, 1941, 28

25. Indira Gandhi, "The Future of Man," *The Theosophist,* April and May 1983, 279 (Besant Lecture, Adyar, Madras [Chennai], India)

26. Olcott, *Old Diary Leaves,* 2:143

27. Blavatsky, *H. P. Blavatsky Collected Writings,* 4:132–36

28. Olcott, *Old Diary Leaves,* 2:21, 24–25; Robert S. Ellwood, Jr., *Alternative Altars: Unconventional and Eastern Spirituality in America,* Chicago, Illinois, University of Chicago Press, 1979, 130; Henry David Thoreau, *Walden,* New York, New York, New American Library, 1942, 198–99

29. [Laura Holloway Langford], "Extracts from Letters Written by William Q. Judge from Paris to a Longtime Friend," *The Word,* New York, New York, April 1912, 23

30. Olcott, *Old Diary Leaves,* 2:42–44

31. Olcott, *Old Diary Leaves,* 2:46–71

32. H. P. Blavatsky, *The Word,* New York, New York, July 1908, 204

33. Jinarajadasa, *Letters from the Masters of the Wisdom*, 2:68–69

34. *The Theosophist*, April 1881, 158–59

35. Vera P. Zhelihovsky, "Helena Petrovna Blavatsky," *Lucifer*, February 1895, 470

36. Blavatsky, letter to Miss Burr, June 18, 1879, de Zirkoff Archives, The Theosophical Society, Wheaton, Illinois

37. Olcott, *Old Diary Leaves*, 2:230–31

38. Blavatsky, *H. P. Blavatsky Collected Writings*, 4:97

39. Mahatmas M. and K. H., *The Mahatma Letters to A. P. Sinnett*, 35; *The Theosophist*, October 1879

40. Blavatsky, letter to Major General Doubleday, July 16, 1879, *The Theosophist*, October 1879; Theosophical Society Archives, Pasadena, California

41. Beatrice Hastings, editor, *New Universe, "Try,"* volume 1, number 2 (December 1937), 18

42. *The Theosophist*, volume 1 (1879–80), reprint by Wizards Bookshelf, P.O. Box 6600, San Diego, California; *The Theosophist*, volume 2 (1880–81), reprint by Eastern School Press, Talent, Oregon, 1983; Edmonton Theosophical Society delux xeroxed edition of vol. 1–6 of *The Theosophist*; Eastern School Press (3185 Boyd Road, Cotopaxi, Colorado 81223), photocopy sets of vol. 3–8 of *The Theosophist*.

43. Michael Gomes, "Damodar—A Hindu Chela," *The Theosophist*, September 1985, 448–49

44. Olcott, *Old Diary Leaves*, 2:212–13

45. Damodar K. Mavalankar, "The Path in India," *The Theosophist*, May 1880, 196–97

46. Judge, *The Ocean of Theosophy*, 7

47. Olcott, *Old Diary Leaves*, 2:28

48. Olcott, *Old Diary Leaves*, 2:114

49. Olcott, *Old Diary Leaves*, 2:129

50. Olcott, *Old Diary Leaves*, 2:131–33

51. Olcott, *Old Diary Leaves*, 2:131–33

52. Eek, *Damodar and the Pioneers of the Theosophical Movement*, 38

53. Eek, *Damodar and the Pioneers of the Theosophical Movement*, 40

54. Damodar K. Mavalankar, "Can Females Become Adepts?," *The Theosophist*, October 1883, 23; T. Subba Row, *Esoteric Writings*, Adyar, Madras, India, Theosophical Publishing House, 1980, 568

55. Olcott, *Old Diary Leaves*, 2:34, 36, 46, 56, 67, 83

56. Olcott, *Old Diary Leaves*, 2:74–75, 138

57. Sangharakshita, *Anagarika Dharmapala, a Biographical Sketch* (booklet), Kandy, Ceylon, Buddhist Publications Society, 1964, 18–20. Sangharakshita, born Dennis Lingwood, was ordained a Buddhist Bhikshu.

58. Blavatsky, *La Revue Spirite*, October 1878; *H. P. Blavatsky Collected Writings*, 1:402

59. *Proceedings of the Blavatsky Association*, London, England, number 1, November 13, 1924, 54–55

60. Edward Buck, *Simla, Past and Present*, 2nd edition, Bombay, India, Times Press, 1925, 162–63

61. Blavatsky, *The Letters of H. P. Blavatsky to A. P. Sinnett*, 353

62. Hume, "The 'Saturday Review' and the 'The Theosophist,'" *The Theosophist*, Supplement, December 1881, 2–4

63. K. F. Vania, *Madame H. P. Blavatsky: Her Occult Phenomena and the Society for Psychical Research*, Bombay, India, Sat Publishing Company, 1951, 65–66

64. Olcott, *Old Diary Leaves*, 2:234

65. A. P. Sinnett, *The Occult World*, London, England, Theosophical Publishing House London Ltd., 9th edition, 1969, 60–61

66. Olcott, *Old Diary Leaves*, 2:365–67

67. Olcott, *Old Diary Leaves*, 2:228–31; *The Theosophist*, June 1929, 214–15

68. Sinnett, *The Occult World*, 70

69. Sinnett, *The Occult World*, 82–83

70. Mahatmas M. and K. H., *The Mahatma Letters to A. P. Sinnett*, 1–4

71. Sinnett, *The Occult World*, 119

72. Blavatsky, *H. P. Blavatsky Collected Writings*, 2:511

73. Blavatsky, *The Key to Theosophy*, 274

74. Blavatsky, *Some Unpublished Letters of Helena Petrovna Blavatsky*, 149–50

75. Wachtmeister, *Reminiscences of H. P. Blavatsky and "The Secret Doctrine,"* 48

76. Janet Oppenheimer, *The Other World: Spiritualism and Psychical Research in England 1850–1914*, Cambridge, England, Press Syndicate of the University of Cambridge, 1985, 173

77. *The Theosophical Forum*, May 1936, 343–46

78. Mahatmas M. and K. H., *The Mahatma Letters to A. P. Sinnett*, 258

79. Blavatsky, *The Letters of H. P. Blavatsky to A. P. Sinnett*, 18

80. Mahatmas M. and K. H., *The Mahatma Letters to A. P. Sinnett*, 6–10

81. Mahatmas M. and K. H., *The Mahatma Letters to A. P. Sinnett*, 13, 38, 455–56

82. "An Important Letter," *Lucifer*, August 1896, 501–6; Jinarajadasa, *Letters from the Masters of the Wisdom*, 1:7–9

83. Blavatsky, *Five Messages to American Theosophists,* 29; *H. P. Blavatsky to the American Conventions: 1888–1891,* 35

84. Blavatsky, "Practical Occultism," *Spiritual Evolution* (H. P. Blavatsky Pamphlet Series), Los Angeles, California, The Theosophy Company, 8

85. Blavatsky, "Is The Desire to 'Live' Selfish?," *Spiritual Evolution* (H. P. Blavatsky Pamphlet Series), Los Angeles, California, The Theosophy Company, 31

86. Blavatsky, "Buddha" and "Buddha Siddharta," *The Theosophical Glossary,* Los Angeles, The Theosophy Company, 1973, 64–67; Sangharakshita, *A Survey of Buddhism,* Bangalore, India, The Indian Institute of World Culture, 3rd edition, 1966, 170

87. Blavatsky, *H. P. Blavatsky Collected Writings,* 1:299

88. Olcott, *Old Diary Leaves,* 2:266–86

89. A. P. Sinnett, *The Early Days of Theosophy in Europe,* London, England, Theosophical Publishing House London Ltd., 1922, 34–37

90. Blavatsky, *The Letters of H. P. Blavatsky to A. P. Sinnett,* Appendix II, 376–86

91. Francesca Arundale, *My Guest—H. P. Blavatsky,* Adyar, Madras, India, Theosophical Publishing House, 1932, 17

92. Mahatmas M. and K. H., *The Mahatma Letters to A. P. Sinnett,* 278–79

93. Olcott, *Old Diary Leaves,* 2:252–60

94. Blavatsky, letter to her relatives; most likely end of September 1882; Russian text in *Russkoye obozreniye,* November 1891, 290; English translation in *The Path* New York, New York, volume 10, (September 1895), 169

95. Blavatsky, letter to Prince Alexander Dondoukoff-Korsakoff, Adyar Archives, The Theosophical Society, Adyar, Madras, India; faulty translation in *H.P.B. Speaks,* 2:95–102

96. Blavatsky, *The Letters of H. P. Blavatsky to A. P. Sinnett,* 38

97. See also D. Mavalankar, "A Great Riddle Solved," *The Theosophist,* December 1883, 61–62

98. Nicholas Roerich, *Shambhala,* New York, New York, Nicholas Roerich Museum, 1978, 16–17

99. "Mahatmas," *The Path,* September 1895, 170–71; Blavatsky, letter to her aunt Nadyezhda Fadeyev, about December 20, 1882, soon after her moving to Adyar; Russian text in *Russkoye obozreniye,* November 1891, 293; English translation in *The Path,* September 1895, 170–71

100. Judge, "Habitations of H.P.B.—No. 2," *The Path,* volume 7 (June 1892), 75

101. Jackson, *The Oriental Religions and American Thought,* 170; Lyman Abbott, "The Parliament of Religions," *The Outlook,* volume 48 (September 30, 1893), 583

102. *The Theosophist,* December 1982, 106–8

103. *The Theosophist,* October 1985, 9–10

104. T. Subba Row, *Esoteric Writings,* xxi

105. Henry Steel Olcott, "The Death of T. Subba Row," *The Theosophist,* July 1890, 576–78; Eek, *Damodar and the Pioneers of the Theosophical Movement,* 602

106. *The Theosophical Forum,* March 15, 1935, 188

107. Mahatmas M. and K. H., *The Mahatma Letters to A. P. Sinnett,* 267

108. Blavatsky, *The Letters of H. P. Blavatsky to A. P. Sinnett,* 95–96; Eek, *Damodar and the Pioneers of the Theosophical Movement,* 664–65

109. *Adyar Bulletin,* May 1909, 156–59; reprinted in *The Canadian Theosophist,* May–June 1983, 26–27

110. Blavatsky, *The Key to Theosophy,* 91–92

111. Blavatsky, *The Key to Theosophy,* 92

112. Blavatsky, "Letters of H. P. Blavatsky IV," *The Path,* March 1895, 415

113. *The Theosophist, Supplement,* September 1883, 6

114. Mahatmas M. and K. H., *The Mahatma Letters to A. P. Sinnett,* 38, 271–72, 299, 341, 365, 392–96, 426

115. Mahatmas M. and K. H., *The Mahatma Letters to A. P. Sinnett,* 394–400; *The Word,* New York, New York, April 1912, 20

116. *Bulletin Théosophique,* Paris, France, July 1974; translated by Boris de Zirkoff, de Zirkoff Archives, The Theosophical Society, Wheaton, Illinois

117. Franz Hartmann, "Autobiography of Franz Hartmann," *The Occult Review,* January 1908, 17

118. Hartmann, "Autobiography of Franz Hartmann," 22–23

119. Hartmann, "Autobiography of Franz Hartmann," 34; Blavatsky, *H. P. Blavatsky Collected Writings,* 8:454–57

120. Emma Coulomb, Anglo-Indian Ceylon *Times,* Ceylon, June 5, 1879

121. *The Word,* New York, New York, April 1912, 18, 19

122. Michael Gomes, "Interview with Madame Blavatsky, Paris, 1884," *The Canadian Theosophist,* November–December 1986, 97–101

123. *The Theosophist,* November 1931, 201

124. Lady Caithness, *The Mystery of the Ages,* London, England, Wallace Publishing, 1887

125. Sinnett, *Incidents in the Life of Madame Blavatsky,* 262–63

126. *The Word,* New York, New York, April 1912, 22

127. Charles Leadbeater, *How Theosophy Came to Me,* Adyar, India, The Theosophical Publishing House, 1930, 43–45; *Theosophical Quarterly,*

October 1910, 110; Bertram Keightley, "Reminiscences of H.P.B.," 2–3; Sinnett, *Early Days of Theosophy in Europe,* 54–57; Arundale, *My Guest—H. P. Blavatsky,* 20–21

128. *First Report of the Committee of the Society for Psychical Research,* 126; Sinnett, *The Early Days of Theosophy in Europe,* 56; Zhelihovsky, "Pravda o Yelene Petrovne Blavatsky," *Rebus,* 1883, 68–69

129. Sinnett, *The Early Days of Theosophy in Europe,* 56

130. Ransom, *A Short History of the Theosophical Society, 1875–1937,* 198

131. Blavatsky, "Letters of H. P. Blavatsky, XII," *The Path,* November 1895, 237

132. Blavatsky, "Letters of H. P. Blavatsky, VI," *The Path,* May 1895, 36

133. Judge, "H.P.B. at Enghien," *Lucifer,* July 1891, 359–61; Wachtmeister, *Reminiscences of H. P. Blavatsky,* 102, for further information on the *Isis Unveiled* index

134. Vera Zhelihovsky's "Report on the Paris Phenomena" sent to a Russian periodical and reprinted in *Rebus,* number 28 & 29 (July 1884), 265, 275, privately translated by Cathy Young, New Jersey

135. "H. P. Blavatsky and the Theosophist" (from a letter to the editor of the *Odesskiy vestnik*), Paris, France, May 25 (June 6), published in *Rebus,* July 15 and 22, 1884, 263–65, 273–75

136. Zhelihovsky, "Pravda o Yelene Petrovne Blavatsky," *Rebus,* 1883, 61

137. Blavatsky, "Is Creation Possible for Man?," *The Theosophist,* December 1881, 80; Blavatsky, *Is Creation Possible?* (Theosophy Company Pamphlet 28), Los Angeles, California, The Theosophy Company, 3

138. "Two H.P.B. Letters," *The Theosophist,* May 1959, 87

139. "Letters of H. P. Blavatsky, VII," *The Path,* June 1895, 73–74

140. Jinarajadasa, *Letters from the Masters of the Wisdom,* 2:111–12

141. Jinarajadasa, *Letters from the Masters of the Wisdom,* 1:34–35

142. Rosa C. Campbell Praed, *Affinities: A Romance of Today,* London, England, Bentley & Son, 1885

143. Arundale, *My Guest—H. P. Blavatsky,* 30–31, 42; Arundale, "Madame Blavatsky and Her Work," *Lucifer,* July 1891, 376–77

144. Blavatsky, *The Letters of H. P. Blavatsky to A. P. Sinnett,* 65

145. Laura Holloway and Mohini Chatterji, *Man: Fragments of Forgotten History,* London, England, Reeves and Turner, 1885

146. William Q. Judge, letter from Paris, France, April 30, 1884, *The Theosophist,* November 1931, 201–2

147. Arundale, *My Guest—H. P. Blavatsky,* 73–74; Jinarajadasa, *Letters from the Masters of the Wisdom,* 1:49–50

148. Olcott, *Old Diary Leaves,* 3:160; xxx

149. Ransom, *A Short History of the Theosophical Society, 1875–1937,* 199

150. Ransom, *A Short History of the Theosophical Society, 1875–1937,* 199

151. *First Report of the Committee of the Society for Psychical Research,* 53 footnote

152. Arundale, *My Guest—H. P. Blavatsky,* 36–37

153. Gregory Bateson, *Mind and Nature,* New York, New York, E. P. Dutton, 1979, 32: "The invention of the microscope or the telescope or means of measuring time to the fraction of a nanosecond, or weighing quantities of matter to millionths of a gram—all such improved devices of perception will disclose what was utterly unpredictable from the levels of perception that we could achieve before that discovery. . . . It follows that what we, as scientists, can perceive is always limited by threshold. That is, what is subliminal will not be grist for our mill. *Science probes; it does not prove.*"; Cranston and Williams, *Reincarnation: A New Horizon in Science, Religion and Society,* 30.

154. W. Anderson, *Open Secrets, A Western Guide to Tibetan Buddhism,* New York, New York, The Viking Press, 1979

155. William Q. Judge, *The Yoga Aphorisms of Patanjali,* Los Angeles, California, The United Lodge of Theosophists, 1967, xvii, 48

156. Mahatmas M. and K. H., *The Mahatma Letters to A. P. Sinnett,* 162

157. Jean Overton Fuller, *Blavatsky and Her Teachers, An Investigative Biography,* London, England, East-West Publications, 1988, 141

158. Jean Overton Fuller, *Blavatsky and Her Teachers, An Investigative Biography,* 141. This book reprints letters first printed in the September and October 1884 issues of *Madras Christian College Magazine.*

159. Blavatsky, *The Letters of H. P. Blavatsky to A. P. Sinnett,* 102

160. Blavatsky, *H. P. Blavatsky Collected Writings,* 6:434–36

161. Arundale, *My Guest—H. P. Blavatsky,* 45

162. *The Theosophist, Supplement,* September 1883, 6

163. James Webb, ed., *The Society for Psychical Research Report on The Theosophical Society,* The Occult, New York, New York, Arno Press, 1976, [xi]

164. Blavatsky, "Letters of H. P. Blavatsky VII," *The Path,* June 1895, 75

165. Sinnett, *Incidents in the Life of Madame Blavatsky,* 289–90

166. Blavatsky, *The Letters of H. P. Blavatsky to A. P. Sinnett,* 115

167. Blavatsky, letter to Henry Steel Olcott, summer 1885, HPB letter file, de Zirkoff Archive, The Theosophical Society, Wheaton, Illinois

168. Francesca Arundale, "Madame Blavatsky, and Her Work," *Lucifer,* July 15, 1891, 376–80

169. "S.P.R. Press Statement," *Theosophical History,* London, England, Leslie Price, ed., April 1986, 127; Vernon Harrison, "J'Accuse: An Examination of the Hodgson Report of 1885," *Journal of the Society for Psychical Research,* London, England, April 1986, 302–3

170. "Je ne pardonnerai jamais dans ma vie . . . je ferai tout le mal que je puis pour elle." *Report of the Result of an Investigation into the Charges against Madame Blavatsky,* 1885, 133–34

171. Blavatsky, *The Letters of H. P. Blavatsky to A. P. Sinnett,* 110

172. Franz Hartmann, *Report of Observations Made During a Nine Months' Stay at the Headquarters of the Theosophical Society at Adyar (Madras), India,* Madras, India, Graves, Cookson and Co., 1884, 32; hereafter called *The Hartmann Report*

173. Jinarajadasa, *Letters from the Masters of the Wisdom,* 1:43

174. *The Hartmann Report,* 35–36

175. *The Hartmann Report,* 38–41

176. R. A. V. Morris, "The Two H. P. Blavatskys," *The Aryan Path,* Bombay, India, The Theosophy Company, January 1932, 56

177. Jinarajadasa, *Letters from the Masters of the Wisdom,* 2:131–32

178. Emma Coulomb, *Some Account of My Intercourse with Madame Blavatsky from 1872 to 1884,* London, England, Elliot Stock, 1885, 111; quoted in Beatrice Hastings, *Defence of Madame Blavatsky,* Volume II, The "Coulomb Pamphlet," Worthing, England, Beatrice Hastings, 1937, 89

179. *The Hartmann Report,* 47

180. William Q. Judge, "Madame Blavatsky in India," *The Arena,* Boston, Massachusetts, March 1892, 472–80

181. William Q. Judge, "Madame Blavatsky in India," *The Arena,* Boston, March 1892, 472–80; "The So-Called Exposé of Madame Blavatsky," *The Index,* Boston, Massachusetts, March 11, 1886, 441–42. Both articles reprinted in *Theosophical Articles by William Q. Judge,* Los Angeles, California, The Theosophy Company, 1980, 2:255–64, 265–67; and *Echoes of the Orient: The Writings of William Quan Judge,* San Diego, California, Point Loma Publications, Inc., 1987, 3:122–24, 198–205

182. Harrison, "J'Accuse: An Examination of the Hodgson Report of 1885," 303, 306. "Incidentally Harrison was in charge of a team of 40 laboratory staff, and learnt much about forgers and their methods. He still works in retirement as an examiner of questioned documents for the legal profession" (*Theosophical History,* London, England, October 1985, 68–69).

183. Blavatsky, *The Letters of H. P. Blavatsky to A. P. Sinnett*, 115–16

184. Vernon Harrison, "H. P. Blavatsky and the Psychical Researchers," March 25, 1984, talk before the Theosophical Society of London, England, printed in *Viewpoint Aquarius*, number 138; see also Harrison, "J'Accuse: . . . ," 288–89, 309

185. William E. Coleman, *Religio-Philosophical Journal*, September 1893, 266

186. *The Theosophist*, February 1985, 185

187. Harrison, "J'Accuse: An Examination of The Hodgson Report of 1885," 310

188. Blavatsky, *The Letters of H. P. Blavatsky to A. P. Sinnett*, 110

189. Hastings, *Defence of Madame Blavatsky*, Volume II, The "Coulomb Pamphlet," 10

190. Adlai E. Waterman, *Obituary: "The Hodgson Report" on Madame Blavatsky 1885–1960*, Adyar, Madras, India, The Theosophical Publishing House, 1963

191. Gomes, "The Coulomb Case, 1884–1984, *The Theosophist*, February 1985, 182–83

192. Fuller, *Blavatsky and Her Teachers: An Investigative Biography*, 150–51

193. Fuller, *Blavatsky and Her Teachers: An Investigative Biography*, 148–53, 240, Appendix

194. Hastings, *Defence of Madame Blavatsky*, Volume II, The "Coulomb Pamphlet," 7

195. "Report of the Committee Appointed to Investigate Phenomena Connected with the Theosophical Society," *Proceedings of the Society for Psychical Research*, London, England, Society for Psychical Research, December 1885, 282–83; hereafter called *The Hodgson Report*

196. Blavatsky, *The Letters of H. P. Blavatsky to A. P. Sinnett*, 98

197. Blavatsky, *The Letters of H. P. Blavatsky to A. P. Sinnett*, 102, 103

198. Harrison, "J'Accuse: An Examination of the Hodgson Report of 1885," 295

199. Harrison, "J'Accuse: An Examination of the Hodgson Report of 1885," 308

200. Blavatsky, *The Letters of H. P. Blavatsky to A. P. Sinnett*, 348–51. In the footnote on 349, the editor mistakenly mentions the handwriting of Master M, when it is in fact that of HPB. See also 250 and 257.

201. Victor A. Endersby, *The Hall of Magic Mirrors: A Portrait of Madame Blavatsky*, New York, New York, Carlton Press, 1969, 89, 132, 160

202. Charles Marshall, "The Mahatma Letters—A Syntactic Investigation into the Possibility of 'Forgery' by Helena Petrovna Blavatsky, a 19th Century Occultist," *Viewpoint Aquarius*, London, England, October 1980, 8–14

203. *The Canadian Theosophist*, Calgary, Canada, November–December 1980, 98

204. *The Hodgson Report,* 313–14

205. *The Hodgson Report,* 314

206. Sinnett, *Incidents in the Life of Madame Blavatsky,* 315

207. Mahatmas M. and K. H., *The Mahatma Letters to A. P. Sinnett,* 465, Appendix

208. Blavatsky, nine-point memorandum to her colleague Henry Steel Olcott, manuscript in Adyar Archives, The Theosophical Society, Adyar, Madras, India; see also Blavatsky, *H. P. Blavatsky Collected Writings,* 6:410; Mahatmas M. & K.H., *The Mahatma Letters to A. P. Sinnett,* Appendix, 466; Blavatsky, *The Letters of H. P. Blavatsky to A. P. Sinnett,* 76, 94

209. Michael Gomes, "The Coulomb Case, 1884–1984," *The Theosophist,* Adyar, Madras, India, January 1985, 143

210. Blavatsky, letter Wednesday, November 1885, from a copy sent to Olcott in Bawaji's handwriting, transcribed from the original in the Adyar Archives, The Theosophical Society, Adyar, Madras [Chennai], India; also available in the de Zirkoff Archives, Theosophical Society in America, Wheaton, Illinois; Henry Steel Olcott, letter to Blavatsky, October 21, 1885, reprinted in *The Theosophist,* January 1933, 402–6; see Olcott letters in *Letters of H. P. Blavatsky to A. P. Sinnett*

211. Blavatsky, "Echoes of the Past," *The Theosophist,* May 1908, 757–58

212. Leslie Price, "Madame Blavatsky Unveiled?: A new discussion of the most famous investigation of The Society for Psychical Research," London, England, Theosophical History Centre, February 1986, 7–8

213. Blavatsky, "Letters of H. P. Blavatsky, VII," *The Path,* June 1895, 78

214. Blavatsky, "Letters of H. P. Blavatsky, VIII," *The Path,* July 1895, 105–7

215. Blavatsky, letter to Henry Steel Olcott, November 1884, Adyar Archives, The Theosophical Society, Adyar, Madras, India

216. Isabel Cooper-Oakley, "At Cairo and Madras," *Lucifer,* June 1891, 278–79

217. Olcott, *Old Diary Leaves,* 3:197; letter to Olcott, November 24, 1884, Adyar Archives, The Theosophical Society, Adyar, Madras, India; see also item by C. W. Leadbeater in *Indian Mirror,* November 28, 1884, on Mrs. Coulomb's nefarious activities in Cairo, reprinted in Eek, *Damodar and the Pioneers of the Theosophical Movement,* 574–76

218. Isabel Cooper-Oakley, "At Cairo and Madras," 279

219. *The Theosophist,* Supplement, March 1885, 5

220. Olcott, *Old Diary Leaves,* 1:97–98

221. Gomes, "The Coulomb Case, 1884–1984," *The Theosophist,* January 1985, 141

222. Gomes, "The Coulomb Case, 1884–1984," 141; Olcott, *Old Diary Leaves,* 3:200–3

223. Olcott, *Old Diary Leaves,* 3:203

224. Hartmann, "Autobiography of Dr. Franz Hartmann," 28

225. Isabel Cooper-Oakley, "At Cairo and Madras," 281–82

226. C. Jinarajadasa, *The Personality of H. P. B.* (pamphlet), Adyar, Madras, India, The Theosophical Publishing House, 1930, 19

227. Harrison, "J'Accuse: An Examination of The Hodgson Report of 1885," 309

228. *The Theosophist,* Supplement, May 1885, 195

229. Blavatsky, "Why I Do Not Return to India," letter of April 1890, reprinted in *The Theosophist,* January 1922; also in the pamphlet *Theosophy and H. P. B.,* Los Angeles, California, The Theosophy Company

230. Richard Hodgson, "The Defence of the Theosophists," *Proceedings of the Society for Psychical Research,* London, England, volume 9 (1894), 135; reprinted in James Webb, editor, *The Society for Psychical Research, Report on the Theosophical Society,* 1976, 135

231. Hodgson, "The Defence of the Theosophists," 135

232. "Letters of H. S. Olcott to Francesca Arundale," *The Theosophist,* October 1932, 48

233. Hartmann, "Autobiography of Dr. Franz Hartmann," 27–28

234. William Q. Judge, *Letters That Have Helped Me,* 267

235. Arundale, *My Guest—H. P. Blavatsky,* 2

236. Blavatsky, "Recent Progress in Theosophy," *The North American Review,* Cedar Falls, Iowa, August 1890; reprinted in *Theosophy and the Theosophical Movement* (HPB Pamphlet Series), Los Angeles, California, The Theosophy Company

Part 6. Horizons Open in the West

1. Hartmann, "Autobiography of Dr. Franz Hartmann," 19–20; Wachtmeister, *Reminiscences of H. P. Blavatsky and "The Secret Doctrine",* 113

2. Mahatmas M. and K. H., *The Mahatma Letters to A. P. Sinnett,* 15, 44, 281; Geoffrey A. Barborka, *The Mahatmas and Their Letters,* Adyar, Madras, India, The Theosophical Publishing House, 1973, 314–16

3. Blavatsky, *The Letters of H. P. Blavatsky to A. P. Sinnett,* 105

4. Blavatsky, *The Letters of H. P. Blavatsky to A. P. Sinnett,* 112

5. Blavatsky, *The Secret Doctrine,* de Zirkoff edition, 1:[12–13]

6. Wachtmeister, *Reminiscences of H. P. Blavatsky and The Secret Doctrine,* 99

7. Blavatsky, "Have Animals Souls?," *The Theosophist,* January–March 1886, 243–49, 295–302, 348–54; reprinted in *Modern Ignorance of Life and Soul* (HPB Pamphlet Series), Los Angeles, California, The Theosophy Company

8. *The New York Times Magazine,* December 31, 1979

9. Muriel Dowding, *Beauty—Not the Beast,* London, England, Neville Spearman, 1980; also Wheaton, Illinois, The Theosophical Publishing House, 1982

10. *The Path,* November 1893, 246–47; *The American Theosophist,* Fall 1937

11. Wachtmeister, *Reminiscences of H. P. Blavatsky and The Secret Doctrine,* 9

12. Wachtmeister, *Reminiscences of H. P. Blavatsky and The Secret Doctrine,* 26–27

13. Wachtmeister, *Reminiscences of H. P. Blavatsky and The Secret Doctrine,* 42–43; Bertram Keightley, in his *Reminiscences of H.P.B.* (Adyar, Madras, India, The Theosophical Publishing House, 1931, 18–19, 26–27) goes into more detail on this method of HPB in training her pupils.

14. Blavatsky, "H.P.B. on the S.P.R. Report," *The Theosophist,* August 1931, 663

15. Wachtmeister, *Reminiscences of H. P. Blavatsky and The Secret Doctrine,* 18

16. Jirah Dewey Buck, *Modern World Movements,* Chicago, Illinois, Indo-American Book Company, 1913, 57

17. Mahatmas M. and K. H., *The Mahatma Letters to A. P. Sinnett,* Appendix, HPB letter to Sinnett dated January 6, 1886, 470–74

18. Blavatsky, *The Secret Doctrine,* de Zirkoff edition, 1:[13–22]

19. Blavatsky, *The Secret Doctrine,* de Zirkoff edition, 1:[13–22]

20. Wachtmeister, "A New Year's Greeting," *Theosophical Siftings,* London, England, 1891, 3:3–4

21. Blavatsky, *The Letters of H. P. Blavatsky to A. P. Sinnett,* 312–13

22. Blavatsky, *The Letters of H. P. Blavatsky to A. P. Sinnett,* 289–90

23. Wachtmeister, *Reminiscences of H. P. Blavatsky and The Secret Doctrine,* 24–25

24. Wachtmeister, *Reminiscences of H. P. Blavatsky and The Secret Doctrine,* 15–16, 22–23

25. Wachtmeister, *Reminiscences of H. P. Blavatsky and The Secret Doctrine,* 42

26. Wachtmeister, *Reminiscences of H. P. Blavatsky and The Secret Doctrine,* 42

27. C. Wachtmeister, "Madame Blavatsky, A Personal Reminiscence," *The Occult Review,* London, England, March 1914, 139, 142

28. "Two H.P.B. Letters," letter to Serguii Alexandrovitch, *The Theosophist,* May 1, 1959, 87

29. Solovyoff, *A Modern Priestess of Isis,* translated by Walter Leaf, London, England, Longmans, Green, and Co., 1895

30. P. D. Ouspensky, *The Fourth Dimension,* 3rd edition, revised, Petrograd, Russia, M. V. Pirozhkov, 1918, 88–96

31. Solovyoff, *A Modern Priestess of Isis,* 10–12, 21, 22, 29

32. Beatrice Hastings, *Solovyoff's Fraud: Being A Critical Analysis of the Book "A Modern Priestess of Isis,"* Edmonton, Canada, Edmonton Lodge of the Theosophical Society in Canada, 1988, 58; hereafter called *Solovyoff's Fraud*

33. Solovyoff, *A Modern Priestess of Isis,* 12, 24, 65

34. Arundale, *My Guest—H. P. Blavatsky,* 29–30; Hastings, *Solovyoff's Fraud,* 59

35. Hastings, *Solovyoff's Fraud,* 59

36. The picture was originally in possession of Judge's wife, who bequeathed his Theosophical effects to the United Lodge of Theosophists in New York City.

37. Eglinton, *A Memoir of Æ,* 13

38. Solovyoff, *A Modern Priestess of Isis,* 15, 22, 27

39. Blavatsky, "Letters of H. P. Blavatsky, VII," *The Path,* June 1895, 76

40. Vera Petrovna Jelihovsky, "Helena Petrovna Blavatsky," *Lucifer,* December 1894, 278–79

41. Solovyoff, *A Modern Priestess of Isis,* 97

42. Zhelihovsky, *Helena Petrovna Blavatskya i sovremenniy zhretz istini* (Helena Petrovna Blavatsky and a Modern Priest of Truth), 52

43. Solovyoff, *A Modern Priestess of Isis,* 173–75

44. Solovyoff, *A Modern Priestess of Isis,* 288–89

45. Solovyoff, *A Modern Priestess of Isis,* xv

46. Solovyoff, *A Modern Priestess of Isis,* 346–47

47. Zhelihovsky, *Helena Petrovna Blavatskya i sovremenniy zhretz istini,* 33

48. Zhelihovsky, *Helena Petrovna Blavatskya i sovremenniy zhretz istini,* 31–32

49. Olcott, *Old Diary Leaves,* 2:373–467

50. Solovyoff, *A Modern Priestess of Isis,* 312

51. Blavatsky, *The Letters of H. P. Blavatsky to A. P. Sinnett,* 172

52. Solovyoff, *A Modern Priestess of Isis,* 313; Zhelihovsky, *Helena Petrovna Blavatskya i sovremenniy zhretz istini,* 123

53. Zhelihovsky, *Helena Petrovna Blavatskya i sovremenniy zhretz istini,* 125

54. Zhelihovsky, *Helena Petrovna Blavatskya i sovremenniy zhretz istini*, 53

55. Blavatsky, *H. P. Blavatsky Collected Writings*, 1:537

56. Edward Kasinec and Boris Kerdimun, "Occult Literature in Russia," in Maurice Tuchman, editor, *The Spiritual in Art: Abstract Paintings 1890–1985*, New York, New York, Abbeville Press, 1986, 361–66

57. Wachtmeister, *Reminiscences of H. P. Blavatsky and The Secret Doctrine*, 94–95

58. Wachtmeister, *Reminiscences of H. P. Blavatsky and The Secret Doctrine*, 50–51

59. Blavatsky, "Letters of H. P. Blavatsky, X," *The Path*, September 1895, 171

60. N. D. Khandalavala, "H. P. Blavatsky and Her Masters," *The Theosophist*, October 1898, 22

61. Wachtmeister, *Reminiscences of H. P. Blavatsky and The Secret Doctrine*, 58

62. *The Theosophical Movement 1875–1950*, 132

63. Buck, *Modern World Movements*, 56

64. Buck, *Modern World Movements*, 56

65. J. D. Buck, "H. P. Blavatsky As Seen Through Her Work," *Lucifer*, June 15, 1891, 308

66. J. Ralston Skinner, *Key to the Hebrew and Egyptian Mystery in the Source of Measures*, (Secret Doctrine Reference Series), San Diego, California, Wizards Bookshelf, 1982; *H. P. Blavatsky Collected Writings*, 13:402–5

67. *The American Theosophist*, July 1979, 247

68. *The American Theosophist*, July 1979, 247

69. Blavatsky, *The Secret Doctrine*, 1:308–9; 2:559–61, 597

70. Blavatsky, *The Letters of H. P. Blavatsky to A. P. Sinnett*, 227

71. "The Mysterious Hand," *The Theosophist*, April 1887, 391–93

72. Wachtmeister, *Reminiscences of H. P. Blavatsky and The Secret Doctrine*, 54–55

73. Wachtmeister, *Reminiscences of H. P. Blavatsky and The Secret Doctrine*, 77

74. Bertram Keightley, *Reminiscences of H.P.B.*, 5

75. Blavatsky, *The Letters of H. P. Blavatsky to A. P. Sinnett*, 205

76. "Theosophy in the West," *The Theosophist*, July 1891, 585 (reprint of Adyar convention lecture by Bertram Keightley)

77. "Extract of a Letter from H.P.B. to a London Group, 1887," *The Theosophist*, July 1988, 387

78. Wachtmeister, *Reminiscences of H. P. Blavatsky and The Secret Doctrine*, 60–62

79. Wachtmeister, *Reminiscences of H. P. Blavatsky and The Secret Doctrine*, 64–67

80. Blavatsky, *The Secret Doctrine*, 1:555

81. NASA, *Jet Propulsion Laboratory* (JPL), December 15, 1982, 82–92

82. Wachtmeister, *Reminiscences of H. P. Blavatsky and The Secret Doctrine*, 78

83. Olcott, *Old Diary Leaves*, 1:26

84. *The Theosophical Journal*, London, England, November–December 1962, 7

85. Bertram Keightley, "Reminiscences of H.P.B.," 10

86. Wachtmeister, *Reminiscences of H. P. Blavatsky and The Secret Doctrine*; 77–82; Keightley, *Reminiscences of H.P.B.*, 13–26

87. "Dr. Keightley Speaks," *The New York Times*, April 29, 1889; reprinted in *Theosophy*, Los Angeles, California, The Theosophy Company, August 1950

88. *The Theosophical Movement 1875–1950*, 123

89. Alexander Fullerton, "Seeing Little; Perceiving Much," *Lucifer*, July 1891, 380; Judge, *The Ocean of Theosophy*, 140

90. W. B. Yeats, *The Collected Letters of W. B. Yeats*, volume 1, *1865–1895*, edited by John Kelly, Oxford, England, Oxford University Press, 1986, 1:319; Śankarāchārya, *The Crest-Jewel of Wisdom and Other Writings of Śankarāchārya*, translated by Charles Johnston, Covina, California, Theosophical University Press, 1946

91. Charles Johnston, "Helena Petrovna Blavatsky," *The Theosophical Forum*, New York, New York, volume 5, number 12, (April 1900); volume 6, numbers 1–3 (May–July 1900); Blavatsky, *H. P. Blavatsky Collected Writings*, 8:392–409

92. Bertram Keightley, *Reminiscences of H.P.B.*, 11–12; Judge, "Habitations of H.P.B. No 1," *The Path*, May 1892, 36–39

93. Blavatsky, undated letter of 1889, de Zirkoff Archives, The Theosophical Society, Wheaton, Illinois

94. Franz Hartmann, "The Talking Image of Urur," *Lucifer*, December 1888–February 1890 (15 installments)

95. Franz Hartmann, *The Talking Image of Urur*, New York, New York, J. W. Lovell & Co., 1890

96. Blavatsky, letter to Count Carl Wachtmeister, *The Eclectic Theosophist*, May/June 1983, 6

97. *Riemann Musik Lexikon*, Sonne, Manz, B. Schatts, 1961

98. *Lucifer*, December 1890, 301

99. Blavatsky, *H. P. Blavatsky Collected Writings*, 9:102–3

100. Alice Leighton Cleather, *H. P. Blavatsky As I Knew Her*, Addendum by Basil Crump, Calcutta, India, Thacker Spink & Company, 1923, 36–37

101. Archibald Keightley, "Reminiscences of H. P. Blavatsky," *Theosophical Quarterly,* October 1910, 107

102. Archibald Keightley, "Reminiscences of H. P. Blavatsky," *Theosophical Quarterly,* October 1910, 117–118

103. *The Canadian Theosophist,* September–October 1991

104. Edmund Russell, "Isis Unveiled: Personal Recollections of Madame Blavatsky," *The Occult Review,* London, England, November 1918, 260–69. Russell incorrectly names the photographer of these pictures.

105. Enrico Resta, "A Link with H.P.B.—Through Her Photographer," *Theosophical News and Notes,* London, England, April 1942, 6. This is the journal of The Theosophical Society in the British Isles.

106. "Theosophical Worthies," *The Theosophist,* September 1911, 897

107. José Xifré, "H.P.B.," *Lucifer,* August 15, 1891, 455–56

108. "Theosophical Worthies," *The Theosophist,* September 1911, 897–99

109. "Theosophy in Spain," *Lucifer,* December 15, 1889, 343–44

110. Blavatsky, *H. P. Blavatsky Collected Writings*, 9:458–61

111. Boris de Zirkoff, "Don José Xifré," *Theosophia,* volume 19, number 2 (Fall 1962), 14–16

112. "'Lucifer' to the Archbishop of Canterbury" appeared in *Lucifer,* December 1887, 242–51, and may have been a collaboration of HPB and Richard Harte, a former New York newspaperman who joined the TS in 1878 and was currently in London (see *H. P. Blavatsky Collected Writings*, 8:268).

113. This three-part work was reprinted in the HPB Pamphlet Series under the title *The Esoteric Character of the Gospels* (Los Angeles, The Theosophy Company)

114. Edward Gibbon, *The History of the Decline and Fall of the Roman Empire,* London, England, John Murray, 1854, 2:163

115. A. A. F. Lamplugh, *Codex Brucianus,* London, England, John Watkins, 1918

116. Carl Jung, *Psychology and Alchemy,* New York, New York, Pantheon Books, 1953, 35

117. Elaine Pagels, *The Gnostic Gospels,* New York, New York, Random House, 1979, xxiv–xxxv

118. Geddes MacGregor, *Reincarnation in Christianity,* Wheaton, Illinois, The Theosophical Publishing House (a Quest book), 1978, 43–44

119. Jean Doresse, *The Secret Books of the Egyptians,* New York, New York, Viking, 1960, 112–13; Sylvia Cranston and Carey Williams, *Reincarnation: A New Horizon in Science, Religion and Society,* New York, New York, Crown, 1984, 219–21

120. G. R. S. Mead, *The Pistis Sophia,* revised edition, London, England, John Watkins, 1921, available from Wizards Bookshelf, P.O. Box 6600, San Diego, California, 92106. See also W. T. S. Thackara, "H. P. Blavatsky Collected Writings, Volume XIII," *Sunrise,* Pasadena, California, Theosophical University Press, August/September 1983, 203–6.

121. Blavatsky, *H.P. Blavatsky Collected Writings,* 13:1–8

122. *Encyclopaedia Britannica,* 1979, 4:530

123. C. G. Jung, *Memories, Dreams, and Reflections,* translated by Richard and Clara Winston, New York, New York, Pantheon Books, 1963, 175–76

124. *Translation of extract from official document*

> The Reichsführer [Heinrich Himmler] and Chief of the German Police of the minister of the Interior
>
> By virtue of article (or paragraph) 1 the decree of the Reichspresident for the Protection of People and State of 2/28/33 (RGBl.I S.83), I dissolve the following named similar to Freemason lodge organizations, as far as they have not dissolved themselves before Aug. 17, 1935 (willingly dissolved). pp. 8. Theosophical Societies [nine listed] . . .
>
> The continuation and founding of these, as well as the founding of camouflaged organizations, will, under threat of order 4 a.a.O. be forbidden.
>
> At the same time, I confirm by virtue of the law of July 7, 1933—RGBl.I S.479, concerning the confiscation of the wealth of the people and of those hostile to the state, that the wealth of the above designated organizations were used or intended for the dispatch (to kill) the efforts (or endeavor, aspiration) of those hostile to the state.
>
>
> Representing:
> for the signed Heydrich
> (signature)
> Employee of the Chancellery
>

What Theosophical teaching so aroused Hitler that Theosophists were among the first to be sent to concentration camps? The first object of the Theosophical movement; to form a nucleus of universal brotherhood, naturally including all human beings, was an alarming concept for a tyrant planning to dominate by eliminating races and groups through genocide. *The Secret Doctrine* has one sentence (2:266) that would inflame the Nazi mentality: "The Aryan and their Semitic

Branch are of the Fifth Race." In Theosophy the fifth race includes (but is not limited to) all that science refers to as Indo-European people, and in HPB's day the preferred name for these groups was "Aryan"—a noble term today become repugnant because of the Nazis' distorted usage. According to philologists, the word is derived from *Arya,* meaning "noble" or "the noble ones" (*Encyclopaedia Britannica,* 1891, 2:672).

Aryan as a technical term has been borrowed from the Sanskrit *ārya* or *arya,* the Zend *airya.* In later Sanskrit *arya* means "of a good family" and is used as a complimentary address. Originally, however, it was used as a national name, and even as late as the time of the Laws of Manu, India was still called Aryavarta, i.e., the abode of the Aryas.

Buddha himself, in his famous Four Noble Truths and Noble Eight-fold Path, uses the word "Aryan" in its high sense of "noble." In Christmas Humphreys's *A Popular Dictionary of Buddhism* we read:

"*Aryan:* From Ārya (Sk.) meaning noble. In Pali, Ariya, e.g., the Aryan or Noble Eightfold Path, or the Four Aryan or Noble Truths. Taken from the Aryan race, the word was used by Buddha as worthy of the race, noble in conduct."

Two teachers, Mary Linne* and Emmi Haerter were imprisoned in Germany because of Theosophical literature found in their house—all of which was burned, including their own translation of *The Secret Doctrine.* This was also the fate of the letters from the Masters to Dr. Hübbe-Schleiden. See the de Zirkoff edition, "Historical Introduction," *The Secret Doctrine,* 1:[16].

125. Blavatsky, *The Secret Doctrine,* 1:563

126. H. P. Blavatsky, "Karmic Visions," *Lucifer,* June 1888, 311–22; *Cycles and Human Destiny* (HPB Pamphlet Series), Los Angeles, The Theosophy Company; also printed in *La Revue Théosophique,* March 21, 1889

127. Blavatsky, *The Secret Doctrine,* 1:vii–viii

128. Blavatsky, *The Secret Doctrine,* 1:272–73

129. Blavatsky, *The Secret Doctrine,* 1:13–17, 20

130. Blavatsky, *The Secret Doctrine,* 1:238, 639; 2:304–5

131. Blavatsky, *The Secret Doctrine,* 2:305

132. Blavatsky, *The Secret Doctrine,* 2:305 and footnote

133. Blavatsky, *The Secret Doctrine,* 1:643

134. Blavatsky, *The Secret Doctrine,* 1:104

135. Blavatsky, *The Secret Doctrine,* 1:104

136. Blavatsky, *The Secret Doctrine,* 1:644, 639

137. Blavatsky, *The Secret Doctrine,* 2:306, 424

138. Blavatsky, *The Secret Doctrine,* 1:266; 2:80, 513

*Letter from Mary Linne, June 28, 1981 to Anita Atkins.

139. Blavatsky, *Transactions of the Blavatsky Lodge of The Theosophical Society,* reprinted verbatim from the original edition, Los Angeles, California, The Theosophy Company, 1923, 148

140. Blavatsky, *The Secret Doctrine,* 1:53-54

141. Robert Crosbie, *The Friendly Philosopher,* Los Angeles, California, The Theosophy Company, 1945, 98

142. Blavatsky, *The Secret Doctrine,* 1:207-8, 208-9 footnote

143. Crosbie, *The Friendly Philosopher,* 98

144. Theodore Roszak, *The Unfinished Animal,* New York, New York, Harper & Row, 1975, 120-22

145. Eglinton, *A Memoir of Æ,* 164-65

146. Wachtmeister, *Reminiscences of H. P. Blavatsky and "The Secret Doctrine,"* 119-20

147. Blavatsky, *The Secret Doctrine,* 1:620

148. Lewis Thomas, *The Medusa and the Snail,* New York, New York, Viking, 1979; selected from a condensed extract published in *Reader's Digest,* October 1979, 98-99

149. Arnold Duncan and Miranda Weston Smith, *The Encyclopaedia of Ignorance,* Oxford, England, Oxford University Press, 1977

150. William R. Corliss, *Mysterious Universe: A Handbook of Astronomical Anomalies,* Glen Ann, Maryland, The Sourcebook Project, 1979

151. Blavatsky, *The Secret Doctrine,* 1:554-60; part 3, chapter 10, "The Coming Force," has a section on Mr. Keely, "an unconscious occultist."

152. W. T. Stead, letter to Blavatsky, Adyar Archives, The Theosophical Society, Adyar, Madras, India

153. Annie Besant, *Annie Besant: An Autobiography,* 3rd edition, Adyar, Madras, India, The Theosophical Publishing House, 1939

154. Arthur R. Nethercot, *The First Five Lives of Annie Besant,* Chicago, Illinois, The University of Chicago Press, 1960, 1

155. Besant, *Annie Besant: An Autobiography,* 308-9

156. Besant, *Annie Besant: An Autobiography,* 310; "Among the Adepts," *Pall Mall Gazette,* April 25, 1889, 3; Besant's review of *The Secret Doctrine;* reprinted in *Theosophical Journal,* November-December 1974, 3-5

157. Besant, *Annie Besant: An Autobiography,* 310

158. "Letters of H. P. Blavatsky to Annie Besant," *The Theosophist,* January 1932, 377

159. Besant, *Annie Besant: An Autobiography,* 311

160. Besant, *Annie Besant: An Autobiography,* 311-13

161. James D. Hunt, *Gandhi in London,* New Delhi, India, Promilla and Company, 1978, 32-33

162. Zhelihovsky, "Radda-Bai: Biograficheskiy ocherk," published in *Zagadochniya plemena na "Golubih Gorah"—Durbar v Lahore*, St. Petersburg, Russia, V. I. Gubinsky, li–lii

163. Olcott, *Old Diary Leaves*, 4:179

164. Original in Adyar Archives, The Theosophical Society, Adyar, Madras [Chennai], India; excerpted in Blavatsky, "She Being Dead Yet Speaketh," *The Path*, July 1892, 121–22

165. Blavatsky, "She Being Dead Yet Speaketh," 121–22

166. Blavatsky, *Letters to Ralston Skinner*, Ralston Skinner Collection, Harvard University, Cambridge, Massachusetts

167. *The Theosophical Movement 1875–1950*, 139

168. Blavatsky, "Letters of H. P. Blavatsky, XII," *The Path*, November 1895, 238

169. "Faces of Friends," *The Path*, June 1894, 90–91

170. Blavatsky, *H. P. Blavatsky Collected Writings*, 11:322

171. Paul Russell Cutright and Michael S. Brodhead, *Elliott Coues: Naturalist and Frontier Historian*, Chicago, Illinois, University of Illinois Press, 1981, jacket

172. Blavatsky, *H. P. Blavatsky Collected Writings*, 11:317–23

173. C. Jinarajadasa, editor, *The Golden Book of the Theosophical Society: A Brief History of the Society's Growth from 1875–1925*, Adyar, Madras, India, The Theosophical Publishing House, 1925, 203

174. Blavatsky, *H. P. Blavatsky Collected Writings*, 11:323, 328; *The Theosophical Movement 1875–1950*, 146–48; Blavatsky, letter to Judge Khandalavala, Adyar Archives, The Theosophical Society, Adyar, Madras [Chennai], India; Jinarajadasa, *Letters from the Masters of the Wisdom*, 1:50

175. *The Theosophical Movement 1875–1950*, 148–49

176. *The Theosophical Movement 1875–1950*, 148–49

177. Gomes, *The Dawning of the Theosophical Movement*, 15

178. De Zirkoff Archives, The Theosophical Society, Wheaton, Illinois

179. William Q. Judge, Archibald Keightley, "'Light on the Path' and Mabel Collins," [New York, New York, June 6, 1889]; Judge, editor. "Dr. Elliott Coues in His Letters," New York, New York, June 14, 1889; letters from Dr. Elliott Coues, *Religio-Philosophical Journal*, Chicago, Illinois, May 11 and June 1, 1889; original in de Zirkoff Archives, The Theosophical Society, Wheaton, Illinois

180. William Q. Judge, "Report of the General Secretary," *Theosophical Society, American Section, Fourth Annual Convention, held at Chicago, Illinois, April 27−28, 1890, Report of Proceedings*, 8−9

181. Blavatsky, "The 'Nine-Days' Wonder' Press," *Lucifer,* August 1889, 444; also in *H. P. Blavatsky Collected Writings*, 11:366−77

182. Cutright and Brodhead, *Elliott Coues: Naturalist and Frontier Historian*, 300

183. Michael Gomes, "Malicious from First to Last" (HPB to Coues), *The Canadian Theosophist,* January−February 1986, 128−29

184. Cutright and Brodhead, *Elliott Coues: Naturalist and Frontier Historian*, 299

185. William Q. Judge, "The Libel Suits Against N.Y. *Sun* and Elliott Coues," *The Path,* March 1891, 390

186. Photostatted documents in the Sylvia Cranston Archives, Santa Barbara, California. These documents were obtained on June 17, 1955, by Walter Carrithers's attorney from the county clerk and the clerk of the Supreme Court, New York County.

187. Walter Carrithers wrote a letter to Don Brown, editor of the Sunnyside, California, *Valley Journal,* dated November 7, 1970, on a letterhead of the Blavatsky Foundation, Fresno, California. When questioned, Carrithers advised him that he had hired a New York attorney, Joseph P. Blechman, to go through the case files in the Hall of Records. It was at this time the proceedings were discovered.

188. Blavatsky, "The 'Nine-Days' Wonder' Press," 441

189. William Q. Judge, "Two Theosophical Events," *The Path,* November 1892, 249

190. William Q. Judge, "The Esoteric She," reprinted in *H. P. Blavatsky, Her Life and Work* (Judge Pamphlet Series number 2), Los Angeles, California, The Theosophy Company

191. Coues Collection, State Historical Society of Wisconsin

192. Blavatsky, "My Books," *Lucifer,* May 1891, 243

193. *Webster's New Collegiate Dictionary,* Springfield, Massachusetts, G. & C. Merriam Company, 1980, 870

194. Solovyoff, *A Modern Priestess of Isis,* 353

195. Emil Ludwig, *The History of a Man,* New York, New York, G. P. Putnam's Sons, 1928

196. Beatrice Hastings, *Defence of Madame Blavatsky,* Volume I, The Hastings Press, Worthing, England, 1937, 10−11

197. HPB took the following six undocumented items: (1.) *SD* 1:2, from Winchell, 553: "Leucippus and Democritus . . . maintained that space was eternally filled with atoms actuated by an eternal motion." Instead

of "an eternal motion," HPB wrote "a ceaseless motion." (2.) *SD* 1:97 footnote quotes from the Reverend W. B. Slaughter's *The Modern Genesis* three sentences that HPB probably took from Winchell, 94 footnote, without mentioning the source. (3.) In *SD* 1:497–98, the words italicized here were taken from Winchell, 553: "The celebrated Kepler, about 1595 devised *a curious hypothesis which made use of a vortical movement within the solar system.* The conception of *attraction and repulsion* had come down from the epoch of *Empedocles,* by whom they were designated *'love' and 'hate.'*" (4.) In *SD* 1:498, three passages are quoted from Winchell, 607; the first is attributed to Winchell, the other two are not. (5.) In *SD* 1:673, the words italicized here were taken from Winchell without attribution, and appear without quotation marks. *"The aphelion of this ring is 1,732 millions of miles beyond the orbit of Neptune, its plane is inclined to the Earth's orbit at an angle of 64° 3' and the direction of the meteoric swarm moving round this orbit is contrary to that of the Earth's revolution."* (6.) In *SD* 2:330 footnote, quotations from *Encyclopaedia Britannica* on the precession of the equinoxes were apparently taken from Winchell, 285–86.

198. Blavatsky, *H. P. Blavatsky Collected Writings,* 13:395–97

199. Blech, *Contributions à l'histoire de la Société Théosophique en France,* 187

200. Jean-Paul Guignette, "Madame Blavatsky at Fontainebleau," *The Canadian Theosophist,* November–December 1985, 101–4

201. Besant, *Annie Besant: An Autobiography,* 352–53; see also Boris de Zirkoff, "How *The Voice of the Silence* Was Written," *The American Theosophist,* November–December 1988, 230–37

202. Gertrude Marvin Williams, *Priestess of the Occult: (Madame Blavatsky);* New York, New York, Alfred A. Knopf, 1946, 11–12

203. Blavatsky, "The Cycle Moveth," *Theosophical Articles,* 1:364

204. Blavatsky, *The Voice of the Silence,* 1, 2–3, 23–24

205. Blavatsky, *The Voice of the Silence,* 52–53

206. William James, *The Varieties of Religious Experience,* New York, New York, Longmans Green, 1925, 421–22; Bhikshu Sangharakshita (Dennis Lingwood), *A Survey of Buddhism,* 3rd edition, Bangalore, India, Indian Institute of World Culture, 1966

207. Bhikshu Sangharakshita (Dennis Lingwood), *Paradox and Poetry in The Voice of the Silence,* Bangalore, India, Indian Institute of World Culture, 1958, 1–2, 4

208. *The Path,* November 1905, 240

209. G. R. S. Mead, "The Last Two Years," *Lucifer,* June 1891, 295–96

210. Adyar Archives, The Theosophical Society, Adyar, Madras, India

211. Blavatsky, *The Key to Theosophy,* 263–71

212. Blech, *Contributions à l'histoire de la Société Théosophique en France,* 198–200

213. Blavatsky, "Letters of H. P. Blavatsky, XIII," *The Path,* December 1895, 267–70

214. Blavatsky, "Letters of H. P. Blavatsky, XIII," *The Path,* December 1895, 269; William Q. Judge, "Mirror of the Movement," *The Path,* July 1891, 131–34

215. Olcott, *Old Diary Leaves,* 4:255

216. "Theosophical Activities," *Lucifer,* July 1890, 428–29; Blavatsky, "Letters of H. P. Blavatsky, XIII," *The Path,* December 1895, 269–70

217. Blavatsky, "Letters of H. P. Blavatsky, XIII," *The Path,* December 1895, 269–70

218. Besant, *Annie Besant: An Autobiography,* 362–63

219. G. R. S. Mead, "The Last Two Years," *Lucifer,* June 1891, 298

220. Nethercot, *The First Five Lives of Annie Besant,* 336–37

221. Blavatsky, "Letters of H. P. Blavatsky to Annie Besant," *The Theosophist,* February 1, 1932, 511–15; Adyar Archives, The Theosophical Society, Adyar, Madras, India

222. Zhelihovsky, "Yelena Petrovna Blavatskaya: Biografichesky ocherk," *Russkoye obozreniye,* volume 6 (December 1891), 608–10

223. C. E. M. Joad, "What Is the Soul?," *The Aryan Path,* Bombay, India, Theosophy Company Ltd., volume 8, number 5 (May 1937), 201–3

224. Blavatsky, *Transactions of the Blavatsky Lodge of the Theosophical Society,* Los Angeles, California, Theosophy Company, 1923; reprinted as *Secret Doctrine Commentary: Stanzas I–IV,* Pasadena, California, Theosophical University Press, 1994

225. Robert Bowen, "The 'Secret Doctrine' and Its Study," *Theosophy in Ireland,* Jan–March 1932; reprinted in Blavatsky, *An Invitation to The Secret Doctrine,* Pasadena, California, Theosophical University Press, 1994

226. G. R. S. Mead, "The Last Two Years," *Lucifer,* June 1891, 295–99

227. Extract from Countess Wachtmeister's Letters as to "HPB's Last Days," *The Theosophist,* May 1929, 125

228. Helena Petrovna Blavatsky, *Nightmare Tales,* London, England, Theosophical Publishing Society, 1892; reprinted as *The Tell-Tale Picture Gallery, Occult Stories,* Bombay, India, International Bookhouse Ltd., no date; *The Tell-Tale Picture Gallery,* Bombay, India, Theosophy Company, 1984

229. Blavatsky and William Q. Judge, *The Tell-Tale Picture Gallery,* Los Angeles, California, The Theosophy Company, 1984

230. HPB's stories in *The Tell-Tale Picture Gallery:* "Karmic Visions," "A Bewitched Life," "Can the Double Murder?," "An Unsolved Mystery," "The Luminous Shield," "The Cave of the Echoes," "From the Polar Lands," "The Ensouled Violin"

231. Blavatsky, *Five Messages to American Theosophists,* Los Angeles, California, The Theosophy Company, 32; *H. P. Blavatsky to the American Conventions 1888–1891,* Pasadena, California, Theosophical University Press, 1979, 33–34, 38–39, 43

232. Blavatsky, *Five Messages to American Theosophists,* 32; *H. P. Blavatsky to the American Conventions: 1888–1891,* 43

233. William Q. Judge, *Notes on the Bhagavad-Gita,* Los Angeles, California, The Theosophy Company, 1956, 152

234. Laura Cooper, "How She Left Us," *Lucifer,* June 1891, 270–71

235. Zhelihovsky, "Yelena Petrovna Blavatskaya: Biografichesky ocherk"

236. Olcott, "Traces of H.P.B.," *The Theosophist,* April 1893, 431

237. "Saladin" [W. S. Ross], "Death of Madame Blavatsky," *Agnostic Journal and Eclectic Review,* May 16, 1891; reprinted as "How an Agnostic Saw Her," *Lucifer,* June 1891, 311–16

238. Reprinted in *Lucifer,* July 1891, 388–89

239. *Borderland,* London, England, October 1894, 511

240. Reprinted in *H.P.B.: In Memory of Helena Petrovna Blavatsky, by Some of Her Pupils,* death centenary edition, Bombay India, The Theosophy Company (India) Private Ltd., 1991, addendum, 195

241. W. B. Yeats, *The Collected Letters of W. B. Yeats,* volume 1: *1865–1895,* 96–7

242. In the following article the same events or observations are sometimes repeated, but in different words. Articles by Edmund Russell on HPB: "As I Knew Her" and "More Recollections of Madame Blavatsky," *The Herald of the Star,* London, England, May 11, 1916, 197–205, and January 1917, 17–22; "Isis Unveiled: Personal Recollections of Madame Blavatsky" and "The Secret Doctrine: Personal Recollections of Madame Blavatsky," *The Occult Review,* London, England, November 1918, 260–69, and June 1920, 332–40

Part 7. The Century After

1. W. Q. Judge, "Yours Till Death and After, HPB," *Lucifer,* June 1891, 291–92

2. Robert Crosbie, *Answers to Questions on The Ocean of Theosophy,* Los Angeles, California, The Theosophy Company, 1974, 190

3. Rick Fields, *How the Swans Came to the Lake: A Narrative History of Buddhism in America,* Boulder, Colorado, Shambhala, 1981, 120–21

4. John Henry Barrows, editor, *The World's Parliament of Religions,* 2 volumes, Chicago, Illinois, The Parliament Publishing Company, 1893, 1:20, 22; Fields, *How the Swans Came to the Lake,* 120

5. Jackson, *The Oriental Religions and American Thought: Nineteenth Century Explorations,* 251–52

6. George E. Wright, "Incidents of the Theosophical Congress," *The Path,* November 1893, 242. The congress was held September 15–17, 1893, and stenographic transcriptions of the talks were printed in the 195-page *Report of the Proceedings of the Theosophical Congress,* published the same year by the American Section Headquarters of the Theosophical Society in New York City.

7. Wright, "Incidents of the Theosophical Congress," 245

8. Barrows, *The World's Parliament of Religions,* 1893, 1:183; Fields, *How the Swans Came to the Lake,* 128–29

9. Jackson, *The Oriental Religions and American Thought,* 251

10. Quoted in *The Lamp,* Canada, December 1895; originally in *Alliance Forum*

11. Privately printed, Calgary, Canada, 1908, 112; quoted in *The Canadian Theosophist,* July–August 1975, 66–67

12. Jerry Hejka-Ekins, "*The Secret Doctrine* in the Light of Twentieth Century Thought," *Sunrise,* April–May 1989, 150, 151

13. Blavatsky, *The Secret Doctrine,* 1:611–12

14. David Dietz, *The New Outline of Science,* New York, New York, Dodd, Mead, 1972, 259–63

15. Robert Millikan, *The Autobiography of Robert A. Millikan,* New York, New York, Prentice-Hall, 1950, 272, 271. Millikan himself played an important role, in 1909, in determining the exact electrical charges of the electron, and in 1923 was awarded the Nobel Prize for Physics for the discovery of cosmic rays.

16. *Science,* January 8, 1937, 598

17. *Theosophia,* volume 4, number 22, November–December 1947, 15

18. Robert Millikan, *Time, Matter and Values,* Chapel Hill, North Carolina, University of North Carolina Press, 1932, 96

19. Raymond F. Yates, *These Amazing Electrons,* New York, The Macmillan Co., 1937

20. Dietz, *The New Outline of Science,* 277

21. A. March and I. M. Freeman, *The New World of Physics,* 1963, 91, 109; quoted in *Sunrise,* November 1975, 81

22. See Preface: EN #11. Robert Millikan was one of the first scientists who may have introduced Einstein to the Secret Doctrine. From 1921 to 1945 he was director of the Norman Bridges Laboratory at the California Institute of Technology in Pasadena; he was also chairman of the executive committee at Cal Tech.

Millikan helped bring Einstein to the United States in the 1930s. For three summers Einstein worked as a chef at Cal Tech, before accepting a position at Princeton.

Millikan was deeply interested in *The Secret Doctrine*. During his tenure at Cal Tech a copy of the book in the school's library was so much in demand that to borrow it, one had to put one's name on a long waiting list. It seems likely Millikan was one of the people who interested Einstein in *The Secret Doctrine*.

Another possible individual was Gustav Stromberg, an astrophysicist at Mount Wilson Observatory in Los Angeles who was a good friend of Einstein's and who worked with him at the observatory. When Stromberg's *Soul of the Universe* was published, Einstein's commendation appeared on the jacket.

It is interesting to note that during this period Boris de Zirkoff, compiler of *H. P. Blavatsky Collected Writings*, visited the observatory frequently and befriended the astronomers there. He said they all were interested in Theosophy, particularly Dr. Hubbell. Stromberg visited the Theosophical Society at Point Loma, and once gave a lecture there; he even wrote the foreword to a book on astronomy by two Point Loma Theosophists. Stromberg states:

"*Star Habits and Orbits* is described as: 'Astronomy for Theosophical Students.' It therefore contains two distinct themes: first, a description of fundamental astronomical facts, and, second, an interpretation of these facts from the standpoint of theosophical teachings. . . . The great edifice of modern science is incomplete without the introduction of a non-physical world from which energy, organization and mind temporarily merge into the physical world of space and time. Modern physical theories show the insufficiency of materialistic concepts which have until recently characterized natural science and point directly to a world in intimate contact with our own consciousness.

"There are many roads to knowledge, and none of them should be overlooked. Knowing, as we do now, that our mind, including our faculty of thinking, has its roots in an unseen but not unknown world, it is conceivable that there may be inspired men and women who have been able to grasp some of the fundamental secrets of life and of the universe without the use of microscopes and telescopes." (Charles J. Ryan and L. Gordon Plummer, *Star Habits and Orbits,* Covina, California, Theosophical University Press, 1944, v–vi).

23. M. R. Crossland, editor, *The Science of Matter,* New York, New York, Penguin, 1971, 76

24. Werner Heisenberg, *Science,* March 19, 1976, 1165

25. Blavatsky, *The Secret Doctrine,* 1:97; see also 1:2, 55, 93 footnote

26. S. Garrett Service, *The Einstein Theory of Relativity,* New York, New York, E. M. Radimann, 1928, 48

27. Millikan, *The Autobiography of Robert A. Millikan*, 273

28. Fred Hoyle, lecture in *The Theosophist*, April 1982, 219

29. *The New York Times*, May 29, 1983, science page

30. Lewis Thomas, *The Medusa and the Snail*, pp. 156–57; selected from a condensed extract in *Reader's Digest*, October 1979, 98–99

31. *Fortune*, January 24, 1983

32. "Strange Stories, Amazing Facts," *Reader's Digest*; "Control Room: The Brain and Its Workings," 42–43

33. Judge, *The Ocean of Theosophy*, 39

34. Judge, *The Ocean of Theosophy*, 41

35. Oliver Sacks, *The Man Who Mistook His Wife for a Hat*, New York, New York, Summit Books, 1985, 64, 66

36. Harold Saxton Burr, *Blue-print for Immortality: The Electric Patterns of Life*, 5th Printing, Great Britain, C. W. Daniel Co., 1991; Fourth Edition, Woodstock, New York, Beekman Publisher

37. Blavatsky, *The Secret Doctrine*, 1:274–75

38. Thomas Huxley, *Some Essays on Controversial Subjects*, New York, New York, Appleton, 1892, 27, 171, 178

39. Alfred Russel Wallace, *Contributions to the Theory of Natural Selection*, New York, New York, Macmillan, 1870, 360

40. *Manas*, June 16, 1982, 1

41. Loren Eiseley, *The Immense Journey*, New York, New York, Vintage, 1957, 94

42. Blavatsky, *The Secret Doctrine*, 2:167, 241–45, 254–55

43. Freeman Dyson, *Infinite in All Directions*, New York, New York, Harper & Row, 1988

44. *Theosophical Research Journal*, June 1986, 43; lecture delivered at the annual Science Seminar held at the Theosophical Society, Wheaton, Illinois, October 19, 1985

45. Charles Darwin, *The Life and Letters of Charles Darwin*, edited by Francis Darwin, New York, New York, Appleton, 1887, 1:282

46. *The New York Times*, February 10, 1981, C2

47. Stephen Hawking, *A Brief History of Time*, New York, New York, Bantam Books, 1988, 5–6

48. "Galactic Changes Startle Astronomers," *The New York Times*, February 26, 1990

49. Judge, *The Ocean of Theosophy*, 23

50. Interview by Barry Rohan, *Detroit Free Press*, October 25, 1983; quoted in *The Eclectic Theosophist*, San Diego, California, May–June 1984, 5

51. Betty Jo Teeter Dobbs, *Alchemical Death and Resurrection: Alchemy in the Age of Newton,* Washington, D.C., Smithsonian Institution Press, 1990

52. *Quantum Questions: Mystical Writings of the World's Great Physicists,* edited by Ken Wilber, Boston, Massachusetts, Shambhala, 1985, 102–4, 108–09, 110–11, back cover

53. *The Universe and Dr. Einstein,* edited by Lincoln Barnett, New York, New York, New American Library, 1950, 105

54. Albert Einstein, *The World As I See It,* New York, New York, Philosophical Library, 1949, 28

55. Millikan, *The Autobiography of Robert A. Millikan,* 287

56. Walter Goodman, "Examining God's Dice with Quantum Mechanics," *The New York Times,* June 6, 1990, C20

57. Roger Penrose, *The Emperor's New Mind,* Oxford, England, Oxford University Press, 1989, vi

58. Penrose, *The Emperor's New Mind,* cover, vi, 226, 280, 298

59. Penrose, *The Emperor's New Mind,* front flap, 402 et seq.

60. Blavatsky, "Kosmic Mind," *Lucifer,* April 1890, 89; Edison quoted in Blavatsky's "The Cycle Moveth," *Lucifer,* March 1890, 8; also in HPB Pamphlet Series, Los Angeles, California, Theosophy Company; *Mind in Nature and in Man,* 5, and *Cycles and Human Destiny,* 11

61. Blavatsky, "Kosmic Mind"; *Mind in Nature and in Man,* 6

62. Heinz Pagels, *Cosmic Code: Quantum Mechanics as the Language of Nature,* New York, New York, Simon & Schuster, 1982, 340; see also Penrose, *The Emperor's New Mind,* 421

63. Blavatsky, *The Secret Doctrine,* 1:246

64. Peter Stenfels, "Beliefs," *The New York Times,* January 20, 1990

65. Francis Merchant, *Æ: An Irish Prometheus,* Columbia, South Carolina, Benedict College Press, 1954, cover

66. Joseph M. Hone, *W. B. Yeats, 1865–1939,* New York, New York, Macmillan, 1943, 130

67. Ernest Boyd, *Ireland's Literary Renaissance,* New York, New York, Macmillan, 1937, 213–15

68. "Special Note," *The Path,* February 1894, 351–52

69. "George William Russell—Æ," *The Canadian Theosophist,* August 1935, 172–73 (taken from Ernest A. Boyd, *Appreciations and Depreciations,* Dublin, 1917, New York, 1918)

70. Blavatsky, letter written in London, late 1880s, de Zirkoff Archives, The Theosophical Society, Wheaton, Illinois

71. William Butler Yeats, *Memoirs,* edited by Denis Donoghue, New York, New York, Macmillan Publishing Company, 1972, back flap

72. William Butler Yeats, *The Collected Letters of W. B. Yeats*, Oxford, England, Oxford University Press, 1986, 1:164 (letter dated May 7, 1889)

73. William Butler Yeats, *Letters to the New Island,* edited by Horace Reynolds, Cambridge, Massachusetts, Harvard University Press, 1934, 83–84

74. Quoted in *W. B. Yeats and Occultism,* by Harbans Rai Bachchan, New Delhi, India, Motilal Banarsidass, 1965, 223

75. Richard Ellmann, *Yeats: The Man and the Mask,* New York, New York, Macmillan, 1948, 66–67; William Butler Yeats, *Memoirs,* New York, New York, Macmillan, 1972, 23–24

76. *Letters to W. B. Yeats,* edited by R. J. Finneran et al., New York, New York, Columbia University Press, 1977, 447

77. William Butler Yeats, *Autobiography of William Butler Yeats,* Garden City, New York, Doubleday Anchor, 1958, 118, 119–20, 123, 197, 199

78. The following sources indicate a direct influence of HPB and Theosophy on Yeats: Bachchan, *W. B. Yeats and Occultism,* many references; Ellmann, *Yeats: The Man and the Mask,* 68–69; Giorgio Melchiori, *The Whole Mystery of Art: Pattern into Poetry in the Work of W. B. Yeats,* London, England, Routledge & Kegan Paul, 1960, 19, 119, 123, 141–47, 161, 165–72, 193, 262–63; Peter Ure, *Yeats and Anglo-Irish Literature,* edited by C. J. Rawson, Liverpool, England, Liverpool University Press, 1974, 49, 64, 124; F. A. C. Wilson, *W. B. Yeats and Tradition,* London, England, Victor Gollancz Ltd., 1958, 55, 56, 143, 235; and F. A. C. Wilson, *Yeats Iconography,* London, England, Victor Gollancz Ltd., 1960, 145, 146, 170, 252.

79. Ellmann, *Yeats: The Man and the Mask,* 67, 68, 69

80. William R. Linville, *Helena Petrovna Blavatsky, Theosophy and American Thought,* doctoral thesis, 1983, 147

81. Yeats, *Memoirs,* 26

82. Yeats, *The Collected Letters of W. B. Yeats,* 1:164

83. Yeats, *Memoirs,* 25

84. *Lady Gregory's Journals,* edited by Lennox Robinson, New York, New York, Macmillan, 1947, 7, 261–63

85. Raynor Johnson, *The Light and the Gate,* London, England, Hodder & Stoughton, 1964, 15, 40

86. Henry Summerfield, *That Myriad-Minded Man,* Totowa, New Jersey, Rowman & Littlefield, 16

87. P. G. Bowen, "Æ and Theosophy," *The Aryan Path,* December 1935, 722–26

88. Bowen, "Æ and Theosophy," 722–26

89. George Russell, letter to B. P. Wadia, October 17, 1922

90. Claude Bragdon, *Merely Players,* New York, New York, Alfred A. Knopf, 1929, 173–75

91. James Pryse, "George William Russell, Poet of the Inner Life," *The Canadian Theosophist,* August 1935

92. Monk Gibbon, *The Masterpiece and the Man, Yeats As I Knew Him,* London, England, Hart Davis, 1959, 54–55

93. Colin Wilson, *The Mysteries,* New York, New York, G. P. Putnam's Sons, 1978, 325

94. James Pryse, "George William Russell, Poet of the Inner Life," *The Canadian Theosophist,* August, 1935; Bowen, "Æ and Theosophy," *The Aryan Path,* December, 1935, 722–26

95. Summerfield, *That Myriad-Minded Man,* 285

96. Richard Ellmann, *James Joyce,* New York, New York, Oxford University Press, 1959, 102–3

97. "After Joyce, There's No World Without Joyce," *The New York Times,* January 31, 1982, E9

98. *Irish Statesman,* November 21, 1925; *The New York Times,* February 27, 1928

99. Stuart Gilbert, *James Joyce's Ulysses,* New York, New York, Alfred A. Knopf, 1952, preface

100. Gilbert, *James Joyce's Ulysses,* 33–34, 36

101. Eugene Jolas, *We Moderns, 1920–1940.* In this anniversary catalogue of the Gotham Book Mart in New York City, well-known authors commented on fellow authors of the day.

102. Leon Edel, *The Last Journey,* New York, New York, Gotham Book Mart, 1947, 42

103. James Joyce, *Portrait of the Artist as a Young Man,* New York, New York, Viking, 1927

104. James Jones, *From Here to Eternity,* New York, New York, Charles Scribner's Sons, 1951, 647–48, 723

105. Russell M. Goldfarb, *Journal of Popular Culture,* Winter 1971

106. William York Tindall, *D. H. Lawrence and Susan His Cow,* New York, New York, Columbia University Press, 1939, 133, 138, 141

107. Tindall, *D. H. Lawrence and Susan His Cow,* 142–43

108. Tindall, *D. H. Lawrence and Susan His Cow,* 141, 146, 147

109. Tindall, *D. H. Lawrence and Susan His Cow,* 156

110. Tindall, *D. H. Lawrence and Susan His Cow,* 143

111. Goldfarb, *Journal of Popular Culture,* Winter 1971

112. T. S. Eliot, *The Waste Land,* New York, New York, Boni & Liveright, 1922

113. Tom Gibbons, *Rooms in the Darwin Hotel*, Nedlands, Australia, University of Western Australia Press, 1973, 134–35

114. Thornton Wilder, *The Eighth Day*, New York, New York, Harper & Row, 1967, 218–19

115. L. Frank Baum, editor of *Aberdeen Saturday Pioneer*, January 18, 1890

116. John Algeo, *The American Theosophist*, August–September 1986, 273; "The Wizard of Oz: The Perilous Journey," *The American Theosophist*, Fall 1986, 291–97

117. Algeo, *The American Theosophist*, August–September 1986, 270

118. Roger Lipsey, *An Art of Our Own: The Spiritual in Modern Art*, Boston, Massachusetts, Shambhala, 1988, 32–34

119. Hilton Kramer, "Kandinsky," *The New York Times*, December 18, 1966

120. Wassily Kandinsky, *Concerning the Spiritual in Art*, translated by M. T. H. Sadler, New York, New York, Dover, 1977, 13–14

121. Laxmi Sihare, *Oriental Influences on Wassily Kandinsky and Piet Mondrian 1909–1917*, New York University, doctoral thesis, 1967, 5, 10, 17, 27, 36, 55, 73, 75, 77, 80–81, 87, 94–96, 100, 121, 122, 125, 131, 152–58, 173, 179–80, 184, 186, 225, 251–54

122. Sihare, *Oriental Influences on Wassily Kandinsky and Piet Mondrian 1909–1917*, 80

123. Sihare, *Oriental Influences on Wassily Kandinsky and Piet Mondrian 1909–1917*, 80; Wassily Kandinsky, *Rückblicke* (autobiography, 1901–1913), 25–26

124. Sixten Ringbom, *The Sounding Cosmos: A Study of the Spiritualism of Kandinsky and the Genesis of Abstract Painting*, Abo, Finland, Abo Academi, 1970, 61–105

125. Frank Elgar, *Mondrian*, New York, New York, Praeger, 1968, 88–89

126. Sihare, *Oriental Influences on Wassily Kandinsky and Piet Mondrian 1909–1917*, 8

127. Édouard Schuré, *The Great Initiates*, translated by Gloria Rasberry, West Nyack, New York, St. George Books, 1961, 17

128. Carel Blotkamp, *The Spiritual in Art: Abstract Painting 1890–1985*, Los Angeles, California, Los Angeles County Museum of Art, 1986 (exhibition catalogue), 103

129. Fred Gettings, *The Occult in Art*, New York, New York, Rizzoli, 1978, 127

130. Robert Knotts, in Kathleen J. Regier, compiler, *The Spiritual Image in Modern Art*, Wheaton, Illinois, Theosophical Publishing House, 1987, 135

131. Thomas Buser, "Gauguin's Religion," *Art Journal*, Summer 1968

132. Paul Gauguin, *Modern Thought and Catholicism,* translated by Frank Lester Pleadwell, privately printed, 1927; original manuscript and translation in St. Louis Art Museum archives, St. Louis, Missouri

133. Lipsey, *An Art of Our Own: The Spiritual in Modern Art,* 2–3

134. John Dillenger, *Los Angeles Times,* February 22, 1987

135. Blotkamp, *The Spiritual in Art: Abstract Painting 1890–1985*

136. Richard Specht, *Gustav Mahler,* Berlin, Germany, Schuster & Loffler, 1913, 39

137. Program notes, recording of Mahler's *Third Symphony,* London Records (CSA 2223), conductor George Solti

138. Joseph Head and Sylvia Cranston, *Reincarnation: An East–West Anthology,* Wheaton, Illinois, Theosophical Publishing House, 1967, 195

139. Faubion Bowers, *The New Scriabin,* New York, New York, St. Martin's Press, 1973, ix–x

140. Gerald Abraham and Michel D. Calvocoressi, *Masters of Russian Music,* New York, New York, Alfred A. Knopf, 1936, 478

141. Faubion Bowers, *Scriabin: A Biography of the Russian Composer (1871–1915),* Tokyo, Japan, and Palo Alto, California, Kodansha International Letters, 1969, 1:87; 2:52, 117, 258

142. Abraham and Calvocoressi, *Masters of Russian Music,* 475

143. Bowers, *Scriabin,* 1:319

144. Bowers, *The New Scriabin,* 53

145. Muriel Daw, "Christmas Humphreys, Theosophist and Buddhist," *The Theosophist,* November 1984, 72

146. "Christmas Humphreys," *The Canadian Theosophist,* May–June 1983, 39

147. Daw, "Christmas Humphreys, Theosophist and Buddhist," 76

148. Christmas Humphreys, "Fifty Years," *The Middle Way,* August 1969, 62–63

149. Daw, "Christmas Humphreys, Theosophist and Buddhist," 69

150. Christmas Humphreys, "A Brief History of the Buddhist Society," *The Middle Way,* November 1974, 9

151. Mircea Eliade, *No Souvenirs: Journal 1957–1969,* translated by Fred Johnson, Jr., New York, New York, Harper & Row, 1977, 208

152. Christmas Humphreys, *Exploring Buddhism,* Wheaton, Illinois, Theosophical Publishing House, 1974, 131

153. Christmas Humphreys, *Karma and Rebirth,* London, England, John Murray, 1959, 10

154. Daw, "Christmas Humphreys, Theosophist and Buddhist," 71

155. Alan Watts, *In My Own Way,* New York, New York, Pantheon Books, 1972, 77

156. Sri Krishna Prem, *Man the Measure of All Things,* London, England, Theosophical Publishing House, 1966

157. Christmas Humphreys, "Helena Petrovna Blavatsky," in Colin Wilson, editor, *Dark Dimensions,* New York, New York, Everest House, 1977, 71–73

158. *Unity,* May–June 1987, 32

159. George Gallup, Jr. *Adventures in Immortality,* New York, New York, McGraw-Hill, 1982, 192–93

160. Gina Cerminara, *Many Mansions,* New York, New York, William Sloane, 1950, 23

161. Thomas Sugrue, *There Is a River,* New York, New York, Henry Holt, 1942, 234–35

162. Thomas Sugrue, *There Is a River,* New York, New York, Dell, 1961, 220–21

163. Cerminara, *Many Mansions,* 44–45

164. Gina Cerminara, *The American Theosophist,* February 1977, 37

165. Ian Stevenson, "Some Questions Related to Cases of the Reincarnation Type," *Journal of the American Society for Psychical Research,* October 1974

166. Bhagavan Das, *The Science of Peace,* 2nd edition, Adyar, Madras, India, Theosophical Publishing House, 1921

167. Ian Stevenson, *Cases of the Reincarnation Type,* four volumes, Charlottesville, Virginia, University Press of Virginia 1971–1983

168. Shirley MacLaine, *Out on a Limb,* New York, New York, Bantam, 1983, 316–17

169. Charles A. Silva, *Date with the Gods,* Huntington, New York, Coleman Graphics

170. Silva, *Date with the Gods,* 401–2

171. "Myrna" is the lifelong Theosophist, teacher, and artist Margaret Geiger.

172. Shirley MacLaine, interviewed by Roderick Townley of *TV Guide*

173. Albert Goldman, *Elvis,* New York, New York, McGraw-Hill, 1991, 364

174. Goldman, *Elvis,* 366

175. Jess Stearn, *Elvis: His Spiritual Journey,* Norfolk, Virginia, Donning Company, 1982, 6

176. Priscilla Beaulieu Presley and Sandra Harmon, *Elvis and Me,* New York, New York, G. P. Putnam's Sons, 1985, 204–5

177. Goldman, *Elvis,* 365

178. Geddes MacGregor, "An Interview with Geddes MacGregor," *The American Theosophist,* August 1978, 199

179. Geddes MacGregor, *Reincarnation in Christianity,* Wheaton, Illinois, Theosophical Publishing House, 1978; *Reincarnation as a Christian Hope*

180. Geddes MacGregor, "Christianity and the Ancient Wisdom," *The American Theosophist,* December 1982, 420, 422

181. MacGregor, *Reincarnation in Christianity*

182. Geddes MacGregor, *The Christening of Karma,* Wheaton, Illinois, Theosophical Publishing House, 1984

183. MacGregor, "An Interview with Geddes MacGregor," 199−204

184. Quoted in "The Author of *The Golden Bough,*" broadcast lecture delivered over the BBC by the Reverend Victor White, and published in *The Listener,* January 21, 1954, p. 137

185. Joseph Campbell, *The Hero with a Thousand Faces* (Bollingen Series 17), New York, New York, Pantheon Books, 1953, 3−4

186. Robin and Stephen Larsen, *A Fire in the Mind: The Life of Joseph Campbell,* New York, New York, Doubleday, 1991, 41, 67, 70, 104, 387

187. Joseph Campbell, *The Power of Myth,* New York, New York, Doubleday, 1988, 58

188. *The Collected Works of C. G. Jung, The Archetypes and the Collective Unconscious,* Volume 9, translated by R. C. Hull, New York, New York, Pantheon Books, 1959, part 1, 3−4

189. C. G. Jung, *Memories, Dreams, and Reflections,* 380, 529

190. C. G. Jung, *Psychology and Religion,* New York, New York, Pantheon Books, 1958

191. Eliade, *No Souvenirs,* 219

192. Ernest Jones, *Sigmund Freud: Life and Work,* New York, New York, Basic Books, 1957

193. H. P. Blavatsky, *Transactions of the Blavatsky Lodge,* Los Angeles, California, The Theosophy Company, 1923, Appendix on dreams, 78

194. Kurt Vonnegut, Jr., *McCall's,* March 1970

195. Blavatsky, "Practical Occultism," *Lucifer,* April 1888, 151; also in *Spiritual Evolution,* (HPB Pamphlet Series) Los Angeles, California, The Theosophy Company, 5

196. David Spangler, *Emergence: The Rebirth of the Sacred,* New York, New York, Dell, 1984, 78−81

197. Spangler, *Emergence: The Rebirth of the Sacred,* 24

198. Spangler, *Emergence: The Rebirth of the Sacred,* 18

199. Tape of a lecture delivered at the Mayflower Bookshop, Ferndale, Michigan, October 15, 1977

200. Rudolf Steiner, *Rudolf Steiner: An Autobiography,* New York, New York, Rudolf Steiner Publications, 1977, 345−48

201. Colin Wilson, *Rudolf Steiner: The Man and His Vision*, Wellingborough, England, The Aquarian Press, 1983, 57

202. H. J. Spierenburg, "Dr. Rudolf Steiner on Helena Petrovna Blavatsky," part 1, and "Dr. Rudolf Steiner on the Mahatmas," parts 1 and 2, *Theosophical History*, July 1986, 159–74, October 1986, 211–23, and January 1987, 23–31

203. Spierenburg, "Dr. Rudolf Steiner on Helena Petrovna Blavatsky," 170

204. Spierenburg, "Dr. Rudolf Steiner on the Mahatmas," part 1, 212–13

205. Spierenburg, "Dr. Rudolf Steiner on the Mahatmas," part 1, 214

206. Spierenburg, "Dr. Rudolf Steiner on the Mahatmas," part 2, 25

207. Spierenburg, "Dr. Rudolf Steiner on the Mahatmas," part 1, 219

208. Spierenburg, "Dr. Rudolf Steiner on the Mahatmas," part 1, 219–20

209. Spierenburg, "Dr. Rudolf Steiner on the Mahatmas," part 2, 25

210. Jean-Louis Siémons, *A Nineteenth Century Scheme for the Interpretation of Near-Death Experiences: The Transpersonal Model of Death as Presented in Madame Blavatsky's Theosophy*, Paris, France, Institut National Agronomique, 7

211. Blavatsky, *The Key to Theosophy*, 162

212. Siémons, *A Nineteenth Century Scheme for the Interpretation of Near-Death Experiences*, 15; R. Noyes and R. Kletti, "Panoramic Memory: A Response to the Threat of Death," *Omega*, volume 7, 1977

213. Siémons, *A Nineteenth Century Scheme for the Interpretation of Near-Death Experiences*, 15; Albert Heim, "Notizen über den Tod durch Absturz," *Jahrbuch des schweizer alpen Club*, volume 27, 1892

214. Carol Zaleski, *Otherworld Journeys*, New York, New York, Oxford University Press, 1987, 130; Albert Heim, letter to Oskar Pfister, "Shocken und Shockphantasien bei Höchster Todesgefahr," *Zeitschrift für Psychoanalyse*, volume 16, 1930

215. Kenneth Ring, *Life at Death*, New York, New York, Coward, McCann and Geoghegan, 1980, 73

216. Raymond A. Moody, Jr., *Life After Life*, New York, New York, Bantam, 1976, 65

217. Moody, *Life after Life*, 60; quoted in Zaleski, *Otherworld Journeys*, 128

218. Ring, *Life at Death*, 73

219. Siémons, *A Nineteenth Century Scheme for the Interpretation of Near-Death Experiences*, 13

220. Ring, *Life at Death*, 240

221. Ring, *Life at Death*, 240

222. Blavatsky, *The Voice of the Silence*, 63

223. Sylvia Cranston and Carey Williams, *Reincarnation: A New Horizon in Science, Religion and Society,* Pasadena, California, Theosophical University Press, 1993, 140-41

224. Kenneth Ring, *Heading Toward Omega,* New York, New York, William Morrow, 1984, 226

225. Ring, *Heading Toward Omega,* 254-55

226. Blavatsky, *The Secret Doctrine,* 2:444-46

227. *The Theosophist,* August 1990

228. Jacqueline Decter, *Nicholas Roerich: The Life and Art of a Russian Master,* Rochester, Vermont, Park Street Press, Inner Traditions International, 1989, 134-135

229. Decter, *Nicholas Roerich,* 134

230. Boris de Zirkoff, "Nicholas de Roerich: A Centenary," *Theosophia,* Fall 1974, 8

231. *The Theosophist,* October 1979, 51

232. Telephone conversation, March 9, 1981

233. *Theosophia,* Fall 1974, 9-10

234. De Zirkoff Archives, The Theosophical Society, Wheaton, Illinois, 50-54

235. William Kingsland, *The Real H. P. Blavatsky,* London, England, John M. Watkins, 1928, v; London, England, Theosophical Publishing House, 1985

Bibliography

Arundale, Francesca, *My Guest: H. P. Blavatsky,* Foreword by C. Jinarajadasa, Adyar, Madras, India, The Theosophical Publishing House, 1932

Barborka, Geoffrey A., *H. P. Blavatsky, the Light-Bringer,* The Blavatsky Lecture, 1970, London, England, The Theosophical Publishing House, Ltd., 1970

Barborka, Geoffrey A., *H. P. Blavatsky, Tibet and Tulku,* Adyar, Madras, India, The Theosophical Publishing House, 1966

Barborka, Geoffrey A., *The Mahatmas and Their Letters,* Adyar, Madras, India, The Theosophical Publishing House, 1973

Besant, Annie, *Annie Besant: An Autobiography,* London, England, T. Fisher Unwin, 1893; 3rd edition, Adyar, Madras, India, The Theosophical Publishing House, 1939

Besant, Annie, *H. P. Blavatsky and the Masters of Wisdom,* Issued as a Transaction of the H.P.B. Lodge, London, England, The Theosophical Publishing Society, 1907

Besant, Annie, *The Theosophical Society and H.P.B.,* Three Articles by Annie Besant and H. T. Patterson, London, England, The Theosophical Publishing Society, 1891

Besterman, Theodore, *Mrs. Annie Besant: A Modern Prophet,* London, England, Kegan Paul, Trench, Trubner & Company, Ltd., 1934

Blavatsky, H. P., *Five Messages from H. P. Blavatsky to the American Theosophists,* Los Angeles, California, The Theosophy Company, 1922

Blavatsky, H. P. (Radda-Bai), *From the Caves and Jungles of Hindostan,* Boris de Zirkoff, translator and compiler, H. P. Blavatsky Collected Writings, Wheaton, Illinois, The Theosophical Publishing House, 1975

Blavatsky, H. P., *Gems from the East: A Birthday Book of Precepts and Axioms,* Pasadena, California, Theosophical University Press, 1983

Blavatsky, H. P., *H.P.B. Speaks,* 2 volumes, edited by C. Jinarajadasa, Adyar, Madras, India, The Theosophical Publishing House, 1951

Blavatsky, H. P., *H. P. Blavatsky to the American Conventions: 1888–1891,* with a Historical Perspective by Kirby Van Mater, Pasadena, California, Theosophical University Press, 1979

Blavatsky, H. P., *H. P. Blavatsky Collected Writings,* 14 numbered volumes and

Cumulative Index, compiled by Boris de Zirkoff, Wheaton, Illinois, The Theosophical Publishing House, 1950–91

Blavatsky, H. P., *H. P. Blavatsky Quotation Book,* Bombay, India, Theosophy Company, 1973

Blavatsky, H. P., *An Invitation to The Secret Doctrine,* Pasadena, California, Theosophical University Press, 1988

Blavatsky, H. P., *Isis Unveiled,* 2 volumes, 1877; reprints Los Angeles, California, The Theosophy Company, 1975; Wheaton, Illinois, The Theosophical Publishing House, 1972; Pasadena, California, Theosophical University Press, reprint 1988

Blavatsky, H. P., *The Key to Theosophy,* 1889; reprints Los Angeles, California, The Theosophy Company, 1973; London, England, The Theosophical Publishing House, 1968; Pasadena, California, Theosophical University Press, 1995

Blavatsky, H. P., *The Letters of H. P. Blavatsky to A. P. Sinnett,* compiled by A. T. Barker, 1925; reprint Pasadena, California, Theosophical University Press, 1973

Blavatsky, H. P., *A Modern Panarion: A Collection of Fugitive Fragments,* London, England, The Theosophical Publishing Society, 1895

Blavatsky, H. P., *Nightmare Tales,* London, England, The Theosophical Publishing Society, 1892; reprint, Theosophy Company, Bombay, India

Blavatsky, H. P., *The Secret Doctrine,* 2 volumes, 1888; facsimile reprint, Los Angeles, California, The Theosophy Company, 1974; Pasadena, California, Theosophical University Press, 1988; reprint, Boris de Zirkoff, editor, Adyar, Madras [Chennai], India, The Theosophical Publishing House, 1978

Blavatsky, H. P., *Some Unpublished Letters of Helena Petrovna Blavatsky,* edited by Eugene Rollin Corson, London, England, Rider & Company, [1929]

Blavatsky, H. P., *Studies in Occultism,* Pasadena, California, Theosophical University Press, 1987

Blavatsky, H. P., *The Theosophical Glossary,* 1892; reprint Los Angeles, California, The Theosophy Company, 1973

Blavatsky, H. P., *Transactions of the Blavatsky Lodge, 1890–91*; reprints Los Angeles, California, The Theosophy Company, 1923; *Secret Doctrine Commentary: Stanzas I–IV,* Pasadena, California, Theosophical University Press, 1994

Blavatsky, H. P., *The Voice of the Silence,* 1889; reprints, Los Angeles, California, The Theosophy Company, 1928; Wheaton, Illinois, The Theosophical Publishing House, 1992; Pasadena, Theosophical University Press, 1992

Blavatsky, H. P. (Radda-Bai), *Zagadochnye plemena na "Golubykh Gorakh," Durbar v Lakhore,* Ishch peshchershch i debrey Indii (*Enigmatical Tribes in the "Light Blue Mountains," Durbar at Lahore,* From the Caves and Jungles of India), St. Petersburg, Russia, V. I. Gubinsky, 1893; includes a biographical sketch by Vera P. Zhelihovsky, English translation by Mary G. Langford, in the Sylvia Cranston Archives, Santa Barbara, California

Blavatsky, H. P., and Judge, William Q., *The Tell-Tale Picture Gallery,* Bombay, India, International Book House, no date

Blech, Charles, *Contribution à l'histoire de la Société Théosophique en France,* Paris, France, Éditions Adyar, 1933

Bragdon, Claude, *Episodes from an Unwritten History,* Rochester, New York, The Manas Press, 1910; 2nd (enlarged) edition, Rochester, New York, The Manas Press, 1910

Brown, W. T., *My Life,* Freiburg, Germany, D. Lauber, 1885

Brown, W. T., *Some Experiences in India,* London, England, Printed under the authority of the London Lodge of the T.S., 1884; *An Explanatory Treatise,* Madras [Chennai], India, The Theosophical Society, 1884

Butt, G. Baseden, *Madame Blavatsky,* London, England, Rider & Company, 1925; Philadelphia, Pennsylvania, David McKay, 1926

Caithness, Marie Sinclair, Countess of (also Duchess of) Pomar, *The Mystery of the Ages Contained in the Secret Doctrine of All Religions,* London, England, C. L. H. Wallace, 1887

Caldwell, Daniel H., *The Occult World of Madame Blavatsky: Reminiscences and Impressions by Those Who Knew Her,* Tucson, Arizona, Impossible Dream Publications, P.O. Box 1844, 1991

Carlson, Maria, *There Is No Religion Higher Than Truth: The Russian Theosophical Movement, 1875–1923,* Princeton, New Jersey, Princeton University Press, 1992

Carrithers, Walter, A., Jr., "Madame Blavatsky: 'One of the World's Great Jokers'" (book review of John Symonds's *Madame Blavatsky, Medium and Magician*), *Journal of the American Society for Psychical Research,* volume 56, number 3 (July 1962)

Carrithers, Walter A., Jr., "Richard Hodgson (1855–1905)," in *Damodar and the Pioneers of the Theosophical Movement* (See Mavalankar, Damodar)

Carrithers, Walter A., Jr., *The Truth About Madame Blavatsky: An Open Letter to the Author of "Priestess of the Occult" Regarding the Charges Against H. P. Blavatsky,* Covina, California, Theosophical University Press, 1947

Cerminara, Gina, *Many Lives, Many Loves,* New York, New York, William Sloane Associates, 1963

Cleather, Alice Leighton, *H. P. Blavatsky: A Great Betrayal,* Calcutta, India, Thacker, Spink & Company, 1922

Cleather, Alice Leighton, *H. P. Blavatsky: Her Life and Work for Humanity,* Calcutta, India, Thacker, Spink & Company, 1922

Cleather, Alice Leighton, *H. P. Blavatsky As I Knew Her,* with an Addendum by Basil Crump, Calcutta, India, Thacker, Spink & Company, 1923

Cleather, Alice Leighton, and Crump, Basil, *Buddhism, the Science of Life,* two Monographs by Alice Leighton Cleather; also "Tibetan Initiates on the Buddha" with explanations and comments by Basil Crump, 2nd edition, revised and enlarged, Peking, China, China Book-sellers, Ltd., 1928

Coleman, William E., "The Sources of Madame Blavatsky's Writings," Appendix C in V. S. Solovyoff, *A Modern Priestess of Isis,* translated by Walter Leaf, London, England, Longmans Green & Company, 1895

Conger, Margaret, *Combined Chronology for use with The Mahatma Letters to A. P. Sinnett and The Letters of H. P. Blavatsky to A. P. Sinnett,* Pasadena, California, Theosophical University Press, 1973

Conze, Edward, *Buddhism: Its Essence and Development,* New York, New York, Harper & Brothers, 1959

Cook, Mabel (Collins), *The Idyll of the White Lotus,* London, England, Reeves and Turner, 1884

Cook, Mabel (Collins), *Light on the Path: A Treatise Written for the Personal Use of Those who are Ignorant of the Eastern Wisdom, and who desire to enter within its Influence,* written down by M.C., a Fellow of the Theosophical Society, London, England, Reeves and Turner, 1885; new edition with notes by author, London, England, George Redway, 1888; many subsequent reprints and editions

Coulomb, Emma, *Some Account of My Intercourse with Madame Blavatsky from 1872 to 1884; with Additional Letters and a Full Explanation of the Most Marvellous Theosophical Phenomena,* Madras, India, Higginbotham & Company, 1884; London, England, Published for the Proprietors of the "Madras Christian College Magazine" by Elliot Stock, 1885

Cox, H. R. W., *Who Wrote the March-Hare Attack on the Mahatma Letters?,* Victoria, Canada, The "H.P.B." Library, 1936

Cranston, Sylvia, and Head, Joseph, *Reincarnation: The Phoenix Fire Mystery,* Pasadena, California, Theosophical University Press, 1998

Cranston, Sylvia, and Williams, Carey, *Reincarnation: A New Horizon in Science, Religion and Society,* Pasadena, California, Theosophical University Press, 1993

Crawford, F. Marion, *Mr. Isaacs: A Tale of Modern India,* London, England, Macmillan, 1882

Crosbie, Robert, *Answers to Questions on The Ocean of Theosophy,* Los Angeles, California, The Theosophy Company, 1974

Crosbie, Robert, *The Friendly Philosopher,* Los Angeles, California, The Theosophy Company, 1923

Dharmapala, Anagarika, *Return to Righteousness: A Collection of Speeches, Essays and Letters of the Anagarika Dharmapala,* edited by Ananda Guruge, Ceylon, Published by the Anagarika Dharmapala Birth Centenary Committee, Ministry of Education and Cultural Affairs, Ceylon, printed at the Government Press, 1965

Eek, Sven, and Zirkoff, Boris de, *William Quan Judge: 1851–1896, The Life of a Theosophical Pioneer and Some of His Outstanding Articles,* Wheaton, Illinois, The Theosophical Publishing House, 1969

Eglinton, John, *A Memoir of Æ,* London, England, Macmillan, 1937

Ellmann, Richard, *Yeats: The Man and the Mask,* New York, New York, Macmillan, 1948; New York, New York, W. W. Norton, 1978

Ellwood, Robert S., Jr., *Alternative Altars: Unconventional and Eastern Spirituality in America*, Chicago, Illinois, University of Chicago Press, 1979 ("Colonel Olcott and Madame Blavatsky: Journey to the East")

Endersby, Victor A., *The Hall of Magic Mirrors, A Portrait of Madame Blavatsky*, New York, New York, Carlton Press (A Hearthstone Book), 1969

Fadeyev, Andrey Mikhaylovich de, *Vospominaniya, 1790–1867* (Reminiscences, 1790–1867), Odessa, Russia, South Russian Society for Printing, 1897

Fadeyev, Nadyezhda, "Helena Pavlovna Fadeyev," *Russkaya starina,* (Russian Days of Yore), St. Petersburg, volume 52, number 12, December 1886, 749–51, English translation in the Sylvia Cranston Archives, Santa Barbara, California

Fields, Rick, *How the Swans Came to the Lake*, Boston, Massachusetts, Shambhala, 1981

Fuller, Jean Overton, *Blavatsky and Her Teachers, An Investigative Biography*, London, East–West Publications, 1988

Gandhi, Mohandas K. *An Autobiography: The Story of My Experiments with Truth,* translated by Mahadev Desai, several editions, reprint, Boston, Massachusetts, Beacon Press, 1957

Gomes, Michael, *The Dawning of the Theosophical Movement*, Wheaton, Illinois, The Theosophical Publishing House, 1987

Gomes, Michael, *Theosophy in the Nineteenth Century: An Annotated Bibliography*, New York, New York, Garland Publishing, 1994

Gribble, J. D. B., *A Report of an Examination into the Blavatsky Correspondence Published in the Christian College Magazine,* Madras, India, Higginbotham Company, 1884

Guenon, René, *Le théosophisme: Histoire d'une pseudo-religion,* Paris, France, Nouvelle Librairie Nationale, 1921; 2nd edition with additional notes, Paris, France, Didier et Richard, 1930

Hanson, Virginia, *Masters and Men: The Human Story in the Mahatma Letters* (foreword by Joy Mills), Adyar, Madras, India, The Theosophical Publishing House, 1980

Harrison, Vernon, *H. P. Blavatsky and the SPR: An Examination of the Hodgson Report of 1885*, Pasadena, California, Theosophical University Press, 1997, includes reprint of "J'Accuse: . . ."

Harrison, Vernon, "J'Accuse: An Examination of the Hodgson Report of 1885," *Journal of the Society for Psychical Research,* London, England, April 1986

Hartmann, Franz, *Report of Observations Made During a Nine Months' Stay at the Headquarters of the Theosophical Society at Adyar (Madras), India,* Madras, India, Printed at the Scottish Press by Graves, Cookson and Company, 2nd edition, 1884

Hartmann, Franz, *The Talking Image of Urur,* New York, New York, J. W. Lovell, 1890

Hastings, Beatrice, *Defence of Madame Blavatsky,* Volume I: 1. Madame Blavatsky and the Mahatma Letters; 2. A Note on the "Kiddle Incident"; 3. The Mahatma Letters and Messrs. Hare; 4. Mahatma K. H. and A. P. Sinnett;

Worthing, England, The Hastings Press, 1937; Volume II: The "Coulomb Pamphlet," Worthing, England, published by Beatrice Hastings, 1937

Hastings, Beatrice, *New Universe "Try,"* a review devoted to the defence of Madame Blavatsky, Worthing, England, July 1937–July 1938 (self-published, 6 issues, July 1937–January 1939)

Hastings, Beatrice, "Solovyoff's Fraud: Being a Critical Analysis of the Book 'A Modern Priestess of Isis', translated from the Russian of Vsevolod S. Solovyoff by Walter Leaf," *The Canadian Theosophist,* July 1943–February 1944; reprint, Edmonton Lodge of the Theosophical Society in Canada, 1988

Hodgson, Richard, "The Defence of the Theosophists," *Proceedings of the Society for Psychical Research,* 1894, London, England, Kegan Paul, Trench, Trubner and Company, Ltd., 1894

Hodgson, Richard, Society for Psychical Research, "Report of The Committee Appointed to Investigate Phenomena Connected with the Theosophical Society," London, England, *Proceedings of the Society for Psychical Research,* 3, Part IX, December 1885

Holloway, Laura, and Chatterji, Mohini, *Man: Fragments of Forgotten History,* by Two Chelas in the Theosophical Society, London, England, Reeves and Turner, 1885

H.P.B.: In Memory of Helena Petrovna Blavatsky, by Some of Her Pupils, London, England, The Theosophical Publishing Society, 1891; centenary edition, London, The Blavatsky Association, 1931; Bombay, India, The Theosophy Company (India) Private Ltd., death centenary edition, 1991

Hume, A. O., *Hints on Esoteric Theosophy. No. 1: Is Theosophy a Delusion? Do the Brothers Exist?* Issued under the Authority of the Theosophical Society, Calcutta, India, Printed by the Calcutta Central Press Company, Ltd., April 1882

Humphreys, Christmas, *Exploring Buddhism,* Wheaton, Illinois, The Theosophical Publishing House (a Quest book), 1974. See chapters entitled "Buddhism and the Esoteric Tradition" and "The Two Concentric Circles of Buddhism in Tibet."

Humphreys, Christmas, *The Field of Theosophy: The Teacher, The Teaching and The Way,* London, England, The Theosophical Publishing House, 1966

Humphreys, Christmas, "Helena Petrovna Blavatsky," in Colin Wilson, editor, *Dark Dimensions: A Celebration of the Occult,* New York, New York, Everest House, 1977, pages 59–76

Jinarajadasa, C., editor, *The Golden Book of the Theosophical Society: A Brief History of the Society's Growth from 1875–1925,* Adyar, Madras, India, The Theosophical Publishing House, 1925

Jinarajadasa, C., editor, *Letters from the Masters of the Wisdom,* 1st series, 4th edition, Adyar, Madras, India, The Theosophical Publishing House, 1948; 2nd series, Chicago, Illinois, Theosophical Press, 1926

Jinarajadasa, C., editor, *The Personality of H. P. Blavatsky* (The Blavatsky Lecture 1930), Adyar, Madras, India, The Theosophical Publishing House, 1930

Johnson, Paul, *In Search of the Masters: Behind the Occult Myth,* South Boston, Virginia, printed by Hadderly-Benton, 1990

Judah, J. Stillson, *The History and Philosophy of the Metaphysical Movements in America,* Philadelphia, Pennsylvania, The Westminster Press, 1967. See chapter 3, "Theosophy and Its Allies."

Judge, William Quan, *Dr. Elliott Coues in His Letters,* New York, New York, 1889

Judge, William Quan, *Echoes of the Orient: The Writings of William Quan Judge,* 3 volumes, compiled by Dara Eklund, San Diego, California, Point Loma Publications, 1975, 1980, 1987

Judge, William Quan, *The Esoteric She, the Late Mme. Blavatsky: A Sketch of her Career,* reprinted from the New York *Sun,* with *The Theosophical Society and H. P. Blavatsky* by Annie Besant, Surat, India, 1893; William Q. Judge PamphletSeries number 2, *The Esoteric She,* Los Angeles, California, The Theosophy Company

Judge, William Quan, *Letters That Have Helped Me,* compiled by Jasper Niemand, New York, New York, *The Path,* 1891; volume 2, 1905; reprint, Semicentennial edition, Los Angeles, California, The Theosophy Company, 1946; Pasadena, California, Theosophical University Press, 1981

Judge, William Quan, *Notes on the Bhagavad-Gita,* Los Angeles, California, The Theosophy Company, 1956

Judge, William Quan, *The Ocean of Theosophy,* 1893; reprint, Los Angeles, California, The Theosophy Company, 1947; Pasadena, California, Theosophical University Press, 1973

Judge, William Q., *Practical Occultism: From the Private Letters of William Q. Judge,* Pasadena, California, Theosophical University Press, 1980

Judge, William Quan, recension of *Bhagavad-Gita,* Los Angeles, California, The Theosophy Company, 1947; combined with *Essays on the Gita,* Pasadena, California, Theosophical University Press, 1978

Judge, William Quan, *The Yoga Aphorisms of Patanjali,* Los Angeles, California, The United Lodge of Theosophists, 1967

Keightley, Archibald, *Reminiscences of H. P. Blavatsky, The Theosophical Quarterly,* New York, New York, October 1910, 109–22

Keightley, Bertram, *Reminiscences of H.P.B.,* Written for H.P.B. Centenary Celebration at Adyar, August 11 and 12, 1931, Adyar [Chennai], Madras, India, The Theosophical Publishing House, 1931, reprinted from *The Theosophist* September 1931

Kingsford, Anna Bonus, and Maitland, Edward, *The Perfect Way: or, The Finding of the Christ,* London, England, Field & Tuer, 1882

Kingsland, William, *The Influence of H. P. Blavatsky's Teachings upon Western Thought,* London, England, The Blavatsky Association, 1926

Kingsland, William, *The Real H. P. Blavatsky: A Study in Theosophy, and A Memoir of a Great Soul,* London, England, John M. Watkins, 1928; reprinted by The Theosophical Publishing House, London, England, 1985; contains as an appendix "A Critical Analysis of the 1885 Report of the Society for

Psychical Research," first published separately under the title *Was She a Charlatan? A Critical Analysis of the 1885 Report of the Society for Psychical Research on the Phenomena Connected with Madame Blavatsky,* London, England, The Blavatsky Association, 1927

Knoche, Grace F., *Report of Proceedings: Secret Doctrine Centenary,* Pasadena, California, Theosophical University Press, 1988

Kuhn, Alvin Boyd, *Theosophy: A Modern Revival of Ancient Wisdom,* New York, New York, Henry Holt, 1930

Leadbeater, C. W., *How Theosophy Came to Me,* Adyar, Madras, India, The Theosophical Publishing House, 1930; 3rd edition, 1967

Leonard, Maurice, *Madame Blavatsky . . . Medium, Mystic and Magician,* London, England, Regency Press, 1976

Lhalungpa, Lobsang P., *Tibet the Sacred Realm: Photographs 1880–1950,* Philadelphia, Pennsylvania, Philadelphia Museum of Art/Aperture, 1983

Lillie, Arthur H., *Madame Blavatsky and Her "Theosophy": A Study,* London, England, Swan Sonnenschein & Company, 1895

M. and K. H., Mahatmas, *The Mahatma Letters to A. P. Sinnett,* transcribed and compiled by A. T. Barker, Pasadena, California, Theosophical University Press, 2nd edition, reprint 1975; Adyar, Madras, India, The Theosophical Publishing House, 3rd edition, 1962

MacGregor, Geddes, *Reincarnation in Christianity,* Wheaton, Illinois, The Theosophical Publishing House, 1978

Magre, Maurice, *The Return of the Magi,* translated by Reginald Merton, London, England, P. Allan, 1931. See section entitled "Madame Blavatsky and the Theosophists."

Maitland, Edward, *Anna Kingsford: Her Life, Letters, Diary and Work,* by her collaborator Edward Maitland, illustrated with portraits, views and facsimilies, 2 volumes, 3rd edition, edited by Samuel Hopgood Hart, London, England, John M. Watkins, 1913

Mavalankar, Damodar K., *Damodar and the Pioneers of the Theosophical Movement,* compiled and annotated by Sven Eek, Adyar, Madras, India, The Theosophical Publishing House, 1978

Mavalankar, Damodar K., *Damodar the Writings of a Hindu Chela,* compiled by Sven Eek, Point Loma, California, The Theosophical University Press, 1940

Mead, G. R. S., *Concerning H.P.B.: Stray Thoughts on Theosophy,* (Adyar Pamphlet number 3), Adyar, Madras, India, The Theosophical Publishing House, 1920

Meade, Marion, *Madame Blavatsky: The Woman Behind the Myth,* New York, New York, G. P. Putnam's Sons, 1980

Merchant, Francis, *Great Images,* Scottsbluff, Nebraska, College Press, 1967. See chapter 7, "Messenger of the Mahatmas: H. P. Blavatsky."

Morgan, H. R., *Reply to a Report of an Examination by J. D. B. Gribble into the Blavatsky Correspondence,* 2nd edition, Ootacamund, India, Printed and published at the "Observer" Press, 1884

Motwani, Kewal, *Colonel H. S. Olcott: A Forgotten Page of American History,* Madras, India, Ganesh & Company, 1955

Murphet, Howard, *Hammer on the Mountain: Life of Henry Steel Olcott (1832– 1907),* Wheaton, Illinois, The Theosophical Publishing House, 1972

Murphet, Howard, *When Daylight Comes: A Biography of Helena Petrovna Blavatsky,* Wheaton, Illinois, The Theosophical Publishing House, 1975

Neff, Mary K., *Personal Memoirs of H. P. Blavatsky,* with 12 illustrations, New York, New York, E. P. Dutton, 1937; London, England, Rider & Company, 1937; Wheaton, Illinois, The Theosophical Publishing House, 1971

Nekrasova, Ekaterina S., "Elena Andreevna Gan, 1814–1842: Biograficheskii ocherk," (Helena Andreyevna Hahn, 1814–1842: Biographical Sketch), *Russkaya starina* (Russian Days of Yore), St. Petersburg, Russia, volume 51 August 1886, 335–54; September 1886, 553–74; English translation in Sylvia Cranston Archives, Santa Barbara, California

Nethercot, Arthur R., *The First Five Lives of Annie Besant,* Chicago, Illinois, University of Chicago Press, 1960

Olcott, Henry Steel, *Buddhist Catechism,* Colombo, Ceylon, Theosophical Society, Buddhist Section, 1881

Olcott, Henry Steel, *A Historical Retrospect 1875–1896 of the Theosophical Society: Extract from the Twenty-first Anniversary Address of the President-Founder of the Society,* Madras, India, Published by the Society, 1896

Olcott, Henry Steel, *Old Diary Leaves: The History of the Theosophical Society,* 6 volumes, 3rd printing, Adyar, Madras, India, The Theosophical Publishing House, 1972–1975

Olcott, Henry Steel, *People from the Other World,* profusely illustrated by Alfred Kappes and T. W. Williams, Hartford, Connecticut, American Publishing Company, 1875; reprint, 1972, Rutland, Vermont, Charles E. Tuttle Company

Olcott, Henry Steel, *Theosophy, Religion and Occult Science,* London, England, George Redway, 1885

Osborn, Arthur W., *The Cosmic Womb: An Interpretation of Man's Relationship to the Infinite,* Wheaton, Illinois, The Theosophical Publishing House, 1969

Pissareff, Helene F., "Helena Petrovna Blavatsky," *The Theosophist,* January 1913

Proceedings of the Blavatsky Association, London, England

Purucker, Gottfried de, *H. P. Blavatsky: The Mystery,* San Diego, California, Point Loma Publications, 1974

Racowitza, Princess Helene Von, *An Autobiography,* authorized translation by Cecil Marr., London, England, Constables & Company, 1910

Ransom, Josephine, compiler, *A Short History of the Theosophical Society: 1875– 1937,* Preface by G. S. Arundale, Adyar, Madras, India, The Theosophical Publishing House, 1938

Report of Proceedings: The Theosophical Congress, held by the Theosophical Society of the Parliament of Religions, World's Fair of 1893, New York, New York, American Section Headquarters T.S., 1893

Roerich, Nicholas, *Shambhala,* New York, New York, Nicholas Roerich Museum, 1978

Roszak, Theodore, *The Unfinished Animal: The Aquarian Frontier and the Evolution of Consciousness,* New York, New York, Harper & Row, 1975. See section entitled "Madame Blavatsky's Secret Doctrine."

Ryan, Charles J., *H. P. Blavatsky and the Theosophical Movement: A Brief Historical Sketch.* Point Loma, California, Theosophical University Press, 1937, 2nd edition with author's corrections and additions, 1975; 2nd edition, San Diego, California, Point Loma Publications, 1975

Sinnett, A. P., *The Early Days of Theosophy in Europe,* London, England, The Theosophical Publishing House, 1922

Sinnett, A. P., *Esoteric Buddhism,* London, England, Trubner & Co., 1883. Many subsequent editions with additional material: reprint, London, The Theosophical Publishing House, 1972; reprint of the 5th edition (1885), annotated and enlarged by the author, San Diego, California, Wizards Bookshelf (Secret Doctrine Reference Series), 1994

Sinnett, A. P. *Incidents in the Life of Madame Blavatsky,* Compiled from Information supplied by her Relatives and Friends, edited by A. P. Sinnett, With a portrait reproduced from an original painting by Hermann Schmiechen, London, England, George Redway; New York, New York, J. W. Bouton, 1886; 2nd edition (incomplete), London, England, The Theosophical Publishing House, 1913; reprint of 1886 edition, New York, New York, Arno Press, 1976

Sinnett, A. P., *The Occult World,* London, England, Trubner & Co., 1881. Many subsequent revised and enlarged editions: 2nd edition, London, England, Trubner & Co., 1882 (includes important preface); new American edition from 4th English edition, with Author's corrections and a new Preface and Appendix, Boston, Massachusetts and New York, New York, Houghton Mifflin, 1885; 9th edition, London, England, The Theosophical Publishing House, 1969

Sinnett, A. P., *The "Occult World Phenomena" and the Society for Psychical Research, with a Protest by Madame Blavatsky,* London, England, George Redway, 1886

Sinnett, Patience, *The Purpose of Theosophy,* London, England, Chapman & Hall, 1885; Bombay, India, The Theosophical Society, 1887

Smith, Warren Sylvester, *The London Heretics, 1870–1914,* New York, New York, Dodd, Mead, 1968. See section entitled "Spiritualism and the London Theosophists."

Society for Psychical Research, *First Report of the Committee of the Society for Psychical Research Appointed to Investigate the Evidence for Marvellous Phenomena Offered by Certain Members of the Theosophical Society* (private and confidential), London, England, 1884

Solovyoff, Vsevolod Sergyeevich, *A Modern Priestess of Isis,* translated by Walter Leaf, London, England, Longmans, Green and Company, 1895

Subba Row, T., *Notes on the Bhagavad Gita,* Pasadena, California, Theosophical University Press, 1978

The Theosophical Movement 1875–1925: A History and a Survey, New York, New York, E. P. Dutton & Company, 1925

The Theosophical Movement 1875–1950, Los Angeles, California, The Cunningham Press, 1951

Vania, K. F., *Madame H. P. Blavatsky: Her Occult Phenomena and the Society for Psychical Research,* Bombay, India, Sat Publishing Company, 1951

Vengerova, Zinaida, "Blavatskaia, Elena, Petrovna," *Kritiko-biograficheskii slovar' russkikh pisatelei: uchenyh,* edited by S. A. Vengerov, St. Petersburg, Russia, 1892

Wachtmeister, Constance, *Reminiscences of H. P. Blavatsky and The Secret Doctrine,* edited by a Fellow of the Theosophical Society, London, England, Theosophical Publishing Society, 1893; Wheaton, Illinois, The Theosophical Publishing House (a Quest book), 1976

Wadia, B. P., *Studies in "The Secret Doctrine,"* 2 volumes, Bombay, India, Theosophy Company, 1976

Waterman, Adlai E., *Obituary: The "Hodgson Report" on Madame Blavatsky, 1885–1960: Re-examination Discredits the Major Charges Against H. P. Blavatsky,* Preface by N. Sri Ram, Adyar, Madras, India, The Theosophical Publishing House, 1963

Williams, Gertrude Marvin, *The Passionate Pilgrim: A Life of Annie Besant,* New York, New York, Coward-McCann, 1931

Williams, Gertrude Marvin, *Priestess of the Occult: Madame Blavatsky,* New York, New York, Alfred A. Knopf, 1946

Yeats, W. B., *The Collected Letters of W. B. Yeats,* Volume 1, edited by John Kelly, Oxford, England, Clarendon Press, 1986

Zhelihovsky, Vera Petrovna de, "Yelena Petrovna Blavatskaya: Biografichesky ocherk" (Helena Petrovna Blavatsky: A Biographical Sketch), *Russkoye obozreniya* (Russian Review), Moscow, number 11 (November 1891), 242–94, number 12 (December 1891), 567–621; privately translated into English by Mary G. Langford, in the Sylvia Cranston Archives, Santa Barbara, California

Zhelihovsky, Vera Petrovna de, *Yelena Petrovna Blavatskaya i sovremenniy zhretz istini: Otvet g-zhi Igrek (V. P. Zhelikhovskoi) g-nu Vsevolodu Solov'evu* (H. P. Blavatsky and a Modern Priest of Truth: Reply of Madame Y (V. P. Zhelihovsky) to Mr. Vsevolod Solovyoff), St. Petersburg, Russia, 1893; privately translated into English by Cathy Young, in the Sylvia Cranston Archives, Santa Barbara, California. The book, in an abridged form, was translated and published as Appendix A of V. S. Solovyoff, *A Modern Priestess of Isis* (see Solovyoff)

Zhelihovsky, Vera Petrovna de, "Yelena Petrovna Blavatskaya i teosofisti" (Helena Petrovna Blavatsky and the Theosophists), letter dated May 25, 1884, to the editor, *Odesskiy vestnik* (Odessa Messenger), Odessa, Russia, number 123 (June 5, 1884), 1–3; reprinted in *Rebus,* St. Petersburg, Russia, number 28 (July 15, 1884), pages 263–65, and number 29, (July 22, 1884), 273–75, and quoted in translation in A. P. Sinnett, *Incidents in the Life of Madame Blavatsky*, 264–69 (see Sinnett)

Zhelihovsky, Vera Petrovna de, *Kak ya bila malenkoy: Iz vospominaniy rannyago dyetstva Veri Petrovni Zhelihovsky* (When I Was Small: From the Reminiscences of the Early Childhood of Vera Petrovna Zhelihovsky), 2nd revised and enlarged edition, St. Petersburg, Russia, A. F. Devrien, 1894; privately translated by Cathy Young, in the Sylvia Cranston Archives, Santa Barbara, California

Zhelihovsky, Vera Petrovna de, *Moyo otrochestvo* (My Adolescence), 3rd edition, St. Petersburg, Russia, A. F. Devriend, 1890; reprint, St. Petersburg, Russia, Editorial Office of *Dyetskoye chteniye* (Readings for Children), printed by P. P. Soikin, 1893; privately translated by Cathy Young, in the Sylvia Cranston Archives, Santa Barbara, California

Zhelihovsky, Vera Petrovna de, "My Sister—H. P. Blavatsky," *The Occult Review* (incorporating *The London Forum*), volumes 60–62 (December 1934–July 1935); translation of "Radda-Bai: Biograficheskiy ocherk" (see below)

Zhelihovsky, Vera Petrovna de, "Neobyasnimoye ili neobyasnenneye: Iz lichnih i semeynih vospominaniy" (The Inexplicable or the Unexplained: From Personal and Family Reminiscences), *Rebus*, St. Petersburg, Russia, volume 3, numbers 43–48 (1884), volume 4, numbers 4–7, 9–11, 13–14 (1885); also published as a pamphlet in 1885 or 1886; privately translated by Cathy Young, in the Sylvia Cranston Archives, Santa Barbara, California

Zhelihovsky, Vera Petrovna de, "Penomeni okul 'ticheskoy sili gospozhi Blavatskoy" (Phenomena of the Occult Force of Madame Blavatsky), *Rebus*, St. Petersburg, Russia, number 50 (1884), 465–67; privately translated by Cathy Young, in the Sylvia Cranston Archives, Santa Barbara, California

Zhelihovsky, Vera Petrovna de, "Pravda o Yelene Petrovna Blavatskoy" (The Truth About Helena Petrovna Blavatsky), *Rebus*, St. Petersburg, Russia, volume 2, numbers 40, 41, 43, 44, 46–48 (1883); also published as a pamphlet; privately translated by Mary G. Langford, in the Sylvia Cranston Archives, Santa Barbara, California. Long excerpts from the articles are quoted, in translation, in A. P. Sinnett, *Incidents in the Life of Madame Blavatsky* (see Sinnett); a translation into English by HPB herself, quite long and in her handwriting, is serialized in *The Theosophist*, May–November 1991

Zhelihovsky, Vera Petrovna de, "Radda-Bai: Biograficheskiy ocherk" (Radda-Bai: A Biographical Sketch), in Radda-Bai (E. P. Blavatskaya), *Zagadochnye plemena na "Golubykh Gorakh," Durbar v Lakhore* (Enigmatical Tribes in the "Light Blue Hills," Durbar at Lahore), St. Petersburg, Russia, V. I. Gubinsky, 1893; privately translated by Mary G. Langford, in the Sylvia Cranston Archives, Santa Barbara, California; article also published in translation as "My Sister—H. P. Blavatsky" (see above)

Zirkoff, Boris de, "How 'Isis Unveiled' Was Written," Introductory, *Isis Unveiled,* volume I, H. P. Blavatsky: Collected Writings, Wheaton, Illinois, The Theosophical Publishing House, 1972

Zirkoff, Boris de, *Rebirth of the Occult Tradition: How the Secret Doctrine of H. P. Blavatsky Was Written,* Adyar, Madras, India, The Theosophical Publishing House, 1977

Index

*Abbreviation used: EN means Endnote: Part of book by number: note number